Restoring a Presence

Restoring a Presence

American Indians and Yellowstone National Park

Peter Nabokov and Lawrence Loendorf

University of Oklahoma Press : Norman

Also by Peter Nabokov

A Forest of Time: American Indian Ways of History (New York, 2002)
Native American Testimony: A Chronicle of Indian-White Relations from Prophecy to the Present, 1492–2000 (New York, 1999)
(with Robert Easton) *Native American Architecture* (New York, 1989)
Indian Running (Santa Fe, 1981)

Also by Lawrence Loendorf

(with Julie Francis) *Ancient Visions: Petroglyphs and Pictographs of the Wind River and Bighorn Country, Wyoming and Montana* (Salt Lake, 2002)

This book is published with the generous assistance of The McCasland Foundation, Duncan, Oklahoma.

Library of Congress Cataloging-in-Publication Data

Nabokov, Peter.
    Restoring a presence : American Indians and Yellowstone National Park / Peter Nabokov and Lawrence Loendorf.
        p.   cm.
    Includes bibliographical references and index.
    ISBN 978-0-8061-5346-9 (paper)
        1. Indians of North America—Yellowstone National Park—History.
    2. Indians of North America—Land tenure—Yellowstone National Park.
    3. Indians of North America—Yellowstone National Park—Social life and customs. 4. Yellowstone National Park—History. 5. Yellowstone National Park—Antiquities. 6. Yellowstone National Park—Environmental conditions.
    I. Loendorf, Lawrence L. II. Title.

E78.Y44N32 2004
978.7'5200497—dc22

                                                                        2004045871

The paper in this book meets the guidelines for permanence and durability of the Committee on Production Guidelines for Book Longevity of the Council on Library Resources, Inc. ∞

Contents

Illustrations

Text ornament is a drawing of the Yellowstone geysers, a detail of a map by Crazy Mule, Cheyenne, circa 1880. Image is reproduced in full on page 221.

Figures

Maps

Preface and Acknowledgments

It is no secret that banning American Indians and appropriating their lands were deemed necessary for the initial establishment and continued security of Yellowstone National Park. Nor should it come as a surprise that subsequent promotional and popular histories of America's inaugural park largely ignored the presence of Indians in the greater Yellowstone landscape, whether as inhabitants, visitors, or wayfarers. When they imagined this Wyoming preserve into being, the park's conceivers projected themselves backward. They *reconceived* this environment as a natural Eden of pristine and pre-human existence, teeming with game, devoid of human meddling or cultural usage. In this primordial scenario, Indians had little place. As the historian Chris J. Magoc writes, "The myth of a virgin Yellowstone long ago removed the park from history and humanity—especially of the native kind."[1]

Although their heritage in the greater Yellowstone region has been established for at least nine thousand years, literally and figuratively Indians had to be "disappeared." This book is but one attempt to restore the presence of American Indian peoples to the cultural history of the greater Yellowstone ecosystem and to the park in particular. As a documentary summary of available information on relationships between Indians and the park, it also covers what little we know about their physical and representational erasure. Paradoxically, however, the acknowledgment of those relationships is a credit to the same powers that denied them years ago. For we have drawn this book from a U.S. Park Service–funded research effort that we conducted between 1994 and 1998 to collect information from Indian peoples and archives about Yellowstone's cultural and ethnographic resources. Its strengths and limitations therefore stem from that mission, which, while an unusual opportunity, was constrained by time, funding restrictions, and the government report genre.

An accompanying irony of this project is the fact that we would have been unable to complete this assignment without the generous assistance of park officials, librarians, researchers, and boosters. We are very indebted to them and to a range of American Indian consultants, to whom we promised anonymity, for discussing issues about which some of them still remain ambivalent. All royalties and proceeds from this work are being donated to the American Indian College Fund.

It is with some trepidation that we add to the voluminous bibliography on Yellowstone National Park's history and position our findings under the high standards established by over a century's worth of chronicles from the likes of Hiram Martin Chittenden, Aubrey L. Haines, Paul Schullery, and Lee H. Whittlesey. Insofar as the human history of the region is concerned, hardly a trail in Yellowstone National Park would seem to have gone undocumented, a ranger station unrecorded, a bridge unmeasured, a place-name unplumbed, or an unusual character even remotely connected with the place unprofiled. This would seem to go equally for the floral and faunal history of this "crown jewel of the nation's park system." But things in Yellowstone are not always as they seem. As with her recently discovered waterfalls that proved mostly invisible from the air, so with her native pasts. The present work is driven by our realization that a major dimension of the culture-and-nature history of the first, largest, and most famous natural reserve in the United States deserves another look.

Chronicles of Yellowstone National Park customarily shuttle between topics associated with the historical or cultural aspects of the park since its exploration and establishment in the late nineteenth century and topics related to scientific features deriving from the park's unique biological, geological, and ecological attractions. Until the present day the subject of American Indians and Yellowstone seems to have fallen into the crack between those two broad areas of inquiry—between, that is, Culture and Nature.

The evolving place of American Indians in the long history of Yellowstone National Park has been underplayed over the years in part because of America's ever-shifting notions and academic debates over how to categorize and characterize the Indians' role in the cultural history of North America in the first place. The answer to the question of whether Indians were to be considered part of the "natural" or "cultural" history of the park seems to have been answered by default, by the implications built into its representations of Indians rather than by any conscious design.

For the most part, commentary on native "historical" relationships to Yellowstone has been confined to one dramatic foray—the Nez Perce adventures of late summer 1877. Until relatively recently, any ties of a "cultural" nature have more often than not been observed in the negative: Indians steered clear of the park's heartland because of their fear of its geysers. Throughout a century and a half of scattered commentaries and uncoordinated representations on Indians and the park, the uncertainty about whether Indians were to be considered more a part of the park's "nature" or "history" or "culture" has underlain the mixed messages concerning the relationships between Yellowstone and its Indians, with any finer tribal distinctions or claims generally ignored in the process.

But this confusion about how to categorize Indians did not arise from nowhere. It grew out of Yellowstone's original mandate, which was to provide a prototype for natural refuges that would save "wilderness," preserving its monumental landscapes that the New World enjoyed as competition with the man-made monuments of Old Europe and, somewhat later, protecting the wildlife from developers and poachers. Yet during roughly the same era as Yellowstone was being conceived, as the historian Mark Spence has perceptively pointed out, another sort of preserve with a different agenda was being created for the American Indians who once lived in or moved through the park. Rather than a refuge for *preserving biological species* and keeping change at bay, the Indian reservation was devoted to *transforming cultural species* and putting their traditional habits behind them. Never should the two forms of containment overlap, or their associated species and symbols intermingle. At Yellowstone most particularly, buffalo had to be kept in, Indians kept out. But it was never quite that simple. As the historian Philip Burnham writes, "For all their obvious differences, however, park and reservation also bore a striking resemblance. They were born of the same era; were both established as havens from unscrupulous private development; and were administered by the swelling bureaucracy ensconced in the Department of Interior."[2]

Under the guiding evolutionary theory of the day, Indians needed to be assimilated into the broader culture and to abandon their ties to nature. In the late nineteenth century this was considered the only humane alternative to brutally killing them off, although their gradual demise might eventuate anyway. The grander role of the park in this triumphal version of western history was quite clear in the mind of Yellowstone National Park Superintendent General S. B. M. Young in 1907, when the report he supervised on the park stated explicitly:

> Looking back a full century we find that the story of the Yellowstone Park is a sequential link in the chain of epochal events which commenced with the purchase by the United States of the then uncharted wilderness called the "Louisiana Territory," the subsequent expedition of Lewis and Clark, the discovery of gold, the conquest of the savages, and all the epic deeds which achieved at last the winning of the west.[3]

From a contemporary perspective, then, the predicament of Indians in any discussion of national parks is a Gordian knot of contradictions. As long as Indians are seen as part of nature, they remain the one species who were not allowed to stay in their natural habitat. When they are considered part of history, they present a threat to the Euro-Americans who had risen sufficiently enough above their "aboriginal" state to develop Culture and keep it distinct from Nature through the very invention of such preserves. But if Indians are to be considered part of human culture, then their claims to the region might compete with those of the Euro-Americans. In this logical stalemate, Indians wind up being placed in no clear category and can claim no stable place in the mind or in the environment.

As scholars who began studying western Indian societies in the late nineteenth century started to delineate the intricacies of and contrasts between different Indian cultures, the ambivalence over how they were to be lumped together became even more problematic. Early park officials were placed in yet another bind: they were government employees with a growing exposure to and appreciation for scholarship, at least in the budding field of "natural" science. It was in their self-interest, therefore, to admit that to some degree Indians were part of culture and hence ineligible for any claims to a natural refuge, as were birds or mammals. At the same time, any claims their culture might have made to the Yellowstone National Park region could threaten the government's insistence that this had always been a pristine natural wilderness.

This philosophical impasse explains, in part, why officials never felt provoked to explain or explore Hiram Chittenden's observations in 1895: "It is a singular fact in the history of Yellowstone National Park that no knowledge of that country seems to have been derived from the Indians. . . . Their deep silence concerning it is therefore no less remarkable than mysterious."[4] Appreciating the awkward place of Indians in Yellowstone National Park's history and ideology helps to clarify why any cultural theories that explained Indian absences from the park region might have been looked upon favorably, why funding for surveying the possible extent and intensity of early Indian occupancy or native uses of the park and environs was never plentiful, and why no full-time park cultural or archaeological advisors were appointed until the 1990s. The reason for this unwritten chapter in Yellowstone Park cultural history is that not until recently was it considered in the park's best interests to research and unravel it. Indeed, early officials went out of their way to get Indians to promise to stay away from the park. As Yellowstone National Park ranger Merrill D. Beal has written:

> These agreements were widely advertised, and in order to further neutralize any fear of Indian trouble a policy of minimizing past incidents was evolved. The recent invasions were represented as unprecedented, actually anomalous. Indians had never lived in Yellowstone, were infrequent visitors because they were afraid of the thermal activity! It was not a conspiracy against truth, just an adaptation of business psychology to a promising national resort.[5]

Changes in the received wisdom regarding the official picture of the relationships between different American Indian peoples and Yellowstone National Park can be attributed to what are now called paradigm shifts in the academic disciplines of social sciences and history. Add to these shifting angles of scholarly focus and interpretation the fact that public agencies, overburdened by meager resources and multiple clientele, are often a half-step behind new paradigms that trickle down from academia, and it becomes clear why our understanding of the roles played by Indians in symbol-dense areas like national parks—Yellowstone above all—might be behind the times.

The questions of how to research and interpret the roles of Indian cultures in the history of the Yellowstone Plateau continue to reflect contradictions at the heart of the park's mission. "Long after Americans have reduced the park to a sedative from modernity," points out Magoc, "we insist on the innocence of Yellowstone."[6] Despite a record of human impact on the Yellowstone ecology that extends back thousands of years, a number of park spokespeople still cling to the vision of an Edenic Yellowstone. "The primary purpose of the Park," said one eminent park biologist recently, "was to preserve this representative natural ecosystem and then we would define 'natural' as 'without human influence.'"[7] This attitude echoed comments of two years earlier, made by the park's chief scientist to the *New York Times*: "If nature is making all the right decisions then you let nature make the decisions . . . [but] if there is something dysfunctional caused by humankind [in the park], then we need to go in and fix it."[8] Given this perspective, it is understandable why, despite mounting evidence to the contrary, the image of a Yellowstone which was relatively devoid of meddlesome Indians, who rarely hunted and never lived there or set portions of the place afire, would continue to find appeal. In a lavishly illustrated 2001 overview of the history of America's national parks, published by the National Geographic Society and with a foreword by former President Jimmy Carter, one reads, "While most national parks would come into existence already impacted by American Indians, Yellowstone was an exception. Being so high and remote, it offered scant hunting opportunities and no winter shelter, and was occupied only by nomadic Indians . . . ."[9] This line of thinking also explains why, as the authors were told by a leading Park official, "when it came to [interpreting] this park, we decided to focus on four themes, and frankly Indians isn't one of them."

In this book we assay other reasons for the dearth of archaeological and ethnographic data on Yellowstone National Park. At the same time, we hope to offer sufficient evidence, teased from myriad sources, to make a case that the cause of at least conceptually reintroducing American Indians into the park's representations of itself is a task that remains worth the trouble. In fact, this approach only enriches the epic of Yellowstone by factoring "human nature" into its equation. We make no pretense that we have produced anything close to a complete composite of the ethnographic resources of Yellowstone National Park. New historical data can always come to light; any ethnohistorical record is under constant revision. For this reason we have consistently hesitated to establish hard and fast criteria for determining which traditional Indian groups should be characterized as "affiliated tribes" where Yellowstone Park is concerned. As this work was reaching completion, for example, new citations turned up regarding Sioux movements into or around the Yellowstone Plateau, whether on raids against other tribes or buffalo hunts. We therefore caution future researchers or writers on Indians and the park to be wary of making definitive statements about which Indians used the park, and about the irrecoverable loss of this or that native tradition, whether it be oral narrative or ritual practice. As suggested by the Kiowa mythic narrative presented in chapter 1 and Plenty Coups' historical buffalo hunt discussed in chapter 3, tattered memories can contain an unusually strong life-force and crop up in unlikely places.

We have depended on the graciousness, patience, experiences, and scholarship of a number of individuals and institutions. Here we would like to acknowledge the work of park officials, other scholars, native advisors and consultants, and additional personnel without whom this work would not have been possible.

We are extremely grateful to National Park Service ethnographer David Ruppert for his constant support, counsel, and patience. We also wish to thank Yellowstone National Park Superintendent Michael Finley for the hospitality and support of his Mammoth staff, with special appreciation to Laura Joss, Chief, Branch of Cultural Resources, a patient and constant supporter; to Lee H. Whittlesey, Archivist, for his tireless responses to phone calls and queries and for his constant encouragement; to Ann M. Johnson, Rocky Mountain Support Office Archaeologist, duty-stationed to Yellowstone National Park, for her solid critiques; to Elaine Hale for her reviews and suggestions; to Vanessa Christopher, Librarian, for her assistance in locating archival sources and photographs; and to Jim Peaco, Park Photographer, for videotaping Dr. Åke Hultkrantz and processing slide requests.

Our project consultants and regional interviewers were indispensable to collecting the raw data from which we have written this book. We are extremely thankful to Dr. Åke Hultkrantz, who with his gracious wife, Gerry, came to Red Lodge for a two-week trip through his old Yellowstone country fieldwork sites. In addition, Dr. Hultkrantz granted permission to select from his photographs as well as to excerpt from his unpublished manuscript on the Sheep Eaters. We are also indebted to the late Aubrey L. Haines for access to his impeccably collated historical notes, for his general readiness to share a lifetime's worth of Yellowstone knowledge, especially his notes on the trail system, and for his prompt written responses. For conducting interviews and independent research, we have relied heavily on the work of alpine ecologist Jan Nixon, who also wrote our summary of plant data related to the park; on the efforts of Dr. Sharon Kahin of Dubois, Wyoming, whose interviews with Shoshone and Bannock consultants provided crucial ethnographic depth to chapters 3 through 5; and on the help of Jeanne Eder, who accompanied our first season's field trips and contributed treaty data.

Although we want this work to reflect the combined voices of many Indian spokespersons and consultants, living and past, we also wish to respect the anonymity of our contemporary American Indian consultants. For now let us just profoundly thank, on the east, DT and SC of the Kiowa tribe, and GB, AS, and JMC among the Crow. For the north, we are grateful to TT, CB, TI, and LA among the Kootenai-Salish, and CCB of the Canadian Blackfeet, and, for the west, to GE, LV, JS, CN, DSC, and JLV. For the south, we thank MG, ZE, FT, MJG, SW, AC, and HW.

We want to particularly thank John H. Furse for a gift to Yellowstone National Park in the name of Kay L. Furse. The donation was used for costs of American Indian participants' travel to Yellowstone National Park for interviews and meetings.

A group of other individuals with special expertise have assisted in many different ways. We offer our gratitude to Walt Allen, Bernard Azure, Gerard Baker, Renee Beltran, Tim Bernardis, Mike Bies, Chuck Branch, Joseph and Elenita Brown, Frances Clymer, Stuart W. Conner, Marcy Culpin, Leslie Davis, David Dominick, Bob Edgar, Ken Fehyl, Paula Fleming, Bill Holm, Richard Holmer, Susan Hovde, Wilfred Husted, Nancy Kreckler, Kevin Kooistra-Manning, Larry Mayer, Tim McCleary, Bonnie Newman, Anibal Rodriguez, Tom Smith, Mark D. Spence, Ken Wade, Deward E. Walker, Jr., and Joseph Weixelman. We are thankful for the editorial expertise, graphic skills, and good humor of Laurie Miller of the *Fine Line*, Cody, Wyoming.

In recent years we have had the able assistance of Rosemary Sucec, who now holds a permanent position in Yellowstone National Park as Cultural Anthropologist for liaison with Native Americans. We are also indebted to Nancy Medaris Stone of Corrales, New Mexico for obtaining copyright permissions. Finally we thank Jo Ann Reece and Marian Stewart of the University of Oklahoma Press for their capable assistance in preparing the manuscript for publication.

Restoring a Presence

Introduction

This overview of the role of American Indians in the region of Yellowstone National Park strives to reevaluate existing literature, probe underused or recently discovered sources of archival, ethnographic, and historical data, and invite a fresh survey of contemporary Indian voices and viewpoints regarding the roles that various Indian peoples played in the human evolution of the landscape and region on which the park now sits. But this is an ongoing saga, which will become more refined as archaeologists explore untested corners of Yellowstone, as ethnohistorians find new primary material or innovative ways to evaluate old data, and as collaborative relations between Indians and ethnographers improve.

In the chapters that follow we itemize and provisionally interpret the life patterns of Indian peoples who neighbored on and acted within Yellowstone National Park. To do so, we have been forced to extend our territorial focus beyond the park proper to include what has been characterized variously as "the Yellowstone ecosystem," the "greater Yellowstone," or "the greater Yellowstone ecosystem." As Mark Spence reminds us, "Yellowstone [Park] is a geographic square that was grafted over native understandings of the place and the region. Consequently, to expect native stories, memories, and actions to precisely distinguish between things and places on either side of current park boundaries is absurd."[1]

Nor can one understand the bureaucratic, military, or environmental history of Yellowstone National Park proper without an appreciation of historical issues related to the western plains and the U.S. park system in general, extending to political decisions made in Washington, D.C. That the adjoining landscape was considered an inherent part of the park ecosystem early on is suggested by the fact that Shoshone National Forest was initially known as "the Yellowstone Park

Timberland Reserve." Hence we are generally adopting the characterization of the Yellowstone ecosystem offered by the lawyer-environmentalist Charles F. Wilkinson:

> [T]he most commonly accepted definition seems to be an area of about thirteen [now eighteen to twenty] million acres. It includes Yellowstone and Teton National Parks, three wildlife refuges, some BLM [Bureau of Land Management] and private lands, part of the Wind River Indian Reservation, and, perhaps most importantly, seven national forests. The ecosystem, as defined in this manner, touches more than two dozen jurisdictions. It also encompasses all of the plateau, the mountain systems that splay out from the park, and the headwaters of all the streams that flow out in all directions.[2]

We have tried to narrate in compelling fashion the results of our ethnographic inquiry and summary of published or archival data as they pertain to the archaeological cultures associated with Yellowstone National Park and its environs; to the so-called Sheep Eater culture, the only recognized "permanent" park inhabitants before and during the historic period; and to the historic tribal groups whose territories overlapped onto or pressed upon the later park boundaries on all four sides.

Yellowstone National Park as Key Symbol

Discussion on practically any aspect of Yellowstone National Park can get one into trouble. This is because the park has become a lightning rod for a wide range of American opinions, beliefs, experiments, attitudes, and desires concerning what is arguably humankind's oldest discourse: the political, technological, economic, philosophical, cultural, and spiritual dimensions of the relationship between culture and nature. As our nation's first, highest-visibility, open-air laboratory where that relationship is constantly being tested, contested, and redefined, what is a calm conversation anywhere else becomes a raging controversy in Yellowstone. This is also because the park's natural properties and cultural history are so dramatic and resonant that they lend themselves to multiple interpretations and repeated, incessant scrutiny. Like the Grand Canyon and Yosemite, or the Alamo and the Vietnam Memorial, they make the place an almost mandatory destination of pilgrimage for every American family. There are many characteristics that converge to create this key symbol for America's paradise lost.

GEOGRAPHY

The lifeblood of the Yellowstone Plateau is the great river that gathers from streams pouring off the Absaroka crest and the Two Ocean Plateau. Then it pools into the largest high-altitude lake in North America before flowing north. There is symbolic importance in the centrality of this spot on the Continental Divide, for Two Ocean Pass Lake is the knot that binds together the continent. One of its outlets, Atlantic Creek, runs into the Yellowstone and thence eventually into the Gulf of Mexico and the Atlantic Ocean; the other outlet, Pacific Creek, replenishes the Columbia River and ultimately enters the Pacific Ocean.

When it is frozen over, the 136 square miles of Yellowstone Lake form the largest ice sheet in the continental United States. As for the Yellowstone River, it extends into the longest undammed stream in the lower forty-eight states, stretching for 671 miles, draining a 70,102-square-mile watershed, and eventually traversing an expanse greater than all of New England. In the initial high-altitude portion of the Yellowstone River's three main sections, it completes more than half its 5,800-foot descent in its first 100 miles. Here is where one can view the great canyons that, in combination with the dramatic effusions of its thermal field, have made it one of the wonders of the world.

GEOLOGY

Both Indians and Euro-Americans recognized the wonders of the Yellowstone Plateau as a spectacular expression of the forces that first produced and still can re-form the earth's topography. This power has less to do with the outer beauty of its lakes, peaks, and valleys than with the ten thousand thermal features that are concentrated within the confines of the park, whose nearly nine hundred geysers contain more than 60 percent of those on the planet. It is appropriate in a survey on Indian relations with and attitudes toward this geological region to remind ourselves of this awe-inspiring force. We say this because Indians have often been charged with giving Yellowstone's thermal field a wide berth in their travels through the region, with dubbing it "taboo," "evil," a place of demonic influences. As observed by historian Robert H. Keller and natural resources specialist Michael F. Turek, however, these claims about Indian attitudes toward Yellowstone would prove merely the first and most strident examples of "[t]he widespread misconception that Indians feared national park areas and had not used the land,"[3] These authors also point out that similar "myths" became attached to Mount Rainier, the interior Olympic Peninsula, and the Southwest's Zion National Park, among other public sites.

But as has been documented by earlier writers and is underscored here, "awesome," "powerful," "dangerous," and "sacred" may be more accurate descriptors for Indian reactions toward the thermal turbulence under Yellowstone National Park. Aside from how such responses were filtered through the Indians' religious belief systems, however, their feelings of amazement and caution are not that different from those of non-Indians. Former Yellowstone Chief Ranger Dan R. Sholly, for example, wrote about a winter tour just west of Canyon Village:

Beneath where we were riding the earth's molten interior was only half a mile down. Yellowstone was born from volcanism and is still being shaped by its forces. About two million years ago, then one million years ago, then again six hundred thousand years ago, tremendously destructive volcanic eruptions occurred right where I was now freezing. The latest alone supposedly spewed out nearly 240 cubic miles of debris. The 28-by-47-mile caldera, or basin, which dominates much of the park's interior, was the result of the earth collapsing from so much lava. . . . To think that just below my snowmobile was a bubble of molten terror as big as a small moon!"[4]

At Yellowstone the landscape rarely sits still. In 1959 one of the strongest tremors ever recorded in the United States, releasing the combined energy of two hundred atomic bombs, shook an area of some 550,000 square miles around the park. For visitors from whatever cultural background, the experience of being in Yellowstone National Park comes as close as anywhere on earth to offering direct witness to the process of primal creation.

ECOLOGY

Just as Father Pierre-Jean De Smet contended in the mid-nineteenth century that "[t]he Yellowstone country abounds in game; I do not believe that there is in all America a region better adapted to the chase,"[5] Aubrey L. Haines would concur nearly a century and a half later that Yellowstone National Park contains "a more representative sample of the primeval fauna of the American West than is now found anywhere else."[6] Whether scientific fact or popular impression, in the American imagination Yellowstone National Park is a place in the country where one seems able to find the full Ark of the West's faunal history, supposedly living naturally in their wilderness habitat, in situ, "as it was" before any humans—Indian or white—took control. This is also the idyllic image that consciously has been promulgated in landscape paintings, photographs, and verbal portrayals of the region and its natural wonders.

As one might expect of the discourse that erupts around any key symbol, however, there are those who contest this view of the greater Yellowstone ecosystem as a natural wilderness overflowing with fauna. Despite the fact that many of the animal species one views grazing throughout the park have had their behaviors modified and have even been partly domesticated by one hundred years of vacillating game management practices, the older image of Yellowstone as the ultimate time capsule game refuge has died hard. Although in other regions of the United States we are gradually realizing the degree to which human interaction, intentional and inadvertent, has affected the ecology, transforming them into culturally constructed landscapes, in the past at least the concept has been resisted at Yellowstone because of its symbolic hold on American consciousness. Especially antagonistic to any notion of Yellowstone as some Garden of Eden has been Charles E. Kay, who has contended, "Historical records do not support the view that the Inter-mountain West once teemed with wildlife."[7] In a series of papers, Kay has argued that many animal and plant species were actually in slim supply in the Yellowstone of pre-Euro-American days. Furthermore, he suggests that "the idea that North America was a 'wilderness' untouched by the hand of man prior to 1492 is a myth created, in part, to justify appropriation of aboriginal lands and the genocide that befell native peoples."[8] And the historian William Cronon also links this illusion of virgin wilderness to the reality of Indian evictions in the West that opened up lands for national parks: "The removal of Indians to create an 'uninhabited wilderness' . . . reminds us just how invented, just how constructed, the American wilderness really is. . . . [T]here is nothing natural about the concept of wilderness. It is entirely a creation of the [non-Indian] culture that holds it dear, a product of the very history that it seems to deny."[9]

To be fair, Kay's opinions have been taken to task by scholars such as Ken Cannon, Paul Schullery, and Lee Whittlesey who criticize what they consider his misreadings and lack of proper historical analysis of procedures for examining primary sources related to observations of animal life, his reliance on minuscule sample sizes for the animal populations assessed,[10] and for his dependence on questionable sources for demographic estimates of early Native Americans in the region. Cannon takes particular issue with using mid- to late-nineteenth-century accounts for reports of earlier game numbers—even though more than 90 percent of observers "expressed belief that game was abundant"—because of the external impact on animal populations that already must have occurred by then.[11] In the entire debate over the time depth of particular interactions between humans and environments across the American West, Schullery sees a mixed blessing:

> This discussion is valuable because it has compelled land managers and public-land users to recognize the important role played by humans in the pre-Columbian landscape. But it has also been used rather like a weapon in land-management debates. What began as an important corrective in our understanding of wild landscapes has become a blanket criticism of all wild-land management. It is now apparently presumed that because Indians had many influences on many North American places, they had all those influences in all those places.[12]

CULTURE

What makes this northwestern corner of present-day Wyoming culturally complex is the fact that three out of Native America's nine broad "culture areas" converge here. Clark Wissler, the first scholar to subdivide American Indians into these native regions, initially saw the Yellowstone Park region as reflecting only the lifestyle of classic, horse-riding Plains Indian peoples.[13] But three years later Wissler refined this continental breakdown so that in addition to this Plains emphasis on the east, he had budged the northwestern Plateau culture region, which he named the Salmon Area, closer towards Yellowstone. Furthermore, Wissler also recognized the influence of the Great Basin peoples, his so-called Wild Seeds area, whose foraging grounds abutted the park on the southwest.[14]

In his 1920 mapping of North American culture areas, the renowned anthropologist Alfred C. Kroeber pushed the Plateau cultural influence even closer to the park,[15] and three years later he placed the entire southwestern half of park territory within the western, or Intermountain, domain, leaving only its northeastern corner associated with the Plains lifestyle;[16] in 1939 Kroeber more decisively identified this western influence as Great Basin.[17] In Julian Steward's classic geographic distribution of Shoshonean groups,[18] however, the park clearly marked the meeting place for all three cultural regions, with Plateau, Plains, and Great Basin peoples using this upper corner of present-day Wyoming at different times and bequeathing different legacies upon it.

Once one factors in the advent of horses, the impact of historical change in and around the park area, the introduction of extractive mining, the territorial adjustments caused by early Indian treaties, the desire of early conservationists to stake out a natural preserve that might remain exempt from further development, and continuing debates between Indians and preservationists over claims to the region's past, the region of Yellowstone National Park is clearly spotlighted as a zone of persistent cultural complexity.

HISTORY

Yellowstone is the oldest and largest "natural" preserve in the United States, carved out of the high lava plateau on March 1, 1872, to protect its 3,448 square miles from poachers and developers and to launch the spirit of natural conservation across the country. As the nation's founding park, it came to occupy almost mythic status and appeal. The historian Richard White has written:

> The [non-Indian] United States was a young nation lacking both an ancient history and a cultural tradition rich in art, architecture or literature. Americans looked to scenery as compensation for the cultural riches they lacked. . . . It became a matter of national pride that the new country set apart areas such as the Yosemite Valley of California or the Yellowstone country of Wyoming as symbols of national greatness. These "earth monuments," proponents claimed, rivaled in grandeur the monuments of Europe's antiquity.[19]

The possibility that regions such as Yellowstone and Yosemite might have already spawned ancient *native* histories, cultural traditions, or literatures was rarely considered. And if any government personnel familiar with these landscapes and their histories harbored misgivings about this erasure of prior cultural impact, they were drowned out by the strident denials and appeals to national identity that have continued to keep Yellowstone in the public eye.

This layer cake of multiple and contentious meanings has made Yellowstone National Park a patriotic symbol of the nation's paradisiacal origins, a lightning rod for the unending American debates between economic development and environmental conservation, and a mirror for self-reflection on how the nation keeps reconstituting its cultural roots and public image. Whether the national discussion is over controlling animal demography, managing human–predator encounters, monitoring mining pollution, reintroducing endangered species, containing buffalo migrations, off-road or snowmobile vehicles, or responding to the moral or legal claims of indigenous peoples, so many hot button issues related to the concept of national parks seem to find their most newsworthy storyline in the Yellowstone Plateau. To the cultural scholar, this constant multisided debate generated by Yellowstone National Park is symptomatic of the fact that from its inception the place was more than the sum of its parts. As the anthropologist Sherry Ortner has written, it is only through a nation's "public symbol system" that members of a society "discover, rediscover, and transform their own culture, generation after generation."[20]

The convergence of unusual factors listed above constitutes Yellowstone National Park as what Ortner calls a "Key Symbol," by which she means it is "'key' to the system insofar as it extensively and systematically formulates relationships—parallels, isomorphisms, complementarities, and so forth—between a wide range of diverse cultural elements."[21] This is to say that Yellowstone National Park seems to occupy a central place in American consciousness where the ongoing relationship between culture and nature is being worked out in uniquely American terms and where the nation redefines itself in the process. Inevitably this book contributes to the complexity of this process by restoring to that discourse information about a host of American Indian cultures that interacted with Yellowstone in practical and spiritual terms.

Researching American Indians in Yellowstone National Park

The different categories of data underlying any diachronic investigation into Indian relationships with Yellowstone National Park calls for an interdisciplinary perspective. This study is ethnographic in that we have reviewed the published literature, have tracked down unpublished field notes produced by scholars who conducted fieldwork among the ten major tribes with cultural or historical associations to the Yellowstone Valley ecosystem, and have sought testimony from a wide range of native consultants. It is ethnohistoric because a great deal of our knowledge of Indian activities and beliefs related to the park springs from documents generated by chroniclers with a greater interest in the historical than the cultural implications of their experiences. This leaves to latter-day ethnohistorians the task of combing through the material to discover whatever it may contain regarding Indian lifeways and worldviews. As our work dipped into the precontact period, it includes archeological data as well. The extensive knowledge of the park by at least two of the major cultural groups we discuss—the Shoshone and the Sheep Eaters—suggests linguistic and other affiliations with precontact populations who moved in and out of the region. Finally, we have employed folkloristic approaches, since vetting and interpreting the wide array of published and unpublished native accounts has required familiarity with oral narrative traditions from Indian groups that have been linked to the Yellowstone region. Let us review the history of these four areas of data in the context of cultural documentation on Yellowstone Park and its environs.

ETHNOGRAPHY

None of the American ethnographers from America's so-called Golden Age of Anthropology, which embraces roughly the 1890–1935 period, focused their research on the greater Yellowstone Plateau. Nor did any of these field-workers seize the opportunity to work with the Numic-speaking Sheep Eaters before or after they were pressured to evacuate from the new park. During Yellowstone's emergent years, when efforts to discourage Indians from trespassing over its boundaries intensified, no scholars staked out the plateau as a center for salvaging old travel routes or reconstructing Indian hunting, foraging, or other cultural practices.

However, a handful of pioneering field-workers collected ethnographic data from tribes in the wider neighborhood—the Plains, Plateau, and Great Basin culture areas. Under government sponsorship, John Wesley Powell recorded aspects of cultural life from the Great Basin cousins of the Numic-speaking Shoshone, James Mooney worked with the Kiowa on their transformation from a northern to a southern Plains people, and James Teit collected folklore and other material among various Salishan peoples of the Plateau. But the self-consciously "scientific" recording of the social worlds of the region had to await the next, second generation of field-workers who dispersed throughout the plains around the turn of the century.

Schooled by the founder-teachers of the emergent discipline of anthropology, such as Franz Boas and Livingston Farrand at Columbia University, and often closely allied with New York's Museum of Natural History, this new cadre was united under the banner of "salvage ethnography." This meant the urgent project of talking with elder Indians about the days, not so far removed, when their peoples freely observed their traditions, foraged for wild plants, hunted buffalo, and raided each other. Like any cohort, these scholars shared blind spots. While visiting the newly established reservations to seek the "memory culture" of old warriors, who were often nostalgic about their free-raiding heyday, they largely ignored women's lives, overlooked internal tensions caused by the impositions of the government's reservation regimen, disregarded the younger Indian generation as irrevocably unaware of their heritage, and frequently failed to record the geographic knowledge of their native consultants.

Their theoretical slant was the "historical particularism" championed by Boas: to reconstruct the past of peoples without archival documents, comparisons must be drawn from neighboring regions where historical association could be substantiated. And to make such comparisons, some kind of logic, no matter how clumsy, had to be devised for characterizing such "culture areas" in the first place. Two additional concepts sprang out of Wissler's concept of the culture area. The first was the proposition that each area had a "center" where the most characteristic people of that area best exhibited its diagnostic features. Although none of Wissler's contemporaries appreciated it at the time, there also appears to have been a localized, high-altitude adaptation to the microhabitat of the Yellowstone highlands that stood sufficiently apart to be singled out on its own—the Sheep Eaters. Second, this cultural hub would also be the generative center for its diagnostic traits, which, like a stone dropping into water, would ripple ever outward, from hand to hand and mind to mind. This "age-area" correlation also suggested that those traits that had the broadest diffusion were probably the region's oldest.

With all the population losses and tribal consolidations and relocations of the late nineteenth century, testing these sorts of secondary propositions in the Plains, Plateau, or Great Basin culture areas was difficult. One of Boas's students, Leslie Spier, made a noble effort in his comparative study of the Plains Indian Sun Dance. But in an environmental refuge such as Yellowstone National Park, whose only full-time native inhabitants had been resettled on the Wind River and Fort Hall Reservation communities, and whose authorities were maintaining the Park as off-limits to all Indians from neighboring reservations, such a study was not considered. So whatever contributions we draw about the Yellowstone region from these early scholars remains peripheral to their main focus and often consists of fragmentary asides in their published works and field notes.

Of these foundational field-workers, the investigations of Robert H. Lowie (1883–1957) are relevant here, for Lowie worked among the Northern Shoshones to the west and south of Yellowstone National Park, as well as among the Crows to the east. A student of both Boas and Kroeber, his efforts went into assembling data but not into advancing overarching theories. This was particularly apparent with Lowie's long-term study of Crow culture, whose southern division, the Mountain

Crow, once enjoyed considerable interaction with the Yellowstone National Park ecosystem. Lowie's work also exemplifies the scholarly goals of his era, which saw the possibilities for collecting linguistic and social data vanishing before the onslaughts of assimilation and modern life. Among other scholars of Lowie's generation working under the same general guidelines and with western tribes historically associated with Yellowstone National Park were Clark Wissler among the Blackfeet, Alfred Kroeber among the Arapaho, and Verne F. Ray in the Plateau.

The ethnographers John C. Ewers and Claude Schaeffer, who worked among the Blackfeet and Flathead, recorded few direct references to Yellowstone National Park, reflecting the lessening familiarity of these peoples with the region. In addition to Ewers's contributions to the record of long-distance travels of the Blackfeet, however, we were fortunate to obtain from the Kootenai-Salish Culture Committee the field notes of Schaeffer, who elicited from Flathead elders a geographically specific sense of their old trail system that led them southward.

The next crop of scholars, trained in subspecialities of anthropology such as religion, folklore, and linguistics, worked closer to the Yellowstone Park region and proved more sensitive to expressions of religious and social change during the reservation period. Robert F. Murphy and Yolanda Murphy studied settlement patterns of the Northern Shoshone and Bannock. Swedish anthropologist Sven Liljeblad collected linguistic, religious, and historical material among the Shoshone-Bannock of Idaho. Demitri Boris Shimkin's studies among the eastern Shoshone touched on many issues related to the park's Indian history. Starting on the Wind River Reservation in 1937, his fieldwork led to highly detailed publications devoted to the ethnopsychology, the ethnogeography, literary forms, and the Sun Dance. Joseph G. Jorgenson focused on the interreservation network responsible for the resurgence of the Sun Dance in the Shoshonean world and interpreted it as a modern "redemptive" movement—a religious expression that continues to evolve on the Wind River, Fort Hall, Crow, and other Indian reservations today. Fred W. Voget provided a tighter ethnographic focus on the Crow segment of this Sun Dance network, retracing how their modern-day rendition was borrowed in 1941 from the Wind River Shoshone and how it still flourishes.

Meanwhile, Deward E. Walker turned from "traditional" religious activities to study the factionalizing consequences of native Christianity among Idaho's Nez Perce, and Omer C. Stewart collated a lifetime's worth of data from Yellowstone Plateau–associated tribes in his capstone history of the revitalizing rituals of the pan-Indian Native American Church. But both Walker and Stewart would devote their ethnographic and ethnohistorical expertise to other park-linked tribes as well, with Stewart providing a useful unscrambling of conflicting assessments of Bannock territoriality and Walker arguing that with the horse the Shoshone-Bannock connection constituted a virtual confederation.

But the scholar whose work most directly targeted the park was neither American nor a Boasian anthropologist. In 1948 the Swedish historian of religions

Åke Hultkrantz began his field studies with the Wind River Shoshone and returned intermittently until 1958; his prodigious output, bibliographic command, and ethnohistorical inclinations make him the most prolific author on Yellowstone's Indians. At the same time, some of Hultkrantz's theoretical orientations may have inhibited fuller appreciation of the roles of Indians in the Yellowstone Basin region. Until the still-unpublished study of Joseph Weixelman, for instance, no one seriously challenged Hultkrantz's thesis that Indians considered the park's thermal field taboo. Yet Hultkrantz must be credited for recognizing that Sheep Eater descendants had not simply vanished; he salvaged many of their traditions through interviews within the Sage Creek enclave of traditional Indians on the Wind River Reservation.

ETHNOHISTORY

Without necessarily broadcasting the fact, the work of most researchers on Yellowstone National Park's Indian connections has inevitably been ethnohistorical. This often misunderstood approach implies little more than the "intent to produce a cultural and/or historical study of an ethnic group as a whole (or a study of some aspect of that culture or history) either at a particular point in time or through a period of years that may extend into centuries."[22] Historicizing an ethnicity is hardest when that group is a preindustrial, small-scale society that transmits its cultural knowledge from generation to generation primarily through oral traditions rather than by written documents and records.

Thus the ethnohistorical approach nearly always entails a sort of cultural translation. One first searches through the archives of one cultural group, which in contexts of Indian–white relations usually means the written records of the dominant society, to glimpse the pasts of other cultural groups. In addition to applying the customary scrutiny and standards that historians use to ascertain their validity, ethnohistorians must also be grounded in anthropological principles and the relevant ethnographic literature to evaluate the accuracy and social import of earlier observations, often made by amateurs, so that they can be interpreted in the light of that other culture's worldview.

Taking an ethnohistorical approach to Indians and Yellowstone National Park has called for frequent oscillation between library and field, compiling and cross-checking archival and ethnographic data, to create three-dimensional portraits of Indian societies "in time." Today this task has been raised to a higher level of complexity, as scholars realize that just because an ethnic group originates from a nonliterate tradition does not mean it lacks its own sense of history or expressive modes for transmitting historical knowledge. To accurately identify and interpret the numerous non-Western ways of doing history entails the skills of the type of researcher the anthropologist Raymond Fogelson has dubbed, only half in jest, an "ethno-ethnohistorian." By this awkward term, he means a scholar whose knowledge of the communicative traditions of particular non-Western, nonliterate societies is sufficiently deep to allow him or her to detect not only when and what that society is remembering of its collective historical experience but also and equally important *why* it chooses to remember certain things in certain ways. Tying this concern for the native point of view to Yellowstone National Park material, the anthropologist Sven Liljeblad found the way in which the Shoshone blended the cultural and historical aspects of their past "truly astounding." He provided the following example:

> There was . . . the old man who described quite accurately and in great detail the complicated manufacture of a sinew-backed bow, and who in the next minute declared that the flint arrowheads picked up by people in the vicinity were made by *nynymbi*, the dwarf who dwells in the mountains. There were those who remembered and could name all camping places along the trail— four hundred miles in length—to the buffalo-hunting grounds in Montana, but who were unable to give even an approximate date for the cessation of these expeditions, even though it occurred in his own lifetime.[23]

But it took a while for American anthropologists to interweave historical perspectives from either Euro-American or Indian points of view into their tribal profiles. As William Fenton has written regarding most of the early-twentieth-century ethnographers working on groups associated with Yellowstone National Park, "The men on [Clark] Wissler's team proceeded as if historical sources were not available to them, and treated Plains culture in flat perspective."[24] Although Lowie, one of that "team" that would produce more than two thousand printed pages on one of Yellowstone's major user tribes, the Crow, confessed that early fur trappers and Indian traders recorded data he had missed, in his own work Lowie actually ignored all but the most easily accessible archival documents and primary sources that mentioned the tribe. Lending a tremendous boost to ethnohistorical studies of Indian groups connected to Yellowstone National Park and elsewhere was the passage by the U.S. Congress, in 1946, of the Indian Claims Commission Act.

Now descriptions rendered by the Lewis and Clark expedition, for instance— which encountered the Northern Shoshone in 1805 and described their subsistence practices, dress style, and political organization—helped to produce a fuller reconstruction of aboriginal life and territoriality. The Claims Commission reports dealing with Yellowstone National Park–related groups covered the Crow, the Shoshone, and the Nez Perce. Soon academia formally recognized this wave of government-funded research by using the term *ethnohistory* more freely and, in 1952, by launching a major journal of that name.

The first generation of Yellowstone National Park scholars, Hiram M. Chittenden, Merrill D. Beal, and Aubrey L. Haines, applied the ethnohistorical method only lightly and largely dispensed with Indians in the early chapters of their books on the park. Then they turned to what more fully engaged their imaginations— the early settlement, changing ecological debates, and administrative developments in park history, with a digression for the seemingly aberrant and sensational Nez Perce intrusion of 1877. Not until the work of Hultkrantz, beginning in the late 1950s, was there an attempt to blend social, historical, and religious data on the park's Indians, and Hultkrantz featured only the Shoshoneans. Besides the noble efforts of Hultkrantz and of David Dominick, an amateur historian, to reconstruct Sheep Eater culture and history, Joel C. Janetski produced a slim handbook summarizing earlier work. Only Mark Spence, from the University of California, did fresh spadework on park-associated archives to make Yellowstone one of three case studies (Yosemite, Glacier, and Yellowstone) in a comparative work on American Indians and national parks.

ARCHAEOLOGY

The most immediate distinction of archaeological research in Yellowstone National Park is its rather early beginnings, which is attributable to the antiquarian interests of the park's second superintendent, Philetus Norris. As early as 1875 Norris was collecting Indian artifacts and describing archaeological sites in the region along the Yellowstone River in Montana between Fort Ellis and the park, and he continued this work throughout his administration.

During the latter quarter of the nineteenth century, Norris's appreciation for archaeology was shared by members of early scientific expeditions in the West. Captain William A. Jones, for example, exploring for the U.S. Army Corps of Engineers, visited Yellowstone National Park in summer 1873. In his travels across Wyoming, Jones also collected Indian artifacts and reported the significance of Indian remains. It was he who reported the favored use of the old stone scraping tools, or *teshoas*, among the Shoshone women for processing hides and the significance of Yellowstone National Park obsidian in the manufacture of artifacts.

On an 1890s expedition to the headwaters of the Jefferson River in Montana, within a few miles of Yellowstone National Park, J. W. Brower, a Minnesota surveyor who sought his fame by discovering the sources of rivers, found an archaeological site where he collected obsidian knives and spear points. In his journal, he pondered the makers of these ancient tools and contemplated that one day we would find evidence for evolving humans, perhaps the oldest in the world, on the North American continent:

The endeavors of ethnologic students . . . utterly fail to determine any correct identification of the original stocks whence the Indian nations of America came, and the best evidence comes from the Indians themselves—"Sponta-neous Man, who sprang from the bosom of the earth."

> The land of America has existed for a much greater time than 500,000 cen-turies, originally producing plant and animal life. . . . Who can truthfully assert that all nations of men sprang from one original parentage, or that the Indians of America did not proceed from the soil of the Western Hemi-sphere? If America has the oldest land, why not the oldest race of men?[25]

We have yet to find any evidence for human evolution in the Western Hemi-sphere before modern *Homo sapiens*. But Brower's reflections remind us how strongly these early scientists were influenced by the evolutionary theories of E. B. Tylor and L. H. Morgan, in which all human cultures were thought to pro-gress through the same stages, from Savagery to Barbarism to Civilization, with common features of material culture such as tools and house types associated with each stage. In his orders to the construction crews who were building Yellow-stone's first roadways, Superintendent Norris alludes to his awareness of such distinctions between "civilized" and earlier peoples:

> As all civilized nations are now actively pushing explorations and researches for evidences of prehistoric peoples, careful scrutiny is required of all material handled in excavations and all arrow, spear, or lance heads, stone axes, and knives, or other weapons, utensils or ornaments; in short, all such objects of interest are to be regularly retained and turned over daily to the officer in charge of each party for transmittal to the National Museum in Washington.[26]

This official alert to his staff brought Norris numerous artifacts, which he care-fully packed and shipped to the Smithsonian Institution. Among them were hundreds of projectile points and other stone-cutting and scraping tools, partial and complete steatite pots, an atlatl weight, and a stone plummet. In the Fifth Annual Report of his tenure as superintendent, Norris described some of these artifacts together with pen-and-ink illustrations.

In a visit to the Smithsonian Institution in August 1996, we found the artifacts sent by Norris, as well as many more. Using the information on the artifact donor cards, it is possible to gain some information regarding the origin of the artifacts. For example, Arnold Hague unearthed a steatite pot and other chipped-stone arti-facts during his geologic research in the mountains along the eastern border of the park and delivered them to the Smithsonian for safekeeping. When W. Hallett Philips studied park administration at Yellowstone in 1885, he must have devoted time to hunting for Indian artifacts, because several dozen stone tools at the Smithsonian list him as donor. In 1908 S. V. Proudfit, an assistant commissioner for the U.S. Land Department who was in Yellowstone surveying boundaries, added more than one hundred artifacts to the Smithsonian collections, many from materials gathered by Edward Fish, an assistant superintendent at the park.

The first half of the twentieth century witnessed the periodic site report from Yellowstone by a trained archaeologist and at least one published account. In 1935 park officials almost teasingly allowed, "We now have evidence in the form of arrow heads, scrapers and other artifacts from almost every part of Yellowstone National Park, indicating that Indians have been at various times in all parts of the Park."[27] But it was not until 1958 that Carling Malouf of the University of Montana directed the first funded research in Yellowstone. Malouf's field-workers located and evaluated well-known sites such as the Lava Creek wickiups and locations subject to high visitor use such as the Fishing Bridge area. At Malouf's request Dee Taylor of the University of Montana took over the direction of the survey in 1959; two years later his field supervisor, Jacob Hoffman, compiled their findings for a master's thesis. More than ninety years after the park was founded, Taylor and Hoffman's two-year survey, published in 1964, became the first professional study on the prehistory of Yellowstone National Park.

Taylor followed a cultural-historical paradigm that described and placed the recovered artifacts in a temporal and spatial framework. Although his crews did not visit a number of sites, 78 of the 195 sites reported on had previously been identified by Wayne Replogle during his reconstruction of the Bannock Trail System. An additional 53 sites were partially recorded by park naturalists, and their surface collections were placed in the Mammoth Visitor Center museum. All in all, 180 of the sites (92%) were surface scatters of chipped-stone detritus with no other defining characteristics, 7 (4%) exhibited tipi rings on their surface, 4 (2%) were areas where chipped stone had been quarried, 2 (1%) were wickiup sites, and the remainder consisted of a single game drive site and a site with ceramics and chipped-stone debris on the surface. Their age ranged from the late Paleo-Indian Period, dating to some 8,000 to 9,000 years before the present, to the still-standing wickiup structures that were almost certainly constructed during the Historic Period. Paul Schullery recently showed how easily such sites could be overlooked:

> A few years ago I was scanning the hills above a meadow near Mammoth Hot Springs. I was looking for grizzly bears, but along a low slope on one side of a small drainage that emptied out into the meadow, two parallel rows of boulders caught my eye. Ranging in size from one to several feet across, the boulders ran downhill in lines so straight and perfect that there could be no doubt they were put there by humans. They had clearly been there a very long time, but nobody, not even the archeologists and historians I later asked, had noticed them. I took an archeologist to see them, just to confirm my suspicion, but the purpose of the boulder lines was pretty obvious to me. Crouching behind them, a hunter would have been well concealed from elk, deer, or bison as they descended through the narrow draw and out onto the meadow on their way to the nearest standing water.

I started spending time in that meadow in 1972, and I glassed those slopes countless times looking for bears, but it took me eighteen years to notice those rocks.[28]

The early 1960s opened a new era in Yellowstone National Park studies when Aubrey Haines was assigned to prepare base maps on archaeology and history for the park's master plan. Frustrated because the University of Montana study was still unreleased, Haines launched his own research program. For the initial phase, he planned to visit artifact collectors and, for the important artifacts, take notes, photographs, and measurements; for the next phase, he envisioned a survey of park areas that had been overlooked by the University of Montana crews.

Haines began by documenting artifacts that were turned up by hunters, guides, and seasonal employees in remote or high-altitude regions outside the northern boundary of the park. A significant number fell into well-known "types" that archaeologists associated with Paleo-Indian societies dating back seven thousand to nine thousand years, when the mountains still retained remnant glaciers. Other stone tools were dated to the altithermal, a hot, dry climatic period that followed the last major glaciers. Aside from the fact that archaeologists were surprised that there were any artifacts at all in the mountains above the timberline, two hypotheses that are still debated today were derived from these findings. One was the idea that high mountain peaks were relatively free of glaciers and might have served as travel routes for Paleo-Indians; the other was the possibility that the hot and dry climate of postglacial times served to create a sanctuary or a retreat in the cooler, moist, mountain region.

Soon after Haines's work, two University of Montana graduate students completed archaeological projects relevant to the park. George Arthur conducted an archaeological survey on the upper Yellowstone River and recorded sites in the vicinity of Gardiner, Montana, that Haines had earmarked as potentially significant. Lewis Napton finished a complementary survey that included the upper reaches of the Gallatin River, excavating in the process a wickiup site on the park's western border. Both surveys yielded similar site types within the same time range as those reported from inside the park and helped to substantiate a 9,000- to 10,000-year record of human use in the southern Montana mountains.

Meanwhile, Larry Lahren, a graduate student at the University of Calgary, Alberta, took a fresh look at the well-stratified Myers-Hindman site near Livingston, Montana. His excavations turned up evidence for more than 9,000 years of intermittent use and produced a chronological profile against which to compare other sites on the upper Yellowstone. Yet it was in the Shoshone River canyon, a few miles east of Yellowstone National Park, that Wilfred Husted of the Smithsonian Institution River Basin Surveys was excavating the most significant archaeological site to be found in the area. The site, named Mummy Cave for the presence of a mummified human burial in an upper cultural layer, contained extremely good stratigraphy, with thirty-six separate cultural levels ranging in age from 9,500 years ago to the Historic Period (post A.D. 1800). In addition to the large numbers of projectile points that provided chronological markers, the cave deposits had ample amounts of charcoal for radiocarbon dating. For the first time, the surface artifacts collected by Haines and many others in the Yellowstone National Park region could be assigned ages with confidence.

George Frison of the University of Wyoming played a major role in identifying high-altitude Indian sites. Among his Yellowstone-linked discoveries was an open-air camp about 25 miles east of the park known as the Dead Indian Creek site. In the Sunlight Basin, an intermontane region about 6,500 feet in elevation surrounded by the Absaroka Range, lay a half-dozen mule deer skulls with the antlers still attached that seemed arranged for a ceremonial activity. Frison now believes that one depression on the site represented a pit house, similar to others that have been turned up over past decades in nearby Wyoming basins. Radiocarbon dated at between 4,200 and 4,500 years ago, the Dead Indian Creek site also yielded McKean-type projectile points that are consistent with this time frame. And based on tooth eruption patterns in their mandibles, most of these mule deer were hunted between October and March, which indicates occupation of the high-elevation site during the winter. Considering all this evidence, the Dead Indian Creek site evokes a group of McKean-period hunters who lived in these mountains more than four thousand years ago. They ate mule deer, elk, and bighorn sheep, processed collected seeds, possibly making flour to thicken soup or to bake a mealy, unleavened bread, and survived at elevations where winter temperatures can drop to life-threatening lows.

Throughout this period, nonacademic archaeologists also conducted serious research in Yellowstone National Park and adjacent regions. Instead of making surface collections and test excavations, their projects were directed toward locating new sites, making sketch maps, and producing a photographic record. Stuart Conner and Kenneth Feyhl of Billings were leaders in these endeavors. Among the sites they recorded along the Bannock Trail was a rectangular outline of stones, possibly used to weigh down the hem of a wall-tent rather than a circular tipi, which led to speculation that it sheltered the Bannock during their final escape through the park in 1878. In addition, Conner documented the year-by-year deterioration of standing timber lodges in the park. He recorded the personal artifact collection of Vern Waples, a game warden who collected hundreds of projectile points and their precise locations in the Beartooth Mountains to the northeast.[29]

In 1966 the face of archaeology in the United States changed dramatically. After passage of the National Historic Preservation Act that year, federal land managers were required to evaluate archaeological and historical sites that might be eligible for the National Register of Historic Places. The Midwest Archeological Center (an archaeological support unit for national parks located in the western states) carried out the mandated research at Yellowstone. Foremost in these efforts were projects directed by Gary Wright and his colleagues. From 1985 to 1995 archaeological studies in Yellowstone National Park concerned sites in the path of proposed construction projects, but after the 1988 forest fires, previously known sites were revisited to assess the fire-caused damage.

A fuller understanding of the Obsidian Cliff site, perhaps the park's best-known archaeological resource, was always a goal for Yellowstone National Park planners. For more than thirty-five years, Leslie Davis of Bozeman studied the area's obsidian quarries, for their potential in dating as well as source analysis, and drafted the cliff's most current evaluative summary.[30] At the same time, Kenneth Cannon worked to identify the numerous sources of obsidian in the Yellowstone region and conducted blood residue studies in order to identify the species of animal blood associated with obsidian blades and points found there.[31]

Though archaeology in Yellowstone was never pursued with the same vigor as studies on animals or plants, the search for evidence of human habitation is nearly as old as the park itself. When funding finally opened up in the past two decades, the research was confined mostly to construction project zones. The most significant archaeological projects, completed outside the tourist areas, have been conducted by avocational archaeologists. It is estimated that approximately 20,000 acres of the 1.5 million acres of Yellowstone National Park have been surface surveyed for archaeological evidence of human activity. Despite this growing interest, in 1982 Gary A. Wright estimated that the park remained "one of the poorest known archaeological areas of North America." He went on to say, "Only 20% of the Park has been surveyed, and there is no adequate synthesis of the archaeological data. . . . The Park's potential is, however, enormous for archaeological research."[32] More than one thousand sites have been recorded, but fewer than sixty have been evaluated through test excavation. Two years after the first full-time National Park Service archaeologist, Anne M. Johnson, was hired in 1995, she reduced Wright's estimate to about 1 percent and admitted, "Our inventories really haven't gotten away from the pavement."[33] It would be hard to find a more promising example of the archaeological record which may still lie "away from the pavement" than Dr. Johnson's own work in 2000 and 2002 at Osprey Beach in the heart of the park. The projectile points, stone flakes, and charcoal which emerged from this eroding river terrace on the shores of Yellowstone Lake dated the site at roughly 10,000 years ago. These excavations revealed Osprey Beach as representative of the so-called Cody Complex, which had been first defined in 1951 at the Horner site near Cody, Wyoming. They provided valuable information on the various sources of stone used for projectile points and tool-making and comparative material for other old sites in the lake's vicinity. And they supported the hypothesis, in the words of park archaeologist Mack W. Shortt,

> that Cody Complex peoples were seasonally adapted not only to the plains
> and intermountain basins as bison hunters, but also to upland/mountain

environs, where a variety of mammalian species were available. The diverse blood residue data indicate that the mountain/plains cultural dichotomy, if it ever existed, was in fact breaking down by the time of the Osprey Beach occupation. . . . It appears, therefore, that early Precontact Period Native Americans at Osprey Beach were versatile hunter-gatherers who sustained themselves in many ways under the various natural resource circumstances they encountered.[34]

FOLKLORE

Of all bodies of cultural data that might reveal or indirectly reflect American Indian connections to the greater Yellowstone River world, oral narratives are the hardest to find and authenticate. The apparent dearth of such material persuaded Lee Whittlesey to maintain, "Other than for this story [the Northern Shoshone narrative "The Old Woman and the Basket of Fish," described in chapter 4], there is little reliable information or documentation on stories, myths or other folklore that may have been told by Indians about present Yellowstone National Park."[35]

One hears various explanations for the paucity of Indian narratives related to Yellowstone Park. Some claim the material is out there but researchers have not been particularly energetic at seeking it out, either from archives or through winning the trust of American Indian communities where it might be elicited. Then again, the environmental settings of many traditional narrative genres, such as the "folktale," are rarely specific enough to pinpoint a locale. Finally, the 125 years of forced separation of Indians from the park's habitat may have lessened the relevance and reinforcement necessary to keep such stories and traditions viable.

An obstacle to assessing the meager amount of American Indian folklore purportedly connected to Yellowstone National Park is distinguishing authentic folklore from what the scholar Richard M. Dorson has labeled "fakelore." By this term, Dorson meant stories or anecdotes that turn up in trade compilations that have been so heavily edited or rewritten, or invented out of whole cloth, as to become "pseudo-fairy tales of dubious value for the serious student." Dorson offered the following advice:

> A couple of minutes handling the book of collected folklore can suffice to inform probing folklorists as to the general character of the goods they hold. Does the collection contain items of folklore as they were actually told, word for word, or are the tales or materials paraphrased? Are the tellers, singers, and carriers of the folklore—the informants—identified, and not just by names with some personal details? And a crucial point, do comparative notes accompany the folklore texts, either as an introductory headnote (preferably) or in an appendix? Are other essential elements of the scholarly apparatus present: tables of motifs and tale types; a classified bibliography, hopefully with descriptive critical comments; a full subject index with a breakdown of key entries; an informative introduction describing fieldwork methods? A few moments

of thumbing through the pages will provide answers to these queries, and the folklorist can judge whether the book is a bona fide work worth serious attention, or one to be used cautiously, or to be disregarded.[36]

The full range of Dorson's three types—bona fide, use cautiously, disregard entirely—turned up during our research. A closer look at the inner constitution of Indian narratives can help us to separate what we might call "authentic fictions" from inauthentic facts. While oral narratives may represent one of the most responsive of all cultural forms to changing historical conditions, different types, such as myth, folktale, and legend, display adaptability or conservativeness in different ways.

"Myths" have been defined by folklorist William Bascom as "prose narratives which, in the society in which they are told, are considered to be truthful accounts of what happened in the remote past."[37] The only clues that we have concerning the authenticity of such narratives possibly linked to Yellowstone National Park, for instance, are (a) the degree to which they are prefaced or concluded with attributions to a sequence of their narrators or to a tribal inheritance that may have been transferred ritualistically from one storyteller to another within a particular family or social connection, and (b) the degree to which we find other credible narratives that either corroborate plot elements (e.g., characters, actions, place-names, or geographic features) or narrative themes.

It was the satisfaction of these admittedly loose criteria that made us include, for example, the Kiowa "Heart of the World" narrative and Crow stories about the origins of Mud Volcano and Dragon Mouth. These renditions of the origins of certain thermal features struck us as sufficiently consonant with contextual data on these tribes' own view of history and mythic events. On the other hand, the myth of world origins, presented as told by "[t]he present-day Indian inhabitants of the Yellowstone and Big Horn valleys, whose ancestors hunted bear, buffalo and elk in the Devil's Land now known as Yellowstone Park," which we discovered in Louis Freeman's *Down the Yellowstone* (1922), seemed at variance with any known Indian belief system or folklore from tribes in the region, and was almost certainly invented by the author. It pits a spirit named Nog, the god of fire, against Lob, the god of rains and snows, in a contest over who will control this "most desirable section of Creation." In his divine wisdom the Great Spirit divides up its tenure into alternating, six-moon intervals controlled by each of them. For millennia, the story goes, their back-and-forth fight has continued, creating in the process beautiful seasons year-round.[38] Clearly Freeman's faux narrative of ultimate origins falls under the genre of "myth," if a preposterous and non-Indian one. What presents us with a problem, however, is that much of the Yellowstone folklore does not neatly fit into Bascom's general categories. The Plateau narratives that present Coyote's earth-creating deeds in the greater Yellowstone region, for instance, seem to fit his definitions of the "folktale" as well as myth.

Holding off discussion of that second narrative form for the moment, Bascom's third category, "legend," clearly displays a more overt flexibility to historical change. According to Bascom, "Legends are prose narratives which, like myths, are regarded as true by the narrator and his audience, but which are set in a period considered less remote, when the world was much as it is today."[39] Yet again, if any park-linked "legendary" narratives are assumed to have come from any Indian's mouth, there should be some kind of corroborative or contextual evidence. In the absence of internal evidence that they possess some formal characteristics of native story-telling practices, and with the lack of external verification, it is difficult to be sure that they ever issued from an Indian's mouth. This consideration is crucial for Indian narratives connected to Yellowstone National Park, because even if they were not originally Indian spoken, there may be a hidden agenda behind the storyline that can lend valuable insights into non-Indian attitudes at the time.

For instance, an early Indian "legend" relating to Yellowstone National Park is found in what is probably the park's first guidebook, Harry J. Norton's *Won-der-Land Illustrated; or, Horseback Rides through the Yellowstone National Park* (1873). On page 31 we find this reassurance to Yellowstone Park visitors: "Dangers from Indians there is none."[40] Norton substantiates this claim by bringing up the pervasive Indian belief that the thermal field is where "Manitou displays his anger towards his red children." But then Norton serves up another piece of Indian lore:

> There is another tradition current among the Sioux and Crows to this effect: Some years ago, the Sioux and Crows, then friendly to each other, were en route to the Upper Yellowstone and Madison Rivers, on a hunting expedition, and while encamped in the second cañon of the Yellowstone, nearly opposite Emigrant Peak, they were hemmed in at both entrances by the Nez Perces, Bannocks, and Flatheads (then, as now, at war with the Sioux and the Crows), and the whole party massacred. For this reason these tribes never ascend the river above the cañon named for fear of meeting a similar fate.[41]

Aside from the fact that we can find no corroboration in Indian narratives or physical evidence for this battle, or any record of these blood enemies, the Sioux and Crow, ever joining forces on a hunt, there is ethnographic evidence of continuous Crow knowledge of the park, as well as the presence of long-used archaeological sites in the Yellowstone Canyon and Emigrant Peak region. One suspects that this so-called legend is a complete fabrication or was plucked from another ethnographic context and distorted to support the reassuring non-Indian profile that Yellowstone National Park sought to present to potential clientele.

A second example of a highly suspicious legendary Indian narrative connected to Yellowstone National Park is entitled "A Yellowstone Tragedy." Published in 1896 by the anthologist Charles M. Skinner with no attribution, it appears to be recycled from a specious article headlined "A Thrilling Event on the Yellowstone," written by Charles Sunderlee for the *Helena Herald* and published on May 18, 1870. Later this story was picked up uncritically by the otherwise able folklorist Ella E. Clark, under the title "Defiance at Yellowstone Falls," for one of her popular anthologies of Indian narratives.[42]

The Skinner rendition, accompanied by an early photograph of Yellowstone Falls, opens with the statement that while "the Indians" feared the "hissing and thundering" spirits of the geyser basin, they regarded the mountains at the head of the river as "the crest of the world" from which they could see the landscape where their deceased still lived on in happiness. It takes a bit of time before we learn the tribal identity of these natives, but eventually we are told that "[t]hey loved this land in which their fathers had hunted[,] . . . and when they were driven back from the settlements the Crows took refuge in what is now Yellowstone Park." But with white soldiers in hot pursuit, "intent on avenging acts the red men had committed while suffering under the sting of tyranny and wrong," only a fugitive remnant of the Crow manage to gather at the end of Yellowstone's Grand Canyon. Just below the upper falls, they hastily build a raft, and in a final suicide run, they plunge down the canyon. The solders suspend fire and watch "with something like dread" as the Indian "death-chant" is drowned out by the roar of the waters.

Apart from the fact that the Crow were well-known for their friendship with whites, there is no supporting evidence for this collective withdrawal by any portion of the tribe into the Yellowstone, or any tribal prototypes for mass suicide, although one does hear of individual warriors engaging in displays of courageous self-annihilation. One must conclude that the story is either another invention or a misappropriation of another tribal narrative set in the park. It is tempting, of course, to consign the story to the dustbin as, in Haines's words, "a gross falsification presented in the romantic manner best termed a Hiawatha treatment."[43]

Despite its questionable origins, however, the narrative is valuable as a reflection of some segment of non-Indian attitudes or wishful fantasies about Indians and Yellowstone National Park at the end of the nineteenth century. It vividly dramatizes one version of the Vanishing Indian theme (see the conclusion) and hence deserves consideration as part of the full cultural history of the park, although without further comparative or contextual data it is useless as documentation of Indian historical connections to the region.

A third, seemingly spurious, Yellowstone National Park "legend" follows the prescription for the geographic fakelore that W. E. Webb characterized, somewhat tongue-in-cheek, over a century ago:

As no remarkable spot in Indian land should ever be brought before the public without an accompanying legend, I shall present one. . . . To make tourists fully appreciate a high bluff or picturesquely dangerous spot, it is absolutely essential that some fond lovers should have jumped down it, hand-in-hand, in sight of the cruel parents, who struggle up the incline, only to be rewarded by the heart-rending *finale*.[44]

The narrative in question, titled "Over the Waterfall," is buried in an early botanical guidebook of the west. It concerns a Bannock Indian named Arropine, who supposedly became Jim Bridger's scout into the Yellowstone. The coauthor of the guidebook, who was charged with supplying Indian narratives, Elizabeth Cannon Porter, asks that we take seriously a romance between Arropine, a captive of the Blackfeet, and Blue Feather, a beautiful Blackfeet maiden. (An equally questionable Indian romance situated in the park is found in William A. Allen's discredited book on the Sheep Eaters.)[45] But Arropine has a rival, the crafty and cunning Blackfeet warrior, Rain-in-the-Face. As the lovers plan to slip away, Arropine says to Blue Feather: "Beyond this lake lies a lake where fire and boiling water burst from the earth. Your people and mine believe that it is haunted by evil spirits so they never go there, but a miserable tribe called the Sheep Eaters hide there because they will not fight and they are less afraid of the spirits than they are of our warriors."[46] The lovers find fish and cook them in the boiling hot springs. They see the geysers spout, and Blue Feather is terrified by them. They watch the rose-colored steam above the lakes and notice the plentiful game. But Blue Feather drinks from a purplish spring and grows sick. They are intercepted by her people, but, unlike the self-destruction motif in the previous example of fakelore, when they must face the test of canoeing over the falls they manage to survive. The story ends: "After resting a little, the two were permitted to take their departure for the Bannocks in the North. Arropine knew all about the Yellowstone, and later acted as a guide for Jim Bridger, when the white trapper went to explore the wonders of geyserland."[47]

Little about this narrative rings true. And contemporary Indians might not take much consolation from the fact that apart from recycling the stereotype about native fear of the geysers, it does not close with symbolic fatalism and death reminiscent of the Vanishing Indian theme mentioned above. For it evokes another demeaning stereotypical role for Indian men that is found in frontier literature, that of the Uncas or the Tonto, the loyal Indian scout who blithely guides the white man to America's natural wonders—in this case the Yellowstone National Park region, which the story informs us they had no use for anyway—for the white newcomers to do with as they may.

A fourth equally problematic legend relating Indians to the greater Yellowstone region and its mountain-dwelling Shoshoneans originates from reminiscences by the popular Idaho historian Charles S. Walgamott, who claimed to have heard it from a Bannock woman named "Indian Mary" whom he met in 1875 at Rock Creek in southern Idaho. Again we have the romantic central plot of an Indian love affair, this one between a lovely Bannock known as "The Beautiful One" and her suitor, the great hunter named Plenty Meat. After her father gives her in marriage to another, her true love mourns in a sacred cave in Snake River Canyon. When the new bride rebuffs her unwelcome husband, she runs away to her first and only love. But the furious mate takes revenge by using magic to age her into an old crone. From their hideaway cave, the lovers relish the beauties of the Sawtooth Mountains, then visit Shoshone Falls, and finally enter a canyon-like "Lover's Lane" where her beauty is restored. They encounter enemy Blackfeet, who pursue them only to come upon a miniature encampment featuring small arrowheads made of black, red, and white obsidian. As the Blackfeet approach a "land that was on fire and so greatly feared by the Indians,"[48] they are so in awe that they leave the couple alone. The two are commanded by the Great Spirit to climb a peak near the Big Wood River until they find a "lake where the fish are red," and there they will establish "a tribe to be known as the Indians of the Clouds."

They live in happy isolation for a long while, until Indians with ponies and rifles enter their world. These are bad Indians, we are told, who fall under the benign influence of these Cloud Indians, who continue to survive on Tukuarikus, or mountain sheep. The Great Spirit shows them where to dig out lead to make their own bullets and where to mine silver for crafting into ornaments. But then "the Beautiful One" has an ominous vision of the coming of the "Pale-Face" and the "Iron Horse." Finally, one of their group, Bloody Hand, reverts to type and kills a white prospector for his horse and belongings. With the demise of the Beautiful One, the hateful Bloody Hand takes charge and the story ends.

The story's conclusion informs us that these people are the Sheep Eaters, presumably of the dangerous Idaho strain who in four years will assault whites. In effect, non-Indian readers now have a prophetic, native explanation for the strong ambivalence they feel about Indians' representations in general, whether as noble red men or as bloodthirsty savages. Although surely a projective fantasy, this specimen has been accepted uncritically as a valid legend of the Northwest.[49]

Once again, this narrative may be useless for examination as a plausible reflection of Indian thought, but it is priceless for its insights into the Euro-American psychology as it pertains to Indians. Some of its implications are patently clear: good Indians stay by themselves and stare at beautiful sunsets; bad Indians adopt white ways and want more of them. The good Indian is too pure to survive the modern world and obligingly becomes extinct in an age in which history has replaced myth. But the bad Indian hangs around to compete with whites and bedevil history.

Some of the publications that purportedly tie together American Indian traditions and Yellowstone National Park also exemplify the fusion of the categories of myth, legend, and folktale. But most of them fail Dorson's prima facie conditions for separating folklore from fakelore. Either they are outright fabrications, or they lack attribution and represent Indian narratives that were so rewritten that their cultural information and valid emotional associations are irrevocably distorted and their links to native sources impossible to reconstruct. It is ironic that the sole mention of Indians in a day-by-day Yellowstone National Park tour script in the mid-1920s drew on such questionable lore. Yet even this tall tale evoked a negative link between Indians and the park, for as the tour moved through the Upper Geyser Basin, the script had the guide summarize some yarns told by the old scout Jim Bridger: "Another one accredited to Bridger is this: A portion of the park was cursed by an Indian chieftain so that everything was petrified, not only the trees and flowers, but also the birds and waterfalls. Even the sunshine was petrified."[50] Other examples of park-related fakelore are to be found in Mary Earle Hardy's collection, *Little Ta-Wish-Indian Legends from Geyserland,* and LaVerne Fitzgerald's *Black Feather: Trapper Jim's Fables of Sheepeater Indians in Yellowstone,* which borrowed heavily from Allen's discredited book. Equally dismissible for bearing any legitimate connection to the history of Indians in the park are such examples of popular culture as the song about the Bannock chief, Pocatello, in Dr. and Mrs. N. W. Christiansen's 1953 publication, *A Trip through Yellowstone Park: Interesting Events Portrayed in Music,* whose lyrics are too insultingly stereotypical to bear repeating.[51]

As for the second narrative genre that we have skipped over, the folktale, Bascom defines them as "prose narratives which are regarded as fiction,"[52] and they may be more responsive than myths to changing historical circumstances. While specificity of place is rarely a strong element in Indian folktales, their everyday function in person-to-person oral exchanges often means that in times of conflict they can carry secret messages or subtexts that indirectly comment on historical change, provide psychological reassurance to Indian listeners, and underscore old Indian values. A good example from Yellowstone National Park–associated Indian tribes is a tale which Lowie collected from the Lemhi Shoshone at Fort Hall in 1909. Lowie complained that when he asked about native lore concerning the visit of Lewis and Clark—after they had secured the invaluable services of their legendary Shoshone guide, Sacajawea, in North Dakota—he was told instead about a contest between Wolf (or Coyote) and Iron Man, known as the "father of the Whites."[53] As he would write later, the experience led him to dismiss the truth-value of Indian notions of history.[54] But a deeper reading of this story shows the classic protagonist of most native folktale genres, the trickster Coyote, defending his Indian peoples against the not-so-overpowering white man.

Although in most of his multiple personalities Coyote functions as a destabilizer of authority and an uncontrollably and hilariously antisocial being, in the folktales of the California, Great Basin, and Plateau culture areas, he is often traditionally manifested in what the linguist William Bright characterizes as his "bricoleur" role.[55] Here Bright refers to Coyote's function as transformer of the world. He defeats a primordial race of monsters and renders the earth safe for human occupancy while creating, through his beneficial deeds, the topographic features of the landscape as we know it today. In this persona, Coyote becomes a culture hero, operating at a time when the topography was still in flux. Perhaps more than any other location in North America, Yellowstone National Park exemplifies this condition of thermal creativity, a fact that Indians, like any peoples who confront the place, would have viewed in accordance with their own conceptual categories.

But how are we to explain the relative absence of folktales in Shoshone Coyote narratives that refer to the park's stupendous natural phenomena? One answer may be that the still-volatile landscape that the park exhibits is testament to the fact that in this unique spot at least, Coyote's task of earth transformation is not yet finished or ready for tidy framing in a narrative memorial. Within the primordial turbulence of Yellowstone National Park, Coyote still has his work cut out for him.

Conditions and Constraints of This Study

Any overview of the ethnographic resources of Yellowstone National Park is bound to be an uphill struggle. First among the obstacles is the aforementioned issue of an inadequate archaeological database on which to build ethnographic data. Our only reference has been scattered reports and professional papers related to the precontact cultures in or immediately around the park.

The second obstacle is the fact that after the late 1870s, federal policy in general sought to abrogate American Indian interests in the greater Yellowstone region (as elsewhere in the west). Although Thomas Jefferson warned in 1812 that any Indians who refused to assimilate or abandon their lands "would relapse into barbarism and misery," whereupon the Euro-Americans would "be obliged to drive them with the beasts of the forests into the stony [Rocky] mountains,"[56] little more than a half century later Indians were about to lose even that mountain retreat. For as far as any traditional hunting, foraging, trading, raiding, or other cultural activities were concerned, by the early 1880s Indians were effectively banned from entry into Yellowstone National Park.

Recovering American Indian memories on Yellowstone proves a difficult, time-consuming, and sketchy process, requiring patience and archival skills as well as the ability to overcome the long-standing stereotypes and resentments of both Euro-Americans and American Indians. As if summarizing pervasive attitudes toward Indians while expressing the degree to which military policy toward them was common knowledge, a stage driver told Eliza and Annie Upham on their ride back from Mud Cauldron in Yellowstone National Park on September 16, 1892, that the local natives were "no more to be trusted than a rattlesnake" and that they were "dirty and lazy." Then he added in no uncertain terms, "Indians are not allowed in the Park."[57]

For tribe after tribe, this suppression of traditional ties to old Yellowstone hunting and traveling grounds precipitated a century of broken connections. Rendering the Yellowstone National Park off-limits to Indians during that time meant that any related Indian traditions of practical use, narrative folklore, or historical memories went unrenewed. Without access to geographic reference points in and around the park by which to anchor and remember them, the stories of mythic origins or legendary events of the Crow, Blackfeet, Flathead, Bannock, Shoshone, and quite likely other Plains Indian groups, as well as detailed accounts of plant foraging, game hunting, medicine acquisition, spiritual activities, or war, were thinned out with disuse or forgotten entirely.

With traditional links between Indians and the park effectively severed so early, the database derived from early anthropologists has also proven meager, the opportunity to recover contemporary ethnographic information is rare, and our reconstruction has often been left to chasing shadows. It must also be stated that this historical rupture between Indians and the park left a legacy of bad feelings. This has clouded our efforts to develop the bonds of mutual trust and collaborative interest that are crucial for effective ethnographic fieldwork.

In the informational vacuum created by these years of Indian absence from Yellowstone, a fourth problem for researchers has been the amount of misguided conjecture and negative stereotyping that has filled the void. From the point of view of scholarship, this situation is not unlike that which the anthropologist Verne F. Ray described for his reconsideration of the cultural importance of northwestern Plateau Indians. By the late 1930s Ray had collected a decade's worth of field and library data so as to challenge the prevailing opinion, largely established by Herbert Joseph Spinden, which held that this culture area of the Columbia Plateau was only a transitional, impoverished patchwork of watered-down and borrowed traits from more influential, neighboring regions. To argue that "Plateau culture could hardly be more grossly misinterpreted,"[58] Ray finally compiled his landmark monograph to demonstrate how quite the reverse was true—but it took a while.

Our overview of the "ethnographic resources" of Yellowstone National Park has developed much the same agenda. Because of misinterpretations about hunting and foraging "Digger" Indian groups that in no small measure were borrowed from derogatory characterizations of native California and Nevada Shoshoneans and applied to the park's original inhabitants, then exacerbated by misinterpretations of ethnohistorical data regarding the attitudes of the park's surrounding native groups toward its unique natural features, the story of the Indians' Yellowstone has remained largely misguided or untold. Any survey of the park's ethnographic resources must therefore wrestle with the following pieces of received wisdom:

1. The park was never more than thinly populated by Indians who had only marginal interest in its resources.
2. The only full-time residents of the park were isolated bands of Sheep Eaters who were timid, impoverished, and culturally underdeveloped.
3. The horse-riding Plains Indians who lived around the park shied away from its thermal areas because they were afraid of the geysers.

4. Once the park was formally established and the Indian wars ceased in the late 1870s, Indians had no further interest in the park.

To their credit, the park and its historians have over the years periodically questioned these propositions and shifted position on them. Too often, however, Indians were simply dropped out of the park equation altogether, summarily ignored, excised from park annals, or briefly profiled in opening chapters before park histories whisked ahead to the more "serious" administrative or environmental sides of the Yellowstone story. This subtler suppression of possible roles and ongoing interests of Indians in the park is a sanitized, modern counterpart to the earlier denial of their physical presence by official coercion.

When governmental recognition of Indians first peaked in the twentieth century, during John Collier's "Indian New Deal" in the late 1930s, ethnographers were assigned to include Indians in their written summaries of the histories of national parks such as that of Glacier National Park.[59] Not once, however, did the official guidebook to Yellowstone National Park mention Indians in its text; it even omitted them when directing visitors to the tourist attraction of Obsidian Cliff. Only its chronological timeline cited General O. O. Howard's pursuit of a lone Nez Perce Indian, Chief Joseph, and the sole book on Indians that was available in the park's bookstore was Laverne Fitzgerald's bogus *Trapper Jim's Fables of Sheepeater Indians in Yellowstone.*

Although it is unfair to apply today's standards for fair representation to yesteryear, what is one to make of a recent semi-popular overview of the park by a cultural geographer? The work purports to reveal "Yellowstone's history as place, as a shared geographic and cultural reality, and its powerful and persistent spirit of place" but devotes only *a single sentence* to the role of Indians.[60] Unable to ignore Joseph Wiexelman's 1992 research that countered the stereotype that Indians were unanimously afraid of the geysers, the sentence reads: "Recent scholarship indicates that Native Americans were the first to recognize the spirit of place unique to the Yellowstone region centuries before whites entered the surrounding areas."[61] Sidestepping the fact that the finding of an Agate Basin point that was traced to Yellowstone National Park and dated to about ten thousand years ago should change "centuries" to "millennia,"[62] the book's dismissal of Indians from further "cultural evolution" of the park is indicative of public and even scholarly opinion. Until recently, this received wisdom has hardly been enlightened by the books, signage, lectures, museum exhibits, or multimedia presentations that were available to the general public in or around the park.

Correcting the Record: New Approaches

A responsible review of Indian–Park relationships requires more than a listing of traits or even a synthesis of hard evidence. It must also take seriously any "representations" of Indians, so as to reveal the stereotypes that, by substituting for that evidence, have affected attitudes and policies relating to the park. It must not ignore circumstantial data and should critically cross-reference data from a host of Indian tribes; reframe them according to the prevailing theories, practices, and presumptions of its times; and reveal how they reflect paradigm shifts in the evolving disciplines of social science and history. This multidimensional and self-reflexive way of contextualizing ethnographic facts also means that any "ethnographic overview" must revisit the historical contexts and possible motivations for earlier representations of tribal groups related to Yellowstone National Park: official park communications, museum exhibits, public signage, pamphlets on Indians for the general public, videos for general consumption, memoirs by park personnel, and so forth. Such self-scrutiny calls for reexamination of the political, economic, and bureaucratic agendas that promoted these portrayals and that influenced any cultural representations they generated in turn. This is cultural anthropology's counterpart to what Gary A. Wright has argued concerning the efforts of archaeologists to understand Yellowstone high-country prehistory: "[T]he first duty of an archaeologist is *not* (despite the dictum from introductory textbooks) to build a satisfactory absolute chronology for a stratigraphic sequence. Rather, it is to realize that the dates themselves are data that may be used for testing hypotheses."[63]

This new awareness means we must always regard culture and our views of "it," in the words of the anthropological critic James Clifford, as "produced historically." Clifford goes on to emphasize, "Culture is contested, temporal and emergent. Representation and explanation—both by insiders and outsiders—is implicated in this emergence."[64] This is what the eminent anthropologist Paul Rabinow meant by entitling his contribution to the same volume in which Clifford made the above remark: "Representations are Social Facts." And Rabinow closes his essay by exhorting today's ethnographers, "[B]e attentive to our historical practice of projecting our cultural practices onto the other. . . . We need to anthropologize the West: show how exotic its constitution of reality has been[,] . . . show how their claims to truth are linked to social practices and have hence become effective forces in the social world."[65] Reviewing Clifford's clarion call for this promising new dimension of contemporary ethnography, it is hard to think of a better laboratory or new dialogical field site than the past and present sets of relationships between American Indians and Yellowstone National Park and their representations:

[H]ow are the truths of cultural accounts evaluated? Who has the authority to separate science from art? realism from fantasy? knowledge from ideology? Of course such separations will continue to be maintained, and redrawn; but their changing poetic and political grounds will be less easily ignored. In cultural studies at least, we can no longer know the whole truth, or even claim

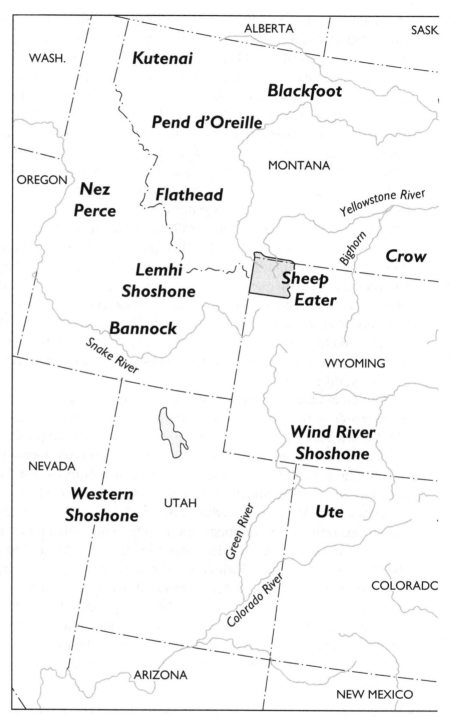

Approximate tribal territories in and around the Yellowstone Plateau.

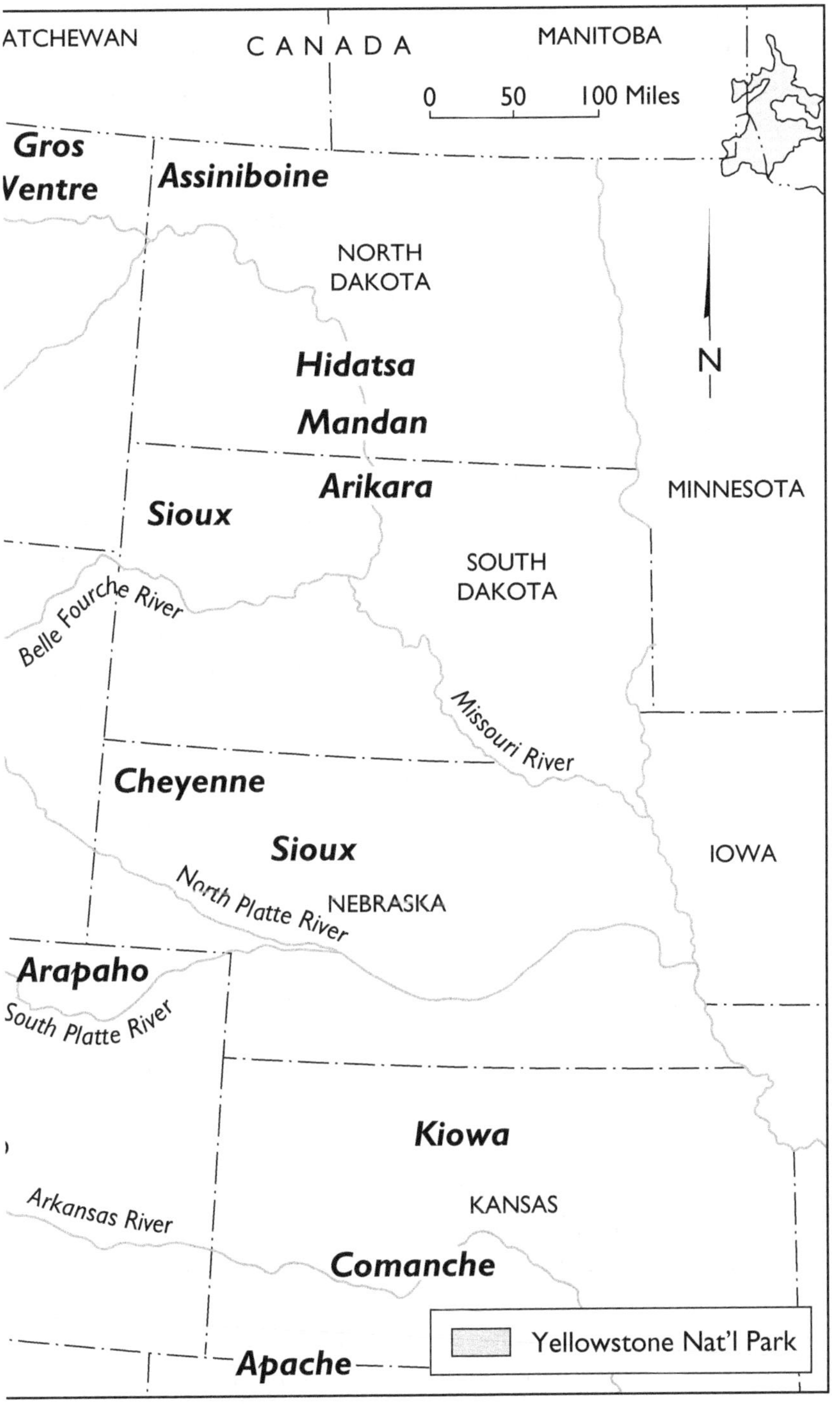

ATCHEWAN　　　C A N A D A　　　MANITOBA

0　　50　　100 Miles

N

Gros Ventre

Assiniboine

NORTH DAKOTA

Hidatsa

Mandan

Arikara

Sioux

MINNESOTA

SOUTH DAKOTA

Belle Fourche River

Missouri River

Cheyenne

IOWA

Sioux

NEBRASKA

North Platte River

Arapaho

South Platte River

Kiowa

KANSAS

Arkansas River

Comanche

Yellowstone Nat'l Park

Apache

to approach it. . . . But is there not a liberation, too, in recognizing that no one can write about others any longer as if they were discrete objects or texts? And may not the vision of a complex, problematic, partial ethnography lead, not to its abandonment, but to more subtle, concrete ways of writing and reading, to new conceptions of culture *as interactive and historical*.[66]

This give-and-take between what was called hard data in the heyday of positivistic ethnography and the discipline's growing awareness that we only know facts through their representation (which itself is always culturally and historically determined) to some degree informs this book.

Yellowstone's Indians in 1872

In the year Yellowstone National Park was established, American Indian tribes of the Rocky Mountain West were in a state of tremendous upheaval, transformation, and insecurity. One year earlier, on March 3, 1871, the Indian Appropriation Act had effectively reversed the government's Indian policy, which had prevailed since the days of George Washington. Whereas the official status of Indians—described variously as "distinct, independent, political communities" or "dependent nations"—had acknowledged their semisovereign ability to sign treaties with the U.S. government, the increasingly criticized and begrudging acknowledgment of Indian autonomy was now considered, in the words of Commissioner of Indian Affairs Francis A. Walker, "a mere form to amuse and quiet savages, a half-compassionate, half-contemptuous humoring of unruly children."[67]

Although the Indian Appropriation Act did not extinguish the lasting terms or obligations associated with the approximately 370 preexisting treaties between the United States and a host of Indian peoples, from that day forward, recognition of Indian tribes as nations or independent powers was outlawed, and the negotiation of additional treaties was forbidden. In terms of Yellowstone National Park history, it is ironic that the last U.S. treaty with Indians to implicitly affirm the political independence of a native group was with the very tribe whose fight to retain that freedom saw the first blood to be shed in a national park. After the signing of that final treaty with the Nez Perce on August 13, 1868 (15 U.S. Stat. 693), what most Indians regarded as sacred pledges on the part of the United States to preserve Indian political authority were now regarded by the government as anachronisms.

The years surrounding the birth of Yellowstone National Park were a major turning point for Indians in U.S. history. Now Indian nations shifted from the status of free-traveling, autonomous tribes to clusters of dependent, remnant natives who were sequestered on reservations administered by the Department of War. In addition, the year 1872 saw the government complete an about-face in its philosophy about how those Indian reservations should be run. The War

Department had been in charge of Indians, but when Ulysses S. Grant ascended to the presidency that year, he instituted the policy of pacifying and assimilating Indians instead of making war on them, which was popularly known as the Peace Policy.

This approach saw the replacement of military officers as Indian agents by members of various religious denominations. By 1872 representatives from a dozen religious groups were functioning as agents for sixty-three of the nation's seventy-five Indian reservations. In the greater Yellowstone ecosystem, Methodists were placed in charge of the Crow, Blackfeet, and Fort Hall Indian agencies, an Episcopalian was running the Shoshone reservation south of the park, the Flathead were allowed to retain their strong ties to the Catholic church, and the Nez Perce were under the control of a Presbyterian.

For Indian peoples whose cultural histories linked them to the Yellowstone region, the conditions of reservation and off-reservation life differed from place to place. But the new environmental, social, and political realities taking shape by 1872 were, to say the least, disruptive for all these tribes. The Crow, Shoshone, Bannock, Flathead, and others now shared the same grim realities: population decline due to disease, warfare, and despair; disarray of established sociopolitical regimes and threats to the authority of traditional chiefs; loss of once reliable buffalo herds; swelling numbers of white ranchers, miners, railroad workers, and settlers, which brought greater opportunities for cross-cultural encounters or misunderstandings to flare into bloodshed; mounting pressures to yield hunting grounds and familiar landscapes; and destabilization of family unity under the policy of removing Indian children to boarding schools and converting parents to Christianity and farming.

In 1872 the quelling of rebellious western tribes was barely under way. The treaty agreed on two years before between the Shoshone and Arapaho was breaking down, leading to Arapaho raids into the central Wyoming region. A number of Lakota groups were flexing their muscles, having temporarily won back through the Fort Laramie Treaty of 1868 their rights to the Powder River country. Within only two years George Armstrong Custer's exploratory expedition into the Black Hills would violate that document, however, and incite the last phase of the Great Sioux War. Meanwhile, the vigorous Sioux war machine was invading Crow country with such ferocity that in 1872 some of their white supporters believed the Crow were on the verge of annihilation.

Not helping the tense atmosphere in the greater Yellowstone region was a widespread anti-Indian sentiment that spread from the muddy streets of Bannack, Virginia City, and Deadwood in the West to the halls of Washington, D.C., in the East. The attitude that Indians were impediments to western expansion had crystallized after the Bear River Massacre of 1863, when volunteer troops descended on Shoshones who were camped near Franklin, Idaho, in midwinter and left an estimated 368 corpses on the frozen ground. Five years later, during a debate in Washington over putting a halt to all treaty making with Indians, a congressman

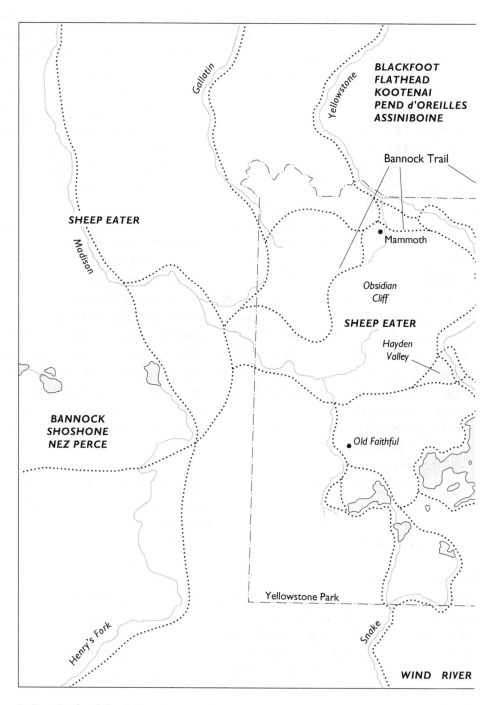

Indian Trails of the Yellowstone region.

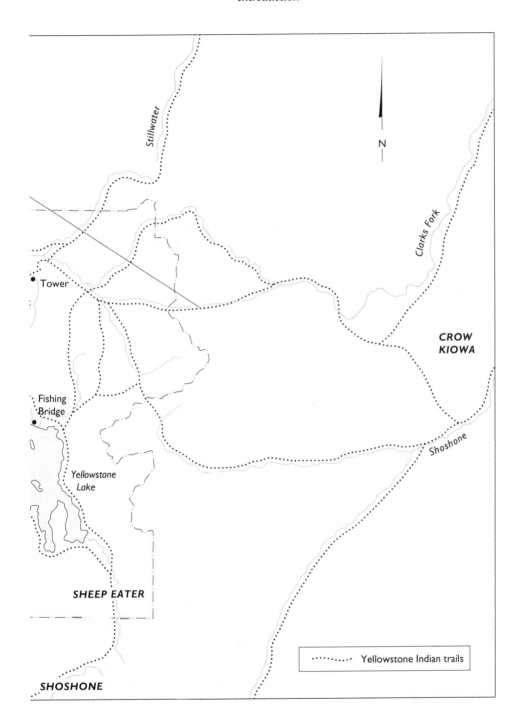

SHEEP EATER

SHOSHONE

CROW
KIOWA

Tower

Fishing
Bridge

Yellowstone
Lake

Stillwater

Clarks Fork

Shoshone

N

.... Yellowstone Indian trails

from Montana, James Michael Cavanaugh, perpetuated the hard-line position: "I have never in my life seen a good Indian (and I have seen thousands) except when I have seen a dead Indian. . . . I believe in the policy that exterminates the Indian, drives them outside the boundaries of civilization, because you cannot civilize them."[68]

A somewhat less strident view was offered in 1872 by Ferdinand V. Hayden, the first surveyor of Yellowstone National Park:

> The present Indian policy, which doubtless looks forward to the localizing and settlement of these roving tribes, is ultimately connected with the agricultural development of the West. Unless they are localized and made to enter upon agricultural and pastoral pursuits they must ultimately be exterminated. There is no middle ground between these extremes. . . . If extermination is the result of non-compliance, then compulsion is an act of mercy.[69]

But there was a third possibility: this was the likelihood that Indians would simply die off. Prevailing in the minds of sympathetic writers was the theory of the Vanishing Indian, which held that their extinction as a race of people was inevitable as a result of the vicissitudes of land loss, warfare, alcoholism, and what one prognosticator called "the natural consequences of one race taking over another." The best that could be hoped for was to treat them humanely in their declining years.

This, then, was the tense climate in western Indian country when Yellowstone National Park was born. As the next two decades unfolded, most of the tribes lost members and freedom until they were left with little more than sheer survival on their minds. A clandestine bolt on a hunting trip might see some Bannock horsemen breach the boundaries of the park, but they were quickly hounded back to their reservations. Little wonder that over the generations Indians felt unwelcome there, and perhaps even blocked their memories and folklore concerning the place.

This book is organized geographically. Starting with the East, in chapter 1 we introduce the Crow, who claimed a sizable eastern portion of the park proper as their aboriginal territory. We also offer unusual data that suggest a possible Kiowa connection to the region, which is interesting given their close early historical friendship with the Crow. In chapter 2 we cover the Blackfeet, Flathead, and Kootenai, who freely penetrated the park for hunting or raiding or resource collecting, and here we also provide general data on buffalo and elk hunting related to the park.

We have placed the Shoshonean people known as the Sheep Eaters in chapter 3, at the heart of this book, because they are believed to be the only Indians who were full-time residents of the high-altitude regions of the park. Here we have benefited immeasurably from Hultkrantz's unpublished field notes. In chapter 4 we discuss the Bannock and Nez Perce, who used the park region as a shortcut to buffalo hunting grounds to the east. But they have a historical affinity as well, for warriors from the Bannock, Northern Shoshone, Nez Perce, and Snake River Sheep Eaters struck against white settlers and were forced to defend themselves against white soldiers in or around the park.

Chapter 5 focuses on the Eastern or Wind River Shoshone. As with the Crow, their connection to the park is territorial; the bottom third of the plateau apparently lay within their traditional territory. In the same fashion that we summarize information on hunting from other tribes in chapter 2, here we compile our diverse tribal data on root-digging practices, and present data from other tribes on the abiding controversy over Indian attitudes toward the park's thermal field.

CHAPTER 1

Occupants on the East

The Crow

The cultural and historical interests of the Crow tribe of Montana have been closely associated with the eastern portion of the greater Yellowstone Plateau. But the fortunes of earlier Indian peoples also touched on the eastern and northeastern flanks of the Absaroka Mountains, such as the little-known archaeological cultures whose lifeways left scraps of evidence that turns up in the compacted earth of, for example, Mummy Cave, just to the east of the park. We also have scattered information on later encounters between other historically known tribes and the eastern Yellowstone region from native oral and pictorial traditions and Euro-American diarists. Among these tribes are the Kiowa, Lakota, and Cheyenne, who interacted with their neighbors both aggressively and amicably. Here, however, we are concerned primarily with tracing the presence of the Crow across this landscape, virtually all of which east of the Yellowstone River and down to the southern Wind River Basin was, until 1868, officially recognized as a piece of their traditional domain.

Through the "Tipi's Doorway" to the Yellowstone Plateau

Rising to a dark profile on the western rim of Bighorn Basin in northwestern Wyoming, the massive ranks of the Absaroka front range face the dry basin and the rising sun. Looming above their green heights, dark clouds promise an interior of rushing streams, wooded draws, and abundant wildlife. The seminomadic bands of Crow Indian kin units who seasonally traveled alongside and through the Yellowstone Plateau were undeterred by the seeming impenetrability of the Absaroka massif.

Crow Indians at the opening ceremony for the East Entrance to Yellowstone National Park, 1927. White Man Runs Him (right) and Max Big Man. (Photo courtesy of Montana Historical Society: Haynes Foundation Collection #H-27006, J. E. Haynes, photographer.)

Although we use the term *seminomadic,* we want to stress that these Plains Indian tribal movements were never aimless wanderings, as early stereotypes of western Indian lifeways often characterized them. They were part of patterned, seasonal circulations that coincided with repeated stopovers at remembered locations for shelter from weather, for obtaining food or other material resources when they were most plentiful, and for the opportunity for various bands to come together at key moments in the tribe's social or ceremonial calendar.

We have little hard data about when, where, and why the first Crows ventured into the Yellowstone Plateau; they may have arrived as early as the seventeenth century. We do know that in the tribe's pre-reservation heyday, a rather brief period between roughly 1620 and 1860, that branch of the tribe known as the Mountain Crow occupied northern Wyoming and southern Montana and hunted east as far as the Powder River and west over to present-day Livingston. Their brethren, known as the Kicked in the Bellies group, preferred to winter along the Wind River basin of south central Wyoming and summer on the eastern flanks of the Bighorn Mountains.

We have gathered enough documentary glimpses from the early nineteenth century of Crow activity in the Yellowstone region to be able to reconstruct some semblance of their movements and territory. And with a strong contingent of old Mountain Crow and Kicked in the Bellies descendants still residing in the Pryor District of today's Crow Reservation, it is no surprise that one still can find the occasional individual with some knowledge of the North Fork of the Shoshone River region, the Absaroka Mountains, and the highland byways that once led the Crow to the Yellowstone.

A few members of the tribe's Mountain Crow division also retain stories and place-names that link the Yellowstone Plateau to their cultural past. They describe how their migratory forefathers of the early nineteenth century wended through the narrow gap that remains the home of their mythic Little People just south of present-day Pryor, Montana, then dragged their travois down the broadening valley through the Arrow Mountains. Before long they passed the immense, V-shaped river canyons that served as portals into the highlands of what would become Yellowstone National Park. Contemporary travelers on Wyoming's State Road 120 heading south toward Cody cannot miss these river canyons, the most dramatic of which is Clark's Fork Canyon, that lead into the Shoshone National Forest.

Today's Crow Indians can also drive on Alternate Route 14 toward the Yellowstone Plateau and see a formation in the McCullough Peaks that is still known for a famous Crow warrior, A Bull Who Could Not Be Pushed Around, and that is therefore referred to as Push's Mountain (Páatchish Awaxaawé). And both roads soon bring one close to Heart Mountain (Awaxaamnaasé), the major landmark and favorite Crow vision-questing spot near present-day Cody. In older times, however, the Crow knew this promontory as "the Foretop's Father" (Ihkapíliilapxe), because a Crow man named Foretop once fasted there. It is said that at one time two points jutted from the crest of Heart Mountain, but, according to one Crow consultant, "an earthquake or something" destroyed the one on the west side.

The story behind the alternative place-name for Heart Mountain relates how Foretop was instructed during his fast that he would live as long as the two points remained on the mountain. Thereafter, Foretop became renowned for his intense battles with Blackfeet, in the Crow effort to push them back into Canada. But after he was killed in the northland and his people returned home, they discovered that there had been a big landslide on one flank of Heart Mountain, leaving only the fanlike uplift that resembles the distinctive brushed-up forelock so associated throughout the plains with Crow identity that it is instantly recognizable on the native "ledger art" produced by many tribes. Afterward, his people commemorated that mountain as being the "medicine father" who had "adopted" the Foretop during his vision quest and helped him to become a successful warrior.[1]

Another important Crow historical site lies just to the west of Heart Mountain. It is the creek near Rattlesnake Mountain, where the famous nineteenth-century Crow chief, Blackfoot, or Sits in the Middle of the Land, is said to have died in battle in 1877 and been placed atop a traditional burial scaffold. A little farther up from the Red Hills (Shichíishe) is the location known to whites as Sunlight Basin but to the Crow as Yellow Crane's Land (Apitshiilishisawe) for a leader who regularly took his band there to hunt elk, deer, bighorns, and buffalo in the winter. South of present-day Cody is Carter Mountain, what the Crow call White Bear Mountain or Bear with White on the Tips of the Fur (Daxpitcheei-iáakeechiate), after a grizzly bear of that description. Facing directly west from Cody, one cannot miss the great canyon of the Shoshone River, or Stinking Water River (Aashíilitche) to the Crow. But in the Crow imagination this avenue into the Yellowstone Plateau was also likened to the east-facing side of one of their buffalo hide lodges, hence their old name for Shoshone Pass (between Cedar and Rattlesnake Mountains), Like a Tipi's Doorway (Bilíiliche), which reminds one of the analogy that struck Jedediah S. Smith in fall 1829 when he described this location as the "back door to the country divines preach about."[2]

Passing by the shadow of Cedar Mountain (Awaxammaalahkape) and through this narrow "doorway," one soon encounters Buffalo Bill Reservoir, about thirty-seven miles east of Yellowstone National Park. Looking down into the gorge's turbulent waters, a Crow consultant pointed to a rim "just below the dam there" overlooking the rapids where the most courageous Crow fasters sought supernatural powers from the dangerous "beings in the water" (Bimmuummaakoolé). Before the creation of the reservoir, according to this consultant, the flat along the Stinking Water was where "the Sheep Eaters used to camp," referring in this case not to the mountain Shoshoneans but to a branch of the Crow tribe known as Those Who Eat Bighorn Sheep (Iisaxpúatduushe).

That these well-watered terraces at the juncture of today's North and South Forks of the Shoshone River were popular with early Crows seems corroborated by statements from early Indians and whites alike. Said the great Crow chief Sits in the Middle of the Land in 1873, "On Sheep Mountain [just southwest of the reservoir] white men come; they are my friends; they marry Crow women, they have children with them; the men talk Crow. When we come from hunting we get off at their doors, and they give us something to eat."[3] Further evidence of the Crow sense that this area was "the Indian's side of the Yellowstone" is found in comments by one "Mea-de-sesh, which, in American, means Two-bellied Woman" (more commonly known as Two Belly), to a man identified only as Allen reported in a 1879 letter to a Bozeman, Montana, newspaper. "My people are hungry," Two Belly complained. "They want to go to the Musselshell to get buffalo to eat. White men drive cattle from Sheep Mountain through the center of my reservation. I do not want it done. They drive all the game out of the country. If they cross the Yellowstone up Sheep Mountain I want them driven back."[4] And on September 6, 1808, George Drouillard, a fur trader, hunter, and interpreter for the Lewis and Clark expedition, drew a map for William Clark and offered some comments that Clark scribbled down. Said Drouillard, "Ap-sha-roo-kee band of Crow Indian winter here [at the convergence of the North and South Forks of the Shoshone River] where there is an abundance of dry grass on which their horses live during the winter. . . . [The band] amount[s] to 280 lodges of dressed leather."[5]

Our main Crow consultant's maternal grandfather had been born near here, at the Place of Chiefs (Ammacheeítche), near present-day Meeteetse, Wyoming, and the origin of that name. A member of the Crow subgroup known as the "Outer Edge People" (Ammitaaashé), he was quite familiar with this reservoir area and showed it to his grandson, who recalled:

> I think there was a trading post on the south side right about where that mountain comes right by the river there. There was an old cabin that was still standing. See those two peaks over there, just below that there was an old cabin right at the edge of the lake. It is probably in the lake now. It was standing in 1948, when my grandfather said that a man named Farthest Up the River had his camp there. . . . There was always a trader here, ever since the early 1800s. . . . [M]y grandfather said that the white people first came into this area right here. They [his grandfather's people, the political band known as "When you Shoot an Arrow at a Buffalo and You Hit a Rib and it Ricochets Off" (Shíiptache)] knew more about white people than the rest of the Crow tribe. So they learned to speak English and learned to adapt to the white man's ways quicker. . . . They were always the translators when they negotiate for treaties. . . . [T]hey first traded with the traders, and then the trappers. So they had more contact with the white people. . . . They intermarried with the Shoshones and were real friendly with them, whereas the other bands didn't get along with the Shoshones. . . . [They wintered at this spot because] there was hardly any snow on the ground in wintertime because of the winds. There were a lot of elk and deer and bighorn sheep.[6]

Past the Stinking Water gorge, the North Fork of the Shoshone valley opens into the funnel that narrows just past present-day Wapiti, as the riverside roadway followed by ancient Indians and today's tourists alike climbs through pine forest. As we drove through this region toward Yellowstone National Park, our consultant recalled that his family carried on an entrepreneurial relationship with Euro-Americans. As a boy, between the ages of eight and thirteen, he wore Indian regalia and danced for tourists outside Cody's Irma Hotel, many of whom were bound for the park. Then, on their own recreational drives into the park proper, his family often enjoyed a rest stop just outside the eastern entrance:

> [T]he Crows used to come to Pahaska Teepee. The old owner way back in the forties and fifties was real friendly with the Crows. They used to come and he

Crow consultant pointing to the Shoshone River gorge, home of supernatural beings, 1995. (Photo by Peter Nabokov.)

would feed them for free. He had a big dining hall for his employees. If you came in there at lunchtime or in the evenings, they would feed you for free and then he would ask them to dance for the tourists. I don't know if they ever do that [anymore]. That was way in the fifties. All of the people in Pryor used to know him. . . . He even had an Indian name.[7]

As he was approaching the park perimeter, this consultant noticed familiar places, as well as plants his family had gathered. To understand how the mobile groups of Plains Indians such as the Crow identified and used the natural resources they found on the Yellowstone Plateau, it is useful to distinguish between those floral, faunal, and geologic resources that were the ostensible objects of their movements and any natural resources they recognized and took advantage of along the way. At a spot where the road cuts between two angled ridges, for instance, our consultant remembered that his parents referred to this spot as Buffalo Fence, or Boundaries for a Buffalo Jump (Binnaxché Bishée), which referred to the way in which the converging ridge lines resembled the drive lines that were demarcated by rock piles or dead-fall fencing into which, in the prehorse days, the Crow would drive buffalo before herding them over a sheer cliff or trapping them for easy shooting in a box canyon or makeshift corral. Recalling this old place-name also caused the consultant to recall an incident that took place deeper inside the park:

> My grandfather told me one time they were chasing some Bannocks. I don't know what the reason was, but I guess they wanted to kill them, . . . and the Bannock got into the Firehole River. They stayed there and they kept chasing them. When they finally came out, the horses' feet were real soft from staying in that water. So that was kind of a trail that they used to hide their tracks. You could take that and get out of the mountains. They called Firehole River the Long Opening in the Ground (Hachkaawúushe)[,] . . . like an entranceway to a cave.[8]

Our consultant pointed to the broomweed that was in flower at that season. This was one of the plants the Crow foraged for as they traveled from the east toward Yellowstone Lake. The Crow call broomweed *(Gutierrezia sarothrae)* "What the Buffalo Won't Eat" (Bishéewaaluushisee). Crow people still store the plant's dried leaves and flowers in jars in kitchen cabinets for brewing teas for any number of purposes, from alleviating sore muscles to helping pregnant women to have an easier childbirth.[9] Other plants that he recalled collecting en route to and in the park were horsemint (Bahpuushé; *Monarda* spp.), which warriors who had counted coup on the warpath would make into crowns to wear on their victorious parades through their home camps; the sweet grass (Bachúate; *Savastana odorata*) that was used for incense; and highly prized forms of tree lichen, such as the compact "yellow plant" (Baaapáashiile; *Everina vulpina*), which served as both headache medicine and perfume, and the "black tree lichen" *(Aletoria fremontii),* whose hairlike tufts were likened by Crows to a buffalo's beard. Other northwestern tribes, such as the Kootenai and Nez Perce, also prized this plant, which they used for flavoring their boiled camas mush and as a curative for upset stomach, indigestion, and diarrhea.[10]

The Crow also collected minerals in the area. Our consultant speculated as to how Crows in the East Yellowstone area may have obtained at a "certain place near the Firehole River obsidian or chert or something like that." He was more specific about "paint":

> There is a bubbling, the Painted Pot, or something like that, that is what it is called. . . . Anyway, it is here in the Yellowstone Park. It is dark brown when it is bubbling, when it is boiling and bubbling. If you get it out, as soon as it is dry it is pure white. That is what they used to refinish the white buckskin. When my mother was still alive that is where she got hers. We harvested certain things here. That is why they would come. It is easily accessible. . . . [W]e just used a coffee can, and then we would just dip it out. We had to ask permission to do that. They finally knew us, because we were there constantly.[11]

Crow women picking berries, 1913. Location unknown. (Photo courtesy of Smithsonian Institution, National Anthropological Archives #79-8487.)

This anecdote about gathering thermal residue for a whitening agent for hides echoes a fuller notation of such practices by the Wind River Shoshone. In the report of Captain William A. Jones of the Corps of Engineers who followed the Shoshone River route into the park in late summer 1873, one reads:

> The material employed [for paint] was usually an ocherous ore, and much of the earthy hematite from the Green Spring locality on Pelican Creek was collected and used for this purpose. The green, slimy cryptogamic vegetation from the same spot was also daubed in stripes and patches on the horses in some instances.[12]

A curious hypothesis about Yellowstone as an inspiration for Indian artistry comes from the writings of Joseph Dixon, chronicler of the "council" expeditions funded by Rodman Wanamaker in 1908–9. Intended to reconcile former warring tribes under the banner of American citizenship, the highly staged, well-publicized Wanamaker events blended the collecting of nostalgic memoirs by battle-scarred veterans of the Indian wars, solemn secular rites of intertribal peace and friendship, and posed photographs that evoked both the "noble savage" and the Vanishing Indian images. Hypothetical and romantic as Dixon's words sound, at the very least they represent a rare example of idealizing rather than demonizing the Indian's relationship to the Yellowstone thermal field and therefore are worth recording as one type of Indian (mis)representation associated with the park. At one point Dixon wonders whether the Plains Indian's "colour scheme" might have originated

> with the dazzling array of colours, beyond the genius of the proudest palette, to be found in the marvelous formations that surround the great geysers of the Yellowstone, colours more exquisitely beautiful than the supremest refinement of art. Every-whither down the cone-shaped mounds are tiny steam-heated rivulets interlacing each other, edged with gold and vermilion and turquoise and orange and opal. Indian trails have been found also interlacing each other all through this wonderland. Deep furrows in the grassy slopes of these ancient footprints are still plainly visible.[13]

To help us picture how the Crow parties pursued their old trails into the Yellowstone mountains, let us turn to the memoir of an early Crow Reservation homesteader, Frank Tschirgi, who watched the tribe's extended families load up for their summer treks into the nearby high country:

> They used to move from their reservation or winter range in long caravans. I have seen these caravans a mile long. Upon arriving at the foot of the mountains they would unpack and discard their tepee poles. They packed their equipment on the backs of ponies and climbed the mountain trails on horseback. The discarded poles left at the foot of the trail accumulated from year to year, and although they were discolored by smoke, they were used by the early settlers for various purposes, such as roofing and corral material.[14]

(This description also resonates with the standing stockpile of used tipi poles that one can still see today nestled in a grove just north of the Soda Butte Creek road in Park's Lamar Valley.)

Background on the Crow

Who were these Plains Indians, and how did they come to claim the territory that became Yellowstone National Park? The Crow are an offshoot of older horticultural ethnic groups who lived along the Middle Missouri in present-day North Dakota. The most recent scenario for Crow ethnogenesis in the West has them striking out from North Dakota in two waves, about 125 years apart.

First to venture West were the Mountain Crow, around A.D. 1550, to be followed more than a century later by the River Crow. It was the combination, then, of these Siouan-speaking divisions and their constituent bands and cross-cutting clans that, say non-Indian scholars, produced the tribe that the French first encountered in the 1740s and named the "beaux hommes" (handsome men), or "gens de corbeaux," from a mistranslation of one of their own self-identifications, "Children of the Large-Beaked Bird" (Apsáalooke).[15] This would have been soon after the Crow acquired horses.

From Crow people themselves, however, one hears a more complicated explanation of how they became a discrete ethnic group on the plains. One of the most common accounts tells of a wandering tribe that eventually came under the leadership of two brothers, No Intestines and Red Scout. In one variant, when they both vision quested together at Devil's Lake, North Dakota, No Intestines was instructed by his vision to search for the seeds of the sacred tobacco, while Red Scout was told to settle his followers along the Missouri River and grow corn.[16] As No Intestines led his people on their wanderings for the promised seeds, they experienced all the corners and climates of the Great Plains. Some versions of the story include possible early knowledge of the Yellowstone National Park area, for it is said that after finding the area around Alberta, Canada, too cold, they headed south, passed the Great Salt Lake, and then traveled the east before swinging back north into Montana, "passing through the place 'where there is fire,' perhaps Yellowstone National Park or a fiery coal pit,"[17] which another respected historian of the Crow calls "land-of-the-burning-ground" or "Land of Vapors" (Awe Púawishe).[18]

Finally, at Cloud Peak, the highest crest in the Bighorn Range, which the Crow call Extended Mountain (Awaxaawakússawishe) and which they consider the center of the world, the fourth of No Intestines's visions told him that the sacred tobacco seeds would be twinkling like stars. That was when the Crow "made their home in Montana and Wyoming, with the Bighorn Mountains as their heartland."[19]

Once in place, these newcomers began to develop regional subdivisions, some of which probably reflected earlier historical or social subgroups within the Crow tribal fold. Of the three social divisions that became more defined in the new landscape, the second-largest, the River Crow (Binnéessiippeele, or Those Who Live Amongst the River Banks), probably had the least cultural knowledge of or subsistence interest in the Yellowstone Plateau and its environs. Although on occasion their fairly independent village groups or subbands might range along their southern boundary, the Yellowstone River, they were generally found farther north, all the way up to the Milk River.[20]

It was members of the tribe's largest division, the Mountain Crow, who considered the region near present-day Yellowstone National Park part of their aboriginal territory (one still hears this claim on the reservation). Among some older Crow people themselves, these Mountain Crow are still referred to as Ashalahó, or Where There Are Many Lodges. The Mountain Crow offshoot that became the tribe's distinctive third group during the historical period are formally called

"Home Away from the Center" (Ammitaalasshé), although a more common and colloquial designation is "Kicked in the Bellies" (Eelalapíio), a name that derives from an incident when the Crow first encountered horses and one member of this sizable band was kicked by a colt.[21]

These three divisions make up the Plains Indian ethnic group that the tribe refers to in most formal settings as Apsáalooke (Children of the Large-Beaked Bird), a translation affirmed by most Crow scholars.[22] In private conversations among themselves, however, they use the term Bíiluuke, which means "Our Side." Lloyd (Mickey) Old Coyote clarified the confusion over the origin of the Crow name:

> [O]ur tribal name in our language is Apsaalooka—of which there are at least sixteen different spellings. French trappers, hearing that we were children of a large-beaked bird, gave our tribe the nickname of Crow, something which we at first resented but in later years have accepted. In reality the large-beaked bird, now extinct, belonged to the raven family, a bird having a long split tail, although some white authors have mistakenly said that the bird was a sparrow hawk.[23]

During the Crow's earliest negotiations with the white man, particular band affinities for certain habitats probably influenced which leaders spoke authoritatively for which territorial claims.[24] Hence it is not surprising that in regard to their interests along the eastern flank of Yellowstone National Park one would hear Mountain Crow spokespeople such as the famous Sits in the Middle of the Land articulating the Crow ties to that landscape. In name if not in social reality, these divisional distinctions continued through the twentieth century, as outsiders learned when the Crow factions that were bitterly opposed to the sale of land rights for Yellowtail Dam on the Big Horn River in the 1960s became publicly identified as Mountain and River Crows.

"Better Than a Book": Earlier Natives of Yellowstone

Long before the eastern migrants who came to be known as the Crow favored the "doorway" outside Cody as their avenue into the Yellowstone Plateau, older generations of Native Americans felt at home there. We are somewhat familiar with these unnamed native occupants thanks to a remarkable episode in American archaeology that captured the world's imagination more than thirty years ago.

In winter 1959–60 the newly hired director of the Buffalo Bill Historical Center in Cody, an art historian and writer named Harold McCracken, visited Washington, D.C., for a talk with the well-known Smithsonian Institution expert on Plains Indian prehistory, Waldo R. Wedel. Based on his excavations a decade before in the Cody vicinity, Wedel confided to McCracken that there was a good chance that promising Indian sites, with very old remains revealing permanent occupation

View of Mummy Cave (dark section of the base of the cliff), at the North Fork of the Shoshone River. (Photo courtesy of Gary J. Westphalen.)

at higher elevations, might be found deeper in the Absaroka range. Two years later, catching rides on fire-fighting helicopters, McCracken cast his eye over the inaccessible high country west of Cody. McCracken and a local trapper, hunter, and amateur archaeologist and historian named Bob Edgar, whose help McCracken had sought, spotted a few old hunting grounds and campsites, including an almost inaccessible elk pasture with arrowheads that Edgar guessed dated to 5000 before the present (B.P.). But it was using ground transportation along the easily accessible U.S. Highway 20 that enabled Edgar to make the discovery that put the Absaroka Mountains on the archaeological map.

In mid-July 1962, only twelve miles from the Park's East Entrance, Edgar pulled into the road shoulder and hiked through underbrush about forty feet to a natural rock shelter overlooking the highway and the North Fork of the Sho-shone River that raced alongside it. Offering natural protection for generations of white trappers, road crews, and picnicking families, the cliff face shadowed a forty-by-eighty-foot patch of ground. Edgar found the dirt kicked up and the walls gouged with graffiti. To one side of the shelter, vandals had recently dug deeply enough to produce a heap of discarded earth. No sooner did Edgar drag his fingers through the pile than they caught a fragment of wooden arrow shaft, apparently sliced off by a shovel. Lashed to one end was a side-notched projectile point that had been chipped from agatized wood about one thousand years earlier.

McCracken and Edgar soon obtained an excavation permit and staked their scientific claim to the site. As they peeled back successive floorings of the cave to the third cultural layer, they came upon a human foot. Soon they had exposed an entire individual, a man buried in a knees-to-chest position who was wrapped in a garment made of mountain sheep skin. This organic material produced a carbon-14 date of about A.D. 724. While the find, which gave the site its popular name, was certainly spectacular, the greater importance of the rock shelter was only revealed over time.

In winter 1965 McCracken contacted the Smithsonian Institution to find an overseer for the final excavation. He was fortunate in finding Wilfred Husted, an archaeologist seasoned by excavating caves in the nearby Bighorn Canyon region. Grid by grid and inch by inch, the floor fill of Mummy Cave was scraped up and sifted. Samples were stored for future analysis. Moving ever downward, they dug through earlier riverbeds and ever older campsites with fire hearths, plant and animal remains, and stone and bone artifacts. By the end of the excavations, they had penetrated 33^1/$_2$ feet into the ground. Their work distinguished thirty-eight culture layers and produced a chronology of twenty-six carbon-dated samples. They established that the most recent Indian builders of fire and cookers of meats camped there about A.D. 1580, and the oldest, which they identified from culture layer 35, used the shelter in about 7280 B.C. This meant that for more than nine thousand almost-continuous years the sun had warmed American Indians who lived beneath the protective west-facing ceiling of this large natural room. When Edgar reflects on this experience of digging back through time, he says it was "better than a book."[25]

Zones of Power: The Crow in the Thermal Field

When a contemporary, traditionally minded Crow arrives at the shores of Yellowstone Lake today, it is not uncommon for him to light a cigarette, puff four times, and pray. In the 1930s and 1940s, according to one of our consultants, a recreational excursion into the park would continue to the geyser region, where this act of supplication might be repeated. When one asks about the older Crow reactions to the geysers, contemporary informants usually prove to be acquainted with the non-Indian idea that their forebears were terrified of the hot, spouting, noisy waters. They regard this image of their forebears as a false stereotype that brands Indians as superstitious or simple-minded.

After more than a century of being discouraged from maintaining an ongoing relationship with the hunting grounds and possibly religious areas of the park, it is not surprising that our data on Crow attitudes toward its thermal features is uneven. Some information can be teased from the archives, as well as from the memories of living Crows once their distrust is overcome about why an institution that once kept them away from Yellowstone would now want to learn about

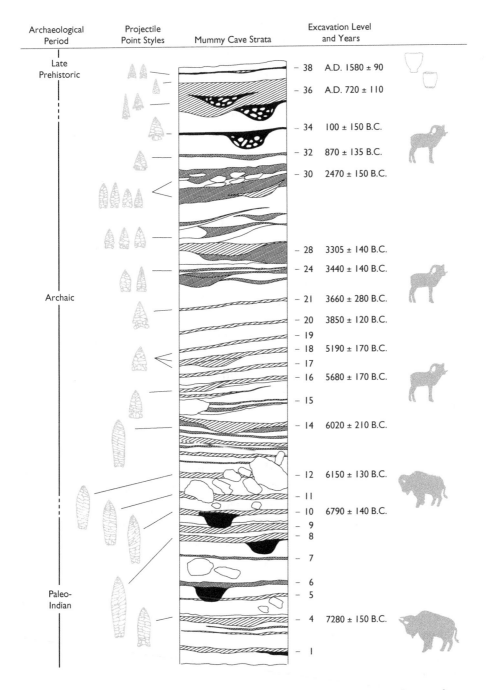

Archaeological Period	Projectile Point Styles	Mummy Cave Strata	Excavation Level and Years	
Late Prehistoric			− 38	A.D. 1580 ± 90
			− 36	A.D. 720 ± 110
			− 34	100 ± 150 B.C.
			− 32	870 ± 135 B.C.
			− 30	2470 ± 150 B.C.
Archaic			− 28	3305 ± 140 B.C.
			− 24	3440 ± 140 B.C.
			− 21	3660 ± 280 B.C.
			− 20	3850 ± 120 B.C.
			− 19	
			− 18	5190 ± 170 B.C.
			− 17	
			− 16	5680 ± 170 B.C.
			− 15	
			− 14	6020 ± 210 B.C.
			− 12	6150 ± 130 B.C.
			− 11	
			− 10	6790 ± 140 B.C.
			− 9	
			− 8	
			− 7	
			− 6	
Paleo-Indian			− 5	
			− 4	7280 ± 150 B.C.
			− 1	

Profile of human occupation layers at Mummy Cave. Projectile points change shape, from Paleo-Indian lance-like forms at the deepest layers up through side notched and then stemmed forms. (Based on a drawing courtesy of Buffalo Bill Historical Center, Cody, Wyoming.)

their traditions regarding it. We first encountered Crow attitudes toward the geyser region in the mid-1960s from the memoirs of a River Crow named Two Leggings. When this old warrior described his youthful war parties to the Dutch-born ethnographer William Wildschut in the 1920s, he recalled one trip into the Yellowstone National Park area. On approaching a hot spring near Yellowstone Lake, Two Leggings and his companions thought that the bubbling sounds and smokey emissions were issuing from an enemy camp. Instead, they were astonished to find the boiling waters, and Two Leggings said that his men "did not like the place."[26] It should be noted that Two Leggings was a member of the more easterly River Crow division of the tribe and therefore may not have been familiar with this volcanic field.

About seventy years later, when Joseph Weixelman sought to test the thesis put forward by Hultkrantz that most Indians were afraid of Yellowstone's geysers, he tried to elicit Crow testimony. Unfortunately, according to the head of the Crow Cultural Commission at the time, John Pretty On Top, the 1989 airing of a segment on PBS's *Sesame Street* had featured the anthropomorphic creature Big Bird visiting the Crow reservation. Many Crows were so insulted by the representation of their community on the program that they suspended communications with outside investigators. Nonetheless, Weixelman chatted with Pretty On Top, who claimed that the geysers and hot springs held little terror for the Crow; he even had heard of elders who recalled traditions involving use of the hot waters, but this was not the time for further investigation.

When it came to recalling personal ties to the Yellowstone region, however, it was often common for nineteenth-century Crows to think personally rather than generically, to consider this or that *place* through identification with specific individuals rather than by overarching characterizations or general proprietary claims. Hence, many Crows, Mountain Crows especially, with personal ties to the generations of the late nineteenth century, when contemplating the entire Yellowstone National Park region and its unique landscape, often recalled one Crow in particular. He was known as the Fringe, and nineteenth-century stories of his powers arouse respect to this day.

This was the case when Frank Bird Linderman asked Plenty Coups, a Mountain Crow leader, "Who was then the most powerful Wise One in your own time?" The old chief immediately responded that it was the Fringe and told Linderman the story of his famous fast on an island in the middle of the healing "medicine water" near the Wind River (Hutchaashe). The Fringe had reached the island "by walking a pole which two friends helped him place from the shore" and then climbed a nearby hilltop to make his fasting bed. His friends noticed that on the third day of his vision quest he had disappeared and that on the fourth he suddenly showed up back on the shore. During that interval, the Fringe had visited the home of a spirit who had given him a patent, water-connected medicine.

Through this experience he received the special powers to heal wounds and thereby to acquire many horses in payment from his patients—powers from the supernatural Otter and White Bear who had appeared to him. Thereafter, Plenty Coups told Linderman, "when we passed the Medicine Water, we each dropped in a bead, or something else very pretty, so that the [dream] Father of The Fringe, and his Woman, might have them."[27]

From one of his key informants, Gray Bull, Lowie obtained this individual's Crow name, Dap'ic (or, in current orthography, Daappish), which he also translated as "the Fringe." In addition, Lowie learned that he was reputedly the most renowned of the category of *akúuwashdiive* (or *akuuwashdiiua*), meaning "wound doctors."[28] One of our consultants identified the Fringe as a Mountain Crow who belonged to Long Horse's band. His name derived from the long fringes that hung down from old-time, rawhide headdress ornaments. The Fringe was born in 1820 and died in the 1860s, during a smallpox epidemic, when he refrained from using his curative powers to heal himself (our consultant speculated that this was because he did not want to live with a scarred, ugly face).

To obtain his powers from the "water beast," our consultant explained, the Fringe was one of those courageous fasters who sought power at present-day Shoshone Dam. Although his vision creature emerged at that time, it was not until a later fast at Thermopolis hot springs that he reappeared and told the Fringe, "You have shown me your fortitude, and your willingness to suffer, so I am going to give you my powers." According to this account, the Fringe would partially immerse his patients in the water so that an otter, his medicine helper and the only water-dwelling animal considered by the Crow to be beneficial for humans, could swim around and bite the wounds and heal them.

In one of his feats, the Fringe even walked on water. He was also said to convene with the chief of all water beasts inside an underwater lodge near the Missouri River headwaters. Two other stories connected with the Fringe revealed his gifts for restoring injured warriors on the brink of death. According to our consultant, it was their preexisting experience with such powers that caused Crows to lend credence to what they heard from the first Catholic priests to arrive in their country: "[T]hey told them about these things, and they could draw parallels about Fringe and what happened. Fringe was actually alive at that time. When they were told about Jesus walking on the water, they thought he was another great medicine man."

Written accounts state that the Fringe's most famous fasting episode took place at Thermopolis and therefore provide only an analogous example of the complexity of Crow reactions to thermal areas in the park. But another story associated with the Fringe places him squarely in the park. This narrative came to light when another nineteenth-century Crow warrior, a competitor of Two Leggings in the search for war honors, was interviewed in about 1915 for photographer-author Edward S. Curtis's volume on the Crow.

Crow Indian Max Big Man and his wife at Yellowstone National Park geyser. (Photo courtesy of Yellowstone National Park Archives, #Yell 37806.)

Curtis's Crow narrator was Hunts to Die, a Mountain Crow who was born in about 1838 and knew the northern perimeter of the park well, having fasted as a young man on Red Lodge Creek in the Beartooth range.[29] With the aid of a Carlisle-educated, mixed-blood Crow interpreter named Alexander Upshaw, Hunts to Die probably talked with a Curtis field-worker, William Meyer, about the man he called simply "Fringes." Although after Frederick Webb Hodge edited Curtis's original writings for his twenty-volume work, *The American Indian*, this portion was not included in the published volume on the Crow, one copy of the original typescript that is housed at the Seaver Center Library of the Los Angeles County Museum of Natural History included the following fragments regarding the Yellowstone National Park area:

> The Great Geysers at Yellowstone are called *Bide-Mahpe* or [Bimmaaxpée, meaning "sacred" or "powerful" water]. Fringes fasted at this place for several days and nights. While fasting at this place the name "Water Old Man," *Bide-issakku* or [Bilísaahke], was given him. The Otter transformed as a medicine-man, and revealed the secrets of doctoring people who are wounded. The medicine otter would take its patient into this sacred water and the different little creatures would work wonders. He had a stuffed otter and would make the animal dive, and also the patient.[30]

Next, Hunts to Die provided some hints about Crow religious concepts that are elusive in early ethnographic writings on the tribe:

The great Yellowstone [Lake] gets its water by waves. There is a little ridge and if the ridge wore away the whole country would be overflowed. The eagles built their nests on the mountains of these lakes. The feathers, breath feathers, would form as driftwood.[31]

Returning to the subject of the Fringe, Hunts to Die recalled how he aquired the water-connected powers at thermal sites such as Thermopolis and Yellowstone:

It was Water Old Man (Fringes) who gave such names among the Apsaroke [Apsáalooke] as Medicine Water, Otter Moves Always (meaning: lives forever), and Otter That Stays in the Water. He would doctor people by taking them to water. He used stuffed otter to do wonders. He claims there are different elements in the water which have life, and it is through them people get well when he doctored them.

The man [Fringes] came back to his people and by his wonderful power as a healer all people loved him and he was regarded a very sacred man. When a person is shot in battle and still has little breath in him he generally pulled through and got them well. He lived to be very old. Not only as medicine man, but was a very able warrior among his people. He died only a short time ago.[32]

Finally, Hunts to Die offered a more general view of the Crow relationship to the Yellowstone geothermal basins. Here we find the old warrior turning the old debate of just who was afraid of whom at the Yellowstone geysers on its head:

The Apsaroke [the Crow tribe] know the great geysers of the Yellowstone National Park. Only few go there to fast. All men who fasted there claimed to have seen many strange beings. *They* [meaning the spirits] would expose themselves when no one was around. *They* seemed to have no fear of the poor people who go there to fast.[33]

For Hunts to Die at least, it was important to emphasize that for the spirits that inhabited Yellowstone National Park—spirits that in his mind are benevolent and helpful rather than malevolent and dangerous—it was their potential "fear" of human beings that was at issue, not the reverse. But this "fear" was allayed when the Crow supplicants presented themselves as "poor" and "pitiful" vision seekers, who momentarily divested themselves of clothing and cultural identity to render their receptivity to "adoption," as Crows generally characterized it, by potential supernatural guardians. According to Hunts to Die, that also appears to have been the condition and context that made the "strange beings" that inhabit the geysers feel comfortable about coming to their rescue. It was then that Crows could harness the inner powers of Yellowstone.

Crow History and the Yellowstone Plateau I (1805–1871)

As was the case in the Bighorn Mountains, in the Yellowstone high country the Crow people found everything they prized on earth. Today's Crows pay homage to the enduring role that mountains play in their sense of identity with a symbolic moment during the final day of their annual Crow Fair, held the third weekend in August. During the afternoon's climactic Parade Dance, a procession of Crows, all in dance regalia, move in stately fashion around the powwow grounds at Crow Agency along the Little Bighorn River. Stopping four times for elaborate giveaways to friends, relatives, clan relations, and special guests, they turn their bodies in unison toward the closest range, the Bighorn Mountains to the south. With great solemnity they then lift their eagle-wing dance fans or raise their arms in salute to the mountains—the original source of all that is good. It is no surprise that the ethnographer Edward S. Curtis characterized the Crow as a "powerful tribe of mountaineers."[34]

An early suggestion of Crow ties to Yellowstone comes from a journal entry for September 14, 1805, by François-Antoine Larocque when he was at the westernmost terminus of his grand tour of the northern plains. Camping on an island in the Yellowstone River a few miles east of Billings, the French trader was told, "[I]n winter they [the Crow] were always to be found at a Park by the foot of the Mountain only a few miles from this or thereabouts. In the spring and fall they are upon this River and in summer upon the Tongue and Horses [Pryor Creek] River."[35]

One Crow teenager who observed Larocque's visit was named Sore Belly (Eelápuash]. A quarter of a century later, then one of the tribe's leading chiefs, he delivered the following, oft-quoted overview of his people's environmental preferences. Though Sore Belly was was a River Crow leader, it is his description of his people's affection for mountain country, such as they found on both sides of the Bighorn Basin, that he emphasized:

> The Crow country is a good country [because] the Great Spirit has put it exactly in the right place. It has snowy mountains[,] sunny plains[,] . . . and all kinds of . . . good things for every season. When the summer heats scorch the prairies, you can draw up under the mountains, where the air is sweet and cool, the grass fresh, and the bright streams come tumbling out of the snow banks. There you can hunt the elk, the deer and the antelope when their skins are fit for dressing; there you will find plenty of white bears and mountain sheep.[36]

During these poorly documented years, one finds mentions of occasional sightings of Crows in Yellowstone. In summer 1830, for example, there is an unconfirmed instance of some fifteen Crow families visiting "wonderful boiling springs" at Mammoth in the company of a Frenchman named Louis Bleau.[37] But a more definitive tie between the tribe and the Yellowstone country comes from the description of Crow territory by the Pennsylvania fur trader, Edwin Thompson Denig. As an employee of the American Fur Company whose posts ranged from Blackfeet country in the northern Rockies down to Fort Union near the mouth of the Yellowstone, Denig interacted with Crow Indians, among other northern Plains Indians, for nearly twenty years—from at least 1837 to 1856, when he moved to Canada where he died in two years later. This is his description of their aboriginal territory:

[They are found] through the Rocky Mountains, along the heads of Powder River, Wind River, and Big Horn, on the south side of the Yellowstone, as far as Laramie's Fork on the River Platte. They also are frequently found on the west and north side of that river as far as the head of the Musselshell River, and as low down as the mouth of the Yellowstone. That portion of their country lying east of the mountains is perhaps the best game country in the world. . . . Some of the springs near the head of the Yellowstone are bituminous, sending forth a substance like tar, which is inflammable. Others are sulfurous, and one or two boiling. The water in the last is hot enough to cook meat well enough to fit it to be eaten. The Indians describe others to be of poisonous nature to animals, 'tho the same water is said not to affect the human species.[38]

In describing Crow territory more precisely, Denig offered what resembles the tribal divisions delineated above. One group headed by one "Big Robber" wintered around the head of the Powder River, "the largest band" led by a "Two Face" clung to the Wind River mountain region, and a third, under the loose control of "The Bear's Head," traveled "along the Yellowstone from the mouth to its head." Denig also added that every summer the Crows enjoyed a major trade fair with the Snake and the Nez Perce "on the headwaters of the Yellowstone."

What lends credibility to Denig's words is that they generally confirm the delineation of Crow holdings that was codified, for the first time, during the great Fort Laramie peace council of 1851. Denig's reputation as an expert on Crow Indian culture made him an advisor to Father De Smet and may have influenced the latter when he attended, with a contingent of Hidatsas, Arikaras, and Assiniboines, the grandest of all Plains Indian gatherings—although the Crow had actually arrived before him in the company of another trader, Robert Meldrum. Because they were anxious about Sioux encroachment along their eastern boundary and because there were no River Crows in attendance, during the Fort. Laramie discussions, the tribe apparently accepted a the Mountain Crow version of their geographic rights and hunting grounds.

As "Crow country" was described in the ratified 1851 treaty, on the west it was bounded by the Continental Divide which, according to U.S. law, annexed to the United States virtually three-fourths of what in about twenty years was to become Yellowstone National Park. Its northern border was the western curve of the Musselshell River, plus a surveyor's line drawn from its mouth on the

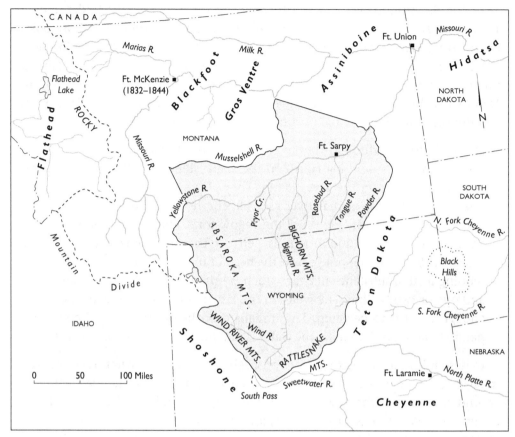

Crow Indian Country, circa 1855. (Based on a map in Edwin T. Denig, "Of the Crow Nation," Smithsonian Institution, Bureau of American Ethnology, Bulletin 5, Anthropological Papers no. 33, 21.)

Missouri River straight to the mouth of the Powder River, where it pours into the Yellowstone. Then the Powder River also served as the primary eastern boundary, while farther down the Rattlesnake Hills of the Sweetwater Uplift at the bottom of the Wind River Basin lay the southern terminus of the Crow domain.

At the time, according to Edwin C. Bearss, "[t]he Crow were undoubtedly pleased with the treaty, because it confirmed them in possession of 'the best game country in the world.'" Today some Crows appear to feel much the same. In an interview with a knowledgeable Crow elder in 1994, Spence found the elder "emphatic that the Crow still have hunting rights based on the 1851 treaty, which they have never given up."

> Sits in the Middle of the Land agreed that the United States could have that area for a price, but the price was never met. The Park area was very important thoroughfare for hunters coming to the Plains. But it was a two-way street. The Crow would go back the other way, meet with Shoshone for games, competition,

hunting, socializing. While they were at their first two reservation agencies, Livingston and Absarokee, the Crow did a lot of hunting in the western portion of their reservation, in Beartooth, Meeteetse and Yellowstone. Bison, elk, deer were all hunted in the Yellowstone area. On a trip into Yellowstone 10 years earlier FS saw lots of knife-sharpening marks for those hunters on their way down to get buffalo. [Here another family member allowed that he would like to "go in there and kill an elk to challenge those hunting laws," and that during the Yellowstone fires he took a buffalo skull from the Park in defiance of the laws against it.]

[In addition,] Yellowstone and surrounding were very important fasting areas. Its an obvious place for this because the mountains are so high. He could see fasting beds on some of the ridges. Very important spiritual place. At this Mrs. FS added that she had the same feeling and knelt down to pray in the Park because "the Maker looks down and he knows that some day we will be hunting there again."[39]

But despite lines drawn on crude maps, in the years following the first Fort Laramie treaty, other enemy tribes did not honor the imposed territorial divisions. The Teton Sioux only intensified their military pressure on Crow country and the white man's trading posts that served Indians in western Montana and Wyoming. Blackfeet raiders were of like mind, viewing the posts in Crow country as a prime target. Indian agent Vaughan wrote in 1854:

Scarcely a day passes but the Crow country is invested with more or less parties of Blackfeet, who murder indiscriminately any one that comes within their reach. At Fort Sarpy so great is the danger that no one ventures even a few yards from his own door without company and being well armed.[40]

Matters got so bad that the American Fur Company felt compelled to close Fort Sarpy the following year. Now Crows were forced to travel many miles north from their homeland, to Fort Union along the upper Missouri in Assiniboine country, for the weapons, tools, and ammunition that had been promised in the 1851 treaty and on which they had grown increasingly dependent. As the fur trade continued its decline in the late 1850s and early 1860s, the tribe's fortunes also declined. They faced mounting Lakota aggression on the east and additional pressure from the influx of gold prospectors and Oregon Trail adventurers to the south.

Yet during these years, the Crow apparently continued to move freely through Yellowstone high country, even staging the occasional raid on outsiders they found there. On his second trip into the park area in 1864, a prospector named John C. Davis first "saw plenty of Indian signs" and then claimed that a "section of [the] party was attacked by a hostile band of Crows, and a man named Harris was killed."[41] If Davis's identification was accurate, this would be uncharacteristic of the generally amiable tribe and perhaps evidence of their desperate straits at the time.

To U.S. authorities, however, the Crow plight was a minor ripple in the alarming instability into which the entire plains had been thrown by the waves of incoming pioneers and miners and by the Indian intransigence that this emigration had aroused. They felt that new methods of pacification, both on the battlefield and at the treaty table, were in order. When the tribe was pressured into attending a second major treaty conference at Fort Laramie, their major spokesperson was the Mountain Crow leader Blackfoot, or Awé Kúalawaachish, meaning Sits in the Middle of the Land.

At six feet two inches, with a muscular build, he was an imposing orator and a fierce defender of his people's aboriginal territory. Today the Crow remember him as their "Chief of All Chiefs" during the diplomatically crucial decade of 1867–77, and identify the geographic significance of his Indian name with their sense of a chosen people who found their promised land in the very center of the Great Plains.[42] This feeling is deeply established in tribal consciousness, as evidenced when the chief's peer and second-in-command, Iron Bull (Uuwatchii-lapish), also known as White on the Temple (Itchúua Chíash), gave William Clark a version of the Crow creation story that climaxed with the Great Spirit leading the Crow to the Yellowstone River landscape and telling them, "This is your country; the water is pure and cold, the grass is good. It is a fine country, and it is yours. . . . I have made all this country round you. I have put you in the center."[43] By another coincidence, Iron Bull was quoted as offering similar sentiments about the sacred establishment of Crow territory:

> This is the earth the Great Spirit made [for] them. The Piegans he put them there, indicating a point in the line of the circle he made, then the Great Spirit made the Sioux, the Snakes [Shoshone]. Flat-heads and many others and located them all around the earth. The Great Spirit put us right in the middle of the earth, because we are the best people in the world.[44]

To lure the Crow to Fort Laramie for the second great council, the government sent them bundles of tobacco. Although while en route to the meeting Sits in the Middle of the Land's group of delegates were attacked by Cheyenne, when they finally sat down to treaty-making business they faced a more serious threat to their territory than they had ever encountered on the battlefield.[45] Despite such convictions about their preeminent position in the plains, in the concluding session of negotiations that stretched into the month of May, the Crow finally agreed to a radically shrunken reservation. Through this Fort Laramie Treaty of 1868 the tribe lost all their lands in Wyoming plus all the territory north of the Yellowstone River and east of the 107th meridian. Giving up 38 million acres they had 8 million acres left for their exclusive use. Soon afterwords Sits in the Middle of the Land complained about how much territory had been surrendered through a "misstatement" of their verbal concessions at Fort Laramie. Were secondhand shirts, rusty kettles, and poor-quality stockings a fair trade for the loss to his Mountain Crows of the bulk of their old Yellowstone hunting grounds? he would ask. Now the great bend of the Yellowstone River itself served as the tribe's northern perimeter—with the domain of their archenemies, the Blackfeet, located much too close for Crow comfort, directly on the river's opposite shore.[46]

Still, along with other Indians, the Crow were not overly impressed by these territorial constraints. When two hunters were killed in the Upper Lamar Valley in 1868, no one was sure which tribe to blame. But when the Washburn expedition entered the park area two years later, they did not hesitate to identify the Indian band of twenty-five lodges that they tracked along the Bannock Trail to its ford at the narrows near Tower Falls as Crows, or to associate the fifteen "wickey ups" a mile from Tower Junction with the "Crow" trails they had been pursuing across the Yellowstone Plateau. Contrary to other reassuring reports that Indians had been cleared out of Yellowstone's thick woods, the expedition also found "recent" camps, freshly used trails, and "old Indian" lodges throughout the region. Obviously Indians felt free to travel in and out of the Yellowstone Plateau as they pleased.

Five years after the Fort Laramie Treaty of 1868, Sits in the Middle of the Land still had second thoughts about the agreement. In the following excerpt from his lengthy remarks he employed a key metaphor for how his people imagined their territory:

> I went to Fort Laramie; the old Indians signed the treaty. We came back to the camp and told the young men, and they said we had done wrong and they did not want to have anything to do with it. . . . *When we set up our lodge poles, one reaches to the Yellowstone, the other is on White River, another goes to the Wind River; and the other lodges on the Bridger Mountains.* This is our land and so we told the commissioners at Fort Laramie, but all kinds of white people come over it and we tell you of it, though we say nothing to them. On this side of the Yellowstone there is a lake; about it are buffalo. It is rich country; the whites are on it; they are stealing our quartz; it is ours, but we say nothing to them. . . . When we were in council at Laramie we asked whether we might eat the buffalo for a long time. They said yes. That is not in the treaty. We told them we wanted a big country. They said we should have it; and that is not in the treaty. . . . They said "Will you sell the Powder River country, Judith Basin and Wind River country?" I told them "No"; but that is not in the treaty. [emphasis ours][47]

Crow History and Yellowstone National Park II: Loss of a Landscape (1872–1996)

During the months that the proposal to establish Yellowstone National Park was debated in the East, there was little discussion about Indian rights to the region and even less about possible cultural remains within the projected "natural" preserve. When the subject did arise, Indian residency was summarily denied. "[T]he Indians can no more live there," argued Massachusetts representative Henry Dawes, a sponsor of the legislation to create the park, "than they can upon the precipitous sides of the Yosemite Valley" (an uninformed comparison, given the long occupancy of Miwok Indians in that very California habitat).[48] And besides, insofar as the Crow Indians of Montana were concerned, the government assumed that any 1851 treaty rights accorded to the Crow to all lands east of their Elk River [Yellowstone] and the Wind River Basin almost down to the Stillwater had been wrested from them during the subsequent, 1868 Fort Laramie treaty. Shrunken by three-fourths, the new map of their reservation pulled their southern perimeter entirely out of the proposed park, running it north of and just parallel to the present-day Montana-Wyoming state line.

Yet in 1871, when the Crow were slowly acclimating to life at their first reservation agency at Mission Creek near present-day Livingston, Montana, they still clung to a sliver of land that would be later accessioned to Yellowstone National Park. Unfortunately, it was to this very region, near the headwaters of the Clark's Fork of the Yellowstone, that prospectors were lured by silver and gold. Since fall 1869 there had been bloody ambushes of miners by Indians furious about outsiders digging into their land; Crows were accused, for instance, of the grisly killing of Jack Crandall, discoverer of the first gold strike, and his companion, Daugherty, in which their severed heads were found impaled on mining stakes.[49] Now an annual council of the tribe concurred about asking the Superintendent of Indian Affairs in Washington for protection from the Sioux, on the one hand, and from prospectors rushing into the Clark's Fork area, on the other.

In 1872 those branches of the tribe more closely connected to the Yellowstone Plateau region—the Mountain Crow and the Kicked in the Bellies—were still smarting from the loss of traditional access to hunting, foraging, and raiding grounds. But there were others reasons why, in 1872, planning in Washington for the country's first national park was not on their minds; at this time the Crows were in an anxious state of division and dislocation. While the Fort Laramie Treaty of 1868 had established reservation boundaries for the division of the tribe known to whites as the Mountain Crow, the less well-to-do division known as the River Crow had only an unratified treaty and were essentially homeless.

So it was understandable that, in 1872, the River Crow saw the Mission Creek Agency as a refuge from the diseases prevalent among the Gros Ventre along the Milk River, as well as from incessant marauding by the Sioux. In 1879 the Indian agent wrote, "This summer, for the first time in their history, the Crows have remained upon their reservation."[50] What was left of Crow holdings within the confines of the fledgling Yellowstone National Park in 1880 was referred to as the "Montana Strip," which Agent Keller advised the government against selling, citing the Crow treaty rights to it and the fact that they "seldom go above the lower canon [first or Rock Canyon] because of the presence of so many whites above the canon which has destroyed the game to the extent that it is impossible for them to live there." Keller continued, "They do, however, go above the Boulder because of that locality being good grazing and the vicinity being one of the best game regions in the Reserve."[51]

As suggested by Keller's communiqué, at this point three factors were impinging on the Crows' free and open use of this area. The first concerned the policy against poaching animals in the park, which was being vigorously enforced by Yellowstone's second superintendent in order to check the dwindling numbers of bear, elk, and deer that had grown increasingly apparent since 1875. White poachers might have been well aware of the rules they were breaking when they trespassed into the park for hunting and trapping. But to the Indians this white man's notion of a "wilderness game preserve" where game and later even plant procurement was banned would have seemed strange indeed.

The second intrusion began less dramatically, but in the long run it would be decisive in the tribe's loss of territory. Already the Union Pacific had been a major factor in the final extinction of buffalo in the southern plains. Now the entrepreneur Jay Cooke, whose wealth had derived from Civil War loans, underwrote the goal of the Northern Pacific to run its trains from Lake Superior to Puget Sound, and railway surveyors had reached the Yellowstone River in 1871.[52] Temporarily stalled by the financial panic of 1873, the Northern Pacific finally penetrated the heart of Crow country in the early 1880s. A prescient promoter, Cooke was soon boosting the visits of famous eastern artists such as Thomas Moran and Albert Bierstadt into the Yellowstone country, whose monumental scenes, one might add, would idealize the landscape while erasing the Indian presence.

At the same time, a third pressure on the Indians was building. This was the influx of miners along the Clark's Fork who had increasingly called for the wholesale eviction of Indians from their sluicing streams. In summer 1862 the first Montana gold strikes were made on Grasshopper Creek, in the western reaches of the territory; within two years mining camps bearing names such as Bear Gulch, Clarks Fork, Emigrant Gulch, and Mill Creek cropped up in the westerly portions of the Crow reservation. After the 1868 treaty, these pockets of frontier industry were more clearly illegal, but the Crow agent still doubted seriously whether there were enough troops in all Montana to keep whites out of the mountains. After Major E. M. Baker's troops and some prospectors attempted to protect the Northern Pacific survey party from the Sioux who were marauding near Bozeman in 1872, prospectors and cattle ranching stirred up the Crow by settling on the Boulder River, further ignoring their reservation boundaries.[53]

But the miners would not be impeded from invading Crow lands or moving up the Rosebud Fork, pursuing their premise that, as the Crow elder Barney Old

Coyote has phrased it, "the bigger the mountains, the more the gold." Yet it was federal policy to encourage such mineral exploitation, so in 1880 the government asked the tribe to sell off the western corner of the reservation, from the Absaroka Range in the west across the Beartooth Plateau and past Rocky Fork. Even before the treaty formally went into effect on April 11, 1882, impatient miners had infiltrated the surrounding valleys and constructed a smelter. And just over the Beartooth Plateau miners had already organized the backwater settlement of thirty to forty cabins into Cooke City—named to entice the great financier, Jay Cooke, into laying a railroad line, which ultimately he failed to do.[54]

Now the "white people," to whom Sits in the Middle of the Land referred in 1873, were firmly in control of the major Crow pass up the Yellowstone River. This 1882 agreement also extinguished Crow rights to that remaining segment of the park north of 45° latitude and east of the Yellowstone River. We may never know exactly the sorts of behind-the-scenes manipulations that caused the eventual capitulation of the Crows and their surrender of northern Yellowstone National Park land.

As if to hammer home the humiliation of the Crow loss of political and territorial authority, when the Northern Pacific Railroad celebrated the completion of its line with a branch connection into Yellowstone National Park, Crow leaders and nearly two thousand followers were invited to attend the last-spike ceremony in full regalia. Their performance of Indian dances at Gray Cliff west of Livingston underscored to Magoc "the emerging role of Native Americans as exotic spectacle in Wonderland tourist culture."[55] But it was also sadly appropriate that the historic tribe with the clearest legal rights to about half of the park proper were represented at the Gold Creek, Montana, celebration in late 1883, for they now became symbolic of the loss to all Indians of this landscape. Observed a visiting British chief justice of the Indians' appearance at the Gold Spike celebration, "Here were the representatives of an old dynasty which was almost dead, and, close by, in the luxurious steam equipage (a compendium of the material civilisation of nineteen centuries) the successful invader, the ruthless, aggressive, all-conquering White man."[56] In the symbolic dramatization of willing capitulation that ensued, it was the genial Crow leader Iron Bull who spoke on September 8 for his people.[57] Second in rank to Chief Sits in the Middle of the Land and well known for his hospitality to whites and indigent fellow tribesmen alike, Iron Bull was assigned to hand the "last" metal spike to Henry Villard, president of the Northern Pacific Railroad. After dutifully fulfilling his role, Iron Bull reportedly told the assembled crowd:

> This is the last of it—this is the last thing for me to do. I am glad to see you here, and hope my people of the Crow Nation are glad to see you, too. There

is a meaning in my part of the ceremony, and I understand it. The end of our lives is near at hand. The days of my people are almost numbered; already they are dropping off like the rays of sunlight in the western sky. Of our once powerful nation there are now few left—just a little handful, and we, too, will soon be gone.[58]

We may never be sure about the possible ironies that underlay Iron Bull's words, or the degree to which the carefully choreographed ceremony whose meaning he says he understood full well was prescripted to fit into the Vanishing American scenario. But the ambivalent presence and double-edged speech of Iron Bull represented the first of various occasions when fully costumed Indians would be invited into or around Yellowstone National Park to grace, perhaps to authenticate solemn occasions such as the opening of gateways or the naming of mountains.

Over time the Crows would be asked to cede more land. In 1891 they felt the full might of the railroad lobby, as the Montana & Wyoming Railroad Company fought for a more direct route to the Clark's Fork mines. While legislators were able to ensure that it would only come within a mile of Yellowstone National Park and no farther, they managed to win full right to lay rails across Crow country.[59] Of Crow feelings about these early land losses in and near the park we have little information. However, it is recorded that in 1907, when the survivor of the Custer fight, Curley, objected to yet another proposal to open up more of the Crow reservation for non-Indian settlement, he revealed to officials the depth of his people's attachment to their traditional landscape:

The soil you see is not ordinary soil—it is the dust of the blood, the flesh and bones of our ancestors. We fought and bled and died helping the whites. You will have to dig down through the surface before you can find nature's earth as the upper portion is Crow. The land as it is, is my blood and my dead; it is consecrated and I do not want to give up any portion of it.[60]

Connections to the Kiowa: Close to "The Heart of God"

An unexpected outcome of our research into Plains Indian views of the Yellowstone's thermal fields was a purported Kiowa connection. According to oral traditions recorded by numerous field-workers, there existed an early, comradely connection between the Crow tribe and the early Kiowa.[61]

The following narrative came to light in late 1994 during our chance encounter with a Kiowa culture researcher and member of the tribe's Business Committee, in the Smithsonian's National Anthropological Archives in Washington, D.C., when we were researching for this project. On learning of our study of the Yellowstone region, this official informed us of a narrative known to the family line of a Kiowa from Anadarko, Oklahoma, which linked the creation of aboriginal Kiowa territory to the Yellowstone Plateau.

Perhaps the knowledge of this northerly region by the early Kiowa, who eventually settled around Rainy Mountain in western Oklahoma, should not have seemed so far-fetched. James Mooney interviewed elderly Kiowa tribal members in the 1890s and learned that their traditions located them "in or beyond the mountains at the extreme western sources of the Yellowstone and the Missouri."[62] Within the oldest memories of these informants were such impressions as an intensely cold region, a place of deep snows, and a people with compressed heads whom Mooney identified as the Flathead. It was while these early Kiowa were living at this location that two rival chiefs got into an argument and the tribe split up. The followers of the one moved to the east, setting up residence near the Crow along the Yellowstone; the second group remained in the mountains.

A closer link between the Kiowa and Yellowstone National Park comes from Hugh Scott, a soldier with the Seventh Cavalry who was stationed at Fort Sill, Oklahoma, in 1889. Scott met many of the old Kiowa warriors who remembered a homeland in what they call Ga'i K'op, or the Kiowa Mountains, at the sources of the Missouri and Yellowstone Rivers. The exact identity of these "Kiowa Mountains" is no longer known, but thanks to Scott we know they lay near Yellowstone National Park:

[The Kiowa came from] [t]he headwaters of the Missouri and Yellowstone Rivers near where the Kiowa Mountains are and the geysers of the Yellowstone Park which they describe as shooting hot water high in the air—and which no Kiowa has seen for some generations—and probably has heard little of from white people but he describes that country in a way it can be recognized.[63]

This strongly suggests that at one time Kiowas were camped near the park and that the nearby range was possibly the Gallatin or Madison Mountains of southern Montana. The broad outlines of this account of Kiowa ethnogenesis are covered by the ethnohistorian Nancy P. Hickerson:

When the Lewis and Clark expedition ascended the Missouri River in the summer of 1805, they reported that the "Kiawa" in seventy tents, were located on the headwaters of the Platte, very near to the Yellowstone Valley, the territories of the Crow, *and the traditional place of Kiowa emergence*. . . . In their early years of trading in the north, the Kiowa could have been witness to a wave of spectacular ceremonial events, as the Sun Dance complex spread through the tribes of the region. They became friends and trading partners of the Crow, lived among them for periods of time, and eventually intermarried. . . . Eventually, the Kiowas also adopted these ceremonies and adapted them to their own needs. This process was completed when the Kiowa Cold People, after sojourning in the north, eventually reunited with their southern congeners. They brought with them a vision of a new type of tribal unity, promoted by

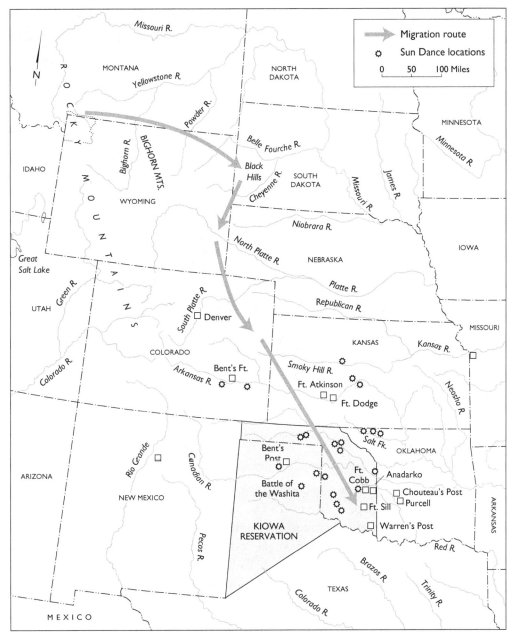

Kiowa tribal migration. (Based on a map in *Handbook of North American Indians*, vol. 13, pt. 2, *Plains*, edited by Raymond J. DeMallie 907. Courtesy of Smithsonian Institution.)

Kiowa consultant and his family visiting Dragon's Mouth, site of the "Heart of God" narrative, 1993. (Photo courtesy of Sherman Chaddlesone, Anadarko, Oklahoma.)

an annual gathering of bands and heightened by the drama of a great ceremonial (emphasis ours).[64]

Native accounts offer some corroboration for this scenario of Kiowa ethnogenesis and intimate knowledge of the north country. In the 1930s, when the military historian W. S. Nye was collecting information from Kiowa elders on the tribe's past, they reversed the chronology suggested by Captain Scott. In their accounts, first the Kiowas lived near Devil's Tower. Then: "We also lived in a country where hot water shot up out of the ground, high in the air. When we first saw this at a distance, we did not know what it was, but when we got nearer, we found that it was boiling water. That was a very dangerous place. We grew up in that hot water country."[65]

Also in the 1930s John Peabody Harrington, a linguist associated with the Smithsonian, interviewed Kiowas in Oklahoma and learned that they retained important place-names for both the Yellowstone and Black Hills regions. Their term Kaaek'oup, for instance, referred to a location in the far north, at least three hundred miles west of the Black Hills, which Harrington conjectured might apply to "the main range of the Rocky Mountains at the Three Forks, and said to be so called because the Kiowas once lived there."[66] As for the Kiowa term for the Yellowstone River itself, most of James Mooney's oldest informants concurred that it was Ts'oousa, meaning "several rocks stand planted," although when Mooney originally noted the word he had unnecessarily added the postpound, -*p'a*, meaning "river," after the place-name. Together with the even more intimate residue of Black Hills topographic knowledge that Harrington found among living Kiowas, it appears highly likely that their northland experiences left an abiding mark on Kiowa cultural memory.

Finally, modern Kiowas claim similar ancestral ties to the Yellowstone region. In writing of his people's origins, the Pulitzer Prize–winning Kiowa Indian novelist, N. Scott Momaday, has said, "Nomads, they had come upon the Southern Plains at about the time of the Revolutionary War, having migrated from the area of the headwaters of the Yellowstone River, in what is now western Montana, by way of the Black Hills and the High Plains. Along the way they had become a people of the deep interior, the midcontinent—hunters, warriors, keepers of the sacred earth."[67] And according to native consultants to the Kiowa Historical and Research Society who were authorized by their Kiowa tribal council to contribute to a collective project on the tribe's cultural history in 1975:

> The Kiowa saga began long ago in the north country. In the land of the Yellowstone the Kiowas felt great personal power. They faced the sun, learned the trails, and conquered the mountains. After many years, however, they became restless in the Yellowstone vastness.
>
> Westward and north the panoramic sweep revealed ranges of mountains stretching against the horizon in shades of green, brown, purple, and misty blues. In that direction the past tribal experience was compatible with the demands of the earth and their friends—the Flatheads.
>
> Eastward and south lay vast unknown prairies and unfriendly tribes, but also millions of life-sustaining buffalo. Though legend recounts that some Kiowas chose the northwest route, the bulk of the tribe turned east and southward for what proved to be their great trek through the land of seemingly limitless prairies abundant with buffalo.[68]

From that point the narrative leads into the story of "why most of the tribe left the plains" and an account of "The 'Pulling-out' Band Legend," which opens with the sentence, "Long ago two chiefs led a Kiowa hunting party in the land of the Yellowstone in the north." After a dispute over the udder of a slain antelope, one of the chiefs leads his faction, the Kuato, or Pulling Out, band, to the northeast, and they are never heard from again, whereupon the victorious chief led his "main body of Kiowas" southeastward toward the Black Hill country.[69]

Yet our investigation turned up a more detailed picture of mythic Kiowa origins that was also more geographically precise in situating the events within the Yellowstone Plateau. This narrative came from a forty-seven-year-old Vietnam War veteran and painter who is an enrolled member of the Kiowa tribe. In winter 1986 his tribe commissioned this man and two other Kiowa artists to illustrate their people's mythohistoric background. Each of the ten panels measured six feet by eight feet; they are currently displayed in the Kiowa Tribal Museum at the Kiowa Tribal Complex in Carnegie, Oklahoma. Among their depictions was "the early history of the Kiowas, the Yellowstone, what we call the Yellowstone period, up until the Kiowas moved down to the southern plains area."[70]

During this mural project, our consultant was approached by a Kiowa elder and tribal historian, now deceased, who "related a story . . . concerning the Yellowstone area and requested that the story be illustrated in a painting." The story sounded very familiar, and our consultant believes he may have heard it earlier, perhaps from his father, a well-known Kiowa storyteller. But this version included "great, great detail." And our consultant said, "[My father] also described the location [in Yellowstone Park] to me." In 1993 our consultant related the following narrative on tape and entitled it "Close to the Heart of God: Kiowa Yellowstone Origins Narration."

> There was a man who the Kiowas say was one of the greatest Kiowas who ever lived, but no one remembers his name so only for the purpose of this story I will call him Kahn Hayn [our phonetic approximation], which means "No Name" in the Kiowa language. Kahn Hayn was orphaned as a young child and he didn't marry. He didn't have any offspring and no immediate family, so his status in the tribe is described as being *kah ah*, or poor. But he was a great hunter and a warrior, and he had a big heart and he was always working for the greater welfare of the Kiowa people and helping to provide for those who were less fortunate than him.
>
> When Doh Ki [also known as Doyem Daw-k'hee, the Earth-maker],[71] or God, put all the people on the earth he placed them here and there in different areas according to how well they could fit in, in those areas. But after that was done there were still several groups of people, different tribes who didn't have places to call a homeland, and the Kiowas were among this group of people. One day a bush spoke to all these people and called them all together in one area. When the Kiowas arrived at this spot they discovered that the voice was the voice of God, or Doh Ki. Doh Ki explained to this gathering that he had one place left on this earth that didn't have anybody living there. But to get to this place, one of them had to go through a very difficult and dangerous journey to arrive there.
>
> Doh Ki then had these people move to a place that Kahn Hayn thought was somewhere near the end of the earth. There was no vegetation there, no animals, no insects. Nothing moved about the ground or in the air. There was only dirt and rough stone formations, and here and there clouds of steam shot out from holes and fissures in the ground. Doh Ki called everyone around one of these steaming pools, and that was the most disturbing sight in

this desolate place. There was a large deep cauldron of boiling water that surged and smashed against the jagged rock walls. It made a loud fearsome thumping noise, the cauldron did. It sounded like a great beast was just below the surface fighting to break free from the cauldron and tossing waters about violently.

Most of the people ran away immediately from the dreadful sight and sounds, and only a handful of chiefs and warriors from the various tribes stayed there, and Kahn Hayn and a few other Kiowa men were among them. Doh Ki then pointed down into the cauldron and told the remaining men that the surrounding land would belong to the tribe of any man who would dive down into the crashing waters. This created a good deal of excited discussion among these men and some began to back away because of fear, and many left because they felt this land, this country was useless and it wasn't worth risking their lives for.

Because of his strong belief and faith in the goodness of God, of Doh Ki, Kahn Hayn knew that there was more to this, to this offer, than what they were seeing and hearing, because Doh Ki didn't play tricks on the people. He constantly tested them, but his rewards were always good and lasting. Kahn Hayn related his feelings to the other Kiowas and said he had decided that he would try this thing, he was Kah Ahn and if this didn't work out right he wouldn't be leaving any family behind, and there would be no one to mourn his passing.

So he stepped over to the edge of the cauldron. He looked around one last time, but there was not much to see in this desolate landscape except his fellow Kiowas watching him with expressions of dread and apprehension. He then looked down into the boiling water, he closed his eyes and pushed himself off and down into the unknown.

Kahn Hayn first felt the extreme heat of the water, this started a small panic within him. The thumping sound that they'd heard was instead above the cauldron now, [there] was a terrible pounding all through his body and made his head feel like it was about to burst. He had a sense that he had dived deep into the hot pool and his thoughts were raised in about what he was supposed to do next. He was wondering if there was something in this pool that he had to reach for, and if so he had to find it real soon because his lungs were beginning to ache, and his skin was getting numb from the heat of the water, and he felt like he was blistering from the intense heat of the water. Now, all of a sudden, while he was going through all these different emotions, something else struck him, just horrified him, and increased his panic. When he entered the water he was tossed about so much that he lost all sense of directions. He wanted to open his eyes to try to find his bearings, but he was afraid that his eyes would be burned like his skin was being burned, and he also felt himself being banged and scraped against the sharp, rough walls. But he couldn't tell, from the angle of the walls, he couldn't tell if he was near to the surface or deeper down into the cauldron, his air was starting to give out and all of the heat and pounding was causing him to lose all hope for his situation.

So just as he felt himself losing consciousness he decided just to let himself go to whatever death had in store for him. So he stopped his moving about, his thrashing, and he let himself go limp and he waited for death to overtake him. He didn't realize that at the time he was near the surface of the water of the cauldron.

When he stopped struggling his body floated up and broke the surface into the cool, sweet air. As he rolled over and began to gulp in the fresh air, he felt himself being lifted from the water by a lot of hands, and the next thing he heard [was] a lot of excited yelling and victory cries that the Kiowas were making.

And then he opened his eyes and he saw the most beautiful sight any human has ever seen. Doh Ki was not around any longer, nor were all the other tribal people who were gathered around as he dove into the cauldron. The only ones that were there were the Kiowas, and they were all trying to explain at once about the miraculous thing that Kahn Hayn had accomplished. The landscape was no longer barren and desolate but was now filled with a thick, rich forest of tall, beautiful trees. The distant mountains were partly covered with snow and small streams and creeks flowed down from the mountains, and they turned into rushing rivers which in turn cascaded into large bodies of water lakes. Also, there were now many large and small animals of all types moving through the forest, across the landscape, and on top and along the waters and waterways. The place that Kahn Hayn left as he dove into the cauldron was now transformed. This became the land that Doh Ki spoke of. This was now the most beautiful and abundant of all places on the earth, and this became the Kiowas' homeland.

Following this journey that Kahn Hayn made, the Kiowas stayed and feasted and celebrated for days and days, and they made many prayers in gratitude to Doh Ki for his gift that he gave to the Kiowas. Kahn Hayn became the chief of the Kiowas, and he had his choice of any young woman from the tribe for wives.

The Kiowas lived in, around this area for many years, and when Kahn Hayn finally died the Kiowas took him back to that cauldron and they buried him nearby. And then, gradually, the Kiowas began to move away from there into other areas.

They say that because of what Kahn Hayn did at that time, and because of the Kiowas' deep faith in God, that the Kiowas would always be preeminent, or paramount, to all other peoples, all other tribes, and that we would always remain closest to the heart of God, Orbah Hah. That's all.

There is corroboration of some aspects of this narrative in the limited corpus of published Kiowa oral traditions. Our consultant had already located one of three variants for the story, "How the Kiowa Became Paramount," which were collected by the noted anthropologist and folklorist Elsie Clews Parsons in the late 1920s. In Parsons's third version, out of nowhere a mysterious voice issues a challenge: "'Whoever jumps into this pool of water, will get something,' and that was, to live in the centre of the world."[72] What is dangerous about the pool are vaguely defined "sharp points" sticking from the water, which are described as "sharp as cattails." Everyone else in the vicinity is too afraid to jump, but when a brave Kiowa leaps into the pool he plunges down and through to "the other side," winning the reward of living in the world's center. The voice went even further and prophesied that if the Kiowa ever died out, "there would be no more life on this earth. When the Indian race and language come to an end, there will be no more life on earth."[73]

According to our consultant, the Kiowa name for where the Yellowstone area where these mythic events occurred "is Tung Sa'u Dah, which means 'hot water,' or 'the place of hot water.'" As for the specific "cauldron" where his protagonist had his near-death experience, he identified it as the Dragon's Mouth, next to Mud Volcano, north of Yellowstone Lake.

Continuing Crow Ties to Yellowstone

Given the estrangement between Crows and the Yellowstone Plateau region that commenced with the Fort Laramie Treaty of 1868, it is unusual to hear of connections in the twentieth century between the tribe and the park. Our principal Crow consultant recalled one form of native enterprise open to Indians in the area: dancing for Yellowstone-bound tourists at Pahaska Tepee or Cody's Irma Hotel. But his family were not the only Indian entrepreneurs who eked out summer earnings by presenting versions of native culture for tourists. The park never encouraged or commercially exploited its romantic association with Indian images in the overt, consistent fashion that Glacier National Park did with the Blackfeet Indians, Yosemite National Park with the Miwok Indians, or Grand Canyon National Park with the Hopi and Havasupai Indians. But over the years there were sporadic attempts to encourage or allow Indians from adjoining reservations to display wares or dance. Although the facts are few and far between, the historical record contains a few glimpses of Indians performing as Indians in the park.

A few hints from the late nineteenth century show that the idea of Indians exhibiting their culture, which became regular practice by the Blackfeet at Glacier National Park, was entertained periodically. Magoc's research uncovered publicity efforts, more ambivalent and less sustained than at Glacier, to join images of "stoically postured" Indians and the Yellowstone "Wonderland." But subtler themes could be read from these publicity depictions, too: some emphasized the Indian-as–U.S. citizen leitmotif; another pictured an iconic Indian with outstretched arm turning the park over to tourists as if he had, as Magoc puts it, "silently acquiesced in their demise."[74] One tawdry instance of park-encouraged Indianist enterprise comes from a letter in the park archives dated July 5, 1896, in which a member of an unidentified tribe complained to a "Captain Anderson" at Fort Yellowstone that he had been ordered to leave the park after being cajoled into buying whiskey for a soldier. To avoid eviction, the Indian took a job cutting wood and doing carpentry offered by a Mr. Waters at "Thumbs." But when some acquaintances asked him to "dance a war dance" and he "got a butcher knife in his teeth and danced" he was fired. His letter pleaded, "[I am] an Indian boy I work for my own living," but a notation penned on his letter says that he was a "deaf and drunk Indian" who was merely excusing "the circumstances that led to his being expelled from the Park."[75]

Three years later E. C. Waters, president of the Yellowstone Lake Boat Company in Fond du Lac, Wisconsin, received permission through the park's acting superintendent from the secretary of the interior "to locate Indians [in their wigwams] on Dot Island in the Yellowstone Lake from June 13th to September 15th, for exhibition to the tourists in the park." But Interior Secretary E. A. Hitchcock also stipulated:

> [The Indians] who may best be secured from the Crow Agency, Montana, are entirely willing to go [and the company will make satisfactory arrangements] for the proper care, protection, and remuneration of the Indians taken, and that it be distinctly understood that the company will pay all the necessary traveling expenses in getting them into the reservation, and returning them promptly to their homes at the close of the season.[76]

We could find no confirming documentation regarding whether any Indians actually pitched tipis on Dot Island. But other opportunities lured Indians to perform as Indians in the park. James Willard Schultz, a well-known writer on the Blackfeet, arranged a "very interesting ceremony" at the Yellowstone geyser region in late spring 1916. Entering by the Cody Road, the Indians were to present "the first ceremony of its kind given by the Crow Indians in the last 20 years"; a proposed film of the proceedings was considered compatible with an ongoing "Shoshone project" related to the "See America First" promotion of recreational tourism in the United States.[77] Then in 1924 a number of Arapahos and other Indians (among them, the elderly warrior Goes in Lodge) participated in the filming of the Hollywood studio production, *The Thundering Herd,* in the park.[78] It is not clear whether this experience was the springboard for a "colorful pageant" that was held the following year near the buffalo ranch in the Lamar Valley between August 30 and September 6. As described in the park's annual report for 1925, each day witnessed a "western frontier round-up celebration":

> The tame buffalo herd of over 700 animals, a score or more of Crow Indians from the nearby reservation dressed in the regalia and war paints of other

Crow Indians during the dedication of Plenty Coups Tablet on Cody Road. (Photo courtesy of Yellowstone National Park Archives, #Yell 37805.)

days, and a few real western cowboys made the round-up a thrilling representation of the old days of the west. Visitors to the ranch during "buffalo plains week," as it was called, were taken from the ranch headquarters to the site of the round-up in the stage-coaches of former days, drawn by four and six horses. The Indian camps were of great interest to visitors. Typical camps with their tepees, open fires, travois, and handiwork of the tribe, and peopled with braves, squaws, and papooses, were a vivid reminder of the fact that not so many years ago the ancestors of these very Indians roamed and hunted over the lands in this vicinity.[79]

A more durable relationship between the park and Indians was under way only two years later, when an enterprising Crow named Max Big Man presented Indian programs for tourists at Yellowstone National Park. Big Man was born in 1886 to a Crow mother and Gros Ventre father and attended the Crow Agency boarding school. After finishing school, Big Man struggled to become an independent rancher, then, in 1926, signed on with the Chicago, Burlington and Quincy Railroad.[80] In addition to his work as a meeter and greeter of visitors to the reservation at the Crow Agency train stop and an aspiring progressive political leader who often escorted Chief Plenty Coups and other old war chiefs to public functions, Big Man was also a promoter of Indian culture presentations for the Custer Battlefield Association and briefly left Montana to participate in a Columbia Broadcasting System radio series for children in the Chicago and New York schools. But in the state he "frequently talked and danced for White men's and women's groups, including visitors to the Crow Reservation and nearby Yellowstone Park."[81] Big Man wrote to Mrs. Jesse Schultz Graham, daughter of the well-known writer on Blackfeet Indians, James Willard Schultz, in early February 1927:

> I am planning now to go to the Park [Yellowstone] this coming summer where I am going to have different dances and little games that would interest the White people. I have a good tepee and I am trying to let the White people see how the Indians used to live in the old days, and lecture on different things. When I was a boy in school, I saw a show, and ever since then, I have taken an interest in shows and plays. I know just about what the White people would like to see and what interests them, because I have talked to different tourists and have learned from the questions they ask me.[82]

Big Man's entrepreneurial relationship with the park continued at least until 1932, when he visited the park to tell stories and his appearance was featured on the cover of the in-house park organ, *Yellowstone Nature Notes.* Perhaps this experience also inspired Big Man to write an article for his local newspaper the following year. Opening with his memories of elders' stories about running buffalo over cliffs, Big Man wrote that a Livingston rancher, Charley Murphy, showed him jump sites near Murphy's Ox Yoke Ranch. Over the following days, attended by Fox Movietone cameramen, Big Man and Yellowstone National Park rangers, including one mixed-blood Flathead ranger who chided him about continuing to wear his hair long, rode their horses to view elk, mountain sheep, and buffalo. "As I was looking down," Big Man mused about the similarity between the old days and the present, "I again thought about the stone age days of my people. . . . As we came down from the mountain, the men were placed all along the trail, so the buffalo would not turn away from us and go over the mountain."[83]

Mrs. Graham, to whom Big Man wrote, was James Schultz's daughter. They appear to have met through Big Man's work on Mrs. Graham's grand pageant, *Masque of the Absaroka,* which hired Crow actors to launch a public dramatization of Crow origin mythology. The pageant's director, Jessie Louise Donaldson, attempted in late 1926 and early 1927 to stage it in Yellowstone National Park.[84]

Planning for the *Masque* began in 1926, when Mrs. Graham and two friends took the train to Crow Agency to solicit the collaboration of the tribe's chief of police, Victor Three Irons, and Max Big Man in a drama that was to be presented "at Montana State College to tell the story of the Crow Indians."[85] After a rocky start, a musical presentation, apparently cobbled together from Crow origin narratives and aspects of Tobacco Society ceremonialism, was staged with a sizable Crow cast in Bozeman, Montana. Although Miss Schultz left the show by this point, it was heavily promoted in the closing months of the year by Miss Donaldson, who managed to win its endorsement by a number of distinguished Indian writers and sympathizers, including George Bird Grinnell and Frank Bird Linderman.

When Donaldson itemized the projected mutual responsibilities and considerable financial and personnel investment involved in mounting the Crow-acted *Masque* in a letter to Yellowstone Park Superintendent Horace M. Albright. But Albright drafted a discouraging reply. Although he admitted apologetically that his earlier letters to Donaldson encouraged the idea, adding that the National Park Service remained "very much interested in productions such as you are planning," he worried that its scale and costs might be prohibitive.[86] But a confidential memo between park officials, affixed to one piece of official correspondence to Donaldson, suggests that park staffers harbored more substantial doubts about the project: "To me, the attached doesn't seem to be suited for presentation in a National Park. I really can't see a great deal of connection it has to the Yellowstone and, of course, the Indian problem is going to be a hard one to solve in case they want to use real Indians. How does it appeal to you?" To this communication, Albright replied, "It can be worked out, I think, although we may have some troubles.[87]

Whatever the private connotations that lay behind this mention of "the Indian problem" and "real Indians," the park avoided the obligations that presenting the *Masque* would have entailed, although Mr. and Mrs. Albright attended its presentation in the less controversial setting of Bozeman on the night of June 6, 1927. As for the National Park Service's participation in other pageants, as Superintendent Albright wrote to Donaldson in greater detail, Washington had appointed a Mr. Garnet Holms as its "Pageant Master" and mounted pageants at other Indian-connected national landmarks such as California's Yosemite and Sequoia Parks, Arizona's Casa Grande National Monument, and southern California. As far as Yellowstone was concerned, however, a behind-the-scenes story of competing pageants and alternating scenarios for the region's crucial history may have contributed to the apparent dropping of the idea of holding the *Masque* there.

For around the same time that the *Masque* was under development by Schultz at the Crow Agency, what appears to be the first attempt to present a historical pageant in Yellowstone National Park did take place. Before an audience of nearly one thousand visitors, the open-air spectacle *Discovery of the Yellowstone Park* featured, according to the *Great Falls Tribune,*

> various times in Yellowstone's history in four scenes. Indians and old-timers—even the Washburn-Langford explorers of 1870—returned to the park. . . . The entire pageant portrays the dream of the old-timer who returns to Yellowstone for the first time since the '70s. First the redskins, with their legends about the formation of the geysers and the Grand Canyon, then the party of exploration and finally the "savages" of today appear in his dreams.[88]

The following summer, 1927, another pageant with a more palatable Indian theme was offered by Old Faithful camp employees. Falling back on Longfellow's *Hiawatha* for its plot, the amateur, non-Indian actors resurrected a story that climaxed with Hiawatha introducing his fellow Indians to a Jesuit missionary. To the strains of Dvorak's "Indian Lament," and with the Indians' embrace of the kingdom of Christ, Hiawatha departed for a final journey toward the setting sun. The melodrama's connection to the prevailing Vanishing Indian motif was not lost on a local newspaper reviewer:

> The curling smoke of the pipe of peace that was offered to the [Jesuit] priest reminds one of the poem by P. W. Norris who was formerly a superintendent of the Yellowstone park, and in it, which was called the Calumet of the Coteau, various pictures of Indian life were depicted, though now the aroma of the kinnikinick has also gone into the quiet places beyond the sun with the passing of the redmen.[89]

Independent Indian craft vending never gained a foothold in the park. Although before the establishment of the National Park Service in 1916 Yellowstone shops sold arrowheads to tourists, we found no direct Indian marketing of cultural identity there until the 1920s, when a few Indians, like Max Big Man, joined commercial ventures. While on March 9, 1937, the newly conceived Arts and Crafts Board of the Department of the Interior attempted to impose an Indian-made-only policy for "Indian jewelry" sold in the national park retail outlets, in Yellowstone there was no stipulation that these "genuine" Indian materials be of local or even regional origin.[90] There is even anecdotal evidence that at least one Indian was discouraged from developing an entrepreneurial presence in the Park. According to a story related to Alston Chase by a former North District ranger in Yellowstone, "not long ago" an Indian businessman wanted to position a tipi-shaped gift shop near Roosevelt Lodge. When the Indian learned that his concession permit had been denied because the building would detract from the park's lodge, which had been nominated the National Register of Historic Places, the Indian is said to have asked in so many words, "How can a white man's building be more historical than an Indian tepee?"[91]

When our principal Crow consultant accompanied his family into the Yellowstone National Park area, they entered as tourists. But that formal category did not mean they had forgotten their oldest cultural memories of the Yellowstone region, which included narratives that explained how the world in its present form was first created.

Among the oldest of Crow story cycles is that which relates the deeds of Old Woman's Grandson (Káalisbaapitua), a character who represents the classic culture hero. Not surprisingly, we also find this important character prominent in the folklore of their old kinfolk, the Hidatsas, to the east, as well as in that of their neighbors, the Mandan. In the Crow version Old Woman's Grandson, the offspring of the Sun and a Crow woman, is usually described as raised by a powerful and often demonic grandmother figure following the death of his human mother.

After maturing to young manhood with remarkable speed, he undertakes the killing of a generation of monsters who rule the world. When he has finally readied the world for human occupation, he turns into the north star, and his grandmother becomes the moon.

Some Crow people believe that a few of the topographical features that define Yellowstone National Park could have come about through the heroic deeds of Old Woman's Grandson. One narrative from the Pryor area discusses the origins of two features possibly from the Mud Volcano area. This version of the basic narrative originates from a southern River Crow man named Sharp Horn, who passed it on to his son, Comes Up Red, who told it to his son, the father of the narrator who provided it for this book. According to our consultant, the following episode belonged to the longer cycle of stories about the mythic deeds of Old Woman's Grandson.

> There was a part where the boy kills a big buffalo bull who sucks in people. A giant buffalo bull that sucks in and eats people. When the boy killed that giant buffalo bull, he turned him into that. That's what he turned into.
>
> Then he put a giant mountain lion right next to it to keep him in check. To keep the bull from coming back. That is what the old people said happened. The old giant buffalo is the one that sucks out the hot blast of air. And then that other hole makes a growling sound. So they say that is the mountain lion that keeps the buffalo bull in check.[92]

A bit later in the interview our consultant elaborated:

> My father was told by his grandfathers that this [the thermal region of the park] was where the Grandchild, the Old Lady's Grandchild, fought all of the beasts and killed them, and turned them into mountains and hills after he killed them. Then he turned the giant buffalo into a geyser's formation. I guess Colter's Hell [consultant later identified Colter's Hell as Mud Volcano and Dragon's Mouth] is the present name for it. It blows hot air out, and for twelve miles windward of it all of the trees are dead. Even animals would die in the old days. But it is not as strong as it used to be. He said I will turn you into this, and then he put another geyser formation there. The other geyser formation roars all of the time. It just makes a sound. He said that was a mountain lion, to keep the buffalo bull in check, from coming back to life again and harass-ing the Crows. That was the reason.[93]

Another mythic Crow narrative that is associated with the park was related on the shores of Yellowstone Lake. It links the earlier death-of-the-monsters theme with the strongest variety of supernatural medicine a Crow can receive—that bestowed by the Thunderbird. In terms of the conceptual categories that constitute the Crow worldview, this story also ties together the three environ-mental forces that still make the Yellowstone region unique: benevolent high mountains, the threatening depths of the great lake, and the hot rocks whose power only a human being can harness. Our consultant received the rights to this story from the man who had adopted him into the Crow Tobacco Society, who had heard it from his own grandfather. But he prefaced it by emphasizing, "Our legends say that the Sun created the first Crow on Yellowstone River, which we call Elk River. The Crows have always lived here." In this narrative and the one that follows Yellowstone Lake becomes essentially a character in the drama. We catch an echo of the relationship between birds and the lake that Hunts to Die mentioned in his equation of driftwood with eagle feathers:

> The story begins when the Crows were camped at the junction of Pryor Creek and the Yellowstone River. A man was sitting on a high hill on the east side of Pryor Creek one day. He was making arrows and looking out. He was the lookout.
>
> Suddenly from out of the sky the Thunderbird came and grabbed him by his hair. When he grabbed him he said, "Do not be afraid." So this man was not afraid when the Thunderbird grabbed him. Then he brought him over here to overlook, Overlook Mountain. It is on the southeast side of the lake where we are at right now.
>
> So the Thunderbird took him to the top of the mountain. His nest was there. So he put him in the nest. He said, "What do you need for food? What do you need to stay alive?" The man said, "Bring me a young buffalo," and he said, "I need water." He [Thunderbird] said, "All the water you need is here." So he brought him a young buffalo calf. When the man finished eating he asked the Thunderbird why he brought him there.
>
> He said, "This is my nest. This is where I live." Then he showed him Yellowstone Lake, which the Crows have no name for except that we call it the Big Lake, the Large Lake. He said, "Down there monsters live in the water and nearby. When I lay my eggs, and the fledglings come out, on the third day that they come out, all of the beasts come and they eat the little ones. I am constantly at war with these beasts."
>
> He said, "I know you are my allies, because I know that you constantly fight these monsters also." He said, "I want you to kill . . . there is one certain one that always comes up and eats the fledglings when they are three days old." He said, "I will bring you anything that you need to kill this water beast that lives in the lake."
>
> So the man fasted, and he didn't know what to do at first. He said, "You have greater powers than I. How is it that you cannot kill this beast?" He [Thunderbird] said, "Our powers are about the same and that is why I cannot kill him." He said, "You have reason, you have your mind to reason. You can think out a way to kill him. That is why I brought you here."
>
> So the man fasted, and thought, and finally he saw in his dream. . . . He was told how he could kill this beast that would eat the three-day-old Thun-

derbirds. He was told to dig pits, and to build big fires, and to put rocks on it. Certain-sized rocks, that he could pick up with a forked stick. He was told that the monster, when he came up the mountain, would open his mouth. He said, "Throw as many hot rocks as he could into his mouth. And then dig another pit and put hides in it. Great big hides, and fill it with water and boil it. When it is boiling, make sure that you have a way to pick it up. Put saplings around it so that you can pick it up. When it is close enough pour the hot water into his mouth. That way you will kill him, you see."

So the eggs were about ready to hatch. When they hatched, they had everything ready. All of the rocks, and all of the wood that they needed for the fire. Then on the third day, they saw the beast coming up the mountain. So they got ready, and they built a big fire and got all of the hot rocks that they needed, and they also boiled water.

Then when the beast came up, the man would pick up the hot rocks with his stick and would throw them into his mouth, as much as he could. Then when he got close enough, he poured this hot water into his mouth. Then steam came out of his mouth, and then he tumbled down into the lake. When he hit the lake the water splashed, and went up about as high as the mountain, when it hit the water.

They say that the man who killed the last dinosaur . . . which doesn't mean anything in our language anymore, it is so old. They say that was the last dinosaur. They have never seen any dinosaurs after that.[94]

Our consultant heard the following narrative from two storytellers, Comes Up Red and George Goes Ahead.

There was a war party. A man named [?]—I don't know what it means, I guess it's too old to translate—led a war party. They came to Yellowstone Lake. Although they were fearful of it, they did not want to go into it, they are drawn to it because of its power, and the mystical quality.

They came to the lake and they saw a swan, way down, almost in the middle of the lake. This war party leader said he needed the feathers of this swan. In his vision he was told to get certain feathers and the swan's feathers fit the description. So he asked if anyone could swim out there and get this swan. All of the men were scared. They did not want to swim out there and get this swan.

But there was one young boy in the war party. He was willing to go out there. He said, "Older brother, let me swim out there. I can swim out there and get that bird for you." But they didn't want him to go. Because all of the men were supposed to be brave and courageous and they showed their fear. They didn't want to be put down by this young boy. They said, "No, don't go out there, you don't know what you are getting yourself into."

Finally he said, "Just let me go out there a little ways. If something bad happens, I can swim back." They said go ahead. The young boy swam into the

Key Crow consultant at Yellowstone Lake, checking the location of cultural sites with Lawrence Loendorf, 1995. (Photo by Peter Nabokov.)

lake and went out there and caught the swan, and came back with it. Then all of the men to show their courage swam to the lake and came back. After that they were not as fearful as they were of the lake.[95]

Although this second story also revolves around a Crow contest with the dangers of Yellowstone Lake, it concerns a more psychological and physical conflict with place than the previous narrative, which dealt with a supernatural encounter with the location's spirit-beings. Goes Ahead set this story "in our time, in our era." But, he said, "My grandfather said it was way back." This shift in temporal context problematizes the issue of whether this story falls into the category of myth, an absolutely truthful and sacred narrative, or in the category of legends, which are generally regarded as true but set in a less remote era, when the world looked as it does today.[96]

When our principal Crow consultant struggled to answer this question and to characterize this story, like many contemporary Indians, he reached for the English category that he believed evoked the greatest truth-value for non-Crow listeners. Of its storyline of the commencement of a new, more equitable relationship between his people and earlier spirits associated with Yellowstone Lake, he stated simply, "It was part of our history."

CHAPTER 2

Wayfarers from the North

The Blackfeet and Flathead

After more than a century of Indian absence from the Yellowstone Plateau, documentation of the trails habitually followed by parties of Blackfeet, Flathead, Pend d'Oreille, and Kootenai through the greater Yellowstone ecosystem is hard to come by. Their place-names for the plateau and its entryways and their oral traditions and cultural practices linking them to the park proper are equally difficult to find. Unlike the Crow to the east and the Shoshone to the south, the hunting territories of the Blackfeet and the Flathead, at least as early treaties delineated them, did not overlap the present park, although these tribes claimed the right to traverse and forage on a vaster landscape than today's reservation boundaries might indicate.

With the exception of the occasionally lost or discarded tools or weapons, these Indian travelers left little evidence of their presence. Even when one is lucky enough to find them, tribal attribution is usually impossible to pin down. During the historical period, moreover, most of those who passed through intentionally sought to cover their tracks. They may have been trying to hunt, gather, or simply travel undetected, and they were quietly alert to steal horses, furs, or weapons from any traditional enemies or non-Indians whose paths they crossed.

Up and Down the Yellowstone: A Northern Entrance

Parties of Flathead and Blackfeet reached the northern rim of the Yellowstone Plateau through the Bridger or Flathead Passes out of present-day Bozeman, or dropped south from the Crazy Mountains by way of the Shields River. These two access trails into Yellowstone's inner sanctum could hardly stand in greater contrast.

Yellowstone National Park Superintendent Horace Albright, adopted by Crow Indians at the Gallatin Gateway opening to the north of the park, 1927. (Photo courtesy of Yellowstone National Park Archives, #Yell 37799-2.)

The first trail opened two-thirds of the way west along the park's northern perimeter and offered a relatively gentle gateway to the high country. In its broad curve between the Absaroka and Gallatin Mountains, here was the long, welcoming corridor of the upper Yellowstone River valley. At this portal, the Flathead, Pend d'Oreille, and Blackfeet, who would have already ventured many days from the upper ranges of present-day Montana, entered the trough of Paradise Valley, about thirty miles long and ten to twelve miles wide, just south of Livingston.[1] Here was also one of those unusual moments when it was necessary to head down in order to go up against the river, as the Yellowstone flows north into Montana.

On foot or horseback, the parties probably then paralleled the river. Moving steadily upstream by means of easy flat terraces, halting occasionally in the shade of cottonwood trees along its banks in summer or feeding their horses from the trees' nourishing inner bark in winter, they were probably well aware of older Indian encampments along the way. Just past Livingston, for instance, they passed between deserted sites positioned on the opposing ridges of the river. One on the western bank was recent enough to contain hearths used by their own relatives, but according to archeological estimates, the site on the opposite ridge had Indian campfires nearly nine thousand years before.[2]

Among the thousands of old Indian sites along this major native trade route into Yellowstone National Park, according to the archaeologist Larry Lahren, is the terrace above the community of Emigrant where one can still pick out miles-long rows of stones—remnants of an old Indian buffalo jump.[3] Such locations would have made Indian travelers like the Blackfeet feel at home; up north their yearly round involved stopping at fixed winter campsites, when the buffalo were fat and prime, and stampeding the animals into the boulder drive lines they called *piskun* and over cliff faces.[4] In one of its rare references to Indians in the Yellowstone valley, an early guidebook to Yellowstone National Park stated that early white settlement in the fertile Paradise Valley attracted "Indian marauders." But since this was only ten years after the Nez Perce troubles in the park, the guide immediately felt obliged to assuage any anxieties with an all-clear advisory: "But fear of Indian attack has now forever passed away."[5]

As early as 1893 William S. Brackett described the "Indian forts" he noticed on the river benches above this stretch of the Yellowstone River and the tipi rings that lay farther into the mountains. He also wrote of other "interesting remains left by Indians who lived and hunted in this fertile valley as late as the year 1876," which he found at local ranches, especially at one that lay "opposite Emigrant Peak, where [he was] writing."[6] Lahren guesses that there are an average of "two or more archaeological sites per square mile" in this Park County corridor. Especially promising locations are found, predictably, wherever drainages such as Six Mile and Tom Miner Creeks offered proximity to water and wood, shelter from wind and sun, or, as in the Tom Miner Basin, topographic conditions for a buffalo jump with attendant tipi rings, stone corrals, drive lines, and kill sites.[7]

Forging beyond Tom Miner Creek, experienced Indian wayfarers heading south would have squeezed through the river's constricted bend at Yankee Jim Canyon, only to spy increasing signs of earlier Indian bivouac and hunting sites. Emerging from this canyon, for instance, they skirted one old camp on the eastern bank, on the valley floor. Since its rock-lined hearth lay beneath twenty-two feet of river silt, the passersby were unaware of the fact that within it lay walnut-sized chunks of charcoal (identified as yew wood) about five thousand years old.[8] At the same time, Flatheads traveling by would have prized the yew (which still grows in the Bitterroot Valley) for bow making. A prominent Flathead elder named Pete Beaverhead remembered the process: season the wood before carving it down to form, varnish it with a concoction of boiled animal muscle and sinew, and then string and hunt with it.[9]

Continuing toward present-day Gardiner, the Indian travelers beat against the cooling winds that regularly sweep down from the upper river channel to replace the rising lowland heat. As the landscape grows progressively drier near the present-day park entrance, they neared a prominent mountain on the right that seemed to attract lighting strikes. Scooped out of the high volcanic talus that overlooks the river trail opposite Electric Peak were remnants of old hunting blinds, of which the scouts flanking out to protect these travelers were surely aware.

Just northwest of the park boundary, the Indian visitors saw the heights of Mount Everts, which they probably knew was another magnet for earlier natives

Probable Indian hunting blind (screen bottom) across from Electric Peak and overlooking Yellowstone River, 1996. (Photo by Peter Nabokov.)

to fast or hunt. Closer to the river trail, among other old sites in the immediate vicinity of Mammoth Hot Springs, lay the 170 foot rock alignment that, strung out along a glacial ridge, indicated a drive line or a religious site. It has been suggested that this area "has the potential to yield important information on Native American life in the Mammoth region."[10] By this time the visitors from the north would find themselves deep in the Yellowstone heartland and surely be on the lookout for other tribesmen who had ventured there, also in search of game, minerals, or the other Indian trails that exited the plateau to the south and east.

Up the Beartooth Pass: A Northeastern Entrance

Beartooth Pass offered more difficult access into the Yellowstone Plateau. Lifting out of Red Lodge not far from the park's northeastern corner, its remnants can still be spotted zigzagging almost straight up alongside today's Beartooth Highway (State Highway 212). To the Crow Indians, the location of present-day Red Lodge was known as Where the Red Lodge Was Annihilated (Ashhishalahaawiio) for the killing by Shoshone warriors of an entire Crow band, thirty lodges strong, which was led by a camp chief whose name was Red Lodge and which included his brother, Yellow Lodge. The tragedy occurred along the banks of Red Lodge's present-day Rock River, which was referred to by the Crow as Fast Current (Biliiliikashee).[11]

Ascending the single-file footpath up the Beartooth Pass, the Crow, Blackfeet, and Assiniboine clambered back and forth for nearly 2,000 feet. After completing this exhausting climb to nearly 11,000 feet above sea level, the subsequent leg to the Cooke City and Silvergate area and the northeastern park entrance was a comparatively easy trek. Today, one can appreciate why early Cooke City miners preferred the lengthier supply route that paralleled the Yellowstone River farther north. It might be a mistake, however, to hypothesize only meager Indian use or occupation of these granite, snowy highlands with their mirror lakes simply because non-Indians today find them cold and forbidding and frequented by grizzly bears. Verne Waples, a former game warden, picked up hundreds of arrowheads and other artifacts around these lakes, and old Indian sites continue to be discovered on the Beartooth Plateau. The archaeologist George Arthur has written of this region:

> Several large private collections of artifacts recovered from high elevation sites in the Beartooth Mountains west of Red Lodge, Montana, add further support for Early Period occupancy throughout this large area. The Early Period artifacts suggest, inferentially, that similar environments and cultural events existed during this period on both sides of the Rockies and throughout the mountains of Southern Montana. A similar cultural homogeneity is inferred for both the Middle and Late Prehistoric Periods, so that the Rocky Mountains may not be considered a barrier to culture.[12]

There has been little archaeological effort to reconstruct the skimpy remains of the steep Beartooth Pass route, but there are other clues that Indians were familiar with this habitat. In 1891, near the head of Little Rock and Bennett Creeks on the plateau and beside one of the numerous bodies of water there, known as Leg Lake, a Red Lodge cowboy found a crude log "stockade" that one U.S. ranger conjectured may have been built by early trappers and their Indian wives who conceivably led them there.[13] In addition, we know that tribespeople around the Yellowstone Plateau could be quite familiar with areas distant from their immediate terrain. Just as it was Crows on the Yellowstone who first informed the mountain man Tom Fitzpatrick about a route (South Pass) through the Wind River Mountains, allowing his trappers to work beaver streams on the other side,[14] so it was Wind River Shoshones who apparently guided Lieutenant General P. H. Sheridan's military expedition across the Beartooth Plateau in August 1882.

Place-names can provide an indirect linkage between cultural groups and geography. Walter F. Columbus, in a 1979 affidavit in which he remembered his work as transit man on a surveying crew between Red Lodge and Cooke City in summer 1920, stated that the sole mountain place-name on their maps was

Beartooth Butte. Columbus testified, "I recall talking to some old-timers in Cooke City, who said that Beartooth Mountain was named by Indians because of a prominent rock which looked like a bear's tooth. They did not say what tribe of Indians but there was a tribe of Sheep Eaters who were familiar with the Yellowstone area."[15] Information provided in 1969 by the Crow tribal historian Joseph Medicine Crow gives us more detail. In response to a request from the Helena National Forest office regarding the origin of this Beartooth place-name, Medicine Crow wrote:

> Unfortunately the old tribal historians, keepers of tribal annals and oral traditions, are gone now and I must find people who had recalled the old story tellers mentioning certain events, etc.
>
> One old lady related that her grandmother used to refer to the whole mountain area around Red Lodge as DAK-PIT-CHAY IGOTUSH, meaning "Bear's Small Teeth." Several other informants agreed with this version; but none of them is certain about the origin of the description. I am inclined to believe that such a description is based on a distant view of the whole area, particularly the jagged looking horizon which may resemble a bear's teeth from a side view.
>
> Another informant, raised by his old grand parents, recalled his grandmother using the words DAK-PIT-CHAY ITAGOTUSH, which means, "Bear's Tusk" or "Bear's Small Tusk." This informant believes that this description referred of a particular rock formation in the mountains but later the whole area was known by singular term. . . .
>
> It is feasible that the original Crow description of a particular rock formation resembling a bear's tusk or fang in time was used to include a general area.[16]

We can add an intriguing bit of Blackfeet data regarding the Beartooth Mountain locale. On a map for which one of their "Chiefs" named Ac Ko Mok Ki, or "the Feathers," provided information to a Hudson Bay Company fur trader in 1801, the Indian offered some interesting glimpses of the extent of Blackfeet familiarity with the plains.[17] Along the eastern side of the Rocky Mountains he clearly indicated Ki oo pe kis, or "Bears Tooth," by which he apparently was referring to the same mountains mentioned by Medicine Crow.

Stuart W. Conner told us a story he heard from Waples that illustrates the pool of local lore that formal studies and surveys too often overlook. In 1936, soon after the Beartooth Highway was completed, Waples was searching for a conical timber lodge that he had heard about from Dominick Reno, who ran a store at Beartooth Lake. Near the U.S. Forest Service fire lookout on the west side of the Beartooth Highway and overlooking the Clark's Fork valley, Waples found a circle of thirteen buffalo skulls "in pretty good shape."[18] No additional information or photographs have come to light about this site. Although none of these circles has been found directly in Yellowstone National Park, such ritual circles of buffalo skulls are known on the high plains; some say Indian hunters laid them out as a magical way to attract buffalo.[19]

We do not mean to suggest that these routes up the Yellowstone River and over the Beartooth Pass were the sole means of native access into the park region.[20] As some northern Indian visitors quietly told Park Service officials when they were visiting in 1993, "We used those major trails, but we had many ways of getting into the Park."[21] Members of tribes as far north as the Canadian border traveled widely and over extremely long distances and entered the park or passed within the rain shadow alongside it. As their own narratives and recorded geographic knowledge (corroborated by non-Indian chronicles) make clear, Blackfeet, Flathead, Kootenai, and Assiniboine penetrated the park's mountainous perimeter and circulated within it at will. Or they skirted its eastern or western boundaries on long-distance ventures farther south, to make the annual Green River trade rendezvous in Shoshone country or to probe still deeper into the Southwest and even beyond to old Mexico.

Blackfeet toward the "Many Smoke"

In the chronicles of Indian–white as well as Indian–Indian relations in the Yellowstone Plateau for the first half of the nineteenth century, few tribes are as associated with hit-and-run raids as the Blackfeet, who came from both sides of the U.S.–Canada border. By at least 1775 this sizable tribe had become a linguistically homogeneous Plains Indian group that was a major player in early European exploration and economic exploitation of the northern plains. Their three politically independent divisions spoke dialects of the same Algonquian stock, but only one of them possessed territories that spilled over the lands of the United States and Canada. Yet distance rarely deterred any of their warriors from going wherever they chose.

Today the members of the tribes collectively but incorrectly known as Blackfeet are increasingly preferring to be known by their old name, Natsitapii. According to Brian Reeves and Sandra Peacock, they are composed of three tribes, the Kainaa, Piikani, and Siksika, with the history of subgroups of these tribes, such as the South Piikani who traditionally hunted, collected plants, camped, and conducted ceremonies in Glacier National Park.[22] The most northerly division of the three tribal groups were the Siksika, whose upper boundary was the Northern Branch of the Saskatchewan River. Between the Battle and Bow Rivers lay the land of the Blood, or Kainawa. But the territory of the third division, the Piikani, stretched along the mountains and dropped well south of the border, past Glacier Park and, according to George Bird Grinnell (1912) and Walter McClintock (1910), actually extending well toward the Yellowstone River.[23] One band of Piikani, known as the Small Robes, developed a special affinity for the southland, intermarrying with Flatheads and settling near the Musselshell River.[24]

Pelican Creek, site of Osborne Russell's 1839 battle with Blackfeet. (Photo courtesy of Yellowstone National Park Archives, #Yell 37880.)

In the late eighteenth century David Thompson heard of a sizable Piegan war party that, unable to locate any Shoshones to raid, ventured farther south to intercept a Spanish column of pack animals and force the whites to flee. The Blackfeet tossed away their cargo, which turned out to be silver ore, and drove the animals an estimated fifteen hundred miles home.[25] The validity of this account is supported by the explorer Alexander Mackenzie, who characterized the Blackfeet of 1800 as an adventuresome, far-ranging people "who deal in horses and take them upon war parties towards Mexico, from which they enter into the country to the south-east, which consists of plains."[26] It is reinforced also by a story reported by James Doty of a Blackfeet trip in the mid-1840s that took three years and transported about five of their chiefs to Taos and Santa Fe, New Mexico.[27]

Clearly, the Blackfeet warriors could strike where they desired, from the Rockies to the Mississippi, from northern Canada down through the southwestern deserts, with stabs into the Yellowstone Plateau in between. And fairly clearly they were familiar with Yellowstone's interior. While accompanying some Blackfeet on a hunt in the Missouri–Yellowstone country in spring 1865, a Jesuit priest, Father Xavier Kuppens, was regaled by a chief named Big Lake "on the beauties of that wonderful spot." His curiosity was so great that Kuppens persuaded some young warriors to guide him into the park area, whereupon they escorted him directly to its "chief attraction," the Grand Canyon and the Firehole basins.[28]

Around 1800, when the Blackfeet made their earliest documented entry into the history of the Yellowstone Plateau, they numbered conservatively 15,000 strong,[29] with one estimate of the size of their available warriors at the time reaching 9,000.[30] By then, thanks to their fortuitous acquisition of the gun (from European traders at the northern plains posts) and the horse (from southern Plains Indian middlemen in the tribal horse trade), they had already succeeded in flexing their muscles on their southeastern borders through Shoshone country and into the Bighorn Mountains of the Crow. This burst of expansionism pushed the Shoshone back into their old Wyoming hunting grounds, as the invaders attempted to occupy the territory in between. "Gradually," writes Hultkrantz, "single bands of Blackfeet reached the Yellowstone Park (probably along the Gallatin and Yellowstone), and in the middle of the 19th century they claimed the plains next to the Rocky Mountains clear down to Yellowstone Park."[31]

Entering the park area to trap beaver but more commonly to maraud the fur caches of American trappers for resale to British traders,[32] the Blackfeet never pretended to call the Yellowstone region their own, in the fashion that they laid spiritual claim to the Rocky Mountain highlands of Glacier National Park and the Badger-Two Medicine region. At the same time, they accorded the area special respect, according to interviews by Joseph Weixelman with Blackfeet elders:

> George Kicking Woman identified the lands of Yellowstone as sacred, although not to the Blackfeet directly. Because they were sacred to others, they were treated as such by them. When passing through Yellowstone on the way to the basins of the Snake or Green rivers, they would stop to pray with their pipes or leave tobacco. Prayers might have especially been said for a safe journey since travel was dangerous in the nineteenth century.[33]

By what routes the Blackfeet made their predatory forays into this landscape we have only a spotty record. But thanks to author James Willard Schultz, we have an intriguing anecdote about a Piegan war party that traveled directly into the heart of what is now Yellowstone National Park. There they are said to have come upon what they took to be the smoke from campfires. But after night fell, they could detect no flickering flames, and only later did they discover that it was steam rising from hot springs. Hence their name for the Park's zone of thermal activity, Aisitsi, or "Many Smoke."[34]

Even some contemporary Blackfeet have heard of long-distance travels. One Blackfeet consultant, on the staff at Calgary's Glenbow Museum, recalled a story told him by a grandfather who belonged to "Chief Old Sun's clan" of the northerly Blackfeet and who died in 1991 at the age of ninety-four:

> One day, he told me, they used to go as far as the Mexicans, go all the way down and come back. I would look at him and think, he was crazy, how could they get there? He said they would start when the grass starts to turn green,

and sometimes they take a whole year to get back. Long, long time ago, a group of them were going south and came upon a huge lake. One old chief was very hot and went to the hills. He was cooling himself—it hardly ever snowed there—when behind him came a ripple. Through his legs came this monster and it burned or did something to him. The chief said to the Thunder God that he didn't do anything. Can you help me in stopping this creature? Then thunder came down, and a huge tornado sucked up that monster, and they left. The following year when they came back by the place where this happened [on the return trip to the north], there was no water left at that place.[35]

Although after considerable searching we have been unable to find more geographically precise descriptions of the trails covered on Piegan adventures to the south, a general picture of Blackfeet long-distance travel comes from Brings Down the Sun, a Canadian Blackfoot man who was interviewed by the amateur scholar and photographer Walter McClintock in 1905. The old man said that his people customarily used two main routes for their major journeys. One led them northward out of Calgary, Alberta, into the Barren Lands of the Northwest Territory and beyond to the Yukon—"as far as people live," in the old man's words. The Old North Trail took them in the opposite direction, along the southern mountains and extending "into the country inhabited by a people with dark skins, and long hair falling over their faces (Mexico)."[36] Fast-moving war parties used these routes, but whole families and bands traversed them as well. Another Blackfeet remembered his tribe's last, unsuccessful journey south to make peace with the Shoshone: "When we traveled, if you were with the head ones, you could not see the last ones, they were so far back. They had more horses than they could count, so they used fresh horses every day and traveled very fast. On the twenty-fourth day they reached the place where Owl Bear had told the Snake [Shoshone] they would camp, and put up their lodges along the creek."[37]

Brings Down the Sun's father told McClintock about one of these long voyages to visit the dark-skinned southerners that was undertaken in the early nineteenth century by Elk Tongue and his wife. The purpose of their trip was neither raiding nor hunting but a quest for powerful medicine. Down in the hot country a "South Man" sold him an extremely sacred "Dancing Pipe," which was to be used on important occasions, in conjunction with its medicine bundle. One feature of this bundle's ceremony was its power to grant practitioners, through gazing into the ritually eviscerated body of a badger, a glimpse of whether they would die young or live to enjoy old age. But because this foreknowledge too often saddened people, the "South Man" discouraged its new Blackfeet owners from trying it out.[38]

On such missions the Blackfeet war parties seized every opportunity to ambush their old enemies, whether they were the Shoshone or the Crow. Brings-Down-the-Sun remembered one "picture writing" created by his father, presumably on buffalo hide, that recorded a far-reaching military expedition led by a young

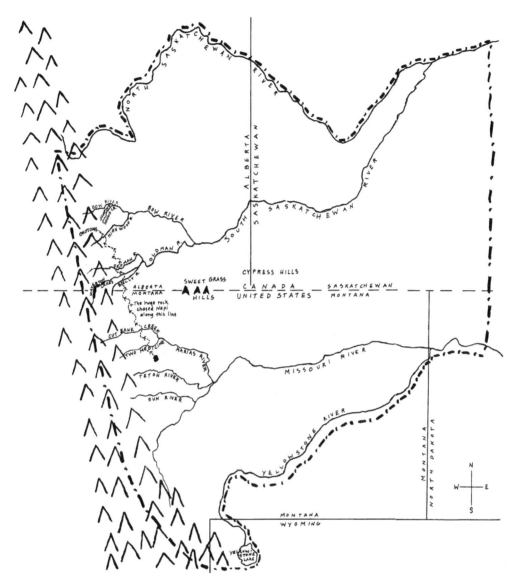

Aboriginal Piegan-Blackfeet hunting territory (shown here by broken border lines), which includes part of the southern portion of Yellowstone National Park. Province and state border lines are shown, even though there were no province, state, or international boundaries during the Piegan-Blackfeet aboriginal time period. (From Percy Bullchild, *The Sun Came Down* [San Francisco: Harper&Row, 1985].)

chief named Calf Robe. After "traveling southward along the Rocky Mountains," Calf Robe's band crossed the Yellowstone and entered "the country of the Snakes," with whom they skirmished, barely escaping with their lives.[39] Thanks again to Schultz, we have another description of a long-distance journey to the south, which he heard firsthand from a Blood chief named Eagle Plume.

The young Eagle Plume departed early one morning for his raid on the Crows. He led nine warriors from their tipis along the "Belly River" to the banks of the "Bear" (Marias) River, which they crossed near a large, sacred red rock on its northern shore "just above Great Northern Railway Branch." After praying to this rock for success on their raid, they then crossed the "Milk" (Teton) River below the breast-shaped butte that lent the stream its name. At the junction of the "Pile of Rocks" (Sun) and "Big" (Missouri) Rivers, the young men, by now very hungry, forded the latter stream and camped for a few nights at "Rock-Ridge-Across," the site of present-day Great Falls, to hunt for buffalo.

Successful at obtaining meat, they then pressed onward, crossing the "Yellow" (Judith) Mountains through the gap and soon reaching the "Dried Meat" (Mussel-shell) River. Shortly after wading across this river, they glimpsed the outline of the north end of the "Bad" or "Unfaithful" (Crazy) Mountains, halting at the head of the "Bad" (Shields) River that they knew flowed into the "Elk" (Yellowstone). Now they were close to their destination, and before long, "where Elk River comes from the mountains [probably near Livingston] into the plain, [they] saw rising the smoke of many lodge fires, of a big Crow camp, of course."[40]

According to Brings Down the Sun, his people might be away on such journeys for many months, which probably led them through or just skirting the Yellow-stone Plateau and eventually brought them into the far southwestern country from whence they brought back exotic materials as proof of their travels. But their absences could also stretch far longer: the journey of a man named Elk Tongue took four years—twelve months of steady traveling to get there and eighteen months just to get back because he chose the longer detour through the "High Trees" or Bitterroot country in order to avoid any Crows, Sioux, and Cheyennes who might be in wait along the North Trail. There was tremendous rejoicing when the Black-feet warriors would finally return home with their spoils.

While on the road the Blackfeet also visited time-honored locations for obtaining natural resources they could not find at home. On the Little Bighorn River (Khpaksi Tuktai, or "Ash River"), for instance, deep in Crow country, they interrupted their raiding long enough to hunt for wood for their bows and arrows and ash for their pipestems.[41] Along the way they also paid special attention to any mineral paint deposits that figured in their mental maps of the countryside.

Another genre that allows us to appreciate the breadth of Blackfeet travels and territorial awareness are visual renderings—either pictographic drawings that usually require interpretation by the original artist or, infrequently, maps. The cartographic document referred to above that was prepared by Ac Ko mok ki, or "the Feathers," may have been sketched in the ground or the snow when he met Peter Fidler, a Hudson's Bay Company trader at his post on the Saskatchewan River in February 1801, possibly in response to a request from Fidler, who then apparently copied it in his notebook.[42] What the Feathers depicted was an area that extended at least five hundred miles south, into central Wyoming. On the east, he illustrated the confluence of the Missouri and Yellowstone Rivers and then indicated his people's range past the Rocky Mountains all the way to the Pacific Ocean. In its entirety this constituted an area of about 200,000 square miles, to which the Feathers then appended a census of the thirty-two Indian groups living in the region, even showing their relative locations and listing the number of tipis for each.

This document offers vivid evidence of Blackfeet trading and warring routes that led them from western Canada down along the Rockies—through or edging along the Yellowstone National Park region—to Shoshone country and the central Wyoming tribes as well as east to the trading rendezvous at the Mandan, Hisatsa, and Arikara villages along the middle Missouri. The full journey from north to south, according to the Feathers, took Blackfeet horsemen thirty-three days. Also, the map reveals tribal names for such sites along the Absaroka front range as "The Rattle" (Rattlesnake Mountain), "The Heart" (Heart Mountain), "Bull's Nose" (the Bull Mountains), and "Warm Water River" (almost certainly the Shoshone River).

Yet even a cursory reexamination of this map suggests that Blackfeet knowledge regarding these and other Yellowstone Plateau–associated tribes might be interpreted a bit more precisely. For example, #17 on the map, the "Fish eating Indians," is probably the Agaidika, or Lemhi; #18, the "root"-eating Indians, very likely refers to the camas eaters or some other Shoshonean group; and #19, the "Wood Indians," could well be the Boise Indians, otherwise known as the Yahandika, or groundhog eaters.

This impulse on the part of Blackfeet to depict the territory known and covered by their forefathers did not cease in the nineteenthh century. As recently as the 1980s, the Piegan Blackfeet storyteller Percy Bullchild, in his collection of traditional narratives, *The Sun Came Down,* included his hand-drawn map of his people's territorial boundaries, boldly positioning a clearly labeled "Yellowstone Park" at its southern extremity. But another way to get a sense of the continuity of Blackfeet awareness of the greater Yellowstone region in the first half of the nineteenth century is to tabulate reports of their incursions into or just past this area, as in this chronology:

1787	Fur trader David Thompson hears from a Blackfeet warrior about his people's first horse-stealing raid into Shoshone territory.[43]
1808	On a branch of the Jefferson Fork, near the Missouri headwaters, fur trapper John Colter barely escapes from a large Blackfeet war party.[44]
1809–10	Blackfeet push Missouri Fur Company trappers from the vicinity of Yellowstone.[45]
July 1826	Northeast of Yellowstone Lake, near West Thumb Geyser Basin, Daniel T. Potts describes two Blackfeet attacks from one "large party."[46]

1826	In area of Yellowstone's springs, a trapper and his party are driven onto the plains by Blackfeet.[47]
1828	En route to a peace parlay with Shoshones in the south, Blackfeet Chief Crowfoot and fourteen warriors ambush a white man.[48]
1829	Between the Yellowstone River and Devils Slide, a party of fur trappers (including young Joe Meek) is attacked by a party of Piegans.[49]
1832	Battle between Blackfeet and fur traders, with Bannock friends, at the Pierre's Hole rendezvous site.[50]
1834	Accompanying Crows for buffalo hunting a half day's travel from No Wood Creek, trapper Zenas Leonard is attacked by Blackfeet.[51]
1839	Near the Pelican Creek outlet into Yellowstone Lake, Osborne Russell's camp is ransacked by Piegans; he never returns to the region.[52]
1839	Just north of Yellowstone Lake, at Indian Pond, the trappers led by Baptise Decharme clash with a large body of Blackfeet.[53]
1844	On the western shore of Yellowstone Lake a large group of trappers from the north battle with Blackfeet.[54]
1845	Reports of Blackfeet leader Painted Wing and 275 warriors pursuing Shoshones who stole their horses into geyser area.[55]
1865	Belgian Jesuit Francis Xavier Kuppens is guided to Yellowstone Grand Canyon and Firehole basins by Piegan warriors.[56]
1867	Prospecting crew and trading post entrepreneurs detect signs of hostile Blackfeet near the Upper Falls of Yellowstone River.[57]

Today, of course, we cannot know whether these Blackfeet parties took advantage of earthen paint deposits along their southern treks. As the Flathead seem to have done, for instance, did they dig into ocher seams near the Missouri River to wrap up in special paint bags for the trip home? Did they stop at one time-honored Blackfeet spot, reportedly near some "warm springs" on the Yellowstone River, to offer the customary prayers before digging into a cutbank for yellow paint?[58]

Once they approached the park, might these Blackfeet have also ventured a quarter of a mile beyond the wood-covered pits on the talus slope opposite Electric peak, just outside the park's northern entrance, to take the premium red and yellow clay from the quarry that local whites would later call Indian Paint Cave, where pick marks indicate the work of other native excavators?[59] And within the present park boundaries and perhaps following Obsidian Creek to Lake of the Woods, did these Blackfeet then turn southeast to Amphitheater Springs, the source of Lemonade Creek, to extract any of the abundant vermilion paint that Indians are said to have obtained there,[60] or use red and yellow paint deposits found in the fissure opposite the mouth of Hellroaring Creek, which Park Superintendent Norris noticed had been visited by Indians in modern times?[61]

The extent to which Indians used these mineral resources may never be learned. But we can be quite sure that the Blackfeet were watchful for edible foods or usable plants along their path. Coming up the Yellowstone River they were probably struck by certain differences between some biotic communities and those back home. In the sagebrush grasslands on the valley bottom in the right season, along Mill Creek, Big Creek, or similar streams, there were bushes of ripe service-berries, gooseberries, raspberries, and chokecherries. In the arid, sun-beaten ground toward present-day Mammoth, there were clumps of prickly pear cactus. And even in the driest portion of the park, around Mammoth itself, there were abandoned "ghost" beaver dams that offered richer soils, more moisture, and ample foraging opportunities.

On the "People's Trail": Flatheads Remember Going South

Other northerly tribes with cultural memories or fragmentary knowledge of the upper Yellowstone and environs were the Flathead, or Salish-speaking people, of Montana and their immediate neighbors. Because there is no evidence that this nation ever flattened their heads—as did their linguistic brethren along the Columbia River—the term *Salish* is often preferred. In Carling Malouf's opinion, their aboriginal center was "Three Forks," the confluence of the Gallatin, Madison, and Jefferson Rivers and the Gallatin Valley to the south, though they hunted and raided as far east as present-day Billings and into the Wyoming Bighorns. James A. Teit placed them as far east as the upper Yellowstone Valley: "Parties of Flathead also visited the mountain Snake, especially the Lemhi, and they also visited Shoshoni bands on the Yellowstone."[62]

The closely associated (Upper) Pend d'Oreille were once part of the Salish nation (the two speak mutually intelligible languages). At the time of Yellowstone National Park was established, they numbered about one thousand and lived around Flathead Lake, the Bitterroot Valley, and the Upper Clark's Fork River between Missoula and Butte. Just west of Salish territory proper lived the linguistically related Coeur d'Alene, who established permanent and temporary camps throughout the Spokane River system but also could be found along portions of the Clearwater and Clark's Fork streams.[63] The Coeur d'Alene numbered only 320 members in 1853, reduced from an estimated 3,000 to 4,000 in 1780. Their foraging grounds probably overlapped in with those of their surrounding linguistic cousins.

One must finally draw into this region of numerous Plateau Indian groups the linguistically unique Kootenai, whose traditional lands north of the Montana Salish extended into Canada but who undertook long-distance buffalo-hunting expeditions into the plains and whose American branch drew closer to the Salish when the Jesuits created the St. Ignatius Mission in 1854.[64] From the early reservation period through today, their historical experience has increasingly been shared with that tribe—except that, as Bill B. Brunton notes, they have "tended to belong to a less-acculturated, traditional group . . . somewhat isolated on the northern end of the Flathead Reservation."[65]

The extent of southern visits by these Salish was made somewhat more precise by Malouf, whose early fieldwork was largely devoted to the tribe and who states unequivocally that "they went as far as Yellowstone National Park."[66] Malouf argues that their motive for relocating in the Bitterroot Valley was the intrusion, as early as the 1600s, of Shoshonean Indians from Idaho and Wyoming who began marauding once they were emboldened by horses and leather armor acquired from the Spanish. Some oral traditions also support Salish knowledge and use of the park. According to interviews by the bilingual Salish interpreter, Pierre Pichette—who talked in the 1930s, on behalf of ethnographer Claude Schaeffer, with such reliable tribal elders as Paul Antoine, Victor and Mortine Vanderburg, and Baptiste and Larse Lumpry—the ancestors of the Salish expressly sought out the obsidian quarries in Yellowstone National Park.[67] Although in 1833 Warren Ferris recalled that his Pend d'Oreille guides were "appalled" by the geysers and that one Indian remarked that "hell, of which he had heard from the white-man, must be in that vicinity," one of Pichette's stories sheds a more positive light on the park. The narrative featured the trickster figure Coyote in his familiar role in the plateau as landscape transformer and protector and culture bearer for human beings.

Before summarizing Pichette's story, which anthologizer Elizabeth Clark entitled "Coyote's Prophecy Concerning Yellowstone National Park,"[68] however, we must first address its authenticity. What we know about Pichette attests to his competence as a traditional narrator. He was born in 1877 on the Flathead Indian Reservation's Jocko Agency near present-day Arlee, Montana. When he died in 1955 it was said, "Pichette had made an enormous contribution to the preservation and understanding of the culture of his people."[69] His cultural knowledge came through his family but was certainly deepened by personal tragedy: at the age of fifteen while a student at the mission boarding school in St. Ignatius, Pichette contracted measles and lost his eyesight.

Thereafter the boy became a tribal intellectual. Pichette had been only a year old when his mother, an enrolled Pend d'Oreille and Kalispell woman named Mary Sabine, passed away. Instead of living with his father, an enrolled Spokane named Modess Pichette, Pierre was raised by his maternal grandmother, also named Mary, who is believed to have been among Chief Arlee's band when it gave up its beloved Bitterroot country and moved to the Jocko Agency after 1872. From his grandmother young Pierre absorbed many narratives—mythic, legendary, and historical. After he became blind, he taught himself to read and use a typewriter in Braille and thereafter became renowned among his people for his bilingual

Folklore from tribes to the north and west of Yellowstone National Park feature the mythic being, Coyote, striving to procure fish for Indians. Although he is successful in providing smaller fish for highland dwellers on the western flanks of the Continental Divide—as illustrated here by the Salish artist Frederick E. Roullier—he fails to provide them for Indians on the mountains' "dawn side." This explains why it is buffalo that these Plains peoples will pursue in the future. (Photo courtesy of the U.S. Department of the Interior, Indian Arts and Crafts Board, Museum of the Plains Indian. From Harriet Miller and Elizabeth Harrison, *Coyote Tales of the Montana Salish,* from narratives recorded from Pierre Pichette [Rapid City, S.Dak.: The Tipi Shop, 1974], 19.)

skills, his clear memory, his gifts as a public orator, and his collaboration and correspondence with numerous scholars on matters of Salish-Kootenai tradition. Furthermore, his reputation for truthfulness and linguistic accuracy made him a valued interpreter for his tribe throughout their eventually successful land claim hearings. This background would seem to validate Pichette's credibility as a trustworthy storyteller, which is reinforced by the fact that the well-respected anthropologist-historian Claude Schaeffer considered him sufficiently knowledgeable to engage him as a key informant.

When questioned about Clark's credentials, we could find no details about her interviewing practices. She was a professor of English at Washington State University in Pullman. Her publications focused on text collections from the Pacific Northwest and the Rockies using her own field interviews and library research.

For a professional evaluation of her work, however, we contacted the two major scholars of Northwest Indian narratives, Jarold Ramsey and, through Ramsey, the dean of American linguistic studies, Dell Hymes. First, from Ramsey:

> Without knowing the details of the charges and biases against Clark's work, I'm afraid I can't give you a very sharp-edged comment. But I'll venture this. In looking at and sometimes consulting her two main collections of Indian narrative texts (from the Pacific Northwest and the Rockies), I have never found any evidence that she "made things up" or even embroidered her materials. . . . My feeling about her work has always been something like this: that she deserves some credit for recognizing and trying to promote the study of traditional Indian oral literature as literature, in a time (30's to 50's) when few scholars were following that line; and she also deserves credit for undertaking quite a lot of folkloric field work—she worked, for example, on the Warm Springs Reservation in Central Oregon, near where I grew up. When I began to work on my own anthology, *Coyote Was Going There: Indian Literature of the Oregon Country*, I thought of her as a worthy predecessor and rival in the cause of gaining serious literary attention for the transcribed oral traditions of the Far West.[70]

Ramsey mentioned our concerns to Hymes and reported the following:

> No sooner had I mailed my letter to you—couple of days ago, then Dell Hymes called from his place in Oregon. He says he never knew Ella Clark, but has always considered her Indian collecting and editing honest, careful, and valuable within what now seem like its limits (re: concern with native literary conventions and assumptions and with questions of translation and textualization). He's as puzzled as I by the opposition you've encountered to her work.[71]

The thrust of these positive testimonials concerns Clark's field collecting, endorsements echoed in Marius Barbeau's review of Clark's *Indian Legends of Canada*.[72] But perhaps her care with vetting received texts left something to be desired. In an August 11, 1998, letter Ramsey added, "[S]he does cast a very wide and sometimes unaccountable net for her materials," and cited a Wasco Indian story that Clark copied from another source, which Ramsey assessed as "romanticized and utterly shaky as to its provenance."[73] We sensed the same discrepancy between stories that Clark collected personally and those she took from other publications. For instance, in our search for Cheyenne materials connected to Yellowstone we were intrigued by a purported Cheyenne creation story for "Land of Great Fire," accompanied by a color photograph of Minerva Terrace at Mammoth Hot Springs, in a 1995 coffee table volume.[74] We discovered from the author that he had lifted it from one of Clark's coedited anthologies.[75] Inspecting that publication led us to a third work from which Clark had uncritically borrowed the story. This pamphlet, *The Flood*, edited by a professor of education at Eastern

Pierre Pichette, Salish-Kootenai oral historian and storyteller. (Photo courtesy of the U.S. Department of the Interior, Indian Arts and Crafts Board, Museum of the Plains Indian. From Harriet Miller and Elizabeth Harrison, *Coyote Tales of the Montana Salish*, from tales narrated by Pierre Pichette, illustrations by Frederick E. Roullier [Rapid City, S.Dak.: The Tipi Shop, 1974], 7.)

Montana College, was first published in 1972.[76] We contacted the author by telephone, and he admitted that the original version from his Northern Cheyenne consultants (he did not audiotape or preserve his handwritten notes) was geographically vague. He told us, "So I think I added those places there, to make it more specific. Yes, I know I did."[77]

Another way to assess such a narrative is to examine its plot and characters and whether it conforms to what we know of Salish and Plateau Coyote storytelling techniques. The Pichette story collected by Clark opens with Coyote leaving a well-known spot in Salish geography: the sacred springs above the medicine tree near the town of Darby in western Montana. This is where Coyote chased a bighorn ram across an arroyo; its horns stuck in a ponderosa pine tree that is still revered by Salish people. The entire narrative, in fact, is anchored by documented Salish places; for at the very end of the story, the plum trees, which Coyote creates out of his horsewhip for the benefit of people, are the origin of the place-name Jocko River, derived from the Salish word. And in the tale Coyote behaves according to type: thin and gaunt, he is relentlessly traveling. We learn that Grizzly Bear has convened a great "gathering of the tribes," but Coyote hears about it too late and must race to the location for this event "in a valley of what is now Yellowstone Park," an area known to teem with these animals.

Instead of walking right in, Coyote stays unnoticed nearby with an old woman. Following the preferred number symbol for Plateau Indian folklore, four times Coyote implores Grizzly Bear: twice for his best food, twice for his best drum.

Finally getting Grizzly Bear's instrument, Coyote then summons supernatural powers to kill him. Although the people want Coyote as their new chief, he promotes Golden Eagle instead. Accepting the gift of a horse, Coyote delivers a glowing portrayal of the thermal region that is at odds with the forbidding image reported by Ferris:

> In generations to come, this place around here will be a treasure of the people. They will be proud of it and of all the curious things in it—flint rocks, hot springs, and cold springs. People will be proud of this spot. Springs will bubble out, and steam will shoot out. Hot springs and cold springs will be side by side. Hot water will fly into the air, in this place and that place. No one knows how long this will continue. And voices will be heard here, in different languages, in the generations to come.[78]

Coyote's fight against grizzly bears, which is echoed in two of Pichette's other narratives,[79] is an extension of the ubiquitous Plateau theme of Coyote conquering dangerous beasts or supernatural monsters to ready the world for human habitation, as compiled in Deward Walker's collection of Coyote-versus-Grizzly stories from the neighboring Nez Perce.[80] As in the Salish story, the Nez Perce even suggest that Coyote tries to use Grizzly's own power against him.[81] With regard to the suggestion that the horse, a "modern" introduction by Euro-Americans, might undermine the narrative's authenticity, Plains Indian folklore contains frequent references to the supernatural origin of horses.

This horse element and Pichette's Yellowstone National Park forecast illustrate a creative mechanism that the Plateau Indian folklore scholar Jarold Ramsay calls "retroactive prophecy." By this term, he means stories that often claim special knowledge, or forecast aspects or consequences of Indian–white interaction or even cataclysmic events that, in reality, have already happened or are already known. However, such stories are recast as prophecies that existed long before and result from "Indian mythologies endeavoring to preserve the continuums of the old ways in the face of their apparent utter disruption."[82] In our example, from a non-Indian point of view, the Salish originator of this story would have retooled information he had heard about the Yellowstone thermal features in order to give his people indirect credit for knowing about this geographic "treasure," since it was *their* culture hero who generously gave it to people from all over the world, who would then flock to it (this can be read as a rare Indian endorsement of a "multiuse policy"). From the Salish perspective, however, the narrator is doing what comes naturally, attributing the world's wonders to this four-legged demiurge who, they always acknowledged, created the known world for them.

Furthermore, like some of Ramsey's examples, this Pichette narrative seems spliced together from two time frames: a "Myth Age" in which Coyote slays the Grizzly Bear and a "Historical Age" in which humans thank Coyote for saving them with the gift of the gray horse. Then comes Coyote's final prophecy about the Park whereby he seems to be reciprocating their gratitude. Just as no one can say that the stories of horses were not grafted onto older narratives on the spot, we cannot be sure whether Pichette himself invented his last section. But what Ramsay argues is that this creative process of trying to make novel phenomena consistent with the tribal worldview has been a persistent impulse throughout the American Indian world since Euro-Americans and Native Americans first began interacting. From the Native American or cultural anthropological perspective, then, the above narrative appears consonant with traditional Indian storytelling mechanisms and motivations, even if historians doubt its chronological accuracy or tidy associations of regions and tribes.

Now we turn from Salish folklore to their history. It has been hypothesized that the tribe split from their linguistic relatives to the west at an early date.[83] Thereafter they became known in Montana for blending key Plains Indian traits, such as use of the horse (which they received from the Northern Shoshone sometime after 1730–40),[84] buffalo hunting, and the conical tipi, with diagnostic Plateau characteristics, such as foraging for tubers with digging sticks and creating collective vision–inspired ceremonies such as the Blue Jay Dance. Never a very large tribe, they numbered only about 600 in 1806, if we believe Lewis and Clark. Largely because of their incessant strife with the more powerful Blackfeet, however, their numbers had been reduced almost by half again by the time they signed the Treaty of Hell Gate in 1855.

The Salish hunters of the early nineteenth century who left the Bitterroot Valley in search of buffalo to the east faced a rougher and longer road to their old hunting grounds than the one they had once undertaken from their earlier homeland at Three Forks, but they surely were acquainted with the route. Their fairly detailed recollections of this long-distance trek, which would have been the major phase of a journey that subsequently could have brought them to the Yellowstone region, were narrated in the 1930s, through translator Pichette, by elders Paul Antoine and Louis Lumpry to Schaeffer.[85]

By about 1800 it had become their customary practice to undertake biannual quests for buffalo meat, following what the Salish called Sinkakatiiwax, or "the People's Trail." For this journey they allowed at least ten days; eventually it took them to the headwaters of the Musselshell River. For the first stretch of such an expedition, the Salish party would bid farewell to their campsites, which were located in the vicinity of Stevensville, Montana. Moving north up the Bitterroot Valley, they headed for the present site of Missoula. There they turned east, following the trail along Petty (Pattee) Creek, which flowed between old Fort Missoula and today's University of Montana campus.

Riding along this creek as it cut through the hills to the "Missoula river" (Clark's Fork of the Columbia), they forded just east of its junction with the Big Blackfoot River and followed its northern banks for a distance of "nine miles

Kootenai-Salish consultant at Obsidian Cliff, 1994. (Photo by Lawrence Loendorf.)

above Bonita." At this point they recrossed the river to its southern shore, rode eastward past Medicine Tree, and finally arrived at present-day Drummond. Still following the southern shore, they dropped about halfway to Garrison before crossing the river once again and pursuing the southern course of the "north fork" (Little Blackfoot River) toward the hamlet of Avon.

Now they forded this river, hugging the southern banks, to Elliston, where they again waded across, to its northern shore, which they followed until they reached a place "where two creeks empty into the river, one from the north and one from the south." At this point the party turned up the northernmost of these creeks (possibly Dog Creek), which they shortly abandoned, however, to head directly east through a pass (possibly Mullen Pass) in the Continental Divide— although Schaeffer's consultants said that they could also have chosen to cut directly east a little earlier so as to use MacDonald Pass through the divide (probably following Tenmile Creek after that). By either route, they soon found the Missouri River, which they crossed just east of the present-day state capital of Helena.

The Missouri River was known to the Salish as *ep iyu ntwe?tkwus,* or "river of the red paint." At a familiar site just north of their Missouri crossing they dug out reddish hematite for face and tipi painting. If this expedition was taking place in the fall, usually they could have forded the river without assistance. But if it was summer, said Schaeffer's narrators, they would have to make "tipi-skin boats."

Had they then wanted to strike out for the Yellowstone Plateau, it would have been an easy matter to continue to follow the Missouri River due south to Three Forks and from there stick with the Madison to the park's present western entrance.

From the Missouri, the hunters headed into the Big Belt Mountains, which they traversed by means of a pass (possibly Deep Creek) before riding by a "Fort Logan," maintaining their course due east so as to cross directly between the Little Belt Mountains (Castle Mountains) and the Crazy Mountains. Picking up the South Fork of the Musselshell in this widening basin, at last the men gained their first sight of the desired buffalo herds. According to the Salish informants, once the party entered this river plain and edged farther along the well-timbered Mussel-shell, they had to remain alert, for surprise attacks by Blackfeet or others might come at any time.

It was at this point, they added, that, had they wished, the Salish hunters (sometimes accompanied by the Pend d'Oreille) might have added a leg to the Yellowstone. This they could accomplished by dropping a bit farther down the Musselshell before turning southeast on their southern trail. Without explanation as to the date's significance, they said that this route was taken "more frequently previous to 1877"—which, however, would have been when these Salish surely knew that military activity over the Nez Perce war was intense and uncomfortably close.

Unfortunately, Schaeffer elicited no further details for the remaining journey to the Yellowstone Plateau, or about any possible routes they followed in the current park. One amusing story told by a Kootenai, however, has Indians from northern Montana at least partway to the park. Remembering humorous "firsts" among his people, Baptiste Mathias told Thain White that it was "down towards Red Lodge" that one traveler to the south picked up a five-pound lard bucket. When he returned home he put a cover on it. As curious onlookers gathered around to see the strange metal container, he whipped off its cover to astound them with reflections of their faces in the metal base. "They offered him all kinds of things but he wouldn't sell it."[86]

Even after all this time of removal from the Yellowstone environs, our recent interview with a Salish elder confirmed the general outline of the Schaeffer claims about southern travels and places his people's geographic knowledge squarely within the park. A forestry technician for the Salish tribe who was born near Arlee about sixty-five years ago, he told us how his elderly relatives gathered in the vicinity of Stevensville, Montana, for the summer. In the fall they scattered into foraging bands made up of two or three families, with some "ending up in Yellowstone."[87]

He believed that if they had gathered enough food during the fall, "they might stay all winter." His explanation: "They liked the hot waters, I guess." They had taken so long to get there, he thought, that they took their time before coming home, since the region provided sufficient elk, buffalo, fish, and roots for their survival. Sometimes, he said, their fellow tribesmen might not see a family for a year or more, occasionally never—"which meant they maybe met up with Crows or Blackfeet." One summer his own family ventured deep into the Bob Marshall Wilderness and came upon a clearing, at the "place of meadows" (L-qul-qo-le-wh), where some Salish families were already camped. Today that memory of a "circle of five or six tipis" remains "like a dream." After talking with the campers for a few hours, his parents returned to their own camp.[88]

When the Salish families returned to the Bitterroot in the fall, they shared what they had seen in the southland; "they talked about this hard stuff like glass" and about the old stone arrow points (*ta-pa-mi*) and spear points (*noo-loo-loo-moo*) they found there. In addition, the consultant remembered three place-names associated with the Yellowstone region: (1) K ali ssens, for "Yellow Stone"; (2) *n' aq es ocq?etKw*, for "Hot Water Coming out of the Ground" or "Hot Springs" (which the Salish were not loath to visit, whether at Lolo Hot Springs or Hot Springs, Montana); and (3) *mo'mo'tu'lex*, for "Smoke from the Ground," presumably associated with steam issuing from the thermal beds.

Indian Hunting and the Greater Yellowstone

In this discussion of Indian use of large mammal resources in and around Yellowstone National Park, we do not wish to suggest that the Blackfeet or others enjoyed any special advantage or claim over other tribes. Quite the contrary, nearly all the native groups featured in this book—and others perhaps as well—probably hunted in and around the Yellowstone Plateau. But for cultural or environmental reasons, some tribes may have had the option to add other staples such as fish or camas into their regular diets. With the exception of pursuing bighorn sheep, however, we collapse much of our hunting information here for reasons of convenience. Yet there may be another justification as well. For as will become clear, it may have been in part thanks to one of these northern tribes that Yellowstone National Park was able to salvage its threatened buffalo population in the first place.

Before turning to this most prominent animal symbol of Yellowstone National Park, however, we touch on information that has come to light during our research regarding Indian hunting of elk in and immediately around the park. One nineteenth-century account comes from Theodore Roosevelt, perhaps the most well known Yellowstone Park booster but also an inveterate hunter. During one elk hunt into the Two-Ocean Pass region of the Wind River Mountains, before the area was protected within the U.S. National Forest Reserve, Roosevelt encountered some horse-riding Shoshones, split into bands of eight or ten members each, who were hunting using the "drive technique":

> [T]he riders strung in lines far apart; they signaled to one another by means of willow whistles, with which they also imitated the calling of the bull elk, thus

Crow and Shoshone Indians driving buffalo in Lamar Valley for the filming of *The Thundering Herd*. (Photo courtesy of Yellowstone National Park Archives, #Yell 27919-1.)

calling the animals to them, or making them betray their whereabouts. As they slew whatever they could but by preference cows and calves, and as they were very persevering, but also very excitable and generally poor shots, so that they wasted much powder, they not only wrought havoc among the elk, but also scared the survivors out of all the country over which they hunted.[89]

Some days earlier Roosevelt had visited an old mountain man with deep knowledge of the Teton country. Richard Leigh, or "Beaver Dick" as he was known, occupied a buffalo-hide tipi with "his comely wife and half-breed children," their sizable herd of horses grazing nearby.[90] British by birth, Beaver Dick came to America as a teenager and ventured west in the early 1850s. Soon after arriving in the Teton country, around 1862, he married a Shoshone woman. Thirteen years later, after Roosevelt's stopover, he lost his wife and six children to smallpox.[91] Beaver Dick's legendary prowess as an outdoorsman found its way into Owen Wister's popular novel, *The Virginian.* The guide seemed "to have had a sense of the importance of his own history with the Indians, for he wished fervently at one point that he could somehow 'give to the world my experience in Indan *[sic]* life and the rocky mountains so that thay *[sic]* could understand it.'"[92]

In 1875, 1876, and 1878, even as most Plains Indians were discouraged from leaving their reservations, Beaver Dick periodically bumped into Indians hunting near the park. Edited by Lee Whittlesey, his comments offer some sense of Indian forays into the general Yellowstone area:

On June 8, 1875, Leigh traveled down Pine Creek in the Snake River Range above present Swan Valley, Idaho, and reported that "Indians [h]ad run the elk and scattered them" there.

On August 25, 1875, Leigh was confronted with four Indians at his cabin and boat near the mouth of South Teton River who wanted passage across the river. They told him that "the [other] indans that was out hunting the teton range [h]as got a big scair [scare] dan thay say thare is war parteys of the seux [Sioux] Indians in the [Teton] range and it is making these Indans go for the[ir] reserve in duble quick [time]." Here we have a rare reference to Sioux Indians in the Tetons and a confirmation of Bannock/Shoshone use of the area for hunting.

Below present Swan Valley Idaho, on September 12, 1876, Leigh ran into two lodges of Indians camped on Snake River: "I talked with them they ware [were] shoshones hunting elk and deer but was making very poor work of it thay [h]ad killed 2 deer and no elk and [h]ad beene out 6 weeks."

On October 12, 1876, while trying to get his cabin built near the mouth of South Teton River (present Rexburg, Idaho), Dick noted that he stopped hunting because "the Indans was hunting all around us."

On September 5, 1878, while at his home near the mouth of South Teton River, Dick mentioned that Indians were "scaterd thrue [scattered through] the timber hunting elk."[93]

Although these Indian sightings of the 1870s involved elk hunting, it is the buffalo whose likeness is emblazoned on the National Park Service official and that symbolizes the park in the eyes of the public. The coin popularly known as the "Buffalo nickel" coupled the symbiotically related symbols of this iconic species and the Noble Indian. At Yellowstone, however, it was vital to send them their separate ways. As civilization "reduced wildlife and natives to emblems of vestigial wilderness," Magoc writes, both might share subjugation to "near-extermination and touristic incorporation," but not side by side. Magoc continues:

> Railroad publicists and Yellowstone Boosters fatalistically linked the vanishing Indian and the disappearing bison as paramount and now picturesque symbols of the vanquished American West. Park officials, although not recognizing the ancient ecological dynamics of the greater Yellowstone environment, vigorously enforced the Indian ban from the reserve and the containment of bison within.[94]

Today one can observe herds of buffalo grazing and switching their tails in broad daylight by the roadside down the Lamar Valley. But in the park of yesteryear, according to a nineteenth-century geologist who knew the place well, it would have been "most unusual, save in midwinter, to find them in open valley or on the treeless mountain slope."[95] This contrast in habitats may be explained, of course, by the adaptive process; today's buffalo have become accustomed to the incessant gazes, even meddling, of gawkers and the intrusion of their vehicles. But it might also be explained by the fact that these were possibly different subspecies of buffalo, as Indians who had personal experience with both strains may have recognized as well.

When wayfaring parties of Indian hunters or raiders pursued buffalo inside Yellowstone National Park or its enfolding mountain ranges they were after an animal, *Bison bison athabascae* Rhoads, whose looks and behavior seemed to contrast with their plains cousins, *Bison bison bison* Linnaeus. These so-called mountain or wood bison appear to have been somewhat smaller, generally tougher and faster, and their fur darker, finer, and curlier.[96] They were skittish and possessed a keen sense of smell. The preferred habitat of the Yellowstone herds was described by Hague when he was working in the park one hundred years ago: "They haunt the most inaccessible and out-of-the-way places[,] . . . living in open glades and pastures, the oases of the dense forest." These woods-adapted bison could have been the subspecies that earlier Indians drove over cliffs eastward into the Bighorn Basin or into catchment pens just south of the park. According to a correspondent for *Live Stock Markets* in 1931, the last of these bison was killed in the Bighorn Mountains in 1885; he added the following description of the breed:

> They grazed largely on willow and browsed on the leaves, shoots, bark, and twigs of trees. This gave the flesh a peculiar aromatic flavor, and you very soon tired of the meat. It was a great source of meat when the overland railroads

were built. The hides made good robes, but the leather was not good. It was spongy.[97]

Not until 1989 did anyone claim to locate an Indian bison kill inside the park proper. Four years after one bull's remains eroded from a cliff of billowing steam vents above Yellowstone Lake at Steamboat Point, a team from the Park Service's Midwest Archaeological Center exposed nearly the entire animal, including bones with apparent butchering marks and obsidian flakes from the cutting tools that made them. The kill site was dated at about A.D. 1200 and quite possibly was chosen by Indian hunters because the steam release made it a warm place to camp, or because they could corner animals against the lakeside cliff.[98] Little is known about when the various Indian groups might have made their last buffalo hunts in the park area, since those forays were clandestine after 1872, and sightings of trespassing Indians were sketchy and infrequent.

The following rare account of a Crow pursuit of buffalo at a known location within Yellowstone National Park was elicited by a Works Progress Administration field-worker in the early 1940s. The telegraphic remarks came from a part-Indian cowhand and former stagecoach driver named Horace La Bree, who in 1929 talked with Crow chief Plenty Coups about what the elderly leader believed was the last Crow hunt to occur in the park.[99] That year the two old men got together when they were both honored guests at a celebration at the park's northern entrance. Plenty Coups was eager to talk with La Bree because the landscape around Gardiner jogged his memory; he wanted to see it with someone familiar with the countryside. About eighty-one years of age at the time, Plenty Coups had retained a boyhood image of long-ago Crow hunters chasing animals up a particular creek that split into two forks and then trapping the buffalo against a high rock or mountain.

Fortunately, La Bree could pinpoint the very stream Plenty Coups was talking about. It was Buffalo Creek, and he also knew where the later-named Hellroaring and Coyote Creeks, the two streams of Plenty Coups's memory, poured into the Yellowstone. Their conversation triggered Plenty Coups's further recollections about the hunt. As it turned out, he had been about twelve years old at the time (ca. 1860):

> The Crows were hungry—in need of meat—food—clothing—The buffalo were becoming scarce—a bunch had gone into the Park—and they could not reach them—they spotted a herd of some two or three hundred—going up—towards these mountains—cross the Yellowstone—This was just what the Indians had hoped they would do.
>
> As Plenticoups explained—that his father [Medicine Bird] knew the lay of the country—where the two creeks came into the Yellowstone—back of which was a high cliff—of a rocky kind(.) The Crows—kept right in pursuit of the bunch of buffalo—running them—between the two creeks—right up against the rocky cliff.

Of course—there was only thing the animals could do that was to mill around at the foot of the Cliff—then try to return—and the Indians had their game corralled.

This was the last hunt of the wild buffalo herd—in that locality. So Plenti-coups told them.[100]

According to the old chief, directly below this hunting location and across the Yellowstone was the expanse known as Buffalo Flat, which one finds just north of the Northeast Entrance Road.[101] One of seven named plateaus that taken together comprise the Yellowstone Plateau, it was in 1870 that a group of prospectors first named it Buffalo Flat, because "we found thousands of buffalo quietly grazing."[102] The description accords with Plenty Coups's memory, for he recalled that in earlier days here "the buffalo would gather—to sun themselves. Often many were killed on this spot."[103]

Aside from its rarity as a description of an uncommon Crow method of driving and hunting bison in Yellowstone, Plenty Coups's account is provocative because of the location it specifies. Where the two creeks run into the Yellowstone River seems about five miles from a buffalo-hunting site identified in the late 1950s during a preliminary archaeological survey of the park by J. Jacob Hoffman, which he designated "The Slough Creek Compound, 48YE420."[104] As Hoffman described the terrain of the half-mile-by-quarter-mile site: "It consists of a series of knolls and terraces overlooking Slough Creek and two intermittent streams that enter the creek from the north."[105]

The combined evidence of rock piles, a rock wall, camping and butchering, and "a natural cul de-sac on the south side" of the creek indicates that Indians had taken temporary advantage of the natural topography to corner buffalo for easier killing and processing. Hoffman also wondered whether some post holes on the creek's northern bank were associated with the animal-drive complex but was not sure they were dug during the historic period. Although the bison bone deposits that protruded out of the Slough Creek banks were not extensive, Hoffman felt this accorded with the characteristically thin animal remains at other northwestern plains game compounds that were associated with late prehistoric or historic times. Suffice it to say that such cross-referencing of personal memory and archaeological reconstruction in the same vicinity is unusual in the annals of Plains Indian cultural history.[106]

Yellowstone National Park was also the setting for another Crow reminiscence about buffalo hunting. In early fall 1932 Max Big Man was visiting the park to participate in the buffalo roundup at Buffalo Ranch. Beforehand he toured the Mammoth museum, helped to interpret an elk hide painting on exhibit, and related the following "real" Crow story, possibly to explain why his wife had not joined him in the park for the roundup. Although he did not indicate whether this account of the vicissitudes of Indian buffalo hunting took place in Yellowstone

National Park proper, park officials considered it interesting enough to publish, and so do we:

My grandfather once told me a real buffalo story. He was not my grandfather, but my grandfather's brother, but he was always kind to me and I call him "grandfather." He said, "I was riding along with my wife and could see the buffalo hunters. Some of the buffalo came very near to us. One of the faster ones, a three-year-old, came right next to us." My wife said, "You had better chase it and get some nice fresh meat."

Very seldom, at that time, was a woman ever on a buffalo hunt. Sometimes a woman cannot keep up with buffalo; sometimes get killed. Woman supposed to stay at home. But I was leading the buffalo off,—a war-whoop—, look to the right of me, and shot an arrow. I did not want to be very far from my wife and because my wife was along I did not have the right skill.

When I wounded the buffalo I was on a little knoll and I looked back to see if my wife was coming. When I turned I stopped and I heard a noise and the buffalo was right at me. I leaned over quick to help my horse start. Too late! The buffalo hit me from behind. Mean fellow! I was thrown. I lay very still. Buffalo might not see me. Alas! he caught me and threw me high. I fell right next to a cut-bank, rolled over, but did not get into that ditch. Buffalo caught me again and struck on my head. Crawled over to deeper place. Got up and gave war-whoop. Wife coming closer.

"Don't come near," I yelled, "buffalo is mad!"

I ran to a nearby tree and climbed it. Buffalo came on. War-whoop given in different places. I look around. In different places I see streaks of dust with spots on the end coming toward me. The riders killed the buffalo, I got down. The blood was streaming from my face and leg and I could see a tendon hanging from my leg. I fainted.

When I came to that night I heard a noise like running water. The Medicine Man was directly over me and his medicine was buffalo meat. Medicine Men had buffalo horns on. I thought it was the buffalo once more and again I fainted. When I came to a second time they had stopped crying and gave me water! I was hungry.

"He must be near death," they said, "asking for food."

No matter how sick an Indian is, he is fed buffalo meat. If he asks for food then he may be going to the Happy Hunting Ground.

The Medicine Man said, "Feed him," and they gave me meat and I ate just like a sound man.

It did not have bad effects; there are my marks. There is the mark on my forehead, touch that, and there is the scar on my leg. Touch that. This is the proof of my story. It is true. Ever since that lesson I make my arrow count.

Never take a wife on a buffalo hunt. Whenever you do a thing, leave out other things. Concentrate![107]

HOW INDIANS SAVED THE YELLOWSTONE BUFFALO I

Roughly before 1750, the mountain buffalo that ranged throughout the Rocky Mountains and their intermountain valleys belonged to a continental buffalo population of all subspecies estimated at between thirty and eighty million animals.[108] Although by the 1840s most of the buffalo were gone from the plains, reports from the Yellowstone Plateau from about 1869 to 1885 suggest a sizable number could still be found, especially in the sequestered domain of the upper Lamar River. In the case of the so-called mountain bison at least, the early vision of Yellowstone National Park as a safety zone for animal species quickly being hunted to the verge of extinction seems valid. Accompanying the Ludlow reconnaissance expedition of 1875, Grinnell encountered hide poachers throughout the area, whose access by new railways set the stage for a final assault against big game all across the Rocky Mountain West. A year later Grinnell urged the U.S. Congress to pay attention to "the terrible destruction of large game, for the hides alone, which is constantly going on in those portions of Montana and Wyoming through which we passed. Buffalo, elk, mule deer and antelope are being slaughtered by thousands each year, without regard to age or sex, and at all seasons. Of the vast majority of animals killed, the hide only is taken. Females of all these species are as eagerly pursued in the spring, when just about to bring forth their young."[109]

The impact of this overkill on Yellowstone's herds would be assessed in 1889. William T. Hornaday's census found only 200 buffalo animals surviving under lax federal supervision,[110] and there were an estimated 1,091 buffalo in North America.[111] Ironically, Hornaday blamed Indians for this decline in the herds, claiming that "up to the year 1880 the Indians of the tribes previously mentioned (Sioux, Cheyenne, Crow, Blackfoot, Assiniboin, Gros Ventre, Shoshoni) killed probably three times as many buffaloes as did the white hunters."[112] But Hultkrantz comments on this quote, "So speaks an inveterate Indian hater, a person who is out to free his white compatriots from the charges of having extinguished the precious American buffalo."[113] When dire predictions of the Yellowstone herd's extinction as a result of rampant poaching reached Congress, the unique power of this park to focus public debate became vigorously evident. Quickly the politicians drafted the first federal law protecting buffalo, and it was signed by President Grover Cleveland in May 1894. It provided for penalties of $1,000 in fines or even imprisonment.

In 1902, when it was estimated that hardly twenty-five animals were struggling for survival, controlled groups of the apparent plains type were introduced into the park. The newcomers were drawn from two sources: a small herd that Charles Goodnight of West Texas had bred from wild strays he found near Palo Duro Canyon in the 1870s; and eighteen cows that belonged to another private refuge for buffalo that was co-owned by two mixed-blood Indians, Michael Pablo and Charles Allard, in northern Montana.

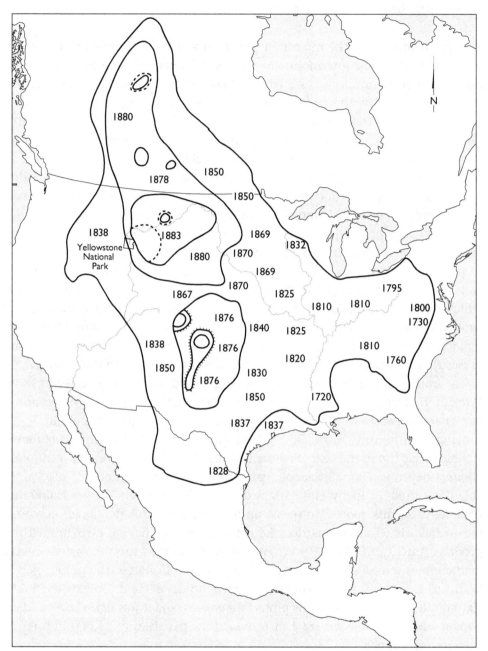

Depiction of the near-extermination of American bison by decades, indicating Yellowstone National Park as one of their last refuges. From an estimated aboriginal population of approximately 80 million their numbers shrank to under five hundred by 1883. (Based on a map from Ernest Thompson Seton, *Animals of North America*).

At first this fresh stock was not intended to replenish the free-range bison who hid out in the upper Lamar Valley. Until at least 1915, these newcomers were relatively quarantined, herded under careful monitoring and corralled together at night. But at about this time, they began to crossbreed; by the 1970s it was estimated that since the preponderance of surviving bulls originated from the mountain population, "the wild strain in the present bison population would seem to be 30-40%."[114]

But how were these plains animals originally rescued from the hunting frenzy that saw the millions of American buffalo reduced to a few hundred by 1900? The following account blends data from Francis Haines,[115] Ernest Thompson Seton,[116] and Martin S. Garretson.[117] Apparently, the Pablo-Allard herd, which by the turn of the twentieth century supplied "more than 80 percent of the buffalo in the United States," was instrumental in rescuing the buffalo from extinction. This was also the group of animals that contributed to the new breeding stock for Yellowstone. And it was these animals whose preservation can be traced to a Montana Indian reservation.

Of the four original breeding herds that ensured the survival of buffalo before the turn of the century, the first two appeared to have been captured and—whether inadvertently or not we will probably never know—preserved by Indians. As Martin S. Garretson of the New York Zoological Society admitted, "It is a singular fact, and contrary to general belief, that we owe much to the Indians for saving the buffalo from extinction."[118] In the first case it was a group of Indians from the Winnipeg area that captured a bull and four calves just north of the Canadian border in Manitoba and sold them to a local trader.

But the other situation involved a member of the Pend d'Oreille tribe named (Sam) Walking Coyote. In spring 1873 Walking Coyote joined a friendly band of Piegan hunters along the U.S.–Canada border near the Milk River, not far from present-day Buffalo, Montana. After killing a number of adults, the men noticed six stray motherless calves plus two bulls and four cows hovering for company around their horses. In tandem with a rancher who was planning to drive a herd of cattle one hundred fifty miles to Salish country, Walking Coyote and his new animals made the mountainous trek south.

When he reached his home in the Jocko Valley, Walking Coyote released his buffalo on open cattle range. Eleven years later, when the herd had grown to thirteen or fourteen animals, he sold ten of them, at $250 a head, to the newly formed partnership of half-Piegan Michael Pablo and the part-Indian Charles A. Allard. By the time of Allard's death in 1896, they numbered about three hundred animals. A portion of this stock were sold to a Kalispell rancher, who provided the startup group for the National Bison Range located in Moise, Montana. Another bunch went to Howard Eaton, the rancher who directly supplied the eighteen cows to Yellowstone National Park. In this roundabout way, then, even the Euro-American accounting for the hybridized Yellowstone buffalo herd acknowledges Indian roots.

Michael Pablo, Flathead Indian rancher and early supplier of buffalo to Yellowstone National Park. (From Martin S. Garretson, *A Short History of the American Bison* [New York: American Bison Society, 1934], 56.)

How Indians Saved the Yellowstone Buffalo II

On the Kootenai-Salish Indian Reservation a story of the saving of some ancestors of the Yellowstone herd has been preserved in a longer, three-part narrative that also fits in an older, more complex tradition of the intimate relationship between Salish Indians and buffalo. Early in 1977 these stories were related on tape by Blind Mose Chouteh, an eighty-seven-year-old elder and famous storyteller, and translated by Dolly Linsbebigler in 1992. A portion is summarized here courtesy of the Kootenai-Salish Culture Committee.[119] All three of these narratives feature the family line of a part-Kalispel, part-Salish man called Blanket Hawk, whose name apparently referred to the protective neckpiece of hawk skins that he habitually wore into battle.

In the first narrative Blanket Hawk is a young man camping with his people away from their protected valley, all of them facing famine on the open plains in the middle of a harsh Montana winter. The chiefs cast around for medicine men with supernatural powers to lure warm weather and make the snow melt. Although Blanket Hawk and his friends propose a Jump Dance, an older medicine man disdains the idea as futile. When the children, who are the last to be given food, are threatened with starvation, the leading chiefs ask Blanket Hawk for help.

In his tipi Blanket Hawk conducts his own Jump Dance to attract the Chinook winds, and afterward predicts that the following morning nine buffalo will enter the camp, to be followed by a larger herd. At sunup the camp is awakened by barking dogs, and everyone emerges from their lodges to find nine buffalo bulls standing and waiting in the midst of camp. They are quickly slaughtered, and warm weather moves in. Everyone is relieved and happy again; according to the narrative, the youngsters throw snowballs. All sit down to meals of boiled and roasted buffalo meat, and the remainder is dried for later use. Then still more buffalo appear, assuring an adequate food supply for the future. The people survive and return home.

By the opening of Chouteh's second story, the character known as Blanket Hawk is a grown man. Again the Salish are out on the plains getting their annual meat supply, but now it is spring—"when the wild roses were in bloom," as they phrase it. On their way home from their successful hunt, they camp for three days in Blackfeet country. It is then that Blanket Hawk gets the idea of initiating a form of animal husbandry. As he explains to his friends and his mother, "I am going to ask the Chief and the people. I am going to tell the Chiefs and leaders if we can bring back some buffalo." After smoking with the chiefs, he shares his plan for having buffalo always close by, so that his people will be safe from distant enemies like the Cree.

But half of the chiefs argue that such long journeys are important, because it is good to be able to fight other tribes and worthwhile to travel so they can hunt and "pass the time." The other chiefs, however, side with Blanket Hawk. When they cannot reach a consensus, Blanket Hawk abandons his idea and pronounces, "I quit asking. I will be silent. The buffalo can stay here on the plains. Maybe you like our people getting killed by the different tribes of Indians. Maybe you like us to get tired by coming here to hunt buffalo for our food."

The following day, when they are breaking camp, "[t]he buffalo surrounded the people who were moving. The buffalo stayed close by, going along with the people; and some stayed near Atatice? (Blanket Hawk) and his friends." But since the other camp members would not allow the buffalo to join them, Blanket Hawk must part with the animals. The story continues:

> His friends mounted their horses. And Atatice? was last. Before he mounted on his horse, he made sounds, saying, "Qeyq, qeyq-eeee." He waved to the buffalo, as if to separate the buffalo. He said to the buffalo, "Go on, it is your destiny, whatever may happen to all of you buffalo. They would not let you go back with me. It is up to you, whatever happens to you and whatever happens to me. That is all." And Atatice cried. His friends also cried. They regretted to part with the buffalo.

The buffalo turned towards the east (rising sun). They went in different directions.

The men were crying as they moved on forward. As they were crossing over the mountains, they looked back and saw the buffalo, saw the black forms of the buffalo moving along.

Thus ended Chouteh's second story. Before moving to his third narrative, he interjected a somewhat shocking anecdote that may shed light on the deeper meaning underlying the unusual affinity between Blanket Hawk and buffalo. Chouteh related that Blanket Hawk's wife brought a buffalo head into their house in order to butcher it and boil it. At the time Blanket Hawk was playing cards with friends and turned to her, aghast at what he saw. Immediately he begged her, "Don't, don't, don't. Take the head outside and fix it, chop it up, because I have always told you all not to prepare it inside of the house. You will hurt me."

Ignoring his plea, she continued cutting away. At first Blanket Hawk suffered from only a nosebleed. But soon he was vomiting blood. When she did not cease sawing on the head, he collapsed to the floor and died.

This taboo against bringing a buffalo head indoors is interestingly similar to that which inhibited a Crow elder from allowing one into his house in Wyola, Montana, in 1986. That was when one of the authors of this book showed up with a large buffalo bull skull from an animal he had hunted in Black Canyon on the Crow Reservation in 1962 while working with the Crow tribe's Fish and Game Division. It was needed for the elder's medicine pipe bundle ceremony, but at the same time the restrictions associated with his rock medicine bundle prohibited a buffalo head from remaining under his roof. In the case of this Salish Indian, Blanket Hawk, we might infer that his close tie with the buffalo world, whether or not it was due to the fact that the buffalo was his personal guardian spirit, was founded on similar respect for the creature as a species, or obligations to it as his supernatural guardian. In the two narratives already cited, such a special relationship was evidenced. But power works for you or against you; in this story the insult shown to the animal in Blanket Hawk's home sealed his gory fate.

Chouteh's third narrative stresses the continuity of the symbiotic relationship between a particular family and buffalo. Now the protagonist is Blanket Hawk's son, a young man named Susep tatati, or "Hawk." As is often the case with more "recent" stories, this one resembles an abbreviated memorandum rather than a well-developed narrative. Without any preamble we learn that Hawk is a "big-sized boy," and we also infer that he seems to have inherited his father's personality or inclinations, for we immediately are told, "He brought back two buffalo from the plains country" and that his intent is to keep them alive. After his father's death, his mother, Sabine Mary, remarries a man named Samuel. It was near their house, just north of the old Dixon Agency, that this particular group of animals began to breed and multiply.

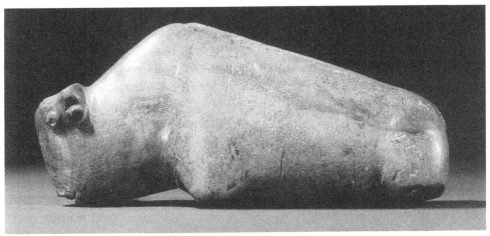

Effigy of a buffalo found in the Absaroka Mountains. (Photo courtesy of Smithsonian Institution, National Anthropological Archives, #77-1330.)

But while the boy was away on a trip, two men showed up at his parents' home and offered to buy the entire bunch. Chouteh gives their names as the aforementioned Michael Pablo and Charles Allard and recalls that they paid a thousand and several hundred dollars for the small herd. The story continues:

The buffalo were herded, going by way of Dixon, Ravalli and came through here. They were driven by way of where the present bridge is now. There were a lot of buffalo.

When the buffalo came over the hill and the Indians here saw the buffalo, they shouted, hollering with excitement. The Indians kept shouting as the buffalo went by.

Charles Allard and Michael Pablo already had a herd of buffalo. They wanted to increase their herd. They were the only two people who had any buffalo.

Maybe it was two days later, maybe it was later that [Hawk] returned and missed the presence of the buffalo. He looked around and found the buffalo gone.

When he got home, he asked his mother, "Where are my buffalo?"

"They are gone," his mother told him. "Your [stepfather] sold them. They were driven off several days ago. You have some money in the amount of a thousand and several hundred dollars. Your stepfather has your money. We are using some of it for food, bought groceries."

[Hawk] cried, he felt so bad. That was the end of that.

Combining this account of the Blanket Hawk family and the earlier story of Walking Coyote, one wonders whether the Pablo-Allard herd, which assisted the reestablishment of buffalo in Yellowstone Park, possibly received two infusions through Plateau Indian donors. But from the rich, latter account, we also get hints of mysterious personal affinities and cultural ties that linked Indians and these animals. Most importantly, as far as the history of Yellowstone National Park is concerned, these narratives help us to appreciate that crucial relationship between American Indians and Yellowstone's buffalo in both biological and cultural terms.

Interactions between Yellowstone's animals and Indians did not end with the founding of the park, though both of them fell under increasing control by the Department of the Interior after 1880. With congressional outcry over the decline of wildlife across the West, uncompromising protection and replenishment of wild stock dominated park policy in the 1890s. Then, during the days of Franklin Roosevelt's "Indian New Deal," came a period of controlled giveaways of elk and buffalo to newly empowered and hungry Indians. A major donation to the Crow tribe in 1934 came after energetic lobbying by their new native superintendent, Robert Yellowtail. Here the Yellowstone National Park herd "paid Indians back" by supplying sixty-nine cows and eight bulls for a new herd to be pastured on rich grassland in the Bull Elk and Black Canyon highlands of the Crow Reservation. Yellowtail furnished the trucks and raised $750 for expenses for the 350-mile trip from Yellowstone to south-central Montana. The Park also provided buffalo to start up another Indian herd at Pine Ridge (Sioux) and for feeding families at Wind River (Shoshone).

But Shoshones were also interested in obtaining Yellowstone buffalo to feed their spirits. As a tourist who visited the Wind River community volunteered in a letter to the park superintendent that same summer of 1934:

> They [members of the Fort Washakie Indian council] remarked how hard it was to get buffalo heads and pelts for their ceremonies; [they said] that you had given them one last year but that they were persuaded not to come asking again this year, even though you would have been more than willing to have given them one from surplus. . . . Fort Washakie Indians wish very much to have a little bison herd of their own. They have blind canyons where they could winter them; plenty of range they say. And since these animals mean so much to these plains tribes, it hits me as something worth talking over with you—this idea of giving them live bison instead of dead 'uns. Maybe just a reasonable start. I think I believe they'd come with pomp and ceremony to drive the bison over the hill and to the tribal lands. It might make a grand story from the park publicity angle; and from the Department of the Interior and its two divisions, Parks and Indian Affairs, angle. New Deal slant.[120]

Further evidence of the close relationship between many Plains Indians and buffalo is an anecdote provided to us by RE, an elderly woman from Fort Washakie. The event she recalls took place in the late 1990s, when she and her late husband made their annual July Fourth camp in the western part of Yellowstone Park.

> So one day we were in camp and my husband said, I think I'll walk this way, he said. I think I'll go with you I said. So we walked down. And there, out of the blue, a great big bison came out, big, big, about that big. Just kept coming

towards us. And I kinda got scared, I thought he was going to maul down there. I stopped. My husband kept walked. He stopped and greeted him. Spoke Indian to him. He looked right at him in the eyes. And like this he touched his forehead. Talking to him. And all that bison did was dig a couple times—like this. Just stood there, and my husband go through talking Indian to him. Says, you roamed this freely like we did. We both roamed this freely. But now we're fenced in. Now look at us, we're run down. Look at your hide. I looked down at his hoofs, man they were about that big. He [my husband] looked so tiny standing underneath it. Talking to it. That buffalo looked at him like he really understood him. Waved his little tail like that. He said, well, give me a good blessing. Told that bison. Turned around, and walked back, and he stopped and looked at him. Starts a little cigarette, put it down, where that buffalo was. That buffalo just turned around and put his head down and turned real easy and started walking. Tourist running around, people just stopped, told not to touch buffalo and here he was touching it on the head. They all got quiet, Chinese people and white people. Ranger drove by and then he walked back. Buffalo just kind of snorted and turned. Chinese people asked, why you touch that buffalo, all kinds of questions—he just smiled. That ranger said I'd like to advise you not to touch any more buffalo cause they might maul you down. But that wasn't what we were thinking.[121]

Nothing came of the tourist's suggestion about the park organizing a "buffalo drive" to Fort Washakie. But in the case of its elk, the park would eventually turn some meat over to Indians, although it took a while. In the process of periodic culling to bring the herd within the constraints imposed by the available winter food supply, early on the park found itself with surplus elk, dead and alive. Initially, live animals and carcasses were parceled out to zoos, state parks, rod and gun clubs, and paternal organizations, with the process starting in 1892 when four elk went to Washington's National Zoological Park.[122] But, according to park records, the earliest elk carcasses provided to feed indigent Indians began with a shipment of about 150 head to Montana's Crow Indian Agency in 1935; the following year that tribe received another 384 head, and the Pine Ridge Sioux received 11.

By the early 1940s efforts intensified to route elk meat to other reservation agencies requesting food assistance. Some of these animals came from the regularly confiscated remains of animals killed illegally, but most originated from park efforts to reduce its northerly herds, estimated at around 13,000 head, so as to bring the stock within the carrying capacity of winter food resources. The 321 carcasses distributed in 1942 wound up on eleven reservations, with Fort Hall getting 16, Wind River getting 50, and the Blackfeet and Crow receiving 70 each. From park correspondence with both the Wind River and Blackfeet Agencies, it also appears that hides and hooves for arts and crafts projects were requested along with meat.[123] The final account we have of elk reduction and meat distribution

Transporting elk carcasses from Yellowstone National Park to nearby Indian reservations, 1930s. (Photo courtesy of Yellowstone National Park Archives, #Yell 28581.)

to Indians occurred in 1961–62, as "Plan 1" in the park's program to reduce the 5,000-member northern elk herd by half involved the distribution of 2,655 animals to nearly forty-one reservations, schools, hospitals, or missions to benefit Indians.[124]

Their older, subsistence and spiritual ties to buffalo were evoked by Indians in winter 1996–97, as losses to Yellowstone National Park's herd as a result of ice storms, freezing temperatures, stray animals, and motor vehicle accidents cut the population by more than two-thirds. About 300 to 400 animals died from the heavy weather, 41 more were struck by vehicles, and another 1,080 wandered outside the Park and were shot by Montana officials or sent to slaughter because of the fear that they might infect neighboring cattle with brucellosis. Of the original 3,436 bison in the park at the beginning of the that winter, only 1,089 animals were found in an aerial count in mid-March 1997. This period represented "the largest slaughter of wild bison this century."[125]

As the magnitude of this crisis in wildlife management and park public relations became clear, Indian groups responded in three ways. One reaction was spiritual. Tribal members joined protestors who gathered on March 6, 1997, to pray for the buffalo's welfare. Representatives of the Intertribal Bison Cooperative convened their National Day of Prayer for the Buffalo in three locations. The Indians selected their date to coincide with the park's celebration of its 125th birthday and with the shooting of the thousandth animal to wander outside the park. One group bowed their heads at the Montana Capitol Building in Helena; in Washington, D.C.,

President Bill Clinton was offered a pipe by tribal elders; and near the Yellowstone National Park's northern entrance in Gardiner, Montana, on the same day that coordinator Rosalie Little Thunder was arrested for trespassing while trying to pray for them, the Montana State Department of Livestock shot fourteen buffalo. The Lakota Gerald Millard summarized the mounting Indian (and non-Indian) sorrow and outrage in his remarks on the Capitol steps in Washington:

> The snow, once white, is yet again red with blood. I am here to speak for the thousand who have passed over to the spirit world and also those yet in danger. I have come to demand the stop of the genocide against my relatives of the Tatanka Oyate, Buffalo Nation.[126]

The second Indian response was equally traditional but was based on subsistence rather than religious impulses. The onetime hunters of Yellowstone Plateau buffalo, the Shoshone of the Wind River Reservation, argued that the park should abolish its old rule against hunting and petitioned for the right of Indians, and only Indians, to cull buffalo inside the park. And given the idea of indigenous breeding suggested by the Salish narratives reviewed above, the third Indian response may be considered equally "traditional," even if couched in modern terminology. About forty-one tribes established the Intertribal Bison Cooperative, spearheaded by its founding president, Fred DuBray, from South Dakota's Cheyenne River Sioux Reservation. This group proposed a $2 million buffalo compound on the state's Fort Belknap Indian Reservation in northern Montana for quarantining all buffalo who tested negative for the brucellosis disease. "To avoid any contamination of tribal cattle," offered a press report on their proposal, "1,280 acres would be encircled by two 8-foot high game-proof fences and a third fence of barbed wire."[127]

The buffalo crisis in Yellowstone National Park made national television news and became the subject of instant documentaries on cable channels. Within the park, it inspired intense discussions. The National Park Service's Intermountain Field Office in Denver contracted with Virginia Ravndal to draft a social-cultural study of Indian and non-Indian opinion about the bison-brucellosis issue. During preparation of an Environmental Impact Statement (EIR) a new bison management plan was discussed with a host of tribal representatives. The park also organized a special three-day course in September 1998 on American Indians and Cultural and Natural Resources Management, reaching out to Indian participants. Greater efforts were made to inform Indian tribes who claimed historical and cultural "affiliation" with Yellowstone National Park about archaeological and ethnographic projects. By 2000, when a final draft of the buffalo management plan was finally signed, "[t]he list of tribes that . . . expressed concern or interest about bison ha[d] grown to 84," according to Laura Joss, outgoing chief of Yellowstone's Branch of Cultural Resources.[128]

Northern Indians at the Geysers

When Joseph Weixelman was interviewing Indians in 1991 for his report on traditional native attitudes toward the Yellowstone geysers, he visited the Assiniboine Reservation at Wolf Point, Montana. There he picked up some of those tantalizing shards of narrative that in the past were conceivably richer in descriptive detail and cultural significance. According to one Assiniboine, a man named Leslie Four Star, the area "where water spouted from the ground" marked the southwestern boundary of his people's traditional territory and where the French had encountered his tribe.

> Four Star had a dim memory of his mother-in-law's grandmother who recalled a trip she took to Yellowstone, which he claimed would have taken place "in the late 1700's or early 1800s" (Her husband, he maintained, was born in 1832). At the place where the water spouted from the ground Four Star speculated that his relatives had probably "prayed[,] . . . thanked the Great Spirit and asked that the water doesn't come any closer."[129]

Weixelman was also able to talk with an eighty-six-year-old Assiniboine named Chief Blue Bird, who was considered a key spiritual leader of the tribe. As a young man he had known a much older fellow tribesman named Walking Bull, said to be the step-grandson of Yellowstone Kelly, who had unwittingly visited the Yellowstone thermal region. According to Blue Bird, Walking Bull once traveled very far, got lost, and was gone for over a year. Eventually he came upon a place where smoke issued from the ground. His instinctive reaction was to pray. Touching some water nearby, he discovered it was hot; putting his hand in another place not far away, however, the water was cold. "Maybe it was Thermopolis," the old man told Weixelman, "maybe it was Yellowstone." Later Walking Bull found a place that was flat and white and tasted like salt. He brought this salt back home. The people put it on their meat, and it tasted good. But his people did not believe the rest of "those wild stories."[130]

The End of Northerly Indian Visits to Yellowstone

Twelve years before the last reports in 1867 of Blackfeet marauding inside the park, the American Blackfeet signed a treaty with the U.S. government that, for the most part, ended the tribe's forays into the Yellowstone highlands. It was Washington Territorial Governor Isaac Stevens whose series of treaty councils throughout the Northwest helped to pacify the region for the railroad. In the so-called Judith Treaty of 1855, the Blackfeet signed a pact with Stevens accepting a hunting ground "from the valleys of the Three Forks of the Missouri River, east to the upper waters of the Yellowstone, an area of 30,000 square miles."[131]

But the treaty merely shoved the sites of increasingly bitter conflict between Blackfeet and settlers farther north. Only smallpox, hunger, and the infamous Baker massacre of Heavy Runner's camp of Piegans in early 1870 finally broke Blackfeet resistance. By the time they agreed to a reservation near Browning, Montana, two years after the establishment of Yellowstone National Park, their intimate memories of its haunts twenty years before were already dimming (although, ironically, in 1920 and 1921 the government would push for using Blackfeet tribal funds to complete a highway linking that reservation and Glacier National Park directly to Yellowstone National Park).[132]

And as for a final word on the association between the Kootenai-Salish people and Yellowstone Park, one of our consultants stated:

> Our people always had a connection with that [greater Yellowstone Region] .... Even in the valley where Bozeman is today, in Belgrade, Manhattan, Livingston, and all that area, Helena, Townsend, Great Falls, all that area, Butte, the Beaverhead, the Dillon area, all those areas are basically Bitterroot Salish aboriginal territories. That's where they lived for thousands and thousands of years. That was before any white contact, before any fur traders got there, before anybody. Basically all the way to where the Crow Indian reservation is, and the Northern Cheyenne Indian reservation is, our aboriginal territories went all the way up to Canada, all the way to Montana and Idaho and Yellowstone Park, a vast, vast aboriginal territory.[133]

CHAPTER 3

Residents in the Highlands

The Sheep Eaters

The mountain-dwelling Shoshoneans, known in their language as Tukudika,[1] Tukuarika,[2] or Tukadudka,[3] meaning "eaters of [bighorn sheep] meat," shared the practice of their linguistic brethren of naming their subgroups after the dominant food source. Two other Shoshone peoples who frequented the greater Yellowstone region were the Agaidika, "salmon eaters," and the Kukundika, "buffalo eaters."

The Euro-Americans who came to the Rocky Mountains imposed new designations. The Lemhi, also known as Northern Shoshone, actually included a western assembly of Sheep Eaters and the "salmon eaters." The Eastern or Plains Shoshone absorbed the "buffalo eaters." The Mountain Shoshone, that is, the Sheep Eaters discussed here, spent the warmer months in Yellowstone National Park and adjacent plateaus but followed the bighorn sheep as they gravitated toward the high country for winter shelter. To further confuse matters, early literature on Shoshoneans often refers to any or all of these groups as "Snakes."[4]

Today, the Eastern Shoshone, together with some Sheep Eater descendants, reside on Wyoming's Wind River Reservation. In Idaho's Fort Hall Reservation one finds the Lemhi, Bannock, and other subgroups of Shoshone and Sheep Eater ancestry. Before reconstruction of Sheep Eater culture history, however, let us compare what we know about them with the legacy of distorted impressions left by early chroniclers.

Shoshoneans of the Mountains

The Sheep Eaters who are associated with Yellowstone Park are often characterized as the most elusive and mysterious Indians of the high plains. With all

Indian pole lodges near Sheepeater Canyon Bridge, Yellowstone National Park, 1915.
(Photo courtesy of Montana Historical Society: Haynes Foundation Collection #H-6066.)

the group mergings, renamings, forced relocations, and population loss that they endured, it is difficult to reconstruct their cultural existence at any point in time. Although our descriptions often seem framed in a "timeless present," like all Native American societies, these purported occupants of Yellowstone National Park were peoples of history. Their adaptations to this highland habitat surely underwent change before the arrival of Euro-Americans and only accelerated afterward. If there is a temporal context for our summary of their hunting, foraging, housing, cooking, tool using, social organization, and religious practices, it would be about 1850. Yet we move back and forth in time to enrich our sometimes circumstantial profile and even pursue the Sheep Eaters into the archaeological past by summarizing competing theories about their earliest development.

Most scholars concur that the Shoshonean groups of present-day Wyoming and Idaho spoke mutually intelligible dialects of the Central Numic division of the Uto-Aztecan language stock, with only minor variation among them. Some suggest that Sheep Eater phonetics were distinct in consisting of a decidedly "slow, singsong speech,"[5] but we have little idea how that actually sounded. The Bannock, a tribe closely related to the Shoshone, speak a northern Paiute language from the western Numic Division of Uto-Aztecan.

These high-altitude-dwelling Shoshoneans inhabited the mountainous regions of Wyoming, northern Idaho, and southern Montana and are often described as the only permanent residents of Yellowstone National Park. But "permanent" does not mean that the Sheep Eaters lived in stationary villages or fixed locations. They were seminomadic hunters whose family bands generally followed the migration of the bighorn sheep in much the pattern described by Yellowstone National Park author Charles Phillips:

> Their distribution in the Park was determined largely by that of the mountain sheep. Col. Norris found a recently deserted encampment in the Lava Creek canyon [on Gardner River south of present Bunsen Peak] and named the basalt wall above Sheepeater Cliffs in consequence. Gen. Sheridan's party which entered the Park at Snake River found them in the vicinity of Mt. Hancock and Mt. Sheridan, but the five who accompanied the expedition had never seen the geyser regions. The shores of Yellowstone Lake seem to have been a favorite summer camping ground where they could vary their diet with fish. The flat open country around Indian Pond ("Squaw Lake") was much frequented and the discovery of a number of obsidian implements and arrowheads during the construction of the Lake Shore road would indicate that the promontory between the Thumb and Lake proper was also used as a camp site.[6]

But when the Sheep Eaters of the 1870s are cited in the literature, we urge caution. In that decade a considerable amount of misinformation was disseminated that tarred two different groups of Shoshonean-Sheep Eaters with the same derogatory brush and created cultural stereotypes and historical confusion in the process.

Stereotypes

Few American Indian groups have been burdened with as many demeaning and dismissive descriptions by non-Indian writers as have the Sheep Eaters of the greater Yellowstone region. Even the California Indians, vilified by the pejorative term "Diggers," did not have it as bad, for they were not incessantly compared to "more advanced" native neighbors. It was as if once the Plains Indians elevated themselves onto horses in the early eighteenth century, they had risen to a higher rung on some evolutionary ladder than their high-country neighbors. True, they would have to be conquered or killed, but astride their horses they were still noble, admirably pugnacious if ultimately doomed adversaries. By contrast, the Sheep Eaters were repeatedly described as reclusive, generally afraid of confrontation, traveling afoot, and dependent on their dogs, and hence were demoted to virtual subhuman status. Even the literature relating to Yellowstone National Park reveals how deeply this evolutionary prejudice underlay common opinion about ethnic distinctions within the greater Shoshonean fold:

The Shoshone Nation was in general characterized by the small stature of the people, who were timid and not of the comparatively high mentality of other neighboring tribes. A few of the tribes of this nation rose over the general plane of development, were mounted, and occasionally met their enemies in open combat. . . . Despite the fact that these Indians were considerably above the average of this nation, they held the Blackfeet to the north in wholesome respect.[7]

This comparison between Plains and Mountain Shoshonean Indians echoed the antiquated nineteenth-century theory of societal development: from savagery to barbarism to civilization, with subphases in between. Each level was associated with such diagnostic categories as social organization, housing, and subsistence practices. In the case of a comparison between Sheep Eaters and Plains Indians, this theory would suggest that the former were an example of arrested development: their pole-wickiup encampments were less evolved than that of hide-tipi circles; their use of dogs placed them beneath the status of their horse-raising neighbors; and their reliance on roots and sheep rendered them less worthy of respect than the meat-eating, buffalo-hunting horsemen. They were considered an example of what early anthropology dubbed a "survival," stone age remnants who never matured beyond an earlier, more primitive stratum of human development.

An early depiction of the Sheep Eaters comes from September 1832, when Captain Bonneville and his party of trappers were searching for a pass over the Wind River Mountains. To the west of present-day Lander, Wyoming, the travelers encountered a band of Sheep Eaters. While editing Bonneville's journal, Washington Irving occasionally embellished the material, so we are not certain to what degree this description is exclusively Bonneville's. But we are aware that Irving was also personally familiar with Sheep Eaters, because he mentions an 1811 run-in with them in the Snake River country,[8] and through conversations with trappers he may have gathered more bits of information. As Irving writes of Bonneville's experience:

Notwithstanding the savage and almost inaccessible nature of these mountains, they have their inhabitants. As one of the party was out hunting, he came upon the track of a man, in a lonely valley. Following it up, he reached the brow of a cliff, whence he beheld three savages running across the valley below him. He fired his gun to call their attention, hoping to induce them to turn back. They only fled the faster, and disappeared among the rocks. The hunter returned and reported what he had seen. Captain Bonneville at once concluded that these belonged to a kind of hermit race, scanty in number, that inhabit the highest and most inaccessible fastnesses. They speak the Shoshone language, and probably are offsets from that tribe, though they have peculiarities of their own which distinguish them from all other Indians. They are miserably poor, own no horses, and are destitute of every convenience to be derived from an intercourse with the whites. Their weapons are bows and stone-pointed arrows, with which they hunt the deer, the elk, and the mountain sheep. They are to be found scattered about the countries of the Shoshone, Flathead, Crow, and Blackfeet tribes; but their residences are always in lonely places, and the clefts of the rocks.

Their footsteps are often seen by the trappers in the high and solitary valleys among the mountains, and the smokes of their fires descried among the precipices, but they themselves are rarely met with, and still more rarely brought to a parley, so great is their shyness and their dread of strangers.

As their poverty offers no temptation to the marauder, and as they are inoffensive in their habits, they are never the objects of warfare; should one of them, however, fall into the hands of a war party, he is sure to be made a sacrifice, for the sake of that savage trophy, a scalp, and that barbarous ceremony, a scalp dance. These forlorn beings, forming a mere link between human nature and the brute, have been looked down upon with pity and contempt by the creole trappers, who have given them the appellation of *"les dignes de pitie',"* or "the objects of pity." They appear more worthy to be called the wild men of the mountains.[9]

Another famous description of Sheep Eaters comes from an articulate Rocky Mountain trapper named Osborne Russell,[10] who encountered a small band in the Lamar Valley of Yellowstone National Park in 1834. He recorded valuable details of Sheep Eater material culture and was generally impressed by their lifestyle:

Here we found a few Snake Indians . . . who were the only Inhabitants of this lonely and secluded spot. They were all neatly clothed in dressed deer and Sheep skins of the best quality and seemed to be perfectly contented and happy. They were rather surprised at our approach and retreated to the heights where they might have a view of us without apprehending any danger, but having persuaded them of our pacific intentions we then succeeded in getting them to encamp with us.[11]

During the night, the trappers traded with these Sheep Eaters, and with charcoal on a whitened elk skin one Indian drew a map of their territory. Following the Lamar Valley on the route depicted by the Indian cartographer, Russell and his companions camped somewhere near the junction of the Lamar and Yellowstone Rivers. That night he rhapsodized about this Sheep Eater landscape:

For my own part I almost wished I could spend the remainder of my days in a place like this where happiness and contentment seemed to reign in wild romantic splendor surrounded by majestic battlements which seemed to support the heavens and shut out all hostile intruders.[12]

So far these early descriptions of Sheep Eaters leave us with contradictory perceptions. On the one hand, they are portrayed as miserably poor, naked, and forlorn "objects of pity," a link between humans and brutes; on the other hand, they are depicted as neatly clothed, contented, and happy, a group with whom it would be enjoyable to share a life. This polarized picture opens our profile of the "mysterious" Sheep Eaters, who throughout literature will be continually represented as either "social outcasts" or "noble savages." As Hultkrantz points out, though early texts presented them as squalid and impoverished, the more romantic image arising from Russell's reminiscences also persisted:

> The story of "the wild men of the mountains," shy inhabitants of the inaccessible mountain vastness, whose footsteps and camp smoke only may be seen, spread rapidly. It was in due time built on with new details: the sheepeaters were pygmies and wild men living like animals, or they were the most dignified and morally "clean" of all Indian tribes. Their disappearance from the ethnographic scene was ascribed to a dramatic disaster of one kind or another. The mystification went so far that the Shoshoni Indians on the Wind River Reservation heard rumors of wild mountain men, and that one investigator of Shoshoni folklore even thought that the belief in dwarf spirits went back to the general picture of the Sheepeaters.[13]

But in the long run, the negative view of Sheep Eaters dominated, as evidenced by the following comments by a Washakie National Forest ranger in 1926:

> They were renegade Indians, who, for the sake of safety and perhaps convenience, with the age old fellowship of man, banded together where possible and lived their lives in the mountain fastnesses. They had evidently violated various tribal laws and did not belong to any fixed tribe, having been compelled on penalty of death to live as fugitives. At times they preyed upon small parties or lone Indians for the purpose of equipping themselves with such implements or weapons as were obtainable, or possibly to steal a squaw, returning at once to their mountain retreats. They were not warlike but were supposed to have been cowardly and shy, which, under the circumstances is easily understood. Plainly they were social outcasts.[14]

Sixty-five years later, these disparaging stereotypes had not changed much. For example, a former chief ranger of Yellowstone National Park wrote in his memoirs:

> Known as the *Tukudikas*, or "Sheepeaters," they had been considered, as I have said, the lowliest of the low in the Shoshone Indian tribes. Lacking either the will or the courage to compete in a world upset by the introduction of the horse and gun, they sought to eke out an existence in the then mostly undesired rugged country. . . . They stayed mostly to themselves, were timid, small in stature. . . . Dirty, destitute, primitive[,] . . . the Sheep eaters were anything but fodder for the Indian romancer.[15]

The range of attitudes toward Sheep Eaters has recently gone so far as to include an argument that they did not really exist.[16] In a postmodern take, the archaeologist

Susan Hughes maintains that fragmentary data on mountain Indians surviving in the Yellowstone Plateau fed into a New World projection of the preexisting medieval "myth" of "wild men" who lived on the fringes of society. Early writers such as Washington Irving creatively merged stereotypical reports of Yellowstone Indians with these figments of European folklore. Promoting the position that Indians never lived permanently in Yellowstone National Park, Hughes cites Togwotee as an Indian who did not know his way around the park and reiterates the opinion that tribes other than Sheep Eaters made its conical timber structures. We submit the data in the following pages as a response to this fashionable academic dismissal of "positivistic" portrayals. A Wind River Shoshone educator recently said:

> My brother, who teaches his fifth-graders about the Sheep Eaters, has often remarked at how surprised his students are to learn about the Mountain Shoshone, Mountain Crow and the lives they had in mountains that are right outside our backdoor. Too often the only Indians they read about in their textbooks or see depicted on television are Crazy Horse and Sitting Bull. It's as though the rest of us, and certainly those that didn't ride horses or chase buffalo, never existed.[17]

Popular conceptions and stereotypes about these onetime dwellers in Yellowstone National Park can be summarized as follows:

1. The Sheep Eaters were pygmies with diminutive limbs and stature.
2. Because the Sheep Eaters were timid and poorly developed as a society and so low on the evolutionary scale, they were probably feeble-minded.
3. Like all the Indian tribes of the region, the Sheep Eaters were afraid of the geysers.
4. The Sheep Eaters were a poor people, living on the edge of starvation, who lacked the appropriate technology to take care of themselves. Coupled with this is the misconception that the Sheep Eaters had no dogs or other beasts of burden.
5. The Sheep Eaters were an ethnically impure, motley crew of renegades whose misdeeds had exiled them from various tribes and who banded together like fugitives to prey on the unwary.

Throughout the historical record each one of these stereotypes had advocates. Often, they were recycled from earlier comments, only cementing the misconceptions in public opinion as well as in the writings of those who might have known better. As recently as 1994, for example, the characterization of Sheep Eaters by a well-known historian was that they were "poor even for Indians."[18] Taking each of the above listed statements in turn, however, one can identify their proponents and debate their accuracy.

1. The first person who described the Sheep Eaters as "pygmies" was the second superintendent of Yellowstone National Park, Philetus Norris. In his annual report of 1880 Norris writes:

The only real occupants of the Park were the pygmy tribe of three or four hundred timid and harmless Sheepeater Indians, who seem to have won this appellation on account of their use of the bighorn sheep for food and clothing.[19]

One wonders how Norris arrived at this conclusion, because he personally visited the Ross Fork Agency of Sheep Eaters, Bannocks, and Shoshones to elicit their pledge not to visit the park.[20] To be sure, the Sheep Eaters as a group were medium to short in stature, resembling the general build of Great Basin Indians. Their bones have been described as more gracile than robust,[21] but one should not take this to mean they were incapable of feats of strength. After all, the Sheep Eaters regularly strung horn bows with a pull strength of about sixty-five pounds, and after witnessing the difficulty today's experienced bow hunters had attempting to use one of his horn bows, the Wyoming bow maker Tom Lucas concluded they had to possess considerable upper body strength.[22]

As with all ethnic groups, however, some Sheep Eaters did not fit the norm. There was Togwotee, for example, perhaps the best-known of the group after he became a subchief under Washakie. Elderly Sheep Eaters told Hultkrantz[23] that Togwotee was tall, slim, crook-nosed, and "looked like a Sioux Indian."[24] If the average height and build of Sheep Eaters was small in comparison to Plainsmen like the Crow—whose Missouri River cousins, the Hidatsa, were famously tall— there was clearly variation among individuals. A clearer understanding of Norris's agenda even suggests that by describing them as diminutive he might have been trying to diminish their presence in "his" park. But the characterization appears in the writings of trusted scholars even when Norris is not credited. Charles G. Coutant, a distinguished Wyoming historian, describes the Sheep Eaters as follows:

> Not cultivating the acts of war, they became a timid and inoffensive tribe, marrying among themselves and at last became dwarfed and were despised by war-like nations.[25]

Here Coutant has added insult to injury by suggesting that their allegedly stunted size was caused by eschewing war and inbreeding. Even the noted Yellowstone National Park historian Hiram Chittenden was coerced into imagining the Sheep Eaters as lacking size and intelligence. Following the Bonneville/Irving line, he describes them thus:

> These hermits of the mountains, whom the French trappers called "les dignes de pitie," have engaged the sympathy or contempt of explorers since our earliest knowledge of them. Utterly unfit for warlike contention, they seem to have sought immunity from their dangerous neighbors by dwelling in the fastnesses of the mountains. They were destitute of even savage comforts. . . . Their rigorous existence left its mark on their physical nature. They were feeble in mind and diminutive in stature, and are described as a "timid, harmless race."[26]

Heartland of the Sheep Eaters, Obsidian Cliff, photographed by F. J. Haynes in 1899. (Photo courtesy of Montana Historical Society: Haynes Foundation Collection #H-3940.)

2. It was also Chittenden who introduced the misconception that the Sheep Eaters were fearful and dim-witted. Following Chittenden, it was not uncommon to hear Yellowstone National Park and non-park commentators refer to the Sheep Eaters as "a weak and degenerate race, wholly unfitted to hold their own."[27] Well acquainted with the Park's interpretive programs over the years, Yellowstone veteran Paul Schullery recently summarized these Chittenden-instigated notions of Sheep Eater mental incompetence and the presumed degree of weakened fortitude that derived from it:

> They are the most maligned of the native groups that used Yellowstone. When I came to work in the park in 1972, park educational programs still presented Chittenden's view that the Sheepeaters were culturally deprived weaklings, hiding in a few remote areas of Yellowstone because they simply couldn't survive anyplace else.[28]

Well into the twentieth century one continued to hear Sheep Eaters characterized as excessively shy and retiring. Nedward M. Frost, writing in 1941, reported that "[e]xplorers left few records concerning these now extinct Indians, probably because their extreme shyness made it difficult to approach them."[29]

This belief in their lack of intelligence led to the conclusion that Sheep Eaters were unable to defend themselves. Again, the subtext seems to have been a sort of dubious equivalence of pugnacity and intelligence. Yet even favorable assessments of the Sheep Eaters have accepted this correlation. For example, Sarah Olden writes, "This band [of Sheep Eaters] was more intelligent, and very warlike."[30] Olden offers no documentation for her declaration, but Hultkrantz located a discussion of Sheep Eater mental capacity in the 1854 writing of a Middle Oregon Indian agent named R. R. Thompson:

> The Mountain Snake Indians are a branch of the Root Diggers, (who, in the extreme south, are presumed to be the lowest order of the aboriginal race) and have a common language. They occupy the country on the north and east of Fort Hall, and to the south to include Bear River valley. These Indians gradually improve in their habits and intelligence as they approach the northern and eastern extremities of their country.[31]

Even when the Sheep Eaters are mentioned in a positive light, the speculations concerning their relative lack of mental ability are couched in pseudoscientific, racist terms, a strategy that has often been used to either denigrate or aggrandize other cultures. If physical and cultural anthropology has taught us anything about modern populations, it is the futility of making such comparisons, especially on the basis of rumor and hearsay. It might be far more worthwhile to examine Sheep Eater adaptations to surviving in the mountains. In their material culture and technology, as we shall see, there is ample evidence of their basic intelligence and good practical sense.

3. Although native people's supposed fear of Yellowstone's geysers has commonly been alleged for other Indian groups that traveled through the park (see chap. 4), the Sheep Eaters were also mentioned in this regard. Hultkrantz championed this misconception in a number of his works,[32] but closer inspection reveals some confusion. In one essay he speculates that "the Sheepeaters shunned the geyser areas—and the reason for this can scarcely have been anything but fear,"[33] but then he offers these comments from George Wesaw, a Shoshone:

> The Indians prayed to the geysers because they believed that there were spirits inside them. Sometimes, when nearing enemies, they let the water from the geysers spray over themselves so they became invisible.[34]

This man was a direct descendant of the "Wesaw" who was Colonel Norris's foremost Indian informant. At one point the older Wesaw had told Norris that the Shoshone, Bannock, and Crow "occasionally visited Yellowstone Lake and river portion of the Park, but seldom the geyser regions, which he declared were 'heap, heap bad,' and never wintered there, as whites sometimes did with horses."[35] We might hear in this mock-Indian English expression "heap, heap bad" an echo of Norris's infamous poetry that more than one writer has declared "unfit for human ears." But more importantly, we should recognize that Wesaw's words were a precise response to Norris's query about whether any tribes wintered near the geysers. The thrust of Wesaw's answer is that the geyser area was a bad place to berth horses over the winter. Behind his response must also have been his awareness, passed on from him to subsequent generations, that spirits lived at the geysers and that places where powerful spirits dwell are rarely suitable locations for the everyday activities of hunting, gathering, and camping.

Hultkrantz knew full well that the Shoshone believed that hot springs and geysers were the abodes of spirits who could help or harm human beings.[36] In addition to those in Yellowstone National Park, the best-known thermal pools are found at Thermopolis. According to the Shoshone, a gigantic "dragon" formerly lived there, as did water creatures known as *pan dzoavits* and water ghosts who made the water boil. As George Wesaw explained to him, such powerful spirits within geysers and thermal pools could be propitiated with prayers. The same essay has Hultkrantz pinpointing these places of religious power as the sites that actually *attracted* Shoshones who were seeking supernatural power:

> [A] centre of religious power having the indifferent character of natural force does not act only negatively; he who knows the secret may turn its destructive activity into useful constructive force. The Shoshone knew that the sacred springs could be utilized for positive purposes. As we have seen, the hot jet of geyser provided invisibility medicine.[37]

Throughout the Shoshone realm were vaporous, multicolored, mysterious spots that contained invisible, spiritual forces. While they were certainly held in healthy respect, even awe, personal contact with them was also a requirement for personal success. It is known that the most respected Sheep Eater leader and medicine man, Togwotee, had this *pan dzoavits* as his personal power; it may not be far-fetched to speculate that, like the Crow Indian medicine man known as the Fringe, he sought the supernatural being out during an arduous fast near the Yellowstone thermal field. If so, certainly Togwotee would have felt some fear as well. Who would not be somewhat anxious about spending three or four days and nights alone beside the thundering geysers, abstaining from food and water, awaiting the wondrous and powerful spirits who lived there? Individuals seeking power often speak of their fear while waiting for a visit from the supernatural, but after the event they feel respect for their powers. Survival in Yellowstone National Park depended on the ability of the Sheep Eaters to live in accord with such "frightening" natural forces as blizzards, grizzly bears, and thunderstorms, as well as geysers. Encountering any one of them required caution and experience, and on occasions when one was transacting with their spirits, respect and prayer.

4. The explanation customarily given for the poverty of the Sheep Eaters is that they were forced into the mountains by more advanced and militaristic

tribes of the lowlands. One even finds this idea in a recent curriculum handbook for the Wind River Reservation: "It is probable that the Sheep Eaters of Yellowstone National Park were stragglers of the Northern Shoshones driven into and forced to live in the high mountains by their enemies."[38] Implicit in the misconception is the image picture of the Sheep Eaters as scrounging for survival in an unforgiving landscape.

The notion that Sheep Eaters were "miserably poor" was prevalent among the chroniclers who had only chance encounters with them. In the north, it apparently originates from the Lewis and Clark journeys, following the killing of a deer by one of the expedition's hunters on Friday, August 16, 1805. According to Meriwether Lewis, after a dash to the spot where the deer had been dressed by the hunter, the Mountain Shoshone (Lemhi)

> all dismounted and ran tumbling over each other like famished dogs, each man tore away at whatever part he could, and instantly began to eat it; some had the liver, some the kidneys, in short no part with which we look with disgust escaped them; one of them who had seized about nine feet of entrails was chewing at one end, while with his hands he was diligently clearing his way by discharging the contents at the other.[39]

This quotation was highlighted in an anthropology text, *Man in the Primitive World,* by E. Adamson Hoebel, which was published in 1949 and read in colleges and universities across America. Hoebel maintained that "fear of starvation constantly haunted the Shoshones."[40] The idea that the hunting-and-gathering cultures that Euro-Americans found throughout aboriginal California, the Great Basin, and the Rocky Mountain highlands lived with the wolf always at their door was not effectively challenged until 1966. That was when an international conference on hunters and gatherers used finer-grained data from ethnographic fieldwork to reappraise the lifeways of band-size hunters and gatherers.

Inspired by the methodology of Richard B. Lee among the San !Kung Bushmen of South Africa,[41] anthropologists followed hunters and gatherers on their daily tasks, paid particular attention to what they ate and drank, and then analyzed their food supply to learn its caloric and nutritional value. They realized that by and large most hunters and gatherers enjoyed a reliable and varied food base, subsisting on plants far more than meat (a ratio of 4:1 in dry environments), working only at intensive intervals to satisfy their food needs, and living to old age with minimal worries about survival.[42] Although some of this groundbreaking research has been reevaluated in recent years, the general conclusion remains viable. Fairly small (30 to 40 individuals), mobile, and socially flexible groups of hunting-and-gathering peoples practiced an impressively successful subsistence strategy that required periodic bursts of effort followed by leisurely intervals for enjoying such freedom from want that the label "the world's original leisure society" was bestowed on them.

Some of Lee's reflections on the subsistence patterns of the native people of South Africa might provide a corrective guide for the reappraisal of a band-based, hunting-and-gathering lifestyle such as that of the Sheep Eaters:

Over the course of a year, the picture of steady work, steady leisure and adequate diet was maintained. . . . In assuming that their life must be a constant struggle for existence, we succumb to the ethnocentric notions that place our own Western adaptation at the pinnacle of success and make all other second or third best. Judged by these standards, the !Kung are bound to fail. But judged on their own terms, they do pretty well for themselves.

If I had to point to one single feature that makes this way of life possible, I would focus on *sharing*. Each !Kung is not an island unto himself or herself; each is part of a collective. It is a small, rudimentary collective, and at times a fragile one, but it is a collective nonetheless. What I mean is that the living group pools the resources that are brought into camp so that everyone receives an equitable share. The !Kung and people like them don't do this out of nobility of soul or because they are made of better stuff than we are. In fact, they often gripe about sharing. They do it because it works for them and it enhances their survival. Without this core of sharing, life for the !Kung would be harder and infinitely less pleasant.[43]

Before painting too rosy a picture of Sheep Eater life, we should point out that at times hunters and gatherers certainly faced extreme food shortages. As we are reminded by Elizabeth Colson,[44] who quotes the research of Burt W. Aginsky,[45] the Indians of central California who formerly inhabited one of the richest biomes in the world had memories of hungry years. But Colson[45] suggests that a fivefold plan helped to alleviate periods of starvation. They relied on a diversified food base whereby the hunters and gatherers exploit multiple animal and plant species; they stored or preserved some foodstuffs; they emphasized and taught their children about the value of what might be called "famine foods"; they converted surplus food into durable articles that could be exchanged for food in times of scarcity; they cultivated strong sets of social relations that could be called upon in hard times. We know that the Sheep Eaters practiced some of these strategies. They exploited a wide array of animal and plant foods; they dried fish and meat as well as root plants and berries; they apparently knew about "starvation foods" such as the cambium of pine trees that was available during the winter; they could have traded surplus food, and they enjoyed access to other valuable resources, such as obsidian, for trade; and they maintained kinship and trade networks on which they could rely in times of scarcity. Of all these the last was probably the most important because the Sheep Eaters lived in such a fluid social organization that they could have moved to a neighboring group when resources were tight.

With the abundant supplies of bighorn sheep, fish, and root plants in their territory, it seems unlikely they were regularly at death's door. During the Standifer gold-prospecting expedition of 1866 into Yellowstone country, A. B. Henderson was dispatched to "hunt up the Sheep Eaters camp for the purposes of trading skins etc. with them, as we knew they had hundreds of fine sheep skins and furs of all kinds." When they finally met the group of some sixty Sheep Eaters, they shared a meal and then traded for the sheepskins and marten furs.[47] Although these Sheep Eaters were certainly eager to obtain the white man's trade goods in exchange, they do not sound impoverished, as Osborne Russell found in his meeting with them in the Lamar Valley:

> Here we found a few Snake Indians comprising 6 men 7 women and 8 or 10 children who were the only inhabitants of this lonely and secluded spot. They were all neatly clothed in dressed deer and Sheep skins of the best quality and seemed to be perfectly contented and happy. . . . Their personal property consisted of one old butcher Knife nearly worn to the back two old shattered fusees which had long since become useless for want of ammunition a Small Stone pot and about 30 dogs upon which they carried their skins, clothing, provisions etc on their hunting excursions. They were well armed with bows and arrows pointed with obsidian. The bows were beautifully wrought from Sheep, Buffalo and Elk horns secured with Deer and Elk sinews and ornamented with porcupine quills and generally about 3 feet long. We obtained a large number of Elk Deer and Sheep skins from them of the finest quality and three large neatly dressed Panther Skins in return for awls axes kettles tobacco ammunition etc. They would throw the skins at our feet and say "give us whatever you please for them we are satisfied. We can get plenty of skins."[48]

If this description represents a people on their last legs, how were they feeding thirty dogs? If they were struggling all day to feed themselves, how did they find time to dress skins of the finest quality and make these beautiful bows? If they were so poor, why would they throw skins at the feet of the trappers in exchange for their goods? The Sheep Eaters themselves answered the last question for us: they could get plenty of skins and, of course, those skins were attached to edible flesh. It is true that they were poor in guns, knives, and horses, but that did not prevent this band of twenty-three Sheep Eaters from living what in their view may well have been the good life.

5. The idea that the term *Tukudika,* or "Sheep Eaters," referred not to a distinct group but to a loose amalgam of ostracized members of different tribes who had only recently banded together in the mountains—a sort of Rocky Mountain version of the infamous Comancheros of the Texas plains—was prevalent in the 1870s. In this incarnation the Sheep Eaters become the flip side of retiring or timid: they are nasty savages who wreak havoc on whites. A member of the William A.

Jones expedition into northwestern Montana in summer 1873 reported that there were stray Sheep Eaters in the park: "There is very little, if any, danger from hostile Indians in the park at present. Small parties of Bannocks, Mountain Crow or Snakes, ('Sheep-eaters'), might try to steal something, but they are arrant cowards."[49]

While omitting the negative commentary, W. P. Clark also transmitted the notion that the Sheep Eaters were a polyglot group:

> They were supposed by many authorities to be a separate tribe, differing in language, habits, and physical peculiarities from all the tribes which surrounded them, while others claimed that they were offshoots from the Shoshones, Bannocks, Flatheads, Pend d' Oreilles, Nez Perces, Crows, and Blackfeet, and that their poverty alone forced them to this peculiar life apart from their tribe.[50]

The fur trader Alexander Ross was of much the same opinion:

> The Ban-at-tees, or mountain Snakes, live a predatory and wandering life in the recesses of the mountains, and are to be found in small bands or single wigwams among the caverns and rocks. They are looked upon by the real Sho-Sho-nes themselves as outlaws, their hand against every man, and every man's hand against them. They live chiefly by plunder. Friends and foes are alike to them.[51]

These comments forecast the general characterization, if not the specific misnomer, expressed by Chief Washakie of the Wind River Shoshone in 1879. The Shoshone Indian agent quoted him complaining about the "many bad Indians," whom whites at the time were often identifying as Sheep Eaters.[52] This take on Sheep Eaters as a cultureless and lawless band of predators remained over the years. T.W. Daniels wrote in 1953, "The origin of the tribe is rather obscure. Some authorities believe them to have been renegades and undesirables who were ostracized from other tribes and ultimately took to the mountains where they banded together to form their own groups."[53]

The negative and inconsistent characterizations may have been based on mistaken identity, as writers confounded two separate groups of "Sheep Eaters." Rather than the Wyoming Tukudika, the people who are the main subject here, they were referring to the aggressive group along the Salmon River country in Idaho that resisted white domination. This mistake was examined by Keith Barrette:

> The Tukudika [Sheep Eaters] are often confused with a small polyglot group of Indians, numbering about 200, who once ranged the Salmon River Mountains of Idaho. . . . The error began in the late 1860s when the Salmon River country was first beginning to be settled. To these early-day prospectors and settlers an Indian was an Indian. They dubbed the band made up of excommunicated Bannack, Shoshoni and Nez Perce as "Renegade Sheepeaters."[54]

It was these "predatory" bands of so-called Sheep Eaters (whom one of Hultkrantz's Shoshone informants distinguished by the term *tidibiano*)[55] that contributed to the hostilities of 1877–78 in the Salmon River district of Idaho. They appear to be only distantly related to the Sheep Eaters of the Wind River and the Yellowstone Plateau. But the confusion between these disparate groups may have been reinforced by the fact that the Idaho marauders were said to have appropriated Tukudika camps, from which they launched the horse-stealing raids and attacks on mining camps on the South Fork of the Salmon River that led to the short-lived "Sheepeater War" of 1879 (see chapter 4).

Whence Came the Sheep Eaters? Competing Theories

The bands and tribes who were related through a common language stock are impossible for outsiders to put into a tidy cultural slot. They tend to irritate those who prefer that Indian tribes have fixed names and identities, live within clear and distinct territorial boundaries, and exhibit lifestyles that fit into predetermined categories of the classic "types" of Indian culture. The Sheep Eaters, for instance, do not seem at all like Plains Indians, and their reputation has suffered by comparison. Nor are they really Plateau Indians, although they share numerous traits of those river-dwelling and root-gathering peoples. And some of their representatives on the fringe of the Numic-speaking world fail to exhibit many of the traits that would grant them a Great Basin identity.

To discover just "what kind of Indian" these Sheep Eaters were, we might begin by asking how they became so. And to investigate that question, we must delve into one of the great conundrums in American prehistory—the spread of the peoples who spoke branch dialects of the Numic language family. Few questions are more intensely debated by American archaeologists, linguists, and anthropologists; conferences have been devoted to Numic origins and dispersal. A proliferating series of scenarios have been put forth for the prehistoric migrations of Shoshonean peoples throughout western North America.[56] Narrowing this broad area of inquiry to the matter of the western and eastern Shoshone Indians proper and to Sheep Eaters in particular, we try to simplify the prevailing arguments into the following four hypotheses, each of which has its own proponents.

A GREAT BASIN SOURCE: RECENT ORIGINS

The theory that argues that Shoshoneans have lived in the north for a relatively brief time has been advanced by the archaeologists B. Robert Butler and Gary Wright. They argue that a date of A.D. 1300 for the arrival of the Shoshone is about twice too old. Citing data from archaeological work in the Teton Mountains on the Wyoming–Idaho border, Wright believes the Eastern Shoshone did not arrive until the historic period;[57] Butler is reluctant to accept any more than a few centuries of time-depth for the Shoshone occupation of Idaho.[58]

To make his case, Butler points out that some offshoots of the southwestern maize-cultivating culture of prehistory, which scholars term the northern Fremont, lived in southern Idaho. Based on ceramic evidence, they also appear to be related to a Fremont division found around the Great Salt Lake. But the Idaho Fremont are believed to have persisted longer than their southern counterparts, as suggested after the analysis of Great Salt Lake Fremont ceramics that were found in Wilson Butte Cave and dated at A.D. 1525 ± 150.[59] Therefore, Butler concluded that the Shoshone, who presumably replaced the Fremont, must postdate this later time period. In this theory the time-depth for the presence of Shoshone peoples in the north could not be any morer than three hundred to four hundred years ago.

Similar conclusions were reached by Wright after several years of archaeological work in the Jackson Hole region. Wright based his belief that Shoshones did not arrive in the until 1400 to 1500 on two supposed diagnostics of their culture: flat-bottom pottery and the shield-bearing warrior motif in rock art.[60] However, it has since been established that this motif is at least as old as 1100 in Montana and Wyoming, and a link has also been established between Wyoming Shoshone cultural beliefs and the Dinwoody petroglyph tradition. More important, further rock research has discounted any relationship between expanding Shoshone peoples and the shield-bearing warrior motif. As for the age of flat-bottom pots, however, often referred to as Intermontane War, their appearance (coincident with that of small, desert side-notched projectile points) in the past five hundred to six hundred years probably associates them with expanding Shoshone populations from the Great Basin and is consistent with the reconciliatory hypothesis we offer below.

A GREAT BASIN SOURCE: OLDER ORIGINS

A theory that pushes the origins for the Northern Shoshone deeper into the past is supported by several well-known archaeologists but is actually premised on advances in another discipline, the historical study of language development. To determine the relative age of the various branches of the Numic language stock, this approach borrows from analysis of rates of change in small elements of a spoken language. Known as glottochronology, this linguistic dating technique develops a rate of word loss for a language that has separated from its parent stock. Adapting this hypothesis to the Numic languages, linguists have proposed that their center or core lay in the southern Great Basin along the California–Nevada border. The various Numic-speaking peoples expanded outward from this heartland into their present-day homelands.

One group of these dispersing peoples spoke dialects of Shoshone proper, and their descendants now live on both the Fort Hall and Wind River Reservations.[61] Study of their evolving vocabulary suggests that their migration was launched around 1000, and their constituent tribes are thought to have reached Idaho and

Wyoming between about 1300 and 1400. In this theory, the presence of the Shoshone people in the north could not have exceeded 750 to 800 years.[62]

A GREAT BASIN SOURCE: ARCHAIC ORIGINS

A third group of archaeologists envision a much longer occupation for Numic-speaking groups in the north. Originally proposed by Earl Swanson and strongly supported by Wilfred Husted, their case is premised on findings from deeply stratified caves and rock shelters that contain artifacts like those used by the Shoshone in the Great Basin for thousands of years. Among the prime sites that offer support for their argument are Birch Creek Cave in Idaho[63] and Mummy Cave in Wyoming.[64] Both of these long-inhabited rock shelters yielded perishable artifacts such as basketry, arrow shafts, and cord netting that are quite similar to those found in Great Basin caves. The assemblages, which include more durable pieces of worked stone, such as net-sinkers and milling rocks, strongly suggest a plant gathering and fishing lifestyle that was practiced in the Great Basin for millennia. Furthermore, these artifacts and associated types of projectile points were repeatedly found at continuous levels of the excavations. This bolsters the case that there were few if any interruptions in the long occupation by a relatively stable cultural group and that therefore the Shoshoneans had made the north their home for 8,000 to 9,000 years.

A "MIDDLE RANGE" HYPOTHESIS

A more recent hypothesis for the antiquity of Shoshonean presence in the north falls between the extremes proposed by Wright-Butler and Swanson-Husted. This "middle range" assessment of Numic origins in the Yellowstone region stems from the work of Richard Holmer, who excavated near Fort Hall, Idaho,[65] in the late 1980s and early 1990s. Holmer's advantage, of course, lay in having three existing hypotheses arrayed before him that he could test through the tried and true direct historical approach.

This approach involves selecting an archaeological site in which there is a high likelihood of evidence of human activity from the recent past and which also was occupied by a specific cultural group. One first excavates the uppermost, recent strata to reveal a diagnostic assemblage of artifacts for that particular group, such as the weight, size, and shape of a stone projectile point, the hafting attributes of a chopping tool, the presence of a root-digging implement, or the decorative characteristics of pottery. As one peels back layers of sediment, debris, and cultural materials, one learns whether the new artifacts coming to light are the same as those above, whether they occur in markedly different shapes, or whether altogether new tools occur that might be grouped in unfamiliar assemblages. If the artifacts remain relatively similar through successive strata, the archaeologist has good reason to suspect that generations of the same cultural group must have occupied the site over time.

The location chosen by Holmer lay in the bottomlands of today's Fort Hall Reservation; he named it Wahmuza, from the Shoshone words *wah'-muza,* meaning "cedar point." It was selected advisedly, for it was known to have been utilized by Shoshones in the historic period. As might have been predicted, the uppermost layers yielded glass trade beads, musket balls, and other objects obtained from Euro-Americans.[66] As the excavations penetrated into deeper levels, they found some variation in artifacts, but their recognizable consistency suggested the presence of a single tradition over time.

At the Wahmuza site, Holmer's crew discovered a distinctive type of lanceolate-shaped spear along with cooking hearths in the topmost levels that reappeared in each successive strata all the way down. It was identified as a lance point used by Shoshone men on a short, thrusting spear (see below). Whereas these so-called Wahmuza spear points near the surface were only a few hundred years old, those found in the lower levels had been chipped more than three thousand years ago.

In an attempt to learn more about the geographic range of such distinctively Shoshonean artifacts, Holmer next excavated a site on the Middle Fork of the Salmon River known as Dagger Falls. His crew recovered 1,400 projectile points, 2,000 complete and broken biface tools, 400 scraping tools, 125 drills, 40 gravers, and approximately 3,300 used flake tools.[67] Once again the characteristic Wahmuza spear points were found at all levels, along with more than 200 potsherds that were crafted much like the ceramics at Wahmuza and represented a continuous time span of 1,200 years. Now Holmer felt confident that the same Shoshonean groups who occupied the Wahmuza site were also living at the Dagger Falls site. Holmer's summary of his results echoes what is known about small hunting-and-gathering band-based societies:

> What we have learned during this exercise is that the Northern Shoshone persisted in what is now eastern Idaho for millennia, perhaps as long as four thousand years. *Their tremendous longevity is a direct product of their technological and social flexibility, being able to respond to rapidly changing and unpredictable situations. For thousands of years they effectively adapted to changing environmental and social conditions without the loss of their cultural identity.* [emphasis ours][68]

To a degree Holmer's work backs up earlier revelations from more deeply stratified cave sites like Birch Creek, Idaho, and Mummy Cave, Wyoming. But whereas those excavations indicated Shoshoneans lived in the north for 8,000 to 9,000 years, Holmer's dates propose use of the region for a little less than half that time. The continuing research of Holmer and others may add years to Shoshonean longevity in the north, or it may support the belief that their original migrations occurred closer to 3,500 years ago.[69]

Other recent research, focused in a restricted area of Wyoming and associated with rock art that is unquestionably of Shoshonean origin, supports Holmer's case for a Shoshone antiquity of more than three thousand years. This focuses on the

Dinwoody petroglyphs, which have been subjected to new dating methods that indicate that at least some of Wyoming's Dinwoody panels were engraved more than three thousand years ago.[70] Because not all researchers accept the validity of the experimental dating methods used to arrive at these age estimates, it is important to recognize there are also traditional radiocarbon dates for cultural deposits in stratified levels that were partially covering a Dinwoody-style image at the Legend Rock site. These traditional dates verify the age of the Legend Rock petroglyph, for instance, at two thousand years[71] and lend credibility to the experimental dates for Dinwoody rock art a thousand years earlier.

A POSSIBLE RECONCILIATION

We suggest yet another approach to the contested issue of Sheep Eater origins. Although hard to test without finer-grained ethnic markers for subgroups in the greater Shoshonean brotherhood, this approach might reconcile the wide temporal range between competing hypotheses for Numic expansion. We begin with the supposition that there were ebbs and flows of Shoshonean migration, that overlapping visits by groups already known to have been highly mobile and singularly adaptive took place, and that a nonaggressive succession of abandonments and reoccupations occurred in sites by peoples who perhaps were only ethnically distinct in nonmaterial aspects of life such as their language dialects, belief systems, or social organization.

To some extent this idea was advanced by C. Melvin Aikens and Younger T. Witherspoon,[72] who suggested that movements of Numic peoples into, out of, and back into the Great Basin may have occurred in the distant past. We believe that the Sheep Eaters could have continued to live in the north after an early expansion that took place by at least 3,500 years ago. Successive spreads of Numic-speaking groups continued to occur, but they were possibly reoccupations of the territory of their ancestors. The most recent of these overlays may have taken place about the time horses were introduced, which would explain the theory of Wright and Butler. Another may have started in about A.D. 1000 when the linguistic data suggest it should have taken place. In this scenario, the Sheep Eaters who had been living in the mountains for millennia would have been joined by linguistic relatives from the Great Basin from time to time.

Similar schemes exist for most of the migrations that are known for other Indian groups in the American West. The Crow, for example, moved in at least two successive waves, the second several centuries after the first.[73] The Athapaskan speakers of the American Southwest are also thought to have moved from north to south, through what is today Montana and Wyoming, at distinct time periods.[74] As our reconstructions of population movements throughout the world grow more sophisticated, we are learning that the collective migrations are not necessarily fixed events. Instead, they are often "time transgressive events"

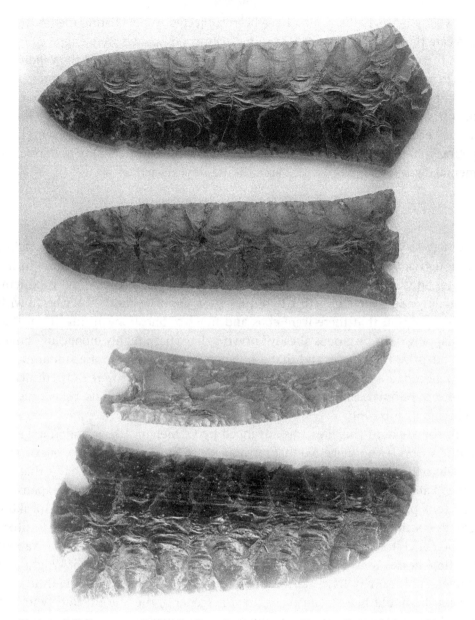

Blades of Yellowstone Park obsidian found in the Hopewell mounds in Ohio.
(Photos courtesy of Field Museum of Natural History, 1922, #31233, #31235.)

that occur in a much more layered or haphazard fashion than the linguistic approach might lead us to believe.

Along with his archaeological work, Gary Wright and Jane Dirks employed traditional narratives to understand the migration of Shoshoneans from the Great Basin to Idaho and Wyoming. In particular, he cites the Shoshone myth of Cottontail's killing of the sun and subsequent exploits as an indigenous accounting of their historical experiences. In the story Cottontail encounters and kills various animals, which Wright and Dirks explain as analogies to their exploitation of new animal species. They interpret Cottontail's use of a magic rock to lure deer over a cliff face as a coded description of the first use of the drive and jump technique for killing bison that is common in Wyoming but not in the Great Basin. Then they cite a sequence in which Cottontail encounters people hunting other cottontails and joining in the killing: "[It] is an odd event. An animal kills and eats its own species. [The description] appears to address a tribe while undergoing environmental change."[75] But it seems equally logical to suggest that the late-arriving Shoshone, represented by Cottontail, are actually meeting other Shoshone, with the suggestion of cannibalism tied to a prohibition related to the deep cultural ties between the incoming Great Basin Shoshone and the older mountain Shoshone. Indeed, at one point Cottontail meets some brush rabbits who are his "uncles," and at another Cottontail is asked to marry the "sisters" of the people he encounters. If the myth reflects the history of the Shoshone migration out of the Great Basin, it seems just as probable to suggest that exploits with uncles and marriages to their sisters represent the socially appropriate way for arriving Shoshones to integrate with resident Shoshones.

To summarize, we find Holmer's research persuasive in suggesting the continued use of the greater Yellowstone ecosystem by Shoshonean peoples. The area of central Montana and Wyoming appears to have been more dynamic, with Athapaskan tribes spending several centuries there before moving out in successive migrations toward the American Southwest. But even if they came and went, it seems plausible that the people historically known as Sheep Eaters could have lived relatively unaltered in the Yellowstone National Park region and the upper reaches of the Wind and Shoshone Rivers for at least 3,500 years.

Diagnostic Features of Sheep Eater Culture

Throughout the glimpses of Sheep Eater lifeways that can be gleaned from ethnohistorical, archaeological, and ethnographic sources, certain aspects of their material world appear again and again. As we pull away from a historical approach to look at the Sheep Eaters' cultural profile, the following discussion fills out a laundry list of the most tangible markers of Sheep Eater identity.

Dogs

During his last visit to Yellowstone National Park in 1994, Hultkrantz was asked what in his opinion differentiated Sheep Eaters from other tribal groups. Without hesitation he responded, "The way they packed their dogs." In their uneven, rocky setting, Hultkrantz explained, a dog dragging a travois was not as efficient as one wearing side packs. Those animals had to be large and sturdy, and he remembered

Though the photograph depicts Assiniboines rather than Sheep Eaters, it suggests how dogs were used by high Plains Indian hunters. (From E. S. Curtis, *The American Indian*, folio 18, plate 630, reproduction courtesy of Buffalo Bill Historical Center, Cody, Wyoming.)

being told that Sheep Eater dogs were noted for "white spots across their chests." Supporting information for the close working relationship between Sheep Eaters and their canine companions comes from the ethnographer Demitri Shimkin, who was told at Wind River that the Sheep Eaters were well known for their dogs. From his key informant, Dick Washakie, son of the well-known chief of the Eastern Shoshone, he learned that the personal names for dogs often derived from their coloring.[76] But Shimkin was also told that the animals were used to both drag travois and carry packs.

> The Mountain Sheep Eaters used dog transport both with parfleche-type packs and with the travois, in which a rawhide case or basket of willow was seated. Food and goods but not children were carried. The dog's harness, it may be noted, was primarily a cinch around the chest, secured by breast and hindquarters straps. There was no leash, the dog being directed entirely by voice.[77]

This close association between Sheep Eaters and their beasts of burden has a solid ethnohistorical basis as well. When Osborne Russell encountered his group of Sheep Eaters (6 men, 7 women, and 8 or 10 children) in the Lamar Valley in July 1834, he counted about thirty dogs "on which they carried their skins, clothing, provisions etc on their hunting excursions."[78] Russell does not elaborate on their appearance, but we have archaeological evidence that the bond between Yellowstone National Park's Indians and their dogs was intended to continue even into the afterlife. The only human burials reported in the park, both found near Fishing Bridge, had dogs interred with them.[79] Workmen digging a sewer line on the Fishing Bridge peninsula of the lake near the outlet of the Yellowstone River first found one of the burials in August 1941. It was an adult male, 5'4" to 5'5" in height and between thirty-five and forty-five years of age.[80] Two adult dogs were interred with him. Another burial, discovered in the Fishing Bridge Campground in July 1956, contained a female, 5' to 5'1" in height and forty to fifty years of age.[81] Two fragments of a single right rib of a human infant were recovered with the adult female skeleton. A single subadult dog accompanied their burial.

While there is no assurance that these burials are the remains of Sheep Eaters, the dogs were probably the same species as those kept by the Sheep Eaters. These animals were of short to medium stature and had blunt muzzles and relatively broad heads. Comparing their jaws to those of coyotes and wolves, Condon learned that the dogs from the first internment were shorter than either a coyote or a wolf, but their breadth was the same as a wolf.[82] When the skeletons were studied by William Haag, an authority on American Indian dogs, he found them similar to the "Siberian-like dogs recovered from archaeological sites on St. Lawrence Island and from parts of the Asiatic mainland,"[83] smaller than Alaskan Huskies and the Plains Indian dogs that approximated and sometimes exceeded wolves in size. Lacking radiocarbon dates but based on their morphological characteristics, he estimated their dates were about A.D. 1000.[84] In a more recent study, Ken Cannon had the bones measured by Danny Walker at the University of Wyoming, who generally agreed with Haag, except that he detected some grinding modification on the teeth, possibly inflicted by their owners to keep them from chewing through leather trappings.[85]

STONE TOOLS

For many years artifact collectors and archaeologists in Wyoming and southern Montana have singled out a distinctive chipped-stone tool, popularly called the "Shoshone knife." Shaped like a willow leaf, these artifacts measure from 3.5" to 5" in length and from 1.25" to 1.5" in width. They are long and narrow and noted for intensive resharpening: blades that demonstrate such extensive use are generally worn away into a pointed shape with a wide base. Frequently the resharpening occurred only along one side, much as was done with old skinning knives. Studies on the wear patterns of Shoshone knives suggest that toward the end of their lives they likely were used for drilling. But when they were in prime condition they were an all-purpose cutting, sawing, and piercing tool.

Once again we must thank Dick Washakie, Demitri Shimkin's key consultant, for enlightening us about these tools in the Sheep Eater kit. In 1937 Washakie said that these knives were usually made of white flint but occasionally of bone. Examples recovered from archaeological sites in Wyoming and Idaho are frequently chipped from obsidian as well.[86] Washakie also described how the knives were wrapped with sinew around the basal end to protect the user's hand and demonstrated how they were held in the palm of the right hand, with the point upward, between the thumb and four fingers. At mealtimes the knives were used by a server to cut cooked meat into large chunks that were laid on rawhide plates.

We have already been introduced to what was probably another important Sheep Eater artifact, the chipped-stone Wahmuza Lanceolate point, which tipped the Shoshone lance. Lances are described by Julian Steward as a distinctively Shoshone tool,[87] but they are best known from archaeological contexts. These well-made stone points often exhibit grinding to smooth the base and lower lateral edges.[88] Presumably this prevented the stone from cutting through the ties of leather or plant fiber that fastened it to the haft. As Torgler notes: "Many of the Wahmuza Lanceolates are missing blades that have snapped off perpendicular to the length of the point near the point base. . . . Typically Wahmuza Lanceolates are made of obsidian and have a distinctive form with parallel oblique flaking on the blades and contracting narrow bases."[89]

These points were fashioned for balance and durability. Many of the surviving points show signs of retouching and sharpening to keep them in use and possibly represent items that were prized and safeguarded. They were used to tip lances or short-spears that were between five and seven feet long, made from hardwood and decorated with feathers.[90] These lances would have been efficient for defense in face-to-face encounters, but their most probable use was for dispatching game already gathered into traps.[91] Although no Wahmuza-style Lanceolate points have been reported from archaeological work inside Yellowstone National Park, K. Torgler notes that they appear in the Carbella site to the north near Gardiner, Montana, and also at a site near Jackson Lake to the south in Wyoming.[92] However, many lanceolate projectile points have turned up in the park[93] and adjoining areas.[94]

The remaining inventory of chipped stone tools used by the Sheep Eaters included arrow points, usually of obsidian. Unlike the Indians of surrounding areas, the Sheep Eaters seem to have used a wide range of stone point styles. In earlier phases they also employed an array of forms, including those identified by archaeologists as Rose Spring as well as the points known as Elko-eared in Nevada, Utah, and Idaho that are better suited for the short darts used with atlatls. Interestingly,

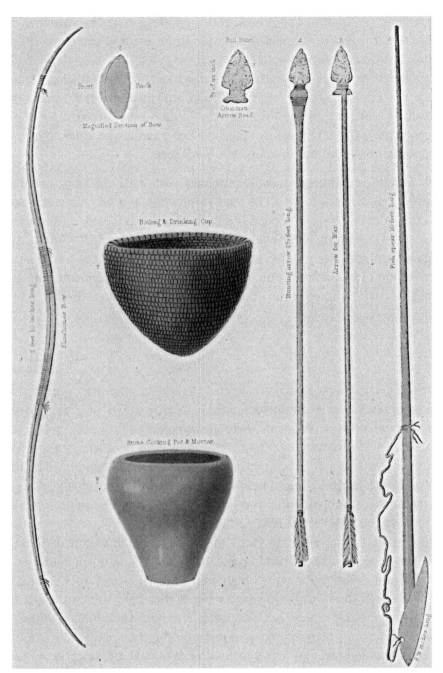

Shoshone horn bow, arrows, steatite pot, basket, and fish spear. Sketches of these artifacts accompanied a letter sent in 1848 by Nathaniel Wyeth to Henry Schoolcraft. Wyeth was in charge of Fort Hall, Idaho and responding to Schoolcraft's query about the Shoshone who inhabited the region. (From Schoolcraft's *Historical and statistical information respecting the history, condition, and prospects of the Indian tribes of the United States.* Vol. VI, 1851–1857, Philadelphia: Lippincott. Reproduction courtesy of William Perkins Library, Duke University.)

these larger types continued to be used throughout later phases when the side-notched points, usually connected with an earlier era and similar to the desert side-notch varieties, predominated.[95]

Since the Sheep Eaters obviously had a need for such tools to clean hides, the absence of scrapers suggests that they accomplished the task with obsidian flakes, using spalls with no defined pattern. Captain Jones noted Shoshone using these points in 1873, and possibly they were being employed in lieu of the turtle-back scrapers more commonly found on the Plains:

> The Shoshones, though mostly provided with tools of iron and steel of approved patterns, are still to be seen employing, as a scraper in the dressing of skins, a mere "teshoa," consisting of a small worn bowlder, thinner at one end, split through the middle in such a manner as to furnish a rough cutting-edge at one side. There seems to be a considerable advantage in this over any form of knife or other tool which has yet reached them from without, and it is probable that it will be retained so long as their present method of preparing hides is in vogue.[96]

Steatite

No artifacts were more unique to Sheep Eater culture than the pots and bowls they carved out of the soft stone described as "soapstone," "talc," or "pipestone," also known as steatite. Although there are approximately twenty minerals that fall under this designation, steatite is a common term for a white to green metamorphic rock that is soft enough to be scratched with a fingernail.[97] The mineral was formed through pressure and heat under the oceans; in the subsequent uplifting of mountains and subsequent erosion, it was exposed in Precambrian metamorphic rocks in the Yellowstone National Park region.

In an experimental effort to learn more about the function of these pots, which heated well without cracking, Richard Adams[98] made one and used it for cooking. From a chunk of steatite obtained from Wyoming, it took Adams about three and a half hours to hollow out a vessel that held somewhat less than a quart. When the pot was placed in red-hot coals the water boiled within eight minutes[99] and continued to boil for four minutes after the pot was taken off the fire. Only twice that long was necessary to cook a double handful of cubed venison.[100]

This stoneware caught the eye of early trappers and explorers. Larocque described a Shoshonean stone pot that he came upon in the Yellowstone region in 1805: "I traded eight Beavers with the Snake Indians in whose possession I saw a kettle or Pot hewn out of solid stone. It was about 1^1/$_2$" thick and contained 6 or 8 quarts."[101]

Lewis and Clark were also struck by the stone pots they found among the Lemhi Shoshone:

Yellowstone National Park historian Aubrey Haines, on the left, inspecting a steatite bowl with Lemuel Garrison, Yellowstone National Park superintendent, 1961. (Photo courtesy of Yellowstone National Park Archives, #Yell 37847-2.)

[T]heir culinary utensils exclusive of the brass kettle before mentioned consist of pots in the form of a jar made either of earth, or of a soft white stone which becomes black and very hard by burning, and is found in the hills near the three forks of the Missouri between Madison's and Gallitin's rivers.[102]

Almost certainly this "solid" and "soft white" stone, which hardens and darkens under fire, is steatite. The Lewis and Clark identification of a well-known source for the material near Dillon, Montana—also identified as the "green pipestone" river by Jim Bridger on a map he made in 1851—was probably an important source of steatite for the Sheep Eaters. Several other sources west and northwest of the park have recently been described by Ken Feyhl.[103]

In Wyoming, however, research on steatite sources is farther along, and approximately twenty quarries have been identified.[104] Although none are known in Yellowstone National Park, a dozen or so lie within a seventy-mile radius. Numerous smaller quarries or secondary deposits of steatite, sometimes only a few meters across, are found in western Wyoming.[105] Dick Washakie told Shimkin that the pots he knew about were made from a stone that was obtained in the mountains, two days' travel to the west of the Wind River Reservation.[106] According to Richard Adams, place-names in the Wind River Mountains immediately south of Yellowstone National Park "read like a Who's Who of steatite: Soapstone Lake, Soapstone Basin, Pipestone Lake, Dish Lake, Soapstone Creek."[107]

It is obvious that steatite was readily available to Sheep Eaters through direct mining or local trade; the historical record testifies to their taking full advantage of it. Nathaniel Wyeth described "a stone pot, holding about two quarts," among the Indians along the Snake River in Idaho.[108] Osborne Russell mentions a "[s]mall stone pot" in use by the Sheep Eaters he encountered in 1835 in the Lamar Valley of Yellowstone National Park.[109] In addition, he describes a pot he found while exploring on the headwaters of the Shoshone River northeast of Yellowstone Lake: "Near the foot of this defile we found a stone jar which would contain 3 gallons neatly cut from a piece of granite well shaped and smooth."[110]

Since granite can resemble steatite, Russell is probably mistaken about the material, but his estimation of its volume suggests an unusually large size for these Sheep Eater vessels. As noted above, Larocque saw Snake Indians using one pot that held 1.5 to 2 gallons. Unfortunately, we find none of these large pots in museum collections today.

Because steatite resists disintegration and decay, the pots, glue jars, cups, and baking platters shaped from it by Sheep Eaters are better preserved than items fashioned from fired clay. What might be called the classic form of their steatite pots is often described as looking like a standard flowerpot. There is the distinguishing flat bottom, straight to outward flaring sides, and rounded lips on undecorated rims. Some may have slightly flanged bases, and none feature any other decoration. These classic pots stand ten to twelve inches high and frequently have more oval than round shapes that measure from seven to eleven inches across. While information on Sheep Eater aesthetics is practically nonexistent, it is worth mentioning that steatite consolidates when heated to become almost porcelain hard and can acquire a shiny luster.

The concentration of this unique ware in and around Yellowstone National Park seems to identify it as an index of Sheep Eater ethnicity. While steatite pots are found throughout the northwestern plains, they are most concentrated in the mountainous region of western Wyoming, a distribution that overlaps the traditional territory of the Sheep Eaters. Marceau suggests that steatite vessels are tightly clustered within sixty miles of Two-Ocean Pass.[111] And Frison suggests that the area of sheep hunting traps and steatite vessels is comparable, citing the discovery of at least three steatite pots in the past three years in the Wind River Mountains, in the center of the largest concentration of sheep hunting traps.[112]

Because few steatite vessels have been recovered from excavated contexts, their time-depth is poorly documented. Frison suggests they are most common in the historic and protohistoric periods,[113] and Adams agrees by noting the telltale steel hatchet and iron tool marks on most vessels.[114] Underscoring the probable recency of these vessels is the fact that our sole radiocarbon date, taken from sooty residue on the inside of one steatite vessel, is 1848.[115] At the same time it should be kept in mind that residue inside a pot only dates its last use and not the time of its original manufacture. There is some evidence indicating that these pots were prized heirlooms among the Sheep Eaters and other Shoshone groups, to be passed on from generation to generation: "The pots were inherited by the daughter of the family, if there were no daughter a son might get one. They were family property. They were never traded."[116]

So long as the pots remained whole, they would probably enjoy years of use, which might also explain why they are not commonly recovered in prehistoric contexts. While Adams has suggested that the pots may have been stashed at campsites, to be used by any traveler, this seems doubtful, given Washakie's suggestion that they had personal value.[117] What seems more likely is that these pots, especially those that could hold one to two quarts, were treasured by families over generations.

We also find steatite beads of various shapes and sizes. One was recovered at the Split Rock site, a pithouse in southwestern Wyoming, in fill that was dated at 5500 before the present.[118] Beads have also been found in precontact contexts; at Mummy Cave, for instance, there were steatite beads and pendants dated at A.D. 734.[119] Other artifacts that definitely indicate the use of steatite in prehistoric contexts include atlatl weights.[120] Although these artifacts are scattered across the state, it is only in the greater Yellowstone region that we find such a concentration of stone pots.

One last category of steatite artifacts is perhaps the most intriguing. These are the tubular pipes and sucking tubes that are carefully cored and smoothed from the workable stone. These cultural items are so prominent among the Shoshone that they have become a diagnostic artifact for archaeologists.[121] Some of the pipes and tubes may have been smoked, but in a surprising recent analysis of forty steatite tubes in Wyoming, none betrayed evidence of tobacco use.[122] In their report on a cache of eight tubular pipes from Coal Draw, George Frison and Zola Van Norman reported that they turned up directly in front of a large petroglyph

Collection of steatite bowls found in Sheep Eater country in 1995, from the Dubois Museum, Dubois, Wyoming. (Photo by Peter Nabokov.)

that depicts an anthropomorphic figure holding a bow.[123] Almost surely belonging to a Shoshone shaman's medicine kit, one of the steatite tubes featured an incised petroglyph of a goose or cranelike waterbird. Based on ethnographic testimony, we might also conjecture that they were used for blowing or sucking functions in rituals of divination, sorcery, or healing to remove the invisible missiles considered to be the cause of human ailments.

OBSIDIAN

Obsidian, or volcanic glass, was found in abundance in the heart of Yellowstone National Park. Its most famous source is the site popularly known as Obsidian Cliff.

In his story of the origin of obsidian arrowheads, a Sheep Eater storyteller named Rupert Weeks told of a smoking contest between E Zhupa, or Coyote, and Beya Ish, Wolf. Initially Wolf continually lost a number of rounds at the pipe, having passed out from the heavy smoking and being revived by Coyote. Here Weeks portrayed the multifaceted, ambivalent character of Coyote in his role as culture giver, always alert for any tips that will assist human beings and ready to put his cunning at their service. The "whirlwind" in this narrative was very likely a malevolent spirit of the dead, or a "ghost":

In the tepee, the coyote saw black-colored objects lying behind the wolf, who had been fashioning arrowheads.

Said E Zhupa, the coyote, "My cousin, who has lost the smoking contest very nobly, let us try another. We will see who can make the most arrows from your obsidian before the whirlwind comes around."

E Zhupa, the coyote, had no knowledge of how to make arrowheads; he wanted to see the wolf make them so that he could learn the technique. The wolf agreed to this contest, for he was ashamed of his defeat in the smoking contest.

He worked feverishly, piling arrowheads beside him in many heaps. The cunning E Zhupa, the coyote, made a great show of working, but all the time he was watching the wolf out of the corners of his eyes. As soon as he was sure he knew the art of making arrowheads, he wished for a whirlwind. The wind blew up the powder from the chipped obsidian that was piled above the wolf's knee, causing him momentary blindness. Putting on the wings he had borrowed from the eagle, Beya Qee Na, the coyote flew back to the home of his nephews, the Shoshones, and taught them the fine art of making arrowheads from obsidian.[124]

This story reflects another, broader theme in American Indian oral tradition, in which key elements of human culture, such as the use of fire or the knowledge of chipping stone, must be wrested from their former ownership in a world of supernatural beings. The narrative also features a mythic prototype for the "shamanic contest," as Wolf's power to work stone is pitted against Coyote's power to control the world of ghosts, represented by the whirlwind—possibly his own supernatural helper or guardian—who performs at his command. Shoshone individuals with powerful spirit helpers would sometimes compete in such displays of supernatural power.

The causal connection between obsidian and blindness in this story was inverted by a number of our native consultants from both the Wind River and Fort Hall Reservations. For instance, one Sheep Eater woman, born in a tipi on the old Ross Fork Agency before it was moved to Fort Hall, remembered her mother using finely ground obsidian mixed with rye grass to treat the onset of blindness from trachoma; others claimed it was a treatment for cataracts. Razor-sharp blades of obsidian were used to bleed patients and to release the pressure of serious headaches and other ills.

Early ethnographers also obtained hints of the tie between obsidian and the spirit world. As described above, both Hultkrantz[125] and Shimkin[126] learned about the class of spirits known as *pan dzoavits*. Among them is a very dangerous, solitary spirit known as "water ghost woman" *(pa:waaip)*. The Shoshone told Shimkin that they always know she is around by obsidian flakes on the ground that represent broken fragments of her body.[127]

Wooden remnants of bighorn sheep trap, Absaroka Mountains. (Photo by Lawrence Loendorf.)

Our Shoshone consultants added that the Sheep Eaters especially prized obsidian for their arrow points because it was sharp and easier to chip and shape "in the way they wanted it." When asked about Obsidian Cliff, one Sheep Eater descendant replied:

> Just like when you go there to get some of the obsidian then it's like a sacrifice, you leave something there, an offering when you get it. It also would be considered a sacred site. Because their prayers were there with whatever we left there. They would offer, like we say now, we give them tobacco, or we leave something there for the spirits to give a blessing for taking it.[128]

The respondent went on to say that obsidian was unobtainable on the Wind River Reservation. Another consultant told us that obsidian scrapers were prized for cleaning hides, and from her description, it seemed that she was referring to the Shoshone split cobble scraping tools.[129] The significance of obsidian was also noted by Polly Shoyo, a consultant to Shimkin in 1937: "After breakfast, the woman would take a rawhide rope, and go to the brush to get wood. She'd pick up branches, or use an obsidian ax to hack them. It was very painful work."[130]

The great-granddaughter of Togwotee, who once had accompanied the old man by stagecoach to Yellowstone National Park, recognized the importance of black obsidian for arrow points. She also updated the spiritual role of the stone to contemporary Shoshoneans by revealing that red obsidian from Yellowstone National Park was used "by peyote people in making the head of waterbirds," a primary symbol of the Native American Church.

Thanks to the dramatic abutment of Obsidian Cliff, this mineral has enjoyed high visibility in the geologic and cultural history of the park. "There is enough obsidian in sight in the Park region to cover the whole of New England, one foot in depth," claimed Orrin Bonney and Lorraine Bonney.[131] Although this may be an overstatement, it is certain that the Yellowstone National Park region contains abundant obsidian.

The famous geologist and artist W. H. Holmes was well versed in Indian stone tool manufacture and paid an early visit to Obsidian Cliff. Noting its importance for stone tools,[132] Holmes went on to describe Yellowstone National Park obsidian in the *Handbook of American Indians,*[133] and later wrote what many still consider an indispensable study of native tool making.[134] Geologists and chroniclers accompanying other early expeditions also reported on Obsidian Cliff.[135] Captain W. A. Jones, for example, described artifacts he and his group found in 1873 and the abundant obsidian near Obsidian Cliff, where they discovered an arrow point still attached to its shaft.[136]

Around the same period, Superintendent Philetus Norris ordered his road builders to watch out for Indian artifacts, which he then shipped to Washington's Smithsonian Institution; materials from Obsidian Cliff were shipped in 1879.[137] Norris first came upon "Obsidian Mountain" in 1878. The following year:

> I . . . traced the mountain of obsidian or volcanic glass from where I discovered it last year, at Beaver Lake, to a branch of the Gibbon, below Lake of the Woods, a distance of some eight miles[,] . . . a vast weapon and implement quarry for the ancient hermit Sheepeaters.[138]

To Norris the volcanic rocks from this site were "unrivaled in quantity, beauty, and variety of color."[139] Smaller fragments of obsidian found along the shores of Yellowstone Lake and Shoshone Lake were said by Norris to "sparkle like diamonds." One of Norris's astute observations, which was frequently overlooked in subsequent years by investigators into the distribution of obsidian, concerned other obsidian sources in Yellowstone National Park. Norris found "large deposits of black and mottled obsidian at the Cascade or Crystal Falls, near the Falls of the Yellowstone, on the Continental Divide near Shoshone Lake, at the Lookout Cliffs, upon the new road over the Madison Plateau, and at other localities."[140]

Several early tourist accounts of trips to Yellowstone National Park included observations of Obsidian Cliff.[141] Coupled with scientific accounts, they led to a false impression that all the North American obsidian, except on the west coast, originated from Yellowstone National Park. And as ably summarized by Davis and colleagues,[142] from the turn of the century until the 1960s, groups ranging from Ohio mound builders to Canadian buffalo hunters were indeed linked in the literature to Yellowstone National Park through the obsidian trade.

Concentrating on Yellowstone National Park as a sole obsidian source, however, put archaeologists and historians in a bind. Certainly there was considerable evidence that obsidian that was sourced to Yellowstone National Park turned up far and wide. But they continued to maintain that most Indians, with the exception of those "reclusive" and "isolated" Sheep Eaters, were supposed to have avoided Yellowstone. If Indians considered the Yellowstone region taboo and were so terrified of its geysers or incapable of traversing the high mountain passes, who quarried and transported all those rocks? One solution was to suggest that "the material was merely quarried and roughly formed by the Sheepeaters who traded it in that condition with the surrounding tribes and by them taken away to be fashioned into final shape."[143]

Because so few actual arrow heads or formed tools were found at Obsidian Cliff, this explanation found support. While we have no evidence that Sheep Eaters controlled the Obsidian Cliff source area, the common method of collecting raw stone material is to quarry it, rough out blanks or preforms, and then transport them to other locations for the finishing work.[144] Sometimes these locations are close by, but preforms are also carried hundreds of miles before being reduced to patterned tools.

One also hears the argument that Obsidian Cliff was a "neutral ground" where brave men went, not to dally or hunt, but primarily to extract the glassy stone. In this view obsidian was so important that its major quarry in the park constituted a sort of sacrosanct zone where, "in timorous truce [Sioux, Blackfoot, Crow and Bannock] made stores of arrowheads from the mountain of black obsidian which looms above the river near its golden gate,"[145] or, as another writer phrased it more simply, where tribes "resorted to temporary peace to make arrow-heads and stone axes."[146] What is interesting about this piece of unsubstantiated geographic folklore is that it is the reverse of the "geyser taboo" idea, suggesting a kind of approach-the-rocks-but-avoid-the-waters contradiction.

Whereas Indians are presumed to have given the forbidden park a wide berth because of their horror of its "demon-haunted fastnesses,"[147] here the region was presumably protected by a kind of intertribal covenant. Possibly originating from Jim Bridger,[148] this notion was disseminated among tourists in early editions of the Haynes guidebooks to Yellowstone National Park, which maintained that "Obsidian Cliff was 'neutral ground' to all the Rocky Mountain Indians and undoubtedly as sacred to the various hostile tribes as the famed Pipestone country of Minnesota."[149] Before continuing this discussion, it should be noted that the primary use of catlinite, found at Minnesota's Pipestone National Monument, was to make sacred pipes, while obsidian was used primarily for utilitarian objects. To be sure, catlinite was sometimes used for nonceremonial objects and obsidian was used to manufacture magnificent ritual bifaces in Ohio, California, and elsewhere. But the making of religious objects from obsidian by Indians who lived in the region surrounding the park was not the norm.

As for substantiating this general "neutral ground" hypothesis, there are other Plains Indian geographic contexts in which the idea has been proposed, but as with the Obsidian Cliff case, too little hard data usually accompanies the assertion. In 1978 Canadian ethnohistorians assessed contentions that the Cypress Hills, overlapping the provinces of southern Saskatchewan and Alberta, was a "neutral ground" or "no-man's land" that different tribes all agreed to avoid so as to protect its wild game. Finding no ethnography to support the idea, the researchers suggested that instead the Cypress Hills, a hunting ground positioned between hostile tribes, were more aptly termed "any-man's-land," since it was generally understood among mutually hostile hunting tribes that you first sought game in your own safe area that you protected against all comers and only ventured out of it when you were willing to pay the price of constant vigilance and possible warfare.[150] Liljeblad heard of a similar region in south-central Montana that lay unclaimed between Crow and Blackfeet territories.[151] Called by the Shoshone *kutsunambihi*, or "the buffalo heart," it was said to serve much the same game park function imputed to the Cypress Hills, with the important difference being that over half a dozen tribes hunted here. "The effect was that the region was somewhat neutral," writes Janetski.[152] Yet another supposed neutral ground, characterized as a multitribal "Peace Valley," supposedly lay to the west of the park and attracted some of its native residents. As Corless and Wells write:

> The Valley where the Boise, Ohyhee, Malheur, Payette, and Welser rivers joined the Snake became a great "Peace Valley" in the Indian world. A legendary fair, or salmon festival, was a yearly intertribal gathering, or rendezvous, held in the summer. It would last for a month or more. Different tribes and bands [Bannock, Nez Perce, Umatilla, Cayuse, Cheyenne, Arapaho, Sheep Eater, Northern Paiute] from throughout the West would meet without fear in order to trade or make treaties and to celebrate the beginning of the fishing.[153]

For the Sweet Grass Hills of north-central Montana, the "neutral ground" claim has taken on a more explicitly spiritual, pacifistic cast. "Many of the tribes who used the Sweet Grass Hills were traditional enemies," contends Emily Cousins, "but the Hills comprised a neutral zone in which no one could be attacked."[154] But unfortunately we are provided with no ethnohistorical, ethnographic, or archaeological evidence to support her assertion that "[a]s long as people did not carry weapons on their journey to the Hills, it was clear they had come to pray."[155]

On the existence of such "neutral grounds" in the greater Yellowstone region or the plains in general, therefore, the jury is still out. And when compared to catlinite, the greater accessibility of obsidian elsewhere would seem to weaken its role in any neutral ground theory in the park. Nonetheless, and despite ample evidence of bloody skirmishing between Blackfeet and other tribes in the park, the notion that Yellowstone was a zone of peace persists; indeed, Weixelman was told by a Shoshone consultant that "as they came for purposes other than warfare, tribes did not fight each other here."[156] The Nez Perce historian Adeline Fredin reported to Weixelman much the same, that at Yellowstone "any hostility was forgotten, and left outside the area."[156] And a Kootenai-Salish consultant contributed to this theme:

> To my understanding, once they went to gather tools, that was kind of a place where they didn't war with each other. It was a common ground where they didn't fight when they were in there gathering their material that they needed for their tools, their projectile points. That is kind of an understanding that I had of that site. That was really special for me to make that positive connection again. To go back there and walk the same land that some of my ancestors walked.[158]

As for Indian access to obsidian, the mineral actually can be found at more than one source in and around Yellowstone National Park. Cannon and Hughes note that the literature on Yellowstone National Park contains references to nearly two dozen sources within its boundaries,[159] and chemical studies for 794 artifacts indicate they were made of obsidian from twelve different sources in and around the park. It is true that about three-fourths of the artifacts were made from Obsidian Cliff obsidian, but this is clearly not the only origin. Eighteen percent of the sample is from Idaho obsidian, while 6 percent comes from obsidian sources in Jackson Hole.[160] As Holmer has stated, "[In] my recent study on obsidian use in the Upper Snake River Basin . . . Obsidian Cliff from Yellowstone is not heavily represented. However, there has been very little work done in the counties nearer to Yellowstone so I suspect the low numbers reflect the nature of the data base more than prehistoric use of the resource."[161]

Once again, we need not duplicate here the recent compilation of information on Obsidian Cliff.[162] For our purposes, the subject of obsidian has allowed us to reinvestigate the role that it and its famous cliff played in the lives of the Sheep Eaters.

Bows

Another intriguing artifact associated with the Sheep Eaters is the bow fashioned from mountain sheep horn or elk antlers. The notion of an extremely powerful killing machine crafted from the strong, curved crown of the creature it was designed to bring down has fascinated anthropologists and do-it-yourself artisans for years.

Horn bows appear to have been prized by all the Plains tribes and used in ceremonial dances as well as for everyday hunting. One appears as a mark of warrior insignia in the famous painting by Karl Bodmer of Pehriska-Ruhpa, a Hidatsa Indian who posed for the artist in his Dog Society costume. It is not known if this bow was made by the Hidatsa or if it was traded to the Hidatsa from the Sheep Eaters or made by another group such as the Crow and traded to the Hidatsa. One of our earliest glimpses of Shoshone bows comes from observations made by Meriwether Lewis of the Lewis and Clark expedition:

> Sometimes, however, the bow is made of a single piece of the horn of an elk, covered on the back like those of wood with sinews and glue, and occasionally ornamented by a strand wrought of porcupine quills and sinews, which is wrapped round the horn near its two ends. The bows made of the horns of the bighorn are still more prized, and are formed by cementing with glue flat pieces of the horn together, covering the back with sinews and glue, and loading the whole with an unusual quantity of ornaments.[163]

The Sheep Eater version of this piece of hunting paraphernalia sounds remarkably similar. After Osborne Russell's visit on July 29, 1835, with the same Lamar Valley group of Indians mentioned earlier, he provided this memorable image:

> They were well armed with bows and arrows pointed with obsidian. The bows were beautifully wrought from Sheep, Bufalloe and Elk horns secured with Deer and Elk sinews and ornamented with porcupine quills and generally about 3 feet long.[164]

Despite the mention of bison horns, usually they were not of sufficient length. But Lowie reported that three pieces of bison horn might be laminated into bows with the help of sinew wrapping.[165] Modern-day bow makers who have worked with elk antlers indicate that it is difficult to remove the branch points and that their quality varies according to the time of the year they were acquired.[166] But the best quality horn bows appear to be crafted from bighorn sheep horns.

Currently on exhibit in the Museum of the Mountain Man of the Sublette County History Society, located in Pinedale, Wyoming, one of these horn bows was originally recovered from a cave high in the Gros Ventre Mountains of western Wyoming.[167] The range was certainly within Sheep Eater territory, and this bow is obviously an authentic example of old horn manufacture. It was donated to the museum by Gene Chapman. The museum label indicates that it is estimated to date from the 1800–1850 period. Its two basic halves are formed from two bighorn sheep horns, very likely from a matched pair from a single animal. Though it is currently missing, the joint was apparently strengthened by another piece of horn that was shaped and glued across it. All the rough outer horn was removed and the horns somehow shaved to create the bow. Then it was backed with continuous pieces of sinew glued down its entire back. Sinew fragments are evident at the ends, and it was also sinew-wrapped where the center joint piece is missing. The entire length measures about 33 inches.

Recently Tom Lucas, an archer and sheep horn bow enthusiast from Lander, Wyoming, has experimented with making these weapons. Although Lucas has neither seen a native-made sheep horn bow nor read any instructions on how to make them, he learned from his trial-and-error approach. After first removing the horns from the skull, he softened them in hot water. Hotter water worked faster, but moderately hot also did the job. Following the outline of the curl, he cut a strip from each horn that retained the outer casing of the horn, to be removed later. To straighten out each end, he dunked them in hot water until they were pliable and then clamped them between two boards. The ensuing drying process in this clamp took seven to ten days.

Shaping began while the straightened horn was still damp, and if needed, it was redipped into hot water. While Lucas fashioned the horn with knife and rasp, he boiled the shavings into glue. In this shaping process, Lucas worked the pliable bow sides with his hands to take out any side curves and then beveled the butt ends until they fit tightly together prior to gluing. For this Lucas first put two small pegs through the butt ends to hold them for the glue. Next he fit two additional pieces of shaped horn over the joint, gluing one on the belly and another on the back. To add tensile strength for the pull, he double-checked that the back of the bow was actually the inside of the horn's natural curl.

Then he glued sinew down the back, letting it dry before layering on additional strips of sinew. He allowed up to thirty days for this important process. Finally, more strips of wet sinew were wrapped around the stock to form the grip and strengthen the all-important center joint. When complete and strung with a twined sinew cord, these efficient, short bows possessed an estimated sixty- to seventy-pound pull.[168]

Another interesting mention of horn bow manufacture among the Shoshone comes from Elijah Nicholas Wilson (affectionately known as "Uncle Nick"), who lived with the Shoshone as a boy in the 1850s.[169] Wilson wrote in his memoirs some sixty years later:

> The bows were sometimes made of mountain sheep horns, which have been thrown *into some hot spring and left there until they were pliable*. Then they were shaped, and a strip of sinew was stuck on the back with some kind of balsam gum that was about as good as glue. This made a powerful bow.[170]

While this account lacks detail, it tends to confirm parts of the Lucas bow-making method, especially the use of hot water and glue, although the mention of balsam gum is confusing because it could not have been obtained in the region. What is most striking, however, is its testimony that Indians took advantage of thermal pools for softening the horns. Considering the availability of hot water in Yellowstone National Park, this exploitation of hot springs seems significant. Another fragment of horn bow lore comes from Lowie, who noted that Northern Shoshone elk horn bows came from a single piece of the horn, backed with sinew and decorated with porcupine quills that were wrapped around the bow limbs. But Lowie also described sheep horn bows:

> Of a different type were the compound bighorn bows, consisting of two parts spliced at the center with sturgeon glue made from boiling rendered fish parts and with deer-sinews wound around the splice and secured by their butt-ends, the small ends bending outward at the ends of the bow. Sometimes the sinews covered the whole width of the back. For ornament, the skin of a snake was glued to the bow.[171]

Lowie's description of the ends as bending outward suggests that this was a recurve bow, pulled against the horn's natural curl, much as Lucas described. Several authors mention decoration with flattened and wrapped porcupine quills, but Lowie's addition of snakeskin sounds novel. Taking two to three months to complete, these bows were highly valued and extensively traded with other tribes. In fact, a well-made Northern Shoshone horn bow was said to go for no less than five to ten horses.[172]

ARROWS

We have archaeological evidence for the missiles fired by these bows. From the excavations at Wickiup Cave, a probable Sheep Eater campsite about thirty miles west of Yellowstone National Park, wooden shafts were recovered that exhibit tenons or ends that are carved to a narrower diameter than the remainder of the shaft. The Sheep Eaters seem to have used compound arrows, which were about 2.5 feet in length, in which the tenon was inserted into the hollow end of the arrow's foreshaft—although Jack Contor was told they were crafted in three sections.[173] Their wooden bodies were used again and again, while the reed foreshafts with their stone points might be replaced whenever they snapped off.

Foreshafts were often manufactured from horse grass (*Equisetum* spp.) and sinew-bound to the tenon. As for the main shafts, the arrows at Wickiup Cave were identified as elm and cottonwood, but Contor was told that the Idaho Sheep Eaters preferred dogwood and mock orange, while Lowie[174] indicates that greasewood was a favorite choice and the field specimens examined by Murphy and Murphy were merely identified as "hardwood."[175] Elsewhere, Lowie has described the Shoshone using service berry wood that they first dried and cured for a year.[176] Stripped of their bark, these raw rods required working out their kinks with a wrench—a hole drilled in an animal rib bone—and possibly limbering over a fire. They were further smoothed by grinding them against sandstone before attaching the feathers, leaving groove marks that can still be seen at some Montana and Wyoming sites.

Fletching on the Wickiup Cave arrows was fastened about five inches beyond the nock end of the shaft, a long style that is associated with Northern Shoshone arrows.[177] Although Dominick indicates that Sheep Eaters preferred owl or eagle feathers because they would not absorb blood,[178] the feather pieces from Wickiup Cave were identified as grouse. Several arrows collected from the Northern Shoshone before 1869 are fletched with feathers from a red-tailed hawk.[179] As with their arrow woods, the Sheep Eaters apparently had considerable leeway in their choice of feathers. Also, their tips might be steeped in a deadly poison concocted from animal spleen mixed with crushed red ants,[180] although we are not aware if this was used in hunting as well as warfare.

The Food Quest I: Hunting the Mountain Sheep

We must not forget that the images of bison-hunting and horse-riding Indians of the Great Plains whose imagery caught the world's fancy in the nineteenth century— and against whose culture the Sheep Eaters were negatively assessed—only represent the thinnest slice of human occupancy of the greater Yellowstone region. While this does not diminish our interest in their uses of the Yellowstone Plateau for hunting, vision questing, shortcuts during long-distance travels, or the place it held in their worldviews, it makes us appreciate more fully the mountain lifeways that developed over thousands of years that supported the Sheep Eaters. To the uninitiated the high mountains appear impassable and harsh, but to people willing to move around and adjust to changing seasonal and climatic realities they could become a storehouse, a church, and a home. For the well-trained forager, the plant and animal bounties of the highlands were especially available in spring and summer. This is because "[m]ountains have one feature which the plains can never claim," write Dale Fredlund and Lynn Fredlund, "a fantastic diversity of ecological zones within a relatively small area." They elaborate on the benefits of this diversity:

> Specific vegetable resources seem to last forever in the mountains. For example, huckleberries begin to bear fruit about the first week of July in sunny areas at low elevations and are finished by the end of that month; but at higher elevations they can still be found at the end of August or the first of September.[181]

Of the animals that can be found year-round in the Rocky Mountain uplands, one of the most easily hunted is the mountain sheep. As their ethnic name suggests, the peregrinations of the Sheep Eaters were symbiotically bound up with migrations of their primary food source, Rocky Mountain bighorn sheep (*Ovis canadensis*). In the late 1800s, before Euro-Americans altered the patterns of bighorn sheep, some herds (or portions of herds) stayed in the park throughout the year, wintering in the vicinity of Mount Everts.[182] Other animals in the park's vicinity apparently moved from one part of their habitat to another during the year in a migration pattern that was affected by the weather and snow depths. Some herds appear to have shifted to lower elevations during the winter, where there was less snow cover, and back to higher elevations in spring and summer.

Whatever their movements, we could expect the Sheep Eaters to position themselves nearby. Their namesake and main staff of life, the sheep on which these Indians depended, were not that hard to kill. But stalking bighorns did require the development of techniques based on close observation of their habits; the Shoshone must have learned early on that they could be approached closely and in plain sight so long as hunters positioned themselves on slopes below the sheep. Hence the hunters climbed toward the animals quietly and steadily, ascending in a zigzag pattern with the sheep watching them all the while, until they drew within arrow range.[183] According to Dick Washakie, during the winter and early spring, solitary hunters or small groups wearing snowshoes and using dogs drove the animals into deep snow. Floundering through the drifts, the sheep were sufficiently slowed down to make them easy prey.[184]

A second hunting method was also premised on familiarity with sheep behavior. To escape from danger the Shoshone knew that bighorn sheep usually retreated from their meadow pasturage by leaping up to rocky precipices and higher outcrops where their sure, quick hooves allowed them to skip rapidly across rough terrain. Hunting in late winter or early spring, the native hunters searched for animals who were grazing in meadows below basalt crags and other dark-colored rocks. Warmed by the sun, the snow on these rocks and talus slopes melted well before the drifts on the flatter slopes. Preparing for this hunting event, the Indians scooped out hiding blinds from the rocky talus, producing circular pits about 5 feet in diameter and 3 feet in depth. Examples of these blinds still can be found inside Yellowstone National Park and in surrounding ranges. On a remote spot high on Mount Everts, for instance, a backpacker friend of the park historian Lee Whittlesey told him of U-shaped and circular rocks and logs that sound much like pits seen on slopes opposite the Gardiner River from Electric Peak.[185] While a portion of the men concealed themselves here, their comrades got into position just below the grazing sheep. At a signal the drivers and their dogs broke out into yells and barking.[186] According to Alexander Ross, the Sheep Eaters were "complete masters of what is called the cabalistic language of birds and beasts, and can imitate to the utmost perfection the singing of birds, the howling of wolves, and the neighing of horses, by which means they can approach, by day and night, all travelers."[187]

Bengt Anell describes the use by western American hunters of yells and calls to drive game into traps, specifically the imitation of wolf howls: "the beaters did their utmost to give a faithful imitation of howling wolves, a trick which in areas where the quarry was torn to pieces by wolves did not fail to produce an effect.[188]

In this wolf habitat it is not impossible to imagine that the Sheep Eaters driving the quarry upward were conceivably howling like wolves. Frightened by the imminent danger, the alarmed sheep rapidly scaled the heights to the talus grade as they sought to escape. The hunters hidden in the pits close by waited until the sheep were within range and then fired arrows at their white bodies that would have been clearly outlined targets against the darker rocks.

More labor intensive was the old Shoshonean technique for hunting bighorns known as the "drive." This called for constructing long fences and corrals from deadfall timber. Still existing in Montana and Wyoming are the remains of fifteen to twenty of these sheep drive sites. Although most of the wood remains of these drives in Yellowstone National Park have disintegrated from decay or wildfire, according to Aubrey Haines, one of them stretched up a hillside across the stream from today's Golden Gate canyon road. He also knew of another to the east of the Gardiner River in the area where an old "elk drive" line was also located, near the Gardiner to Jardine road. A third stood in the vicinity of Mammoth Hot Springs.[189] If Superintendent Norris's comments in his 1881 annual report are any indication, at one time these sheep drives must have been fairly common in the park, though he apparently mistakes them all for circular breastworks:

> Four of these were discovered during this season, viz., one beside our camp, in a grove north of the crossing of Willow Creek, some three miles below Mary's Lake. . . . It is about thirty feet long by twenty wide, and constructed of fragments of logs, stumps, poles, and stones, with ingenuity and skill proverbial to the beaver; nearly weather, wind, and bullet proof; about breast high, which is certainly less than when built, and situated, as usual, in a wind-fall then screened by a thicket of small pines, which are now large enough for bridge or building timber.[190]

Norris found three other drives as well. One lay east of Yellowstone Lake in the Stinkingwater drainage, another was found near Bridger Lake, and the third stood on a branch of Barlow Fork of the Snake River. Since these do not correlate with any of the drives known historically in the Mammoth area, we get the impression that these sheep drive lines and corrals were not rare in the park. Thus when we discovered Norris's mention that his artist companion, Albert Bierstadt, sketched an Indian deadfall corral and breastwork near Mary's Lake, we made every effort to hunt for the illustration.

We learned that Bierstadt's Yellowstone sketchbook had "surfaced briefly in 1965 and ha[d] been unlocated since. A single note concerning it, `Yellowstone Camp, August 1881,' is all that remains a part of recorded history."[191] However, our further inquiries revealed that a dealer in western art, William Bertsche, then of Great Falls, Montana, had written the New York Public Library on June 25, 1965, to ask for background information about "two sketch books that were found among some paintings of Albert Bierstadt" that were now in his possession. As Bertsche described their contents: "There are sketches of the Madison River in Montana, Yellowstone Lake, geysers, buffalo, elk and mountain scenes. One sketch is dated 'Yellowstone Camp, August, 1881.'"[192] Two weeks later the library responded to Bertsche with "only rather negative evidence concerning the date of Bierstadt's visit to Yellowstone," although it did turn up one reference to a dated Bierstadt painting, "Geysers, 1883."[193] In the October 28, 1881, edition of the *New York Express*, an interview with Bierstadt briefly describes his Yellow-stone experiences, but there is no mention of these Indian structures or artifacts. Before Bertsche's death in a Kalispell rest home in 1996, he personally informed Tom Minckler, a western art and rare book dealer in Billings, Montana—at the express request of our Yellowstone project—that he had turned over Bierstadt's Yellowstone sketchbooks to the Montana Historical Society.[194] We then asked Peter H. Hassrick of the Buffalo Bill Historical Center to make a formal query to the Society, but he was notified by Society Registrar Janet Sperry that their review of the "maps, manuscripts and diaries" that Bertsche had donated in 1976 to their archives did not turn up the elusive Bierstadt Yellowstone sketchbook(s).[195] Though extremely desirous of obtaining the Bierstadt sketch for this document, time constraints forced us to halt further investigation at this point.

It is certainly possible that some of the man-made structures described by Norris had not served that purpose; fortifications, corrals, and other types of deadfall timber structures are found throughout the Mountain West. Although there have been numerous archaeological projects in Yellowstone National Park over the past thirty years, it is a lamentable oversight that these corrals, breastworks, or fortifications were not mapped and recorded. While photographs of the wickiups (tipi-shaped pole lodges) are fairly common, drawings and photos for other man-made timber remains are rare. One photograph of some decayed drive lines across from Golden Gate Canyon was taken by Hultkrantz in the 1960s, but the ground scrap was scanty.

Fortunately, however, old sheep traps of the same general style are fairly well represented in the mountainous regions adjoining Yellowstone National Park. About a dozen were recorded by George Frison in the Absaroka and Wind River ranges, which still lie well within Sheep Eater territory.[196] Another sheep trap found a few miles west of the park was protected by local outfitters during the 1988 forest fires,[197] and more have been identified in the Bighorn Mountains, Wyoming,[198] the Lemhi Mountains, Idaho,[199] and the Bitterroot Mountains of southwestern Montana.[200] In the sites for these traps we see additional evidence of the keen observation by Sheep Eaters of animal behavior, for the great major-ity are constructed near sheep-bedding grounds.[201] When the animals congregate in late November during the rutting season and throughout the following winter months, they prefer to bed on open, bare ridges where they can see long distances. If frightened, they will usually dart a short distance downslope before veering uphill to escape. The lengthy, V-shaped drive fences, which were stacked from deadfall with intermittent rock cairns filling the gaps, were laid so that these escape routes funneled between the fencing. Once inside the drive lines the sheep were chased into catch-pens and easily killed with clubs or spears.

Among the six sheep traps located adjacent to a major sheep-bedding area on the Wiggins Fork of the Wind River, Frison distinguished two types. The simplest variety had drive lines extending along the side of a ridge and over a steep decline.

At the base of the decline, often hidden in the trees, a rectangular-shaped catch-pen constructed of logs laid into tiers awaited the animals. As measured by Frison and colleagues,[202] these pens range from 14.8 feet to 23.9 feet long and 8.2 feet to 13.5 feet wide; usually they are positioned at a lower elevation than the sloping entry ramps, which are built of logs leaning into the pens on their high side at the apex of the drive lines. Covered with soil and vegetation to help conceal their traps, their inward-leaning logs prevent the sheep from leaping out once they have been driven inside. Although the catch-pens examined by Frison have eroded, the tallest ones remain standing to a height of five feet. The side walls lean into the structure as a further hindrance against any sheep escaping. Frison and colleagues report that one even had a log in its bottom that could be swung out, like a pole corral gate, probably to allow for removal of the sheep carcasses.[203]

The larger, more elaborate type of trap added a circular or oval corral near the terminus of the V-shaped drive lines, where the sheep were contained before they were sent into the catch-pen. Frison believed that this allowed the hunters to control the number of sheep they had in the catch-pen at any one time. Perhaps more importantly, it let the hunters cull those animals they wanted for slaughter and those that they perhaps wanted to release. A third type, described by Forest Ranger A. G. Clayton, combined features of sheep traps and buffalo jumps. Based on the remains of one that Clayton observed on the east wall of the West Fork of Torrey Creek near its mouth (in the Yellowstone National Park Timber District, which later became Washakie National Forest and later Shoshone National Forest), this type featured two drive fences of wood that converged at an opening through which the game could pass. "But the opening would probably lead out onto a ledge over which the game could not go," Clayton believed, "and they would then be rushed from behind."[204]

The second type of trap probably took more time and effort to construct. Based on the condition of timbers in their catch-pens, Frison and colleagues[205] believe that these larger traps are more recent and that sheep hunting technology improved through time. Might this be evidence of a game management system by which the Sheep Eaters controlled the numbers and types of animals they took from the herds? By freeing pregnant females and the very young, they would have assured themselves of a resource for the future.

Once the sheep were in the catch-pen, Frison et al. suggest, they were dispatched with clubs.[206] This conclusion is based on the absence of projectile points in the catch-pens, where one might expect to find them if the hunters were shooting the penned animals with arrows. Short spears could have been jabbed at the animals, but the recovery of several hardwood clubs near sheep traps indicates they were more efficient killing tools. One of these clubs has a flanged end, runs about the length of a billy club or softball bat, and features holes where a wrist strap would have facilitated hanging onto it during hefty swings. Of two other sticks found by Frison, one was simply a heavy stick with a rawhide wrapping, the other was a pine limb with a weighty burl on one end.[207]

Among surrounding tribes Sheep Eaters were rumored to possess a powerful medicine that allowed them to control whole herds of sheep.[208] Shoshones of the Great Basin used charming practices during communal antelope hunts,[209] while among the Wind River Shoshone hunting shamans coaxed antelope into wooden traps that sound remarkably similar to those used by the Sheep Eaters.[210]

Frison, always on the lookout for any inkling of hunting magic among Wyoming's mountain dwellers, noticed the occasional presence of small circular structures that were either incorporated into drive lines or positioned on ridges near the traps but always with commanding views of both the drive complex and the approaching sheep. Might they have been special booths for shamans to make their magic during the hunt? More persuasive evidence of supernatural practice came from his discovery of ram skulls placed in trees near the catch-pens.[211] Some had rested in the crotches of branches for so long that bark had grown around them, and it was necessary to cut them down for safeguarding in museums. All told, nearly a dozen of these elevated skulls were found, many exhibiting broken crania for the removal of brains.[212] Early trappers had reported the veneration of these ram's skull trees by the Flathead, a tribal group whose territory was adjacent to the Sheep Eaters on the north and west,[213] and hence Frison has wondered whether the Sheep Eaters learned this magic from their neighbors or vice versa.[214]

Clearly these Shoshoneans were intimately acquainted with the habits of bighorn sheep and were capable of hunting them efficiently. Much like bison to Plains Indians, bighorn sheep were their staple, and they used them in many ways. The meat, of course, was their main food supply, the hides became clothing, and the horns were turned into bows, spoons, and arrow shaft straighteners. The activity of acquiring them must have been so much a part of Sheep Eater identity that it comes as no surprise that they believed it would continue forever. As Hultkrantz has written of the Sheep Eater worldview:

> In religious beliefs spirits take the form of surrounding animals, and their haunts are supposed to lie at difficult passages—overhanging cliffs, narrow passageways, etc.—or in places where tradition tells they appear. The geysers and hot springs are residences of supernatural powers. Life after death is supposed to lie in a mountainous region where mountain sheep hunting is part of the daily occupation.[215]

The Food Quest II: Fishing

The Sheep Eaters did not subsist by sheep alone. Their appetite for fish set them dramatically apart from their Plains neighbors like the Crow and the Blackfeet.

Much of the following information on fishing derives from Shimkin's interviews with Wind River Shoshone in 1937, most prominently Dick Washakie. Since Washakie was a Plains Shoshone we might ask whether his comments are relevant for the Mountain branch. But it seems that fishing techniques were fairly standard across Northern Shoshone territory, and most likely Sheep Eaters practices followed suit. Fish were obtained throughout the year, but during the spring runoff (June), when fish congregated in shallow waters, was the optimal time. Like their neighbors who lived along the Columbia and other plateau streams, the Sheep Eaters could rely on an annual fishing surplus, since the waters of the Yellowstone region were subject to the dramatic spawning runs of cutthroat trout. The Indians fished in Yellowstone Lake as well as other basins, and along the mountain rivers as well.

According to Dick Washakie, fish were second only to bison as a preferred food source among his people, and one need only substitute "sheep" for bison to speculate that the same was true for the Sheep Eaters. Early trappers and travelers in Idaho describe fishing among the Sheep Eaters' linguistic cousins, the Northern Shoshone and Lemhi Shoshone who were known historically as Agaidika, or "salmon eaters."[216]

Evidence of earlier fishing in the park comes in the form of stone net sinkers, made by chipping notches into the sides of water-worn pebbles, randomly found along the shores of Yellowstone Lake.[217] These distinctive artifacts also turn up in such Sheep Eater related sites throughout the wider region as Mummy Cave along the Shoshone River.[218] One well-made plummet (an elongated, torpedo-shaped stone with a hole through its top) was found by Norris[219] in the park and may have been a fishing accessory, but to our knowledge, no net sinkers have been dug from park sites. There is speculation that remains of a stone wall in the shallows of Bridge Bay were part of a fish weir,[220] but it could also be a natural phenomenon. At the same time, there is strong evidence for eating fish from recent excavations along the Gardiner River, where fish bones intermixed with charred earth have been recovered from cooking pits.[221] Because of the virtual taboo against fish among the Blackfeet and Crow,[222] these remains are more likely of Salish or Shoshonean origin.

Historically, the most abundant fish species in Yellowstone Lake were cutthroat trout, and that was probably the case in earlier days. In the Yellowstone River, however, Indians went after whitefish and suckers, while they probably pulled grayling and other species out of streams and smaller lakes. Early references to fishing in the greater Yellowstone ecosystem are few and far between. On June 17, 1860, Captain W. F. Raynolds noted, "We were visited by Indians today, among who was Cut-Nose. . . . I made him a small present, and from the others the men purchased some capital trout."[223] Although the Sheep Eaters were familiar with hooks and lines, they probably caught more fish with dams, weirs, and fish basket traps. Wherever the water channeled through a narrows, at lake inlets or

Dick Washakie, Shoshone, with a string of fish caught in Yellowstone National Park while guiding Owen Wister in 1887. (Photo courtesy of American Heritage Center, University of Wyoming, Laramie, Owen Wister Collection, #290.)

stream shallows, they positioned temporary weirs or brush dams. Driving the fish into them, it was easy to spear or scoop them out with basket nets. Quickly assembled of perishable brush on the spot, these weirs do not survive very long, but they were probably quite effective, if one extrapolates from Norris's experience of building one on June 3, 1881:

Wishing a supply of trout . . . Rowland, Cutler, and myself rode to Trout Lake, and, after pacing around and sketching it, with brush and sods I slightly obstructed its inlet near the mouth. Within eight minutes thereafter the boys had driven down so many trout that we had upon the bank all that were desired, and the obstruction was removed, allowing the water to run off, and within three minutes thereafter we counted 82 of them from 10 to 26 inches in length. Of these, 42 of the larger ones, aggregating over 100 pounds, were retained for use, 30 of the smaller ones returned to the lake unharmed, and the remaining 10 were, together with a fine supply of spawn, distributed in Long-fellow's and other adjacent ponds, which, although as large, and some of them apparently as favorable for fish as Trout Lake, are wholly destitute of them.[224]

From Norris's fishing memoir we also learn that in 1881 three men could catch one hundred pounds of fish with minimum effort in a short time; smaller ones were released to maintain the supply. While fish were not uniformly distributed from lake to lake, the Sheep Eaters had sufficient places to fish with the ease described by Norris in order to meet their needs. Not far from Trout Lake is Soda Butte, which stands close to the spot where Russell[225] describes a small camp of Sheep Eaters in late July 1835 who may have been fishing as well as sheep hunting to fill their larders. We might suspect Norris of a fisherman's talltale except that in 1880 an army surgeon remarked that the soldiers in his escort took so many trout from Trout Lake, each weighing about five pounds, that his boat was nearly swamped.[226] Trout Lake continued to supply fish to the miners in Cooke City who took large numbers with explosive powder and nets until the practice was stopped through the game laws protecting animals and fish in the park.[227]

Sheep Eater check dams made of rocks and brush were probably much like that described by Norris, but perhaps they employed the Northern Shoshone style of conical-shaped fish basket that Dick Washakie told Shimkin about.[228] Their dams blocked the small streams, while weirs were constructed by pushing pointed willows into soft mud and interlacing them with other willows to form a crude latticework fence. The baskets they measured five feet long, with an opening diameter of three feet, and were woven from willow splints using a simple over-one and under-one checkerboard pattern. Strips of bark finished the upper rim, bending the warp over and lashing it across the uppermost weft splint. The small end was finished in the same way, except that the opening was only about an inch in diameter.

The basket was positioned in the center of a rock dam so that the stream current flowed through the basket's wide mouth and incoming fish had no alternative but to swim into it. Then the basket was lifted out and dumped on the ground, or the fish were removed by hand. They could also be extracted from dams and weirs with the help of an eight- to ten-foot-long spear tipped with a single barb carved out of greasewood. The barb's butt end was inserted into the spear's split end, then bound in place with glue and sinew. The spears were thrust down using two hands, releasing with one and retaining hold with the other.

Certainly the Sheep Eaters favored convenient spots for dipping and spearing, but we have no indication that families owned rights to repeatedly used holes or shorelines. In winter the traps would be abandoned, with new ones tied together in spring. Couples usually fished togther, with men constructing the dams and extracting the catch, women cleaning the fish for drying (smoking fish was apparently not a Shoshonean practice). After removing the viscera the back was split to remove the bones and head. Then the fillets were lined up to dry on a willow rack five to six feet high and about sixteen feet in length. Into a boiling pot went the bones and heads for immediate consumption, while extra fish heads were tossed to the dogs. Another method of drying was to simply lay the fish on grass mats on the ground, but they had to be watched carefully lest the dogs get them. Depending on the amount of sun and the weather, the drying process could take from one to two months. Once they were ready, the dried fish were stored in parfleches or baskets for use over the winter.

Dipnets made of willow were used to scoop up squirming bunches of minnows, which went into soups that were consumed almost immediately. Although this might be considered a secondary food pursuit, in October 1811 a small village of Shoshone, probably near Fort Hall, Idaho, were observed drying small fish, about two inches long, along with roots and seeds.[229] In this case cleaning was unnecessary, and their small bodies were eaten as is or pounded in mortars to make a fish flour.

Although fish may have played a much greater role in the Sheep Eater diet than previously suspected, the activity does not leave the sort of abundant evidence that archaeologists recover from large game hunting and processing sites. And while fish bones do preserve in some locations, it has only been in recent years that sophisticated flotation techniques have been used to recover their minuscule bones. If the drying of fish took up to two months, it would have restricted the movements of the Sheep Eaters until it was completed. It is also apparent that fish would dry best during the summer or autumn when there was abundant sunshine and less chance of rain or snow. Using these parameters, we might hazard a guess that the best fishing occurred between late May and late July, and the optimal times for drying them in Yellowstone National Park were from August to the end of September.

As a region of overlapping influences for Great Basin and Plateau subsistence traditions, the greater Yellowstone ecosystem may still be underrecognized where fish utilization by Sheep Eaters is concerned. Walker believes, for instance, "that prior estimates of Lemhi Shoshone-Bannock reliance on fish have been too conservative" and that his initial review of their fishing practices "supports Swanson's argument for deep Plateau–Great Basin cultural linkages" that are evident in art, mythology, technology, and social organization.[230] The Shimkin and Hultkrantz

Pawagap, meaning "Water Bush," was also known as Pearl Cody. One of Åke Hultkrantz' key Sheep Eater consultants and close to one hundred years old in 1955, she had been born in the mountains. From her Hultkrantz obtained "direct experience of the old Sheep Eater pre-reservation life." (Photo courtesy of Åke Hultkrantz and The Lucius Burch Center for Western Traditions.)

material suggests that women and children joined in fishing—and that Shoshonean fishing was exempt from the restrictions and magic that preoccupied hunters of big game. Whereas Hultkrantz downplays spirits of fish or medicine men with special powers over the catch for the Plateau region, Walker argues that "[t]here appear to be quite similar religious practices regarding fishing throughout the Plateau and Great Basin," and "[t]he presence of fish leaders (chiefs), fish shamans, and veneration of the rivers and falls in both areas have been verified ethnographically."[231]

The Food Quest III: Foraging

Although the name "Sheep Eaters" reflects a bias toward a meat diet, plants, much like fish, probably satisfied a greater part of the Sheep Eater nutritional needs than is usually credited. Ethnographic information on subsistence practices of hunting-and-gathering groups in the Great Basin suggest that roots, seeds, nuts, and berries constituted from 30 percent to 70 percent of their diet.[232] On the other hand, hunters and gatherers who live in subarctic environments not too different from Yellowstone National Park use few plants for food.[233] Perhaps a more appropriate comparison is the Northern Shoshone, who obtained their subsistence in the same region as the Sheep Eaters. According to Lowie,[234] these foragers relied heavily on plants, and it seems reasonable to assume the Sheep Eaters also incorporated them into their diet.

Since archaeologists tend to recover large mammal bones and associated stone tools, this often skews their interpretations toward a meat-biased economy. Except for a few manos and metates, archaeologists working in the Yellowstone National Park region seldom find tools specifically associated with plant collection and processing. The perishable nature of the wooden sticks used for digging roots and the baskets used in collecting seeds may account for this, but the techniques for processing and preparing plants are not well researched and some evidence is probably overlooked. For example, nuts from both the limber pine and the white bark pine are excellent food sources in the Yellowstone National Park area, and both were probably eaten by Sheep Eaters. The cones could be roasted slightly to open them, or if the cones were taken after the first frost, the bracts opened naturally to release most of the seeds. As described by Fowler and Liljeblad,[235] the next step was to extract any remaining seeds by beating a pile of cones with sticks or tapping individual cones with a small hand stone while holding it on an anvil stone. As they were picked up locally, used for this single purpose, and not kept for another season, it would be very difficult for any archaeologist to specify these rocks as pine nut–harvesting tools. Based on Fowler's Great Basin Shoshonean material, however, other items used for seed-processing might be more easily identifiable:

> Once extracted, the seeds were given a preliminary parching in an open twined fan-shaped tray to make the seed coats brittle. They were then shelled using a flat metate and, depending on the area, differing types of large hullers. The seed coats were removed by winnowing in a fan-shaped tray. A final parching in twined or circular coiled trays prepared the seeds for grinding.[236]

Fragments of baskets in association with stones that could have been used for hulling in this fashion were recovered from Mummy Cave,[237] and radiocarbon testing assigned them a date of A.D. 734. Similar tools have not been identified in Yellowstone National Park, but site environments in the area where basketry preservation is most likely (caves or rock shelters) have never been searched and the hullers may not be recognized.

Seeds from many other plants, like sunflowers *(Helianthus annus)*, knotweed *(Polygonum* sp.*)*, and lamb's quarter *(Chenopodium)* were also collected and eaten without additional processing, crushed with manos and metates and used as flour, or boiled and added to soups.[238] Stews made in steatite pots were probably the centerpiece of daily sustenance for the Sheep Eaters. Meat or fish and water would form the base, but many other ingredients would add nutrition and taste. Wild onions *(Allium sibiricum)*, wild carrots *(Leptoaenia multifida)*, and wild turnips *(Psoralea esculenta)*, for example, would add distinctive flavor when they were in season, while pounded chokecherries *(Prunus melanocarpa)* and service berries *(Amelanchier alnifolia)* would contribute a different, sweeter taste when they were available. Soups were probably also thickened with a flour made by grinding the seeds from a variety of Chenopodium and Amaranth plants.

Dug and processed roots were probably the most important plant foods in the Sheep Eater menu. Species and subspecies of plants like bitterroot *(Lewisia rediviva)*, balsamroot *(Balsamorhiza* sp.), biscuitroot *(Lomatium* sp.), yampa *(Carum gairdneri)*, camas *(Camassi* sp.), sego lily *(Calochortus nuttalli)*, and tobacco root *(Valeriana* sp.) could have been important foods in the Yellowstone National Park region. When they were plentiful some of these roots were probably eaten raw and any excess dried in the sun, stored in hide bags, and reconstituted in soups. Dried roots were also ground into a mealy flour, mixed with water, and formed into flat cakes that were placed on hardwood trays or flat slabs of rock and set in the ashes of a fire to bake. The name "biscuitroot" derives from these biscuitlike cakes that early trappers saw Indians consuming.[239] Yampa is another root that was eaten in its raw form, boiled in soups, or dried and pounded into flour.

C. A. Geyer, who collected information on Indians' preparation and use of Bitterroot during a trip from St. Louis, Missouri, to the Pacific Ocean (across South Pass, Wyoming) in 1843 and 1844, writes:

> The root is dug during flower-time, when the cuticle is easily removed; by that it acquires a white colour, is brittle, and by transportation is broken into small pieces. Before boiling, it is steeped in water, which makes it swell, and after boiling it becomes five or six times larger in size; resembling a jelly like substance. As it is so small a root, it requires much labour to gather a sack, which commands generally the price of a good horse.[240]

As Lewis and Clark[241] describe the roots that were in the possession of Shoshone (Lemhi) women in August 1805:

> The roots were of three kinds, folded separately from one another in hides made of buffalo made into parchment. The first is a fusiform root six inches long, about the size of a man's finger at the largest end, with radicals larger than is usual in roots of the fusiform sort. The rind is white and thin; the body is also white, mealy, and easily reducible by pounding to a substance resembling flour, which it thickens by boiling, and is of an agreeable flavor; it is eaten frequently in its raw state, either green or dried.[242]

This root is probably not yampa, because Lewis and Clark were familiar with yampa, having learned about it, including its Shoshone name, from their guide, Sacajawea, so it may be biscuitroot. As for the second root, Lewis and Clark describe it as fibrous with a cylindrical form. According to the Indians, it was always boiled before eating, and when the explorers tried it they learned that it readily softened and was edible but that it had a bitter taste; almost certainly it was bitterroot *(Lewisia rediviva)*. The third root, a small tuber with a round shape and nutty flavor, was most likely sego lily.

In addition to the parfleches or rawhide containers described by Lewis and Clark, they noted two bags made of silk-grass, which is derived from yucca and was presumably braided to make a strong fiber.[243] They were also sizable, one holding about a bushel of dried service berries and the other about the same amount of dried roots. Because of their identification as "bags" they were apparently flexible, with an open weave, perhaps something like the fiber sacks used to package onions today. Lewis and Clark encountered these Mountain Shoshone along the Jefferson River, about 50 miles northwest of Yellowstone National Park, in August 1805. Their plants were dug with elk antler tines or wooden sticks that had fire-hardened ends. A cross piece, made of an antler, was sometimes fitted over the end and pushed with the hands to facilitate the digging. Their journals also mention several locations in the vicinity where holes in the ground were probably left by Indians who were collecting and drying plants for winter.

Other plants, including roots, nuts, berries, and seeds that were eaten raw or dried without additional processing, added significantly to the Sheep Eater food supply. (See chapter 5 for a discussion of camas, their paramount tuber resource.)

Dwellings of the Sheep Eaters

The largest and most obvious indicators of Indian occupation in Yellowstone National Park, which always caught the eye of visitors and photographers, are their houses. Standing mute and skeletal, those conical timbered lodges that have withstood the ravages of fires, windstorms, bugs, and vandals seem to evoke a special sympathy. Perhaps this is because we know that in these camping spots other living and breathing human beings socialized, worked, ate, argued, told stories, loved, slept, and planned their days. As to the exact origins and ethnic identification of these buildings that acquired the Algonkian-language term *wickiups,* however, there has been some debate.

After 1750, when horses were in general use throughout the plains, the Crow, Blackfeet, Shoshone, and Bannock built conical-shaped, hide-covered tipis as their preferred dwellings. But their long lodgepole pine frames and weighty hide covers required horses to transport them. Lacking horses, the Sheep Eaters were not able to transport such heavy houses. Instead, they lived in semipermanent shelters or temporary houses that, from their scattered remains, seem to be of three kinds. The first type of impermanent shelters were made by leaning timber poles into conical-shaped structures, the aforementioned wickiups. The second form of structure was built inside a rock shelter and featured poles leaning against a crude frame that backed up against the rear of a cave wall. A third building type was made by stacking deadfall timber into cribbed walls with four or five sides that stood about five feet in height.

Because all northwestern Plains tribes made both the conical and cribwork shelters, it is difficult to differentiate their use by one tribe or another; hence, when an archaeologist finds these temporary dwellings they are customarily assigned to the cultural groups closest to their location.[244] Associated artifacts

Åke Hultkrantz at Sheepeater Cliffs, July 1994. (Photo by Peter Nabokov.)

may be a more reliable indicator of their cultural affiliation, but these are often problematic as well. Given the usual association based on proximity, it is interesting that in the opinion of Aubrey Haines, the wickiups found in Yellowstone National Park were *not* the work of Sheep Eaters:

> George Bird Grinnell long ago identified the Yellowstone wickiups as Crow hunting lodges, and Dr. Malouf recently came to the same conclusion as a result of his archaeological investigations, which showed only a very transient use and none of the household debris that would have remained from even a seasonal use by Sheepeaters.[245]

To identify the wickiups as Crow, Haines cites a letter from Grinnell to Phillip Martindale, a park ranger, in 1927,[246] which suggested that they were built by hunting and raiding groups with poles that stood close together to conceal fires. The Malouf reference stems from work undertaken as part of a preliminary archaeological survey in the park prior to the research of Jake Hoffman and Dee Taylor. Yet when Hoffman reviewed the evidence collected by Philetus Norris regarding park wickiups, he[247] assigned them to the Sheep Eaters.[248] Hoffman may have been wise not to take Norris's work lightly, for the superintendent drafted maps of sites in the park, selected park artifacts for the Smithsonian Institution, and steeped himself in the archaeological knowledge of his day. In Norris's view the cribbed-style dwellings and conical wickiups were the work of Sheep Eaters, and he reached this conclusion after considerable discussion with others while visiting the sites. And a principal consultant to Hultkrantz agreed. Were the diameters of park wickiups once larger when they were brand-new, and were they made by Piegans? Hultkrantz asked Jack Haynes. Haynes replied, "Yes the wickiups in the park had considerably wider bases originally. I doubt they are Piegan. They were identified as Sheepeater as early as the 1870's."[249]

Research among the Shoshone Indians, including inquiries made of Sheep Eater descendants, reveals ample knowledge of these house types. From the Northern Shoshone, for example, Lowie[250] learned that before they used hide tipis they lived in small, conical-shaped dwellings made of timber and covered with brush. The crudeness of the dwellings led to outsiders referring in sign language to the Shoshone as "Bad Lodges."[251] When the Wind River Shoshone described these shelters to Lowie they said they were both grass and brush covered, stood seven to eight feet high, and faced east and that inside there were no fixed seating assignments.[252] Among the Northern Shoshone Murphy and Murphy[253] obtained a photograph of one taken circa 1900, which was made of interwoven rushes and willows on a conical frame and identified as a "summer tipi." Without the brush covering, it would look almost identical to the conical-shaped wickiups found in the park.

More recent interviews of the Shoshone also tie the park wickiups to the Sheep Eaters. When David Dominick[254] interviewed Wind River Shoshone consultants they claimed that the conical wickiup remains were the work of both Plains Shoshone and Sheep Eaters. But more than one claimed that the mountain-dwelling Sheep Eaters laid more tightly fitted poles into the cone so that they were "waterproof" and added that they sheltered one or two families.[255]

While some timbered shelters may have been used by the Crow, the foregoing discussion makes a strong case that most of the conical wickiups and other pole dwellings in Yellowstone National Park were the work of the park's more permanent residents, the Sheep Eaters.

WICKIUPS

Since the creation of Yellowstone National Park in 1872 dozens of wickiup sites have come to light. Hardly an annual report of Superintendent Norris neglected to comment on the abundant wickiups in the "sheltered glens and valleys" of the park. In his report for 1880, for example, Norris describes a Sheep Eater camping spot on the divide between Hoodoo Creek and Miller Creek where a single wickiup stood among the remains of more than forty others that had collapsed.[256] According to Jack Haynes, this site was still visible in 1924:

In the fall of 1924 in company with Superintendent Horace M. Albright, Samuel T. Woodring, chief ranger, and Ed Bruce I saw a large, ancient Indian camp ground northeast of Parker Peak across the gully between there and Hoodoo Peak. It was on the bank, sheltered by the southern ridge and about 1/4 mile west of the rim of the gully. The area consisting of three or four acres was covered with tepee poles—hundreds of them—flanked at the west by a grove [of] aspen trees.[257]

Haynes believed that this was the largest wickiup site in the park. Actually his father, Frank Jay Haynes, had already seen it in 1894 in the company of Acting Superintendent Captain George S. Anderson and scout George Whittaker. But Frank Haynes failed to indicate whether any structures were standing at the time.[258] When Stuart W. Conner, Kenneth J. Feyhl, and Dan Martin visited this region in 1977, they recorded a site known as the Parker Peak site, 48YE506, but they did not notice any fallen wickiups; probably the collapsed poles had decayed and decomposed in their relatively wet environment. Nonetheless, the record of this site attests to the popularity of free-standing wickiups as Sheep Eater houses, especially in summer.

The remains of dwellings in Yellowstone National Park whose claim to Sheep Eater manufacture seems most plausible are the conical-shaped pole structures a short hike off the Mammoth-to-Tower road. Recognized for more than a century and assigned site number 48YE2, these structures stand relatively close to the road between Mammoth Hot Springs and Tower Falls in a location near the park headquarters, where they have received considerable attention.[259] A series of picture postcards were made of the structures in about 1900 by an unidentified photographer. According to a letter from Jack Haynes to Park Superintendent Rogers in 1940, in 1905 his mother, Lily V. Haynes, provided the following caption for one of those cards:

> Tepees put there by Indians forty years ago. Near 3 mi. post on way to E. Gardiner Falls. Papa saw them years ago (3 of them) thought they had been torn down. Hunter found them early this year. Are 1/4 mile E. of road.[260]

This pictorial collection includes two views of unidentified hunters holding an elk head in front of the most prominent wickiup and separate views of two of the wickiups standing alone. One image reveals a third wickiup barely visible to the rear of a prominent one. Based on an estimated height of 5.5 feet for the hunters themselves, the prominent wickiup appears to be standing about 12 feet high.

Another photograph showing two wickiup structures and dated 1915 is found in the F. J. Haynes collection with the caption "Indian tepees (aspen) above road east of Sheepeater Canyon Bridge. YNP." When Stuart Conner[261] compared this photograph to ones he has of the site taken in 1937, 1963, 1964, and 1991 in order to be certain it was the Lava Creek site, 48YE2, he noted that the photograph was from a glass plate in the F. J. Haynes collection at the Montana Historical Society but that the photographer was unknown. When the scene was photographed at least a decade after the postcard series, the site showed little change.

J. M. Shippee saw this site twice, in 1947 and 1950, when he was working for the Smithsonian Institution River Basin Survey. [262] During his first visits, three structures were standing and a fourth was collapsed. The upright structures had inside height measurements of about 9 feet and base diameters of 14 feet, the poles were fir with a basal thickness of 2 to 3.5 inches, and fifty-five of them were counted in one structure while another had sixty-five in its walls. Shippee adds:

> All four wikiups had small shallow fireplaces at their centers. In one fireplace, an obsidian spall was found. Obsidian flakes also occurred in the cutbank of the highway, but around the lodges the litter of the forest floor hid all camp debris except for several large leg bones of animals.[263]

The Shippee notes represent the first systematic attempt to describe the size and character of these wickiups. It is noteworthy that this recording did not take place until nearly a century after Superintendent Norris described the site in his annual report of 1880. In 1958, eleven years after Shippee's first visit, Jake Hoffman[264] recorded the site and found two standing and two collapsed wickiups, all arranged in an arc with the open side facing downhill to the northwest. According to Hoffman, the wood was both aspen and lodgepole pine, with the poles measuring about 4 inches in diameter. The largest standing wickiup was 12 feet in height, with an ellipsoidal base that measured 6 by 10 feet; the smaller standing structure measured 10 feet in height with a circular base diameter of 8 feet. Discussing their interior features, Hoffman wrote:

> The center of each wickiup floor (standing and fallen) has been dug out by unknown persons. However, stones and charcoal still left inside the wickiups reveal the presence of true hearths. We recovered several large pieces of elk bone consisting of a femur, vertebrae and scapula from inside the wickiups. No other occupational debris lay within the wickiups, but we found small amounts of obsidian 25 yards north of the structures within the sites area.[265]

The "animal" bones mentioned by Shippee are probably these elk remains identified by Hoffman and are not necessarily contemporaneous with the wickiups since they may be from the trophy elk shown with hunters in the early postcard. When Hoffman spotted a single large pole resting on top of the wickiup's other crossed poles, he suggested that its weight "exerted at the poles' common focus creates a downward force and increases the stability of the shelter's framework."[266] Using a pole weight across the top of the structures is reminiscent of the long pole used in the construction of the Sheep Eater dwelling in the cave on Big Sheep Creek.

TIMBER-POLE HOUSES

The so-called timber-pole house, also used by the Sheep Eaters, is found in caves and rock shelters throughout their territory. In smaller caves one finds them with walls of rocks and timber across the openings; in larger caves or rock shelters they are made by leaning timbers, brush, and then rocks against the rear walls. A probable Sheep Eater structure of this variety was discovered in a limestone cave, now called Wickiup Cave, on a tree-covered slope at 7,400 feet elevation, in Big Sheep Creek Canyon at the southern end of the Tendoy Mountains about 110 miles west of Yellowstone National Park.[267]

The structure was built of timbers, branches, pine boughs, and rocks. Its main frame was two long poles that were braced against the rock shelter's back wall, which were supported by a forked, upright post. More than thirty timber poles leaned against this framework so as to enclose a semicircular area 17 feet in diameter and 10 feet high. Many of the poles had burned ends, suggesting they were felled or cut to length with fire. For added protection smaller tree branches and pine boughs were interwoven into walls, while around the exterior sides a rock wall was constructed by stacking limestone blocks to a height of 2 feet, with a break for an entryway.[268]

In its prime the timber-pole house fit tightly against the rear wall, with rock walls snugly flanking it on the sides. The natural rock ceiling afforded protection from snow and rain while the woven branch and pine bough walls deterred the wind and cold. Inside lay a 4-by-8-foot bed, outlined with rocks and mattressed with pine boughs and giant wild rye grass. Archaeologists found no interior fire hearth, but the site had been disturbed by relic hunters who may have destroyed the cooking remains. The estimated date for this structure was most likely about 1850, but the discovery of a square nail, an unidentifiable metal fragment, and a hammered lead pendant suggest that the cave had also seen human use in the protohistoric period one hundred years or more before that. Unfortunately, vandals had scattered nearly all the artifacts from the site, but the archaeologist Carl Davis tracked many of them down and was able to reconstruct a representative inventory[269] of some thirty small triangular arrow points, a few with side notches, others with side and base notches, and a collection of simple triangular points lacking notches. Although its shaft was broken, one of those points was tied by wrapped sinew to an arrow fragment. Other pieces of shaft, smoothed from cottonwood and elm, exhibited narrowed ends and presumably were the main bodies of compound arrows whose points, as described earlier, were attached to hollow reeds and fitted over the narrow tenon. One arrow piece even retained a feather, attached with sinew, about four inches below the nock end, and although it was not identifiable, other bits of feather fletching were identified as blue grouse and sage grouse.[270]

In the assemblage were also chipped stone artifacts for cutting, scraping, and drilling. One long and narrow blade, shaped like a willow leaf and measuring 6.5

inches in length by 1.5 inches in width, was a typical Shoshone knife that had been extensively resharpened. There were also two bone awls, one made from a splinter of straight bone shaft, the other from the scapula of an unidentifiable mammal. Under the mattress of rye grass and pine bough matting two beads were recovered, presumably carved from bird bone.

In addition, the Wickiup Cave site yielded more than one hundred ceramic sherds, only two of which remained for Davis to identify as "undecorated Intermountain," a ware typically associated with Shoshones of Wyoming and Idaho. The relic collectors indicated that they had found them beneath the cave floor, but the disturbance from illegal digging was so great that the exact placement of the pottery in the deposits could not be determined.[271] Since this Intermountain Tradition pottery has recently been recognized as having far greater antiquity than previously believed,[272] it is possible the ceramics represent a still earlier cultural use of the rock shelter.

From the trapper Alexander Ross we hear of the use by "mountain Shoshone" of such caves. Describing the different Indians that inhabit the mountainous region surrounding Yellowstone National Park, Ross identifies one group as the "Ban-at-tees," or "mountain Snakes" who "live a predatory and wandering life in the recesses of the mountains, and are found in small bands or single wigwams among the caverns and rocks."[273]

According to Davis, these Indians are thought to be Sheep Eaters, and the reference to their "wigwams among the caverns" suggests houses constructed in caves.[274] Much like the Big Sheep Creek example, timber lodges constructed inside caves may have been a preferred seasonal type of lodging for the Sheep Eaters. Superintendent Norris[275] mentions Sheep Eater occupation of caves but does not describe houses in them. Hikers and tourists have reportedly stumbled upon similar-sounding structures in Yellowstone National Park,[276] but unfortunately none have been recorded. Haines[277] has pointed out that one advantage of pole lodges in caves is that fires built against the back wall of the cave would radiate heat. While this may have been a factor in cold weather, during the warmer months and when they were traveling in areas that lacked these overhangs, Sheep Eaters undoubtedly sought shelter in other types of housing, including crib-style structures made of stacking horizontal layers of timber, usually deadfall trees, into layers up to a height of five or six feet.

To summarize, we have a speculative picture of Sheep Eater architecture in which wickiups, such as those formerly standing between Miller and Hoodoo Creeks, were most likely used in summertime, while the rock shelters featuring leaning pole structures were probably preferred for high-elevation winter use, and the cribbed style of shelter would most likely have been used in the lower valleys during the colder months.

Exhibition on Yellowstone Park's Sheep Eaters in the Albright Visitor Center, employing blown-up and cutout photograph of Shoshone-Bannocks taken in 1871 by William Henry Jackson along Idaho's Medicine Creek Lodge, more than one hundred miles southwest of West Yellowstone. (Photo courtesy of Yellowstone National Park Archives, #Yell 34259.)

Sheep Eater Social and Political Life

How did the Sheep Eaters organize their interpersonal existence? How did they govern themselves; how did they reach decisions concerning when and where to hunt; did they have leaders and how did they select them; how did they choose their husbands and wives; how did they resolve quarrels among themselves; how did they relate to outsiders? And how can we possibly answer any of these questions?

The difficulties of compiling the circumstantial montage of Sheep Eater life that we have attempted so far are only compounded when we submit a picture of their nonmaterial beliefs and practices. There is no getting around the fact that we have very few recorded accounts revealing their social structure and political organization. Even after his interviews with elder Sheep Eaters in the late 1940s and the 1950s, Hultkrantz lamented the fact that he still had a minimal idea of Sheep Eater sociopolitical life. To fill the gap, he felt one was forced to extrapolate from data obtained from neighboring Plains Shoshone.[278] In what follows we have added to Hultkrantz's information from the writings of Robert Lowie;[279] Julian Steward,[280] Demitri Shimkin,[281] and Carling Malouf,[282] with supporting material from trappers' and explorers' journals. But in most cases we have had to reconstruct Sheep Eater lifestyle patterns by reference to other Shoshone groups, a second-best recourse that may not be as risky as it seems, for as Steward reminds us:

> A very fundamental feature of Basin-Plateau society is the remarkable absence of any traditional institutions other than the nuclear families. There were no men's initiations or secret societies, no marriage-regulating clans, moieties, segments or lineages, no age grade or women's societies, and no ceremonials, recreational activities, or warfare that united all members of what were later called "bands."[283]

Steward's negative checklist may be relevant to the sociopolitical organization of those cousins to the Basin-Plateau Shoshoneans with whom we are concerned, the Sheep Eaters. Certainly the most applicable feature of Steward's characterization is the fact that Sheep Eater society was also founded on the native nuclear family—father, mother, a grandparent or two, and immediate offspring. Two or three of these related families might live and work together for weeks at a time during their annual food pursuits, and more families might periodically convene to activate their large sheep traps. But generally these groups did not rely on help from secondary sources, except when a lone shaman or medicine man was needed in the event of illness or stress.

In the day-to-day activities of any Sheep Eater encampment, the clearest social distinction visible to any outsider would probably have been a sexual division of labor. Men hunted and fished; women gathered tubers, seeds, and berries. Since plants were a significant part of the Shoshone diet in the Great Basin, it was women who supplied as much as 75 percent of their food supply. But in the higher elevations, where sheep and fish were abundant, this ratio dropped to about equal time devoted to meat and fish, on the one hand, and to plant foraging, on the other. Yet this does not mean that men and women put the same amount of energy into camp tasks, for women completed additional chores such as preparing meals, working hides, drying fish, and gathering wood in addition to their responsibility as primary caretakers of children. Men certainly had their gender-specific jobs, too, including the procurement of suitable stone and steatite, manufacturing finished tools from them, and crafting the specialized items such as horn bows. So even though most anthropologists might classify Sheep Eater society as "egalitarian" and lacking in class distinctions, in the final analysis the lioness's share of daily tasks probably fell to the women.

Lamentably, we know next to nothing about the psychological and emotional dimensions of Sheep Eater existence. None of the ethnographers who were in a position to elicit a Sheep Eater "life history" ever did so, and the purported Sheep Eater "marriage ceremony" described by Allen is patently absurd.[284] More likely, as judged by Hultkrantz, marriages were sealed without much ceremony. And based on Shoshonean customs in the Great Basin and the plains, we suspect that there was not even gift exchange to publicly formalize the union, although a young man who was considered a good hunter and provider would certainly be highly valued by his new in-laws.

While the family unit was almost certainly the building block of Sheep Eater society, it was commonly augmented by a larger, loosely knit amalgam of families. To characterize this mutually supportive cluster Malouf coined the term *kin and clique*.[285] By this he meant the primary subsistence, social, and political unit of the Great Basin Shoshone, which was composed of nuclear families who were linked by various combinations of blood relatives, in-laws, adoptees, and possibly friends. In Malouf's concept, these food-gathering, kin and clique groups varied so greatly in size and composition from year to year that it is difficult to give them any firmer definition:

> There were no social compulsions which gave the kin and clique a permanent identity. Friends, especially, were apt to change their affiliations for practical or emotional reasons. A quarrel or the prospects of a more favorite food quest in another area might entice some of the group away.[286]

Not until the introduction of horses did the Shoshone transform some of these socially fluid and highly mobile kin and clique units into more permanent organized hunting bands.[287] Originally Steward[288] assigned many northern Shoshone groups to the political designation "bands," but after more comparative research was available on hunters and gatherers throughout North America and the world he changed his mind and suggested that bands were so variable that his own term had lost much of its definitional value.[289] This debate about "bands" aside, the Sheep Eaters, who never possessed horses, do not appear to have felt the practical, diplomatic, or social need to organize themselves beyond the kin and clique level.

As for selecting their leaders, it was probably repeatedly successful hunters or charismatic individuals who got along with everybody—or could intimidate them—who initiated decisions regarding the movement of Sheep Eater camps. While these leaders were often as not men, women undoubtedly played a significant role in scheduling and guiding the foraging parties in their search for vital plant staples like camas and biscuitroot. At all times, we can guess that consensus was a desired ideal. Malouf offers this description of the inner workings of a kin and clique:

> Politically the *kin and clique* group was basically democratic. An informal council of adults made the decisions. Men of good reputation for knowledge or strength, or persons with potent shamanistic powers were consulted or even asked to lead a temporary drive, a gathering venture, or a ceremony, but there office was not permanent. Some older persons were regarded as important to the *kin and clique* because of their knowledge of places where plant and animal foods could be found, but they never held a place of prestige.[290]

Based on the practices of generally equivalent Great Basin groups, we suspect that quarrels between individuals outside the nuclear family were easily adjudicated, since the disputing party simply moved apart to align with another kin and clique. But arguments within the immediate family were probably not so easily resolved. Separation was an option, and certainly after children reached an age when they could travel on their own they were free to join relatives elsewhere.

We recall that the Sheep Eaters encountered by Osborne Russell in Yellowstone National Park in July 1835 included six men, seven women, and eight or ten children.[291] This would have been a plausible size for a kin and clique in midsummer, when there was no need for extra hands for hunting or processing meat. At least three or four of the men and women were probably married, and one or two of the men may have had more than one wife. Again relying on Shimkin's research among Plains Shoshone, the other adults in the group possibly included widowed or divorced women, elders, and two or three unmarried but related males. It is also likely that the group trading with Russell included more than a single family, who converged for this special occasion out of curiosity and the chance to trade with these exotic trappers.

In contrast to the smaller band met by Russell, a large gathering of sixty Sheep Eaters feasted and traded with white trappers in 1866 near the head of the Greybull River: "Squaws, dogs, papooses and all. They was all loaded down with skins and furs, besides a large Jackass loaded down to the guards and the only animal these beings possessed."[292] The size of the group suggests that this meeting occurred around the time of a communal hunt, perhaps just as the Sheep Eaters were emerging from the mountains for trading or hunting. That Henderson's meeting occurred thirty-six years after the Russell encounter may also signify some acculturation that led to a change in group dynamics and practices, underscored by mention of the "Jackass," or mule. Still, the picture of such a large kin and clique group laden with furs to trade suggests they were successfully inhabiting their mountain homes.

Further evidence that these Mountain Sheep Eaters were surviving and trapping efficiently in the following decade comes from a newspaper editor and Yellowstone traveler named Spencer Ellsworth. Lee Whittlesey suspects he entered their stronghold sometime in the 1870s. As Ellsworth wrote of the encounter:

[T]heir camp was in a most secluded and inaccessible part of the Madison Range, but guided by certain signs [I] succeeded in reaching it the second day. There was [sic] a dozen or more lodges, the inmates of which were sitting or lying indolently about, when unexpectedly I appeared. I am not considered particularly ferocious, but at the sight of me every soul started and ran like so many rabbits . . . For twenty minutes or more I waited, when a very old woman came up and seeing she was not hurt the others stole timidly out of the brush. Their only firearms were two old muskets of the Hudson Bay pattern, for which they had no powder and did not even know how to use them. Game was killed with bows and arrows or trapped with snares. There is a sort of sign language common to all nations, by which I made my wishes known, and having arranged to meet them two days later for trade, I departed. At the agreed upon time I was there again with a supply of sugar, coffee, and various things for trade, but fear again had taken possession of they, and they were not to be found. Taking their trail however, I followed it for twenty miles and found their camp. My adventure was very successful for I returned with two horses loaded down with valuable furs worth one dollar a pound.[293]

Descriptions of trading between Sheep Eaters and trappers can also offer oblique insights into social customs. In these dealings, according to Russell, the Indians simply threw their tanned hides and skins on the ground, as if ready to accept whatever the trappers thought was a fair price. From their exchange with Henderson somewhat later, we get the more explicit impression of innocent Sheep Eaters ripe for the picking. To better understand the Indians' negotiating posture, however, we should probably explore such economic transactions from the native viewpoint. Their asking for a "fair price" was likely an overture to what is identified by economic anthropologists as a form of "balanced [if delayed] reciprocity," in which parties to such transactions are expected to honor debts at a later date. As we might understand from the combinations of people in their kin and clique relationships, in Sheep Eater reckoning such a debt would be honored in a time of need. When Sheep Eaters tossed their tanned skins on the ground and traders returned items deemed of lesser value, it conceivably meant that when Indian families found themselves without food in the next year, they could then rely on the traders, who they still had in their debt. Trade to a Sheep Eater was probably never a quick and fast "done deal"; instead, as a more drawn-out engagement between parties, it initiated important social and political bonds. Trading times were an opportunity for all kinds of social business to take place and for meeting new people, and, even when cross-cultural engagements might be intimidating to the individuals involved, trade offered a mutual language for human interaction, an opportunity for exchange of news and input of fresh ideas.

In this regard it is important to recognize that the Sheep Eaters were historically noted for their trade engagements. Trade to the east was with the Plains Shoshone, to the west it was with other Shoshone and the Nez Perce and Flathead, who, in turn, had received some of their wares from other tribes. Horn bows, obsidian preforms, tailored clothing, and sheep and elk hides were commodities that Sheep Eaters brought to these native trading rendezvous, while they sought Pacific marine shells, bison robes, salt, seeds, roots, salmon, and dried crickets.[294] Although the Sheep Eaters did not trade for horses, the value of trade items was usually reckoned in horses, and in the mid-1800s Lowie[295] tells us that ten sheepskins or two bearskins were worth one horse, while Jack Contor learned that a sheep horn bow was worth five to ten horses.[296]

Sheep Eater Worldview and Religion

Most scholars who conducted ethnographic fieldwork among the host reservations where remnants of the park-dwelling Sheep Eaters found refuge did not make an effort to elicit whatever diagnostic data might set them apart from the Wind River or the Lemhi Shoshones. Thanks to the notable exception of the historian of religion, Åke Hultkrantz, however, we have a better understanding of the conceptual life of these "elusive" mountain people than we do of their sociopolitical organization. But in striving to sort out what made the Sheep Eater cultural inheritance unique, Hultkrantz had to peer through "the common religious pattern on the [Wind River] reservation."[297]

During his fieldwork in the 1940s and 1950s, Hultkrantz tried to locate every elder of Sheep Eater ancestry. But he also talked with knowledgeable, conservative Shoshone medicine people whose houses clustered around the Sage Creek corner of the Wind River Reservation as he sought to construct "a theoretical pattern, a structure in which the fragmentary facts [of Sheep Eater beliefs] find their natural place."[298] For Hultkrantz, a fundamental dimension of such a pattern was "religious ecology," a concept whose influence he explained at the outset of his unpublished manuscript on Sheep Eater lifeways and religion:

> There are three steps in the ecologist's investigation. First, he analyzes the interrelationship of exploitative or productive technology and environment. Second, he investigates the behavior patterns associated with this technology. Third, he tries to find out to what extent these behavior patterns affect other aspects of culture, such as society and religion.
>
> The religio-ecological approach proceeds from these premises.[299]

This quotation clarifies the conceptual framework that organizes many of Hulkrantz's glimpses into the Sheep Eater belief system.[300]

WORLDVIEW, COSMOLOGY, AND SACRED GEOGRAPHY

Hultkrantz opened his sketch of Sheep Eater religion with their worldview. He emphasized that while the Sheep Eaters lived in both the supernatural and natural worlds,

[a] conscious distinction between them was never made, at least not verbally. Some of the phenomena of the supernatural world belonged to the diffuse upper part of the world, the sky; or they were just as distant by belonging to the remote past, the days of Coyote and his associates, or they represented a different existence, the afterlife.[301]

A trinity of sorts occupied the highest, most generalized tier of Sheep Eater cosmology. All of Hultkrantz's Sheep Eater consultants were unanimous in their conviction that Tam Apo, or "Our Father," was a pre-Christian concept. But the Sun also figured in a supreme position. As to the relationship between them, one of his informants tried to explain:

> We pray to Our Father, not to the Sun, although we direct the prayers to the Sun. We thank the Father for our lives, and for the fact that the sun shines over us. We do not pray every day facing the Sun, only at certain occasions, for instance, at the Sun Dance. Memories from the past indicated that we have never prayed to any other being than the Father above *(tam pa ant)* and the Sun. The father has created the Sun; Sun is a superior being, therefore we pray both to the Sun and to the Father.[302]

Hultkrantz explained that when Sheep Eaters prayed they often actually faced the Sun, which was at once the symbol for Our Father (also called *oyo k tam nuy-wonaip,* or "all us people he made") and "a divine being in its own right."[303] At the same time, his Indian friends also cited the importance of the third, semidivine character, Coyote, or *tzi isapo.* Although they admitted that he had assisted Our Father in creating life on earth, one Sheep Eater woman added, "Coyote is a treacherous animal, he even tried to copulate with his mother and his daughter."[304] But when referring to their cosmology, Sheep Eaters stressed the more formal, constructive side of Coyote's personality, his time-honored role of creator and transformer rather than transgressor.[305]

Most of the other Sheep Eater spirits were more down-to-earth entities, who constantly interferred with or facilitated their hopes and dreams. There were the beings associated with the "diffuse" and "superior" supernatural world, whom they invoked in times of peril or during storytelling or in meditation. Then there was an "inferior" domain of spirits, closer at hand, a possible source of supernatural assistance or of immediate danger, and yet somewhat more susceptible to human supplication and manipulation.

According to Hultkrantz, the "scene of the interaction" between Sheep Eaters and their spirits was the *"wooded mountain areas of the Yellowstone Park,* the Absarokas, the Wind River Mountains and, possibly, the Big Horn Mountains."[306] This was the landscape that, to the medicine men with whom Hultkrantz interacted, was "by definition the home country of the spirits."[307] Of all the guardian spirits available to human beings, they said, the power *(pukka* or *puha)* known specifically as "mountain-medicine" *(toyawo)* was the strongest and most dangerous, and one Sun Dance leader, Hultkrantz's closest Wind River Shoshone consultant, added:

The fellow who wants it has to bathe, paint himself, make cedar smoke, smoke tobacco and pray. He may pray in any language, like *pukka* understands all kinds of languages. He must be alone, he is without the help of the medicine-man. Now, *pukka* has drawn its signs on the rocks, and in tall trees—you can see them drawn in the bark high up on the trees of the mountain areas. There are many rock-drawings in the mountains round about [the Wind River Valley] where you can seek *pukka*. One place is just under the Teton peak, another north of the hot springs in Yellowstone Park, close to the boundary line to Montana.[308]

Some of Hultkrantz's Sheep Eater informants refined this notion by claiming that spirits withdrew into the mountains during the summer but returned to the rock drawings in lower altitudes in September, when the weather turned cold.[309] In a sense, then, the movements of spirits paralleled those of the Sheep Eaters, many of whom passed their summers in the mountains and spent much of the rest of the year in the Wind River country. Hultkrantz explained this "spirit nomadism" by recalling that in older days, summer was the only proper time for receiving the power-visions at the rock drawings, through the practice known as *puhawilo,* or "sleeping at medicine-rock."[310] Because the rock drawings are all at lower elevations, this suggests that late summer, the *yuvat mua* or "elk breeding moon" of late September and October, would have been a prime time for the vision-seeking ritual.

Hultkrantz was also told that the spirits actually lived *within* the mountains. One Sheep Eater claimed that some people were invited inside a peak behind Bull Lake (known to the Wind River Shoshone as "water buffalo lake" and a special haunt of water spirits, whose buffalo-like sounds can be heard in the spring when the ice cracks),[311] located in the northern Wind River Mountains, to play a hand game with them.[312] When Hultkrantz wanted to know if the Sheep Eaters considered their hunting grounds "sacred," he found no satisfactory equivalent in the Shoshonean vocabulary. Their closest term was *igaunt,* or "full of wonder," which referred less to the sanctity of place than to the efficacy of supernatural powers who lived there.[313]

Rock-drawing places were definitely *igaunt,* in part because they were considered evidence of the work of sacred lightning, or *eygagu ce,* "red light." Hultkrantz was able to visit such places throughout Sheep Eater territory—at Dinwoody Lake, different points along the North Fork of the Popo Agie River, "Washakie's meadows" west of Fort Washakie, the South Fork Canyon of the Little Wind River, the Sage Creek foothills and Medicine Butte, sites in the Owl Creek Mountains, on the slopes of the Absarokas, and in the Tetons.

SOULS, SPIRITUAL GUARDIANS, AND SPIRITS

Hultkrantz's inquiries also delved into the uncharted terrain of Sheep Eater ontology. He learned that each Sheep Eater possessed at least three types of "soul." First was the *suap,* or "ego-soul," which was embodied by one's breath. Second, they had a closely related "free-soul," or *navushieip,* the soul that might abandon the body during dreams, trances, and comas. During a particularly powerful dream of this kind, known as *puhanavuzieip,* one also might encounter a guardian spirit who would remain an ally throughout one's life. Third, there was the "body-soul," or *mugua,* which activated the body during one's waking hours. Hultkrantz's Sheep Eater informants likened this third soul to a thin, strong thread, and one said it was situated "between the eyebrows. Breath is a part of *mugua.* The heart keeps you alive; it stops, *mugua* leaves the body [through the top of the head], only skin and bones remain."[314]

Hultkrantz found it more difficult to obtain stories of Sheep Eater vision quests than he had among the Wind River Shoshone, but "the tradition of vision quest" among them was still alive. It was hard to find out about them "perhaps because some would-be medicine men secretly practice spirit seeking, perhaps because medicine-men have done so in recent times." [315] Their visions might earn men the power of invulnerability; such was the consequence of a power-dream that was received by a Sheep Eater in which he shot at three bears in his dream, only to have the bullets twist and stop like mud clots in their fur. Thereafter he believed he had acquired that power of self-protection as well.

Sheep Eaters sought their visions through a process that was not radically different from their Plains and eastern Basin-Plateau neighbors. According to Hultkrantz, the pattern went as follows:

> There is the frightening trial, the manifestation of the spirits who tends to change forms—now a man, now an animal—, the imparting of supernatural power, the conditions for the ownership of this power, and the regulations concerning ritual paraphernalia.[316]

The category of spirits to which Sheep Eaters might become allied through such life-changing experiences were what Hultkrantz called "particular nature types, such as the water spirits." Lakes, rivers, springs, and thermal pools were all potential locations for this group of spirits who possessed great supernatural power, with which the Sheep Eaters sometimes transacted for good or ill. Hultkrantz took pains to distinguish these spirits from the spirits "associated with the dangerous places—mountains tops, geysers," supernatural beings that he believed usually played little role as guardian spirits. Under extraordinary circumstances it appears that some of the following generally malevolent beings might be associated with an especially powerful medicine man:

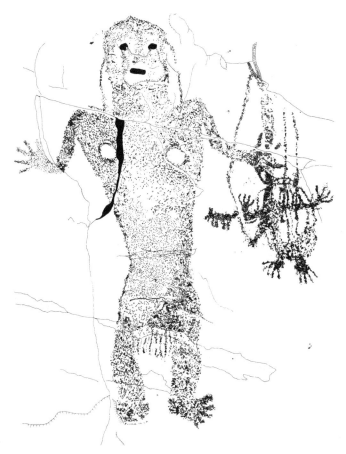

Rock art image identified as Shoshonean spirit known as Water Ghost Woman. (Drawing by Linda A. Olson.)

1. *pa:unha*—evil "children of the water," or "water babies," who lived in creeks, rivers, and lakes.
2. *pandzoavits*—large, tough-skinned "water ghosts," ogres who occupied lakes and hot springs and drowned people so as to eat them.
3. *pa:waip*—a female "water ghost" whose special prey were men.
4. *tundzoavits*—a "rocky-skinned ghost" who also belonged to the "water" specter category; his body was made of stone, with the exception of soft face and hands.
5. *tundzoavaip*—"stone ghost woman," the female counterpart of the above, who had a reputation for snatching babies.

Another group of supernaturals were the mischievous or evil spirits who hovered around human habitations. But Hultkrantz confessed to finding it difficult to clearly differentiate between what he called the "pedagogic ficts," or frightening spirits that figured in stories told children so as to make them behave; the "true spirits," which haunted and even hurt adults; and the "ghost" spirits of the living dead. The following is a partial list of the second group of "true spirits" that Sheep Eaters identified for Hultkrantz:

1. *wokaimumbic*—a giant, cannibalistic owl. It talks and behaves like a human being but resembles an enormous butterfly. It grabs children, flies away with them, and then eats them.
2. *toxabit narukumb*—an evil spirit of the night, who may have been identical to the owl and whose shrieking sounds, "tchi-tchi-tchi-tchi," terrify people.
3. *nimrika*—dangerous ogrelike spirits who are often difficult to distinguish from human beings, except that they eat human flesh and live in old-style brush houses. Unlike the fearsome owls, they can bestow power on humans.
4. *ninimbi*—spiritually powerful, usually invisible "little people" who are often associated with the Sheep Eater homelands in the mountains and are prominent in Sheep Eater religious thought. Humans can help them and vice versa.

The third group of spirits, the ubiquitous *dzoap,* or "living ghosts," might brush up against the living without warning. As one of Hultkrantz's Sheep Eaters informants recalled such an encounter:

> I have heard that almost every day the spirits of the dead are around us. The ghosts who walk round appear as whirlwinds. Not long ago I and some other women met a whirlwind, and one of these women got angry and threw a slur towards it. The whirlwind turned and went against her, destroyed her tent into pieces and broke her leg. That was three years ago [1945]. That woman is still alive.[317]

INDIVIDUAL CURING AND GROUP CEREMONIES

The oldest and most common form of interaction between Sheep Eaters and their supernatural realm was probably more individual than collective. The mediator of this relationship was generally a medicine man, or *puhagant,* who was known to have a powerful *puha* (or *pukka*) and used that dream-derived power to heal or harm. Possessing a lesser power might grant one a "gift," such as the ability to outrun deer, but it did not qualify one as a medicine man who could effect a cure or have an impact on the natural world. That level of supernatural voltage only came through a power-dream.

There were two primary techniques by which Sheep Eater healers cured illnesses. If they determined that someone was sick because their soul had fled, the medicine man put himself into a trance to search for the "fugitive soul," hopefully restoring it to the body and their patient to health. But if the ailment was revealed as coming from an object having been "shot" or inserted into the patient's body through witchcraft or a malicious spirit, then the medicine man's job was to suck or blow out the infecting object. But some Sheep Eater medicine men possessed other specialized powers as well—to charm game, cause storms, induce rain, and so forth. Unfortunately, the few purported examples of Sheep Eater oral tradition that might tell us more about their supernatural practices appear to be inauthentic,[318] and little has come down to us regarding the careers of their medicine men.

When it came to discussing collective rituals of the Sheep Eaters, Hultkrantz admitted he was dealing with "very brittle" documentation. Relying on comparative material from neighboring Shoshone groups, Hultkrantz pieced together a case for the so-called Father dance as having been their onetime annual ceremony. This appears to have been an older form of the "round dance" known in Shoshone as *naraya ndo narayar,* literally, "shuffling sideways," and which Shimkin identified as one of the special dances of the mountain Sheep Eaters.[319] And that suggests that Sheep Eaters, whose descendants acted as consultants for both Shimkin and the ethnomusicologist Judith Vander, were at least in part responsible for the Naraya, also referred to later as the Ghost Dance, the Shoshonean rendition of the revitalization movement whose intense focus was to reverse the order of the world in the Indians' favor once again. As late as 1927, Yellowstone National Park officials conveyed the U.S. government's general attitude toward this ritual: "The Ghost Dance is more recent [than the Sun Dance] and far more dangerous from a disciplinarian point of view."[320] Yet despite this negative attitude, the Shoshones managed to retain the song literature from their unique, Great Basin form of Ghost Dance (as differentiated from the Plains form) on the Wind River Reservation into the mid-twentieth century.[321]

The Wind River Shoshone told Hultkrantz that the old-time "round dance" existed "way back when Coyote was ruling the world." But the older form of the round dance was known as *apo noka,* or "Father Dance." During his early fieldwork on the Wind River Reservation in 1912, the name "Father Dance" was explained to Lowie. As Vander[320] has pointed out, Lowie's comment indicates a close relationship between the Father Dance and the Naraya as well as the almost multiple-personality relationship between Coyote as Creator and Father:

> After the Father *(a'po)* had created the world, there was a man with his wife and two children. Coyote came along and said, "I am your father and made all these hills and trees. Now I will give you this *a'po noqa.*" [*a'po,* father; *noqa,* dance] So he taught them the *na'roya* dance. Coyote was merely fooling the people.[323]

From Hultkrantz's description, this ceremony sounds like a grander version of the category of foragers' celebration that anthropologists sometimes label a First Fruits ritual, the expression of collective gratitude for the seasonal availability of a primary, natural food source. The Shoshone of Grouse Creek in Utah, directed by a shaman, staged such a thanksgiving dance when the first pine nuts were ready for picking. They then thanked *apo*, the Father, setting aside some pine nut mush for him. According to Shimkin, it took place at night in fall, winter, and spring, and both men and women joined in as sacred songs were sung.[324]

After the introduction of the Sun Dance from the Comanche—also known as "Standing Alone in Thirst"—this earlier round dance appears to have been demoted in importance for most Plains Shoshoneans. As the Sheep Eaters drew closer for comfort and protection to their lowland cousins, Hultkrantz speculated that their version of this annual thanksgiving ritual was gradually replaced first by the Shoshone-style Sun Dance and subsequently by the Ghost Dance. According to one of Hultkrantz's female Sheep Eater consultants, the Sheep Eaters staged their first Sun Dance with the Bannock in the Jackson Hole country sometime before 1896 (where they also remembered the Plains Shoshone holding theirs).[325] They emphasized that the ceremony was held in the mountains and that they sang the same songs as were heard at regular Shoshone Sun Dances.

However, Sheep Eater consultants who talked with Hultkrantz claimed an independent origin for their own particular Sun Dance, and said it first gained currency in their culture after the turn of the nineteenth century. One man told Hultkrantz:

> According to what we have learnt from the old timers we did not get the Sun Dance from any other tribe. It happened this way. Many years ago there appeared a Shoshoni warrior. He had left his people [for some time]. During the night he rested on a hill, and the Father appeared to him in a vision and instructed him to go back to his people and to build a round enclosure [i.e., the Sun Dance lodge]. He should tell the people to go there, to dance and to pray. Those who believed in the Dance would be cured from diseases.[326]

In this chapter we have interwoven direct, indirect, and circumstantial information on the lifeways of the Sheep Eaters. But it must be regarded as an interim account of the only Indian group who are generally acknowledged, even by park officials, to have been "the only permanent residents of the Park."[327] Our overview has also committed three sins of representation: we have been obliged to take a largely ahistorical "snapshot" of Sheep Eater life, to some degree casting them in a timeless amber. And lacking any full-bodied ethnographies or life histories of Sheep Eater life in the mountains, we have also surrendered to a "trait list" profile of their cultural life. Finally, in the absence of enough information on individual variation, we have perforce "essentialized" their cultural practices, a sin we hope to redress, at least partially, when we provide a historical updating of the Sheep Eater story in chapter 5.

CHAPTER 4

Visitors on the West

The Bannock and Nez Perce

Other branches of the Shoshonean Indian family migrated seasonally into Yellowstone National Park from the west, as well as the Bannock, a Northern Paiute offshoot from the Snake River and Blue Mountain area in eastern Oregon whose fortunes intertwined with those of the Northern Shoshone from the early 1700s onward. Today these Shoshone-Bannocks (sometimes referred to as "Sho-Bans") dwell on the 544,000-acre Fort Hall Indian Reservation, about one hundred miles southwest of the park's West Yellowstone entrance.

Through unusual circumstances, a Columbia River people, the Sahaptian-speaking Nez Perce, also played an important role in the park's early history. Although the Yellowstone Plateau lay somewhat beyond their cultural hearth, Nez Perce hunters and raiders freely crisscrossed this landscape in the past. But a key phase of the tribe's dramatic bid for freedom in 1877 was their passage through Yellowstone National Park only five years after its establishment; an event which would leave an indelible stamp on the park's relations with Indians down to the present day.

Trails into Yellowstone National Park from the West

From the rim of the Yellowstone caldera one gazes west across the gray-green tree cover of the geologically younger Madison Plateau and notices how the gradually sloping country grows progressively drier—down to an average rainfall of under fifteen inches a year. And descending from the western side of the Yellowstone Plateau one cannot miss the emerging features of the Columbia Plateau physiographic province. Stands of lodgepole pine give way to forests of fir and wind-beaten

Park historian Wayne F. Replogle standing on the remnants of the Bannock Trail. (Photo courtesy of Yellowstone National Park Archives, #Yell 37838-1.)

aspens, which in turn are replaced by stunted juniper before leveling out into low brush and spotty grasslands. Away from the river valleys, the broken landscape can appear inhospitable, with erodible slopes and an extremely rocky surface, especially where the Snake River courses deeply through the broken-up lava beds as it heads for the Columbia River.

The different ways that early Indians lived here reminds us that anyone tracing the wide range of Shoshonean sociopolitical worlds must always clarify *where* and *when* cultural or historical descriptions are situated. It is necessary to know *where* because a prime feature of their mobile, small-scale, prehorse way of life was its adaptability to a variety of ecological niches. The highly localized nature of basic foods—seeds, fish, small mammals, and so on—could influence band size, migratory patterns, and tool inventory. As these Indians were so responsive to their surroundings, it is not surprising to learn of their custom of naming groups by their dominant food supply.[1]

When is bound up with *where*. After adopting horses in the late 1700s, the eastern Great Basin and southern Plateau Shoshoneans underwent internal transformations. Fringe bands or elderly people may have continued seed and root gathering and hunting for small mammals, but most of these peoples came to revel in the equestrian lifestyle of their Plains Indians neighbors. According to Omer C. Stewart, the liberation from having one's survival constrained by local food supplies, plus the sudden access to war booty and surplus game, produced new class, age, and even personality divisions within the Northern Shoshone world, as highly intelligent or charismatic leaders rose to chiefly prominence.[2] At the same time, a number of Shoshonean-speaking enclaves of south-central Idaho, northern Utah, and eastern Oregon continued to prefer rabbit hunting, fishing, and gathering seeds, nuts, roots, and berries.[3] To further complicate this picture, some bands developed what might be termed "seasonal identities," alternating between the buffalo-hunting and ground-foraging ways of life.

At one time the carpet of grasses that was thick along the Snake and Columbia River basins supported buffalo that grazed up the Lemhi Valley and upper Snake region and which, until the mid-nineteenth century, were pursued by Indians all the way into present-day Montana. This was also a landscape whose valleys supported a host of edible roots. As one moves northward from the Great Basin piñon nut region and into the Columbia Plateau proper, the all-important native food was camas, which, along with other tubers, provided sustenance for many of these western peoples (see chapter 5).

Even before entering the Madison River valley that provides a principal westerly portal into Yellowstone National Park, one has traversed Indian-occupied country of considerable antiquity. In recent years the windswept sagebrush flats of southeastern Idaho have been revealing evidence of dense native occupation over a considerable time-depth. Within the sprawling lava plateau are such recently discovered sites as Scaredy Cat Cave, which, it is hypothesized, was utilized by early Shoshoneans or their forebears as a meat locker for possibly four thousand years. Located only about one hundred fifty miles southwest of the park's West Yellowstone entrance, this dark, cool, natural chamber has revealed to Bureau of Land Management archaeologists old picks made from elk antlers, which may have been used to dislodge the stored bison meat from the ice; decaying remains of sagebrush stalks, which probably helped to insulate the cool food stores; and fragments of woven baskets and broken stone pestles.[4]

About fifty miles closer to West Yellowstone and more directly on the Snake River corridor that led many Shoshoneans to the Yellowstone is the region's archaeological counterpart to the spectacular Mummy Cave site just over the park to the east. This is the Wahmuza site, one of a cluster of early Numic in the bottomlands near today's Fort Hall Indian Reservation. The considerable time-depth of the site that R. N. Holmer named Wahmuza, from the Shoshone word for "Cedar Point," indicated a similar sort of long-term record of material culture change among Yellowstone National Park–connected Indians to the west that Mummy Cave revealed for the east.[5]

But our reconstruction of eastern Great Basin precontact history is by no means complete. It may be some time before we can synthesize a full picture of aboriginal movements along the western boundary of Yellowstone National Park. To glimpse those movements today, one may be on firmer ground if one follows the tracks left by historical Indians, always keeping an eye open for signs that they, too, might have been traveling in the footsteps of their own or other ancestors.

All around the park, as already observed in previous chapters, were old trails that led Indians to various, familiar locations within, through, and around the park. Hints of the presence of such well-worn pathways come from the faint remains of what appear to be trail cairns or rock piles,[6] which may have guided travelers along the way. Blaze marks on trees probably prevented early Indian wayfarers from taking wrong turns in the road. The comments of early trappers and explorers frequently refer to this or that "old Indian trail" they ran across; Chittenden's early history of the park is replete with such comments, such as the important trail "in the vicinity of Conant Creek leading from the Upper Snake Valley to that of Henry Fork."[7] While "Beaver Dick" Leigh apparently named the creek for a white man who almost died there,[8] it was familiar enough to the mixed-blood Indian boys who accompanied Ferdinand V. Hayden's 1872 trip into Yellowstone that they were able to provide Sidford Hamp with its (untranslated) Indian name: *pom-pya-mena* creek.[9]

For the most part, the early exclusion of Indians from the park seems to have left present-day Shoshone and Bannock consultants with few surviving memories of the precise routes pursued by their ancestors—or perhaps they prefer to keep such information to themselves. And searching for mention of these century-old trails in the documentary record is problematic, because inevitably one tends to privilege the best-known pathways of the late historical period. Thus, when Haines attempted to reconstruct from his array of old government reports, explorers' diaries, and trappers' journals the system of old Indian trails into and out of the park area (see map 2), because of its historical importance during the Nez Perce War he felt compelled to highlight the Bannock Trail as the park's preeminent native roadway, acknowledging, "Essentially, the Bannock Trail was a system of trailways, which, together, made up a complex route."[10]

Yet in aboriginal days this now-famous Bannock Trail complex may not have experienced any greater amount of foot traffic than other native roadways in the region. As to their use over a considerable period, however, a strong piece of circumstantial evidence comes from what we can infer of early obsidian trade, which also includes hints at the directional flow of such commerce, as nicely summarized most recently by Leslie B. Davis and his study group:

> The mechanisms by which obsidian was translocated from the Obsidian Cliff plateau source to geographically distant destinations are not known. Overland transport along trails or over water are usually suggested. That the Yellowstone River would have been the gateway or passageway is likely, with continuation via one or more exchange events to a downstream corridor (or corridors) leading to the Mississippi. Obsidian may have been traded 'utilizing a generalized regional exchange system involving trading partners'.[11] To date, materials exchanged

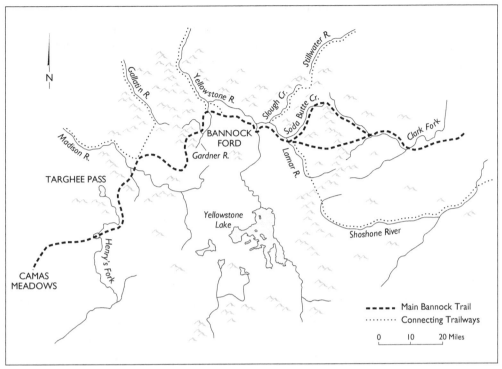

The Bannock Indian Trail and associated Indian hunting areas. (Based on a map from Aubrey L. Haines, *The Bannock Indian Trail* [Yellowstone National Park, Wyo.: Yellowstone Library and Museum Association, 1964], 4–5. Courtesy of U.S. Department of the Interior, National Park Service, Yellowstone National Park.)

or traded for the obsidian which are known to be diagnostic for Hopewell, i.e, Snyders points and Havana Ware, have not been found in the Yellowstone drainage, on the Obsidian Cliff plateau, or in the vicinity.[12] That void may reflect the transfer of obsidian from the source eastward by indigenous peoples who quarried it and transferred it to the middlemen.

Or Hopewellian traders went to the quarries and in a single procurement event, acquired sufficient obsidian to meet their needs. . . . [13] The 300 kg (660 lbs) of obsidian found cached at the Hopewell site, for example, attests to the importance, value, and energy involved in moving this high density raw material over distances, in this case over more than 680 km (1500 mi).[14]

The likelihood of such long-distance trade would also testify to the probable Indian awareness, via oral traditions, of the intervening topography and to the existence of a repeatedly used trail system. In his description of the density of such aboriginal park pathways, Chittenden opens with two lesser-known routes before addressing the more renowned west-to-east Bannock road:

Indian trails, though generally indistinct, were every-where found by the early explorers, mostly on lines since occupied by the tourist routes [which would also have contributed to the obliteration of their traces]. One of these followed the Yellowstone Valley entirely across the Park from north to south. It divided at Yellowstone Lake, the principal branch following the east shore, cross Two-Ocean-Pass, and intersecting a great trail which connected the Snake and Wind River valleys. The other branch passed along the west shore of the lake and over the divide to the valleys of Snake River and Jackson Lake. This trail was intersected by an important one in the vicinity of Conant Creek leading from the Upper Snake Valley to that of Henry Fork. Other intersecting trails connected the Yellowstone River trail with the Madison and Firehole basins on the west and with the Bighorn Valley on the east.[15]

Of all the numerous Indian pathways that threaded over the Yellowstone Plateau from all sides, it still remains the Bannock Trail, cutting across the two-hundred-mile width of the park from Henry Lake to the Shoshone River, that has captured the imagination of historians and Indian buffs alike. For western Indians, it possessed the practical virtues of steering clear of dangerous Blackfeet country and offering open, grassy oases dark with meandering buffalo, and its linkage of valleys and climb-overs promised the smoothest traveling to be expected in such a mountainous region. To outsiders, however, its fame undoubtedly derived from its prominent role during the so-called Nez Perce War of 1877, and because some of its overgrown furrows, originally gouged by generations of tipi poles tied to the sides of files of Indian ponies with their ends dragging along the ground, can be detected to this day.

A fairly comprehensive reconstruction of this Bannock Trail is possible because of the work of park naturalist Wayne F. Replogle and his wife, Marian, who devoted eight years, from 1948 to 1956, to reconstructing the winding path followed by the Bannock Trail and its branches,[16] and park historian Aubrey L. Haines, who built on Replogle's efforts eight years later. Here we provide Haines's condensed description, written in 1964:

> That portion of the Bannock Trail which lay across what is now Yellowstone Park can yet be traced on the ground almost throughout, and it will give a better idea of the nature of the route to trace it in detail. From the point near Horse Butte in the Madison Valley, where the main trail from the Camas Prairie, via Targhee Pass, was joined by branches up the Madison and Gallatin Rivers, the trail entered what is now the Park by way of the Duck Creek drainage, approximately ten miles north of West Yellowstone, Montana. It then followed the edge of the valley in a southward swinging arc almost to Cougar Creek, before doubling abruptly northward to pass over the Gallatin Range west of Mount Holmes, at an elevation of over 9,300 feet (2,750 feet of climb from Horse Butte).

Once over the top, the trail followed down Indian Creek to its junction with the Gardner River, where there was a branching; the main trail crossing Swan Lake Flat and descending through Snow Pass to the vicinity of the present Park headquarters at Mammoth, while a cut-off passed between the Gardner River and Bunsen Peak to rejoin the main trail below the present high bridge over the Gardner.

At Mammoth, near where the hydro-electric powerhouse now stands, the main trail was joined by an Indian trail ascending the Gardner River from the Yellowstone (an exit which gave access to the buffalo range in the valley between Yankee Jim Canyon and Livingston, Montana.)

Southeast of Mammoth, the trail crossed the Gardner River and ascended the east bank of Lava Creek to the vicinity of the present campground, then crossed Blacktail Deer Creek, where it was joined by two minor Indian trails, one from the mouth of the Gardner (later known as the "Turkey Pen Trail"), and one to the ford over the Yellowstone River below the mouth of Oxbow Creek. From the junction on Blacktail Deer Creek, the main trail continued across the high meadows to Crescent Hill, which it rounded on the south side through a narrow ravine later designated as The Cut. Descending steeply to the site of Yancy's Ranch, the trail crossed Pleasant Valley to the Yellowstone River, and passed upstream, over the top of Overhanging Cliff to a crossing of Tower Creek at the present automobile campground.

Where the trail crosses Antelope Creek, it is plainly visible from the road, and it was there joined by an Indian trail from the Canyon area, via the western flank of Mount Washburn. Continuing down the Yellowstone River, a crossing was made at the ford near what are now called the "Sulphur Beds."

Once over the river, the trail climbed out of the canyon to enter the Lamar Valley through the "Horseshoe." From there the route held close to the foot of Speciman Ridge and Amethyst Mountain, branching off another minor Indian trail to the Stillwater and Rosebud Rivers by way of Slough Creek. At the mouth of Soda Butte Creek, the main trail itself branched; one fork passing the Clark Fork River by way of Soda Butte Creek, and the other reaching that river more directly by following up the divide between Cache and Calfee Creeks. An Indian trail from the Upper Lamar and Shoshone rivers joined the route at the mouth of Cache Creek.[17]

Another controversial topic connected with this western flank of the park, the relationship between Indians and fire, deserves mention. Anyone retracing the winding route of the historical Bannock Trail from west to east today runs into the burned-over countryside around West Yellowstone, left over from the ravaging fires of summer 1988, which began on July 22 with an illegal woodcutter tossing out a cigarette butt on the Moose Creek Plateau. Most extensive of the seven major burns that eventually destroyed about a million acres of park ground cover was the North Fork blaze.[18] Even before that recent conflagration, however, some observers sought to bring Indian data to bear on the debate over whether to "resume an ancient approach of using fire to accomplish multiple objectives."[19]

Those advocating the environmental benefits of such man-made fires often point to evidence, especially strong for America's eastern woodlands[20] and for California,[21] that the habitats encountered by the first Europeans had already undergone considerable alteration, much of it by fire.[22] Indeed, there are arguments that intentionally using fires to drive game into concentrated bunches for easier hunting—and perhaps to expand rangeland for buffalo or to encourage the growth of browse to attract deer—occurred in and around Yellowstone National Park.[23]

But opinions differ strongly as to the utilization of fire by Indians in the park. The fire ecologist George Wuerthner contends:

> Though Indians occasionally passed through Yellowstone, and one small group called the Sheepeaters lived there year-round, it is uncertain how many fires they may have caused in the Yellowstone ecosystem. Because of their overall low numbers and the infrequency with which they passed through the area, the Indian influence on fires [in the Park] is likely to have been less than it was in other places, such as the Great Plains, for example.[24]

This position seems premised on the lighter use of the park by Indians than that proposed by Spence, who, contrary to Wuerthner, has recently suggested:

> Seasonal burns opened up broad savannas favored by ungulates, created "open districts" in the forest that eased travel, and encouraged the growth of valued grasses, shrubs, and berries, and tubers. Smaller fires kept favored camping sites free of underbrush and insect pests and served as an important hunting tool.[25]

Direct evidence still remains too thin to make a solid case about the degree to which Yellowstone National Park proper was subject to alteration by intentional Indian fires, although some scholars have tried.[26] At the same time there do exist scattered, circumstantial data on the widespread practice of Indian-set fires, serving multiple purposes, throughout the greater Yellowstone ecosystem. To the east, for instance, it was on August 23, 1805, while traveling west through the Beaverhead Valley, that Captain Meriwether Lewis weighted his canoes with rocks and dunked them in a pond to protect them from "the Fire that is Frequently kindled in these plains by the natives."[27]

To the west, the Nez Perce also significantly altered their regional environment this way. The anthropologist Alan G. Marshall writes:

> The use of fire by the Nez Perce to improve game habitats . . . was noted in 1900 by John Leiberg, a forest ecologist. His studies of the Bitterroot Forest Reserve showed that two-thirds of it had been burned at least twice in the previous 150 years. Nez Perces both then and in the present have maintained

that such burning increases game populations, especially elk and deer. Thus, the very character of this region's forests was affected by the Nez Perce management practice. Fire was similarly used on the region's prairies; reportedly, camas meadows were also burned.[28]

To the north, the Flathead, Pend d'Oreille, and Kootenai ignited the lichens hanging from trees so as to kill insects, halt the spread of tree diseases, help to prevent the spread of wildfires, and improve forage for grazing.[29] But apparently these particular Plateau peoples set their fires in an ad hoc, nonpatterned way, or whenever their movements prompted them to clear trails, to encourage the growth of browse for deer, elk, and horses, to create signals to communicate over long distances, and even as a shamanic technique for influencing the weather—all of which, the Indians maintain today, would simultaneously have bolstered the growth of pasturage for deer, elk, and horses.[30]

Lieutenant Gustavas C. Doane may have identified a hunting technique when he reported a fire in 1870 along the Gardiner River, closer to the park's northern entrance, with apparently multiple points of origin; he believed the fire had been set by Indians "to drive away the game."[31] Even as late as 1887, a newspaper report entitled "Indian Marauders" testifies to Indians along the western boundary of the park employing this fire-drive technique:

A serious danger menaces the game and forests of a portion of the Yellowstone National Park. This danger arises from the invasion of the country to the south and west of the reservation by Indian hunting parties, principally Bannocks and Shoshones from the agencies at Fort Hall, Lemhi and Washakie.

These Indians leave their reservation and proceed toward the borders of the Park, where they destroy great numbers of elk, drying the meat for winter use, and carrying it and the hides to their home. A far more serious injury than the destruction of game which thus takes place, is caused by the forest fires which these Indians kindle to drive the game from one place to another, or to prevent it from going to certain directions. In this way thousands of acres of living forest are frequently burned over, and an amount of harm is done that the growth of a quarter of a century cannot repair.

Captain Harris has known of this state of things for years, and has done everything in his power to keep the Indians away from the Park. He has repeatedly notified the interior department of these depredations but the agents in charge of these Indians have met his remonstrances with demands of facts which are perfectly well known to all travelers in the southern portion of the Park.[32]

Yet Indians who relied on fish and traveled on foot through the mountains could also maintain a healthy wariness of fire. Some Sheep Eaters of central Idaho told G. A. Thompson that it was actually their practice to fight wildfires because of their "great fear" of the devastated canyons left in their wake.[33] Today, managers of what remains of American Indian cultural resources in the park have good reason to feel threatened by fires. When the flames of 1988 drove through the Mammoth Hot Springs and Tower Junction areas, they quickly consumed whatever dried-wood remains of old Indian dwellings, pole storage locations, or fenced game drives lay in their path.

Western Indians and the Greater Yellowstone Region

The Bannock

The Bannock, speakers of a Shoshonean dialect that springs from the great Uto-Aztecan language family, called themselves Bana'kwut, or "Water People," although others knew them by more pejorative titles, such as "Diggers" or "Robber Indians."[34] Hailing from northern Paiute stock with an aboriginal homeland located possibly in the eastern Oregon plateau, these Bannock obtained horses in the late 1600s from Ute Indian traders to the south; their lives were never the same. Under the widespread, group-naming tendency that we have described for their new Northern Shoshonean allies, in the early days the Bannock names for their various subgroups betrayed an intimate association with localized ecosystems. For instance, there were Bannocks known as Kutsshundika, or "buffalo eaters"; Penointikara, meaning "honey eaters"; and Shohopanaiti, or "cottonwood Bannock."[35] With the rapid spread of their horse culture, however, it was the first group, "buffalo eaters," who bloomed into the Bannocks of historical chronicles, and whose fortunes left their imprint on the history of the greater Yellowstone ecosystem.

As these early Bannock shifted their base of operations into the Snake and Lemhi River valleys and the Bridger Basin, they formed a close affiliation, some maintain a virtual "confederation" that not infrequently was sealed through intermarriage, with the already resident Shoshone. From here they launched their eastern forays in search of buffalo to be found in especially plentiful numbers in the plains dubbed by them "Buffalo House," around Laramie.[36] And while en route there, crossing the Yellowstone before dropping down the Big Horn valley, these Sho-Ban were not averse to exploiting raiding opportunities along the way. Indeed, relations between these two tribes grew so interdependent that Deward E. Walker Jr.'s most recent argument is that "[t]he artificial distinction between the Bannock and the Shoshone as separate cultures must be discarded. The two groups comprised one social system during the protohistoric and historic periods."[37]

Despite Walker's recent comments on the indivisibility, starting with their earliest days together, of the Shoshone and Bannock and the fact that non-Indians often found it difficult to tell the two tribes apart, one does discover commentary on psychological and physical differences between them. While some non-native observers found the Bannock more "aggressive,"[38] a few Indians today will confide that the Bannock were "always the bigger people, taller."[39] And based on his fieldwork,

Bannock Indian brush lodge, circa 1900. (Photo courtesy of Idaho State Historical Society, Catalog #77-69.4.)

Liljeblad believed that although prior to the Shoshoni-Bannock merger the Bannocks were not known for their sociopolitical development on a level much larger than the "band," once they allied with the Shoshoni they "tended to be a dominating group whenever they settled with the Shoshoni."[40] It was also Liljeblad's impression that whereas the Shoshone could be characterized as "extreme individualists," the Bannock appeared more willing to "sacrifice their personal differences and to follow their leaders in achieving concerted action."[41] At the same time, the old internal distinction between the mounted and "walker" members of the Sho-Ban world continued to provide grist for interethnic stereotyping, as the horse-riding Fort Hall Indians joked about their pedestrian bands who were so poor they became cannibals in destitute times and "could only keep themselves upright by placing forked sticks under their chins." But in retaliation, descendants of the Sheep Eaters would complain about "the haughtiness, quarrelsomeness, and clannish egotism" exhibited by the horse-owning bands.[42]

Once they were on horseback, the entire Yellowstone Plateau sat in the lap of Bannock territory, for their tribespeople of the late eighteenth and early nineteenth century freely hunted through southeastern Idaho and western Wyoming but could also be found down the Snake River, up the Salmon River, and into southern Montana. The eventual residence of these peoples was forecast five years later, when Nathaniel Wyeth established Fort Hall in 1834. However, it would take until 1878 for the freedom-loving tribe to be forcibly ensconced on the Fort Hall Reservation. Never a numerous nation, their population is estimated at 1,000 members in 1845, and, according to the Indian agent for the Eastern District of Oregon, only 700 by 1859.[43]

Until the mid-1830s the countryside of eastern Idaho covered by Bannock hunters was home to ample numbers of buffalo, on which tribes from the Rocky Mountains all the way west across the plateau to the California Sierras could survive. As Russell wrote in 1841, "In the year 1836 large bands of buffalo could be seen in almost every little valley on the small branches of this stream." Indeed, four years ago representatives of the Bannock tribe claimed that "Buffalo Country" was their original name for the Yellowstone National Park area.[44] However, the intensity of buffalo hunting, white settlement, and mounting overland use of the trails heading west meant that five years later it was a much different story, as "the only traces which could be seen of them were the scattered bones of those that had been killed."[45]

With almost no adequate meat supply left on the Snake River plain by the early 1840s,[46] Bannock hunters were forced to range wider and to undertake lengthier journeys. Now these long-distance hunting trips became annual affairs, and increasingly the tribe was accompanied by its associates, the Northern Shoshone. On occasion, for reasons of collective security on these far-flung ventures, the Flathead, Lemhi, and Wyoming Shoshone might join them as well.[47] As Crowder writes of the Lemhi at this time, "As the buffalo were practically extinct in Idaho by 1840, the Indians of the Lemhi area had to cross the Continental Divide into Montana and travel into the Three Forks country, north and east of what is now Yellowstone National Park."[48] Along the way they might utilize any resources in their path—plants, smaller game, and minerals—and possibly they even stockpiled tipi poles en route, such as the cache of still-standing tipi poles leaning in the crotches of cottonwood trees that one finds just off the Bannock Trail in the Lamar Valley today.

The extended reach of these hunting expeditions also meant that these mixed Bannock and Shoshone parties probably had greater contact with non-Indian communities than other Plateau Shoshoneans and hence greater opportunities to raid for food and horses in order "to compensate for the loss of game and key resources."[49] Faulkner describes the broadening yearly movements of Bannocks and Shoshones that developed in the 1841–63 period following the virtual extinction of their local buffalo resources:

Families or bands began their annual quest in the spring, moving down the Snake River to Camas Prairie or to the area of the junction of the Boise and the Snake rivers. After digging camas roots and trading with other Indians, they returned upstream fishing or trading for fish on the way home. In the autumn when the leaves were turning, the Shoshoni and Bannock migrated to Yellowstone River or Green River, where they spent the fall hunting in the buffalo country, not only because they desired additional hunting in the spring, but also because of the comparably milder winters of the Yellowstone Valley. Usually, however, most of them returned to their winter camps on the Snake River.[50]

These new, more dangerous—and, to younger warriors, more exhilarating— conditions of life affected criteria for tribal leadership. They propelled to positions of authority those Bannock and Shoshone leaders with proven abilities in battle.[51] The climate of heightened mobility produced other transformations as well. Excellent horsemen, these tribes built up horse herds that numbered in the thousands, and for their relatively brief heyday, from 1820 to 1840, they lived life to the fullest, enjoying the white man's goods by trade or theft as they hunted and raided at will. At the same time, these increasingly abrasive interactions with whites, although begun on an equal and promising footing, soon encouraged a battle-ready outlook that prepared the Bannock and Northern Shoshone to strike out whenever they felt the government had reneged on promises of compensation for remaining at peace.

Contributing to their aggressive mood was one of the worst mass killings of Indians in the history of the United States. This was the annihilation of a band of northwestern Shoshone on the Bear River north of Cache Valley in Utah, on January 29, 1863. Every native member of the northern Great Basin Indian world would have heard word-of-mouth how "California Volunteers" under Colonel O'Conner had mowed down nearly two hundred fifty men, women, and children in an encounter that Madsen calls "unnecessary and cruel" and an outright "massacre" [52] and which the noted historian Alvin E. Josephy Jr. calls "one of the largest, most brutal, and, because of its eclipse by other Civil War news, least-known massacres of Indians in American history."[53] As Josephy explains, word of the tragedy spread quickly throughout the area's Indian communities, inspiring some to revenge and intensifying in others an apprehension about their survival.

At the same time, the Bannocks and their allies were more clearly grasping what they had to lose as they watched the mounting volume of emigrant traffic on the various roadways—the Oregon Trail, California Road, Lander's and Hudspeth's cutoffs—that pointed west along the various lush river valleys that spilled out of Wyoming Territory and over their old hunting and foraging grounds.

For their part, the attitudes of Euro-American emigrants, local settlers, and townsfolk from areas surrounding Yellowstone National Park began to stiffen toward

Indians, as if importing from California the discriminatory posture nurtured in the gold country over the previous two decades. Only a few months before the Bear River killings a local man in Bannack, Montana, "bought a Sheep-Eater squaw; but she refused to live with him, alleging that she was ill treated."[54] When an elderly tribesman came to her defense, some barroom toughs immediately "declared, while drinking, that if the d——d cowardly white folks on Yankee Flat were afraid of Indians, they were not" and fired at point blank range into the tipi, killing the chief, a boy, and a baby. Before they were completely exonerated by a local jury they explained that this was revenge for the killing by Indians of their friends during the 1849 California gold rush.[55] Others would continue to draw unflattering associations between Great Basin Indians of California and Utah and the horseless Shoshoneans they found in and around the park. Wrote Dr. A. C. Peale, a mineralogist who accompanied F. V. Hayden's 1871 survey to Yellowstone, after discovering clear evidence of Indians in the northeastern corner of the park:

> We concluded that the Indians must belong to the same class as the Diggers. When Utah was settled by the Mormons, the Ute, Bannack, and Snake Indians were driven out, and as the game disappeared they were obliged to separate into small bands. Some were driven to the mountains [and] having no ponies they are very poor, and live principally by stealing.[56]

It is necessary to evoke this general climate of ethnic animosity west of Yellowstone National Park in the 1860s and 1870s if we are to understand the context and motivations for the Nez Perce, Bannock, and Sheep Eater outbreaks that now were about to affect park history. For some citizens to the west in Idaho Territory, for instance, an often-quoted editorial from a Boise newspaper in fall 1867 expressed the widely shared sentiment about Indians at this time:

> This would be our plan of establishing friendship on an eternal basis with our Indians: Let all the hostile bands of Idaho Territory be called in (they will not be caught in any other manner) to attend a grand treaty; plenty of blankets and nice little trinkets distributed among them; plenty of grub on hand; have a jolly time with them; then just before the big feast put strychnine in their meat and poison to death the last mother's son of them.[57]

The words of Montana congressman James Cavanaugh, uttered the following year during debate on an "Indian Appropriation Bill," echoed how many locals north of the park felt about free-roaming western Indians:

> [I]n my judgement, the entire Indian policy of the country is wrong from its very inception. . . . The gentleman from Massachusetts may denounce the sentiment as atrocious, but I will say that I like an Indian better dead than living . . . I believe in the Indian policy which was taught by the great chieftain of Massachusetts, Miles Standish.[58]

To the east and south of the Yellowstone Plateau, a large measure of public opinion regarding any native obstacle, Shoshone, Bannock, or otherwise, to Wyoming's incoming pioneers, was reflected in this editorial from a major Wyoming newspaper only two years later:

> The Indians must stand aside or be overwhelmed by the ever advancing and ever increasing tide of emigration. The destiny of the aborigines is written in characters not to be mistaken. The same inscrutable Arbiter that decreed the downfall of Rome, has pronounced the doom of extinction upon the redmen of America. The attempt to defer this result by mawking sentimentalism in favor of savages is unworthy of a great people. . . . If these Indian treaties have got into such a tangled knot that they cannot be untied, the sword of the pioneer will sever them.[59]

THE NORTHERN SHOSHONE

When the early linguist and folklorist James Teit collected ethnographic information among the Salishan peoples of the eastern Oregon plateau from 1907 to 1917, they gave him the strong impression that, in their view, "to the south, both east and west of the rockies" there were no tribes *that were not* branches of the 'Snake,'" or Shoshone. As for the country "[e]ast of the Rockies," his Indian informants led Teit to believe the following:

> Shoshonean tribes occupied the Upper Yellowstone country, *including the National Park*, and they are said to have extended east to the Big Horn Mountains or beyond. . . . Farther north Shoshonean bands occupied the country around Livingston, Lewiston and Denton. How far east and down the Yellowstone they extended is not known; but they are thought to have at one time held the country around Billings, and most, if not all, of the country where the Crow Indians now have a reservation.[60]

Apart from the critical but characteristic neglect of a time frame in this Salish-oriented description of Shoshone territory, and ignoring for the moment the important question of whether "holding" is the most accurate term to characterize land use customs of highly mobile Shoshonean bands, the quoted passage at least provides an Indian perspective on the virtual encompassment of the greater Yellowstone ecosystem by members of the Shoshonean peoples all along the southern half of the park. Among their Siouan and Algonquian-speaking enemies, these Shoshoneans were maligned far and wide as "Snake Men" (Chippewa) or "Rattlesnake Men" (Yankton Dakota). At the same time, other Plains tribes, who enjoyed better on-again/off-again trading relations with the Shoshone, often adopted the more neutral name for them of "Grass Lodges" (Crow), or "People that use grass or bark for their houses or huts" (Arapaho).[61] As for self-designations, the Fort Hall Shoshone came to know themselves as Bohogue, meaning "Sage-brush Butte," tying them to a promontory northeast of Fort Hall. Although their Lemhi Valley and lower Snake River linguistic kinfolk adopted this term as well, the Bannock knew the Fort Hall people as Wi:nakwut, which probably meant "Iron Knife."[62]

Because of their wide geographic range and highly changeable social and political organization, the total Shoshonean population was almost impossible to tabulate over these early decades. Whereas in 1845, according to the rough estimate of Indian agent Jacob Forney, the combined numbers of Shoshones and Sheep Eaters was about 4,500 souls,[63] this figure overlooked the highly localized, independent nature of their subgroups. One of the largest of these Shoshonean populations were the group known as Pa:dai, or "Water," because its 200 families, who foraged over a 27,000-square-mile area, had their base camps along Idaho's Lemhi River, around present-day Salmon.[64] A portion of this group identified themselves as Sheep Eaters, but the influence of the horse, which the Lemhi Shoshone obtained from Spaniards, was significant in attracting many of these independent mountaineers to relocate in the larger, horse-riding villages, with their centralized control and authority under permanent chiefs. When the Lemhi hosted Lewis and Clark in 1806, the explorers counted about four hundred horses and also noted the presence of Spanish bridles and brands.

As for how the Indians employed these mounts, according to Steward, an annual seminomadic pattern soon arose. Conducting the tedious task that was common among mid-nineteenth-century anthropologists of extracting lists of diagnostic cultural traits and then comparing them, Steward also found little distinction between these Northern Shoshone and Bannock, although he distinguished them from their brethren who remained on foot, such as the northerly Sheep Eaters. As Steward summarized the new lifestyle:

> The two [Shoshone and Bannock] seem to have wintered together and pastured their horses in and near the lush bottomlands of the Snake River since prehistoric times. They usually made hunting expeditions together on horseback, *sometimes going east to Wyoming for buffalo*, west to Camas Prairie and beyond to trade and gather roots, and down the Snake River below Shoshone Falls for fishing. The foot Shoshoni, along the Snake River gorge below American Falls, especially on the south bank, were, in contrast to the Fort Hall Shoshoni and Bannock, impoverished, primitive in their culture, restricted in their movements, and unorganized. Few of them owned horses.[65]

When reading ethnographies that describe such "seasonal rounds" of traditional American Indian societies, however, one should not underestimate the degree to which economic opportunism dictated survival strategies, and Shoshoneans were nothing if not master survivalists. With conditions of life west of Yellowstone

National Park shifting radically year by year, these Northern Shoshoneans changed their lifestyle accordingly. When a combination of factors such as fear of Blackfeet raiders, scarcity of buffalo in the Snake River country, and greater efficiency of communal hunting made larger groups mandatory, they had no hesitation about creating multiethnic bands of Fort Hall Shoshone, Bannock, Lemhi, Nez Perce, Flathead, and Wind River Shoshone members who traveled together en masse. As sizable large parties moved eastward, they always scoured the landscape for any familiar seeds, roots, and berries they could find in the mountains. In the Yellowstone National Park vicinity, for instance, Steward notes that "they sometimes stopped briefly to gather nuts of the 'white pine' variety, known as *wongoduba*, which they either ground and carried to the plains in buckskin sacks or cached to assure food for their return trip."[66]

During that optimistic interval when horse herds were multiplying and before the imposition of government pressure to consolidate on Idaho and Wyoming reservations, one of the favorite Northern Shoshone campgrounds lay near the Menan Buttes, two old volcanic craters southwest of the junction of the Snake River and Henrys Fork.[67] As the Northern Shoshone of Idaho made the horse a mainstay of their life, the journeys launched from such camps extended. Much like descriptions of long-distance travels of Blackfeet explorers and raiders (see chapter 2), there are early references to "Pannacks" and even Shoshoneans from as far south as the Great Basin (Salt Lake) participating in hunting expeditions to the headwaters of the Missouri and the Yellowstone—journeys as great as twelve hundred miles.[68]

At the same time, for reasons of caution or cultural or environmental preference, those pockets of mountain Shoshoneans mentioned by Steward clung to their highland outposts, remaining on foot and relying on their dogs—in locations such as the headwaters of the Henry River, a tributary of the Snake, where Hunt's Astoria party came upon them in 1811.[69] Right into the days of forced consolidation on the reservation, these subgroups often retained their older Shoshonean identity. "Although the Fort Hall Bannock and Shoshoni were probably comparatively well amalgamated into a band by 1840," writes Steward—an amalgamation that Deward Walker would maintain was tantamount to a formal confederation—"there is little doubt that a few small groups continued for many years to live in isolation."[70]

But the Shoshone-Bannocks could not avoid the irony that descended on all newly equestrian tribes of the plains. Just as one loan item from Euro-American society was allowing them to cover ground and hunt more effectively and extend their tribal territories, expanding settlement by Euro-American society was closing this window of freedom. Each year after the informal opening of the Oregon Trail in 1841 the consequences of additional wagon trains trundling through their country on a proliferating number of trails and cutoffs and toll roads were not lost on the Shoshone. In 1858 Chief Washakie of the Wind Rivers described their impact to Captain Frederick Lander: "Before the emigrants passed through my country, buffalo, elk, and antelope could be seen. . . . Now, when I look for game, I see only wagons with white tops and men riding upon their horses. My people are very poor and have fallen back into the valleys of the mountains to dig roots and get meat for their little ones."[71]

Fifteen years earlier the opening phase of this traffic saw an estimated one thousand people pass through Fort Hall. Two years later that number had trebled. By 1863 the Bear Valley featured a permanent white town, with more ranches and fences crowding around the Fort Hall area with each passing year. As the distance between Indians and whites closed up, the desires of new residents for more pasturage, railroad rights, and homesites, together with anxieties about threatening Indians at large in the region, caused Idaho's territorial governor, Caleb Lyon, to establish the Fort Hall Reservation in 1867.[72]

The same year President Andrew Johnson signed an executive order that gave federal sanction to the Fort Hall Reservation, a development that was accepted by the Indians in the Fort Bridger Treaty of 1868. Initially, this document set aside 1.8 million acres of the former Bannock homeland for a separate reservation for that tribe alone. Despite the paper document, however, the Bannocks were not moved from Fort Hall, and in 1872, because of "a surveying error," a shared reservation centered at Fort Hall for both the Bannock and the Northern Shoshone was reduced to 1.2 million acres.

Meanwhile, there was another 1868 treaty that was never ratified, although it had been drafted and signed on September 24 at Virginia City, Montana Territory, between Indian Commissioner W. J. Cullen and Acting Montana Governor James Tufts. The agreement saw twelve members of "the mixed Shoshone, Bannacks and Sheepeaters" accept two townships on the North Fork of the Salmon River about twelve miles above Fort Lemhi.[73] In his accompanying remarks to the treaty, Commissioner Cullen described the threesome as a "mixed nation" scattered "from the Yellowstone to a mountain between the Bitter Root and Big Hole, running through Montana into Idaho."[74]

What makes this document valuable is how it sheds light on the cultural territory and desired lifestyle of these Bannock and Shoshone. Most important to the Indians was their clearly stipulated right to travel to their Camas Prairie and to continue long-distance trips to the buffalo country. According to Doty, while the Shoshones had described their eastern boundary at the Virginia City conference as the crest of the Rocky Mountains, "it is certain that they, as well as the Bannacks, hunt the buffalo below the Three Forks of the Missouri, and on the headwaters of the Yellowstone and Wind rivers. . . . [T]hey wander over an immense region, extending from the fisheries at and below Salmon Falls, on the Shoshonee [Snake] river, near the Oregon line, to the sources of that stream, and to the buffalo country beyond."[75]

A year later, in another treaty finally signed on February 24, 1869, between the United States and the Bannock, it was stipulated that the tribe "shall have the right to hunt upon the unoccupied lands of the United States so long as game may be found thereon, and so long as peace subsists among the whites and Indians on the borders of the hunting districts."[76] But when Wyoming Territory was admitted into the Union as the forty-fourth state on July 10, 1890, there was an express declaration that it should have all the powers of other states over its lands, and make no special provisions for Indians, whether or not they had a treaty.[77]

Despite the presumed pacification and confinement of these Indians on the Fort Hall Reservation, however, white relations with their neighbors remained uneasy over the next three decades. In 1873 ranchers in the area were reported as increasingly "annoyed," as Special Commissioners John P. C. Hanks, T. W. Bennet, and Henry W. Reed reported to the secretary of the interior about "roving bands of Indians . . . near whitemen's homes [which] causes distrust and fear on the part of women and children, and their universal custom being to carry all their effects with them, their horses turned upon the prairies encroach on the inclosures of the whites."[7]

THE NEZ PERCE

At first it seems only a twist of fate that linked the geographically distant Nez Perce tribe with the history of Yellowstone National Park. We are referring, of course, to their famous evasive maneuvers through the region in 1877, as described below. But no sooner did the Nez Perce acquire horses after 1700 than they apparently began exploring the wider world to the east, as hunters, traders, and raiders. This exploration gained them the geographic knowledge to which an old Nez Perce warrior known to whites as Hemene Moxmox, or "Yellow Wolf," testified, when long after the 1877 war he insisted in his autobiography:

> My grandfather [maternal], Homas, son of Seeloo Wahyakt, died on a buffalo hunt in Yellowstone Park. I am not mistaken. It was at Sokolinim [Antelope] where he was buried. This is north of some hot springs. Not over or beyond any big mountain, but is above where two rivers meet. . . . *We knew that Park country, no different* [matter] *what white people say.* And when retreating from soldiers [during the Nez Perce War of 1877] we went up the river and crossed where are two big rocks. The trail there is called Pitou Kisnit, meaning Narrow Solid Rock Pass. This is on the south side of Pahniah Koos. We did not enter the Park by our old trail when on war retreat.[79]

At the turn of the eighteenth century Yellow Wolf's Plateau Indian tribe, some of whom today prefer to call themselves Nee-Me-Poo, were largely concentrated in present-day western Idaho, in the heart of their aboriginal territory, and occupying

communities of reed-mat or buffalo-hide lodges that lay north and south of the
Clearwater River. While James Mooney estimated their aboriginal population at
about 4,000 members strong and spread across some 130 villages in this area,[80] in
1805 their numbers were believed to be as high as 6,000 by Lewis and Clark.
However, less than fifty years later warfare and disease had withered their population to an estimated 1,700.[81]

Within the Nez Perce communities of this prereservation period, the primary
social groupings were known as "camps," or *wi.se.s,* which according to Walker
constituted "the smallest customarily associated group of persons tending to be
found on a seasonal basis in a given named geographical locale."[82] These camps
differed from the more sizable Nez Perce "village," or *tew?yeni.kes,* in that they
only possessed usufruct privileges over the environment, whereas the village was
considered to "own" its geographic territory. The highest level of Nez Perce
sociopolitical grouping was the "band," which was composed of several villages
located along a larger stream into which each of the village streams emptied.[83]
However, this one-dimensional picture of a static social hierarchy and structural
sameness over the Nez Perce landscape must be altered by two real-life facts of
their existence.

The first concerned cultural diversity within the Nez Perce world across space,
for throughout the southeastern plateau the bands of Nez Perce "were clearly
distinguished from one another and had well-known dialectical, ecological, and
economic differences."[84] The second was their evolving character over time, for
though always in a state of some flux, the lifestyle of these Nez Perce began to
change dramatically as the different historical exposures of separate bands to the
horse culture of the plains after 1700 only widened the subtribal specializations
among them. Living in deep riverine canyons, for instance, the two main bands
of the Salmon River Nez Perce, often derogatorily known as *eneynu ti.to.qam,*
which Walker translates as "provincials," kept relying on their fish and root diet
despite the intrusion of horses.

However, those bands north of the Clearwater, who were more influenced by the
Plains culture and took to horses early on, became known as *k'usaynu ti.to.gan,* or
"sophisticated people." They would mock their pedestrian kinfolk with humorous
imitations of their eating dogs, and make fun of their preference for huckleberries
rolled in salmon fat over the more manly buffalo flanks.[85] Thanks in part to their
commercial and social interactions with the Flathead and especially with the Crow,
it was these Nez Perce who greatly expanded their worldview. As to the degree to
which this cultural cross-fertilization expanded their geographic freedom as well,
the leading expert on the tribe, Deward E. Walker Jr., asserts:

> The Nez Perce had a pretty full knowledge of that area that would include
> present Montana, Wyoming, South Dakota, probably Nebraska, and the river
> systems, the mountain systems, the locations of the different tribes. . . . The

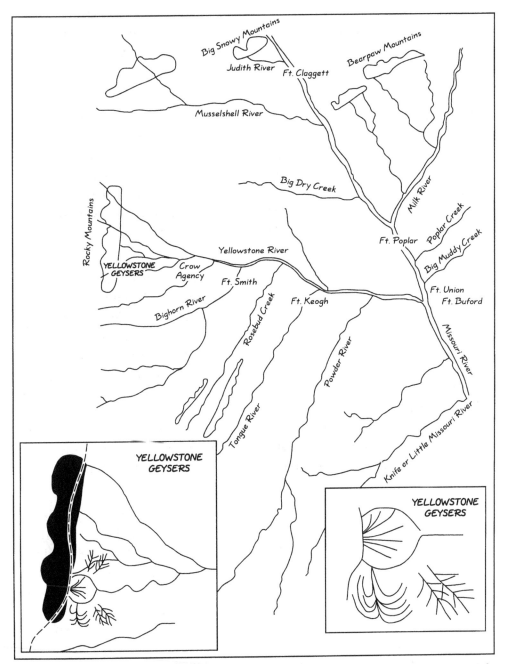

Map of the Yellowstone–Milk River country drawn by the Cheyenne scout Crazy Mule during the Nez Perce campaign; the more detailed insert shows the Yellowstone geyser field. (Based on a map from G. Fredlund, L. Sundstrom, and R. Armstrong, "Crazy Mule's Maps of the Upper Missouri, 1877–1880," *Plains Anthropologist* 41, no. 155 (1996): 14–15. Courtesy of Joslyn Art Museum, Omaha, Nebraska.)

Crow came over to Idaho to trade horses often and there's a lot of exchange back and forth. You know, I think anthropologists have got themselves much too limited in their thinking about tribal movements. I've always run into this with archaeologists especially; people erect boundaries that tribes never understood, recognized, or even now agree with, concerning the range of their movements.[86]

Although the violent interchange in Yellowstone Park in 1877 only involved rebellious remnants of the Lower Snake and Salmon-Wallowa groups of the tribe, and the park lay somewhat to the southeast of their traditional range, it is probable that a general Nez Perce awareness of routes across the greater Yellowstone preceded those exploits. During his forty years of fieldwork among Plateau tribes, Walker took road trips on both sides of the Rocky Mountain uplift in the company of Nez Perce, Kootenai, Flathead, and Wind River consultants. He summarizes the experience:

In the process it became apparent to me that there were a number of fairly well established pathways or trail systems that they followed. Lolo [Pass] of course, which goes to Flathead country, and then the southern pass that they would go through, or the southern trail that they would take is now the one that goes across Bannock Pass, not far from Leadore, Idaho. They would go up and over there *and down into the Park area on a regular basis*, sometimes even accompanied by some of the Lemhi. . . . They usually went in pretty big [multi-tribal] parties because they were afraid of the Lakota and they were afraid of the Blackfeet. . . . I would say that the Nez Perce . . . looked upon the Park as a friendly place, a place where there was good hunting, none of this stuff that the Swedish ethnographer [Åke Hultkrantz] talks about, no fear of the geysers or any of the other stuff he said worried other tribes. I don't think he's right about that. I think that's all nonsense.[87]

Occasionally one runs across older documents to back up Walker's assertions about Nez Perce interaction with other tribes. Their friendly trade with, intertribal marriage among, and artistic influence on Crow culture has been well studied.[88] They also enjoyed a clearly marked, eight-hundred-mile trail from Lapwai across the Salmon and Boise Rivers to the Wind River country, where they hunted for buffalo and returned to the Columbia River with hides for trade with those fisherman groups.[89] But these same sources also touch on the potential drawbacks of such adventures, such as the report of a clash with the Sioux east of Yellowstone Park around 1867. Eight of the Nez Perce were killed, and under cover of night they wrapped the corpses in raw buffalo hides, lashed them to the backs of their ponies, and rode for thirty days before returning safely to Lapwai, Idaho.

To get within range of the easterly trails leading into and bordering the park, the Nez Perce of Idaho might well have turned east from their own "ancient Nez Perce Indian Trail," which headed into the Snake River country "by way of the Seven Devils [Mountain], crossed over the mountains, and wound down into the

Wester River drainage," a major route for the horse trade used by Spokanes, Flatheads, and Cayuse as well.[90] Before finding themselves that far south, however, the Nez Perce hunters would probably have headed west, skirting the northern rim of Lemhi and Shoshone-Bannock territories, to hasten through the Yellowstone Plateau in search of the buffalo herds. That they might not have been inhibited from striking through the center of the park area itself was suggested by the Nez Perce historian Adeline Fredin to Joseph Weixelman. As she wrote to him, "[The] geysers/hot springs were a ceremonial and religious part in our history/prehistory . . . It was one place where the Great Spirit existed and we could bath the body and spirit directly."[91]

Indian "Wars" of the West and Yellowstone National Park

Some 1,470 incidents of military action are officially enumerated by the U.S. War Department against American Indians between the years 1776 and 1907. Only two of these actions were ever formally elevated to the status of "war" under U.S. Army typology: the Nez Perce "war," which lasted from May 14 to October 1, 1877, and covered a theater of skirmishes that encompassed 1,170 miles, and the 1878 Bannock Indian "war" in Idaho, Washington Territory, and Wyoming Territory. Another action, often referred to as the Snake or Sheep Eater Indian campaign or "troubles," took place from August to October 1879 in Idaho.

Before summarizing these three conflicts and their connections to Yellowstone National Park in particular, an introductory word on what the historian Frederick E. Hoxie has called the "self-justifying rhetoric" of violence in the history of Indian–white relations seems in order.[92] As we have already seen, traditional historians of the Indian wars of the West generally adopted terms such as *raid, skirmish,* and even *feud* to characterize the intrusions by parties of Blackfeet and other tribes into the Yellowstone Plateau during the early fur-trapping and "mountain man" years. In those instances the terms usually evoked stealthy, hit-and-run attacks by adventuresome Indian warriors on the prowl for guns, horses, or furs from whomever they might encounter, Indians or non-Indians. These terms covered the glancing encounters and hand-to-hand combat necessary to acquire the war honors and booty that would win heightened status for tribesmen once they returned home.

So we might well ask if the conflicts discussed here were in fact full-fledged wars, or are they more aptly characterized on an individual basis as "a military version of that childhood game known as blind man's buff," which is how Aubrey Haines described the Yellowstone Park chapter of the Nez Perce War of 1877,[93] or "a summer of fox-and-hounds chase," as Brigham Madsen referred to the Bannock War of 1878,[94] or a "pathetic affair . . . committed to memory by Idaho historians under the presumptuous title of 'the Sheep Eater War'" of 1879, in the words of Sven Liljeblad.[95]

What is similar about the violence of this action, however, is that the anxieties raised by the native peoples moving freely in and around the park's western boundary presented opportunities for military authorities to argue for their own protective necessity to the park. They provided justification for park officials' efforts to persuade Indian agencies to keep tighter rein on their Indians. We also detect a semantic shift in terminology. Instead of *raid* or *attack,* we now have the formalized introduction of that inflammatory word *war* and the intrusion of a logic of military retaliation that it kicked into gear.

Throughout the history of Indian–white relations we often get the impression that this shift from "raid" to "war" reflects the spirit of the times, when an emotional vocabulary was needed for military strategists and their supporting politicians to respond to public outcry for redress against perceived threats to its security. On the other hand, might not this rhetorical shift have also quite accurately reflected new terms of engagement, in which native peoples had decided to resist diplomatic or other maneuvers to shrink their territory or to remove them altogether, or to mount a last-ditch form of collective defiance against perceived oppression? In the brief span of three years, the park experienced this semantic shift as it bore witness to outbreaks by invading Nez Perce (1877) and neighboring Bannocks (1878) as well as overblown problems with the western group of Sheep Eaters (1879).

Another incidental commonality among these hostilities was that they all drew the involvement of the same veteran Indian fighter, General Oliver Otis Howard. In the general's own mind, suggests the historian Robert M. Utley, there may even have been a deeper connection, for "the Bannock-Pauite War enable[d] the one-armed 'praying general' to gloss over the stains left on his reputation by the Nez Perce War."[96]

A third common feature was that none of these hostilities appear to have been directed against the park's existence or its authorities per se. But their most profound shared causes were the similar losses to each of these American Indian peoples of their ways of life and land tenure. A surprising appreciation of this deeper background shared by the Nez Perce, Bannock, and Sheep Eater conflicts was offered by Emma Carpenter Cowan, spiced with a little cultural critique of her own society. What makes her statement so unaccountably charitable is that this is the same twenty-four-year-old woman who was captured, along with her husband, George Cowan, on her second wedding anniversary, August 23, 1877, by the Nez Perce rebels in Yellowstone National Park. Despite watching her wounded husband nearly die and enduring fears for her own fate, she later wrote:

> [A] tribe of Indians is located on a reservation. Gold is discovered thereon by the prospector. A stampede follows. The strong arm of the government alone prevents the avaricious pale face from possessing himself of the land forwith. Soon negotiations are pending with as little delay as a few yards of red tape

will admit. A treaty is signed, the land is ceded to the government and opened to settlers, and "Lo, the poor Indian" finds himself on a tract of a few degrees more arid, a little less desirable than his former home. The Indian has few rights the average white settler feels bound to respect.[97]

As for their impact on Yellowstone National Park, the trio of hostilities that we profile below would rattle its public relations image for years to come. They would also leave an indelible mark on the park's management policy regarding Native Americans.

THE NEZ PERCE WAR OF 1877

Following the park's formation in 1872, there were occasional expressions of concern by its employees about poaching by Indian hunters. But it was the Nez Perce outbreak of 1877 that aroused a feeling of vulnerability among potential tourists and official concern about the park's ability to protect its borders. The immediate origins of this campaign, whose denouement included a clumsy but bloody dash through Yellowstone National Park, can be traced back to the mid-1850s. That was when an energetic governor of Washington Territory, Isaac I. Stevens, extracted millions of acres from Plateau and Columbia River Indian tribes through the most intense period of treaty making in which the U.S. government would ever engage. Among the forty-five treaties that Stevens and his aides hastily drafted and managed to authorize with Indian "signatures" was one signed in May 1855 with the Nez Perce.

The thrust of this document was the turnover by the Nez Perce of their mountains, valleys, and rivers of southeastern Washington, northeastern Oregon, and north-central Idaho and the acceptance of a 5,000-square-mile reservation in Idaho. But tribal feelings about this treaty were by no means unanimous, since it demanded the surrender of their beloved Wallowa Valley. Already splits within the tribe had been exacerbated by Christian missionaries, with the result that outsiders, at least, divided the Nez Perce into "Christian" and "pagan" factions. With the dissent over the 1855 land cessation, however, there was now an added gulf between the viewpoints of progressive, or "treaty," and traditional, or "nontreaty," members of the tribe.

In the early 1860s, after gold was discovered on the new reservation's land, some Nez Perces were pressured into accepting an even smaller reservation along the Clearwater River. However, the nontreaty group shunned both agreements, with one segment camped on the lower Salmon River under the leadership of White Bird and the other clinging to the Wallowa country, located across the Snake River in eastern Oregon. Heading the latter community was the Nez Perce named Heinmot Tooyalakekt ("Thunder Coming from Water Over Land") but who had been baptized "Joseph" at the age of three.[98] According to the Nez Perce themselves,

Nez Perce warriors revisiting the site of Baronett Bridge, which they partially destroyed in 1877. (Photo courtesy of Yellowstone National Park Archives, Catalog #Yell 37810.)

Joseph was actually a "civil chief" rather than a "war chief" whom circumstances soon thrust into military leadership. Although the fertile Wallowa Valley was opened up to white settlement and these nontreaty leaders reluctantly accepted removal, an outburst by some of White Bird's young warriors in June 1977 left four white settlers dead.

Expecting the worst, the antitreaty Nez Perce gathered their forces and took off. Within weeks a series of Indian-white clashes began to move eastward across western Idaho. Eventually the insurgent Nez Perce covered more than twelve hundred miles until their rebellion came to its denouement on October 5 on

Montana's Snake Creek, less than forty miles from the U.S.–Canada border. During a five-day portion of that exhausting chain of heated fights and nightly maneuverings, as the outnumbered Nez Perce feinted and clashed in their race for freedom, described by Utley as "one of history's great—and tragic—odysseys,"[99] the rebels were inside Yellowstone National Park. The story of their traversing of the park under Chief Joseph has been told often and requires no more than brief summary here, drawn from the accounts of William Lang, Robert M. Utley, and Cheryl Wilfong.

Some time around August 22 Nez Perce scouts are believed to have first crossed into the park, moving along the Madison and then the Firehole River and, on the morning of August 24, taking prisoner the Frank Carpenter party of tourists. The scouts returned to the main body of Nez Perce with their captives. Initially the whites were freed, but a subsequent tense encounter saw one of them severely wounded and three others escape into the trees. Riding along Trout Creek the next day, the Indians headed on to what became known as Nez Perce Ford, and on August 26 released the rest of their prisoners.

But these Nez Perce were splintered into somewhat separate groups, and one band of independent-minded warriors engaged in two more attacks on tourists, near Mud Volcano and just north of Mammoth Hot Springs, leaving two dead victims behind them. As if anxious about the consequences, the Indians quickly headed north, burning James Henderson's ranch house and then trying to put the seven-year-old Baronett Bridge at Junction Butte, at the junction of the Lamar and Yellowstone Rivers, out of commission behind them. Aside from yanking out some beams, however, and ineffectually lighting it on fire, the runaways caused only a three-hour delay as General Howard, pressing on their rear, waited for the span to be repaired.

Generals Howard and William T. Sherman then geared up their forces for a pincer movement to grab the Indians once they emerged from the Clark's Fork canyon on the park's eastern slopes. But Nez Perce scouts seem to have second-guessed their strategy. Riding to the crest of the Clark's Fork canyon, the Indians first crossed the eastern end of Sunlight Basin and then performed one of their most cunning maneuvers of the campaign. It was as if in finding a way to outsmart the whites by escaping from the Yellowstone Plateau they were making up for their fumbling around for the most efficient Madison River entry into it, which had caused that initial run-in with the tourists a week before.

Instead of exiting from Sunlight Basin in plain sight of the soldiers—headed by Colonel Samuel D. Sturgis—the Nez Perce party diverted onto a little trail that led from Dead Indian Hill, as if making for the Shoshone River. But then they doubled back and abandoned this trail altogether, descending instead down a narrow, heavily shaded, rocky draw on the east side of Dead Indian Hill, before hurriedly returning to the Clark's Fork. By this time the impatient Colonel Sturgis had repositioned his troops from the Clark's Fork over to the Stinking Water. But soon General Howard was back at the Clark's Fork canyon entrance where he discovered, to his chagrin, that the Indians were long gone. According to Nez Perce themselves, accusations that Joseph's Nez Perce were initially lost in the park are erroneous. They maintain that a man named Ho-to-toe-e, who "was familiar with the country east of the Rocky Mountains . . . he always live there, raised there," had led them through.[100]

After his exhaustive study of the Nez Perce experience in the Yellowstone Plateau, the historian William L. Lang suggests that the hungry, weary Indians most likely tarried in the park to get some much-needed rest, to hunt the grass-fattened elk, and to enjoy the meadows and groves that reminded them of home. He concludes:

> The Nez Perces wanted to stay in the Park. In other words, they decided to remain in the Park; they were not there because of disorientation or incompetence. . . . Throughout their ordeal, the Nez Perces had pursued the same strategy: avoidance of conflict with whites and attainment of sanctuary. What they wanted was their true and just homeland and an end to harassment. Those days in the Park may have been the closest they came to their goals during their heroic flight.[101]

The Nez Perce claim of long experience with this terrain is buttressed by the fact that the pass over Dead Indian Hill, at least, had experienced traffic over many years. First it was a well-known game migration route;[102] then it was part of the Bannock Trail used by different Indian groups for countless decades, after which it became known as the precipitous "Beaver Slide" stretch of an early wagon route. But we might interject here that its place-name has on occasion been erroneously associated with the Nez Perce War. The story goes that a Nez Perce insurgent was slain on top, when in fact the killing of the Indian for which it was remembered occurred the following year, during the Bannock campaign. First wounded by U.S. troops during General Miles' opening assault on the Bannocks south of Clark, Wyoming, on the following day he was said to have been killed and scalped by Crow Indian scouts. His grave was marked by a pile of stones with an upright steel bar sticking out of one side.[103]

Such was the chapter of the Nez Perce "war" that was staged in Yellowstone National Park. One still hears folklore about a clandestine meeting on the Sunlight Basin between Chief Joseph or his subchief Looking Glass and the Crow leader, Chief Plenty Coups, during these anxious days, when the Nez Perce unsuccessfully sought Crow allies in their struggle. There are also unverifiable stories that a few Nez Perces asked some friendly Crows to adopt their children in order to keep them out of harm's way. But the Crow would stick with their tried and true posture of neutrality—which did not prevent them, however, from signing on as occasional U.S. government scouts against both the Bannock and their old trading partners, the Nez Perce.

It is interesting that the climactic Nez Perce escape maneuver was conducted in the shadow of an important if enigmatic American Indian cultural feature to the north and east of the park. This is the semicircle of angular boulders atop the 8,673-foot Dead Indian Hill, which the Billings researcher Ken Feyhl recorded on July 3–4, 1976, as "Bicentennial Rock Structure #48PA44." Conjectures for its function include vision quest structure, fortification, or, most plausibly in Feyhl's opinion, an observation post.

A valuable reflection of native topographic knowledge is indigenous mapping, but finding Indian maps has proved elusive for Yellowstone. One depiction on a buffalo hide by unidentified Indians, including "among other things a little incredible, a Volcano . . . distinctly described on Yellow Stone," was collected by the governor of Louisiana Territory, James Wilkinson, and sent to Thomas Jefferson, who thereupon deposited it at the University of Virginia, where it was destroyed by a fire.[104] The only native-drawn "name glyph," or pictographic representation, for Yellowstone National Park or its geyser field that we were able to find was an indirect product of this Nez Perce campaign. It appears on a pictorial map of the 1877 war's stage of operations drawn by a Northern Cheyenne Indian scout named John Crazy Mule who was stationed at Fort Keogh in Montana Territory between 1877 and 1890.[105] One of two drawings made by this individual with red lines on lined ledger book paper in about 1880, the document was discovered among the papers of the military ethnographer, John Gregory Bourke, that are deposited in the archives division of the Joslyn Art Museum in Omaha, Nebraska.

Crazy Mule's map focuses on the Yellowstone, or "Elk," and Milk River drainages. Especially interesting are his details of the battles on Rosebud Creek and in the Bearpaw Mountains. But he also indicates a skirmish on the Nez Perce escape route near the extreme left side of the map, where the headwaters of the Yellowstone are shown branching out as they flow downward from the mountain range and past the Yellowstone geyser field. As Glen Fredlund and colleagues decipher the sprays of encircled and isolated lines beneath the isolated mountain range located here:

A knowledge of Northern Plains Indian pictography allows a rough interpretation of these pictographs; however, their specific references rely on historic sources, discussed below. Following the first trail down the left side of the map, one finds a pictograph at the foot of the mountain range on one of the upper branches of the Yellowstone River. The pictograph consists of a circle enclosing a series of short lines. Trees surround the circle. A figure apparently representing a geyser. . . . The closest interpretation this glyph allows is "they were surrounded in a grove near geysers."[106]

The Nez Perce warpath had hardly cooled before one of two typical responses by would-be tourists to Yellowstone National Park set in. Then as today there was a fascination to view the actual scene of the tense encounters, as evidenced during the tour made by the H. W. Hutton party in September 1881, which generally retraced the Nez Perce route into the park by way of the Madison Valley. After an overnight stay at Driftwood along the bank of the West Fork, the group of five female and four male visitors was thrilled to be shown the very spot "where a party of citizens from Willow camped; their object was to steal horses from Joseph band of Nez Perce. The Indians made their appearance on the bluff above their camp, fired on them and stampeded their horses, so they were compelled to go home on foot."[107]

But doubt about the government's invincibility had been cast by the ease with which those renegade Nez Perce had penetrated the sanctity of America's first national park. Even as late as 1900, the park's acting superintendent, a captain of the lst Cavalry, felt compelled to reassure a prospective visitor who had written anxiously about rumors of hostile Indians and about the whereabouts of hot springs to assuage his rheumatism: "There are no Indians in the park, and no more outlaws that may be found in any other part of the West; you would be as safe in the park as in your own home."[108]

THE BANNOCK WAR OF 1878

If the greater Yellowstone region is to be remembered for its historical role in any Indian–white hostilities, the Bannock War would actually seem a more suitable candidate than the Nez Perce affair. While the Bannock hostilities did not see any bloodshed directly within the park boundaries, its fighting raged all around it, its origins were more steeped in the region's history, and, like the Nez Perce the year before, the Bannock rebels would dash through the northern reaches of the park in the hope of joining up with Sitting Bull in Canada.[109] And finally, aftershocks from this flareup would reverberate the longest, as rumors of Bannocks on the loose in the park would be heard well into the 1890s.

In the fall of 1868 two government officials made an optimistic assessment of Bannock and Sheep Eater receptivity to settling down to constructive reservation life. "They are peacefully disposed towards the whites," wrote Commissioner W. J. Cullen and Acting Governor of Montana James Tufts in their notes to a treaty they had negotiated with these Indians. "They are tractable and intelligent, receiving instruction quite readily."[110] In no small measure it was official neglect and empty stomachs that forced the Bannocks and Shoshones at the Fort Hall Reservation to continue to break the rules. In 1875 agent W. H. Danilson, an apparently sympathetic man with a respect for the limited survival options open to his charges, reported with nonjudgmental candor:

> Owing to the small amount appropriated for their support the majority of the Indians have been obliged to resort to the mountains in quest of game for their subsistence. . . . Quite a number of the Bannacks, who have heretofore

Buffalo Horn (at far left, on horseback), a leader during the Bannock War, is shown with Bannock Indians at Fort Hall, Idaho. (Bureau of American Ethnology, Smithsonian Institution, L. Tom Perry Special Collections, Harold B. Lee Library, Brigham Young University, Neg. #P80, W. H. Jackson, photographer.)

gone to the Yellowstone country to spend the winter hunting buffalo, concluded last fall to forgo their annual hunt and spent the winter on the reservation. Unfortunately the supply of beef became exhausted about the 1st of January, and they, together with the Shoshones, were here all winter with scarcely any meat at all. They became thoroughly disgusted with the reservation, and early this summer struck out for their old hunting-grounds.[111]

The following year Danilson reported that conditions had not improved. Rations were insufficient, and even ran out completely before the year was done. Then heavy snow prevented the Indians from going out to hunt on their own, and they were forced to beg at his door to avoid starvation.[112]

So it was probably little surprise to Danilson that when the next hunting season rolled around he counted nearly half of the 1,052 Indians under his responsibility as absent from the reservation, "on the road to and from" their buffalo-hunting grounds—by which he very likely meant the Bannock Trail through Yellowstone National Park. Meanwhile, at Fort Hall rumors of troops coming to quell the Nez Perce had caused his Bannocks to be "rather restless."[113]

The provocation often cited as the match that ignited this unstable situation was non-Indian invasion of the Indians' favored grounds for digging their staff of life—bulbs of the camas plant. After the treaty of 1868 failed to protect this expanse in eastern Idaho, white stockmen and farmers took over. When herds of domesticated pigs rooted out these plants, the Bannocks became furious. In Indian oral history, this resentment was fixed in a story that held that the war actually erupted after their disturbed camas pastures were discovered in 1878; they took to the warpath immediately after the harvest. Liljeblad maintains that the insurgents actually rose up beforehand, on May 30,[114] possibly because the outrage had rendered the harvest futile and they were inspired to retaliate without delay.

The Nez Perce and Bannock outbursts shared some interesting features. First was a geographic connection. Against the background of unrest at home, it did not take much for angry Shoshones and Bannocks, fewer than two hundred strong, to break north and east, with the last surviving insurgents following much the same Yellowstone National Park route pursued by the Nez Perce the year before. A second, curious tie-in between the Nez Perce and Bannock hostilities is that whereas the Lemhi Shoshone Chief Tendoy cautioned restraint among his people, it fell to the Bannock successor to Chief Pocatello, a young warrior named Buffalo Horn, who had actually served as a government scout during the Sioux and Nez Perce campaigns, to assume command.

But the third and perhaps more important link between these hostilities was their shared spiritual ideology. Behind both flareups loomed the influence of anti-Euro-American nativistic movements, originating in spirit from the 1870 California and Great Basin Ghost Dance prophets but more directly from the new religion spawned by the Columbia River Dreamers, spearheaded by the Wanapum holy man, Smoholla.[115] The Nez Perce called their take on this Dreamer religion "Turning Around Oneself." It emphasized visions acquired in dreams, a single deity, cleanliness, and respect for the female earth.[116] Just as Chief Joseph of the Nez Perce had the Dreamer-influenced religious advisor named Toohoolhoolzote constantly by his side throughout their escape trek through the park to the eventual showdown in the Bear Paw Mountains, so did the Bannock uprising have a Northern Paiute shaman, named Oytes, from the Malheur Agency in Oregon, with his militant interpretation of Smoholla's doctrine.

As the succession of bloody clashes between a few hundred Bannock, Paiute, and Umatilla insurgents and white farmers, volunteer patrols, government surveyors, and military troops unfolded across southern Idaho and into Wyoming, the rebel leaders were picked off one by one.[117] First, Buffalo Horn was killed on June 6 in an encounter with armed Silver City, Idaho, civilians. About two weeks later, the Paiute leader, Egan, who had filled his moccasins, died in another fight on his own Malheur Reservation in eastern Oregon. As the hostile Indians then fell under the leadership of Oytes, the Bannocks and Paiutes split into smaller bands, but Oytes finally surrendered on August 12. Only a greatly reduced group of Bannock rebels remained at large.

Pursued by forces under various U.S. military officers, the rebels rustled livestock and exchanged glancing blows with soldiers as they broke for the east. In late August a group that was now down to no more than sixty to seventy Bannocks sought their old entryways into Yellowstone National Park.[118] The Indians headed over Targhee Pass and across the Madison and Gardiner Rivers, then rode up the Lamar Valley and eventually dropped down the Sunlight Basin to camp along a sharp bend where the Clark's Fork emerges onto the Bighorn Basin—about a mile from today's Belfry-to-Cody road. Embarked on a leisurely pack trip toward Yellowstone National Park, the famous Indian fighter, General Nelson A. Miles, got word of the Bannock uprising and quickly transformed from tourist to commander. Driving his troops hard toward the Heart Mountain area so that they could position an ambush from the cover of some piney hills near Bennett Creek, on September 4 Miles gave the order for the two-hour surprise attack on the unsuspecting Bannocks, who were scattered within two hours.[119]

By the time Miles had corralled about 250 Indian horses and 32 prisoners, buried the dead, and cared for the wounded, the Bannock breakout had cost at least 80 Indian lives, about 40 non-Indian casualties, and a bill to the U.S. Treasury of over $556,000. But for the park it was another blow to its image as a safe and secure vacation attraction. This new flurry of military activity in and around the plateau only reinforced an uneasiness that the region was not entirely purged of its potentially dangerous original inhabitants.

As for the captured insurgents, some were marched to Fort Brown (later Fort Washakie), others were dispersed to "allotments within the Territories," and a handful escaped only to ultimately wend their way to Fort Hall to blend in with their fellow tribespeople.[120] For the military, the Bannock affair was more of a public relations success than a military triumph. After the larger Sioux campaigns of 1876 and 1877, the outbreak cinched the arguments made by General Sheridan and others that their depleted forces needed significant reinforcement. Two years later new appropriations of money and manpower for the military poured into the northern plains.[121]

THE SHEEP EATER WAR OF 1879

One year after the Bannock War a smaller band of Idaho Shoshoneans, known as Mountain Snakes or Sheep Eaters, who lived along the Salmon River, got embroiled in what became officially listed as a "trouble," or the "Sheepeater Campaign." Although the government's problems with these Sheep Eaters involved those who resided in central Idaho and not the Wyoming–Montana hunters of high-altitude mammals discussed earlier (see chap. 3), any Shoshonean bands known by that name, such as had resided in Yellowstone National Park, were stigmatized by this conflict. Of this particular group of Sheep Eaters it is said they had greater affinities with the Plateau rather than with the Great Basin culture area. A number of them had taken up horses and buffalo hunting, although Madsen maintains that they "hunted buffalo in a seasonal cycle different from the Fort Hall pattern."[122] Long after other Shoshones settled on reservations, "a small remnant of culturally conservative Sheep Eaters kept up their old mountain life."[123]

The spark for these troubles were the killing of five Chinese on Loon Creek, a tributary of the Middle Fork of the Salmon River, and the discovery of two dead white settlers on the river's South Fork. While it was rumored around Bonanza, Idaho, that the Chinese murders may have been the work of whites disguised as Indians, it was the white deaths that prompted General O. O. Howard to investigate. Howard had already been wanting to subdue what was said to be the last holdout of hostiles from the Bannock War along the Middle Fork of the Salmon.[124] But according to Colonel W. C. Brown, who was second in command during the Sheep Eater episode, the local Indians had some justification for resisting military intrusion into their country:

> They [the Salmon River Sheep Eaters] had been in this unexplored and almost inaccessible region for generations, with apparently no hostility to the Whites, and they might be there now but for the fact that in an evil day they were joined by a few refugees from the Bannock War of 1878, and it seems probable that the murders of the Chinamen at Oro Grande (Casto) and [Hugh] John and [Peter] Dorsey on the South Fork of the Salmon in May were instigated by these new additions to the small tribe.
>
> The real Sheepeaters, the old residents, resented [Lieutenant Henry] Catley's invasion. He was trespassing on *their* country—theirs and their ancestors before them from time immemorial. They fought to repel the invader—and who would not?[125]

Looked at today, the episode seems more like a mopping-up police action than a major military campaign. Soldiers guided by Umatilla Indian scouts entered the isolated, rough country of today's Frank Church–River of No Return Wilderness Area. When snipers picked off one trooper, the Boise newspaper editorialized, "These Indians are enemies to mankind, and have no more right to live than Guerilla highway men. To shoot them down would be an act of justice to the human family."[126] The renegades seized every opportunity to ambush their pursuers, but eventually, with the Indians flushed out family by family, the soldiers accumulated forty-four "prisoners of war." It turned out that the mounted troops and their Indian mercenaries had been pursuing an enemy force whose entire artillery consisted of four carbines, one breech-loading and two muzzle-loading rifles, and a double-barreled shotgun.[127] But this campaign did not locate all of these conservative Salmon River Sheep Eaters, for according to Madsen, "Eagle Eye's band of Sheep Eaters finally settled in Dry Buck Basin in the Payette River country until the end of the nineteenth century before relinquishing their independent existence as nonreservation Indians."[128]

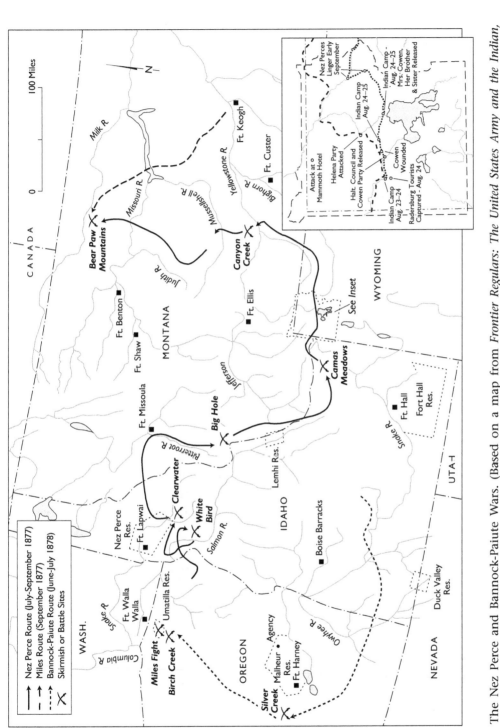

The Nez Perce and Bannock-Paiute Wars. (Based on a map from *Frontier Regulars: The United States Army and the Indian, 1866–1891* by Robert M. Utley, by permission of The University of Nebraska Press. Copyright 1973 by Robert M. Utley.)

Discouraging Indians in Yellowstone National Park

The rolling sputter of Indian–white hostilities during this 1877–79 period seemed to bear out earlier worries by park officials that the presence of Native Americans might be "a potential deterrent to tourist traffic in the Park," as Joel C. Janetski has phrased it.[129] Today we may more aptly describe these encounters as "outbreaks" or "police actions" rather than full-fledged wars, but local rumors and newspaper reports at the time raised the specter of Indian marauders lurking behind every Yellowstone tree and mountain. To minimize such bad publicity in the wake of the admittedly lethal Nez Perce actions, Superintendent Norris drew on various kinds of data about Indians and the park:

> The lamentable Indian raid, burning of houses, bridges, and massacre of inno-cent tourists within the park, soon after my leaving there, is as anomalous as unexpected; the first, and probably the last of the kind, as it is wholly aside from all Indian routes, and only chosen in the desperation of retreat by the Nez Perces, who have acquired sufficient civilization and Christianity to at least overpower their pagan superstitious fear of earthly fire-hole basins and brim-stone pits.[130]

Norris's efforts to reassure the public are interesting for a number of reasons. They can be seen as the opening salvo in what Janetski has called "the very effec-tive campaign to characterize the Park as taboo to the 'superstitious' indigenous peoples" (see chapter 5 for a fuller discussion).[131] Of this personal crusade, Spence has written:

> Norris always believed his biggest problem lay with the Shoshone, Bannock, and Sheep Eater. After meeting with the Crow he traveled directly from Wash-ington to Idaho to personally elicit a "solemn promise from all [the] Indians to abide by the terms of their treaty in Washington, and also that thereafter they would not enter the park."[132] After meeting with the acting agent for both the Fort Hall and Lemhi reservations, and then holding council with tribal leaders, Norris felt assured of the Indians' "faithful adherence." The following year he again renewed these unofficial agreements and happily reported to the Secretary of the Interior that the Indians had "sacredly observed" their pledges not to enter the park. While he never met personally with tribal leaders at the Wind River reservation, Norris apparently corresponded with the agent at Fort Washakie and felt satisfied that his concerns would be equally respected among the people living there.[133]

Norris's comments on the heels of the Nez Perce affair are also significant because here was the first time that a highly placed park official invoked any knowledge about the inner workings of Indian culture in order to exploit the stereotype that Indians were afraid of the park because of their beliefs concerning its thermal features.

Norris also drew on some knowledge of Nez Perce history, for he apparently was aware that French (and Iroquois) Catholic missionaries had successfully converted significant numbers of the tribe in the early 1800s—which was when the group's leader, Joseph, had received his Christian name. But he sounds ignorant of the fact that these Nez Perce marauders belonged to the self-consciously anti-Christian faction that had come under the influence of the Plateau Prophet movement. To these hostiles Christianity was anathema; they were in the process of consciously reviving those "pagan" beliefs that restored powers to the very Mother Earth whose actions were so awesomely apparent in the park.

Finally, despite his erroneous comment that the Nez Perce escapees had blazed a brand-new trail, Norris would grow fascinated with the density of archaeological remains in the park and evidence of widespread "Indian routes" through the region, especially the well-traveled thoroughfare followed by the Nez Perce that would be used again by Bannock renegades the following year.

Attempts to reassure visitors that the park was purged of Indians proved to be a bit premature. Since the Nez Perce and Bannock–Sheep Eater disturbances, wrote tourist George W. Wingate in 1886, after he and his wife rode horseback through the park, "the Indian difficulty has been cured, the Indians have been forced back on their distant reservations, and the traveler in the park will see or hear no more of them that if he was in the Adirondacks or White Mountains."[134] But when a *Billings Gazette* correspondent visited John Yancey's well-known stopover ranch near the mouth of present-day Yancy's Creek in February 1887, the story he heard about some Bannock families still passing through the park's northwestern corner seems like a visitation from an earlier era. His informants were Vic Smith, an old-time scout and buffalo hunter, and Dick Rock, a bronc rider, and they were recalling an event at their hunting camp on Hellroaring Creek located northeast of today's Tower Junction. Despite the obvious racial slurs and insulting characterizations of Indians in the following article that appeared on the newspaper's front page, the account confirms the continuing Bannock use of trails in the park, even in winter, as well as their reliance on dogs for transport.

About a month ago [January 1887] it seems that a dozen Bannock Indians and squaws passed this camp with toboggans on which they had meat, hides and papooses attached and dogs harnessed to haul with. The Indians, not receiving much of a welcome, they soon struck out. About half an hour after they passed on, one large dog returned bringing his sled with a pappoose strapped on it. Some poison had been distributed around the shack to kill magpies. Of course the dog took a lunch of the same and soon succumbed.

The boys had a friend from St. Paul sojourning with them. He went out and unhitched the sled from the defunct and brought the sled in, as it was bitter cold, and excavated the kid from the blankets and skins in which he was wrapped. It soon commenced to cry and as none of them had even been a father or mother they were in a dilemma. A bacon rind and then a sugar teat were given it, but it was no go, for the squalling still continued. The St. Paulite tapped his Henry Clay forehead (more clay than Henry) and cried "Eureka," and rushed out and unchained a large Newfoundland canine of the female persuasion, belong to Rock, and led her in, while Vic carried the two pups, and Rock was walking the floor with young Lo [a derogatory epithet for Indians of this period, derived from the phrase, "Lo, the Poor Indian"] and singing, "baby mine." The dog was muzzled and thrown down on the marble floor, and the two pups and young aborigine scrambled for the fullest teats. By a unanimous vote they called the kid Romulus.

In about an hour the squaw returned and claimed the maverick. As the boys did not have the youngster branded they cheerfully parted with it.[135]

Despite the public relations efforts of Norris and his successors to downplay the cultural and historical roles of various Indian groups in the park area, and their strategy of quietly pressuring the relevant Indian agencies to keep their native charges under stricter surveillance, the increasingly impoverished western Indians had minds of their own. At the same time, conservationist pressure to ban Indian interlopers often exaggerated their impact. "On the northern plains in the spring of 1883," writes Magoc, "with market hunters and sportsmen about to annihilate the last great herd of bison, *The Yellowstone Journal* furiously decried the 'slaughter' of 'our mountain bison' by 'the red ones.'"[136]

In 1886 the U.S. Army assumed control over the park in order to stop any and all threats to its animals and forests. No sooner was its first military superintendent, Captain Moses A. Harris, at his new desk, however, than his annoyance fixed on these western Indians for repeatedly trespassing into the park to camp and hunt. Harris's irritated missives to the commissioner of Indian Affairs, the secretary of the interior, and various reservation agents, as well as concerned conservationists, ignited something of a bureaucratic name-calling controversy while arousing popular eastern magazines such as *Forest and Stream* and *Frank Leslie's Illustrated* to write alarmingly in 1889 about "Indian marauders" and "the deviltry" of the Indian hunting by fire-drive method in Yellowstone.[137]

As revealed by the research of Spence and Magoc, fears of Bannock and Shoshone poachers on the loose in Yellowstone National Park were heard well through the 1890s.[138] To counter these "invasions of Indians" cutting across the southwestern corner of the park to hunt elk in Jackson Hole, a cluster of white vigilantes conspired, as the commissioner of Indian Affairs later put it, "to kill some Indians and thus stir up sufficient trouble to subsequently get United States troops into the region."[139] Spence summarizes what happened next:

Yellowstone's hot springs threaten to turn into rivers of blood when "Easy" declares the area off limits!

Indian "wars" along the western flank of Yellowstone National Park have influenced popular thinking about the historical role of Yellowstone's Indians down to the present day. This cover of a pulp novel set in the park features warlike Indians and the U.S. Cavalry company assigned to drive them out. (Cover from *Easy Company in Colter's Hell* by John Wesley Howard [New York: Jove Publications, 1981]. Used by permission of Berkley Publishing Group, a division of Penguin Group (USA) Inc.)

When a large posse arrested some thirty Bannock from the Fort Hall reservation in 1895, killing one and seriously injuring several others, their actions did far more than bring troops in to quell an Indian uprising that never happened. Within a year the Supreme Court would become involved in the question of native rights to hunt off-reservation in the state of Wyoming, and decided firmly in favor of the Jackson Hole residents. In the case of *Ward v. Race Horse*, the Court ruled that all treaties guaranteeing native rights to hunt on public lands were predicated on "the disappearance of those [public lands]." Consequently, a posse could enforce state laws that banned native hunters from lands expected to be settled sometime in the future. While it is not clear whether Yellowstone officials lobbied the court, they were certainly pleased with the ruling since it effectively restricted the Shoshone and Bannock to their reservations under penalty of law.[140]

The impact of *Ward v. Race Horse* on the legacy of American Indian relations with the Park, and its wider consequences for Indian peoples in general, derived from the fact that this was when U.S. Supreme Court Associate Justice Edward Douglas White cited legislation that had established the Park in the first place "as the legal foundation for any efforts to keep Indians off public lands."[141] Although smaller bands of Indians would continue to slip in and out of the park for various reasons over the following years, the *Ward v. Race Horse* verdict gave state and federal agencies the power to keep Indians on their reservations and out of places like Yellowstone National Park.[142]

Greater Yellowstone in Far Western Indian Memories

The shadow of historical conflict and interethnic distrust between tribes on the western and northwestern boundaries of Yellowstone National Park and Euro-Americans continues to color communications and mutual understanding in Idaho and Wyoming. The backdrop of intense hostilities and rampant frontier settlement, unratified treaties, and territorial evictions negatively affected twentieth-century attitudes of Indians toward the federal government and park authorities. Initially, for instance, our overtures to the culture committee of the Shoshone-Bannocks at the Fort Hall Indian Reservation in spring 1994 to commence interviews for this project were frustrated. Before Indian representatives at Fort Hall would make themselves available to us, they insisted on a face-to-face meeting with Yellowstone National Park Superintendent Michael Finley. Two park staff members, Laura Joss, chief of cultural resources and Susan Kraft, curator, traveled to Fort Hall to confer with tribal representatives and provide assistance with the Fort Hall Museum. Superintendent Finley met with tribal representatives at Fort Hall in November 1995. While we continued to build preliminary working relationships with Fort Hall tribal members, we passed on their requests to park officials for such an interchange at the earliest opportunity.

It was also difficult to convince Indian officials and residents from the Wind River and the Fort Hall communities that they had anything to gain from participating in a government-sponsored, fact-finding project on a federally owned and protected landscape from which they felt estranged and which never seemed to welcome their presence. During the scarce time left for our ethnographic survey, however, project consultants Sharon Kahin and Jan Nixon were able to obtain interviews with knowledgeable Fort Hall elders. As mentioned in the introduction, another consequence of the hundred-plus years of enforced unfamiliarity with the park has been the gradual erosion of tribal memory regarding any traditions and memories that fall under our category "ethnographic resources."

ORAL NARRATIVES: MYTHS AND TALES

It was especially rare to elicit from Northern Shoshoneans examples of traditional narrative genres relating to the greater Yellowstone region. However, consultant DS, an eighty-nine-year-old Bannock woman who was born in a tipi on Ross Creek in Idaho, shared what apparently was a widespread Shoshonean narrative about the old woman with the basket of salmon and the origin of certain landscape features—in this case, the origin of certain drop-offs and obstructions along the Snake and Columbia Rivers. This account would seem to belong to the category of Shoshonean narrative that tribespeople themselves knew as *l_ap_nabeguyap*, or "stories about the coyote."[143] She began:

> There's a lot of stories but I can't remember. When my grandpa and all of them started telling stories, I didn't pay attention to them. . . . About this old lady with her basket. Had salmon in it. That Fox kept going around and she told him, leave it alone. Finally, he tipped it over, and that's where that river started, came down there. That Fox kept running, and that water followed him all the way, everywhere he went, it followed him, and that's what the Snake River started. . . . Oh [remembering more details], the Fox carried that basket trying to hold the water back, and every time the water go over, and that's what Idaho Falls dam, American Falls dam, Shoshone dam, all that was caused by from that he'd trying to hold that basket, you know, so water won't go over it, then water make falls. Then he'd go another way, and he'd try it, and that make American Falls and Shoshone Falls. Finally, he got tired way down then and he just threw that basket in the river. That's what's sitting in the middle of Columbia River or Snake River.[144]

Not surprisingly, it was through a man who happened to be a direct ancestor of our Bannock consultant that anthropologist Robert Lowie, during his career's inaugural field trip for New York's American Museum of Natural History in 1909, collected two other versions of this same story at Idaho's Lemhi Reservation. The first version takes place "below Teton Basin,"[145] and the protagonist is Coyote rather than Fox. As Coyote upsets the old woman's willow fish basket, he frees the salmon. Then he performs the second important deed, which is to erect two rocks "below Ross Fork" creek, so that the fish could not descend any farther. He instructs the salmon that they must now come upstream every spring.

In Lowie's second version, the old woman treats Coyote to his first taste of salmon flesh, whereupon he first steps on the basket to spill out its fish and then constructs the dam. Only this second version follows the Bannock account above, in that "the water broke the dam," causing Coyote to dash downstream and create another dam. After this, he instructs the salmon, "Every spring you must go up the mountains and spawn."[146]

Perhaps the most elaborate version of this basic narrative was collected in 1953 from a Northern Shoshone named Ralph Dixey, who was then living in south-eastern Idaho. Dixey related the narrative to folklorist Ella E. Clark, who added in the published version that Dixey's wife, a Bannock, had also heard the story from members of her family. Unlike the foregoing variants, it directly draws topo-graphic features of Yellowstone National Park into its narrative. Here is the Dixey narrative:

> Long ago there was no river in this part of the country. No Snake River ran through the land. During that time a man came up from the south. No one knows what kind of person he was, except that among his people he was always nosing around, always sticking his nose into everything.
>
> He came through this valley, traveled north past Teton, and then went up on a mountain in what is now called the Yellowstone country. He looked around there and soon found an old lady's camp. She had a big basket of fish in water—all kinds of fish—and the man was hungry. So he said to her, "I am hungry. Will you boil some fish for me?"
>
> "Yes, I will cook some for you," the old lady answered. "But don't bother my fish," she warned, as she saw him looking into the basket.
>
> But he did not obey her. While she was busy cooking, he kept nosing around, kept monkeying around. At last he stepped on the edge of the basket and spilled the fish. The water spread all over.
>
> The man ran fast, ahead of the water, and tried to stop it. He piled some rocks up high, in order to hold the waters back. But the water broke his dam and rushed over the rocks. That's where Upper Yellowstone Falls are now. The man ran ahead of the water again, and again he tried to stop it. Four or five miles below Yellowstone Falls he built another pile of rocks. But that didn't hold the water back either. The rush of water broke that dam, too. That's where Lower Yellowstone Falls are today. The water kept on rushing and formed the Yellowstone River.
>
> Then the man ran to the opposite side of the fish basket, to the other side of the water emptying from it. He built another dam down the valley where

Idaho Falls are now. By the time he got there, the flood had become bigger and swifter. And so, though the man built a big dam, the water broke it and rushed on down the valley.

Again he ran, overtook the water, and built another dam. "Here's where I'm going to stop it," he said to himself. But the water had become bigger and bigger, swifter and swifter. So it broke that dam and left the American Falls where they are today.

The man rushed ahead and built two piles of rocks in the form of a half-circle, one pole where Shoshone Falls are now and one where Twin Falls are now. "I'll really stop the water this time," he said to himself. But the water filled the dam, broke it, and rushed over the rocks in giant waterfalls.

The man ran ahead, down to near where Huntington, Oregon, is today. There the valley narrows into a canyon. "Here's where I'll stop the water," he said, "here between these high hills."

So he built a dam and walked along on top of it, singing and whistling. He was sure he had stopped the water this time. He watched it coming toward him, sure that he would soon see it stop. It filled the dam, broke it, and rushed on down the canyon. Hell's Canyon, it's called today.

Just before the dam broke, the man climbed up on top of the canyon wall.

"I give up," he said, as he watched the water rush through the gorge. "I won't build any more dams. They don't stop that water."

After the river left Hell's Canyon, it became wide again and very swift. The water went on down to Big River and then on down to the ocean, taking with it the big fish that had spilled out of the old lady's basket. That's why we have only small fish up here. Salmon and sturgeon were carried on down to the ocean, and they have never been able to get back up here because of the waterfalls. Salmon used to come up as far as Twin Falls, a long time ago, but they don't come now.

The big fish basket that the man tipped over is Yellowstone Lake. The water that he spilled ran off in two directions. Some if it made the Snake River, as I have told you, and finally reached the Columbia and the Pacific. Some of it ran the other way and made the Yellowstone River and then reached the Missouri River.

Who was the old lady with the basket of water and fish? She was Mother Earth. Who was the man who wanted to see everything, who was always sticking his nose into everything? He was *Ezeppa*, or Coyote.[147]

What is curious about Dixey's fuller version of the origin of the Snake and Yellowstone Rivers is how it seems to be a reversal of other, Plateau narratives in which the protagonist Coyote—the "man from the south," the narratives say, as if to emphasize that this is a Shoshonean and not a Salish or Sahaptin Coyote— is involved with maximizing the fishing opportunities for his Indian people. In all of these stories we are witnessing Coyote in his role as transformer and protector of Indians, the aspect of Coyote's multiple personality that the scholar William Bright describes as "Coyote the Bricoleur," when the more positive accomplishments of this trickster figure may include "the slaying of monsters, the theft of natural resources for the benefit of man, the teaching of cultural skills, and the ordaining of laws."[148] The folklorist Jarold Ramsey sets such activities in the middle stage of the three loosely defined and overlapping time periods of Plateau Indian narratives—the Myth Age, the Age of Transformation, and the Historical Age.[149]

But in most Plateau stories where Coyote is meddling with dams in the Age of Transformation for the benefit of his Indian people, his efforts are devoted either to unsuccessfully securing salmon for those "dawn people" on the eastern side of the Continental Divide who lack the benefit of well-stocked streams[150] or to tearing down preexisting obstructions so that western "sunset" Indians can have access to the spawning runs of salmon and other fish. In the Nez Perce version of "Coyote Breaks the Fish Dam at Celilo," for instance, Coyote is en route from fishing country of the plateau to the buffalo-hunting country of Montana and stops at a waterfall along the Snake River. When he breaks a fish dam used by five sisters, he admonishes them: "You have deprived all the people of salmon and fish for such a long time by keeping them from going upstream. Now the people will be happy to get the salmon. Now salmon will go straight upriver and spawn, and the people will have salmon to eat." The narrative continues: "This is how Celilo [Oregon] originated, where the Wasco people are today. Because Coyote tore down the fish dams, salmon could come upriver and spawn."[151]

As if Coyote were attuned to the different ecological niches in which different tribes find themselves, however, in the Dixey and Lowie variants above he tries unsuccessfully to engineer exactly the *opposite effect*. On behalf of these Shoshone or Bannock ancestors of the higher altitudes, he tries to construct a series of lasting dams that will contain what precious fish Indians could find in these upstream, more mountainous regions. As with the reversals and inversions that the French anthropologist Claude Lévi-Strauss says are quite common among the Sahaptin-speaking Nez Perce, whose intermediate geographic position between "true" Plateau and Plains cultures is expressed in the fluctuating symbols of their stories, here we may be seeing another subtle reflection of the attempt by Shoshoneans to rationalize why their high country contains smaller and fewer fish than those enjoyed by both the Salish and the Sahaptin farther downstream—and at the same time an explanation for distinguishing features of the landscape that would become Yellowstone National Park.[152]

Oral Narratives: Encounters with Government Officials

In the following accounts we do not make an effort to ascertain "historical truth" since these Indian memories of brief encounters with government officials would have little evidentiary confirmation in the archival record. They constitute part of the neglected "attitudinal history" that forms much of the "ethnographic resources" associated with the greater Yellowstone ecosystem and provide some neglected Indian commentary on the uncomfortable background of Indian–white relations in the region.

One of our principal Fort Hall consultants, for instance, GE, a sixty-three-year-old woman, described her memories of the gathering of yampa in the area "starting from the Tetons clear up into Togwotee and clear up into Montana." She added quietly that "people still gather it when they know they are not going to get caught." To illustrate the conflict between her people and government authorities, she provided the following family anecdote:

See, my grandmother used to do that and we got chased out one time. We were gathering over in West Yellowstone. It was back up in those mountains over there and we were gathering yampa. She was sitting on the ground and she had me with the shovel. She said I know we are going to get caught so hurry up. So I dug as much as I could and she sat down. Then she said put the shovel down. So I put the shovel down and she was sitting there with her back to the road. She was maybe fifty feet away from the road, the main highway. She was sitting there, she was just cleaning them and putting them in a sack. I said Grandma, here comes a Ranger. She said don't say anything. Pretend like you can't understand him. I said o.k. So I sat down with her and we were sitting there and he asked us what we were doing? Grandma looked at him. He kept talking to me and I just sat there and looked at him too. Then finally he motioned us to get off and go. She used to do some goofy things, I swear, but that is what we were doing. We were gathering some yampa, because we were going to bring it home.[153]

This prompted further discussion of relations between the park and her people. Another of our Fort Hall female consultants, LV, recalled a woman named Circle Forehead who had been a Bannock and had helped to raise her "like [her] Grandmother."[154] Without specifying whether the following anecdote transpired within or outside Park boundaries, she shared her mother's recollection of an occasion when this Bannock woman and her mother were picking berries:

They went in the buggy with all of us kids, mother used to always pick up orphan kids too, put them under her wing and take them too. Here was this white man, and he said, "You Indians get out of here. Get out of here." Oh she was angry with him for telling them to leave. She told him in broken English, she said, "This was our land, our place before you came. Before you came this was ours, these were our berries. They are still our berries." Mother said she just went into a rage. She was this nice, tall, good-looking Bannock lady. Mother said they went on picking the berries but then not to cause any trouble they left. My mother used to pull that same trick that her [GE's] grandmother pulled. Non-Indians would come to the place and ask questions, this or that or whatever, and she would just sit there with her Indian face. Sorry, she didn't know a word, not a thing that they were talking about. She could talk Bannock fluently, Shoshone fluently, and English fluently, [but] she always pulled that "No Savvy."[155]

Another interview, with a male consultant, CN, also from Fort Hall, yielded fragmented, broken-English memories of unpleasant interactions between Indians from the region and government officials.[156] Indeed, he grew visibly upset when he recollected, "They wouldn't let Indians hunt any place, just the white people, that's the only thing." As for his own experiences, "[I] never been to Park to stop—just traveled through," "get off like the white people, walk around." But "its too slow going through there. . . . Uncle went through once long time ago, he's lucky." But he also remembered, "[A] lot of Indians stopped going when they made them pay. Prior to that we used to go . . . certain times of year to gather but seems like we were always going to Yellowstone, two or three times in summertime, spring and fall. All we had to do was show the blue card from the superintendent . . . But after they started charging everybody, people kind of stopped going—another government promise broken."

The eighty-nine-year-old Bannock consultant who related the story of the old woman and the fish basket, DS, also had a family memory that, she maintained, illustrated why the Bannock no longer traveled through Yellowstone: "People got so they didn't want to go out there anymore [toward the Yellowstone region] because they got scared. This one whole family was killed. . . . After that people sneak around but they won't go out in the open. Whole tribe found out about it and they were afraid to go back and hunt." The event is said to have taken place around Jackson when the consultant's mother was about five years old:

> One time a man came at night and he had a little baby with him. He told them, "I just came from my camp had the white men just killed all my family, all of them. I came late from hunting," he said, "and I saw their dead bodies laying around so I sneaked away. I was afraid and as I was coming I heard a little baby crying in a cradleboard hanging in a tree. You fellas were the closest so I came here."[157]

Her mother continued, "So we packed up the same night. We just packed everything [and] traveled by night, hid by day, no fire, anything." The young girls were tied behind the horses and hidden in the packs. [They] hid and traveled until they reached Monspelon, they stayed with Mormons who "were very good to us, that's how we got away from there."

Gathering Mineral Resources in the Park

Obsidian was a prized resource collected by Indians in the greater Yellowstone ecosystem. Of Nez Perce rock gathering, Walker claims: "They regard the Park as a healthy place, they went there, they took the baths, they gathered certain kinds of obsidian in that vicinity. I can't tell you exactly where, but there's some pretty decent obsidian in the Park area."[158]

The Shoshone-Bannock put obsidian to medical use, as one consultant from Fort Hall explained:

I know she [an older healer] used obsidian to poke your head with, because that is what she did for my headaches. She kept it very carefully. She had a little tin, like used to have chocolates in a long time ago, she always carried it in that. She had about four or five different sizes and shapes that she used to poke heads with . . . poke your head in different areas to drain the blood. . . . It was her specialty to do that to other people. Just special people did that. . . . Finally, something started dripping, like this color [dark blue] came out. Big blots, she kept pressing my head like that and pretty soon it started flowing, red.[159]

During our Fort Hall interviews, the topic of obsidian periodically cropped up in unexpected ways. Women recalled hearing older Shoshone-Bannock men complaining "about not being able to go into that [park] area to get [obsidian]— mainly for skinning—because they said that you couldn't control the [metal] knives because they would cut the skin. But the obsidian was good because you didn't cut the skin like the knives did." In another interview, after sharing her version of the old woman and the basket of fish narrative given above, the Bannock storyteller said that after contracting the eye disease trachoma at the government boarding school in Sherman, California, she was sent home. She recalled that to use the outhouse she had to keep her hands on a rope to lead her there. Her mother treated the disease with grass (described as "wye grass" in other interviews, which the Paiutes knew as *kawonoo*)[160] and "powder" made from crushed obsidian.[161]

But the Shoshones and Bannocks exploited other Yellowstone rocks as well: "There were certain rocks that they used for certain things were in the Park . . . like for doing their hides there were certain rocks. They hit them and then they would break and then they would clean their hides with these rocks. One was for cleaning and the other was for going this way."[161] Here the Bannock storyteller seemed to be describing different lithic bifaces for the two separate tasks of fleshing and scraping a skinned, raw buffalo hide. As another Fort Hall interviewee, GE, added about her own grandmother during this same discussion:

She needed a certain kind of rock to do her hides at the certain time of the drying. The other rock was for when she was trying to get part of the membrane off. [She would use] the cold rocks, I call them cold rocks, and they would be cold and the warm rocks would be kind of warm . . . the warm rocks would be from the heated areas, and the cold rocks would be from the Salmon area or from the Blackfoot or Snake River where they have those boulders. . . .

Sometimes the rocks that have been heated through the geysers or the mud-pots break differently from rocks in the cold water that you get along the riverbeds. Sometimes they will break like a slice of bread, across a plane. Those rocks are generally used for aches and pains. If the rock breaks on an angle that rock is used for scraping or for grinding or pounding. Grandma used to teach me how to do those things. I haven't done those things for a long time so I don't remember.[163]

CHAPTER 5

Sojourners from the South

The Shoshone

The Indian nation whose relationships with the greater Yellowstone ecosystem are the focus of this chapter is that eastern branch of the Shoshonean people who today occupy the 2,268,008–acre Wind River Reservation in Fremont and Hot Springs Counties in west-central Wyoming. As discussed in chapter 4, the earlier history of the numerous Shoshonean peoples whose many treaties eventually situated them on reservations not far from the western and southern boundaries of Yellowstone National Park is complex. The extensive sway of their linguistic community and its numerous dialects, combined with the small-scale nature of their autonomous social units and their regionally distinctive interactions with Euro-Americans, has left Shoshoneans scattered across at least six states.

These Shoshone were closely related to the Shoshone-Bannock but during the treaty-making period of 1863–68 they became distinguished as the "Washakie band" because of their popular chief. Today they are officially the Eastern Shoshone Tribe. Here we provide an overview of their activities in and around the park and end with the role of their Wind River Reservation as a final refuge for the onetime Yellowstone residents, the Sheep Eaters.

Southerly Trails into the Yellowstone Plateau

Few dramatic landscape features announce the southern boundary of Yellowstone National Park. For many travelers heading toward the park, any appetite for drama has already been satisfied by the awesome skyline of the Grand Tetons and their jagged reflection in Jackson Lake. Visitors are startled to find themselves suddenly

Indian tipis near Togwotee Pass, circa 1922. (Photo courtesy of Yellowstone National Park Archives, #Yell 37784.)

braking at the park's southern entrance, for the buffer zone outside this edge of the greater Yellowstone ecosystem almost imperceptibly becomes Yellowstone National Park proper. Intermittently gleaming with lakes but thick with forest, at eye level it can be hard for newcomers to get their bearings. That is one reason why early travelers relied on Indian trails and Indian guides.

On September 1, 1873, when the military engineer Captain William A. Jones and his exploratory party found themselves not far from the marshy inlet, where the Yellowstone River empties into the lake, one of his scouts, a Sheep Eater (possibly the famous Togwotee), had no problem remembering "the way back to Camp Brown by the head of the Wind River."[1] Throughout Jones's summer-long reconnaissance of the park and its southeastern environs, he was constantly crossing back and forth over a tracery of old Indian pathways.

Jones took pains to record the native routes that wound in and out and across Yellowstone National Park proper. Commencing at Fort Washakie (known until then as Camp Brown), he then followed the Wind River Valley nearly to its head, crossed the Continental Divide and continued to where the Gros Ventre Fork splits from the Snake River. According to Jones,

> [Here the trail forked,] sending one branch down the stream as far as Jackson's Hole, where it forks in turn, one portion leading down the Snake River to Fort Hall, and the other, bending sharp around to the northeast, follows up Pacific and down Atlantic Creeks to the Yellowstone River, down which it follows,

passing, to the east of Yellowstone Lake, to the Crow country in Montana—a branch of it following Lewis Fork and the west side of the lake and river; the other branch leaves the Gros Ventre near its head, and bending to the south, crosses a low pass in the Wyoming Mountains to the headwaters of Green River, which it follows down to the open country and thence to Fort Bridger.[2]

But Jones learned more about the old Indian trail to which his Sheep Eater pathfinder had apparently referred, an arduous passage that required the ascent and descent of two divides. Taking off from today's Fort Washakie in the direction of the North Fork of the Wind River, it swung over the headwaters of the Snake River until it finally reached the headwaters of the Yellowstone, at which time it paralleled the river to Yellowstone Lake, so as to tie into the first trail linkage.

Especially appealing to Jones was a third route, apparently of considerable antiquity, that led his party into the inviting, secret "park" of Owl Creek canyon in the shadow of the Owl Creek Mountains. Here, surrounded by rugged and unprepossessing scenery, they descended into a well-watered little ecosystem featuring splendid sheep-hunting terrain and replete with signs of "numerous trails, old lodge-poles, bleached bones of game, and old camps of Cheyennes and Arapahoes,"[3] though Jones's Indian guides claimed ignorance of the small canyon. To find this "luxurious" spot, Jones had headed from the "big bend" of the Wind River, following its left bank to Dry Fork, which he pursued to its head, surmounting a low divide to reach the headwaters of Owl Creek near the Washakie Needles, a stream he then traced into the hidden canyon.

Jones also discovered that Camp Brown was the starting point for yet another, fourth Indian trail that climbed northward over the Owl Creek Mountains. This is the range that curves down the northeastern sector of the Wind River Reservation. Leading hunters to the buffalo herds of Bighorn Basin, this route could also direct them north-northwest, where they soon entered the Shoshone River country with its distinctive landmark, Buffalo Heart Mountain. From there a splinter trail veered up the North Fork of the Shoshone River, lifting Indian travelers over the divide and intersecting with the path that drew them into Yellowstone National Park via its eastern entrance and the great lake.

In addition, Jones noted other early Indian trailways that sprang from these origin points, such as (1) the route possibly ridden by Shoshone raiders into Sioux country, which headed directly eastward from the Wind River's big bend and hugged the northern flank of the Sweetwater Valley before following the Powder River toward the plains east of the Bighorns; or (2) the native road that dropped south from the Wind River Valley across the mountains above Union Peak and then led to the headwaters of the Green River; or (3) another Indian trail that led from Camp Brown to the head of the Wind River, then lifted up and over Togwotee Pass before taking the northerly drainage of the Snake River and finally reaching Pacific Creek whereupon Indian wayfarers could take advantage of the route that connected the Tetons to the eastern shores of Yellowstone Lake.

The curiosity of the William Jones expedition of 1873 about evidence of Indian travel routes in the Yellowstone National Park environs stood in contrast to the Hayden party's relative disinterest in native ethnography the previous year. And Jones also remained alert to any signs of what Indians made with their hands or expressed with their words. He also may have been open to learning about the Shoshone's belief system, but they appear to have been ambivalent about allowing whites to view their rituals. When Chief Washakie was at his hunting camp in 1873, members of the Jones expedition were first invited to a forthcoming "buffalo dance," which involved abstaining from water on the part of both men and women. Suddenly, however, the Indians changed their minds about the foreign presence and made up an excuse to renege. Yet when some Shoshones returned from the Crow Reservation with a captured Sioux scalp the Crow had given them, they not only staged an impromptu scalp dance inside the new park, on the southwestern arm of Yellowstone Lake, but also welcomed the Jones crew into their celebration around the "disgraced" scalp.[4]

Abetted by a native informant identified only by the name Pinatsi—whom we might assume was a Shoshone—Jones sought information about their distant past, as evidenced by his surface collections of lithic artifacts. But he also interviewed Shoshones about their native language and compiled a working vocabulary. Also uncommon among Yellowstone explorers was the credit Jones gave to abiding ties between Indians and landscape. When Indians led him to "a perfectly practicable passage to the Yellowstone Valley, via Wind River Valley and the head of Wind River," Jones shortly dubbed it Togwotee Pass, explaining that he preferred "to attach easy Indian names, wherever possible, to the prominent features of the country."[5] Ten years later, visitors were still counting on local Indians to guide them through the region. Five years after the Arapahoes had joined the Shoshones at Wind River, one of their elders, Old Man Sage, recalled such a request:

> [T]he President of the United States came here [President Arthur's visit to Wind River in 1883] and we all remember and understood what he said, 'Friends that is your land, all of it, but I would like to have three young men to go with my command and guide my command to Yellowstone Park,' and that was complied with.[6]

Domain of the Eastern Shoshone in the Era of Ethnogenesis

We might expect these Shoshoneans, who lived along the southern fringes of the greater Yellowstone region, to be familiar with this landscape. When Omer Stewart began in 1952 to reconstruct for the Shoshone Land Claims Case the boundaries of aboriginal Shoshone territory, he painstakingly plotted onto a series of maps the known locations of the five major groups of Shoshone from more than four dozen sources.[7] Insofar as these northeastern Shoshoneans were concerned, with the exception of James Doty's 1863 map, all Stewart's major documentation agreed that in aboriginal times these peoples claimed a portion of present-day Yellowstone National Park, as had been decreed in the Fort Laramie Treaty of 1851.[8] While most of his sources concurred that at least the lower southwestern third of the park was Shoshone territory, both Kroeber[9] and Steward[10] pushed that boundary even farther north, placing more than two-thirds of the present-day park within the aboriginal Shoshone holdings.

Among the Flathead it was generally understood, according to the well-informed pioneer ethnographer James Teit, that "Shoshonean tribes occupied the Upper Yellowstone country, *including Yellowstone Park*." As Teit wrote, reflecting the Flathead view of Shoshone territoriality: "Farther north Shoshonean bands occupied the country around Livingston, Lewiston, and Denton. How far east and down the Yellowstone they extended is not known; but they are thought to have at one time held the country around Billings, and most, if not all, of the country where the Crow Indians now have a reservation."[11]

Brigham Madsen has described the broader Shoshone and Bannock historical (nineteenth-century) domain as follows:

> In the beginning they claimed and roamed over a territory extending from the Wind River Mountains, *the Yellowstone Park country*, and the buffalo plains of Montana on the west to the Weiser-Boise-Bruneau valleys of the west, and from Great Salt Lake and Bear Lake on the south to the Salmon River of the north. The twin hearts of this immense area were Camas Prairie and the Portneuf-Snake River bottoms, the first a summer home and the latter a sheltered haven against winter storms.[12]

As suggested by our parenthetical qualifier, "nineteenth-century," however, to more accurately reflect historical and sociopolitical realities, Madsen's territorial assignment for the Shoshones should be placed in a number of contexts. This domain was not "owned" in the Euro-American sense of land tenure. Only the natural resources of this habitat could be claimed by Indian families who, at any given time, found themselves in an auspicious situation for harvesting them. And in the egalitarian ethic of these hunters and gatherers, it was only practical to share, as Sally Jean Laidlaw describes for the Fort Hall Shoshones:

> When there were good crops in any locality, they ripened so fast and fell to the ground so quickly that the people who ordinarily lived in the area could not possibly gather them all. When a good harvest was promised they therefore spread the news abroad, so that people whose crops had failed could come to share their bounty with them.[13]

Second, *despite* Madsen's phrase that this land area was what the Shoshone claimed "In the beginning," any representation of the tribe's territory must be positioned within a historical frame. Somewhat earlier than this purported "In the beginning," the Shoshoneans were probably situated somewhat south of this area. In his attempt to summarize the protohistoric migrations of the early Shoshone, Carling Malouf sees them concentrated in the "great reservoir" of the southern Great Basin, by which he means the large area we now know as southern Nevada and adjoining portions of Utah, California, and Arizona.[14]

And instead of imagining these Shoshones moving en masse northward in some wholesale migration, Malouf has them percolating in small groups both eastward into Wyoming and northward up the Snake River system where he envisages pockets of Shoshonean settlers putting down roots, with one of the Wyoming offshoots even venturing still farther to become the Comanche. In the days before the horse, still others ventured "up the North Fork of the Snake River, and through Targhee Pass and Raynolds Pass into the Madison and Jefferson river systems. . . . When horses did arrive, Shoshoni power to wage war increased, and soon they had reached as far north as Canada."[15] By this point, according to Alfred Kroeber, the "pretty pure" foundation of Great Basin culture began to assume "an overlay of Plains culture."[16] After this the inventory of Plains-style markers such as "war bonnets, war honours, dancing societies and the Sun Dance now became parts of the Eastern Shoshone culture."[17]

Before long, however, Shoshonean expansionism seems to have been checked on the north and the east. Although evidence is strong concerning their extensive forays into Canada, by 1800 they clearly became outnumbered and outarmed by newly mounted Blackfeet who began to force their southern retreat. That is around the time when the land base described by Madsen seems to have been established. Scholars also point to this as the time when the Crow put a halt to any further Shoshonean spread into their territory on the east. Interestingly, after this adjustment of their mutual boundary, the Crow and Shoshone began forming a fairly durable, long-term intertribal friendship, which even saw a joint Shoshone-Crow trading expedition visit the Mandan in 1805[18] and the transfer from the Crow of the idea of reconstituting the Wind River mens' warrior societies (now known as "dance groups") in 1878.[19]

Given their close proximity, it is not surprising that a review of historical relations between Shoshones and Crows discloses this alternating picture of antagonistic territorial competition and amicable cultural exchange. It was already thanks to the Shoshones that the Crows had obtained their horses in the early eighteenth century, and it would be from the Wind River Shoshone that more than two hundred years later, in 1938, they would receive a revived form of Sun Dance that still binds the two tribes on a summer ceremonial circuit.[20] At the same time, as neighbors who shared strong military codes in the midst of the volatile arena of nineteenth-century Plains Indians jockeying for economic, political, and territorial advantage, their warriors periodically drew the line against one another. According to Larry G. Murray, an Eastern Shoshone member of the Economic Development Committee and a tribal historian:

> By the 1850s the Crows began hunting regularly in central Wyoming, and the Eastern Shoshones, under the leadership of Chief Washakie, challenged their right to hunt and camp there. In March 1866 the Crows were camped near the present site of Kinnear, Wyoming, on the north side of the Big Wind River, when the Eastern Shoshones drove them out of the valley, and thus ended the Crow intrusion into Shoshone country.[21]

Any realistic portrayal of this "Shoshone country" must also factor in a third context. We need a more dynamic, situational appreciation of how rapidly Shoshone forms of sociopolitical organization could adapt to changing circumstances. For it is safe to say that before the horse and the treaty-making era there was no widely shared notion of overarching Shoshonean nationality or collective territory, as the Madsen quote above misleadingly suggests. Rather, in aboriginal times any Shoshone's political and economic allegiance would likely be to his immediate subsistence-based "kin and clique" group, or band, which would probably be named for the colloquial designation of its primary food (see chapter 4).

With the spread of horses and then, equally important, the bureaucratic reorganizations of Indian groups during and after the treaty era, an altered sense of collective identity took over. In place of identification by primary food source came a notion of group solidarity organized around specific, named leaders, or "chiefs." In former, more "traditional" years these notables might have only been what political anthropologists know as "big men," forceful personalities who retained control of distributing food and resources so long as they enjoyed continued success in the hunt. But under the white-initiated demands that these select individuals negotiate with U.S. emissaries, ratify treaties, and make choices about providing native mercenaries for their Indian wars, they suddenly found themselves elevated to the status of political figureheads for their ethnic flocks.

Around the 1860s we begin to hear of Shoshonean groups who were located on the borders of Yellowstone National Park or were implicated in the region's history becoming publicly identified by the personalities of such leading chiefs, with their group's reputation often stamped by the degree to which their particular leader was friendly or hostile to whites. For instance, there were the accommodating followers of Taghee (or Tyhee) of the Bannocks, whom Chief Washakie permitted to live with his Eastern Shoshone people at Wind River but who preferred to relocate to Fort Hall in Idaho instead. Initially aggressive toward white emigrants, Taghee agreed to land cessation treaties, became a successful farmer, and sat out the 1878 Bannock War. There were also the Indians attached to Pocatello, who had achieved chieftainship of his Western Shoshones at about the same time as Washakie but whose attitude toward white intruders was far more militant until his imprisonment in 1859. And there were friendly bands that gravitated toward Tendoy of the Lemhi Shoshone (whose father was a Bannock and mother a Sheep Eater), who has been described as "probably one of the last Bannock-Shoshone leaders to cross Yellowstone National Park on the Great Bannock Trail."[22] Tendoy shared Washakie's conciliatory strategy with regard to whites, despite enticements in the 1860s to join Ute upstarts or northwestern hostiles under the command of Pocatello and Bear Hunter.

By aligning themselves behind such leaders, tribespeople declared both their ethnic and political allegiances. But none on this roster of celebrity chiefs enjoyed so long a reign or achieved the widespread prestige as the man named Gourd Rattle, or Washakie. If ever the historical trajectory of an American Indian tribe's relations with the United States were dominated by a single larger-than-life individual, this was he.

Wind River Shoshone History: The Washakie Years

From his birth in 1804 to a Flathead father and part-Lemhi Shoshone (and possibly part-Sheep Eater as well) mother[23] to his old age and death at the very start of the twentieth century, Washakie's life would symbolically and literally be linked with the history of the greater Yellowstone environment. He was born only a year before his fellow tribesperson, the famous Shoshone woman named Sacajawea, or "Birdwoman," became attached to the exploratory expedition led by Lewis and Clark. Their triumphal journey would just bypass the Yellowstone National Park area as it linked the fledgling Republic from sea to sea. And nearly four score years later Washakie would host the president of the United States, Chester Arthur, during his fishing and sight-seeing trip through Yellowstone National Park in 1883.

For many of the decades in between those benchmark dates, Washakie served as his people's unquestioned leader. In the major transformation of the Shoshone from a free-foraging society of hunters and gatherers to subjects sequestered on a government reservation, Washakie would become one of the most important "transitional" chiefs in the Great Plains. During his rough-and-ready warrior days, between 1820 and 1840, the youthful Washakie reveled in guerrilla warfare with Blackfeet.[24] The battlefield honors he earned during this period, plus his physical charisma and oratorical gifts, elevated Washakie to the position of principal chief in the 1840s on the death of the brother-chiefs, Padashawaunda and Moowoomhah.

The renown gained by Washakie for his loyalty to Euro-Americans grew out of the largely amicable trading "rendezvous" era of the early fur trade, when isolated Rocky Mountain fur trappers, whose swaggering lifestyle had borrowed heavily from Indians, exchanged horses, furs, muskets, knives, beads, and kettles with Shoshones along the Green River. Later in life, Washakie enjoyed recalling when he herded the trappers' horses, learned to become a marksman with their firearms,

Eastern Shoshone Indians at Fort Washakie, August 1883. Chief Washakie, on horseback, is at the far right. (Photo courtesy of Montana Historical Society: Haynes Foundation Collection #H-1011, F. Jay Haynes, photographer.)

and developed a taste for their bread and coffee.[25] But just as overtrapping of fur-bearing mammals and decline in the beaver hat market caused this frequently romanticized "mountain man" era to wane, other social, economic, and political forces began to influence the Shoshonean world.

The loosely organized Shoshones fell under threat of tribal expansionism from other quarters, as their archenemies, the Sioux and Cheyenne, acquired the white man's weapons and horses and began aggressively pushing into Crow and Shoshone territories. Discoveries of gold in California as well as closer to home—just north of South Pass—intensified the traffic across the rutted wagon roads that ran south of their country. As an estimated 155,000 people and 100,000 head of stock crossed South Pass between 1849 and 1851, this not only increased the danger of angry brushes between Shoshones and settlers, more important, it motivated the government to construct military posts along the Oregon and other trails to protect travelers from the Sioux and Cheyenne raiders, as well as to consider a national policy of consolidating Indians on reservations. The permanent Mormon settlements that arose along the southern rim of Washakie's hunting grounds eventually forced Washakie to choose between his allegiance to these solicitous new neighbors and to the United States, which soon found itself at odds with the Mormon challenge to its sovereignty.

Over the decades of trying to keep his more impetuous tribesmen in check, Washakie also shepherded his Eastern Shoshone followers through the series of road widenings, railroad track openings, valuable mineral discoveries, peace treaties, and land cessation agreements that, one by one, curtailed Shoshone freedom of movement and reduced their land base. It was during the tribe's first treaty, the grandiose Fort Laramie Council of September 1851, that Washakie's significance as paramount chief came to light. Outsiders saw the chief's cool demeanor in the face of one Sioux's direct challenge to hand-to-hand combat as a highlight of the Shoshone appearance.[26] Although the territorial boundaries assigned by U.S. officials in 1851 were rather loose, it may have been the Shoshones who lost most during this convocation, for the Crows were rewarded for friendship with the whites by receiving the Bighorn Basin clear down to the Shoshones' Wind River mountains.

The following year the Mormons served as intermediaries for Washakie's peace treaty with the Utes. But it was not until 1863 that Washakie was invited to Fort Bridger for the next important treaty signing with the U.S. government; among the five peace treaties negotiated with Shoshonean peoples that year was one he signed at Fort Bridger on July 2. In exchange for the right to clear roads, establish military forts, and open telegraph lines, stage routes, and railheads across Shoshone lands, the government promised $20,000 worth of goods (which the U.S. Congress quickly cut in half) for twenty years. Despite delays in receiving the promised goods, under Washakie's influence his people prospered and largely adhered to the peace treaty. The next U.S. treaty with Washakie and other Shoshone and Bannock leaders, negotiated five years later, also at Fort Bridger, gave the chief the secure reservation for which he had been petitioning. Later this agreement would also allow Congress to allocate funds for the building of a road in 1898 between Fort Washakie and the Buffalo Fork of the Snake River, so as to hasten troops from Fort Washakie into the Jackson Hole area in the event of possible clashes between Shoshone hunters and white outlaws and game wardens.

Through the terms of the Fort Bridger Treaty of 1868 Washakie also allowed his Eastern Shoshone to be drawn into the government's new assimilation policy. Now heads of Shoshone families were encouraged to choose 320 acres for their farms and receive seeds and agricultural implements; a building and teacher were to be provided for every thirty children, and every Indian was to receive cotton and flannel goods. Yet Washakie warned the treaty commissioners at Fort Bridger that he would not accept the new reservation until the government proved it could protect his people from the Sioux, Cheyenne, and Arapaho. His insistence forced the government to establish Camp Augur (named for its builder, General Christopher C. Auger) on June 28, 1869, at the present site of Lander, Wyoming, whose name was changed to Camp Brown (for Captain Federick Brown, who was killed in the Fetterman Massacre) on March 28, 1870. So it seems appropriate that the old chief was honored on December 30, 1878, after the garrison had been relocated to the center of the reservation, with its new name, Fort Washakie.

Two other major land cessation negotiations were thrust upon Washakie. With the discovery of gold at South Pass, he was pressured to sanction the sale of all Shoshone lands south of the Popo Agie in December 1874. It was also fairly clear that Washakie was personally profiting from such agreements; this 1874 sale saw the United States promise annually $5,000 worth of cattle for five years, with an additional $500 a year earmarked for Washakie himself. In 1896, with much greater reluctance, the ninety-four-year-old chief agreed to share negotiating rights with Sharp Nose of the Arapaho as they sold the ten square acres housing the precious hot springs of the Thermopolis area to the government for $50,000. That was the last time Washakie would affix his "X mark" to an official document. By then the only faint reminders that tied Shoshone Indians to the Yellowstone environment were a handful of park place-names derived from their language, such as Dunanda Falls, Gwinna Falls, Ponuntpa Springs, Wahb Springs and Wahhi Falls.

Safeguarding his followers' political neutrality through these years was not easy. Younger upstart warriors decamped to join less conciliatory Shoshone and Bannock leaders, such as Bear Hunter or Pashego, as they swooped down on pioneers and ranchers along the Utah–Idaho border. Despite Washakie's stance of alliance with whites, which extended to lending warriors to serve as U.S. scouts, he was constantly being asked to concede more land and authority. In 1878, when he was originally forced to accept a contingent of almost a thousand, near-destitute Arapahos on the Shoshone reservation, he reminded the governor of Wyoming Territory what it felt like to lose political freedom and larger homeland: "The white man, who possesses this whole vast country from sea to sea, who roams over it at pleasure, and lives where he likes, cannot know the cramp we feel in this little spot."[2/]

One of Washakie's last government-sanctioned escapes from that little spot had actually occurred four years earlier, in fall 1874, when the Commissioner of Indian Affairs allowed him to lead a buffalo hunt. Accompanying the old-style expedition would be a "roaming school" for Indian children, with instructor (and later Indian agent) James I. Patten packing along a circus-size tent to serve as his mobile classroom, "a comfortable place for 25 to 35 scholars." On October 16 the large party of pack and hunting horses and outlying scouts departed from Fort Washakie to ford the Big Wind River just south of the present Diversion Dam. After waiting three days for their scout reports, they discovered that the Bighorn Basin was teeming with game. Yet when they spied numerous signs of a large hostile group of Indians they struck out on the Red Canyon Trail across the Owl Creek Mountains. Snowbound for another four days, they eventually descended into the basin to camp at Red Springs.

It was then that schoolteacher Patten "saw the Indians in another light." What follows is Patten's eyewitness to Shoshones relishing a taste of the old days. Here was the sort of communal hunt they must have conducted throughout the greater Yellowstone ecosystem for centuries:

They were not the same people who a few days earlier had left the agency complacent and mild. Huge fires were burning throughout this camp. Harangues were made by old men, incantations made by medicine men, drums were beaten, and rattles shaken. Washakie himself seemed another being on this wild and weird camping ground. His voice, loud and clear, rang out on the night air as he addressed his people. His face lighted up and caused great enthusiasm among the young and old and they joined in singing their old war and hunting songs.[28]

After Shoshone runners located some buffalo about forty miles west of present-day Worland and just southeast of Meeteetse, the hunters readied their special buffalo horses and gave chase. In less than an hour they had killed 125 animals, and shortly crossed the Shoshone River a few miles west of present-day Emblem to continue on to the Bighorn River. On their return home about a month after they had left, they crept up on a small buffalo herd about eighteen miles from the Wind River Agency. As Patten and his Indian friends watched from hiding, the animals rolled on their backs in a muddy buffalo wallow. According to Patten, "This was the last herd of bufalo seen near the [Wind River] agency for already the vast herds of buffalo were beginning to disappear."[29]

The best evidence we have that intimate knowledge of the greater Yellowstone ecosystem was being transmitted from generation to generation are the hints of Shoshone Indians functioning as hired hunting guides, or even as hunt predators, during visits by white sportsmen. In the winter of 1880–81, for instance, William Baillie-Grohom noticed that when he left Fort Washakie for the "Sierra Shoshone," hungry Indians often pursued and butchered those wounded deer that he found too troublesome to track down on his own.[30] Packing in with his elk and bear hunting party in 1887, Owen Wister was led first over the Continental Divide for some elk and bear hunting in Jackson Hole and then up into the southern reaches of the park all the way to Mammoth Springs by his guide, a "full-blood Shoshone" named Tighee, or Tigi. Wister evoked Tighee's woodsmen skills in a journal: "But it was necessary to follow Tigi like his shadow. I tried to make as little noise as he does. Whipping by jagged rotten boughs, letting his shoulder go an inch from them and stepping over twigs that lay thick in the timber. His moccasins slipped over them with never a crack."[31]

When the British hunter Edward Buxton wanted to locate game around the Jackson Hole and southern Yellowstone region he sought out local Indians because he had heard that they still hunted up there. But he had to be satisfied with second-best in the person of the white man named "Indian Dick" who had been raised by the Wind River Shoshone.[32] Other information suggests that well into the twentieth century, if times got tight the Eastern Shoshone could fall back on their older hunting expertise and topographic knowledge of the greater Yellowstone ecosystem.

Dick Washakie (left) guiding Owen Wister party into Buffalo Fork, just south of Yellowstone National Park, 1887. (Photo courtesy of American Heritage Center, University of Wyoming, Laramie, Owen Wister Collection, #290.)

As late as fall 1929, for instance, when the Shoshones and Arapahoes were suffering slim government rations on their reservation, they conducted what almost sounds like a repeat performance of Washakie's 1874 hunt. About twenty-five to thirty Indians slipped away from their agency and trespassed on the Washakie National Forest, pitching their canvas tents on Green Creek, which lay just to the west of Trapper Creek. While on his regular patrol, a timber sale ranger named Carl G. Krueger spied the band and felt he was glimpsing "the way they had been preparing meat for hundreds of years." As Krueger recalled the scene of this Shoshone food-processing encampment:

> They came by team and wagon, and had a bunch of extra horses, so made quite a procession. They built pole racks at their camp, and it looked as if a half an acre of land was covered with strips of meat hanging in the sun to dry. This was fairly early in the fall; there were still lots of flies, and around their camp there was also a good strong odor. I expect this was the way they had been preparing meat for hundreds of years. Moose were protected at that time too, but I think some of them got on the drying racks; there seemed to be fewer of them around after the Indians left. I did not take any pictures of this; maybe I thought the Indians wouldn't appreciate it. There are both Shoshone and Arapahoes on the reservation, but I don't know which tribe these belonged to.[33]

Washakie's waning years as principal chief of the Wind River Shoshone witnessed increasing impoverishment and collective uncertainty, as government rations were trimmed, the agricultural promise that saw Shoshones managing their own farms with some success by 1872 turned sour within a few years, and a measles epidemic killed many of their children.[34] Faith in their old modes of maintaining psychological balance and physical health began to falter. Many were attracted to the messages of Mormon and Episcopalian missionaries, as well as to new native ceremonies like their version of the Ghost Dance, the Native American Church, and a form of Sun Dance that blended old beliefs and Christian symbols and placed special emphasis on curative rituals.[35]

All three of these rituals still survive in various forms on the Wind River Reservation, with Sun Dancing and Peyotism actually flourishing.[36] But the tribe's wider domain has shrunk, with the surrounding federal lands largely off-limits to hunters. The Camas Prairie, where their northern brethren once harvested the onionlike roots is now under agribusiness cultivation; the only stray camas to be found sprout out of roadside ditches.[37] Yet the Shoshone-Arapaho land base, extending seventy miles from east to west and fifty-five miles from north to south just east of the Continental Divide, is still a sanctuary where a handful of elder Eastern Shoshone and Sheep Eater descendants retain some knowledge of religious and social practices that link them to the greater Yellowstone ecosystem. Surrounding the river valley settlements occupied by these Indians is an encircling wall of snow-capped mountains. Within their embrace this cultural world exists apart, and in it, writes the anthropologist Loretta Fowler, "[t]here is a pervasive stillness and, despite the clusters of extended family settlements, a sense of great space."[38]

Camas among Yellowstone's Indians

Although many natural plant resources were harvested by Shoshoneans along the southern reaches of the greater Yellowstone ecosystem, such as the tiny leaves from thistles and heath for their tobacco mixtures,[39] we focus here exclusively on the widespread use of the *Camas* bulb—reputed to be "the great northern Plateau staple"[40] or the "queen root of this clime"[41]—in and around the park region. Our information on camas originates from archaeological, historical, ethnographic, and folkloristic sources.

ARCHAEOLOGY

The preponderance of our archaeological data about camas comes from around the skirt of the Yellowstone Plateau in the form of the pit roasting hearths in which it was cooked. Not far south of the Park, for instance, at the Henn site in the southern Jackson Hole region—one of the most recent and sophisticated archaeological investigations in the region—University of Wyoming archaeologists in 1992 discovered nine of these rock-filled hearths.

According to the Henn investigators, "pit roasting is an extremely labor intensive, messy, space consuming activity that typically requires 1–3 days to complete. As a result such activities are often conducted in areas peripheral to the main habitation area."[42] Because almost none of the hearths betrayed evidence of animal remains, the archaeologists David J. Rapson, Marcel Korfeld and Mary Lou Larsen concluded that in all probability they were evidence for the reliance of Indians on plant resources such as camas for at least three hundred years during the Late Prehistoric and Protohistoric periods. As their work pointed out, however, blue camas was only one of many edible root and tuber resources eaten by Indians in the area; among that others are white mules ears, arrowleaf balsamroot, Wyeth biscuitroot, wild hyacinth, sego lily, tobacco root, arrowhead, wild onion, cattail, and yampa.[43]

By the time of the Henn excavations, botanical archaeology in the Jackson Hole–Yellowstone National Park ecosystem had been under way for a dozen years. In 1980 Stuart A. Reeve perceived that native food-foraging practices of this region reflected a blend of the Great Basin–Shoshone, Plateau–Salish, and Plains–Blackfeet traditions. Of the many plant species used by early Indians here, he believed that the blue camas found in the lowland meadows was most popular, whose gathering "focused migratory patterns and structured band territories."[44] Over the course of his doctoral research, Reeve realized that while "the number of potential plant resources [is] vast . . . the task of attributing prehistoric significance to one or more plants can be risky."[45] Despite other scientific opinions to the contrary,[46] he still felt confident enough about pinpointing camas as a key plant for prehistoric peoples "occupying the Snake River headwaters of northwestern Wyoming" to devote his dissertation to the topic.[47] Examining the Lawrence site at the northern end of Jackson Lake, he speculated on the gender division of labor for native food-gathering:

> [T]he eastern biogeographic boundary of the liliaceous root crop blue camas *(Camassia quamash)* provided an ecological context for surplus root harvest and for social aggregating. Female root gathering activities may have provided economic and ideological bases for ceremonialism, trade and political alliance central to the reemergence of a high country adaptive system since perhaps 10,000 B.P. in the mountains of north-western Wyoming. . . . Lithic assemblages from meadow and non-meadow sites are compared to demonstrate both the sequence of seasonal subsistence and settlement patterns, and to differentiate work activities at female-oriented meadow sites and presumed male fishing sites.[48]

When Reeve's next assignment moved into Yellowstone National Park, he kept his eye out for evidence of camas use. The only promising meadows for gathering lay in the southwestern corner of the park, but he turned up earth ovens at a Fishing Bridge site (48YE304). The cracked rock features used to cook large quantities of roots and the grinding stones for reducing them to flours or cakes that mobile Indians could carry as they moved, made him wonder again whether, since plant gathering was largely women's work, the residential camps "may have allowed direct access to female exploitative environments."[49]

But the hundreds of large cobble-filled fire pits found in Wyoming's upper Green River Basin, on the southern fringes of the greater Jackson Hole–Yellowstone ecosystem, provide a better sense of the extent of Shoshonean dependence on wild plants.[50] It is to these wet meadow environments that the mountain dwellers probably would have descended on foraging expeditions in spring and fall. Analysis of one of their roasting hearths was conducted in 1991 by Wyoming State archaeologists as part of a Wyoming Department of Transportation survey. It yielded a detailed glimpse of the nutritional value to Indians of the Yellowstone Plateau of not only camas but also other edible roots and tubers such as wild onion, biscuitroot, and yampa.[51]

Near Duck Creek, a tributary of the New Fork, the archaeologist Julie Francis worked on a cooking pit, known as "feature 5," a little more than one hundred miles south of the park, which would have held about nine bushels of roots. When Francis examined ethnographic writings on the Flathead and other Plateau groups, she discovered that it was estimated that a single root digger could collect about one bushel of camas roots a day[52] but that an average of only 0.7 bushels of biscuitroot might be collected each day. This meant that it would take one person about nine days to fill the cooking pit with camas and thirteen days to fill it with biscuitroot.[53]

Next Francis wanted to learn how beneficial this cooking oven might have been to its Indian users. Already she knew that Hunn had estimated that 0.1 kilogram of fresh camas roots yielded 113 kilocalories[54] and therefore that 200 kilograms of camas cooked in the pit she had excavated would yield about 226,000 kilocalories. She continued:

> Assuming an average [human] requirement of 200 kcal/day, camas cooked in feature 5 would have supplied the total caloric needs of one person for 113 days or a family of four for nearly 30 days. One must also consider that roots processed in feature 5 would have constituted only a portion of the total diet. For a family of four, camas cooked in feature 5 would supply 56,500 kcal/person. Spread out over one year, this would amount to 8% of the daily caloric requirement.[55]

From the lack of animal and other plant remains, Francis concluded that this hearth had been devoted exclusively to roasting root products. She believed that this hearth and others like it were not necessarily associated with a residential camp of any duration but were more likely reflective of Indians who organized themselves to undertake food-gathering expeditions with specific products in

A camas plant. (Illustration by Hannah Hinchman.)

mind that they would process on site and then transport to their homes at other locations.

HISTORY

For the region west and northwest of Yellowstone National Park, much of our information about this crucial food source is historical in nature. It was Lewis and Clark who first named the camas plant on September 20, 1805, during their trek through the country of the Nez Perce Indians. Finding it growing at "Quawmash" Flats in northern Idaho, where they learned that it was a vital part of the native food supply, they named it accordingly.[56]

Subsequent visitors to Shoshone and Bannock country did not overlook these Indians' special dependence on camas. While visiting Fort Hall in 1839, T. J. Farnham learned that Indians to the west of Fort Hall "are said to subsist principally on roots" and then, on the Bear River divide, got a chance to see for himself that "[t]his valley is the grain-filled and root-garden of the Shoshonie Indians; for there grow in it a number of kinds of edible roots, which they dig in August, and dry for winter use."[57] And traveling across the same landscape only a few years later, Theodore Talbot met Shoshones bearing "Kooyah or Black root" to trade. Talbot looked with some distaste at the "black, sticky, suspicious looking compound, of a very disagreeable odor," until he was told that "when you have overcome the prejudices which its appearance and smell create . . . it is a very palatable and soon a favorite mess."[58]

During the historical period, the horse-riding Shoshone and Bannock Indians were distinguished from other Plains peoples by their seasonal alternation between hunting for large mammals and foraging for plant staples. Indeed, their favored areas for harvesting tubers, roots, and seeds appear to have been as important as were their big game hunting grounds. Only nine months before the establishment of Yellowstone National Park, in June 1871, families from the Idaho Bannock tribe undertook their customary spring expedition to their favored camas meadows west of Fort Hall. They were bent on foraging for camas roots, which they knew as *pasigo,*[59] and which they habitually unearthed using antler digging sticks and leather sacks and then dried before leaving on their spring buffalo hunts.

Already these Bannocks were aware that the Oregon Trail was cutting across the fertile bottomlands of the Bear, Snake, and Portneuf Rivers, where they were accustomed to finding camas. But what the Indians discovered on the Camas Prairie that spring brought home the consequences of white penetration like never before. Great swatches of the moist rich loam where they expected to find two-foot-high stalks, supporting delicate blue flowers that lifted out of sweet-tasting, highly nutritious bulbs, had been torn up and the plant remains strewn about by the white man's hogs.

Since their earliest treaty discussions, the Bannocks and Shoshones had insisted that this food-gathering region be set aside for them. And during treaty negotiations with the Fort Hall Bannock and Shoshone in 1868, the government vowed to allow the Indians

> retention of "reasonable portions" of the Portneuf River valley and the Big Camas Prairie, the best root-digging grounds in southern Idaho. Their chiefs had been firm on this point; whatever else they would have to give up, the habitats of their most important food plants they would not give up. . . . The Fort Hall band leaders took great pains to convince the agent that Camas Prairie was essential to the economy which he wanted them to maintain.[60]

The heavy concentration of camas in the Bannock and Northern Shoshone region seems to have led to the importance of the Camas Prairie as a trading center, in addition to the fact that it was also a good staging place from which to launch their large-scale buffalo hunts.[61] As Statham has written, "Although surpluses sufficient to foster the emergence of a well-developed trade were unusual for the native people of the Great Basin,[62] the localized abundance of camas in the northern Great Basin made the potential of trade a reality."[63] Because the well-watered Big Camas Prairie, which extends north of present-day Mount Bennett Hills in south-central Idaho, was such a first-rate foraging ground, it also became a crossroads where Bannocks, Shoshones, Nez Perces, Flatheads, and Pend d'Oreilles exchanged deer hides, horses, buffalo robes, pine nuts, seeds, otter furs, and tanned buckskins, along with a variety of root resources, camas foremost among them.[64]

But in 1871, after the Bannocks complained of the hog invasion into their camas fields, they were informed that a clerical error in the written transcription of their Fort Bridger Treaty had actually altered the wording of "Camas Prairie" to "Kansas Prairie," and thus the region had not been protected. We have no record of what the Indians thought of this feeble explanation. Even their own government agent, M. P. Berry, later confessed, "White men were merely using the mistake as a subterfuge for claiming the Camas Prairie as open for settlement and use by the whites."[64]

Not long afterward dignitaries such as Idaho governor W. J. McConnell and U.S. Army general and Indian fighter George Crook admitted that the Bannocks considered their traditional ties to this Portneuf–Camas Prairie region so vital to their food supply that it was perfectly understandable why, seven years later, they would take up arms to defend this stretch of ground—which could be likened to their bread basket.[66] Indeed, a former Yellowstone National Park official also compared the importance of the plant for tribes in and around Yellowstone National Park to that of "bread" for the non-Indian.[67] While other causes can be cited for instigating the Bannock and Northern Shoshone hostilities of 1878, today's Fort Hall Indians often point to this wanton destruction of their fundamental food source as the major catalyst.

Our emphasis on historical information should not give the misleading impression that nothing is known about Northern Shoshone or Bannock gathering and preparation practices for camas. Although there has not been a systematic ethnographic review of the root and bulb resources exploited by the Shoshone-Bannock peoples,[68] the ethnographic literature contains such frequent references to its use in the Great Basin and Plateau that by historic times it must have been a staple of the Shoshonean diet for centuries if not millennia.[69]

During springtime any Bannocks or Shoshones moving into the southwestern corner of the Yellowstone Plateau would ascend the broad grand steps of the Bechler meadows alert for its telltale blue flowers. Most northern Plains and western Plateau peoples responded with gratitude when that bloom announced that their abundant food staple, the camas root, was ripe for the digging. But flats of flowering camas and yampa could also be found intermittently throughout the plateau. For instance, one probable harvesting place lay alongside Fishing Bridge, in the very core of the present-day park. Wherever the Shoshones moved in the months of June and July, a large part of their attention was paid to favored spots for digging out these hyacinth-shaped, bulbous roots, which were generally buried no more than about four inches into the ground. They unearthed them with the aid of fire-hardened wood or antler digging sticks—later to be replaced by metal hay rake tines with metal, horn, or wood pushing handles.

ETHNOGRAPHY AND FOLKLORE

For more fine-grained ethnographic detail on how camas was gathered, prepared, and celebrated, it seems more fruitful to return to literature on tribes to the north of Yellowstone National Park. From such material we get a sense that dependence on camas and other ground tubers was not uniform. While the Blackfeet did not rely on camas to the extent of the so-called West-Side tribes like the Kootenai, Salish, and others, they too occasionally roasted them in stone-lined pits.[70] Yet some anxiety seems to have attended its processing ,which, although camas was abundant in their region, may have inhibited its use by the Blackfeet, as explained by Schultz and Donaldson:

> It was a belief of the Blackfeet that, if a pit of camas proved to be improperly roasted, overcooked or undercooked, death would soon come to the roasters or to their relatives. For that reason they did not gather and roast it. But when at peace with the West-Side tribes, as sometimes happened, they eagerly traded buffalo robes and buffalo leathers for all of it that they could possibly obtain.[70]

While a wide range of Yellowstone-connected Indian peoples depended to some degree on this plant, the most detailed account concerns camas use by the Flathead and their neighbors.[71] Attempting to understand the place of Flathead camas practices within their annual subsistence pattern, anthropologist Richard Malouf quotes Indian agent R. H.Lansdale from around 1860:

> They go to buffalo every year—first in April, "to Bulls," as it is called, returning the latter part of June; the second, or fall hunt, "for Cows," they start in August, and get back generally in December or March following. The "bitter root" is dug and cured in May; the "camash" in June and July.[73]

These bulbs, known by a number of terms to delineate whether the plant was raw, cooked, or of the smaller, sweet subspecies, were so vital to the Flathead diet that they dubbed the month of June "Camas Moon."[73] That was when the wet meadows became covered with carpets of swaying flowers that looked "like a blue lake,"[74] and when Indians kept on the lookout for the ripening of the black seeds in their pods. For some tribes around Yellowstone National Park, such as the Shoshone and the Flathead, the harvest was generally a family affair; for others, like the Nez Perce, it was communal, with up to one hundred or more Indians joining together in a summer root-digging camp.[76]

When the petals began to wilt the pods indicated that the bulbs' stored energy was at its peak, and that their black skin was easiest to peel off.[77] As Flathead families returned each year to their favored digging grounds, it was largely women who did the work, with much of the effort by grandmothers and their grandchildren poking two-and-a-half -foot-long elk antler or fire-hardened digging sticks made from serviceberry wood to loosen the ground around the bulbs and uproot them.[78] From sunrise to late afternoon each woman covered about a half acre a day and could accumulate a bushel's worth of roots that they stored in special baskets or rawhide bags.[79]

Once stripped of their onionlike skin, the crisp bulbs could be enjoyed raw on the spot, but the bulk of their crop was cooked in round roasting pits dug at their temporary gathering camps. These underground ovens could range from 14 to 235 cubic feet.[80] Exactly how they were preheated depended on whether the firewood or river boulders came first, or whether the rocks were heated elsewhere before being laid inside. Once the firewood had burned down, however, and the floor was cleared of ashes, some grass or other foliage was laid on the hot rocks that were left inside, and the camas roots were laid upon them, with black tree moss (*Alectoria* sp.) sometimes added for flavor. Often the camas were placed in layers, with intervening tiers of grass and moss, the whole topped by moistened moss, bark, or rocks and a final cap of a buffalo robe to seal in the steam. A final fire sometimes burned atop the pit as well.

From the summary by Richard Malouf we know that any of the moist, soft, and sweet camas that were not eaten immediately were dried—often pounded first with pestles—in the form of loaves or cakes.[81] If kept dry, camas could be stored in rawhide bags indefinitely; the explorer David Thompson remembered some that were edible after thirty-six years on the shelf.[82] But the plant could also be boiled and eaten in a gelatinous stew, or when boiled with meat broth or powdered with black moss and simmered in blood it made a prized hot beverage. All these methods yielded a starchless, fructose-rich, energy-intensive food source for Indian peoples.

Among the Flathead, Salish, and Kootenai, the cycle of camas harvesting and processing culminated in special ceremonies. Immediately after the harvest, the Flathead staged an outdoor thanksgiving Camas Dance back in their home village. But a more important celebration associated with the plant opened their Midwinter Festival in January and was immediately followed by the Bluejay Dance. An anticipatory ritual for maximizing an adequate supply from the camas meadows the next June, this celebration also provided an opportunity for sealing marriages and social interaction.[83]

Malouf found narrative traditions connected with the plant hard to come by. Wherever he did learn of folklore, however, the origin of camas was always attributed to the culture hero, Coyote. An unpublished M.A. thesis by Ron Stubbs contains the Flathead comment that as Coyote traveled along he distributed their bulbs across the landscape out of a bag he carried, an Indian version of Johnny Appleseed.[84] But the more common motif has Coyote creating them out of his backside, from his excrement. The Blackfeet word for *camas*, noted Edward Curtis, also means "dung."[85] Then Richard Malouf repeats a story heard from a Kootenai in which the places where Coyote defecated become camas prairies.[86] From the same tribe, Teit had already collected a tale, "Coyote Goes Visiting," in which Moose "slapped his backside," boiled up the camas that came out, and fed it to Coyote.[86] The fullest version of this puzzling equation of camas and excrement was published by W. J. Hoffman in 1883,[88] which Willard rewrote in 1992 as follows:

> Coyote and his five sons went traveling one day to visit Elk, who also had five sons. When they arrived at Elk's lodge they found no one home and nothing to eat. They were quite angry and put out because they were very hungry. Shortly Elk arrived and after greeting his guests leaned over and picked up a stick and started digging his backside with it. Out came camas roots. Coyote was very disturbed. He felt it was impolite to serve one's guest dung and so he loudly complained. Elk said, "that is not dung but delicious camas root. I often carry them that way when I travel." Coyote tried them and found them quite tasty. He and his sons ate their fill.
>
> When Coyote departed, he asked Elk to visit him some day. The next day Elk showed up. Coyote went over and picked up a stick to dig at his own backside, only to cause a wound. Elk said that only he could do it so he took the stick and produced another feast of camas from his backside. As a form of friendship, Elk spread material from his backside all around the area to form camas roots.[89]

The two explanations for this association of excrement and camas might be termed the mimetic and the psychoanalytic. Willard offers the explanation based on mimesis, or similarity, when he adds at the end of his rendition of the narrative, "To this day, camas roots appear a little bit like elk or moose dung when they are first dug up, and after they are roasted." While Malouf concurs that from such narratives "one could conclude that the allusion was due to the similar appearance of cooked camas bulbs and the excrement of large members of the deer family," he remains bewildered by the fact that the Stubbs comment mentioned above refers less to Coyote's excrement than to the camas prairie landscape where his defecation took place.[90]

The psychoanalytic interpretation of such a story is less concerned with similarities in physical appearance than with psychological mechanisms for responding to cultural dynamics. Whether it relates to the creation of human beings or to their most precious foodstuffs, the "creation out of excrement" motif has been noted by folklorists in a number of American Indian narratives.[91] Folklorist Alan Dundes has tried to make sense of the overwhelming number of narratives in which human beings are also created by men out of their anal passages.[92] To a psychoanalytically minded folklorist, the explanation for this recurrent motif is that this is the male form of "penis envy"; that is, men are jealous of the female power to give birth and hence through such stories they project a fantasy of being able to do so on their own. In the narrative above, this line of explanation might suggest that men are envious of the prerogatives women enjoy in Plateau or Great Basin societies in regard to supplying the primary foodstuffs. This explanation would even equate the "stick" mentioned in the above story with a male organ, and it would argue that in the kind of autoerotic act for which Coyote is hilariously famous in American Indian folklore,[93] he manages to impregnate himself with it and "give birth" to the precious substance that is camas, thereby reclaiming for men both the power to give life and the credit for this life-supporting plant. Most native people, it must be added, would probably disavow such an explanation as a ridiculous example of non-Indian theorizing. For them, Coyote is simply performing one of his defining tasks on their behalf, offering laughter along with sustenance.

Rise and Reconsideration of the Yellowstone "Taboo" Theory

It was while working among the Wind River Shoshone whose traditions had an impact on the southern and the southeastern reaches of Yellowstone National Park that Hultkrantz first developed his theoretical position that valued the ecological dimension of Indian belief systems. His Eastern Shoshone and Sheep Eater researches began in 1948, when the Swedish Society for Anthropology and Geography's Vega Fund provided him with a stipend for fieldwork in Wyoming over that summer and fall. The following year Hultkrantz wrote a brief comment, "Cultural Formations among the Wyoming Shoshone Indians," for the European publication *Ymer* (1949), and an essay on Shoshone concepts of the soul for *Ethnos* came out two years later. But his summary treatment, "The Indians and the Wonders of Yellowstone," for *Ethnos* would first appear in 1954.

Realizing that it would take more than a few months in the field to do justice to the Shoshones' social and religious culture, Hultkrantz applied for additional Vega funding, and also received a grant from the States Social and Law Scientific Research Council. Returning to work in Wyoming from June 1955 to January 1956, Hultkrantz focused his interviews on the Wind River community, especially the so-called Sage Creek group of Sheep Eater descendants and traditionalists. Yet he also spent time with the neighboring Arapaho in the community of Ethete and accompanied the experienced Yellowstone hand, Jack E. Haynes, around the mountain haunts of the Sheep Eaters. At the same time he conducted archival research at the Indian agencies of Fort Washakie and Fort Hall, dug into the Yellowstone National Park files at Mammoth Hot Springs, the Library of Congress materials in Washington, D.C., and the Wyoming state archives in Laramie. Robert F. Murphy of the University of California, who with his wife, Yolanda, had conducted a study of Shoshonean bands, helped Hultkrantz to obtain hard to get documents.

From this data base, Hultkrantz launched a prolific and distinguished writing career, reconstructing the subtle differences among the lifeways of fishing and buffalo- and sheep-hunting Shoshoneans, interpreting their oral traditions, and refining what he called an "ecological" interpretation of native religious practices. Hultkrantz remained fixated on the impact that the Yellowstone geysers had on the belief systems of Indians, and undisuaded from his conviction that they considered the park region taboo because of their fear of its natural thermal phenomena. "And this tabooing rendered impossible, *inter alia*," he concluded, "a more intensive exploitation of the Park for transit and for settlement."[94]

Hultkrantz became aware that the greater part of what he termed American Indian "popular tradition" regarding Yellowstone National Park had come from Shoshone peoples, most particularly from the Eastern Shoshone at Wind River.[95] However, his opening example of secondhand ethnohistorical data was actually vague as to tribal derivation, and contained some internal contradictions. It was a quote from a letter he found in Hiram Chittenden's famous history of the park, which the Jesuit missionary Pierre De Smet wrote from St. Louis in January 1852, where the priest described the geysers he had heard about but never seen:

> The hunters and the Indians speak of it with superstitious fear, and consider it the abode of evil spirits, that is to say, a kind of hell. Indians seldom approach it without offering some sacrifice, or, at least, without presenting the calumet of peace to the turbulent spirits, that they may be propitious. They declare that the subterranean noises proceed from the forging of warlike weapons; each eruption of the earth is, in their eyes, the result of combat between their infernal spirits, and becomes the monument of a new victory or calamity.[96]

A dozen years later De Smet reiterated this impression of Indian attitudes toward the region:

> The Indians pass these places in profound silence and with superstitious dread. They regard them as "the abode of underground spirits always at war with one another, and continually at the anvil forging their weapons." They never pass without leaving some offering on a conspicuous point of that mysterious region.[97]

For all his familiarity with Shoshone belief systems, Hultkrantz never analyzed the inconsistencies in De Smet's remarks. For example, we did not hear whether the Shoshone cosmology included any kind of "hell," if there was any ethnographic documentation that their "infernal spirits" fought against each other (most epic wars in American Indian mythology are between protohumans and supernatural beings), in what way such evil spirits might be also "propitious," or how they might have had metal weapons that required "forging" before the advent of white society.

These problems with De Smet's report lead one to wonder how much of this picture might have been a projection of Euro-American society rather than any reflection of Indian thought. Indeed, even before the park's infancy and early years it is not exactly clear which ethnic group may have treated these hot pools and spouts with greater trepidation and terror.

Euro-American Demonizing of Yellowstone's Thermal Field

The following series of comments by early non-Indians visiting Yellowstone underscore attitudes that might well have been projected onto native cultures.

Item. In what Leroy R. Hafen calls the "fictionalized history" of George Ruxton's western travels in the late 1840s, there is an account of white responses to the country just over the divide from the deep Yellowstone Canyon, which was "full of beaver, as well as abounding in the less desirable commodity of Indians." Ruxton continued:

> This was the valley lying about the lakes now called Eustis and Biddle, in which are many thermal and mineral springs, well known to the trappers by the names of Soda, Beer, and Brimstone Springs, and regarded by them with no little awe and curiosity, as being the breathing places of his Satanic majesty— considered, moreover, to be the "biggest mind" of "Medicine" to be found in the mountains. If truth be told, old Bill hardly relished the idea entering this country, which he pronounced to be of "bad medicine" notoriety.[98]

Item. Just before his comments above on the unspecified Indian fears regarding hot spots in the general Yellowstone region, Father De Smet wrote of the "Colter's Hell," probably DeMaris Springs, near Cody, Wyoming,[99] "This locality is often agitated with subterranean fires. The sulphurous gases which escape in great volumes from the burning soil infect the atmosphere for several miles, and render the earth so barren that even the wild wormwood cannot grow on it. The beaver-hunters [Euro-American mountain men] have assured me that the underground noises and explosions are frightful."[100]

Item. During his expedition of 1870, Nathaniel Langford could not avoid similar language in his description of a thermal area south of Mount Washburn:

> The spring lying to the east, more diabolical in appearance, [was] filled with a brownish substance of the consistence of thin mucilage, emitting fumes of villainous odor. . . . This was a most perfect realization of Shakespeare's image in Macbeth-and I fancied the "black and midnight hags" concocting a charm around this horrible cauldron.[101]

Item. Lord William Blackmore, a British anthropologist, thought the thermal springs he saw during his 1872 trip through the park were "horrible and appalling." He could well understand the impression "that you have at length come to the entrance to the infernal regions." He continued, "I have never seen anything so thoroughly diabolical in my life."[102]

Item. During the Jones reconnaissance expedition into the park in summer 1873, the scout who seemed most afraid of the geysers turned out to be a white man, not an Indian. And Jones invoked Christian and not pagan cosmology as a way to contextualize the man's reaction: "The spot has most of the physical characteristics of our best authenticated conceptions of hell; and one of our guides, who discovered it, did not tarry, for he felt certain that 'the devil was not far off'."[103]

Item. Should we deduce anything about America's ambivalent relationship to "wilderness" from the fact that few locales in the United States are as plastered with demonic place-names as this symbolic center of our national park system? Writes Merrill D. Beal, "Surely [the park founders'] concepts of Christian theology rendered them acutely conscious of the attributes and environment of His Satanic Majesty" when they provided such place-names as Devil's Slide, Hellbroth Springs, Brimstone, Devil's Hoof, Devil's Den, Devil's Kitchen, Hell's Half Acre, and Hell Roaring Mountain,[104] among the more than fifty diabolic toponyms once used in the park that were tallied by Lee Whittlesey.[105]

Item. Reviewing such early comparisons between these thermal hot spots and Christian cosmology led the Yellowstone aficionado Gary Ferguson to conclude:

> Clearly, infatuation with hell and evil is much more a trait of white visitors and explorers than Native Americans. And given the Christian preoccupation with wickedness, it's easy to see how one might interpret the offering of gifts [by Indians] to a geyser basin as an attempt to please an angry, fearsome god. Indeed, this tendency to project a European view of the cosmos on other cultures is found in much of our so-called "Indian lore."[106]

ATTITUDES ABOUT YELLOWSTONE IMPUTED TO INDIANS

What is revealing about the Euro-American citations above is how many of their analogies, rhetorical turns, and moral implications are reflected in attitudes about the Yellowstone thermal area that are attributed, often by the same writers, to Native Americans. For a sense of this similarity, here is a representative sample of comments about American Indians and their alleged feelings about the area.

Item. Contended Walter Trumbull, a member of the Washburn expedition of 1870, "[T]he unscientific savage finds little to interest him in . . . places [like the thermal hot spots]." Instead, Trumbull argued, Indians "would give [such places] wide berth, believing them sacred to Satan."[107]

Item. When General Philip Sheridan was contemplating visiting the park in 1877—the very same year that the Nez Perce would cause havoc as they cut through the place—he reassured his superiors that he envisioned no problems with Indians

Cover of Yellowstone National Park guidebook, published by the Northern Pacific Railway in 1917, suggesting Indian timidity as opposed to fur trapper's confidence. (Photo courtesy of Yellowstone Research Library.)

because the region was "to their superstitious minds associated with hell by reason of its geysers and hot-springs."[108]

Item. Looking back on her tragic experience with the Nez Perce in the park in 1877, Mrs. G. F. Cowan reiterated the prevailing opinion at the time:

We are told that the Indian is superstitious. To him anything out of the ordinary must be possessed of the Evil One. The phenomena of the geysers account for the fact very probably that this land is not now and never has been an

Indian country. Few Indian trails are found within the boundaries of the Park, as they are in other parts of the West. Yet, this year, of all others, the Indians are very much in evidence in the National Park, as we found to our evidence.[109]

It is possible that after her park experience Mrs. Cowan accepted what she was "told" and made exactly the causal connection between Indian beliefs about the park and the lack of Indian presence there that Superintendent Norris hoped for in his soothing annual reports.

Item. Norris's construal of Indian beliefs for his own purposes is evident in his comments in 1880, when he claimed that the Shoshone and Bannock were "deterred less by these natural obstacles [the high mountains and deep snows] than by a superstitious awe concerning the rumbling and hissing sulphur fumes of the spouting geysers and other hot springs."[110]

Item. Entering the park from the south with their Shoshone guide seven years later, the Owen Wister party "sealed [their] rifles" because of the ban on hunting and then "took [their] way into the haunted land, the domain possessed of devils, shunned by the Indians of old."[111]

Item. In his 1907 historical sketch of the park, John H. Raftery attempted to synthesize Indian attitudes toward the region:

> Out of the vague, unwritten lore of Indian tradition come the remote rumors of an enchanted land among the mountains where the rivers boiled, the earth burned and haunted lakes tossed spectral plumes of scalding steam into the zenith. Here in cauldrons of gypsum or jasper or jade the evil spirits mixed their war paint, and from peak and promontory, in the valleys, and on the hills could be seen the spiral smoke of their bale fires. The nomads of the Northwest shunned it as a land of evil haunt of prowled around its margins in awesome fear and reverence.[112]

Item. We are informed by the historian Grace Hebard that the Shoshone, along with "all other tribes who knew of the mysterious nature of the Yellowstone National Park, believed that the geysers, paint pots and weird rumblings were a real conflict of the evil spirits as they fought within the recesses of the earth; for this reason, the wonder of the park was shunned and feared by the red man."[113]

Apparently recycling De Smet's comments without any cultural critique or contextualization, Hebard here compounds her errors of (1) lumping "all" tribal beliefs in the area and then (2) without any documentation, stating that they share some belief in combat between underworld evil spirits by (3) the following implausible scene almost certainly borrowed from Father De Smet:

> When acting as escorts or scouts for military or exploration forces marching into the Yellowstone country, the Shoshones always offered up a sacrifice before entering the land where were "the rumbles within the earth that heralded the geyser eruptions, which the red man regarded as the forging of warlike

weapons by the spirits; each eruption bespoke a victory or defeat of one band of spirits."[114]

As we have seen, well before Hultkrantz entered the debate, this matter of Indian reactions to Yellowstone's thermal fields and geyser basins became politicized. Early park boosters used the dubious comparisons to substantiate the idea that superstitious, terrified Indians steered clear of geyser basins and detoured around the heart of the park.[115] By the late nineteenth century the notion of Indians staying away from the park because they feared its spirits had become a truism of Yellowstone history. It permeated popular consciousness and was often invoked when the topic of Indians in the park came up. Potential tourists need not worry about Indians, declared Yellowstone concessionaire Charles Gibson in an interview with a *New York World* reporter, for the following reason:

> There are none [Indians] within the Park. They believe it is the abode of evil spirits and don't like to go there. In fact, they will not even talk about it. . . . The Northern Pacific Railroad, however, runs through the Crow Reservation this side of the Park, and of course there are Indians there, but they are so well guarded by the soldiers that there is no danger to be apprehended from them.[116]

So far we have briefly sketched the spectrum of Anglo-European emotional attitudes toward Yellowstone's hot spots and their portrayals of Indian responses to those same places. Now let us resume the efforts we have made in chapters 1 and 3 to see its thermal wonders through Indian eyes.

NATIVE BELIEFS AND PRACTICES REGARDING HOT SPRINGS AND GEYSERS

We begin this review with our recent inquiries into Plains, Plateau, and Great Basin Indian attitudes toward hot springs and geysers. With regard to thermal pools, virtually all the Shoshonean consultants to our study concurred that they held positive, curative benefits.

SW, a Shoshone elder from Fort Washakie, said that the thermal outlets such as those at Thermopolis, Wyoming, "got some kind of good power." He went on to emphasize that different tribes passing through would camp there because its hot waters were "good for the bones" and alleviated the pains of rheumatism and arthritis. Furthermore, he said, "if you can swim in here with the muskrats you'll never get a cold." This consultant also perceived a subterranean connection between the Yellowstone geysers—specifically, "that place where the water came out," or Old Faithful—and other thermal pools farther away. "This [the Fort Washakie hot spring] is a branch of it [Old Faithful]," he claimed, "and [also] down through Thermopolis." Or, as he would later elaborate regarding Old Faithful, "it's a vein."[117] Indeed, their waning strength was to him a portent of greater disturbances and imbalance in the wider, white-controlled world.

According to other Eastern Shoshone advisors, soaking in such waters—known in their language as *bow-we-ran,* or "steaming water"—not only assuaged aches in the bones, but drinking the liquid also alleviated problems with ulcers and gall stones. "Even today," we were told, "when they have the reenactment for the Gift of Waters, they drink that water in the reenactment."[118] The earthen by-products at the hot springs were also considered healthy. Said FT, "[Our grandparents] even told us that they would go down there just to be in that water. There is also what they call mud-bath, in Thermopolis, by the river. They would go in there and cover themselves with mud. That used to cure sores or things on your body; it would bring out that sickness in your body."

That interview session revealed other uses of minerals at hot springs. The pastelike "white clay buildup" found there was used to whitewash buckskins, or was packed around swollen joints to draw out the pain. Mixed with water it, was ingested—"like Alka-Seltzer" or "Milk of Magnesia"—for indigestion. And it was part of a decoction drunk when water is permitted for the fasting participants at a Sun Dance:

> And then for a religion that meets secretly, they also took that clay, and mashed it up into a fine clay powder. After Sun Dance they put that in their fresh drinking water. . . . Then you don't get sick and get cramps in your stomach after your first drink. . . . [They collected it] in the special place. Most of the people here either get it in Idaho now and in Yellowstone ["At Mammoth Springs. That is where they usually get it at, at Mammoth Springs"—MJG]. . . . But you have to get permission from the Park Service. . . . It takes quite a lot to get permission.[119]

Conversations with contemporary Eastern and Northern Shoshones disclosed the personal use of these thermal areas. After some warmup discussion with Fort Hall elders, one consultant, who maintained that her great-grandfather was buried in Yellowstone National Park, confided:

> In some of those areas, too, up in the high country Yellowstone area, people buried Bannock in those areas. Some of the people, depending on who the individual was, his ranking in the band or the tribe or the group, whoever he was with[,] . . . they would bury them right in the springs, the hot springs. . . . They would just drop them down in there. Then, depending on who it was and what kind of ranking they had, whether they were a warrior or just an elderly person or one with medicine powers or other powers, they were buried in the springs, up in the hills, in lava beds. . . . Generally, the chiefs were the ones who were dropped into the hot springs, the leaders you might say, because that was the quickest way for them to get where they were going.[120]

Joseph Weixelman learned from a Shoshone consultant that the hot springs were "a natural jacuzzi for us. . . . It's healthy . . . there is a lot of value to these springs."[121] When consultants suggested to him that offerings, such as arrowheads, might be left at such sites, with the understanding that they were to remain there undisturbed, Weixelman wondered whether that might explain the stone point found by George Marler while cleaning a hot spring in the Firehole Geyser Basin in 1959.[122]

Such contemporary statements have their resonance in the ethnographic and ethnohistorical literature on the Shoshone and their neighbors, which is peppered with observations on the positive value of springs, both hot and cold. The affinity of the Wind River Shoshone for the "healing waters" at Big Spring and Washakie's Plunge is well documented. Here at the northern end of the reservation, Chief Washakie and his people bathed to relieve their rheumatism and muscular pains.[123] While working among the Northern and Gosiute Shoshone, Steward learned that "a hot spring near Yellowstone was favored [for obtaining powers], but was dangerous because of proximity to Blackfoot," and that "Powers whose identity were unknown to SB [his consultant], were acquired, however, at Soda Springs near Lava Hot Springs" in Idaho.[124]

While researching in the Bureau of Indian Affairs archives at Salt Lake City, Hultkrantz learned that the Shoshone Indians known as "Walkers" were noted for seeking out hot springs for their warmth. As the Salt Lake Valley Indian agent wrote to the secretary of the interior in 1849: "There are many warm and hot springs throughout this country, and it is said to be no uncommon thing to see the Indians sheltering themselves and their children from the bleak and terrible storms which prevail in these grand and rugged mountains, by lying during a great part of the day and perhaps night too in water."[125]

In the broader plains region, the mutual recognition of a sacred spring could, temporarily, quell animosity between blood enemies. In the late 1840s the chronicler George Ruxton heard the following story from a Brule Lakota:

> One evening he drew near a certain "medicine" spring, where, to his astonishment, he encountered a Crow warrior in the act of quenching his thirst. He was on the point of drawing his bow upon him, when he remembered the sacred nature of the spot, and making a sign of peace, he fearlessly drew near his foe, and proceeded like-wise to slake his thirst. A pipe of kinnik-kinnik being produced, it was proposed to pass away the early part of the night in a game of "hand."[126]

Here we might reiterate the suggested Crow Indian use of such healing springs described in chapter 1. In 1830 a Frenchman named Henri Bleau heard from a fellow countryman, known only as Robaire, about some "wonderful boiling springs, not far distant, whose waters he said were a cure for all diseases that man was heir to."[127] Their conversation occurred on today's Henrys Lake in Idaho, but Whittlesey believes this location sounds more like Mammoth Hot Springs. Along with some fifteen Crow Indian families, who may or may not have been his guides, Robaire went to the springs:

[H was so badly crippled up with rheumatism that he could not take a step without crutches, and now he was as straight and active as a young man. There were several in our party who had been suffering from this disease, and I was among the number. We were delighted and determined to visit the medical springs and test their healing qualities before another month had elapsed.[128]

We also have documentary support for assertions by our consultants that Shoshones chose hot springs for human burials. Before his death in October 1884, the noted Shoshone chief Pocatello made arrangements for his internment at a sacred spring near the American Falls. As Judge Walter T. Oliver described this remarkable ceremony,

First we took the chief and wound all his clothing around him, then tied his guns, knives, and all his hunting equipment and relics to the clothing with willow things and tossed him out into the middle of the spring, and he went to the bottom quickly. Then the Indians took the eighteen head of horses, killed them one by one and rolled them into the spring on top of the old man, and they too were soon out of sight, for the spring is said to have no bottom.[129]

An astonishing example of a similar burial on Utah's Shoshone–Ute boundary was reported in 1855 by George W. Bean, a Mormon missionary to the Indians. Leaving Redden's Springs and heading for the Rush Valley, Bean and his group came upon a warm saltwater spring that was used for burial by Indians whose camp remains Bean could detect on nearby hillsides. What Bean saw underneath the warm waters was almost unbelievable:

This crust of elevation had been formed by the continuous overflow of the mineral water, hardened by its contact with the cold air and projecting over at the top. What was most curious, was the six Indian bodies standing bolt upright and crusted over with the salty deposit in this lake, giving them the appearance of mummies. It was evident that they had heavy weights attached to their lower extremities, thus keeping them perpendicular with their heads three or four feet below the surface of the water. It appeared that other corpses were back of these.[130]

Additional support for this practice comes from the Wind River Shoshone elder, Rupert Weeks. At the end of a story about obsidian, Weeks described a trade between his father and white men in which knives and flintlock rifles were exchanged. As for the ultimate deposition of the rifle, Weeks told his grandchildren: "It is buried with your great-grandfather near Wonzee Kawdee, the place where male antelope feed on top of a high plateau south of Dea Pa Qee Wuana, the little hot springs. We lowered him into a deep hole and covered him with stones, so that the coyotes and wolves would not dig up his resting place."[131]

Early Indian fascination for the process of calcification is underscored by a curious anecdote from a Washington, D.C., architect who in 1839–40, at the age

Old Indian campsite in Yellowstone thermal area, near Lone Star Geyser. (Photo courtesy of Yellowstone National Park Archives, #Yell 37824.)

of twenty-five, accompanied a trading expedition that explored the volcanic field around the headwaters of the Yellowstone. E. Willard Smith wrote in his journal entry of December 20, 1839:

> Mr. Vasquez told me he went to the top of one of these volcanoes, the crater of which was filled with pure water, forming quite a large lake. There is a story told by an Arapahoe chief of the petrified buffalo standing in the lake on the east side of the mountains. It was in a perfect state of preservation, and they worship it as a great medicine charm. There are also many moccasin and buffalo tracks in the solid rock along the side of the lake. Nothing would induce this Indian to tell where the sacred buffalo is to be found. Great presents were offered to him in vain.[132]

It may be because the Indians were actually inspired rather than repelled by the Mammoth Hot Springs, hints Yellowstone ranger Dan R. Sholly, that outsiders had to discover them for themselves: "It was easy to see why the Indians had never told the white man of such spectacles. They looked supernatural, especially with their vapors writhing so thickly in the cold."[133]

Finally, there is the conjecture of the geologist George Marler that one important Indian hot bath was located directly in the Lower Geyser Basin, a circular pool about sixty feet in diameter. Marler believed that the thickness of its mineral deposit suggested it had been purposefully constructed sometime before 1870, known variously as Tank Pool, Ranger Pool, or Old Bath Lake. He considered it one of the park's "most important archeological sites."[134]

In the face of this evidence and persuaded by Carling Malouf's archaeological evidence that Indians had not shied away from Yellowstone's hot spots, Hultkrantz tempered his "Yellowstone taboo" hypothesis to draw a distinction between geysers and hot springs. As he narrowed his argument for a 1979 reappraisal, Hultkrantz wrote, "The indications of dangerous spots in Yellowstone Park *all refer to the geysers, not to the less dramatic hot springs.*"[135] Let us ignore the fact that sensible members of many cultures might be expected to experience awe, apprehension, caution, and even fear in the face of boiling hot waters, steaming vapors, and lifelike growling sounds that emerge out of deep holes in an ashen-colored ground that breaks like crust beneath their feet. And if they had children with them, they might be expected to agree that such places are just as dangerous as the Yellowstone National Park signs with slashed red circles warn us that they are today.

As with hot springs, however, so with geysers. Once again, documentary information suggests that when they wanted, Indians could approach Yellowstone's most volatile thermal locations. We know, for instance, that George Harvey Bacon, a miner from Montana, was led to the Upper Geyser Basin by "a friendly band of Indians" in 1865.[136] On August 12, 1935, a seventy-four-year-old Nez Perce from Idaho named White Hawk visited the park to reminisce about the old days and to visit key sites associated with Chief Joseph's famous retreat. At the time White Hawk had been a teenager in charge of herding and feeding the rebels' horses. With him on this nostalgic return was Many Wounds, whose father had been present when the Nez Perce attempted to burn down Baronett's Bridge. In Yellowstone National Park naturalist W. E. Kearns's description of their tour, at one point the old man was questioned about Indian reactions to the thermal areas:

> When asked if the Indians were afraid of the Geysers or hot springs, Chief White Hawk replied that they were not, and implied that the Indians used them for cooking food. They were a source of wonder, undoubtedly, but even these startling manifestations of "Mother Earth" did not alarm them.[137]

White Hawk's comment echoed the Nez Perce reaction to the area that was made by the warrior Yellow Wolf ("The hot smoking springs and the high-shooting water were nothing new to us").[138] It also followed the observations of Indian attitudes made by Frank Carpenter at the time of the Nez Perce invasion of the park. To Carpenter it seemed that the Indians had no hesitation being in the vicinity of geysers in Firehole Basin, and one man even "sprang from his horse and picked up a piece [of smelly hot sulphur] and began a critical examination of it."[139] For further evidence that Indians were not adverse to this Firehole vicinity, we have signs that, for some purpose or other, Indians converged here five years earlier. In an article he wrote for a Montana periodical, James H. Mills recalled his party of travelers meeting with the "Helena Press Expedition" just north of the Upper Basin on the Firehole River:

> Expressing some astonishment at our having come through "the Indian country on the Madison" we learned they had encountered two trappers bound down the Yellowstone with hair on end and horses on the run, who had "seen two Indians and counted twenty ponies grazing at the mouth of the Fire Hole."[140]

Hultkrantz himself heard about their popularity from J.G., one of his part–Sheep Eater consultants, whose grandfather, Rabbit Feet, had been a well-known band chief and who had regularly summered inside the park:

> They raised their tents close to the Firehole Geyser Basin (the geysers there as well as the other hot springs were called pa:gusuuinot "water-steam-standing up"). They watered their horses down at the river. The men themselves bathed in the geysers whilst they directed their prayers to the spirits. J.G. had not heard they were afraid of the geysers, but could not maintain the opposite either.[141]

Contemporary Indians often respond with a chuckle when they are told of the theory that their ancestors cowered before these places. As our leading Salish-Kootenai consultant said:

> These white historians stated a long time ago when Yellowstone Park first opened up that the Indian people were afraid of the geysers, that they just couldn't understand them and that they'd run and hide whenever these things would go off. I talked to some of our elders when I got back (from the park) and they just laughed. They thought that was funny. Because the only reason an Indian person would move away from that area is maybe they had children with them, and they didn't want them to be burnt by that hot scalding water. Our people had a very good common sense. Once one person got burnt they didn't go back and stick their hand back in it again.[142]

Despite the mounting evidence that argues for ancient and historical Indian travel through most corners and core locations of Yellowstone National Park, the question of Indian relations to its thermal fields remains debatable. To a great extent this is because of the tenacity of Hultkrantz, who nonetheless has modified somewhat in recent years his earlier insistence that Indians held the entire geyser region as a taboo area. Both his strident and softened viewpoints are combined in one of his most recent statements about this issue. Hultkrantz offered the following comment on videotape during a tour he and his wife were making of the park on July 26, 1994, hosted by our project:

> The other [Plains Indian] tribes were very much surprised [at the geysers] when they came into the park, many of them at least, while the Sheep Eaters were quite familiar with the features here. . . . The information I received from the

last Sheep Eaters still alive who had roamed up in the mountains was that they were afraid of the geysers. This was quite definite. And I don't think that this is a late superstition that was introduced among them. This is what they thought. And we know from the early sources, practically all early sources, that the Sheep Eaters had this respect and fear for the geysers and consequently they didn't live exactly close to the geysers but out more in the woodlands. This didn't stop them from visiting the geysers now and then. And I think particularly for religious purposes, to have visions there, to give offering to the spirits, because they believed in spirits in the geysers.[143]

But Yellowstone National Park officials were already backing away from their nineteenth-century notion that Indians feared the geysers and had no traditional presence in park's heartland. In 1927 the Ranger Naturalist Manual reminded park employees and interpreters that in 1870 the Washburn-Langford expedition had found along the east bank of the Yellowstone River an old dismantled pit or trench (which could have been an Indian hunting blind of the sort described in chapter 3).[144] By 1949 Yellowstone ranger and writer Merrill Beal no longer accepted the notion that Indians stayed away from Yellowstone because of their fear of the place. Something of a romantic where Indians were concerned, he argued:

After all, Indians were children of nature; the earth was their mother. In Yellowstone Mother Earth was especially intriguing. They might not understand her; they might entertain great respect for her strange manifestations, but cringing trepidation? Hardly![145]

By summer 1961 the park's official approach had advanced to the point that a press release, announcing the donation of a soapstone pot to the Mammoth museum, added the following statement:

The National Park Service now believes that the Yellowstone Park Area may not have been taboo to the nomadic Indian tribes which frequented the Northwest in prehistoric times. Evidence collected over the past several years seems to indicate that many tribes have been more or less permanent residents of this geologically mysterious area.[146]

This declaration may have been drafted by Aubrey Haines himself. He had been sufficiently impressed by Malouf's preliminary conclusions after his survey of the park in summer 1958—when he identified over forty native occupation sites near thermal areas, at, for example, Sulphur Mountain, Gibbon Basin, Norris Basin, Thumb, the confluence of the Lewis and Snake Rivers, Mammoth, along the Firehole River, and even behind the Inn at Old Faithful[147]—to state for an in-house draft of his *History of Yellowstone National Park:*

There is no indication as to how the restlessness of the Late Prehistoric Period affected life on the Yellowstone Plateau. According to Dr. [Carling] Malouf, the evidence indicates that the people who occupied the northern part were culturally associated with sequences characteristic of Montana, while the occupancy of the southern part appears to have had its origin in Western Wyoming and Southeastern Idaho. He points out that use was continuous and relatively heavy, and that it *included the thermal areas.*[148]

A more cohesive summary of evidence against the Hultkrantz thesis came in late 1991 when the Yellowstone Association, with funding from the Wyoming Council for the Humanities, assigned Joseph Weixelman, then a Montana State University graduate student, to conduct a short-term ethnographic and ethno-historical study of the relationships between Indians and the thermal features of the park. Under the direction of park historian Tom Tankersley, Weixelman interviewed representatives from various tribes and researched the historical literature on Yellowstone National Park from October 1991 to July 1992. His carefully footnoted, 101-page report concluded:

[T]he thermal wonders of the Park did not frighten the native peoples of the region. Euro-Americans originated this idea and it must be dispelled before we can understand the true nature of Yellowstone's human past. Native peoples held varied beliefs concerning Yellowstone and different tribes used its resources differently. Each tribe found something of value here. The religious beliefs of a tribe and their proximity to the park shaped individual responses to the geysers. Many tribes approached Yellowstone as a sacred land for prayer and meditation. Some tribes found the thermal waters useful for healing, bathing, cooking and other activities.[149]

The Fate of the Sheep Eaters

We now return to the subject of the fate of the Sheep Eaters, the group of that designation who were presumably at one time the only year-round residents of Yellowstone National Park. We add to our discussion here a sixth misperception about these mountain-dwelling Shoshone (see chapter 3). This misperception remains alive and well today; it is the impression that the Sheep Eaters died out from smallpox, were totally annihilated by aggressive Plains tribes, or lost their separate identity through intermarriage with other Indians—in other words, that they "vanished" or became "extinct."

As early as 1870 the broader Yellowstone region was witnessing a get-tough policy toward any and all surrounding Indians. When a fairly implausible rumor of possible Crow raids in the Gallatin and Yellowstone Valleys reached James Stuart, for instance, he seized the opportunity to advocate no quarter against Indians: "I would like it better if it was a fight from the start; we would then kill every Crow that we saw, take [away] the chances of their rubbing us out."[150] Around the same time the fabricated story in the *Helena Daily Herald* of the slaughter of eighteen Indians at the Falls of the Yellowstone also revealed the tenor of the times. According to Haines, anti-Indian sentiment was "common among the prospectors," who were swarming into the northern reaches of the park. In this false report the Sheep Eaters were singled out as the target of both white rifles and inflammatory rhetoric:

> We felt no great uneasiness however, knowing full well that with our improved firearms, we would be enabled to overcome fifty of the sneaking red devils. It is proper to add, that the 'Sheep Eaters' are those of the Snake and Bannack tribes, who would not live with their brethren in peace with the whites. . . . A body of savages who would gladly welcome death in preference to capture.[151]

In 1871, with animosity toward Montana Indians in the air, J. A. Viall was appointed superintendent for Indian Affairs in Montana for the Shoshone, Bannock, and Sheep Eaters. This mixed group of mountain Indians, banded together for survival, subsisted by fishing in the Salmon River region during the spring and summer before moving to the Yellowstone region to hunt buffalo in fall and winter. Viall first tried to relocate these Indians with the Crow, an arrangement to which the Crow agreed. He dispatched A. J. Simmons to "Stinking Water Valley, Virginia City, Beaverhead, and other places, to gather together the scattered remnants of these tribes, who were prowling around the country half starved, and in deplorable condition, for the purpose of taking them to the Crow reservation."[152]

Apparently a few families joined the Crow, but the majority, especially the Bannock, were not welcome because during the fall and winter buffalo hunt of 1870, they stole some Crow horses, and the deal was off.[153] So Viall had Simmons escort the assembled group instead to a valley about twenty miles above the mouth of the Lemhi Fork of the Salmon River. Although not identified as such by Viall in his annual report to the Commissioner of Indian Affairs, the location was probably within the two townships of land described in the 1868 unratified treaty as the Shoshone, Bannock, and Sheep Eater reservation. It was also important as a pass through the mountains via Lemhi Pass, and not far from the route taken by Lewis and Clark when they crossed the Continental Divide. Simmons entrusted the Indians to agent A. I. Smith, who set to building fencing and plowing about four hundred acres. Smith reported that the Indians were willing workers and that in the year they had dug nearly two miles of irrigation ditches, erected three log dwellings, and dug two root cellars.[154] The fruits of their labor were reported as 3,000 bushels of potatoes, 160 bushels of wheat, and about 160 bushels of barley.[155] In addition, they had caught, dried, and stored 30,000 pounds of fish.

The "Lemhi farm," as it was sometimes called, was an auspicious beginning for its group of only six hundred mountain Indians. But in 1872, the crops were severely damaged by grasshoppers. A new agent, J. C. Rainsford, complained that obstructions on the Columbia River were limiting the number of fish.[156] Then the crops were again destroyed by grasshoppers in 1875,[157] and the agency buildings were moved a few miles in 1876.[158] Nonetheless, the Lemhi Valley Agency, also known as the Ross Fork Agency, remained in existence until 1880, at which time the mountain Indians were instructed to move to Fort Hall. Tendoy, a Shoshone leader and the person usually recognized by the U.S. government, was infuriated by this order, threatening to go to war before moving to Fort Hall.[159] In 1907, one year after the noted anthropologist Robert Lowie visited them, the last of the Shoshone, Bannock, and Sheep Eaters finally moved from the Lemhi Valley Agency to Fort Hall.[160]

But other Sheep Eaters remained in Yellowstone National Park and eventually joined Chief Washakie's Eastern Shoshones.[161] One has only fragmentary hints concerning who instigated this later Sheep Eater removal. Haines, citing a letter from the Wind River Reservation agent of August 12, 1929, claims that at least some of the Sheep Eaters who had become isolated in the Yellowstone region entered the Wind River Reservation in about 1871, but we are given no details.[162] There is Washakie's strongly worded objection during a council meeting called by agent James Patten in June 1879 to propose the transfer of Tendoy's band of Western or Lemhi Shoshone to Wind River. "Washakie rose and without hesitation," recalled Patten, to express his vehement opposition to the plan.[163] According to the old chief, the Tendoy group "are mixed up with the Bannocks and there are a good many bad Indians in his band," and all his subchiefs concurred with their leader. Possibly some of these "bad Indians" were also Sheep Eaters, but they would have hailed from the Western group.

Yet from a letter by Park naturalist Dorr Yeager, dated 1929, which Hultkrantz perused in the Wind River Reservation files, one gathers that there was no such objection to the removal of the last Sheep Eaters from Yellowstone National Park to join the Washakie group at Wind River in 1879, but again no details are provided concerning the group's size or the transfer.[164] One learns from the anthropologist Joel C. Janetski that as both a consequence of the "Sheepeater War" and the worries of Superintendent Norris, "the presence of Sheepeaters was perceived as a potential deterrent to tourist traffic," most of the Yellowstone Sheep Eaters were relocated at Wind River and Fort Hall, with a few quite likely transferred (presumably on or after 1879) to the Lemhi reservation on the Idaho–Montana line,[165] but again specifics remain absent.

Following the Sheep Eater removals, Norris and subsequent superintendents remained concerned about maintaining an Indian-free environment. As Norris wrote in his Fifth Annual Report:

The recent sale of the National Park and adjacent regions by these Indians insures future freedom from any save small horse-stealing bands of these tribes also. To prevent these forays, in council at their agency on Ross Fork of Snake River, in Idaho, and in Ruby Valley, in Montana, early in 1880 I obtained a solemn pledge from them to not thereafter go east of Henry's Lake, in Montana, or north of Hart Lake, in Wyoming, to which, as stated on page 3 of my report of 1880, they faithfully adhered. This pledge was renewed at Ross Fork when I was en route from Washington this year, and has again been sacredly observed.[166]

Although these hints of Sheep Eater dispersal present a different picture from that of some mysterious extinction, we still need to know more precisely when, why, and how the evacuation of Sheep Eaters from Yellowstone National Park took place. But what is almost as interesting as what actually happened to the Sheep Eaters, is what writers, bureaucrats, and the general public wanted to think about what happened. The absence of hard facts about their fate provided ample opportunity for the image of the Sheep Eaters to become absorbed into iconic representations and self-serving stereotypes of Indians that were part of American consciousness during the late nineteenth century.

SHEEP EATERS AS "VANISHING INDIANS" AND THE "LAST OF . . . "

In the Euro-American imagination, the end of the old western frontier was often equated with the end of old Indian ways of life. In print and picture, the latter offered a poignant, sentimental symbol for the former: sad paintings and moody photographs depicting various renditions of Indians as a "vanishing race" became commonplace images, trickling down from fine art to mass-produced advertisements. The theory of the vanishing Indian fit the wishful thinking of government bureaucrats, social planners, and popular writers alike.[167] It held that the demise of traditional Indian culture was a natural consequence of disease, depopulation, depression, an innate inability to evolve beyond the level of savagery, and, as U.S. Senator James R. Dolittle put it in 1867, "the natural effect of one race replacing another."[168]

The romantic lament for bygone Indian days was an artistic accompaniment to this cultural and political prediction. But this vanishing Indian theme was actually turned around so that some early representations often portrayed the Indian as lamenting his own demise. This sentimental image in American popular culture can be heard in the "Rising Glory" genre of nationalistic poetry, such as the example written for the opening of the New York Theatre on September 1, 1821, in which Charles Sprague rhapsodized about the growth of America, during which "The startled Indian o'er the mountain flew/ The wigwam vanish'd, and the village grew."[169]

Although the 1820s were so replete with such sentiments that the literary scholar Klaus Lubbers calls it the "last-of-the-Mohicans' decade," he documents that this icon of the "Indian's lament" over an irretrievable past had already been in the air for decades. Popular nostalgia for the red man as a as dying race was also reiterated in the visual arts.[170] Fine paintings, such as "The Last of the Race," an oil by Tompkins Harrison Matteson in 1847, showed dislocated Indian families looking disconsolately over the Pacific Ocean, having been rendered homeless at the very edge of the continent. Or their demise was often pictorially equated with that of their mainstay, the doomed buffalo (as Joseph Dixon would lament in his *Vanishing Race:* "The buffalo has gone from the continent, and now the Indian is following the deserted buffalo trail").[171]

A closely related icon, the "Last of His Tribe," often allowed for the localization and personalization of this "vanishing Indian" stereotype. Poets revisited the birthplace of a famous local Indian chief, or described an old graveyard or pond where the ghosts of departed Indians evoked their vanished past, as Isaac McLellan Jr. wrote in "The Fall of the Indian": "Yet sometimes in the gay and noisy street/Of the great City, which usurps the place/Of the small Indian village, one shall see/Some miserable relic of that race."[172] But it was novels that most powerfully engraved this image into American consciousness, especially, of course, James Fenimore Cooper's *Last of the Mohicans* (1826), although N. M. Hentz's less well written *Tadeuskind, the Last King of the Lenapes* had come out the previous year. Even into the twentieth century, this theme continued to fascinate non-Indians, as the story of "Ishi, the Last of the Yahi Yana" captivated readers from 1911 until the present day. Ishi, the nearly naked, sole Indian survivor of his band's virtual extermination, turned up in a slaughterhouse corral in Oroville, California.[173] Across the nation these "Last of . . . " Indians continued to function as protagonists of novels, or the stuff of local legends, as still today one hears about or sees evocative photographs depicting the "last" Indian full-blood, the "last" speaker of an Indian language, the "last" Indian medicine man.

These images offered a psychological mechanism for outsiders to symbolically justify the physical removal or elimination of Indians that had occurred or that appeared imminent. With such sentimental requiems for the "passing of the Redman," by offering praiseworthy laments for their nobility and indulging in nostalgia for their heyday as Noble Savages and poignance at their extinction, non-Indians at the same time paved the way for their physical elimination and freed themselves of any guilt for it. One might predict how well the fuzzy and mysterious finale to the Sheep Eater story could be configured into these preconceived themes and images.

Writing of his guide and key informant, Wesaw, Yellowstone National Park's second superintendent, P. W. Norris, was one of the first writers to hint at how the Sheep Eater situation might fit into the "vanishing Indian" model. In his first report he wrote:

Owing to the isolation of the Park, deep amid snow mountains, and the superstitious awe of the roaring cataracts, sulphur pools, and spouting geysers over the surrounding pagan Indians, they seldom visit it, and only a few harmless Sheepeater hermits, armed with bows and arrows, ever resided there, and even they now vanished.[174]

MAGAZINE

The Billings Gazette

THE SOURCE

Coming Monday in The Gazette

History of Yellowstone

Section **E**

Sunday, June 29, 1997

A sacred place

prayers buffalo visions

& Yellowstone Park

By LORNA THACKERAY
Of The Gazette Staff

IN THE DEEP quiet that settled over the Sun Dance site in the back country of Yellowstone Park last Sunday night, H.P. Fritz dreamed of bison running through camp.

"It was so vivid I woke expecting to see buffalo around us," he said.

And then he felt the ground beneath him move, rumbling as if a vast herd approached.

"I could have been all these buffalo that have been killed," speculated Fritz, an Independence, Mo., hospital administrator. "Maybe they were trying to tell us something."

A few yards away, John Potter ran with wolves in a dream that has probably simmered beneath the surface for the two years The Billings Gazette artist has been planning the ceremony with Sun Dance Chief Scott Frazier.

"The three of us were running with them, and, as we ran, their radio collars fell off," Potter said.

The Sun Dance was a promise made to Yellowstone's wolves when Potter, of Ojibway and Seneca descent, and Frazier, whose ancestors are Sioux and Crow, adopted them in March 1995.

"Since they are our family, we wanted them to know our songs and be a part of our ceremonies," he said.

When the sun had risen and the praying was done on Wednesday, the third and final day of the Sun Dance, Potter could hear the wolves calling.

"They let me know they were there and that they heard our songs and that they were with us," he said.

Frazier, too, had a good feeling about what he, Potter and Fritz had accomplished.

"I think the Sun Dance we just did is going to open something up that was covered," he said. Now they must wait and see what it is.

Patience

They are patient men — they do not expect sudden revelations or cataclysmic events. But they hope that, through time, their good will and their prayers will help restore the harmony between animals and man and men and the earth, that they believe has been disrupted by recent events such as the killing of bison who wander out of the park.

Indian rituals return to Yellowstone National Park. In an effort "to restore the harmony between animals and men and the earth," which an Ojibwa, a Sioux-Crow, and a non-Indian friend of theirs believed had been "disrupted by recent events such as the killing of bison who wander out of the Park," they were permitted to hold a Sun Dance above Blacktail Deer Creek in late June 1997. (Reprinted with permission of the *Billings Gazette*, Sunday Magazine Section, June 29, 1997, 1E–2E.)

In another official report three years later Norris added a reason for their absence:

[My Indian guide] had made several trips before the one with Captain Jones, one of which was, as I understood him, to assist some friends who had inter-married with the Sheepeaters to leave the Park after the great small-pox visitation some twenty years ago.[175]

Following Norris, explanations that Sheep Eaters' numbers had dwindled because of smallpox would become widespread. One principal proponent of the "smallpox extinction" theory was W. A. "Doc" Allen, whose book for general readers, published in New York in 1913, became the source for other publications that reproduced its misinformation. Nearly every summer a Montana newspaper carries a story about the "extinct Sheep Eaters" and their demise from smallpox. Allen quotes an old Indian woman about their final days thus:

White man got lost and his ponies come into our camp. White man very sick. Medicine man put him in big tepee and take care of him, give much bath in hot water. Man got very red like Indian man, face much all over spots. By and by he die. Then sickness all over camp. Sheep Eater run off in forest and die. Sheep Eater all much scared and run away. Many tepee standing alone, all dead inside.[176]

Allen explains that a handful of survivors descended into the valleys and were given refuge by other tribes. Other authors merely stated that the Sheep Eaters were extinct, without providing any further explanation. As "Bill" Daniels wrote in 1953, "There are no known survivors today, but small bands of the Sheep-Eaters were common as late as 1880."[177] Hebard gave intertribal warfare as an explanation for their disappearance:

They were a timid and fugitive people, who lived in the most inaccessible part of the Absaroka, Ten Sleep and Teton mountains, and who, in their rare con-tacts with whites, showed themselves generally friendly. Ultimately the Sioux penetrated to their recesses and virtually exterminated them. Of their history we know little, for though they left on the mountain walls many engravings and bright-colored paintings that may tell their story, the characters have never been interpreted.[178]

The magazine journalist Keith Barrette offered the sort of sentimental eulogy to which other "vanishing" Indians like Mandans of North Dakota or Indian enclaves of California have been subjected:

Civilization proved too much for the Tukudeka. . . . The plague was thorough—so thorough that the only memorials remaining are the empty campsites, the conical skeletons of abandoned lodges, the empty and silent sheep traps. Not even the saga of a battle has come down to us. The names of their great chiefs, or elders, if they had any, are unknown. The Tukudeka stand in the vague mists of western history, ghostly, almost formless shapes. Only the mountains are their remaining glory.[179]

This sentimental message, which writes an epitaph to Sheep Eater society so as not to be forced to deal with their intermixed history, continues to be recycled today. In a feature article headlined "Sheepeaters Were Doomed by Smallpox" in the July 9, 1979, *Billings Gazette,* John Bonar wrote: "Beware of the white man's smallpox. The terrified cry echoed through what is now Yellowstone National Park. It was the early 1800's. This warning came from a shy tribe of small Indians known as the Sheepeaters."[180] The "smallpox extinction" idea promulgated by Allen is also perpetuated in a video entitled "The Sheepeaters: Keepers of the Past,"[181] which is sold in Yellowstone National Park. A softer variant on the theme, in which most Sheep Eaters reportedly succumbed to European diseases once they were moved onto reservations, is also found in a recent newspaper feature.[182] The story's final scene has Sheep Eaters losing their separate identity as they are absorbed into the general population—despite the fact that the Idaho census continued to list them separately for years after they moved onto the reservation and that when Hultkrantz and others conducted fieldwork among the Shoshones, everyone on the reservation knew which tribal members claimed Sheep Eater ancestry.

When Allen's *The Sheep Eaters* was reprinted in 1989, it lacked any updating or critical commentary. Its front matter contained a brief note informing the reader that the book concerned Wyoming Sheep Eaters and referred anyone interested in the Sheep Eaters of Idaho to the University of Idaho archivist. The new edition did include—without the author's permission—a reprint of "The Sheepeaters," a reliable article written by David Dominick and originally published in *Annals of Wyoming* in October 1964. It should be noted that Hultkrantz discredited the Allen book,[183] but perhaps because Hultkrantz referred to these Indians by their Shoshone name, the Tukadika, instead of as Sheep Eaters, his critique has been ignored.

Along with entering the Sheep Eater story under the "vanishing Indian" category, Allen added his own version of the last-of-his-tribe stereotype. He claimed that the Indian-spoken account of the tragic end of the Sheep Eaters—the quote reproduced above—came from a woman named "Woman Under the Ground" who was the last living Sheep Eater Indian; he even provided a frontispiece photograph of her. Allen claimed to have met her through the Crow Chief Pretty Eagle. Known locally as "Doc Allen," William Alonzo Allen practiced dentistry in Billings, Montana, at the turn of the century, but by trade he was a blacksmith.[184] He was born in 1848 and arrived in Montana Territory about 1876. Shortly after his arrival, he claims to have heard of a Sheep Eater woman still living in the mountains and to have finally stumbled upon her by chance, while hunting in the Bighorn canyon in 1877 and living among the Crow. Through sign language she reportedly communicated the sad tale of her tribe, "the ancient Sheep Eaters."

During photographic research for this book, we probed the origin of the uncredited photograph of "The Woman Under the Ground" that appeared in Allen's book. In the Montana Historical Society we found a duplicate of the same image, but according to handwriting by O. S. Goff himself on the back of the historical print it was identified as his image of an "Old Crow Squaw." Goff had shot the picture in Fort Custer, Montana, where he served as the post photographer. Were we to assume that Goff was actually wrong, and she was indeed a Sheep Eater, there would then be a problem with her age. For Allen informs us that Woman Under the Ground was 115 years old in 1877 and thus would have been 126 in 1888 when Goff made his picture, which seems highly unlikely. It is more probable that Allen found a photograph of an old Indian woman to match his "invented Sheep Eater" and used it to enhance his credibility. Because Goff retired from the photography business in 1900 and moved to Idaho, where he remained until his death in 1917,, perhaps Allen felt the photographer would never dispute his claims that she was the last living representative of her people.

So smitten was Superintendent Norris, too, by the sad demise of these mountain dwellers that he weighed in with his own poetic treatment. In his assortment of odd writings that swing between allusions to the "bloody raids" by Yellowstone's "superstitious" Indians and condemnations of white greed for Indian lands, one finds in these verses, under the title *The Mystic Lake of Wonderland,* a sense of guilt about Sheep Eater treatment at the hands of their evictors:

And here by lonely rill I find—
Sad trace of race to pale-face kind,
But feeble, few, and shy of men—
A wick-e-up of brush in glen,
And (blanket-robed for want of grave),
Last of his band, "Sheep-Eater" brave.

And now I pause and sadly think
Of cruel scenes ne'er traced in ink;
Of kindly words and acts of those
We curse and treat as savage foes,
Yet practice crimes that dark disgrace
Our Christian creed and bearded race.[185]

SURVIVAL OF THE SHEEP EATERS

Misrepresentations to the contrary, the Sheep Eaters did not vanish or become extinct. Three years after the "Sheepeater War" of 1879, General Philip Sheridan was guided through Yellowstone Park by Sheep Eater scouts, by then confined to

Wind River consultants of Åke Hultkrantz who were either Sheep Eaters or in-laws of Sheep Eaters. (Photo courtesy of Åke Hultkrantz and The Lucius Burch Center for Western Traditions.)

the reservation, who "were greatly excited in getting back to their old country."[186] Among other refutations of premature declarations of Sheep Eater extinction was the continued presence in southern Wyoming of the Sheep Eater guide and renowned medicine man named Togwotee. Prominent among the Sheep Eater contingent that was granted refuge on the Wind River Reservation around 1872 by Chief Washakie, Togwotee periodically appears throughout the early record of the Wind River Reservation. Yet in the following summary of our documentation on this somewhat mysterious individual we also have an illustration of the contrast between outside, or public, knowledge regarding an Indian figure that has been gleaned from written documents and the inside, private, or even "esoteric" information providing an Indian perspective that has been compiled largely from oral sources.

From the written record, we know that Togwotee was among the Sheep Eater minority of Shoshonean guides who led William A. Jones of the Corps of Engineers into northwestern Wyoming in summer 1873. With Togwotee personally leading the way, the Jones party navigated the mountain pass between the head of the Wind River and a small tributary of the Snake River. During the journey, one of the group's members, a geology professor named Theodore B. Comstock, got the impression that when his "mountain Shoshone," or Sheep Eater, status caused other Indians to look down on him or make derogatory remarks, the man known as Togwotee merely looked "annoyed" and generally paid them little mind, for "he was then of much importance on account of his superior knowledge of the country through which he was guiding us."[187]

Clearly this Sheep Eater guide also made a favorable impression on the expedition's leader, for Jones made sure the man's name would live on. After being led across the pass known to Shoshone Indians as simply *pia wia:wi*, or "Big Gap," Jones renamed it "Towgwotee Pass," in line with his preference for attaching easy Indian names, wherever possible, to the prominent features of the country.[188] Another story for this place-name harkens back to the literal meaning of Togwotee's Indian name: *togoti* is said to translate as "Shoots with a Spear," referring to his keen marksmanship. When he guided the Jones expedition through the "Big Gap," it was said to be as though he was sighting the white men toward a "bull's eye" with the same skill that made him always strike the center of his target.[189] This information ties the name to the arrow-throwing contest, a form of Indian competitive sport that is still practiced in Crow Indian reservation districts of south-central Montana each spring. To play the game, the Sheep Eaters first hurled a target arrow, which usually landed from fifty to seventy-five yards away. Then each contestant threw three javelin-sized arrows tipped with heavy, unbarbed heads, aiming as close to the target as possible. According to one account, Togwotee was exceptionally adept at the game, and during a particular meet, all his throws were said to actually touch the target arrow.[190]

In 1878, despite their assistance to Jones, Togwotee and his followers were accused of participating in the Bannock War in Jackson Hole and were rounded up by U.S. authorities. Since they were discovered in a large camp at the "Big Gap" pass, not far from the scene of those hostilities, it was assumed they had joined the Bannock rebels. In fact, they were only hunting elk. But a decade later Togwotee was characterized by an Episcopalian minister as a "veteran mountaineer," "reliable guide," "sub-chief" and "old scout of the Indian wars, trustworthy and intelligent," and cited by name as among the "Mountain-Sheep-Eating Shoshones" who helped to guide President Arthur on his horse ride from Washakie Springs to Yellowstone National Park along Indian paths and wild game trails "through the primeval Forests and mountain passes."[191] Not long afterward, Togwotee was assigned the job of chief of the Indian police at the Shoshone Agency.

That exhausts the written record for Togwotee. When it comes to what we can glean from oral traditions, however, the emphasis is less on physical prowess or scouting skills than on metaphysical knowledge or the inner, supernatural dimensions of his personality. From Hultkrantz's interviews with Wind River Reservation consultants we learn that among his own people Togwotee had a darker reputation as "both a medicine-man and witch doctor" rather than as a "chief." Only an especially strong and brave Sheep Eater might seek *puha,* or medicine power, from among the category of dangerous water spirits. And Togwotee was especially noted for his association with the most fearsome of this supernatural company, the *pandzoavits* or "water ghost woman."

Hultkrantz's Shoshone friends described Togwotee as "tall, slim and crook-nosed." He also learned that the man had two other names: *pa:yorowo,* or "making mark in the water," and *suga b ganigent,* meaning "home in the middle of the bush." When she was working among the Wind River Shosohone from 1977 to 1988, Judith Vander gathered that Togwotee might have been instrumental in transforming the older Shoshonean round dance into the tribe's expression of the Ghost Dance, which was called the Naraya (see chapter 3). Central to the early version of Shoshone Ghost Dance doctrine was the theme of the resurrection of the dead. As described by one of Vander's elder Wind River consultants, who was well into his eighties, Togwotee devised a trick to recruit his people for this new dance.

> One ole man, he was going to make them believe that there is something to that. So I guess he—that was old Togwotee—he's the one. They said they was having a Round Dances and he was kind of with them ones that's have that, in that belief. I guess one time he went and got old rotten wood. He took all that rotten stuff—the top was alright—rotten stuff out, that loose stuff, he push it out. He must of made it just part of it. And he made a hole and he cut eyes in it, where the nose is and the mouth. He must of made some kind of a thing in it so it would hold up that light, I guess, in there—candle. He put that in brush somewhere where he lived. I believe close there they have that Naraya—where they see it themselves. I guess there was a Naraya. And they saw that. Light down in the eyes, somebody down that. And then he told them, "You people dance hard," he said, "The dead is coming back. That's the leader over there."
>
> Vander: "He fooled them."
> Consultant: "Old Togwotee."[192]

Togwotee also possessed special powers that he employed during the Sun Dance. According to Hultkrantz, it was actually Togwotee's use of his destructive rather than curative powers that embroiled him in the sort of "shamanic duel" that has been reported from other parts of Native America as well. The following story, from Hultkrantz's unpublished manuscript on the Sheep Eaters, also accounts for Togwotee's death:

He used to carry a doll that was clad in buckskin and tied to his necklace. He used his power to injure people, for example, by depriving them of [their] *navuzieip* ["free soul"]. His guardian spirit was *pandzoavits* ["water ghost"]. He was also feared in the Sun Dance. If he [someone] danced forward [he became afraid], for then Togwotee might take his *navuzieip*. Especially was he feared when he stood at the center pole and whistled eagerly. His doll represented *pandzoavits*. Many good men and women were killed with this medicine. There was only one way of overcoming Togwotee and thus curing his victim: to call for a medicine-man who had still stronger medicine.

Now Togwotee was living in the vicinity of [the present town of] Dubois. After many appeals from people a Ute [*yu;ta*] medicine man promised to out maneuver Togwotee. The Ute arrived at Fort Washakie, rolled up his sleeve and suck his arm, with his gaze steadily fixed in the direction of Dubois [about 50 miles to the northwest]. In this way [he] deprived Togwotee of his medicine. The Ute sucked the medicine into his body, both the necklace and the doll.

He then vomited up the two objects and held them out in his hands, so that all those standing round about could see them. At his request he was now handed by my grandfather an old muzzle-loader used in buffalo hunting. With a knife he cut the doll into little pieces, loaded the gun with powder, stuffed the doll into the barrel of the gun, and fired. People could then hear the shriek of a child.

The Ute said, however, that this was Togwotee's own voice, and he also said that Togwotee's *puha* was now destroyed, and that Togwotee himself would now fall ill little by little, turn blue and waste away. This actually happened. The name of the Ute Indian was Little Doctor, and he was known as a very clever medicine-man.[193]

Togwotee may have been the best known of the Sheep Eaters who survived on the Wind River Reservation. But other Sheep Eater families sustained themselves in relative obscurity for generations. At least one federal employee reported rumors of Sheep Eater persistence; former Washakie National Forest ranger, A. G. Clayton, wrote in 1926:

Several theories are advanced as to the final disappearance of the sheepeater. One is that diseases of various sorts entered their ranks; another that tribal Indians destroyed them, but it appears that the most likely one is the coming of the white man who, in subduing their enemies the lowland Indians, made it possible for them to return to their former homes and take up the life of the normal Indian. It is said by some that a few are still living on the Wind River

Indian Reservation. In any event these people can justly be considered as the first users of the Washakie National Forest.[194]

Completing research on the Wind River Reservation twenty-eight years later, Hultkrantz interviewed a half-dozen self-identified Sheep Eaters, including the old woman, pictured in chapter 3, who was said to have been born in the mountains. Although today their numbers are not large, descendants of these individuals continue to live and work on both the Wind River and Fort Hall Reservations. As a reminder of this fact, we close with a telling moment that occurred during our third and final ethnographic season.

On June 25, 1996, with the help of the Branch of Cultural Resources, we sponsored at park headquarters in Mammoth a round-table discussion between Yellowstone National Park officials and twenty members of the Fort Hall Shoshone and Bannock and the Wind River Shoshone Indian communities. At the outset of our morning session, each of the Indian visitors was asked to introduce himself or herself by name and identification. When this well-intentioned request was made we were in innocent ignorance of their deep-seated reluctance to expose this sort of personal information. "The Wind River Shoshone do not like to tell their names," wrote Demitri Shimkin, the anthropologist who had interviewed the parents of some of those very same Wind River individuals who were now struggling with the assistant superintendent's invitation. "A man rarely does so—more readily if alone than in the presence of other tribesmen—a woman never."[195] And while working among the Lemhi Shoshone to the west, then residing on the Fort Hall Reservation, Lowie also learned that "[t]he Lemhi people still show great reluctance in divulging their native names; a middle-aged man who had lived with the whites for many years obstinately denied having a Shoshone name, though it was subsequently discovered by chance."[196]

Realizing that we were uninformed about their forms of etiquette and wanting to avoid starting off on the wrong foot, the Indian visitors graciously complied with the official's request. But when they introduced themselves, it is noteworthy that a number of them not only stated that they hailed from this or that Shoshone or Bannock community. About a half-dozen of the visitors also volunteered that they were of mixed descent—" . . . *and Sheep Eater,*" both men and women added emphatically. It was as if this ethnic identification, which for so long had occupied the most denigrated Indian status in the Euro-American literature on Shoshone peoples, was now holding its head high and claiming its rightful place as an indigenous presence in the Yellowstone heartland.

Conclusion

We have assembled enough bits and pieces of data from archaeological, ethnographic, and ethnohistorical sources, collected largely between 1994 and 1998, to challenge prevailing misconceptions about the relations between American Indians and Yellowstone Park. We have questioned the long-standing suggestion that the Yellowstone Plateau was a *terra incognita* before the coming of Euro-Americans. We now know that Indian peoples have visited and utilized practically every corner of the park area off and on for almost ten thousand years. We have documented that during the historic period, Plains and Plateau Indian peoples knew the Yellowstone ecosystem with varying degrees of intimacy, and we have argued that geyser activity did not deter them from exploring and exploiting its habitats. Furthermore, we have proposed that the "Sheep Eaters" were neither the figments of anti-Indian imagination, as some revisionist writings now maintain, nor the timid, stunted outcasts skulking in their mountain haunts as portrayed in the early literature. We have also reported the contemporary interest that most of these same Indian nations retain in their historical experiences in the park, and we have communicated their concerns about strengthening special, "traditional" relationships with its many resources.

Instead of imagining and representing the Yellowstone region as an Edenic wilderness, we have implored the park to reconceive its environment as a multicultural habitat that has been visited, inhabited, shaped, and instilled with meaning by American Indians for millennia and Euro-Americans for centuries. The summary message of our investigations is that the Indian role in the cultural history of the greater Yellowstone ecological system deserves to be restored.

Assessing which of the Indian peoples might have stronger or weaker historical or cultural affiliations with or claims to Yellowstone National Park was never our task. We suspect that the state of knowledge will remain far too fragmentary to ever accurately determine these differential relationships. Like many studies whose limited resources and time frames are unequal to the magnitude and complexity of their charge, our research should be considered an interim report, a provisional contribution. Just because we describe certain Indian peoples as having particular relationships with the park must not preclude the emergence of new ethnographic, archaeological, or archival information that might identify other Indian nations with such claims, or which might corroborate, challenge, or expand our proposed reconstruction of tribal activities in the region.[1] Research remains to be done in government records, in regional newspapers, in field notes of earlier ethnographers, in the folk histories and other narratives still circulating within tribal communities, and, of course, within the strata that contain Yellowstone's underinvestigated archaeological resources.

Despite the scattered and inferential nature of some of our data, early on we developed the conviction that a collection of narrative summaries rather than a "checklist of sites" was the best strategy for presenting this material. Only that way could we call attention to the human nature of the "data beneath the data"—the cultural backgrounds and historical contexts and societal motivations by which any of it made sense. Only then could we provide park interpreters with meaningful frameworks for making storytelling use of facts and figures whose significance to the cultural history of human beings is what excites the imaginations of visitors. And only then could we also educate everyone in the behind-the-scenes struggle of creating, challenging, and updating such explanatory narratives, and thereby demonstrate how the representation of any cultural history is inevitably a work-in-progress.

When these chapters were in their former incarnation as a U.S. government report on the ethnohistory of Indian and Yellowstone Park relations, our conclusion was cast as a list of ten recommendations to park managers and interpreters of Yellowstone's culture and history. We spelled out these recommendations with some care, supporting each with short narratives that functioned almost as documentary affidavits.

We reiterated the incompleteness of our study, and we strongly encouraged the park to continue its ethnographic research projects and update its ethnographic archives. We stressed the need for a long-term, methodically phased archaeological survey and site-sampling campaign for the entire park, and we urged that the park enlist American Indian elders and students as collaborators and interns in this effort.

We pleaded that outmoded museum exhibitions and interpretive programs be totally revamped to fully review and entertainingly illustrate the ten-thousand-year associations between various American Indian peoples and the greater Yellowstone region.[2] We suggested that instead of shying away from controversial topics

Archaeological excavation at the ancient campsite on Osprey Beach in Yellowstone National Park. (Photo by Ann Johnson, 2001.)

the park interpreters might "teach the debates" about sensitive or timely Indian issues, such as access to sacred sites, procurement of culturally important natural resources, proper treatment of buffalo, and respect for and reburial of human remains found in archaeological sites. We supported improving communication with Indian communities by appointing an Indian advisory committee, hiring Indian staff and interns, and instituting cross-cultural workshops. And most important to many Indians, we urged revisiting the issue of entrance fees and hunting and plant foraging policies for native petitioners.

Since our project commenced in 1994, and accelerating after early drafts of our report were submitted, we applauded as the park undertook a number of these initiatives. After some fishermen noticed human remains eroding from the lakeshore in the park in 1996, the Branch of Cultural Resources met with representatives from seven tribes to mutually decide how to handle the "inadvertent discovery." That same year we were also pleased to learn that the secretary of the interior designated Obsidian Cliff as a National Historic Landmark, recognizing it as one of North America's "first industrial areas," a source of tool-making material for nearly twelve thousand years and a dispersal center for intercultural transactions across hundreds if not thousands of miles.

In 1998 Yellowstone National Park hosted a three-day workshop, "American Indians and Cultural and Natural Resources Management: The Law and Practice Regarding Federal Lands," taught by an American Indian lawyer, and a separate "Archeological Resources Protection Program" in which half a dozen tribal members participated. It also invited representatives of those tribes deemed historically and culturally "affiliated" with the park to visit four sites along the Tower-to-Canyon highway that were earmarked for archaeological testing.

To its credit, the park turned the Indian activism that was galvanized by the Yellowstone bison controversy of 1997–98 into an opportunity to liaison in a new, cooperative fashion with approximately eighty-four concerned tribes. Indian perspectives for surveys of park cultural resources, such as Obsidian Cliff or the soon to be reconstructed road between Norris Junction and Mammoth Hot Springs, were elicited through tribal consultations, with similar cooperative research on the Bannock and Nez Perce (Nee-Mee-Poo) trails planned for the future.

In 1999 the park invited representatives from approximately twenty-five tribes to attend its recently instituted twice-yearly consultation meetings. Under discussion were such issues as bison management, enhancing diversity recruitment, building the park's tribal heritage program, and updates on its archaeological, ethnographic, and archival projects. In recent years tribes have also requested permission to collect items including buffalo skulls, plants, and obsidian for traditional, ceremonial purposes. The requests have been handled on a case-by-case basis, with some permissions granted and others met by offering alternatives outside the park where such items could be obtained.

In 2001 Yellowstone continued to strengthen Indian–park relations. It changed its entrance fee policy to allow those "affiliated" tribes to enter the park for traditional purposes without paying the recreation fee. It hosted a round-table for Nez Perce elders and park staff to share perspectives about the 1877 Nez Perce trek through the park. It welcomed a Lower Brule Sioux tribal delegation from South Dakota for a four days of discussion on bison management, reintroduction of wolves, sacred sites, fee waivers for religious and other traditional purposes, and employment opportunities. As of 2002, with the permission of tribes, the park began holding only one annual meeting at Yellowstone, with park managers traveling to various regions to meet with tribes on their home ground, also on a yearly basis. It cooperated with the Confederated Salish and Kootenai in producing "Before Yellowstone," a film about the Salish presence in the Park before 1870. And finally, the park has assured us, "[It] continues to spend time consulting with Native Americans to identify traditional cultural properties, issues of concern or interest, and appropriate ways to handle the protection, interpretation and research of ethnographic resources."

During our years of study of the park, the future for an organized archaeological research program in Yellowstone also brightened. In departing remarks by the chief of Yellowstone's Branch of Cultural Resources, Laura Joss, before her transfer in 2000, she was more conservative than earlier commentators in her estimation of what had been accomplished thus far:

> Maybe 2 to 3 percent of the park has been inventoried for archeology. . . . We have inventoried along the roads and that's often where the tribal people traveled prehistorically. We may be inventorying the highest use areas, but there probably will be a systematic method for inventorying within the park, particularly the back country. Along rivers or lakes, logical campsites for us would have been logical campsites for people prehistorically, too.[3]

Reinforcing Joss's optimism about archaeology's promise in the park were the important discoveries of summer 2001. One was what park archaeologist Ann Johnson extolled as "the oldest intact cultural deposit in the park found thus far." She was referring to the discovery, by a Wichita State University student team conducting a weeklong surface survey under the direction of Don Blakeslee, of two chipped obsidian pieces whose knifelike form has been associated with bison-hunting peoples who utilized much of the greater Yellowstone ecosystem from 9400 to 9600 B.C. These so-called Cody Complex peoples camped and hunted in the Osprey Beach vicinity where those blades turned up, along the park's eastern boundary down into Jackson Hole, throughout eastern Idaho, and along the Madison River.

During that same season, archeologists located agate and chert veins inside the park's Hellroaring Valley, with chipping debris that indicated precontact peoples mined there. Summarizing the five years of archaeological research in Yellowstone's canyons conducted by Bozeman's Museum of the Rockies (MOR), Mack W. Shortt reported that by the end of the 2000 field season MOR teams recorded a total of 224 precontact sites. The evidence strongly suggested that nearly all segments of the Yellowstone River valley were utilized by early American Indians.[4]

As archaeological work progresses in and around the park, we hope that the role of American Indians as ethical guides, content consultants, and student-interns will become regarded as essential and routine. Precedents for collaborative field schools and coauthored research design, such as occurred between the Shoshone-Bannock from Fort Hall and Idaho State University in 1970, and Alaska's Tlingit and Haida Tribes together with the U.S. Forest Service's Tongass Forest Project in 1993, have demonstrated the advantages of native and governmental professionals, tribal elders, and elected officials sharing knowledge and learning together about the past in an atmosphere of trust, respect, and mutual investment.[5]

Perhaps the most important change in Yellowstone National Park administration is the hiring of Rosemary Sucec, a cultural anthropologist who is working toward better relationship between Indians and the park. Rosemary is a very energetic and hard-working advocate for the Indian rights and her presence signals a change in the park's attitude with Indian issues.

In the later stage of researching and writing this book, it slowly dawned on us that Indian experiences with the Yellowstone Plateau echoed within a broader frame of reference. By sheer coincidence the decade of our work coincided with a spate of studies on interactions within the United States and around the globe between native peoples and national parks or game preserves. Truth be told, most of our document was produced in ignorance of this emergent discourse. The downside was a discernible lack of sophistication in our general statements; the upside was independent verification of our references to contradictory cultural definitions of nature and culture and the influences of cultural attitudes and historical processes in the park's immediate region and from the late nineteenth century through the twentieth. For instance, the maneuvers we described to physically distance Indian peoples from Yellowstone National Park and to underplay their historical and cultural associations with the region foreshadowed the modern environmental movement's efforts "to save landscapes from people who live in them," according to the French anthropologist Simone Dreyfus. "Many of them [environmentalists] seem to care more about animals and plants than about people."[6]

Up until the early 1990s, one searched in vain for writings on America's park system that discussed Indian issues and interests, and the same could be said for much discussion of indigenous peoples and natural resources preserves around the world.[7] With the arrival of the last decade of the millennium, however, this neglectful attitude changed dramatically. From the perspective of the case studies in Patrick C. West and Steven R. Brechlin's *Resident Peoples and National Parks: Social Dilemmas and Strategies in International Conservation* (1991), which profiled conflicts between non-native and indigenous game management strategies in or close to national preserves in North America, Africa, and Australia, our Yellowstone findings could be viewed as precursor to what some anthropologists were now characterizing as "green imperialism." When West and Brechlin wrote that "all too many in the international conservation community viewed resident peoples as a clear evil, a 'weed' to be plucked from the purity of wild nature," the nineteenth-century century attitudes of Yellowstone officials and locals alike sprang to mind.[8]

When we discovered Theodore Catton's *Inhabited Wilderness: Indians, Eskimos and National Parks in Alaska* (1997), a detailed investigation of the impact on local native peoples of the establishment of Glacier Bay, Denali, and Gates of the Arctic National Parks, we could have been reading a hypothetical update on Yellowstone's aboriginal peoples, had they not been banned early on from the park. As we encountered Nora Danenhauer and Robert Danenhauer's assertion, which also cited Catton's Alaskan research, that "[t]o the Tlingits [of Alaska] park regulations seem to screen Indian people systematically out of the national park, and since national parks were dedicated to the preservation of nature, they screen Indian people out of nature as well," the resemblance to our own conclusions was unmistakable.

A 2002 advisory meeting of Yellowstone National Park personnel and American groups "affiliated" with the park. (Photo by Rosemary Sucec.)

We were reviewing galleys of our original Yellowstone report, conducted for the park service, when this string of new publications bolstered our sense of the deeper clashes of cultures, ideologics, and representations that lay beneath its surface. From Robert H. Keller and Michael F. Turek's *American Indians and National Parks* (1998), a collaboration between a historian and a natural resource specialist, we were reminded how earlier disputes between native peoples and parks over fishing and hunting rights across the West had set the stage for present intercultural tensions throughout the U.S. National Park system. Although we were unaware of his work, Roderick P. Neumann's *Imposing Wilderness: Struggles over Livelihood and Nature Preservation in Africa* (1998), which analyzed the struggle between Arusha National Park officials and local Meru peasant communities in Tanzania, would have provided an apt comparative case of how colonial-era environmentalism and the symbolic importance of landscape to native peoples often stood at odds. Indeed, Jim Igoe's *Conservation and Globalization: A Study of National Parks and Indigenous Communities from East Africa to South Dakota* (2004) makes explicit comparisons of Tanzanian and American Indian case studies.

After his graciousness in sharing with us unfinished drafts of his chapters, Mark David Spence's completed work, *Dispossessing the Wilderness: Indian Removal and the Making of the National Parks* (1999), more definitively profiled the official machinations by which Indians lost rights to Yosemite, Yellowstone, and Glacier

National Parks. Philip Burnham's *Indian Country, God's Country: Native Americans and the National Parks* (2000) further highlighted land use conflicts in Glacier, Badlands, Mesa Verde, Grand Canyon, and Death Valley National Parks. Regarding the ironies arising from Indian relationships with America's parks, Burnham observed, in the words of Montana reviewer Jeffrey M. Sanders, that:

> [T]he national parks ultimately become rich people's playgrounds, and in some cases economic ventures, at the expense of Indians . . . that the national parks as presented by NPS [National Park Service] as scenic wonders and home to various wildlife, but not for indigenous human inhabitants whose conditions were an embarrassment to NPS and whose traditional land use practices were no longer allowed; and . . . that in the second and third decades of this century, as wealthy Americans were being eschewed from touring Europe and encouraged to come to national parks, Indian people still needed permits to leave their reservations.[9]

Karl Jacoby's carefully researched *Crimes against Nature: Squatters, Poachers, Thieves and the Hidden History of American Conservation* (2001) expanded the cultural frictions caused by the park conservation movement to include the non-native communities in its case studies of the early years of the Adirondacks, Yellowstone, and Grand Canyon parks.

Although these critical perspectives retroactively reinforced the pervasive themes we were articulating within the sometimes inhospitable framework of a government report, they rarely engaged one important topic. That topic is the ways in which parks and their like *represented* and *interpreted* the claims and experiences of their indigenous neighbors or residents. To be sure, as the debate over establishment of the Pajarito or Cliff Dweller's National Park demonstrated years ago, national parks designed around the allure of American Indian culture, prehistoric and historic, have had a hard time appealing to the legislators who must fund them.[10] But the failure of the Parajito proposal occurred in another era (1900–1920), when Indian history and culture were not of widespread interest. We would hope that today, with Americans receptive to "a dramatic new park ethic,"[11] Yellowstone would become a pioneer in viewing its custodianship of a well-aged, multi-stranded American Indian past as an educational and promotional asset.

Set within this growing subset of literature on native peoples and parks, the historical relationships we have reconstructed between Yellowstone and its earlier residents and neighbors seems positioned at the most estranged pole. The Indian peoples who once seasonally exploited the region, who felt free to travel its trails and passes, or who lived there for extended periods paid the highest price in terms of forced removal from the park proper as well as from the stories that the park told outsiders about itself.

This separation of native peoples and natural environments was not always the idea. In fact, George Catlin's 1832 description of the sorts of American parks that the government ought to establish envisioned "[t]he native Indian . . . galloping his wild horse . . . amid the fleeting herds of elks and buffaloes. What a beautiful and thrilling specimen for America to preserve and hold up to the view of her refined citizens and the world, in future ages! A *nation's Park,* containing man and beast."[12] And about twenty-five years later, Henry David Thoreau endorsed the proposal for "natural preserves . . . in which the bear and panther, and some even of the hunter race, may still exist, and not be 'civilized' off the face of the earth? . . . Or should we, like villains, grub them all for poaching on our own national domains?"[13] These vanguard statements did not even insist that this indigenous presence be permanent; it was merely sufficient that they traditionally enjoyed usufruct privileges to the region.

In reality, Catlin's and Thoreau's visions were pipe dreams. Through federal policy, official park practices, and distorted representations of its Indians, quite the opposite sort of approach evolved at Yellowstone and other preserves. They caused over a hundred years of estrangement between living Indians and the park and the "disappearing" of native peoples from park history and interpretation. To the credit of a more enlightened generation of federal policies, park administrators, and Indian peoples willing to forget the past and conceive of new partnerships, this separation is gradually being reversed.

But this is no easy task. For park supervisors, researchers, and interpreters, it calls for abandoning old attitudes and approaches and developing new skills of intercultural communication—which Yellowstone has begun to initiate. For Indians, it asks that the entrenched suspicion and knee-jerk resistance to park initiatives be softened. May the constructive imaginations of Indian representatives and park planners continue to ensure that the presence of Indians past, present, and future in the ongoing history of Yellowstone National Park regains its proper place in a landscape that Indian forebears knew and used and respected for a very long time.

Notes

Preface

1. Magoc, *Yellowstone*, 140.
2. Burnham, *Indian Country, God's Country*, 58.
3. Raftery, "Historical Sketch of Yellowstone National Park," 102.
4. Chittenden, *The Yellowstone National Park*, 8, 99.
5. Beal, *The Story of Man in Yellowstone*, 91.
6. Magoc, *Yellowstone: The Creation and Selling of an American Landscape, 1870–1903*, 190.
7. Cole, "Oral History Interviews," 15.
8. *New York Times*, June 23, 1998, p. B9.
9. Carter, Foreword to *An American Idea*, 161.

Introduction

1. Personal communication, June 17, 1999.
2. Wilkinson, *The Eagle Bird*, 176.
3. Keller and Turek, *American Indians and National Parks*, 24.
4. Sholly and Newman, *Guardians of Yellowstone*, 43.
5. Chittenden and Richardson, eds., *Life, Letters and Travel of Father De Smet*, 243.
6. Haines, *Yellowstone Places Names*, xix.
7. Kay, "Aboriginal Overkill and Native Burning," 121.
8. Kay, "Systems Then and Now," 84.
9. Cronon, "The Problem with Wilderness," 79.
10. Scullery and Whittlesey, "Greater Yellowstone Carnivores," 20.
11. Cannon, "A Review of Archaeological and Paleontological Evidence," 1–158.
12. Schullery, *Searching for Yellowstone*, 314–15.

13. Wissler, "The Influence of the Horse in the Development of Plains Culture," pl. 33.

14. Wissler, *The American Indian*, 8.

15. Kroeber, "California Culture Provinces," 167.

16. Kroeber, *Anthropology*, fig. 41.

17. Kroeber, *Cultural and Natural Areas of Native North America*, map 6, 55.

18. Steward, *Basin-Plateau Aboriginal Sociopolitical Groups*.

19. White, *It's Your Misfortune and None of My Own*, 410.

20. Ortner, *Sherpas through Their Rituals*, 94.

21. Ibid., 97.

22. Wedel and DeMallie, "The Ethnohistorical Approach in Plains Studies," 110.

23. Liljeblad, "The Old Traditions of the Shoshoni and Bannock Indians of Idaho," 7.

24. Fenton, "The Training of Historical Ethnologists in America," 329.

25. Brower, *The Missouri River and Its Ultimate Source*, 131.

26. Norris, *Fifth Annual Report of the Superintendent of the Yellow National Park*, 7.

27. *Yellowstone Nature Notes* 12, nos. 5–6 (May–June 1935): 1.

28. Schullery, *Searching for Yellowstone*, 6.

29. Stuart N. Conner, personal files and records.

30. Davis, Aaberg, and Schmitt, *The Obsidian Cliff Plateau Prehistoric Lithic Source*.

31. Cannon, "Blood Residue Analyses of Ancient Stone Tools Reveals Clues to Prehistoric Subsistence Patterns in Yellowstone."

32. Wright, "Notes on Chronological Problems on the Northwestern Plains and Adjacent High Country," 11–12.

33. *Billings Gazette*, July 20, 1997.

34. Shortt, "Record of Early People on Yellowstone Lake," 9.

35. Whittlesey, "Yellowstone's Horse-and-Buggy Tour Guides," 4.

36. Dorson, "Teaching Folklore to Graduate Students," 463.

37. Bascom, "The Forms of Folklore," 9.

38. Freeman, *Down the Yellowstone*, 1–3.

39. Bascom, "The Forms of Folklore," 9.

40. Norton, *Wonder-Land Illustrated*, 31.

41. Ibid., 31.

42. Clark, *Indian Legends from the Northern Rockies*, 323–24.

43. Haines, *The Yellowstone Story* I, 339.

44. Webb, *Buffalo Lands*, 308–401.

45. Allen, *The Sheep Eaters*, 52–74.

46. Paul, Barnes, and Porter, *Farm Friends and Spring Flowers*, 70.

47. Ibid., 72.

48. Walgamott, *Six Decades Back*, 116.

49. Salmonson, *Phantom Waters*, 123–40. Although we have declared this a specious narrative, which Salmonson's anthologized version entitles "Spirit of the Grey Wolf: The Idaho Legend of Red Fish Lake," it should be mentioned that a shorter version, "The People of Redfish Lake," appears in Heady's collection of narratives that she claims to have collected from Fort Hall Reservation residents (Heady and Stewart, *Sage Smoke*, 89–94). In the Heady account the tribe created by the lovers at Redfish Lake—who were first heading for "the Rocks of Fire" to establish their new homes before a white deer led them "to a big river, over a high mountain, up the Valley of the Salmon, to a blue lake at the foot of a rocky cliff"—is not explicitly identified as Sheep Eaters, as in the Salmonson version. However, the experience of the western Sheep Eaters and their Bannock allies is evoked when we learn that, "as the white deer had

predicted, strange men came, white men with cattle that ate the grass and drove away the game. The Indians grew hungry, for the camas meadows lay trampled and the fish no longer leaped from the waters of the lakes in the moonlight." After a brief resistance, which may be a limning of the Sheepeater War, the Redfish Lake Indians are scattered into the mountains as whites take over their valley. And in an evocation of how they still haunt the region that reminds one of the poetic lamentations of Yellowstone's own Philetus Norris, we are told, "Now, if you stand very still in the mountain forests, you may hear the voices of the wandering people of this land. They sing in the sighing pine trees and along the rippling shores of the blue, clear lakes of the red fish. They cry in the hoot of the owl, the wail of the Coyote, the scream of the eagle. Listen—you may hear their voices weeping for a lost land" (Heady and Stewart, *Sage Smoke,* 94).

50. Yellowstone National Park Archives, File N. 154.31, Lectures, Fiscal Year 1925, 1925, 1927.

51. Madsen, *Chief Pocatello,* 121.

52. Bascom, "The Forms of Folklore," 8.

53. Lowie, "The Northern Shoshone," 251 f.

54. Lowie, "Oral Tradition and History," 161–67.

55. Bright, *A Coyote Reader,* 35.

56. Letter of Jefferson to John Adams, March, 1912, in Foley, *The Jefferson Cyclopedia,* 422–23.

57. Buffalo Bill Historical Center Archives, "Eliza A. and S. Annie Uphams' Excursion with the Raymond Party to The Yellowstone Nation Park in September, 1892," 37–39.

58. Ray, *Cultural Relations in the Plateau of Northwestern America,* 3.

59. For example, see Beals, *History of Glacier National Park.*

60. Meyer, *The Spirit of Yellowstone,* 114.

61. Ibid., 32.

62. Cannon, "Paleoindian Use of Obsidian," 8.

63. Wright, "Notes on Chronological Problems," 158.

64. Clifford, *Writing Culture,* 18–19.

65. Rabinow, "Representations Are Social Facts," 241.

66. Clifford, *Writing Culture,* 25; emphasis added.

67. In Prucha, *The Indian in American Society,* 16.

68. *Congressional Globe* 1868, 2638.

69. Hayden, *Preliminary Report of the U.S. Geological Survey of Montana,* 263–64.

Chapter 1

1. Interview, July 16, 1995.

2. Bearss, *Bighorn Canyon National Recreation Area,* 71.

3. House Executive Document No. 89, 43d Cong., 1st sess., 28.

4. *Bozeman Avant Courier,* June 19, 1879, A2.

5. Skarsten, "George Drouillard," 265.

6. Interview, July 16, 1995.

7. Ibid.

8. Ibid.

9. McCleary, "Plants Utilized by the Crows," 2.

10. Hart, *Montana - Native Plants and Early Peoples,* 11.

11. Interview, July 16, 1995.

12. Jones, *Report upon the Reconnaissance of Northwestern Wyoming,* 278.

13. Dixon, *The Vanishing Race,* 22.

14. Tschirgi, *The Tenderfoot,* 31.

15. These origin scenarios are discussed in Voget, *The Shoshoni-Crow Sundance,* 3–10; Hoxie, *Parading through History,* 36–42; and throughout Nabokov, "Cultivating Themselves."

16. McCleary, *The Stars We Know,* 16–18.

17. Voget, *The Shoshoni-Crow Sundance,* 7.

18. Bradley, *The Handsome People,* 42.

19. McCleary, *The Stars We Know,* 18.

20. Ibid., 2.

21. Ibid., 2–3.

22. Medicine Crow, *From the Heart of Crow Country,* 2; Hoxie, *Parading through History,* 122; Lowie, *The Crow Indians,* 3; Frey, *The World of the Crow Indians,* 11.

23. Old Coyote and Smith, *Apsaalooka, The Crow Indian Nation Then and Now.*

24. For a historical overview of Crow association with Yellowstone Valley, see Heidenreich, "The Native Americans' Yellowstone."

25. For updates on Mummy Cave interpretation, see Hughes, "Mummy Cave Revisited" and "Synthesis of the Mummy Cave Materials."

26. Nabokov, *Two Leggings,* 20.

27. Linderman, *Plenty Coups,* 299–307.

28. Lowie, "The Religion of the Crow Indians," 376–78.

29. Curtis, *The North American Indian,* vol. 4, 201.

30. Los Angeles County Museum, Seaver Center Library, Curtis Papers, Box 4B, Unlabeled Pile #1, Folder #14.

31. Ibid.

32. Ibid.

33. Ibid.; emphasis ours.

34. Curtis, *The North American Indian,* vol. 4, xi.

35. Larocque, *Journal of Larocque,* 45.

36. Bradley, "Lt. James H. Bradley Manuscript," 306–7.

37. Whittlesey, *Yellowstone Place Names,* 94, after Sharman, *The Cave on the Yellowstone.*

38. Denig, *Five Indian Tribes of the Upper Missouri,* 139–41.

39. Mark Spence interview, July 8, 1994, courtesy of the author.

40. Annual Report of the Commissioner of Indian Affairs to the Secretary of the Interior, 1854, 85.

41. *Louisville* (Ky.) *Courier Journal,* April 18, 1884, 12.

42. Bernardis, *Crow Social Studies,* 50–52.

43. Clark, *The Indian Sign Language,* 137–38.

44. Father Prando to Cataldo, September 26, 1883, Gonzaga College Jesuit Archives, translation from the Italian by Paul Gehl, Newberry Library, Chicago, courtesy of Dr. Frederick E. Hoxie, Director, McNickle Center for Indian History, Newberry Library, Chicago, 5.

45. Bradley, *The Handsome People,* 94.

46. Ibid., 96.

47. House Executive Document No. 89, 43d Cong., 1st sess., 28–42; emphasis ours.

48. U.S. Congress, House *Congressional Globe,* 42d Cong., 2d sess., February 27, 1872, p. 1243.

49. Hansen and Funderburk, *The Fabulous Past of Cooke City,* 2–3.

50. Augustus R. Keller to Hon. E. A.Hayt, 1879, Yellowstone National Park Archives.

51. Ibid., June 19, 1879.

52. Bradley, *The Handsome People,* 100.

53. Ibid., 102.

54. Ibid., 114; Haines, *The Yellowstone Story,* vol. 2, 267; Aubrey L. Haines, pers. comm., October 15, 1999. See also Larson, *Jay Cooke.*

55. Magoc, *Yellowstone,* 58.

56. Russell, *Diary of a Visit,* 74-74.

57. For a profile of this Crow leader, see Bernardis, *Crow Social Studies,* 52–53.

58. *Livingston Enterprise,* March 28, 1884.

59. Haines, *The Yellowstone Story,* vol. 2, 40.

60. Garber, "Facts Concerning the Bozeman Trail," 28.

61. Mooney, *Calendar History of the Kiowa Indians,* 153–56; Scott, "Notes on the Kado"; Lowie, "Alleged Kiowa-Crow Affinities," 357–68; Old Horn and McCleary, "Apsaalooke Social and Family Structure"; Parsons, *Kiowa Tales,* xix; Voeglin, "Kiowa-Crow Mythological Affiliations," 470–74.

62. Mooney, *Calendar History of the Kiowa Indians,* 153.

63. Hugh Scott Papers, National Anthropological Archives, no date, no pagination.

64. Hickerson, "Ethnogenesis in the South Plains," 86–87; emphasis ours.

65. Nye, *Bad Medicine and Good,* vii.

66. Harrington, "Anthropological Miscellany," 167.

67. Momaday, *The Way to Rainy Mountain,* 28.

68. Boyd, *Kiowa Voices,* 9.

69. Ibid., 9–10.

70. Pers. comm., July 17, 1995.

71. Boyd, *Kiowa Voices,* 2.

72. Parsons, *Kiowa Tales,*15.

73. Ibid.

74. Magoc, *Yellowstone,* 142–45.

75. Yellowstone National Park Archives, Document #2586.

76. Yellowstone National Park Archives, Letters Sent, vol. 8, April 15, 1899.

77. National Park Service Archives, 1912–18 Roads/Trails, Folder #342 "Opening Roads 1916," from letter by C. J. Blanchard, Statistician for the United States Reclamation Service, to P. S. Eustis, Passenger Traffic Manager of the Burlington Railroad, May 6, 1916.

78. *Wind River Mountaineer* 7, no. 1 (January–March 1991).

79. Yellowstone National Park Archives, *Annual Report for Yellowstone National Park, 1925,* 16.

80. Hoxie, *Parading through History,* 329.

81. Heidenreich, "The Beaver Dance and the Adoption Ceremony of the Crow Indians," 55.

82. Ibid., 45.

83. *Hardin Tribune,* January 13, 1933.

84. Yellowstone National Park Archives, PAGEANTS Folder, #139.91, Fiscal Year 1927, 1928.

85. Heidenreich, "The Beaver Dance and the Adoption Ceremony of the Crow," 43.

86. Yellowstone National Park Archives, Albright to Donaldson, January 20, 1927.

87. Yellowstone National Park Archives, Albright file, December 29, 1926.

88. *Great Falls Tribune,* August 24, 1926.

89. *Livingstone Enterprise,* July 31, 1927.

90. Yellowstone National Park Archives, Memos and Correspondence, 1942–51, Box #C-33, J. C.McCaskill to Eleanor K. Geary, April 28, 1950.

91. Chase, *Playing God in Yellowstone,* 107 fn. 48; Chase remembers hearing the story from ranger David Spirtes, pers. comm., July 30, 1995.

92. Narrated July 16, 1996.

93. Ibid.

94. Ibid.

95. Ibid.

96. Bascom, "Forms of Folklore," 9.

Chapter 2

1. According to Rosemary Sucec and Dan Reinhart, "Called 'pointed hearts' by the French for the exactness with which they traded, the Coeur d'Alene have oral accounts of traveling with some bands of the Salish and Kootenai and the Nez Perce to hunting grounds that encompassed the mountain plateaus of Yellowstone National Park."

2. Lahren, "Archaeological Investigations in the Upper Yellowstone Valley."

3. *Billings Gazette,* July 6, 1995, 4B.

4. Barrett, "Collecting among the Blackfoot Indians," 23.

5. Hyde, *Official Guide to the Yellowstone National Park,* 18–19.

6. Brackett, "The Shoshones or Snake Indians," 127.

7. Lahren, "Archaeological Investigations in the Upper Yellowstone Valley."

8. Ibid., 170; Haines, "The Rigler Bluffs Site."

9. Hart, *Montana - Native Plants and Early Peoples,* 49.

10. Sanders, Adams, and Wedel, "The 1995 Class III Cultural Resource Inventory," 39–42.

11. Old Coyote and Old Coyote, "Crow Stories," 7.

12. Arthur, "Southern Montana," 53.

13. Rollinson, *Hoofprints of a Cowboy,* 138–39.

14. Hafen, *Broken Hand,* 339.

15. Columbus, Affadavit, November 6, 1979.

16. Medicine Crow to Helena National Forest, February 20, 1980, Carbon County Historical Society, Red Lodge, Mont.

17. Moodie and Kaye, "The Ac Ko Mok Ki Map."

18. Stuart Conner, pers. comm., August 11, 1993.

19. See painting of buffalo skull circles by Alfred Jacob Miller, in Barsness, *The Bison in Art,* 86.

20. Another possible access to the Yellowstone area was south of Big Timber, along the rugged trail that paralleled the Boulder River.

21. David Ruppert, NPS Regional Ethnographer, pers. comm., August 9, 1996.

22. Reeves and Peacock, *Our Mountains Are Our Pillows,* 3.

23. Steward, *The Blackfeet,* 3.

24. Ewers, *The Horse in Blackfoot Indian Culture,* 216–17.

25. In Ewers, *The Blackfeet,* 197.

26. Quoted in McClintock, *The Old North Trail,* 3.

27. Ewers, *The Horse in Blackfoot Indian Culture,* 198–99.

28. Kuppens, "On the Origin of the Yellowstone National Park," 7.

29. Mooney, "The Aboriginal Population of America North of Mexico," 13.

30. Jenness, *The Indians of Canada,* 324, quoting Alexander Mackenzie in 1801.

31. Hultkrantz, "The Indians in Yellowstone National Park," 142, corroborated by Schultz, *The Sun God's Children,* 27.

32. Spence, "Dispossessing the Wilderness," 22.

33. Weixelman, *The Power to Evoke Wonder,* 55.

34. Schultz, *Blackfeet and Buffalo,* 377.

35. Telephone interview, August 22, 1996.

36. McClintock, *The Tragedy of the Blackfoot,* 435.

37. Grinnell, *Pawnee, Blackfoot and Cheyenne,* 130.

38. McClintock, *The Tragedy of the Blackfoot,* 435–36.

39. Ibid., 469.

40. Schultz, *The Sun God's Children,* 217–24.

41. Schultz, *Blackfeet and Buffalo,* 373.

42. Ruggles, *A Country So Interesting,* 62–65. Information courtesy of Mark Warhus and the Newberry Library, Chicago, from exhibit descriptions for A. N. Arrowsmith's "A map exhibiting all the New Discoveries in the Interior Parts of North America, January 1st, 1795, additions to 1802."

43. Thompson, *David Thompson's Narrative,* 342–43.

44. Chittenden, *The Yellowstone National Park,* 28–29.

45. *American State Papers* VI, Indian Affairs II, 451,453.

46. Haines, *Yellowstone Place Names,* 52.

47. Hultkrantz, "The Indians in Yellowstone Park,"142, after letter in the *Philadelphia Gazette,* September 1927.

48. Dempsey, *A Blackfoot Winter Count,* 8.

49. Chittenden, *The Yellowstone National Park,* 39–40.

50. Replogle, *Yellowstone's Bannock Indian Trails,* 37; Norris, *Report upon the Yellowstone National Park,* 988.

51. Brown, *Plainsmen of the Yellowstone,* 55–56.

52. Russell, *Journal of a Trapper,* 101–5.

53. Hamilton, *My Sixty Years on the Plains,* 94–95.

54. Chittenden, *The Yellowstone National Park,* 45.

55. Linford, *Wyoming,* 251.

56. Haines, *Yellowstone Place Names,* 89.

57. Haines, *Yellowstone National Park,* 37; Brown, *Plainsmen of the Yellowstone,* 170–71.

58. For Blackfeet paint-collecting practices, see McClintock, *The Old North Trail,* 207–24.

59. Walt Allen, Gallatin National Forest Archaeologist, pers. comm., August 15, 1996.

60. Bach, *Hiking the Yellowstone Backcountry,* 165.

61. Norris, *Fifth Annual Report,* 54.

62. Teit, "The Salishan Tribes of the Western Plateaus," 269, 303–06.

63. Palmer, *Handbook of North American Indians,* vol. 12, 313–26.

64. Brunton, *Handbook of North American Indians,* vol. 12, 223–37.

65. Ibid., 234.

66. Malouf, "Historic Tribes and Archaeology," 4.

67. Clark, *Indian Legends from the Northern Rockies,* 87.

68. Ibid., 86–90.

69. Miller, Harrison, and Pitchette, *Coyote Tales of the Montana Salesh,* 7.

70. Jarold Ramsey, pers. comm., August 11, 1998.

71. Dell Hymes, pers. comm., August 13, 1998.

72. Barbeau, Review of *Indian Legends of Canada.*

73. Ramsey, pers. comm., August 11, 1998.

74. Milne, *Sacred Places in North America,* 89.

75. Edmonds and Clark, *Voices of the Winds.*

76. Galliland, *The Flood.*

77. Pers. comm., August 13, 1998.

78. Clark, *Indian Legends from the Northern Rockies,* 89.

79. Miller, Harrison, and Pichette, *Coyote Tales of the Montana Salesh,* 46–49, 54–57.

80. Walker, *Blood of the Monster,* 103–20.

81. Ibid., 107–9, 116.

82. Ramsey, *Reading the Fire,* 164.

83. Turney-High, "The Flatheads of Montana," 11-21.

84. Ewers, *The Horse in Blackfoot Indian Culture;* Malouf, "Louis Pierre's Affair."

85. Claude Schaeffer Papers, Glenbow Museum, Calgary, courtesy of the Kootenai-Salish Culture Committee.

86. White, "'Firsts' among the Flathead Kutenai," 4.

87. Interview, June 4, 1996.

88. An Indian food-procuring camp hidden inside a designated "wilderness area" in Western Salish country is the subject of native author Louis Owens's memoir, "Burning the Shelter."

89. Roosevelt, "An Elk Hunt at Two-Ocean Pass," 718.

90. Ibid., 714.

91. Whittlesey, "Yellowstone's Horse-and-Buggy Tour Guides," 23.

92. Dick entry for September 12, 1878. We are particularly grateful to Park Historian Lee Whittlesey for providing us with a typed summary of Dick's journal notations on Indian hunting in the Pierre's Hole/Henry's Fork areas adjoining the park.

93. Schullery and Whittlesey, *History of Large Mammals on the Yellowstone Plateau.*

94. Magoc, *Yellowstone,* 139.

95. Hague, "The Yellowstone National Park as a Game Preserve."

96. Meagher, *The Bison of Yellowstone Park,* 14–15.

97. Burnett, "White Hunters and the Buffalo," 23.

98. *Lincoln Star,* September 24, 1993, 1, 6.

99. Howard, *Livestock and Buffalo History,* 3–5.

100. Ibid.

101. Whittlesey, *Yellowstone Place Names,* 29.

102. Yellowstone National Park Archives, A. Bart Henderson Diary, 50.

103. Howard, *Livestock and Buffalo History,* 5.

104. Hoffman, *A Preliminary Archaeological Survey,* 28–30.

105. Ibid., 24.

106. For a Crow Indian account of buffalo jumps and the importance of the legendary leader, Running Coyote, in initiating the first Crow technique of driving buffalo over embankments, see Medicine Crow, *From the Heart of the Crow Country,* 86–99.

107. *Yellowstone National Park Nature Notes* 9, nos. 10–11 (October–November 1932): 45–46.

108. Thornton, *American Indian Holocaust and Survival,* 52.

109. Grinnell, *The Cheyenne Indians,* 118.

110. McHugh, *The Time of the Buffalo,* 294.

111. Thornton, *American Indian Holocaust and Survival,* 52.

112. Hornaday, "The Extermination of the American Bison with a Sketch of Its Discovery and Life History," 505 f.

113. Hultkrantz, *Belief and Worship in Native America,* 133.

114. Haines, *The Buffalo,* 29.

115. Ibid., 6, 34, 148, 219–22.

116. Seton, *Lives of Game Animals,* 658.

117. Garretson, *American Bison.*

118. Ibid., 215.

119. The following excerpts are from Tape 95, FCC Transcripts, Courtesy of the Kootenai-Salish Culture Committee, used with the understanding that they shall not be reproduced without express approval of the Kootenai-Salish Culture Committee, and that no one shall profit financially from their use.

120. U.S. National Archives, General Administrative Records, Denver, Record Group 75 BIA, NA-RMR, Wind River Agency, 1890–1960, Box 237, folder 920.

121. Videotape interview with RE by Sharon Cahin, at Fort Washakie, Wyoming, June 20, 2001.

122. Yellowstone National Park Archives, Box N-6, 4, File: Distribution of the Elk Shipments."

123. Yellowstone National Park Archives, Animals (cont.), Box N-20.

124. Yellowstone National Park Archives, Final Reduction Report, 1961–62, Northern Yellowstone Elk Herd.

125. Ravndal, "A General Description of the Social and Cultural Environment Surrounding the Bison/Burcellosis Issue," April 6, 1997 draft, 1.

126. *Casper Star-Tribune,* March 20, 1997.

127. *New York Times,* April 13, 1997, 18.

128. "The Evolution of Cultural Resources Management in Yellowstone: An Interview with Laura Joss," *Yellowstone Science* 9, no. 1 (winter 2001): 13.

129. Welxelman interview, September 15, 1991, Wolf Point, Montana.

130. Weixelman interview, September 14, 1991, Wolf Point Lutheran Rest Home, Wolf Point, Montana.

131. Lewis, *The Effects of White Contact upon Blackfoot Culture,* 62.

132. Kappler, *Indian Affairs.*

133. Interview, August 22, 1995, Pablo, Montana.

Chapter 3

1. Murphy and Murphy, "Northern Shoshone and Bannock," 306.

2. Hodge, *Handbook of American Indians North of Mexico,* vol. 2, 835.

3. Steward, *Basin-Plateau Aboriginal Sociopolitical Groups,* 186–87.

4. Explanations for the name "Snakes" vary, with one possibility that the name Shoshone was from their word for grass (*sonip*) because they lived in grass-covered lodges. Sign language for grass was a waving hand and this sign was misinterpreted for a similar sign for snake. Another explanation is that the name is linked to extensive use of Ling fish by the Shoshone, and when seen skinned in their camps the fish looked like snakes.

5. Liljeblad, *Indian Peoples in Idaho,* 95.

6. Phillips, "The Indians of the Yellowstone Country," 38–39.

7. Mills, 'The Bannocks of Yellowstone National Park," 22.

8. Irving, *Astoria,* 271.

9. Irving, *The Adventrues of Captain Bonneville, U.S.A.,* 192–93.

10. Russell, *Journal of a Trapper,* 26.

11. Ibid., 26.

12. Ibid., 27–28.

13. Hultkrantz, "The Sheepeaters of Wyoming," vol. 1, 12, n.d.

14. Clayton, "A Brief History of the Washakie National Forest and the Duties and Some Experiences of a Ranger," 277–78.

15. Sholly and Newman, *Guardians of Yellowstone,* l06–7.

16. Hughes, "The Sheepeater Myth of Northwestern Wyoming," 63–83.

17. Sharon Kahin, pers. comm., based on interview with Wind River Shoshone educator, May 17, 2001.

18. Aubrey Haines lecture, Mammoth, Yellowstone National Park, 1994.

19. Norris, *Annual Report of the Superintendent of the Yellowstone National Park, to the Secretary of the Interior, for the Year 1879,* 35.

20. Ibid., 45.

21. Gill, "Human Skeletal Remains on the Northwestern Plains."

22. Pers. comm., July 8, 1995.

23. Hultkrantz, "The Sheepeaters of Wyoming," vol. 1, 18, n.d.

24. Ibid., vol. 1, 61, n.d.

25. Coutant, *The History of Wyoming,* 705.

26. Chittenden, *The Yellowstone National Park,* 11.

27. Phillips, "The Indians of the Yellowstone Country," 32.

28. Schullery, *Searching for Yellowstone,* 24.

29. Frost, "The Sheep Eaters," 17.

30. Olden, *Shoshone Folk Lore, as Discovered from the Rev. John Roberts, a Hidden Hero, on the Wind River Indian Reservation in Wyoming,* 13.

31. Thompson, "First Annual Report—Oregon Territory—South Side of the Columbia River between the 46th and 44th degrees Latitude between the Summits of the Rocky and Cascade Mountains," 490.

32. Hultkrantz, "The Indians and the Wonders of Yellowstone"; "The Fear of Geysers among Indians of the Yellowstone Park Area."

33. Hultkrantz, "The Indians and the Wonders of Yellowstone," 46.

34. Ibid., 44.

35. Norris, *Fifth Annual Report,* 38.

36. Hultkrantz, "The Indians and the Wonders of Yellowstone," 49.

37. Ibid., 49–50.

38. Anonymous, "Wonderland: A Journey through the Yellowstone National Park," 9.

39. Lewis and Clark, *Original Journals of the Lewis and Clark Expedition, 1804–1806,* 401.

40. Hoebel, *Man in the Primitive World,* 102.

41. Lee, *Subsistence Ecology and the !Kung Bushmen;* Lee and DeVore, *Man the Hunter.*

42. Lee and DeVore, *Man the Hunter.*

43. Lee, *The Dobe !Kung,* 55.

44. Colson, "In Good Years and in Bad."

45. Aginsky, "Population Control in the Shanel (Pomo) Tribe."

46. Colson, "In Good Years and in Bad," 20.

47. Henderson, "Journal of the Yellowstone Expedition of 1866 under Captain Jeff Standifer," 19–20.

48. Russell, *Journal of a Trapper,* 26–27.

49. Jones, *Report upon the Reconnaissance of Northwestern Wyoming, Including Yellowstone National Park, made in the Summer of 1873,* 22.

50. Clark, *The Indian Sign Language, with Brief Explanatory Notes,* 334.

51. Ross, *The Fur Hunters of the Far West,* 240–41.

52. James I. Patten, U.S. Indian Agency, Shoshone and Bannock Agency, to Hon. E. A. Hayt, Commissioner of Indian Affairs, Washington, D.C., June 11, 1879.

53. Daniels, "Food for the Sheep-Eaters," 24.

54. Barrette, "Ghost Tribe of the West," 330.

55. Hultkrantz, "Configurations of Religious Belief among the Wind River Shoshoni," 187.

56. Madsen and Rhode, *Across the West.*

57. Wright, *Regional Assessment, Archeological Report.*

58. Butler, *When Did the Shoshoni Begin to Occupy Southern Idaho?*

59. Butler, "The Pottery of Eastern Idaho,"131–33.

60. Wright, *People of the High Country,* 95–99.

61. Miller, "Numic Languages."

62. Lamb, "Linguistic Prehistory in the Great Basin."

63. Swanson, *Birch Creek Human Ecology in the Cool Desert of the Northern Rocky Mountains 9,000 B.C.–A.D. 1850.*

64. Husted and Edgar, "An Archaeology of Mummy Cave, Wyoming."

65. Holmer, "Prehistory of the Northern Shoshone"; "In Search of the Ancestral Northern Shoshone."

66. Holmer, "Prehistory of the Northern Shoshone," 45.

67. Ibid., 48.

68. Ibid., 57; emphasis ours.

69. Ibid., 453.

70. Francis, Loendorf, and Dorn, "AMS Radiocarbon and Cation-Ratio Dating of Rock Art in the Bighorn Basin of Wyoming and Montana."

71. Walker and Francis, *Legend Rock Petroglyph Site (48H04), Wyoming.*

72. Aikens and Witherspoon, "Great Basin Numic Prehistory."

73. Hoxie, *Parading through History.*

74. Biddle, quoted in Opler, "The Apachean Culture Pattern and Its Origins."

75. Wright and Dirks, "Myth as Environmental Message," 166.

76. Shimkin, Unpublished field notes on the Eastern Shoshone.

77. Shimkin, "Eastern Shoshone," 320.

78. Russell, *Journal of a Trapper,* 26.

79. Willey and Key, *Analysis of Human Skeletons from Yellowstone National Park.*

80. Ibid., 17.

81. Ibid., 22.

82. Condon, "American Indian Burial Giving Evidence of Antiquity in Yellowstone National Park."

83. Haag, "Aboriginal Dog Remains from Yellowstone National Park," 1–2.

84. Ibid., 4.

85. Kenneth Cannon letter to Larry Loendorf, September 2, 1996.

86. Larson and Kornfeld, "Betwixt and Between the Basin and the Plains," 202–3; Holmer, "In Search of Ancestral Northern Shoshone," 184.

87. Steward, "Culture Element Distributions," 314.

88. Holmer, "Dagger Falls: A Preliminary Report"; Holmer, "Prehistory of the Northern Shoshone"' Holmer and Ringe, "Excavations in Wahmuza," summarized in Holmer, "In Search of the Ancestral Northern Shoshone"; Torgler, "Continuous Artifact Tradition from the Middle Archaic to the Historical Present."

89. Torgler, "Continuous Artifact Tradition from the Middle Archaic to the Historical Present," 87.

90. Shimkin, Unpublished field notes on the Eastern Shoshone.

91. Dominick, "The Sheepeaters," 156.

92. Torgler, "Continuous Artifact Tradition from the Middle Archaic to the Historical Present," 91–92.

93. Hoffman, "A Preliminary Archaeological Survey of Yellowstone National Park"; Taylor, Wood, and Hoffman, *Preliminary Archeological Investigations in Yellowstone National Park.*

94. Haines, *The Bannock Indian Trail.*

95. Torgler, "Continuous Artifact Tradition from the Middle Archaic to the Historical Present," 98; Holmer, "A Compilation of Projectile Point Data from Southwestern Idaho," 119.

96. Jones, *Report upon the Reconnaissance of Northwestern Wyoming, Including Yellowstone National Park, made in the Summer of 1873,* 261.

97. Adams, *Pipes and Bowls,* 20.

98. Ibid., 152–53.

99. Ibid., 153–54.

100. Ibid.

101. Wood and Thiessen, *Early Fur Trade on the Northern Plains,* 185.

102. Thwaites, *Original Journals of the Lewis and Clark Expedition 1804–1806,* 19.

103. Feyhl, "Steatite."

104. Frison, "Sources of Steatite and Methods of Prehistoric Procurement and Use in Wyoming"; Adams, *Pipes and Bowls.*

105. Adams, *Pipes and Bowls,* 33.

106. Shimkin, 1937 interview.

107. Adams, *Pipes and Bowls,* 33.

108. Schoolcraft, *Historical and Statistical Information Respecting the History, Condition and Prospects of the Indians of the United States,* 211.

109. Russell, *Journal of a Trapper,* 26.

110. Ibid., 23.

111. Ibid., 91

112. Frison, "Sources of Steatite and Methods of Prehistoric Procurement and Use in Wyoming," 285.

113. Ibid., 284.

114. Adams, *Pipes and Bowls,* 114.

115. Ibid., 116.

116. Shimkin, 1937 interview; Dick Washakie interview.

117. Adams, *Pipes and Bowls,* 120.

118. Eakin, Francis, and Larson, "The Split Rock Ranch Site."

119. Husted and Edgar, "An Archaeology of Mummy Cave, Wyoming," 204–5.

120. Adams, *Pipes and Bowls,* 143–44.

121. Malouf, "The Shoshonean Migration Northward," 7.

122. Adams, *Pipes and Bowls.*

123. Frison and Van Norman, "Carved Steatite and Sandstone Tubes."

124. Weeks, *Pachee Goyo*, 27.

125. Hultkrantz, "The Religion of the Wind River Shoshoni," 49.

126. Shimkin, "Eastern Shoshone," 325.

127. Shimkin, "Wind River Shoshone Literary Forms," 334.

128. Interview, February 4, 1996.

129. Jones, *Report upon the Reconnaissance of Northwestern Wyoming, Including Yellowstone National Park, made in the Summer of 1873*, 261.

130. Shimkin, "Wind River Shoshone Ethnogeography," 318.

131. Bonney, *Battle Drums and Geysers*, 485.

132. Holmes, "Notes on an Extensive Deposit of Obsidian in the Yellowstone National Park."

133. Holmes, "Obsidian."

134. Holmes, "Handbook of Aboriginal American Antiquities, Part 1: Introduction. The Lithic Industries." (1919).

135. Hayden, *Twelfth Annual Report U.S. Geological and Geographical Survey of the Territories, Part II*; Iddings, "Obsidian Cliff, Yellowstone National Park."

136. Jones, *Report upon the Reconnaissance of Northwestern Wyoming, Including Yellowstone National Park, made in the Summer of 1873*, 262.

137. Norris, *Report upon the Yellowstone National Park, to the Secretary of the Interior, for the Year 1879*, 7.

138. Norris, *Prehistoric Remains in Montana, Between Fort Ellis and the Yellowstone River: Annual Report of Regents of the Smithsonian Institution . . .* , 16.

139. Norris, *Annual Report of the Superintendent of the Yellowstone National Park, to the Secretary of the Interior, for the Year 1880*, 15.

140. Ibid.

141. Gerrish, *Life in the World's Wonderland*, 196; Synge, *A Ride through Wonderland*, 120; Dudley, *The National Park from the Hurricane Deck of a Cayuse, or the Liederkranz Expedition to Geyserland*, 47; Kipling, *From Sea to Sea*, 79.

142. Davis, Aaberg, and Schmitt, *The Obsidian Cliff Plateau Prehistoric Lithic Source, Yellowstone National Park, Wyoming*, 6–7.

143. Skinner, *The Yellowstone Nature Book*, 191.

144. Loendorf et al. "The Proposed National Register District in the Knife River Flint Quarries in Dunn County, N.D."

145. Raftery, "Historical Sketch of Yellowstone National Park," 102; emphasis ours.

146. Skinner, *The Yellowstone Nature Book*, 190.

147. Raftery, "Historical Sketch of Yellowstone National Park," 102.

148. Alter, *James Bridger, Trapper, Frontiersman, Scout and Guide*, 381.

149. Guptill, *Practical Guide to Yellowstone National Park*, 34.

150. Bonninichsen and Baldwin, "Cypress Hills Ethnohistory and Ecology," 35–39.

151. Liljeblad, *Indian Peoples in Idaho*, 63–65.

152. Janetski, *The Indians of Yellowstone Park*, 60.

153. Corless, *The Weiser Indians*, 14.

154. Cousins, "Mountains Made Alive," 505.

155. Ibid.

156. Weixelman, "The Power to Evoke Wonder," 59.

157. Ibid.

158. Interview, August 22, 1995.

159. Cannon and Hughes, "It's Not Just Obsidian Cliff."

160. Ibid.

161. Richard N. Holmer to Peter Nabokov, pers. comm., February 27, 1997.

162. Davis, Aaberg, and Schmitt, *The Obsidian Cliff Plateau Prehisotric Lithic Source, Yellowstone National Park, Wyoming.*

163. Lewis, *History of the Expedition of Captains Lewis and Clark 1804-5-6,* vol. 1, 451.

164. Russell, *Journal of a Trapper,* 26–27.

165. Lowie, "Notes on Shoshonean Ethnography," 246.

166. Anonymous, "Sources of Bow Material," 6.

167. Frison, "A Composite, Reflexed, Mountain Sheep Horn Bow from Western Wyoming," 173.

168. For another modern experiment with making horn bows, see Bill Holm's "On Making Horn Bows," 116–30.

169. Wilson, *The White Indian Boy; or, Uncle Nick among the Shoshones,* vi.

170. Ibid., 107; emphasis ours.

171. Lowie, "The Northern Shoshone," 192.

172. Fowler and Liljeblad, "Northern Paiute," 439; Dominick, "The Sheepeaters," 156.

173. Dominick, "The Sheepeaters," 156.

174. Lowie, "The Northern Shoshone," 192.

175. Murphy and Murphy, "Northern Shoshone and Bannock," 301.

176. Lowie, "Notes on Shoshonean Ethnography," 246.

177. Lowie, "The Northern Shoshone," 192.

178. Dominick, "The Sheepeaters," 156.

179. Murphy and Murphy, "Northern Shoshone and Bannock," 301.

180. Lowie, "The Northern Shoshone," 192, quoting Lewis and Clark.

181. Fredlund and Fredlund, "Archaeological Survey of the Three Forks of the Flathead River, Montana," 48.

182. Caslick, "Bighorn Sheep in Yellowstone," 6.

183. Barrette, "Ghost Tribe of the West," 22.

184. Shimkin, Unpublished field notes on the Eastern Shoshone.

185. Lee Whittlesey to Laura Joss, pers. comm., n.d.

186. Lowie, "The Northern Shoshone,"185; Steward, *Basin-Plateau Aboriginal Sociopolitical Groups,* 37.

187. Ross, *The Fur Hunters of the Far West,* 241.

188. Anell, *Running Down and Driving of Game in North America,* 116–17.

189. Stuart Conner letter to Bonnie Hogan, December 9, 1973.

190. Norris, *Fifth Annual Report of the Superintendent of the Yellowstone National Park to the Secretary of the Interior,* 36.

191. Hendricks, *Albert Bierstadt,* 270.

192. Bertsche to New York Public Library, June 25, 1965.

193. New York Public Library, Art and Architecture Division, to Bertsche, July 6, 1965.

194. Pers. comm., August 24, 1995.

195. Sperry to Hassrick, January 30, 1996.

196. Frison, Reher, and Walker, "Prehistoric Mountain Sheep Hunting in the Central Rocky Mountains of North America"; Frison, *Prehistoric Hunters of the High Plains.*

197. Frison, *Prehistoric Hunters of the High Plains,* 257.

198. Frost, "The Sheep Easters."

199. Barrette, "Ghost Tribe of the West."

200. Hogan, "Two High Altitude Game Traps Sites in Montana."

201. Frison, Reher, and Walker, "Prehistoric Mountain Sheep Hunting in the Central Rocky Mountains of North America," 251.

202. Ibid., 218.

203. Ibid., 226.

204. Clayton, "A Brief History of the Washakie National Forest and the Duties and Some Experiences of a Ranger," 278.

205. Frison, Reher, and Walker, "Prehistoric Mountain Sheep Hunting in the Central Rocky Mountains of North America," 222.

206. Ibid.

207. Ibid., 230–31.

208. Barrette, "Ghost Tribe of the West," 22.

209. Lowie, "Notes on Shoshonean Ethnography," 303; Steward, *Basin-Plateau Aboriginal Sociopolitical Groups,* 34–37.

210. Shimkin, "Eastern Shoshone," 386.

211. Frison, Reher, and Walker, "Prehistoric Mountain Sheep Hunting in the Central Rocky Mountains of North America," 232–34.

212. Ibid., 234.

213. Ferris, *Life in the Rocky Mountains;* Wiesel, "The Rams Horn Tree and Other Medicine Trees of the Flathead Indians."

214. Frison, Reher, and Walker, "Prehistoric Mountain Sheep Hunting in the Central Rocky Mountains of North America."

215. Hultkrantz, "The Sheepeaters of Wyoming," vol. 2, 119.

216. Steward, *Basin-Plateau Aboriginal Sociopolitical Groups,* 186–87; Murphy and Murphy, "Northern Shoshone and Bannock," 306.

217. Yellowstone National Park collections in the Smithsonian Institution.

218. Husted and Edgar, "An Archaeology of Mummy Cave, Wyoming."

219. Norris, *Fifth Annual Report of the Superintendent of the Yellowstone National Park to the Secretary of the Interior,* 34.

220. Interview, March 13, 1994.

221. Ann Johnson, pers. comm., July 1995.

222. McAllester, "Water as a Disciplinary Agent among the Crow and Blackfoot," 602–4.

223. Raynolds, *The Report of Brevet Brigadier General W. F. Raynolds on the Exploration of the Yellowstone River and the Country Drained by that River,* 95.

224. Norris, *Fifth Annual Report of the Superintendent of the Yellowstone National Park to the Secretary of the Interior,* 30–31.

225. Russell, *Journal of a Trapper,* 26–27.

226. S. Weir Mitchell, quoted in Haines, *The Yellowstone Story,* vol. 2, 398.

227. Haines, *The Yellowstone Story,* vo. 1, 304.

228. Interview notes, 1937.

229. Irving, Astoria II, 18, in Steward, *Basin-Plateau Aboriginal Sociopolitical Groups,* 205.

230. Walker, "Lemhi Shoshone-Bannock Reliance on Anadromous and Other Fish Resources," 246.

231. Ibid.

232. Fowler and Liljeblad, "Northern Paiute," 91–92.

233. Rogers and Smith, "Environment and Culture in the Shield and Mackenzie Borderlands," 134.

234. Lowie, "Notes on Shoshonean Ethnography," 195.

235. Fowler and Liljeblad, "Northern Paiute," 65.

236. Ibid.

237. McCracken et al., *The Mummy Cave Project in Northwestern Wyoming,* pls. 26, 34.

238. Steward, *Basin-Plateau Aboriginal Sociopolitical Groups,* 189.

239. "Range Plant Handbook."

240. Geyer, "Notes on the Vegetation and General Character of the Missouri and Oregon Territories", quoted in Range Plant Handbook, W105.

241. Coues, *History of the Expedition under the Command of Lewis and Clark,* vol. 3, 543–44.

242. Ibid., 543.

243. Ibid.

244. Kidwell, "The Conical Timbered Lodge on the Northwestern Plains"; Loendorf and Klinner, *Deadfall Timber Structures in the Bighorn Canyon National Recreational Area, Montana;* Frison, *Prehistoric Hunters of the High Plains,* 122–27; Larson and Kornfeld, "Betwixt and Between the Basin and the Plains," 204–5.

245. Haines, *The Yellowstone Story,* 25.

246. Martindale, "The Old Wickiups of the Gallatin," 4.

247. Hoffman, *A Preliminary Archaeological Survey of Yellowstone National Park,* 39.

248. Ibid., 39.

249. Jack E. Haynes to Åke Hultkrantz, January 6, 1956.

250. Lowie, "The Northern Shoshone," 183.

251. Ibid.; Clark, *The Indian Sign Language, with Brief Explanatory Notes,* 337.

252. Lowie, "Notes on Shoshonean Ethnography," 221.

253. Murphy and Murphy, "Northern Shoshone and Bannock," 294.

254. Dominick, "The Sheepeaters,"163.

255. Ibid., 164.

256. Norris, *Report upon the Yellowstone National Park, to the Secretary of the Interior, for the Year 1879,* 7.

257. Jack E. Haynes to Åke Hultkrantz, October 23, 1955.

258. Ibid.

259. Norris, *Report upon the Yellowstone National Park, to the Secretary of the Interior, for the Year 1879,* 10; Replogle, *Yellowstone's Bannock Indian Trails;* Hoffman, *A Preliminary Archaeological Survey of Yellowstone National Park,* 35–40; Shippee, "Wickiups of Yellowstone Park," 74–75; Haines, *The Yellowstone Story,* 24–25.

260. L. Haynes in J. Haynes letter to Superintendent Rogers, 1905, Yellowstone National Park Archives.

261. Conner, "Letter Report on Lava Creek Wickiups."

262. Shippee, "Wickiups of Yellowstone Park."

263. Ibid., 74.

264. Hoffman, *A Preliminary Archaeological Survey of Yellowstone National Park.*

265. Ibid,. 38.

266. Ibid., 36.

267. Davis, "Wickiup Cave."

268. Ibid., 298–99.

269. Ibid., 301–2.

270. Ibid., 301.

271. Ibid.

272. Torgler, "Continuous Artifact Tradition from the Middle Archaic to the Historical Present," 98.

273. Ross, *The Fur Hunters of the Far Wests,* 240.

274. Davis, "Wickiup Cave."

275. Norris, *Report upon the Yellowstone National Park, to the Secretary of the Interior, for the Year 1879,* 35.

276. Interview, March 14, 1994.

277. Haines, *The Yellowstone Story* 24.

278. Hultkrantz, "The Sheepeaters of Wyoming," vol. 1, 59.

279. Lowie, "The Northern Shoshone"; "Notes on Shoshonean Ethnography."

280. Steward, *Basin-Plateau Aboriginal Sociopolitical Groups.*

281. Shimkin, "Childhood and Development among the Wind River Shoshone"; "Wind River Shoshone Ethnogeography."

282. Malouf, "Ethohistory in the Great Basin."

283. Steward, "The Foundations of Basin-Plateau Shoshonean Society," 115.

284. Allen, *The Sheep Eaters,* 62–71.

285. Malouf, "Ethnohistory in the Great Basin," 4–5.

286. Ibid., 4.

287. Steward, "The Foundations of Basin-Plateau Shoshonean Society," 114–16.

288. Steward, *Basin-Plateau Aboriginal Sociopolitical Groups.*

289. Steward, "The Foundations of Basin-Plateau Shoshonean Society," 115.

290. Malouf, "Ethnohistory in the Great Basin," 4.

291. Haines, "A Supplementary Report on High-Altitude Indian Occupation Sites near the North Boundary of Yellowstone National Park," 26.

292. Henderson, "Journal of the Yellowstone Expedition of 1866 under Captain Jeff Standifer," 20.

293. Ellsworth, "A Visit to Wonderland."

294. Shimkin. "Chilhood and Development among the Wind River Shoshone," 269–70; Steward, *Basin-Plateau Aboriginal Sociopolitical Groups,* 203; Lowie, "The Northern Shoshone,"191; Dominick, "The Sheepeaters," 155.

295. Lowie, "The Northern Shoshone," 191.

296. Dominick, "The Sheepeaters," 156.

297. Hultkrantz, "The Sheepeaters of Wyoming," vol. 2, 9.

298. Ibid.

299. Ibid., 14.

300. Referred to as Hultkrantz, n.d. II.

301. Hultkrantz, The Sheepeaters of Wyoming," vol. 2, 22.

302. Ibid, 60.

303. Ibid.

304. Ibid, 63.

305. See Bright, *A Coyote Reader,* for a full treatment of Coyote's multiple personalities.

306. Hultkrantz, "The Sheepeaters of Wyoming," vol. 2, 22; emphasis ours.

307. Ibid.

308. Ibid., 23.

309. Ibid., 46.

310. Ibid., 23, 46, 49, 50.

311. Hultkrantz, in Earhart, *Religious Traditions of the World,* 293.

312. Hultkrantz, "The Sheepeaters of Wyoming," vol. 2, 23–24.

313. Ibid., 25.

314. Ibid., 35.

315. Ibid., 50.

316. Ibid., 51.

317. Ibid., 57.

318. Allen, *The Sheep Eaters.*

319. Shimkin, Unpublished field notes on the Eastern Shoshone.

320. Phillips, "The Indians of the Yellowstone Country," 35.

321. For exhaustive analysis on this Shoshonean Ghost Dance and its Great Basin origins, see Vander, *Shoshone Ghost Dance Religion.*

322. Vander, "Ghost Dance Songs and Religion of a Wind River Shoshone Woman."

323. Lowie, "Dances and Societies of the Plains Shoshone," 817.

324. Shimkin, "Eastern Shoshone," 325.

325. Hultkrantz, "Configurations of Religious Belief among the Wind River Shoshoni," 187.

326. Hultkrantz, "The Sheepeaters of Wyoming," vol. 2, 76.

327. Phillips, "The Indians of the Yellowstone Country," 38.

Chapter 4

1. Because the Shoshoneans were so dependent upon their immediate environment, it is unsurprising to learn of their custom of naming groups by their dominant food supply, as already mentioned by Walker, "Lemhi Shoshone-Bannock Reliance on Anadromous and Other Fish Resources," 141. At first the list of food-named groups or "hunting districts" by which these Shoshoneans are distinguished—Jack Rabbit Eaters, Salmon Eaters, Ground Hog Eaters, Yampa Eaters, and the like—sounds suspiciously like a non-Indian's shorthand for labeling a bewildering array of local Indians. But apparently this pattern was an indigenous tradition, since when the Shoshones first encountered the Peyote religion, for instance, they dubbed it Wogwedika, "Peyote Eaters," and when the ritual was defamed as being a drug cult, they upgraded the name to Natsundika, or "Medicine Eaters"; from Vander, "Ghost Dance Songs and Religion of a Wind River Shoshone Woman," 68.

2. Stewart, "The Shoshoni," 4.

3. Ibid.

4. (Twin Falls, Idaho) *Times-News,* Sunday, September 15, 1996, 1.

5. Holmer, "Prehistory of the Northern Shoshone."

6. Chittenden, *The Yellowstone National Park,* 14.

7. Ibid., 12.

8. Urbanek, *Wyoming Place Names,* 43.

9. Brayer, "Exploring the Yellowstone with Hayden," 273.

10. Haines, *The Bannock Trail,* 7.

11. Anderson, Tiffany, and Nelson, "Recent Research on Obsidian from Iowa Archaeological Sites."

12. Holmes, "Aboriginal Pottery of the Eastern United States," to the contrary.

13. Griffin, "Hopewell and the Dark Black Glass."

14. Davis, Aaberg, and Schmitt, *The Obsidian Cliff Plateau Prehistoric Lithic Source, Yellowstone National Park, Wyoming,* 57.

15. Chittenden, *The Yellowstone National Park,* 11–12.

16. Replogle, *Yellowstone's Bannock Indian Trail.*

17. Haines, *The Bannock Indian Trail,* 6–7.

18. Morrison, *Fire in Paradise.*

19. Barrett and Arno, "Indian Fires as an Ecological Influence in the Northern Rockies," 650.

20. For a useful summary of this material, see Cronon, *Changes in the Land.*

21. For a comparative discussion on Indian fires among western Great Basin and Californian hunter-gatherers, see Blackburn and Anderson, *Before the Wilderness.*

22. Pyne, *Fire in America*.

23. Chase, *Playing God in Yellowstone*, 92–97.

24. Wuerthner, *Yellowstone and the Fires of Change*, 7.

25. Spence, "Dispossessing the Wilderness," 44.

26. Kay, "Aboriginal Overkill and Native Burning."

27. De Voto, *The Journals of Lewis and Clark*, 222.

28. Marshall, "Euro-American Attitudes and the Native American Experience," 171.

29. Barrett, "Indians and Fire," 18.

30. Ibid., 19–20.

31. Doane, *Report of Lieutenant Gustavus C. Doane upon the So-Called Yellowstone Expedition of 1870*.

32. Incomplete photocopy, *Billings Gazette*, 1887, Bob Edgar Collection, Cody, Wyoming.

33. Thompson, "Fire in Wilderness Areas."

34. Swanton, *The Indian Tribes of North America*, 398

35. Ibid.

36. Interview, April 2, 1997.

37. Walker, "The Shoshone-Bannock," 154; see also Steward, "Linguistic Distribution and Political Groups of the Great Basin Shoshoneans"; Jorgenson, *The Sun Dance Religion*, 66–69.

38. Spence, "Dispossessing the Wilderness," 15.

39. Interview, November 18, 1995.

40. Liljeblad, *Indian Peoples in Idaho*, 90.

41. Ibid.

42. Liljeblad, "The Old Tradtions of the Shoshoni and Bannock Indians of Idaho," 7.

43. In Ulebaker, "The Sources and Methodology of Mooney's Estimates of North American Indian Population of the Americas in 1492," 285.

44. Yellowstone National Park Archives, Shoshone-Bannock Tribes Tribal Tax Commission to Superintendent Robert Barbee, October 7, 1993.

45. Russell, *Journal of a Trapper*, 123.

46. Steward, *Basin-Plateau Aboriginal Sociopolitical Groups*, 191, 204.

47. Ibid., 191; Haines, *The Bannock Indian Trail*, 6.

48. Crowder, *Tenday Chief of the Lemhis*, 18.

49. Spence, "Dispossessing the Wilderness," 16.

50. Faulkner, "Emigrant-Indian Confrontation in Southeastern Idaho," 48.

51. Liljeblad, *Indian Peoples of Idaho*, 41.

52. Madsen, *The Shoshoni Frontier and the Bear River Massacre*, 222–23.

53. Josephy, *The Civil War in the American West*, 259.

54. Dimsdale, *The Vigilantes of Montana or Popular Justice in the Rocky Mountains*, 33.

55. Ibid., 34–35, 38.

56. From the diary of Dr. A. C. Peale, entry for August 21, 1871, in Merrill, *Yellowstone and the Great West*.

57. *Idaho Statesman*, Boise, October 6, 1867.

58. *Congressional Globe*, May 28, 1868, 2638.

59. *Cheyenne Daily Leader*, March 3, 1870.

60. Teit, "The Salishan Tribes of the Western Plateaus," 268; emphasis ours.

61. Swanton, *The Indian Tribes of North America*, 403.

62. Steward, *Basin-Plateau Aboriginal Sociopolitical Groups*, 198.

63. Ulebaker, "The Sources and Methodology for Mooney's Estimates of North American Population of the Americas I 1492," 285.

64. Steward, *Basin-Plateau Aboriginal Sociopolitical Groups,* 188–189.

65. Ibid., 200; emphasis ours.

66. Ibid., 204.

67. Beal, *History of Southeastern Idaho,* 49.

68. Steward, *Basin-Plateau Aboriginal Sociopolitical Groups,* 201.

69. Irving, *Astoria,* 12–13.

70. Steward, *Basin-Plateau Aboriginal Sociopolitical Groups,* 202.

71. Report to the Commissioner of Indian Affairs, U.S. House Executive Document 108, 35th Cong., 2d sess., no. 1008.

72. Shoshone-Bannock Tribes, Idaho Centennial Celebration Brochure, Fort Hall, Idaho, 1968, p. 5.

73. Kappler, *Indian Affairs: Laws and Treaties,* 707.

74. Ibid., 709.

75. Doty, *Report of July 18, 1963,* 174–75.

76. Kappler, *Indian Affairs: Laws and Treaties.*

77. *Supreme Court Reporter,* 16 (1891): 1076-77.

78. Shanks, Bennett, and Reed, "Report of Special Commission to investigate the condition of the Indians in Idaho and adjacent Territories," 157–58.

79. McWhorter, *Yellow Wolf: His Own Story,* 26; emphasis ours.

80. Walker, *Conflict and Schism in the Nez Perce Acculturation.*

81. Swanton, *The Indian Tribes of North America,* 402.

82. Walker, *Conflict and Schism in the Nez Perce Acculturation,* 9.

83. Ibid., 13.

84. Ibid., 14.

85. Ibid.

86. Interview, April 2, 1997.

87. Interview, April 2, 1997; emphasis ours.

88. Data summarized in Galante, "East Meets West"; Lessard, "Crow Indian Art"; Loeb, "Classic Intermontane Beadwork of the Crow and Plateau Tribes."

89. *Report on Indians Taxed and Indians Not Taxed in the United States at the Eleventh Census: 1880,* 627.

90. Corless, *The Weiser Indians,* 13.

91. Weixelman, "The Power to Evoke Wonder," 53.

92. Pers. comm., May 20, 1997.

93. Haines, *Yellowstone Place Names,* 219.

94. Madsen, *Chief Pocatello: The White Plume,* 108.

95. Liljeblad, "The Idaho Indians in Transition," 39.

96. Utley, *Frontier Regulars* 329.

97. Cowan, *Reminiscences of Pioneer Life,* 169–70.

98. Halfmoon, "Joseph (Heinmot Tooyalakeet)," 309.

99. Utley, *The Indian Frontier of the American West, 1846–1890,* 190.

100. Lang, "Where Did the Nez Perce Go," 22, cites unpublished interviews with historian Lucullus McWhorter; the Nez Perce movements through Yellowstone National Park are expertly summarized in Lang, and a day-by-day itinerary of Nez Perce movements written for park visitors is in Wilfong, *Following the Nez Perce Trail,* 226–72.

101. Lang, "Where Did the Nez Perce Go," 29.

102. U.S. National Archives—Rocky Mountain Region, Record Group N-95, Records of the Forest Service Historical files, 1900–1965, Box 15, Folder #81, Narrative by J. K. Rollinson, May 15, 1935.

103. Shoshone National Forest, 7; Rollinson, "Northern Pacific Transport Company," 7.

104. Haines, *Yellowstone National Park,* 4.

105. Fredlund, Sundstrom, and Armstrong, "Crazy Mules Maps of the Upper Missouri, 1877–1880."

106. Ibid., 13.

107. Yosemite National Park Archives, H. W. Hutton Account of Trip through Yellowstone National Park (1881), Typescript, p. 2.

108. Yosemite National Park Archives, Letters Sent, vol. 9, October 2, 1899, to September 9, 1890; May 4, 1900.

109. Thompson and Thompson, *Beaver Dick,* 106.

110. Kappler, *Indian Affairs: Laws and Treaties,* 709.

111. Danilson, "Report of the Fort Hall Agency, Idaho, Sept. 7, 1875," 258; emphasis ours.

112. Danilson, "Report of the Fort Hall Agency, Idaho, 1876."

113. Danilson, "Report of Fort Hall Agency, Idaho, August 15, 1877."

114. Liljeblad, "The Old Traditions of the Shoshoni and Bannock Indians of Idaho," 8.

115. Ruby and Brown, *Dreamer-Prophets of the Columbia Plateau,* 68–69.

116. Aoki, *Nez Perce Texts,* 84–85.

117. Much of the following data comes from the historian Kyle V. Walpole's recent reconstruction of the Bannock campaign for the Buffalo Bill Historical Center, especially his research into its climax on Bennett Butte east of Yellowstone National Park; Walpole, "Bennett Butte, 'Bivouc of the Dead.'"

118. This is apparently when the J. H. Schoenberger Jr. party, touring the park and enjoying a hot spring interlude, were spotted by "a party of Bannack Indians" and barely escaped a repeat performance of the Nez Perce encounter a year before; all the Indians got were two buffalo robes, scooped up without even dismounting, before disappearing into the woods. *Bozeman Avant Courier,* November 28, 1878.

119. Walpole, "Bennett Butte, 'Bivouc of the Dead,'" 32–36.

120. Thompson and Thompson, *Beaver Dick,* 107–9.

121. Burlingame, *The Montana Frontier,* 242–44.

122. Madsen, *The Northern Shoshoni,* 19.

123. Ibid.

124. Corless, *The Weisner Indians,* 116–17.

125. Brown, *The Sheepeater Campaign,* 14.

126. *Idaho Statesman,* September 25, 1879, 3.

127. Janetski, *The Indians of Yellowstone Park,* 54, citing Madsen, *The Lemhi, Sacajawea's People,* 104.

128. Madsen, *The Lemhi, Sacajawea's People,* 24.

129. Janetski, *The Indians of Yellowstone Park,* 54.

130. Norris, *Report upon the Yellowstone National Park, to the Secretary of the Interior, for the Year 1877,* 842.

131. Janetski, *The Indians of Yellowstone Park,* 85.

132. Norris, *Report upon the Yellowstone National Park, to the Secretary of the Interior, for the Year 1878,* 985.

133. Spence, "Dispossessing the Wilderness," 58-59; P. W. Norris to R. E. Trowbridge, April 26, 1880, Record Group 75, Records of the Bureau of Indian Affairs, "Letters

Received by the Office of Indian Affairs, 1824–1831" [Microfilm Series M234, Roll 352, Frame 322]; Norris to Carl Schurz, June 21, 1880; Norris to Harry Yount, June 21, 1880, Record Group 48, "Records of the Office of the Secretary of the Interior Relating to Yellowstone National Park" [Microfilm Series M62, Roll 1, Frames 288-9].

134. Wingate, *Through the Yellowstone Park on Horseback,* 140.

135. *Billings Gazette,* March 2, 1887, 1.

136. Magoc, *Yellowstone,* 147.

137. See the discussion and citations from the October 1997 version of Mark Spence's essay, "First Wilderness: Indian Removal from Yellowstone." In his *Yellowstone,* chap. 6, "Indians, Animals, and Yellowstone Defenders," Magoc is especially informative on comparing Indian and white hunting in the Yellowstone region.

138. Magoc, *Yellowstone;* Spence, *Dispossessing the Wilderness,* 63.

139. *Annual Report of the Commissioner of Indian Affairs, 1894,* 63–68, 76–77.

140. Spence, "Dispossessing the Wilderness," 10, and his lengthier treatment in his subsection, "The First Cavalry to the Rescue," Spence, "Dispossessing the Wilderness," 62-70; see also Ward, Sheriff v. Race Horse, May 25, 1986, Supreme Court Reporter, vol 16, pp. 1076-1082].

141. Spence, "Dispossessing the Wilderness," 68.

142. Harring, *Crow Dog's Case,* 204–6; see also Czech, "Elk Hunting in the Shadow of Ward vs. Racehorse."

143. Hultkrantz, "An Ideological Dichotomy: Myths and Folk Beliefs among the Shoshoni Indians of Wyoming," 345.

144. Ibid.

145. Lowie, "The Northern Shoshone," 278.

146. Ibid.

147. Clark, *Indian Legends from the Northern Rockies,* 174–77.

148. Bright, *A Coyote Reader,* 35.

149. Ramsey, *Coyote was Going There,* xxiv.

150. Miller, Harrison, and Pichette, *Coyote Tales of the Montana Salish,* 16–19.

151. Walker, *Blood of the Monster,* 49.

152. Lévi-Strauss, *Anthropology and Myth,* 64–67.

153. Interview, November 18, 1995.

154. Interview, November 18, 1995.

155. Interview, November 18, 1995.

156. Interview, November 18, 1995.

157. Interview, December 15, 1995.

158. Interview, April 2, 1997.

159. Interview, November 18, 1995.

160. Murphey, *Indian Uses of Native Plants,* 32.

161. Interview, December 15, 1995.

162. Interview, November 18, 1995.

163. Interview, November 18, 1995.

Chapter 5

1. Jones, *Report upon the Reconnaissance of Northwestern Wyoming,* 39.

2. Ibid., 54.

3. Ibid.

4. Ibid., 276.

5. Ibid., 55.

6. Anderson, *One Hundred Years*, 93.

7. Stewart, "Tribal Distributions and Boundaries in the Great Basin," 167–238.

8. Citing Royce, "Indian Land Cessions in United States"; Powell, "Indian Linguistic Families of American North of Mexico"; Kroeber, *Handbook of the Indians of California;* Steward, "Linguistic Distribution and Political Groups of the Great Basin Shoshoneans"; Stewart, "Tribal Distributions and Boundaries in the Great Basin."

9. Kroeber, *Handbook of the Indians of California.*

10. Steward, "Linguistic Distribution and Political Groups of the Great Basin Shoshoneans."

11. Teit, "The Salishan Tribes of the Western Plateaus," 304; emphasis ours.

12. Madsen , *The Northern Shoshoni,* 223; emphasis ours.

13. Laidlaw, "Federal Indian Land Policy and the Fort Hall Indians," 1–4.

14. Malouf, "Historic Tribes and Archaeology"; also Johnson, "The Enos Family and Wind River Shoshone Society," 16–18.

15. Malouf, "Historic Tribes and Archaeology,"130.

16. Kroeber, "Cultural and Natural Areas of Native North America," 80, 82.

17. Hultkrantz, "Shoshoni Indians on the Plains," 72.

18. Ibid., 57.

19. Shimkin, "Dynamics of Recent Wind River Shoshone History," 457.

20. Voget, *The Shoshoni-Crow Sundance.*

21. Curriculum Development Workshop, *The Wind River Reservation Yesterday and Today,* 587.

22. Whittlesey, *Yellowstone Place Names,*153.

23. Crowder, *Tenday, Chief of the Lemhis,* 41.

24. Fowler, "Notes on the Early Life of Chief Washaki Taken Down by Captain Ray."

25. Wright, "High Country Adaptations."

26. Hebard, *Washakie: Chief of the Shoshones,* 698–70.

27. Ibid., 212.

28. Patten, "Buffalo Hunting with the Shoshone Indians," 298–99.

29. Patten, "Last Great Hunt of Washakie and His Band," 34.

30. Baillie-Grohman, *Camps in the Rockies,* 263–77.

31. Wister Notebook, Tuesday, August 16, 1887, University of Wyoming, Special Collections, Accession #290.

32. Buxton, *Short Stalks: Or Hunting Camps N, S, E and W,* 75.

33. Krueger, *Eighteen Months in a Wyoming Tie Camp,* 11..

34. Vander, "Ghost Dance Songs and Religion of a Wind River Shoshone Woman," 5.

35. See Shimkin, "Dynamics of Recent Wind River Shoshone History," 456–61, for Shoshone religious change.

36. Liljeblad, "The Religious Attitude of the Shoshonian Indians," 41.

37. Statham, "A Biogeographic Model of Camas and Its Role in the Aboriginal Economy of the Northern Shoshoni in Idaho," 65.

38. Fowler, *Arapahoe Politics,* 228.

39. Nickerson, "Some Data on Plains and Great Basin Indian Uses of Certain Native Plants," 49–50.

40. Turney-High, 'Ethnography of the Kutenai," 33.

41. Father Pierre De Smet, in Chittenden and Richardson, *Life and Letters and Travels of Father De Smet,* 488.

42. Rapson, Kornfeld, and Larson, "The Henn Site Today and in Prehistory," 235–36.

43. Ibid., 77.

44. Reeve, "Ethnobotany and Archeology in Yellowstone and Grand Teton National Parks," 378.

45. Pers. comm., December 4, 1993

46. Conner, "Jackson Lake Archaeology Project 1985," 247.

47. Reeve, *Root Crops and Prehistoric Social Process in the Snake River Headwaters, Northwestern Wyoming*, iii.

48. Ibid.

49. Reeve, *Prehistoric Settlements at the Yellowstone Lake Outlet*, 32.

50. Francis, "Root Procurement in the Upper Green River Basin," 2.

51. Ibid.

52. Malouf, *Camas and the Flathead Indians of Montana*, 26; Ray, "The Sanpoil and Nespelem," 98.

53. Hunn, "On the Relative Contribution of Men and Women to Subsistence among Hunter-Gatherers of the Columbia Plateau,"129.

54. Ibid., 13.

55. Francis, "Root Procurement in the Upper Green River Basin,"10.

56. Thwaites, *Original Journals of the Lewis and Clark expedition 1804–1806*, vol. 5, 119.

57. Ibid., 293.

58. Carey, ed., *The Journals of Theodore Talbot 1843 and 1949–52*, 45.

59. Statham, "A Biogeographic Model of Camas and Its Role in the Aboriginal Economy of the Northern Shoshoni in Idaho," 60.

60. Liljeblad, *Indian Peoples in Idaho*, 70.

61. Steward, *Basin-Plateau Aboriginal Sociopolitical Groups*, 328; Murphy and Murphy, "Shoshone-Bannock Subsistence and Society," 320.

62. Murphy and Murphy, "Shoshone-Bannock Subsistence and Society," 321.

63. Statham, "A Biogeographic Model of Camas and Its Role in the Aboriginal Economy of the Northern Shoshoni in Idaho," 78.

64. Ibid., 78–79.

65. Report of the Commissioner of Indian Affairs, 1871, 540–43; Berry to Walker, Fort Hall Agency, January 1, 1872, in Fort Hall Agency Letter Book, quoted in Madsen, *The Bannock of Idaho*, 182–83.

66. Madsen, *The Bannock of Idaho*, 228–29.

67. Beal, *History of Southeastern Idaho*, 46.

68. Statham, "A Biogeographic Model of Camas and Its Role in the Aboriginal Economy of the Northern Shoshoni in Idaho," 60.

69. Anastasio, "Intergroup Relations in the Southern Plateau," 18; Liljeblad, *Indian Peoples in Idaho*, 15, 26, 65; Curtis, *The North American Indian*, vol. 7, xi; Steward, *Basin-Plateau Aboriginal Sociopolitical Groups*, 10, 167; and "Culture Element Distributions," 364; Kroeber, *Cultural and Natural Areas of Native North America*, 49; Murphy and Murphy,"Shoshone-Bannock Subsistence and Society," 319, 321.

70. For the Blackfeet method, see Schultz and Donaldson, *The Sun God's Children*, 42–43.

71. Ibid., 43.

72. Malouf, *Camas and the Flathead Indians of Montana*.

73. Weisel, *Men and Trade on the Northwest Frontier as Shown by the Fort Owen Ledger*, 112.

74. Curtis, *The North American Indian*, vol. 7, 185; Turney-High, "The Flatheads of Montana," 24, 252.

75. Murphey, *Indian Uses of Native Plants,* 14.

76. Curtis, *The North American Indian,* vol. 8, 43.

77. Malouf, *Camas and the Flathead Indians of Montana,* 15.

78. Ibid., 19.

79. Ibid., 26.

80. Ibid,, 31.

81. Ibid,, 34.

82. White, "David Thompson's Journals Relating to Montana & Adjacent Regions," 57a.

83. Malouf, *Camas and the Flathead Indians of Montana,* 41.

84. Stubbs, "An Investigation of the Edible and Medicinal Plants Used by the Flathead Indians," 53.

85. Curtis, *The North American Indian,* vol. 6, 169.

86. Malouf, *Camas and the Flathead Indians of Montana,* 41.

87. Boas, *Kutenai Tales,* 11.

88. Hoffman, "Selish Myths," 24–40.

89. Willard, *Edible and Medicinal Plants of the Rocky Mountains and Neighbouring Territories,* 48.

90. Malouf, *Camas and the Flathead Indians of Montana,* 41.

91. See Thompson, *Tales of the North American Indians,* 356, Motif #285, for a summary of Indian citations involving "Trickster creates men of excrement."

92. Dundes, *Sacred Narrative.*

93. Bright, *A Coyote Reader,* 70–72.

94. Hultkrantz, "The Indians and the Wonders of Yellowstone," 66.

95. Ibid., 42.

96. Chittenden and Richardson, *Life, Letters and Travels of Father De Smet,* 661.

97. Ibid., 1377–78.

98. Ruxton, *Life in the Far West,* 117.

99. Mattes, "Behind the Legend of Colter's Hell."

100. Chittenden and Richardson, *Life, Letters and Travels of Father De Smet,* 79.

101. Langford, "Diary of the Washburn Expedition to the Yellowstone and Firehole Rivers in the Year 1870," 97.

102. Blackmore, "Diary—Fourth Visit to the United States."

103. Jones, *Report upon the Reconnaissance of Northwestern Wyoming,* 28.

104. Beal, "The Story of Man in Yellowstone," 122.

105. Whittlesey, *Yellowstone Place Names,* xxxix, a figure that the author has currently updated to "56 devil, 6 hell, and 3 satan place names"; pers. comm., July, 1999.

106. Ferguson, *Walking Down the Wild,* 137.

107. Trumbull, 'The Washburn Yellowstone Expedition No. 1," 436.

108. Quoted in Ferguson, *Walking Down the Wild,* 136.

109. Cowan, *Reminiscences of Pioneer Life,* 159.

110. Norris, *Report upon the Yellowstone National Park, to the Secretary of the Interior, for the Year 1879,* 35.

111. Wister, "Old Yellowstone Days," 473.

112. Raftery, "Historical Sketch of Yellowstone National Park," 101–2.

113. Hebard, *Washakie: Chief of the Shoshones,* 307.

114. Ibid.

115. See early park guidebook entries following this line, such as Norton, *Wonder-Land Illustrated,* 31; Wingate, *Through the Yellowstone Park on Horseback,* 139; Guptill,

Practical Guide to Yellowstone National Park; Hough, *Yellowstone,* 13; and the more recent Schreier, *Yellowstone Explorers Guide.*

116. Quoted in Magoc, *Yellowstone,* 141–42.

117. Interview, November 14, 1995.

118. Interview, February 4, 1996.

119. Interview, February 4, 1996.

120. Interview, November 18, 1995.

121. Weixelman, "The Power to Evoke Wonder," 57.

122. Ibid., 55; Marler, "Plants Utilized by the Crow Indians."

123. Trenholm and Carley, *The Shoshonis,* 286–311.

124. Steward, *The Blackfoot,* 286.

125. Letter of John Wilson, quoted in Hultkrantz, "The Fear of Geysers among Indians of the Yellowstone Park Area," 34.

126. Ruxton, *Life in the Far West,* 101–2.

127. Sharman, *The Cave on the Yellowstone or Early Life in the Rockies,* 31.

128. Ibid.

129. Quoted in Madsen, *Chief Pocatello,* 112–13.

130. Horne, *Autobiography of George Washinton Bean,* 114.

131. Weeks, *Pachee Goyo,* 31.

132. Barry, "E. Willard Smith Journal 1839–1840," 36.

133. Sholly and Newman, *Guardians of Yellowstone,* 37.

134. Marler, "Inventory of Thermal Features of the Firehole River Geyser Basins and Other Selected Areas of Yellowstone National Park," 462.

135. Hultkrantz, "The Fear of Geysers among Indians of the Yellowstone Park Area," 35, emphasis ours.

136. J. H. Bacon, "Letter regarding George Harvey Bacon's visits to Yellowstone area from 1864 to 1873," Yellowstone Research Library, in Weixelman, "The Power to Evoke Wonder," 70.

137. Kearns, "A Nez Perce Chief Revisits Yellowstone," 41.

138. McWhorter, *Yellow Wolf: His Own Story,* 30

139. Carpenter, *Adventures in Geyserland,* 128.

140. Mills, "The Grand Rounds."

141. Hultkrantz, "The Fear of Geysers among Indians of the Yellowstone Park Area," 37.

142. Interview, August 22, 1995.

143. Yellowstone National Park Archives, Interview with Ake Hultkrantz, July 26, 1994.

144. Ranger Naturalist Manual of Yellowstone National Park, 19.

145. Beal, *The Story of Man in Yellowstone,* 89.

146. Department of the Interior Memorandum, National Park Service, Yellowstone National Park, August 4, 1961.

147. Malouf, *Preliminary Report, Yellowstone National Park Archeological Survey,* 5–6.

148. Haines, "History of Yellostone National Park," 87, original emphasis.

149. Weixelman, "The Power to Evoke Wonder," 60.

150. Quoted in Haines, *Yellowstone National Park,* 63.

151. Ibid., 41; *Helena Daily Herald,* May 18, 1870.

152. Viall, "Annual Report of the Commissioner of Indian Affairs 42d Congress, 2d Session House exdoc (42-2), SN-1505," 831.

153. Pease, "Report on Crow Agency, Montana," 836.

154. Smith, "Lemhi Valley, Montana Territory," 848.

155. Viall, "Annual Report of the Commissioner of Indian Affairs 42d Congress, 2d Session House exdoc (42-2), SN-1505," 832.

156. Rainsford, "Lemhi Farm, Montana Territory," 666.

157. Fuller, "Lemhi Valley Indian Reservation," 813.

158. Fuller, "Lemhi Special Indian Agency," 448.

159. Wright, "Lemhi Indian Agency, Idaho," 160.

160. Clemmer and Stewart, "Treaties, Reservations, and Claims," 53.

161. Thompson and Thompson, *Beaver Dick,* 96.

162. Haines, *Yellowstone Place Names,* 29, 333.

163. Patten to Commissioner of Indian Affairs E. A. Hayt, June 11, 1879.

164. Hultkrantz, "The Indians of Yellowstone Park," 145.

165. Janetski, *The Indians of Yellowstone Park,* 54.

166. Norris, *Fifth Annual Report of the Superintendent of Yellowstone National Park, to the Secretary of the Interior,* 45.

167. Dippie, "This Bold But Wasting Race."

168. Quoted in Nabokov, *Native American Testimony,* 188.

169. Quoted in Lubbers, *Born for the Shade,* 214.

170. Berkhofer, *The White Man's Indian,* 537.

171. Dixon, *The Vanishing Race,* 5.

172. Quoted in Lubbers, *Born for the Shade,* 220.

173. Kroeber, *Ishi in Two Worlds.*

174. Norris, *Report upon the Yellowstone National Park,* 842.

175. Norris, *Fifth Annual Report of the Superintendent of the Yellowstone National Park to the Secretary of the Interior,* 38.

176. Allen, *The Sheep Eaters,* 74.

177. Daniels, "Food for the Sheep-Eaters," 25.

178. Hebard, *Washakie: Chief of the Shoshones,* 118.

179. Barrette, "Ghost Tribe of the West," 58.

180. Bonar, "Sheepeaters Were Doomed by Smallpox," 6.

181. Smith, *The Sheepeaters: Keepers of the Past.*

182. Bellinghausen, *Sheepeater People.*

183. Hultkrantz, "The Source Literature on the 'Tukudika' Indians in Wyoming."

184. Wagner and Allen, *Blankets and Moccasins,* 150.

185. Norris, *The Calumet of the Coteau and Other Poetical Legends of the Border,* 47.

186. Quoted in Janetski, *Indians in Yellowstone National Park,* 24. Report, Philip Sheridan to Brigadier General R. C. Drum, November 1, 1882, M-62, Reel 1, Record Group 48, National Archives Record Administration.

187. Jones, *Report upon the Reconnaissance of Norethwestern Wyoming,* 275.

188. Ibid., 55.

189. Sharon Kahin, from Charlie Beck, pers. comm., July 15, 1996.

190. Esther Mockler manuscript, 15, Dubois Museum, courtesy of Sharon Kahin, Museum Director.

191. Reverend John Roberts manuscript, quoted in Hultkrantz, "The Sheepeaters of Wyoming" II: 87. Ms. in possession of Roberts family.

192. Vander, *Shoshone Ghost Dance Religion,* 210.

193. Hultkrantz, "The Sheepeaters of Wyoming" II: 88–89; also in Hultkrantz, "The Concept of the Soul Held by the Wind River Shoshone," 36-37.

194. Clayton, "A Brief History of the Washakie National Forest and the Duties and Some Experiences of a Ranger," 278.

195. Shimkin, "Childhood and Development among the Wind River Shoshone," 303.
196. Lowie, "The Northern Shoshone," 211.

Conclusion

1. One such relationship has been hypothesized by the linguist Donald Bahr based on a comment in a Tohono O'odham (Papago) migration narrative about that Arizona tribe's ancestors coming to a place "where the ground was boiling," which Bahr suggests might be Yellowstone.

2. We advocate that the park explore the "interpreted environments" approach outlined by Michael Southworth in his *Landscapes for Learning*.

3. "The Evolution of Cultural Resources Management in Yellowstone: An Interview with Laura Joss." Joss's estimate contrasts with Gary A. Wright's comment, about twenty years earlier: "Yellowstone Park is one of the poorest known archeological areas of North America. Only 20% of the Park has been surveyed, and there is no adequate synthesis of the archeological data." "Archeological Research in Yellowstone National Park." Yet it is more optimistic than the 1 percent estimate provided by the Yellowstone National Park archaeologist Ann N. Johnson in 1997, who added, "Almost no archaeology has been conducted in the park. Our inventories haven't gotten away from the pavement," which, of course, was the intent of Joss's hopes for the "back country" phase of Yellowstone archaeology still ahead.

4. Mack W. Shortt, "Museum of the Rockies Archaeological Research in the Canyons of the Yellowstone."

5. Jack Edmo provides a Shoshone-Bannock perspective on how the collaborative project between Idaho State University's Archaeological Research Project and twenty-four young people from his reservation worked out in "Native Archaeologists: The Bannock-Shoshone Program in Study of Man." The Tongass Forest example of Indian and non-Indian collaboration on an archaeological project is described by David Hurst Thomas in the epilogue to his *Skull Wars: Kennewick Man, Archaeology, and the Battle for Native American Identity*, while Indian perspectives on such partnerships in California are found in the thirteen articles collected in a special "California Indians and Archaeology" issue of *News from Native California*, summer 1996.

6. Quoted in "In the 'Greened' World, It Isn't Easy to Be Human," by Alexander Stille, *New York Times*, July 15, 2000, A17.

7. One searches in vain for any discussion of Indian concerns related to national park access for subsistence or religious purposes, for a higher American Indian profile in all interpretive representations of their historical or cultural ties to parklands, or any mention of the impact of such protective legislation as the American Indian Religious Freedom Act (AIRFA) or the Native American Graves and Repatriation Act (NAGPRA) in the following overviews: Ronald A. Foresta, *American's National Parks and Their Keepers;* John C. Freemuth, *Islands under Seige: National Parks and the Politics of External Threats;* John C. Miles, *Guardians of the Parks: A History of the National Parks and Conservation Association.* Even the high-level symposium convened by Secretary of the Interior Bruce Babbitt in Vail, Colorado, in October 1991, on the National Park Service's seventy-fifth anniversary, which produced thirty-seven recommendations covering "challenges and strategies for the 21st century," totally any indigenous historical involvements, environmental concerns, or continuing legal or cultural interests in NPS-administered lands *(National Parks for the 21st Century: The Vail Agenda)*. The same neglect is largely true for pre-1990 assessments of natural reserves globally; in the

700-page document report on a 1982 conference titled *National Parks, Conservation, and Development: The Role of Protected Areas in Sustaining Society* (edited by Jeffrey A. McNeely and Kenton R.Miller) only one six-page article, by Raymond F. Dasman, discussed the relations between protected areas and native peoples.

8. West and Brechlin, *Resident Peoples and National Parks*, xix.

9. Sanders, "Review of Indian Country," 198.

10. See "The Pajarito or Cliff Dwellers' National Park Proposal, 1900–1920," by Thomas L. Altherr.

11. *Los Angeles Times*, August 3, 1997, M4.

12. Catlin, *North American Indians*, vol. 1, 2.

13. Thoreau, "Chesuncook."

Bibliography

Reports and Federal Documents

Arno, S. F. *The Historical Role of Fire on the Bitterroot National Forest.* Forest Service Res. Paper INT-187. Intermountain Forest and Range Exp. Station, Ogden, Utah, 1976.

Bearss, E. C. *Bighorn Canyon National Recreation Area, Wyoming-Montana, History Basic Data Study, Vol. 1.* Submitted to the National Park Service, Office of History and Historic Architecture, Eastern Service Center, Washington, D.C., 1970.

Blauer, A. C., A. P. Plummer, E. D. McArthur, R. Stevens, and B. C. Giunta. "Characteristics and Hybridization of Important Intermountain Shrubs: I, Rose Family." Research Paper INT-169. Ogden, Utah: USDA Forest Service, Intermountain Forest and Range Experiment Station, 1975.

Cannon, K. P. "A Review of Archaeological and Paleontological Evidence for the Prehistoric Presence of Wolf and Related Prey Species in the Northern and Central Rockies Physiographic Provinces." In *Wolves for Yellowstone. A Report to the United States Congress*, Vol. IV, Research and Analysis, edited by J. D. Varley and W. G. Brewster. Yellowstone National Park, Wyo., 1992.

Cannon, K. P. and P. Phillips. "Post-fire Inventory and Evaluation in Yellowstone National Park, Wyoming: The 1989 Field Season." Midwest Archeological Center Technical Report No. 24. Submitted to the National Park Service, Rocky Mountain Regional Office, Denver, 1993.

Chittenden, H. M. "Construction, Repair, and Maintenance of Roads and Bridges in the Yellowstone National Park." *Annual Report of the Chief of Engineers for 1902.* Washington, D.C.: Government Printing Office, 1902.

Cummings, L. S. "Appendix C: Pollen and Macrobotanical Analysis at 24YE353 and 24YE366 along the Yellowstone River, Montana." In *Post-Fire Inventory and Evaluation in Yellowstone National Park, Wyoming, The 1989 Field Season*, by K. Cannon and P. Phillips, 229–237. Midwest Archeological Center Technical Report No. 24. Produced for the Rocky Mountain Region, National Park Service, 1993.

Danilson, W. H. "Report of the Fort Hall Agency, Idaho, September 7, 1875." In *Papers Accompanying the Annual Report of the Commissioner of Indian Affairs*. Accompanying the Annual Report for the Secretary of the Interior for the Year 1875, 258–60. Washington, D.C.: Government Printing Office, 1875.

———. "Report of the Fort Hall Agency, Idaho, 1876." In *Papers Accompanying the Annual Report of the Commissioner of Indian Affairs 1876*. 44th Congress 2nd Session, House Executive Document. Washington, D.C.: Government Printing Office, 1876.

———. "Report of the Fort Hall Agency, Idaho, August 15, 1877." In *Papers Accompanying the Annual Report of the Commissioner of Indian Affairs 1877*. 45th Congress 2nd Session, House Executive Document 1, 474–75, Serial 1800. Washington, D.C.: Government Printing Office, 1878.

———. "Report of the Fort Hall Agency, Idaho, August 28, 1878." In *Papers Accompanying the Annual Report of the Commissioner of Indian Affairs*. 45th Congress 3rd session, House Executive Document 1, 545–47, Serial 1850. Washington, D.C.: Government Printing Office, 1879.

Davis, L. B., S. A. Aaberg, and J. G. Schmitt. *The Obsidian Cliff Plateau Prehistoric Lithic Source, Yellowstone National Park, Wyoming*. Selections from the Division of Cultural Resources No. 6. National Park Service, Rocky Mountain Region, Denver. Report submitted by Museum of the Rockies, Montana State University, Bozeman, Contract No. PX-1200-8-PO52, 1995.

Doane, G. C. *Report of Lieutenant Gustavus C. Doane Upon the Socalled Yellowstone Expedition of 1870*. 41st Congress 3rd Session, Senate Executive Document 51. Washington, D.C.: Government Printing Office, 1871.

Dorson, R. M. *The Historical Validity of Oral Tradition: First Report*. Presented Nov. 1961, Indian Claims Commission. Justice Department. Bloomington, Ind.: Lilly Library, Indiana University, 1961.

Doty, J. D. *Report of July 18, 1863*. 38th Congress 1st Session, House Executive Document, Serial 1182. Washington, D.C.: Government Printing Office, 1864.

Fuller, H. "Lemhi Valley Indian Reservation." *Annual Report of the Commissioner of Indian Affairs*. 44th Congress 1st Session, House Executive Document 44-1, Serial 1680. Washington, D.C.: Government Printing Office, 1875.

———. "Lemhi Special Indian Agency." *Annual Report of the Commissioner of Indian Affairs*. 44th Congress 2nd Session, House Executive Document 44-2, Serial 1749. Washington, D.C.: Government Printing Office, 1877.

Gilmore, M. R. "Uses of Plants by the Indians of the Upper Missouri River Region." In *33rd Annual Report of the Bureau of American Ethnology for the Years 1911–1912*, 43–154. Washington, D.C.: Smithsonian Institution, 1919.

Gregory, Lieutenant Colonel J. F. *Report of Lieutenant General P. H. Sheridan . . . of his Expedition Through the Big Horn Mountains*. Washington, D.C.: Government Printing Office, 1882.

Haines, Aubrey L. *Yellowstone National Park: Its Exploration and Establishment*. National Park Service. Washington, D.C.: Government Printing Office, 1974.

Hatton, C. "Report of Shoshone and Bannock Agency, Wyoming." In *Annual Report of the Commissioner of Indian Affairs to the Secretary of the Interior for 1881*. Washington, D.C.: Government Printing Office, 1881.

Hayden, F.V. *Preliminary Report of the U.S. Geological Survey of Montana and Portions of Adjacent Territory*. Washington, D.C.: Government Printing Office, 1872.

———. *Twelfth Annual Report. U.S. Geological and Geographical Survey of the Territories, Part II*. Washington, D.C.: Government Printing Office, 1883.

Holmes, W. H. "Aboriginal Pottery of the Eastern United States." Bureau of American Ethnology Twentieth Annual Report for 1898–1899, 1–201. Washington, D.C.: Government Printing Office, 1903.

———. "Obsidian." *Handbook of the American Indians North of Mexico.* Part 2. Bureau of American Ethnology Bulletin 30 (1910): 102.

———. *Handbook of Aboriginal American Antiquities, Part 1: Introduction. The Lithic Industries.* Bureau of American Ethnology Bulletin 60, Washington, D.C.: Government Printing Office, 1919.

Hornaday, W. T. "The Extermination of the American Bison with a Sketch of its Discovery and Life History." *Report of the U.S. National Museum*, Part 2, 367–548. Washington, D.C.: Government Printing Office, 1889.

Iddings, J. P. "Obsidian Cliff, Yellowstone National Park." *Seventh Annual Report of the United States Geological Survey to the Secretary of the Interior, 1885–1886.* Washington, D.C.: Government Printing Office, 1888.

Indians South of the Yellowstone: Cheyennes, Arapahoes, Kiowa, Crows. 1824. *American State Papers, VI, Indian Affairs* II.

Jones, W. A. *Report upon the Reconnaissance of Northwestern Wyoming, Including Yellowstone National Park, Made in the Summer of 1873.* 43rd Congress 1st Session, House Executive Document 285. Washington, D.C.: Government Printing Office, 1875.

Keller, Augustus R. Report to Hon. E. A. Hayt, Commissioner of Indian Affairs, 1 July 1879. Box 9, Records of the Crow Indian Agency, Federal Records Center, Seattle, Wash., 1879.

Lahren, L. A. *Archeological Salvage Excavations at a Prehistoric Indian Campsite (2AVE344) in Yellowstone National Park.* Submitted to the National Park Service, Contract #PX-6860-3-1618, 1973.

Loendorf, L. and D. Klinner. *Deadfall Timber Structures in the Bighorn Canyon National Recreational Area, Montana.* Report on file with Bighorn Canyon National Recreation Area, Fort Smith, Mont., 1995.

Malouf, C. *Preliminary Report, Yellowstone National Park Archeological Survey.* University of Montana, Missoula, 1959.

Marler, G. "Inventory of Thermal Features of the Firehole River Geyser Basins and other Selected Areas of Yellowstone National Park." Washington, D.C.: Report of the U.S. Geological Survey, 1993.

National Parks for the 21st Century, The Vail Agenda. Report and Recommendations to the Director of the National Park Service. National Park Service Document #D-726. Post Mills, Vt., 1993.

Norris, P. W. *Annual Report of the Superintendent of the Yellowstone National Park, to the Secretary of the Interior, for the Year 1880.* Washington, D.C.: Government Printing Office, 1881.

———. *Fifth Annual Report of the Superintendent of the Yellowstone National Park to the Secretary of the Interior.* Washington, D.C.: Government Printing Office, 1881.

———. "Prehistoric Remains in Montana, Between Fort Ellis and the Yellowstone River." *Annual Report of Regents of the Smithsonian Institution, 1878*, 327–328. Washington, D.C.: Government Printing Office, 1880.

———. *Report Upon the Yellowstone National Park, to the Secretary of the Interior, for the Year 1877.* Washington, D.C.: Government Printing Office, 1877.

———. *Report Upon the Yellowstone National Park, to the Secretary of the Interior, for the Year 1878.* Washington, D.C.: Government Printing Office, 1879.

———. *Report Upon the Yellowstone National Park, to the Secretary of the Interior, for the Year 1879*. Washington, D.C.: Government Printing Office, 1880.

Noste, N. V. and C. L. Bushey. "Fire Responses of Shrubs of Dry Forest Habitat Types in Montana and Idaho." USDA Forest Intermountain Research Station, General Technical Report INT-239, 1987.

Parker, P. L. and T. F. King. "Guidelines for Evaluating and Documenting Traditional Cultural Properties." National Register Bulletin No. 38. National Park Service. Washington, D.C.: Government Printing Office, 1990.

Parry, C. C. "Botanical Report: List of Plants Collected." In *Report upon the Reconnaissance of Northwestern Wyoming, Including Yellowstone National Park, Made in the Summer of 1873*, by W. A. Jones, 308–318. 43rd Congress 1st Session, House Executive Document 285. Washington, D.C.: Government Printing Office, 1875.

Pease, F. D. "Report on Crow Agency, Montana." *Annual Report of the Commissioner of Indian Affairs*. 42nd Congress 2nd Session, House Executive Document 42-2, Serial 1505. Washington, D.C.: Government Printing Office, 1871.

Rainsford, J. C. "Lemhi Farm, Montana Territory." *Annual Report of the Commissioner of Indian Affairs*. 42nd Congress 3rd Session, House Executive Document 42-3, Serial 1560. Washington, D.C.: Government Printing Office, 1872.

Range Plant Handbook. Washington, D.C.: Forest Service, United States Department of Agriculture, 1937.

Ranger Naturalists Manual of Yellowstone National Park. Yellowstone National Park: U.S. Department of the Interior, National Park Service, 1927.

Rapson, D., M. Kornfeld, and M. L. Larson. "The Henn Site Today and In Prehistory." In *The Henn Site, 48TE1291: Early Archaic to Protohistoric Occupation at the Jackson National Fish Hatchery, Wyoming*, edited by M. L. Larson, 234–239. Technical Report No. 7. University of Wyoming, Laramie: Department of Anthropology, 1995.

Raynolds, W. T. *The Report of Brevet Brigadier General W. F. Raynolds on the Exploration of the Yellowstone River and the Country Drained by that River*. 40th Congress 1st Session, Senate Executive Document 77. Washington, D.C.: Government Printing Office, 1868.

Reeve, S. A. "Ethnobotany and Archeology in Yellowstone and Grand Teton National Parks." In *Proceedings of the Second Conference on Scientific Research in the National Parks*, San Francisco, Calif., November 26–30, 1979. Vol. 1, 362–380. National Park Service.

———. *Prehistoric Settlements at the Yellowstone Lake Outlet, Yellowstone National Park, Wyoming*. Jefferson Patterson Park and Museum, Maryland Division of Historical and Cultural Programs. Submitted to the National Park Service, Midwest Archeological Center, Lincoln, Contract No. PX-6115-7-0115, 1989.

Reeve, S. A., T. E. Marceau, and G. A. Wright. *Mitigation of the Sheepeater Bridge Site, 48YE320, Yellowstone National Park*. Submitted to the Midwest Archeological Center, Lincoln, Nebr., 1980.

Reeves, B. and S. Peacock. *Our Mountains Are Our Pillows: An Ethnographic Overview of Glacier National Park*, 2 vols. Calgary, AB, Canada. Submitted to the National Park Service, Rocky Mountain Regional Office, Denver, 1995.

Royce, C. C. "Indian Land Cessions in the United States." *18th Annual Report of the Bureau of American Ethnology for the Years 1896–1897 (Pt. 2)*, 521–964. Washington, D.C., 1899.

Sanders, P., R. Adams and D. Wedel. "The 1995 Class III Cultural Resource Inventory of a Black Survey near Mammoth Yellowstone National Park." Project 254G. Laramie:

Office of the Wyoming State Archaeologist, 1996. Typescript report on file, Yellowstone National Park.

Schullery, P. and L. H. Whittlesey. "Early Wildlife History of the Greater Yellowstone Ecosystem: An Interim Research Report Presented to the National Research Council, National Academy of Sciences Committee on Ungulate Management in Yellowstone National Park." Yellowstone National Park, Wyo.: Yellowstone Center for Resources, 1999.

Sebastian, L. "Protecting Traditional Cultural Properties Through the Section 106 Process." In *Federal Register* 61(104), 1993.

Shanks, J. P. C., T. W. Bennett, and H. W. Reed. "Report of Special Commission to Investigate the Condition of the Indians in Idaho and adjacent Territories, Salt Lake City, Utah, November 17, 1873." In *Papers Accompanying the Annual Reports of the Commissioner of Indian Affairs, 1873.* 46th Congress 3rd Session, House Executive Document 1, 525-27, Serial 1601. Washington, D.C.: Government Printing Office, 1873.

Shoshone National Forest. United States Department of Agriculture, Forest Service. Washington, D.C.: Government Printing Office, 1941.

Smith, A. I. "Lemhi Valley, Montana Territory." *Annual Report of the Commissioner of Indian Affairs.* 42nd Congress 2nd Session, House Executive Document 42-2, Serial 1505. Washington, D.C.: Government Printing Office, 1871.

Sowers, T. *Final Report of the Wyoming Archaeological Survey.* Cheyenne, Wyo.: Works Progress Administration, 1941.

Statham, D. S. *Camas and the Northern Shoshoni: A Biogeographic and Socioeconomic Analysis.* Archaeological Reports No. 10. Idaho: Boise State University, 1982.

Taylor, D. C. K. Wood and J. J. Hoffman. *Preliminary Archeological Investigations in Yellowstone National Park.* Montana State University, Missoula. Submitted to the National Park Service, Yellowstone National Park, Contract No. 14-10-232-320, 1964.

Teit, J. A. "The Salishan Tribes of the Western Plateaus." *45th Annual Report of the Bureau of American Ethnology for the Years 1927–1928,* 23–296. Washington, D.C., 1930.

Thompson, R. R. "First Annual Report—Oregon Territory—South Side of the Columbia River between the 46th and 44th degrees Latitude between the Summits of the Rocky and Cascade Mountains." Washington, D.C.: Government Printing Office, 1854.

U.S. Bureau of Indian Affairs. Letter from James I. Patten, U.S. Indian Agent, Shoshoni and Bannock Agency, to E. A. Hayt, Commissioner of Indian Affairs, referring to the transfer of Ten Doy's Band to that reservation, 11 June 1879. National Archives, Record Group 75, Washington, D.C.: Government Printing Office, 1879.

———. Letters Received by the Office of Indian Affairs, 1824–1831. National Archives Record Group 75. Washington, D.C.: Government Printing Office, 1880.

———. "Report of Ft. Hall Agency." In *Annual Report of Commissioner of Indian Affairs to Secretary of Interior W. H. Danilson.* Washington, D.C.: Government Printing Office, 1875.

U.S. House Committee on Expenditures for Indians and Yellowstone Park. *To Provide for the Appointment of a Commission to Inspect and Report on the Condition of Indians, Indian Affairs, and for Other Purposes,* Report No. 1076. To accompany bill H.R. 6973. 49th Congress 1st Session, 1886.

U.S. Indian Claims Commission. "Commission Findings on the Shoshone Indians." 11 Indian Claims Commission 387, 16 October 1962. In *Shoshone Indians.* New York: Garland, 1974.

U.S. Office of the Secretary of the Interior. Records relating to Yellowstone National Park. Record Group 48, 1880.

U.S. Statutes at Large 78:890–96. Public Law 88-577.

Viall, J. A. Montana Superintendency. Office of the Superintendent of Indian Affairs. *Annual Report of the Commissioner of Indian Affairs.* 42nd Congress 2nd Session House Executive Document 42-2, Serial 1505. Washington, D.C.: Government Printing Office, 1871.

Wright, G. A. *A Preliminary Report on Jenny Lake II (48TE576): A Posthorse Shoshone Site in Grand Teton National Park.* Department of Anthropology, State University of New York, Albany. Submitted to the National Park Service, Midwest Archeological Center, Lincoln, 1977.

Wright, G., T. Marceau, F.A. Calabrese, and Melodie Tune. *Regional Assessment, Archeological Report.* Greater Yellowstone Cooperative Regional Transportation Study. Submitted to the National Park Service, Midwest Archeological Center, Lincoln, 1978.

Wright, J. A. "Lemhi Indian Agency, Idaho." *Annual Report of the Commissioner of Indian Affairs.* 46th Congress 2nd Session, House Executive Document 46-2, Serial 1910. Washington, D.C.: Government Printing Office, 1897.

Books and Articles

Aginsky, B. "Population Control in the Shanel (Pomo) Tribe." *American Sociological Review* 10, no. 2 (1939): 209–16.

Aikens, C. M. and Y. T. Witherspoon. "Great Basin Numic Prehistory." In *Anthropology of the Desert West: Essays in Honor of Jesse D. Jennings,* edited by C. J. Condie and D. D. Fowler. Salt Lake City: University of Utah Press, 1984.

Allen, W. A. *The Sheep Eaters.* New York: The Shakespeare Press, 1913; Fairfield, Wash.: Ye Galleon Press, 1989.

Alter, J. C. *James Bridger, Trapper, Frontiersman, Scout and Guide: A Historical Narrative.* Salt Lake City: Shepard Book Co., 1925; Columbus, Ohio: Long's College Book Company, 1951.

———. "The Indian's Pathway to Yellowstone (Cody Gateway)." *Motor* 27 (1917): 82–83, 140.

Altherr, T. L. "The Pajarito or Cliff dwellers's National Park Proposal 1900–1920." *New Mexico Historical Review* 60, no. 3 (1985): 271–94.

Anderson, D. C., J. A. Tiffany, and F. W. Nelson. "Recent Research on Obsidian from Iowa Archaeological Sites." *American Antiquity* 51, no. 4 (1986): 837–52.

Anderson, Jeffrey D. *One Hundred Years of Old Man Sage: An Arapaho Life.* Lincoln: University of Nebraska Press, 2003.

Anell, B. *Running Down and Driving of Game in North America.* Studia Ethnographica Upsaliensia 30. Lund, Sweden: Berlingska Boktryckeriet, 1969.

Aoki, H. *Nez Perce Dictionary.* Vol. 122, *Publications in Linguistics.* Berkeley: University of California Press, 1994.

———. *Nez Perce Grammar.* Vol. 62, *Publications in Linguistics.* Berkeley and Los Angeles: University of California Press, 1974.

———. *Nez Perce Texts.* Berkeley and Los Angeles: University of California Press, 1979.

Arthur, G. "An Archaeological Survey of the Upper Yellowstone River Drainage, Montana." *Agricultural Economics Research Report* 26. Bozeman: Department of Agricultural Economics and Rural Sociology. Montana Agricultural Experiment Station, 1966.

———. "Southern Montana." In *Northwestern Plains: A Symposium,* edited by Warren W. Caldwell, 51-78. Occasional Papers, No. 1. Billings, Mont.: Rocky Mountain College, 1968.

Bach, O. E., Jr. *Hiking the Yellowstone Backcountry*. 2nd rev. ed. San Francisco: Sierra Club Books, 1979.

Bahr, D. *The Short Swift Time of Gods on Earth: The Hohokam Chronicles*. Berkeley and Los Angeles: University of California Press, 1994.

Baillie-Grohman, W. A. *Camps in the Rockies*. London: Sampson Law, Masston, Searle, and Rivington, 1882; New York: Charles Scribner and Sons, 1898.

Ball, S. H. "The Mining of Gems and Ornamental Stones in American Indians." *Anthropological Papers 13, Bureau of American Ethnology Bulletin* 128 (1941): 1–78.

Balls, E. K. *Early Uses of California Plants*. Berkeley and Los Angeles: University of California Press, 1941.

Barbeau, M. "Review of Indian Legends of Canada by Ella Elizabeth Clark." *Journal of American Folklore* 15 (1962): 65–66.

Barrett, S. and S. F. Arno. "Indian Fires as an Ecological Influence in the Northern Rockies." *Journal of Forestry* 80, no. 10 (1982): 647–51.

Barrett, S. A. "Collecting Among the Blackfoot Indians." *Milwaukee Public Museum Yearbook* 1 (1921): 22–28.

Barrett, S. W. "Indians and Fire." *Western Wildlands* (Spring 1980): 17–21.

Barrette, K. "Ghost Tribe of the West." *Frontier Times* (Nevada), Oct.-Nov., 1963.

Barry, J. N. E. "Willard Smith Journal 1839–1840." *Annals of Wyoming* 11, no. 1 (1939): 31–41.

Barsness, L. *The Bison in Art: A Graphic Chronicle of the American Bison*. Fort Worth, Tex.: Northland Press with the Amon Carter Museum of Western Art, 1977.

Bartlett, R. A. *Nature's Yellowstone*. Albuquerque: University of New Mexico, 1974.

———. *Yellowstone: A Wilderness Besieged*. Tucson: University of Arizona, 1985.

Bascom, W. "The Forms of Folklore: Prose Narratives." *Journal of American Folklore* 78 (1965): 3–20.

———. "The Forms of Folklore: Prose Narratives." In *Sacred Narrative: Readings in the Theory of Myth*, edited by A. Dundes. Berkeley and Los Angeles: University of California Press, 1984.

Beal, M. D. *History of Southeastern Idaho*. Caldwell, Idaho: Caxton Printers, 1942.

———. *The Story of Man in Yellowstone*. Caldwell, Idaho: Caxton Printers, 1949; rev. ed. Yellowstone National Park, Wyo.: Yellowstone Library and Museum Association, 1960.

———. *The Story of Man in Yellowstone*. Yellowstone Interpretive Series, No. 7. Yellowstone National Park, Wyo.: The Yellowstone Library and Museum Association, 1956.

Beal, S. M. "Indian Camps in the Lower Geyser Basin." *Yellowstone Nature Notes* 23 (Jan.-Feb. 1949): 10–11.

Beals, R. L. "History of Glacier National Park, with Particular Emphasis on the Northern Developments." Berkeley: National Park Service Field Division of Education, 1935.

Beckwourth, J. *The Life and Adventures of James P. Beckwourth*. Lincoln: University of Nebraska Press, 1972.

Berkhofer, R. F., Jr. *The White Man's Indian: Images of the American Indian from Columbus to the Present*. New York: Alfred Knopf, 1978.

Bernardis, T. *Crow Social Studies: Baleeisbaalichiwee History, Teacher's Guide*. Crow Agency, Mont.: Bilingual Materials Development Center, 1986.

Biddle, N., ed. *The Journals of the Expedition Under the Command of Capts. Lewis and Clark to the Sources of the Missouri, Thence Across the Rocky Mountains and the River Columbia to the Pacific Ocean Performed During the Years 1804–5–6*. 1814. Reprint, New York: Heritage Press, 1962.

Big Man (Chief Max). "The Story of a Certain Buffalo Hunt." *Yellowstone Nature Notes* 9 (1932): 45–46.

Blackburn, T. C. and K. Anderson, eds. *Before the Wilderness: Environmental Management by Native Californians.* Menlo Park, Calif.: Ballena Press, 1993.

Blackmore, W. "Diary—Fourth Visit to the United States, 1872." Mammoth, Wyo.: Yellowstone National Park Library. Photocopy.

Boas, F. *Kutenai Tales.* Together with texts collected by Alexander Chamberlain. Smithsonian Institution, Bureau of American Ethnology, Bulletin 59. Washington, D.C.: Government Printing Office, 1918.

Bonney, O. H. and L. Bonney. *Battle Drums and Geysers.* Chicago: The Swallow Press, 1970.

Bonnichsen, R. and S. J. Baldwin. "Cypress Hills Ethnohistory and Ecology." Occasional Paper No. 10. *Archaeological Survey of Alberta.* 1978.

Boyd, M. *Kiowa Voices.* Fort Worth, Tex.: Texas Christian University Press, 1981.

Brackett, A. G. "The Shoshones or Snake Indians, Their Religion, Superstition and Manners." In *The Annual Report of the Smithsonian Institute for 1879,* 328–33.

Brackett, W. S. "Indian Remains on the Upper Yellowstone." In *The Annual Report of the Smithsonian Institution for 1892,* 574–81.

Bradley, C. C., Jr. *The Handsome People: A History of the Crow Indians and the Whites.* Billings, Mont.: Council for Indian Education, 1991.

Bradley, J. H. "Lieut. James H. Bradley Manuscript." *Contributions to the Montana Historical Society* 9 (1923): 306-307.

Brayer, H. O. "Exploring the Yellowstone with Hayden, 1872." *Annals of Wyoming* 14 (1942): 253–98.

Bright, W. *A Coyote Reader.* Berkeley and Los Angeles: University of California Press, 1993.

Brower, J. Vradenberg. *The Missouri River and its Utmost Source; Curtailed Narration of Geologic Primitive and Geographic Distinctions Descriptive of the Evolution and Discovery of the River and its Head-waters.* 2nd ed. St. Paul, Minn.: Pioneer Press, 1897.

Brown, B. "The Buffalo Drive." *Natural History* 32 (1932): 75–82.

Brown, M. *Plainsmen of the Yellowstone.* Lincoln: University of Nebraska, 1961.

———. *The Flight of the Nez Perce.* New York: G. P. Putnam's Sons, 1983.

Brown, Col. W. C. *The Sheepeater Campaign.* 1879. Reprint. Boise, Idaho: Idaho State Historical Society, 1926.

Bruchac, J., comp. *Native Plant Stories.* Golden, Colo.: Fulcrum Publishing, 1995.

Brunton, B. B. "Kootnenai." In *Handbook of North American Indians,* Vol. 12 of *Plateau,* 223–37, edited by D. E. Walker, Jr. Washington, D.C.: Smithsonian Institution, 1998.

Bullchild, P. *The Sun Came Down.* San Francisco: Harper & Row, 1985.

Burlingame, M. G. *The Montana Frontier.* Helena, Mont.: State Publishing Company, 1942.

Burnett, E. "White Hunters and the Buffalo." *Wind River Mountaineer* 4, no. 2 (1988): 22–24. Originally published in *Live Stock Markets,* August, 1931.

Burnham, Philip. *Indian Country, God's Country: Native Americans and the National Parks.* Washington, D.C.: Island Press, 2000.

Butler, B. R. "The Holocene or Postglacial Ecological Crisis on the Eastern Snake River Plain." *Tebiwa* 15, no. 1 (1972): 49–63.

———. "The Pottery of Eastern Idaho." In *Pottery of the Great Basin and Adjacent Areas,* edited by Suzanne Griset, 37–57. Salt Lake City: University of Utah Anthropological Papers No. 111, 1986.

———. *When Did the Shoshoni Begin to Occupy Southern Idaho? Essays on the Late Prehistoric Cultural Remains from the Upper Snake and Salmon River Country.* Occasional Papers of the Idaho Museum of Natural History, No. 32. Pocatello: Idaho Museum of Natural History, 1981.

Buxton, E. N. *Short Stalks: Or Hunting Camps N, S, E and W.* New York: G. P. Putnam's Sons, 1892.

"California Indians and Archaeology." *News from Native California* 9, no. 4 (Summer 1996).

Cannon, K. P. "Blood Residue Analyses of Ancient Stone Tools Reveals Clues to Prehistoric Subsistence Patterns in Yellowstone." *CRM* 2 (1995): 14–16.

———. "Paleoindian Use of Obsidian in the Greater Yellowstone Area." *Yellowstone Science* (Summer 1993): 6–9.

Cannon, K. P. and R. Hughes. "It's Not Just Obsidian Cliff: Diversity of Obsidian Source Use in Yellowstone National Park." Paper presented at the Second Biennial Rocky Mountain Anthropological Conference, Steamboat Springs, Colo., 1995.

Carey, C. H., ed. *The Journals of Theodore Talbot 1843 and 1949–52.* Portland, Oreg., 1931.

Carpenter, F. D. *Adventures in Geyserland.* Caldwell, Idaho: Caxton Printers, 1935.

Carter, Jimmy. Foreword to *An American Idea: The Making of the National Parks*, by Kim Heacox. Washington, D.C.: National Geographic Society, 2001.

Catlin, George. *North American Indians: Being Letters and Notes on their Manners, Customs, and Conditions, Written during Eight Years' Travel amongst the Wildest Tribes in North America, 1832-1839.* Vol. 1. London: n.p., 1880.

Catton, Theodore. *Inhabited Wilderness: Indians, Eskimos, and National Parks in Alaska.* Albuquerque: University of New Mexico Press, 1997.

Chalfant, S. A. and V. F. Ray. *Nez Perce Indians: Aboriginal Territory of the Nez Perce Indians.* New York: Garland Publications, 1974.

Chase, A. *Playing God in Yellowstone: The Destruction of America's First National Park.* Boston: Atlantic Monthly Press, 1986; San Diego: Harcourt Brace Jovanovich, 1987.

Chittenden, H. M. *The American Fur Trade of the Far West.* Vol. 1. 1902. Reprint, Stanford, Calif.: Academic Reprints, 1954.

———. *The Yellowstone National Park*, edited by Richard A. Bartlett. 1895. Reprint, Norman: University of Oklahoma Press, 1964.

———. *The Yellowstone National Park: Historical and Descriptive.* Cincinnati, Ohio: The Robert Clark Company, 1895.

———. *The Yellowstone National Park: Historical and Descriptive.* 1915. Cincinnati, Ohio: Stewart and Kidd, 1918.

Chittenden, H. M. and A. T. Richardson. *Life, Letters and Travels of Father De Smet.* 4 vols. 1905. Reprint, New York: Francis P. Harper, 1969.

Clark, E. E. *Indian Legends from the Northern Rockies.* Norman: University of Oklahoma, 1966.

Clark, F. W. "Analysis of Rocks." *Bulletin of the United States Geological Survey* No. 148, 1896.

———. "Analysis of Rocks." *Bulletin of the United States Geological Survey* No. 168, 1900.

Clark, W. *The Indian Sign Language, with Brief Explanatory Notes.* Philadelphia: L. R. Hamersly, 1885.

Clayton, A. G. "A Brief History of the Washakie National Forest and the Duties and Some Experiences of a Ranger." *Annals of Wyoming* 4, no. 2 (1926): 277–81.

Clemmer, R. O. and O. C. Stewart. "Treaties, Reservations, and Claims." In *Handbook of North American Indians.* Vol. 11 of *Great Basin*, edited by Warren L. D'Azevedo, 525–57. Washington, D.C.: Smithsonian Institution, 1986.

Clifford, J. *Writing Culture: The Poetics and Politics of Ethnography*. Berkeley and Los Angeles: University of California Press, 1986.

Cole, Glen. *Yellowstone Science* 8, no. 2 (2000): 15.

Colson, E. "In Good Years and in Bad: Food Strategies of Self-Reliant Societies." *Journal of Anthropological Research* 35, no. 1 (1979): 18–29.

Columbus, W. F. Affidavit, Carbon County, Mont. 6 November 1979.

Condon, D. "American Indian Burial Giving Evidence of Antiquity Discovered in Yellowstone National Park." *Plains Anthropological Conference Newsletter*, Vol. I, 1949.

Connor, M. A. "Jackson Lake Archaeology Project 1985. An Interim Report." Manuscript on file Lincoln, Nebr., National Park Service. Mammoth, Wyo.: Midwest Archaeological Center, Cultural Resources Division, Yellowstone National Park, 1986.

Cooper, J. F. *The Last of the Mohicans, A Narrative of 1757*. Philadelphia: H. C. Carey, 1826.

Corless, H. *The Weiser Indians: Shoshone Peacemakers*. Salt Lake City: University of Utah Press, 1990.

Coues, E. *History of the Expedition under the Command of Lewis and Clark*. Vol. III. New York: Dover Publications, 1965. Originally published by Francis Harper in 1893.

Coulter, J. M. and A. Nelson. *New Manual of Botany of the Central Rocky Mountains (Vascular Plants)*. New York: American Book Company, 1937.

Cousins, E. "Mountains Made Alive: Native American Relationships with Sacred Land." *Cross Currents* 46, no. 4 (1996/1997).

Coutant, C. G. *The History of Wyoming*. Vol. 1. Laramie: Chaplin, Spafford & Mathison, 1899.

Cowan, Mrs. G. F. "Reminiscences of Pioneer Life." *Montana Historical Society, Contributions* 4 (1903): 156–87.

Crampton, L. C. *Early History of Yellowstone National Park and the Relationship to National Park Policies*. Washington, D.C.: Government Printing Office, 1932.

Cronon, W. *Changes in the Land: Indians, Colonists and the Ecology of New England*. New York: Hill and Wang, 1983.

———. "The Problem with Wilderness." In *Uncommon Ground: Toward Reinventing Nature*, edited by William Cronon. New York: W. W. Norton, 1995.

Crowder, D. L. *Tenday Chief of the Lembis*. Caldwell, Idaho: Caxton Printers, 1969.

Curriculum Development Workshop. *The Wind River Reservation Yesterday and Today: The Legends—The Land—The People*. Workshop directed by Larry Murray, Wind River Agency, Fort Washakie, Wyo., 1996.

Curtis, E. S. *The North American Indian: Being a Series of Volumes Picturing and Describing the Indians of the United States, and Alaska*. Edited by F. W. Hodge. 20 vols. New York: Johnson Reprint, Harcourt Brace Jovanovich, 1907–1930.

———. *The North American Indian*. Vol. 9. Norwood, Mass.: Plimpton Press, 1909.

Czech, Brian. "Elk Hunting in the Shadow of Ward vs. Racehorse: Ten Bear and the Crow Tribe." *Journal of Wildlife* 39, no. 1 (2000): 64-71.

Czeczuga, B. and S. Eversman. "Carotenoids in Lichens from Yellowstone National Park and Adjacent Forests in Montana and Wyoming." *The Bryoligist* 96, no. 1 (1993): 102–105.

Daniels, T. W. "Food for the Sheep-Eaters." *Wyoming Wildlife* 17, no. 4 (1953).

Dasmann, Raymond F. "The Relationship Between Protected Areas and Indigenous Peoples." In *National Parks, Conservation, and Development*, edited by Jeffrey A. McNeely and Kenton R. Miller, 667-72. Washington, D.C.: Smithsonian Institution, 1984.

Dauenhauer, Nora Marks and Richard Dauenhauer, eds. *Haa Kusteeyi, Our Culture: Tlingit Life Stories*. Seattle: University of Washington Press, 1994.

Davis, C. M. "Wickiup Cave." *Plains Anthropologist* 20, no. 70 (1975): 297–305.

Dempsey, H. A. "A Blackfoot Winter Count." Glenbow Foundation Occasional Paper 1. Calgary, Alberta: Glenbow Foundation, 1965.

Denig, E. T. *Five Indian Tribes of the Upper Missouri*. Norman: University of Oklahoma, 1961.

Despain, D. G. *Field Key to the Flora of Yellowstone National Park*. Mammoth, Wyo.: Yellowstone Library and Museum Association, 1975.

———. *Yellowstone Vegetation: Consequences of Environment and History in a Natural Setting*. Boulder, Colo.: Roberts Rhinehart, 1990.

De Voto, B. *Across the Wide Missouri*. Boston: Houghton Mifflin, 1947.

———. *The Journals of Lewis and Clark*. Boston: Houghton Mifflin, 1953.

Diamond, K. B., G. R. Warren, and J. H. Cardellina II. "Native American Food and Medicinal Plants." *Journal of Ethnopharmacology* 14 (1985): 99–101.

Dimsdale, T. J. *The Vigilantes of Montana or Popular Justice in the Rocky Mountains*. Norman: University of Oklahoma Press, 1982.

Dippie, B. W. "This Bold But Wasting Race: Stereotypes and American Indian Policy." *Montana Magazine of Western Research* 36, no. 86 (1973): 2–13.

———. *The Vanishing American: White Attitudes and U.S. Indian Policy*. Middletown, Conn.: Wesleyan University Press, 1982.

Dixon, J. K. *The Vanishing Race: The Last Great Indian Council*. Philadelphia: National American Indian Memorial Association Press, 1925.

Dockstader, F. J. "Museums and the American Indian." In *Indian Voices: The Native American Today*, 191–212. The Second Convocation of American Indian Scholars. San Francisco: The Indian Historian Press, 1977.

Dominick, D. "The Sheepeaters." *Annals of Wyoming* 36, no. 2 (1964): 131–68. Also published in *The Sheep Eaters* by W. A. Allen, pp. 79–116, Fairfield, Wash.: Ye Galleon Press, 1989.

Dorn, R. D. *Vascular Plants of Montana*. Cheyenne, Wyo.: Mountain West, 1984.

———. *Vascular Plants of Wyoming*. 2d ed. Cheyenne, Wyo.: Mountain West, 1992.

Dorsey, G. A. "Pawnee War Tales." *American Anthropologist* 8 (1906): 337–45.

———. *The Pawnee: Mythology (part I)*. The Carnegie Institution of Washington, Publication no. 59. Washington, D.C.: The Carnegie Institution, 1906.

Dorson, R. M. "Ethnohistory and Ethnic Folklore." *Ethnohistory* 8, no. 1 (1961): 12–20

———. *Folklore Research Around the World; a North American Point of View*. Indiana University Folklore Series No. 16. Bloomington: Indiana University Press, 1961.

———. "Teaching Folklore to Graduate Students: The Introductory Proseminar." In *Handbook of American Folklore*, edited by R. M. Dorson, 463–69. Bloomington: Indiana University Press, 1983.

Downing, G. R. and L. S. Furniss. "Some Observations on Camas Digging and Baking Among Present-day Nez Perce." *Tebiwa, the Journal of the Idaho State University Museum* (Pocatello) 11, no. 1 (1968): 48–53.

Dudley, W. H. *The National Park from the Hurricane Deck of A Cayuse, or the Liederkranz Expedition to Geyserland*. Butte, Mont.: Frederick Loeber, 1886.

Dundes, A. *Sacred Narrative: Readings in the Theory of Myth*. Berkeley and Los Angeles: University of California Press, 1984.

Eakin, D., J. Francis, and M. L. Larson. "The Split Rock Ranch Site: Early Archaic Cultural Practices in Southcentral Wyoming." In *Changing Perspectives on the Archaic on the Northwestern Plains and Rocky Mountains,* edited by M. L. Larson and J. Francis. Vermillion: University of South Dakota Press, 1997.

Earhart, H. B., ed. *Religious Traditions of the World.* San Francisco: Harper, 1993.

Ebeling, W. *Handbook of Indian Foods and Fibers of Arid America.* Berkeley and Los Angeles: University of California Press, 1986.

Edmo, Jack. "Native Archaeologists: The Bannock-Shoshone Program in Study of Man." *The Indian Historian* 3, no.4 (1970): 23-25.

Edmonds, M. and E. E. Clark. *Voices of the Winds: Native American Legends.* New York: Facts on File, 1998.

Erichsen-Brown, C. *Medicinal and Other Uses of North American Plants.* Unabridged republication. New York: Dover Publications, 1989. Originally published as *Use of Plants for the Past 500 Years* (Aurora, Ontario, Canada: Breezy Creeks Press, 1979).

Ewers, J. C. *The Blackfeet: Raiders on the Northwestern Plains.* Norman: University of Oklahoma, 1958.

———. *The Horse in Blackfoot Indian Culture.* Reprint, Washington, D.C.: Classics of Smithsonian Anthropology, Smithsonian Institution, 1969. Originally published in Bureau of American Ethnology Bulletin No. 159 (Washington, D.C.: Government Printing Office, 1955).

Faulkner, Mont E. "Emigrant-Indian Confrontation in Southeastern Idaho, 1841–1863." *Rendezvous: Idaho State University Journal of Arts and Letters* 24 (1988): 43–58.

Fenton, W. N. "The Training of Historical Ethnologists in America." *American Anthropologist* 54, no. 3 (1952): 328–39.

Ferguson, G. *Walking Down the Wild: A Journey through the Yellowstone Rockies.* San Francisco: Harper Collins West, 1995.

Ferris, W. A. *Life in the Rocky Mountains, 1830–1835,* edited by P. C. Phillips. Denver: Old West Publishing, 1940.

Feyhl, K. S. "Steatite: Some Sources and Aboriginal Utilization in Montana." *Archaeology in Montana* 38, no. 2 (1997): 55–83.

Fitzgerald, L. H. *Black Feather: Trapper Jim's Fables of Sheepeater Indians in the Yellowstone.* Caldwell, Idaho: Caxton Printers, 1933.

Flathead Cultural Committee. *A Brief History of the Flathead Tribes.* Polson, Mont.: Gull Printing, 1993.

———. *Flathead Language: Common Names.* Polson, Mont.: Gull Printing, 1981.

———. *Flathead Language Vocabulary: Word List.* Polson, Mont.: Gull Printing, 1976.

Fogelson, R. D. "On the Varieties of Indian History: Sequoyah and Traveller Bird." *Journal of Ethnic Studies* 2, no. 1 (Spring 1974): 106–107.

Foley, J. P., ed. *The Jefferson Cyclopedia.* New York: Funk and Wagnells, 1900.

Folsom, D. E. *The Folsom-Cook Exploration of the Upper Yellowstone in the Year 1869.* St. Paul, Minn.: H. L. Collins, 1894.

Foresta, Ronald A. *American's National Parks and Their Keepers.* Washington, D.C.: Resources for the Future, 1984.

Fowler, C. "Subsistence." *Handbook of North American Indians: Great Basin* 11, 64–97. Washington, D.C.: Smithsonian Institution, 1986.

Fowler, C. S. and S. Liljeblad. "Northern Paiute." *Handbook of North American Indians: Great Basin* 11, 435–65. Washington, D.C.: Smithsonian Institution, 1986.

Fowler, D. D., ed. "Notes on the Early Life of Chief Washakie Taken Down by Captain Ray." *Annals of Wyoming* 36, no. 1 (1964): 34–42.

Fowler, L. *Arapahoe Politics, 1851–1948: Symbols in Crises of Authority*. Lincoln: University of Nebraska Press, 1982.

Francis, J. E., L. L. Loendorf, and R. I. Dorn. "AMS Radiocarbon and Cation-Ratio Dating of Rock Art in the Bighorn Basin of Wyoming and Montana." *American Antiquity* 58 (1994): 711–37.

Frantz, D. G. and N. J. Russell. *Blackfoot Dictionary of Stems, Roots and Affixes*. Toronto, Ontario: University of Toronto Press, 1989.

Fredlund, D. E. and L. B. Fredlund. "Archaeological Survey of the Three Forks of the Flathead River, Montana." *Archaeology in Montana* 12, nos. 2–3 (1971):1–58.

Fredlund, G., L. Sundstrom, and R. Armstrong. "Crazy Mules Maps of the Upper Missouri, 1877–1880." *Plains Anthropologist* 41, no. 155 (1996):5–27.

Freeman, L. *Down the Yellowstone*. New York: Dodd, Mead and Co., 1922.

Freemuth, John C. *Islands Under Siege: National Parks and the Politics of External Threats*. Lawrence: University Press of Kansas, 1991.

Frey, R. *The World of the Crow Indians*. Norman: University of Oklahoma Press, 1987.

Friedman, I. and R. L. Smith. "A New Dating Method Using Obsidian: Part I, The Development of the Method." *American Antiquity* 25 (1960):476–522.

Frison, G. C. "A Composite, Reflexed, Mountain Sheep Horn Bow from Western Wyoming." *Plains Anthropologist* 25, no. 88 (1980): 173–5.

———. *Prehistoric Hunters of the High Plains*. New York: Academic Press, 1978; 2nd ed., 1991.

———. "Shoshonean Antelope Procurement in the Upper Green River Basin, Wyoming." *Plains Anthropologist* 16, no. 54 (1971): 258–84. (Memoir 8 pt. 1.)

———. "Sources of Steatite and Methods of Prehistoric Procurement and Use in Wyoming." *Plains Anthropologist* 27, no. 1 (1982): 273–86.

———. "The Chronology of Paleo-Indian and Altithermal Cultures in the Big Horn Basin, Wyoming." In *Cultural Change and Continuity: Essays in Honor of James Bennett Griffin*, edited by Charles E. Cleland, 147–73. New York: Academic Press, 1976.

Frison, G. C., R. L. Andrews, J. M. Adovasio, R. C. Carlisle, and R. Edgar. "A Late Paleoindian Animal Trapping Net from Northern Wyoming." *American Antiquity* 51, no. 2 (1986): 352–61.

Frison, G. C., C. A. Reher, and D. N. Walker. "Prehistoric Mountain Sheep Hunting in the Central Rocky Mountains of North America." Chap. 12 in *Hunters of the Recent Past*, edited by L. B. Davis and B. Reeves, 208–240. One World Archaeology 15. London: Unwin Hyman, 1990.

Frison, G. C. and Z. Van Norman. "Carved Steatite and Sandstone Tubes: Pipes for Smoking or Shaman's Paraphernalia?" *Plains Anthropology* 38, no. 143 (1993): 163–76.

Frome, M. *Regreening the National Parks*. Tucson: University of Arizona, 1992.

Frost, N. M. "The Sheep Eaters." *Wyoming Wildlife* 6, no. 8 (1941): 17–19.

Galante, G. "East Meets West: Some Observations on the Crow as the Nexus of Plateau Upper Missouri River Art." *Crow Indian Art*, edited by F. Dennis Lessard. Mission, S. Dak.: Chandler Institute, 1984.

Garbes, Mrs. A.L. "Facts Concerning the Bozeman Trail and Adjacent Territory." *The Teepee Book*, September 1916, 17–28.

Garretson, M. S. *American Bison: The Story of Its Extermination as a Wild Species and Its Restoration Under Federal Protection*. New York: New York Zoological Society, 1938.

Gerrish, T. *Life in the World's Wonderland*. Biddeford, Maine: n.p., 1887.

Geyer, C. A. "Notes on the Vegetation and General Character of the Missouri and Oregon Territories, made during a Botanical Journey from the State of Missouri, across the South-Pass of the Rocky Mountains, to the Pacific, during the years of 1843 and 1844." *Journal of Botany* 5 (1846): 285–310.

Gill, G. "Human Skeletal Remains on the Northwestern Plains." In *Prehistoric Hunters of the High Plains*, edited by G. C. Frison. New York: Academic Press, 1991.

Goodwin, Cardinal. "Larger View of the Yellowstone Expedition." *Mississippi Valley Historical Review* 4 (1917): 299–313.

Griffin, J. B. "Hopewell and the Dark Black Glass." *Michigan Archaeologist* 11 (1965): 115–55.

Grinnell, G. B. *Pawnee, Blackfoot and Cheyenne: History and Folklore of the Plains*, selected by Dee Brown. New York: Charles Scribner's Sons, 1912.

———. *The Cheyenne Indians: Their History and Ways of Life*. Lincoln: University of Nebraska Press, 1972.

Guidley, M. *Indians of Today*. Chicago: Lakeside Press, 1936.

Guptill, A. B. *All About Yellowstone Park: A Practical Guide*. St. Paul, Minn.: Jay Haynes Publishing, 1894.

———. *Practical Guide to Yellowstone National Park*. St. Paul, Minn.: Jay Haynes Publishing, 1890.

Gunther, E. *Ethnobotany of Western Washington: The Knowledge and Use of Indigenous Plants by Native Americans*. Rev. ed. Seattle: University of Washington, 1973. Originally published in University of Washington Publications in Anthropology 10, no.1, 1945.

Hafen, L. R. *Brokenhand: The Life of Thomas Fitzpatrick: Mountain Man, Guide and Indian Agent*. Lincoln: University of Nebraska Press, 1981.

Hagan, W. T. "United States Indian Policies, 1860–1900." In *History of Indian-White Relations*, edited by W. E. Washburn. Vol. 4, *Handbook of North American Indians*, general editor W. C. Sturtevant, 51–57. Washington, D.C.: Smithsonian Institution, 1988.

Hague, A. "The Yellowstone National Park as a Game Preserve. In *American Big Game Hunting*." New York: Forest and Stream Publishing Company, 1893.

Haines, A. L. *The Bannock Indian Trail*. 1964. Reprint, Yellowstone, Wyo.: Yellowstone Library and Museum Association in cooperation with the National Park Service, 1980.

———. "The Bannock Trails of Yellowstone National Park." *Archaeology in Montana* 4 (1893): 1–8.

———. "The Indians in Our Past." In *A Manual of General Information on Yellowstone National Park*. National Park Service, 1963.

———. "The Rigler Bluffs Site: 24PA401." *Archaeology in Montana* 7, no. 2 (1966): 5.

———. *The Yellowstone Story: A History of Our First National Park*, 2 vols. Rev. ed. Yellowstone: Wyo.: Yellowstone Association for Natural Science, History and Education; Niwot, Colo.: University Press of Colorado, 1996.

———. *Yellowstone Place Names: Mirrors of History*. Niwot, Colo.: University Press of Colorado, 1996.

Haines, F. *The Buffalo: The Story of American Bison and Their Hunters from Prehistoric Times to the Present*. Norman: University of Oklahoma Press, 1970.

———. *The Nez Perces: Tribesmen of the Columbia Plateau*. Norman: University of Oklahoma Press, 1955.

Halfmoon, O. "Joseph (Heinmot Tooyalakeet)." In *Encyclopedia of North American Indians*, edited by Frederick B. Hoxie, 309–11. Boston: Houghton Mifflin Co., 1996.

Halmo, D. B., R. W. Stoffle, and M. J. Evans. "Paitu Nanasuagaindu Pahonupi (Three Sacred Valleys: Cultural Significance of Gosiute, Paiute, and Ute Plants)." *Human Organization* 52, no. 2 (1993): 142–50.

Hamilton, W. T. *My Sixty Years on the Plains*. New York: Forest and Stream Publishing, 1905.

Hansen, V. and A. Funderburk. *The Fabulous Past of Cooke City*. Billings, Mont.: Billings Printing, 1962.

Hardy, M. E. *Little Ta-Wish-Indian Legends from Geyserland*. Chicago: Rand McNally, 1914.

Harring, S. L. *Crow Dog's Case: American Indian Sovereignty, Tribal Law in the Nineteenth Century*. Cambridge: Cambridge University Press, 1994.

Harrington, H. D. *Edible Native Plants of the Rocky Mountains*. Albuquerque: University of New Mexico, 1967.

———. *Western Edible Wild Plants*. Albuquerque: University of New Mexico, 1967.

Harrington, J. P. "Anthropological Miscellany." In *So Live the Works of Men, Seventieth Anniversary Volume, Honoring Edgar Lee Hewett*, edited by D. D. Brand and F. E. Harvey, 159–76. Albuquerque: University of New Mexico, 1939.

Harris, B. *John Colter: His Years in the Rockies*. New York: Charles Scribner's Sons, 1952.

Hart, J. *Montana—Native Plants and Early Peoples*. Helena, Mont.: Montana Historical Society and Montana Bicentennial Administration, 1976.

Hartman, R. L. "Additions to the Vascular Flora of Yellowstone National Park, Wyoming." *Madroña* 37, no. 3 (1990): 214–16.

Haynes, J. *Haynes' Guide: Handbook of Yellowstone National Park*. Bozeman, Mont.: Haynes Studios, 1940.

Heady, Eleanor B. *Sage Smoke: Tales of the Shoshoni-Bannock Indians*. Chicago: Follet, 1973; Morristown, N.J.: Silver Burdett Press, 1993.

Hebard, G. R. *Washakie: Chief of the Shoshones*. Lincoln: University of Nebraska Press, 1995.

Hedberg, I. "Botanical Methods in Ethnopharmacology and the Need for Conservation of Medicinal Plants." *Journal of Ethnopharmacology* 38 (1993): 121–28.

Heidel, B. "Questions and Answers about Sweetgrass." *Kelseya, Newsletter of the Montana Native Plant Society* 9, no. 4 (1996): 7.

Heidenreich, C. A. "The Beaver Dance and the Adoption Ceremony of the Crow Indians by Max Big Man." In *Lifeways of Intermontane and Plains Montana Indians*, edited by Leslie B. Davis, 43-56. Occasional Papers of the Museum of the Rockies, no. 1. Bozeman, Mont.: Museum of the Rockies, 1979.

———. "The Native Americans's Yellowstone." *Montana: The Magazine of Western History* 35, no. 4 (1985): 2–17.

Heinerman, J. *Spiritual Wisdom of the Native Americans*. San Rafael, Calif.: Cassandra Press, 1989.

Hellson, J. C. and M. Gadd. *Ethnobotany of the Blackfoot Indians*. National Museum of Man Mercury Series, Canadian Ethnology Service Paper No. 19. Ottawa, Ontario: National Museums of Canada, 1975.

Hendricks, G. *Albert Bierstadt: Painter of the American West*. New York: Harry N. Abrams in association with the Amon Carter Museum of Western Art, 1974.

Hentz, N. M. *Tadeuskund: The Last King of the Lenape*. Boston: Cummings, Hilliard, 1825.

Hickerson, N. P. "Ethnogenesis in the South Plains: Jumano to Kiowa?" In *History, Power and Identity: Ethnogenesis in the Americas, 1492–1992*, edited by J. D. Hill, 70–89. Iowa City: University of Iowa Press, 1996.

Hitchcock, C. L., A. Cronquist, M. Ownbey, and J. W. Thompson. *Vascular Plants of the Pacific Northwest*. 5 vols. Seattle: University of Washington, 1961.

Hodge, F. W., ed. *Handbook of American Indians North of Mexico.* 2 vols. Bureau of American Ethnology Bulletin 30. Washington, D.C.: Smithsonian Institution, 1907–1910.

Hoebel, E. A. *Man in the Primitive World: An Introduction to Anthropology.* New York: McGraw Hill, 1949.

Hoffman, J. J. "The Yellowstone Park Survey." *Archaeology in Montana* 1, no. 2 (1958): 24.

Hoffman, W. J. "Selish Myths." *Bulletin of the Essex Institute* 15 (1883): 24–40.

Holm, Bill. "On Making Horn Bows." In *Native American Bows*, by T. M. Hamilton, 116–30. Columbia, Missouri: Missouri Archaeological Society, Special Publications 5, 1982.

Holmer, R. "A Compilation of Projectile Point Data from Southwestern Idaho." *Tebiwa, Journal of the Idaho Museum of Natural History* 25, no. 1 (1995): 115–21.

———. "Dagger Falls: A Preliminary Report." *Idaho Archaeologist* 12, no. 1 (1989): 3–13.

———. "In Search of the Ancestral Northern Shoshone." In *Across the West: Human Population Movement and the Expansion of the Numa*, edited by David Madsen and David Rhode, 179–87. Salt Lake City: University of Utah Press, 1994.

———. "Prehistory of the Northern Shoshone." *Rendezvous, Idaho State University Journal of Arts and Letters* 26, no. 1 (1990): 41–59.

Holmer, R. N. and B. L. Ringe. "Excavations in Wahmuza." In *Shoshone-Bannock Culture History*, edited by Richard N. Holmer, 69–203. Swanson-Crabtree Anthropological Research Laboratory Reports of Investigations 85-16. Pocatello: Idaho State University, 1986.

Holmes, W. H. "Notes on an Extensive Deposit of Obsidian in the Yellowstone National Park." *The American Naturalist* 13, no. 4 (1879): 247–50.

Horne, Flora Diane Bean. *Autobiography of George Washington Bean: A Utah Pioneer of 1847, and His Family Records.* Salt Lake City: Utah Printing Company, 1945.

Hough, J. "The Grand Canyon National Park and the Havasupai People: Cooperation and Conflict." In *Resident Peoples and National Parks*, edited by P. C. West and S. R. Brechiu. Tucson: University of Arizona Press, 1991.

Houston, D. B. *The Northern Yellowstone Elk: Ecology and Management.* New York: Macmillan Publishing, 1982.

Hoxie, F. E. *Parading Through History: The Making of the Crow Nation in America, 1805–1935.* Cambridge: Cambridge University Press, 1995.

———. *The Crow, Indians of North America.* New York: Chelsea House, 1989.

Hughes, S. "Mummy Cave Revisited." *Annals of Wyoming* 60, no. 2 (1988): 44–54.

———. "The Sheepeater Myth of Northwestern Wyoming." *Plains Anthropologist* 45, no. 171 (2000): 63–83.

Hultkrantz, Åke. "Accommodations and Persistence: Ecological Analysis of the Religion of the Sheepeater Indians in Wyoming, U.S.A." *Temenos: Studies in Comparative Religion* (Helsinki, Norway) 17 (1981): 35–44.

———. "An Ecological Approach to Religion." *Ethnos* (Stockholm, Sweden) 31, nos. 1–4 (1966): 131–50.

———. "An Ideological Dichotomy: Myths and Folk Beliefs Among the Shoshoni Indians of Wyoming." *History of Religions* 11, no. 4 (1972): 339–53.

———. "Attitudes to Animals in Shoshoni Indian Religion." *Temenos: Studies in Comparative Religion* (Helsinki, Norway) 4, no. 2 (1971): 70–79.

———. *Belief and Worship in Native America*, edited by Christopher Vecsey. New York: Syracuse University, 1981.

———. "The Concept of the Soul Held by the Wind River Shoshone." *Ethnos* (Stockholm, Sweden) 16, nos. 1-2 (1951): 18–44.

———. "Configurations of Religious Belief Among the Wind River Shoshoni." *Ethnos* (Stockholm, Sweden) 21, nos. 3-4 (1956): 194–215.

———. "The Ethnological Position of the Sheepeater Indians in Wyoming." *Folk* (Copenhagen, Denmark) 8–9 (1966-1967): 155–63.

———. "The Fear of Geysers Among Indians of the Yellowstone Park Area." In *Lifeways of Intermontane and Plains Montana Indians*, edited by Leslie B. Davis, 33–42. Occasional Papers of the Museum of the Rockies, no. 1. Bozeman, Mont.: Museum of the Rockies, 1979.

———. "The Indians and the Wonders of Yellowstone: A Study of the Interrelations of Religion, Nature and Culture." *Ethnos* (Stockholm, Sweden) 19, nos. 1–4 (1954): 34–68; In *Belief and Worship in Native North America*, edited by C. Vecsey. New York: Syracuse University, 1981.

———. "The Indians in Yellowstone Park." *Annals of Wyoming* 29, no. 2 (1957): 125–49. First published in *Ymer* (Sweden) 2 (1954): 112–40. Also published in *Shoshone Indians*, translated by A. Liljeblad (New York: Garland, 1974), 215–56.

———. "The Masters of the Animals Among the Wind River Shoshone." *Ethnos* (Stockholm, Sweden) 26, no. 4 (1961): 198–218.

———. "The Origin of Death Myth as Found Among the Wind River Shoshoni Indians." *Ethnos* (Stockholm, Sweden) 20, nos. 2-3 (1955): 127–36.

———. *Prairie and Plains Indians*. Iconography of Religions 10, no. 2. Leiden, The Netherlands: E. J. Brill, 1973.

———. "Religio-Ecological Approach." In *Science of Religion, Studies in Methodology*, edited by L. Honko. Proceedings of the Study Conference of the International Association for the History of Religions, held in Turku, Finland, August 27–31. New York: Mouton, 1973.

———. "Religion and Mythologie der Prarie-Schoschonen." In *Proceedings of the 34th International Congress of Americanists*. (Vienna, 1960) 546–54.

———. "The Religion of the Wind River Shoshoni: Hunting, Power, and Visions." Chap. 3 in *Native Religions of North America: The Power of Visions and Fertility* 16, nos. 1–2 (1987): 18–44.

———. "Religious Aspects of the Wind River Shoshoni Folklore Literature." In *Culture and History: Essays in Honor of Paul Radin*, edited by S. Diamond, 552–69. New York: Columbia University, 1960.

———. "The Shoshones in the Rocky Mountain Area." Translated by Arne Magnus. In *Shoshone Indians*, 173–214. New York: Garland, 1974.

———. "The Shoshones in the Rocky Mountain Area." *Annals of Wyoming* 33, no. 1 (1961): 19–41.

———. "Shoshoni Indians on the Plains: An Appraisal of the Documentary Evidence." *Zeitschrift fur Ethnologie* 93, nos. 1–2 (1968): 49–72.

———. "The Source Literature on the "Tukudika" Indians in Wyoming: Facts and Fancies." In *Languages and Cultures of Western North America: Essays in Honor of Sven S. Liljeblad*, edited by E. H. Swanson, Jr., 246–64. Pocatello: Idaho State University, 1970.

———. "Tribal Divisions within the Eastern Shoshoni of Wyoming." In *Proceedings of the 32nd International Congress of Americanists*. (Copenhagen, 1956) 148–154.

———. "Yellow Hand, Chief and Medicine-man Among the Eastern Shoshone." In *Proceedings of the 38th International Congress of Americanists*. (Stuttgart-Munchen, 1968), Vol. 2, 293–304.

Hunn, E. S. "On the Relative Contribution of Men and Women to Subsistence Among Hunter-Gatherers of the Columbia Plateau." *Journal of Ethnobiology* 1, no.1 (1981): 124–34.

Hutchens, A. R. *Indian Herbalogy of North America.* Boston: Shambhala, 1973.

Huth, H. *Nature and the American: Three Centuries of Changing Attitudes.* Lincoln: University of Nebraska Press, 1950.

Hutton, H. W. "Account of a Trip through Yellowstone Park in Sept. 1881." In *Yellowstone and the Great West: Journals, Letters and Images from the 1871 Hayden Expedition,* edited by M. D. Merrill. Lincoln: University of Nebraska Press, 1999.

Hyde, J. *Official Guide to the Yellowstone National Park, A Manual for Tourists.* St. Paul, Minn.: Northern News Company, 1887.

Igoe, Jim. *Conservation and Globalization: A Study of National Parks and Indigenous Communities from East Africa to South Dakota.* Belmont, Calif.: Thompson Learning, 2004.

"Indian Marauders." *Forest and Stream* (April 4, 1889) 32: 209.

"Indians and the National Park." *Forest and Stream* (May 2, 1889) 32: 296.

Irving, W. *The Adventures of Captain Bonneville, U.S.A.,* edited by Edgeley W. Todd. Norman: University of Oklahoma Press, 1961; New York: J. B. Miller, 1837; 2 vols., Philadelphia: Carey, Lea and Blanchard, 1885.

———. *Astoria.* Norman: University of Oklahoma, 1964; Philadelphia: Carey, Lee and Blanchard, 1836.

Jacoby, Karl. *Crimes Against Nature; Squatters, Poachers, Thieves, and the Hidden History of American Conservation.* Berkeley and Los Angeles: University of California Press, 2001.

Janetski, J. C. *The Indians of Yellowstone Park.* Salt Lake City: University of Utah, Bonneville Books, 1987.

Jenness, D. *The Indians of Canada.* Canada Dept. of Mines. National Museum of Canada. Bulletin 65. Anthropological Series, no. 15. Ottawa: F. A. Acland, printer to the King, 1932.

Johnson, A. M., K. J. Feyhl, S. W. Conner, and M. B. Bryant. "The Cremation of Two Early Historic Timbered Structures in the Bull Mountains." *Archaeology in Montana* 29, no. 2 (1988): 1–17.

Johnston, A. *Plants and the Blackfoot.* Occasional Paper No. 15. Alberta, Canada: Lethbridge Historical Society, 1987.

Jorgensen, J. G. *The Sun Dance Religion.* Chicago: University of Chicago Press, 1972.

Josephy, A. M., Jr. *The Civil War in the American West.* New York: Alfred A. Knopf, 1991.

Joss, L. "The Evolution of Cultural Resources Management in Yellowstone: An Interview with Laura Joss." *Yellowstone Science* 9, no. 1 (2001): 13–16.

Kappler, C. J., ed. *Indian Affairs: Laws and Treaties.* 2 vols. Washington, D.C.: Government Printing Office, 1904.

Karp, I., C. M. Kreamer, and S. Lavine. *Museums and Communities: The Politics of Public Culture.* Washington, D.C.: Smithsonian Institution Press, 1992.

Karp, I. and S. Lavine. *Exhibiting Cultures: The Poetics and Politics of Museum Display.* Washington, D.C.: Smithsonian Institution, 1991.

Kay, C. E. "Aboriginal Overkill and Native Burning: Implications for Modern Ecosystem Management." In *Sustainable Society and Protected Areas: Contributed Papers of the 8th Conference on Research and Resource Management in Parks and on Public Lands,* edited by Robert M. Linn, 107–18. Hancock, Mich.: George Wright Society, 1995.

————. "Systems Then and Now: A Historical-Ecological Approach to Ecosystem Management." In *Proceedings of the Fourth Prairie Conservation and Endangered Species Workshop* (February 1995), 79–87. Occasional Paper No. 23. Alberta, Canada: Curatorial Section, Provincial Museum of Alberta, 1996.

Kearns, W. E. "A Nez Perce Chief Revisits Yellowstone." *Yellowstone Nature Notes* 12 (June-July 1935): 41.

Keller, R. H. and M. F. Turek. *American Indians and National Parks.* Tucson: University of Arizona Press, 1998.

Keyser, J. "A Shoshonean Origin for the Shieldbearing Warrior Motif." *Plains Anthropologist* 20, no. 69 (1975): 207–15.

Kidwell, A. S., Jr. "The Conical Timbered Lodge on the Northwestern Plains: Historical, Ethnological, and Archaeological Evidence." *Archaeology in Montana* 10, no. 4 (1969): 1–49.

Kindscher, K. *Edible Wild Plants of the Prairie: an Ethnobotanical Guide.* Lawrence: University Press of Kansas, 1987.

————. *Medicinal Wild Plants of the Prairie: An Ethnobotanical Guide.* Lawrence: University Press of Kansas, 1992.

King, C. "Fuel Use and Resource Management: Implications for a Study of Land Management in Prehistoric California and Recommendations for a Research Program." In *Before the Wilderness,* edited by Thomas C. Blackburn and Kat Anderson, 279–98. Menlo Park, Calif.: Ballena Press, 1993.

Kipling, R. *From Sea to Sea.* Garden City, N.Y.: Doubleday Page, 1920.

Kreitzer, Matthew E., ed. *The Washakie Letters of Willie Ottogary: Northwestern Shoshone Journalist and Leader, 1906-1929.* Logan: Utah State University Press, 2000.

Kroeber, A. L. *Anthropology.* New York: Harcourt Brace, 1923.

————. "California Culture Provinces." *University of California Publications in American Archaeology and Ethnology* 17, no. 2 (1920): 151–69.

————. *Cultural and Natural Areas of Native North America.* Berkeley and Los Angeles: University of California Press, 1953.

————. "Cultural & Natural Areas of Native North America." *University of California Publications in American Archaeology & Ethnology* 38 (1939).

————. *Handbook of the Indians of California.* Smithsonian Institution, Bureau of American Ethnology, Bulletin 78. Washington, D.C.: Government Printing Office, 1925.

Kroeber, T. *Ishi in Two Worlds.* Berkeley and Los Angeles: University of California Press, 1961.

Kuhnlein, H. V. and N. J. Turner. "Traditional Plant Foods of Canadian Indigenous Peoples: Nutrition, Botany and Use." *Food and Nutrition in History and Anthropology,* Vol. 8, edited by S. H. Katz. Philadelphia: Gordon and Breach, 1991.

Kuppens, F. X. "On the Origin of the Yellowstone National Park." *The Jesuit Bulletin* 41 (1962): 6–7, 14.

Kvasnicka, R. M. "United States Indian Treaties and Agreements." In *Handbook of North American Indians,* Vol. 4, *History of Indian-White Relations,* edited by W. E. Washburn, pp. 195–201. Washington, D.C.: Smithsonian Institution, 1988.

Lahren, L. A. "Archaeological Investigations in the Upper Yellowstone Valley, Montana: A Preliminary Synthesis and Discussion." In *Aboriginal Man and Environments on the Plateau of Northwest America,* edited by A. H. Stryd and R. A. Smith, 168–182. Alberta, Canada: University of Calgary Archaeological Association, 1971.

Laidlaw, S. J. "Federal Indian Land Policy and the Fort Hall Indians." Occasional Papers of the Idaho State College Museum 3. Pocatello: Idaho State College Museum, 1960.

Lamb, S. "Linguistic Prehistory in the Great Basin." *International Journal of American Linguistics* 24, no. 2 (1958): 95–100.

Lang, W. L. "Where Did The Nez Perce Go?" *Montana, The Magazine of Western History* 40 (Winter 1990): 14–29.

Langford, N. P. "Diary of the Washburn Expedition to the Yellowstone and Firehole Rivers in the Year 1870." St. Paul, Minn.: F. J. Haynes, 1905.

———. *The Discovery of Yellowstone Park, 1870*. St. Paul, Minn.: J. E. Haynes, 1923.

Larocque, F. "Journal of Larocque from the Assiniboine to the Yellowstone, 1805." Canada Archives Publication, No. 3, 1910.

Larson, Henrietta. *Jay Cooke: Private Banker*. Cambridge: Harvard University Press, 1936.

Larson, M. L. and M. Kornfeld. "Betwixt and Between the Basin and the Plains: The Limits of Numic Expansion." In *Across the West: Human Population Movement and the Expansion of the Numa*, edited by D. Madsen and D. Rhode, 200–10. Salt Lake City: University of Utah, 1994.

Lee, R. B. *Subsistence Ecology of the !Kung Bushmen*. Ph.D. diss., University of California, Berkeley, 1965. University Microfilms, Ann Arbor, Mich.

———. *The Dobe !Kung*. New York: Holt, Rinehart and Winston, 1984.

Lee, R. B. and I. De Vore. *Man the Hunter*. Chicago: Aldine, 1968.

Lessard, F. D. "Crow Indian Art: The Nez Perce Connection." *American Indian Art* (November 6, 1980): 54–63.

Levi-Strauss, C. *Anthropology & Myth: Lectures 1951–1982*. Translated by Roy Willis. New York: Basil Blackwell, 1987.

Lewis, H. T. "Maskuta: The Ecology of Indian Fires in Northern Alberta." *Western Canadian Journal of Anthropology* 7, no. 1 (1977): 15–52.

———. *Patterns of Burning in California Ecology and Ethnohistory*. Pomona: Ballena Press, 1973.

Lewis, Meriwether. *History of the Expedition of Captains Lewis and Clark, 1804-5-6*, 2 vols. Chicago: A. C. McClurg & Company, 1902.

Lewis, M. and W. Clark. *Original Journals of the Lewis and Clark Expedition, 1804–1806*, 8 vols., edited by R. G. Thwaites. New York: Dodd, Mead, 1904–1905; Reprint, New York: Antiquarian, 1959.

Lewis, O. *The Effects of White Contact Upon Blackfoot Culture, with Special Reference to the Role of the Fur Trade*. American Ethnological Society Monograph 6. Seattle: University of Washington, 1942.

Liljeblad, Sven. "The Idaho Indians in Transition, 1805–1960." Pocatello: Special Publications of the Idaho State Museum, 1972.

———. "Indian People of Idaho." In *History of Idaho*, Vol. 1, edited by S. Beal and M. Wells, 29–59. New York: Lewis Historical, 1959.

———. *Indian Peoples in Idaho*. Pocatello: Idaho State University, 1970.

———. "The Old Traditions of the Shoshoni and Bannock Indians of Idaho." *Rendezvous: Idaho State University Journal of Arts and Letters* 6, no. 1 (1979): 1–11.

———. "The Religious Attitude of the Shoshonean Indians." *Rendezvous: Idaho State University Journal of Arts and Letters* 4, no. 1 (1969): 47–58.

Linderman, F. B. *Plenty Coups, Chief of the Crows*. 2nd ed. Lincoln: University of Nebraska, 1962.

———. *Pretty-shield: Medicine Woman of the Crows*. Reprint, Lincoln: University of Nebraska, 1972. Originally published as *Red Mother*, 1932.

Linenthal, E. T. *Sacred Ground: Americans and Their Battlefield.* Urbana and Chicago: University of Illinois Press, 1993.

Linford, V. *Wyoming: Frontier State.* Denver, Colo.: Old West Publishing Company, 1947.

Loendorf, L. L., S. Ahler, and D. Davidson. "The Proposed National Register District in the Knife River Flint Quarries in Dunn County, N.D." *North Dakota History* 51, no. 4 (1984): 4–20.

Long Standing Bear Chief. "Prairie Sage: The Healing & Purifying Plant." *Spirit Talk* (Browning, Mont.) 2 (n.d.): 40.

Lowie, R. H. "Alleged Kiowa Crow Affinities." *Southwestern Journal of Anthropology* 9, no. 4 (1953): 357-68.

———. *The Crow Indians.* Lincoln: University of Nebraska, 1983.

———. *The Crow Indians.* New York: Holt, Rinehart and Winston, 1956.

———. "Dances and Societies of the Plains Shoshone." *Anthropological Papers of the American Museum of Natural History* 11, no. 10 (1915): 803–35.

———. "The Northern Shoshone." *Anthropological Papers of the American Museum of Natural History* 2, no. 2 (1909): 165–306.

———. "Notes on Shoshonean Ethnography." *Anthropological Papers of the American Museum of Natural History* 20, no. 3 (1924): 185–314.

———. "Notes on the Social Organization and Customs of the Mandan, Hidatsa, and Crow Indians." *Anthropological Papers of the American Museum of Natural History* 21, no. 1 (1917): 1–99.

———. "Oral Tradition and History." *Journal of American Folklore* 30 (1917): 161–67.

———. "The Religion of the Crow Indians." *Anthropological Papers of the American Museum of Natural History* 25, no. 2 (1922): 309–444.

Lubbers, K. *Born for the Shade: Stereotypes of the Native American in United States Literature and the Visual Arts, 1776–1894.* Amsterdam and Atlanta: Editions Rodopi B.V., 1994.

Lurie, N. O. "Ethnohistory: An Ethnological Point of View." *Ethnohistory* 8 (1961): 78–92.

Madsen, B. D. *The Bannock of Idaho.* Caldwell, Idaho: Caxton Printers, 1958.

———. *Chief Pocatello: The White Plume.* Salt Lake City: University of Utah Press, 1986.

———. *The Lemhi: Sacajawea's People.* Caldwell, Idaho: Caxton Printers, 1979.

———. *The Northern Shoshoni.* Caldwell, Idaho: Caxton Printers, 1980.

———. *The Shoshoni Frontier and the Bear River Massacre.* Salt Lake City: University of Utah Press, 1985.

Madsen, D. B. and D. Rhode, eds. *Across the West: Human Population Movement and the Expansion of the Numa.* Salt Lake City: University of Utah Press, 1994.

Magoc, Chris J. *Yellowstone: The Creation and Selling of an American Landscape, 1870–1903.* Albuquerque: University of New Mexico Press, 1999.

Malouf, C. "Ethnohistory in the Great Basin." In *The Current Status of Anthropological Research in the Great Basin: 1964,* edited by Warren L. d'Azevedo et al., 1–38. Reno: University of Nevada, Desert Research Institute Social Sciences and Humanities Publications 1, 1966.

———. "Flathead." In *Handbook of North American Indians,* Vol. 12, *Plateau,* edited by D. E. Walker, Jr., 297–312. Washington D.C.: Smithsonian Institution, 1998.

———. "Historic Tribes and Archaeology." *Archaeology in Montana* 8, no. 1 (1967): 1–16.

———. "Louis Pierre's Affair." In *Historical Essays on Montana and the Northwest. In Honor of Paul C. Phillips,* edited by J. W. Smurr and K. Ross Toole, 224–30. Helena: The Western Press, The Historical Society of Montana, 1957.

———. "Preliminary Report: Yellowstone National Park Survey, Summer, 1958." *Wyoming Archaeologist* 8, nos. 3 & 4 (1965): 21–27.

———. "The Shoshonean Migration Northward." *Archaeology in Montana* 9, no. 3 (1968): 1–12.

Malouf, C., and Å. Hulkrantz. *Shoshone Indians: The Gosiute Indians*. New York: Garland Publishers, 1974.

Malouf, R. T. *Camas and the Flathead Indians of Montana*. Contributions to Anthropology No. 7. Missoula: Department of Anthropology, University of Montana, 1979.

Mann, L., Jr. Letter to James Duane Doty, Acting Supt. Indian Affairs. Fort Bridger Agency, 20 June 1864. In "Washakie and the Shoshoni: A Selection of Documents from the Records of the Utah Superintendency of Indian Affairs." *Annals of Wyoming* 29, no. 1 (1957): 101.

Manning, S. *American Pictures Drawn with Pen and Pencil*. London: Religious Tract Society, 1876.

Marshall, A. G. "Euro-American Attitudes and the Native American Experience." In *Interpreting Local Culture and History*, edited by J. Sanford Rikoom and J. Austin, 167–74. Boise: Idaho State Historical Society; Moscow: University of Idaho Press, 1991.

Martindale, P. "The Old Wickiups of the Gallatin." *Yellowstone Nature Notes* 4 (1927): 8.

Mathias, Baptiste and T. White. "'Firsts' Among the Flathead Lake Kutenai, as told to Thain White." Anthropology and Sociology Papers No. 8. Missoula: Montana State University, 1952.

Mattes, M. J. "Behind the Legend of Colter's Hell: The Early History of Yellowstone National Park." *Mississippi Valley Historical Review* 36, no. 2 (1949): 251–82.

Mayes, V. O. and B. Bayless Lacy. *Nanise': a Navajo Herbal, One Hundred Plants from the Navajo Reservation*. Tsaile, Arizona: Navajo Community College, 1989.

McAllester, D. P. "Water as a Disciplinary Agent Among the Crow and Blackfoot." *American Anthropologist* New Series 43, no. 4 (1941): 593–604.

McCleary, T. P. *The Stars We Know: Crow Indian Astronomy and Lifeways*. Prospect Heights, Illinois: Wavelend Press, 1997.

McClintock, W. *Old Indian Trails*. New York: Houghton Mifflin, 1923.

———. *The Old North Trail; or, Life, Legends and Religion of the Blackfeet Indians*. London: MacMillan and Co., 1910. Reprint, Lincoln: University of Nebraska, 1968.

———. *The Tragedy of the Blackfoot*. Southwest Museum Papers No. 3. Los Angeles: Southwest Museum, 1930.

McCracken, H., W. R. Wedel, R. Edgar, J. H. Moss, H. E. Wright, Jr., W. M. Husted, and W. Mulloy. *The Mummy Cave Project in Northwestern Wyoming*. Cody, Wyo.: Buffalo Bill Historical Center, 1978.

McDougall, W. B. and H. A. Baggley. *The Plants of Yellowstone National Park*. 2d. rev. ed., Yellowstone Interpretive Series No. 8. Yellowstone Park, Wyo.: Yellowstone Library and Museum Association, 1956. Originally published Washington, D.C.: Government Printing Office, 1936.

McHugh, T. *The Time of the Buffalo*. New York: Alfred A. Knopf, 1972.

McNeely, Jeffrey A. and Kenton R. Miller, eds. *National Parks. Conservation, and Development: The Role of Protected Areas in Sustaining Society*. Washington, D.C.: Smithsonian Institution, 1984.

McWhorter, L. V. *Yellow Wolf: His Own Story*. Caldwell, Idaho: Caxton Printers, 1940.

Mead, M. and R. Banzel. *The Golden Age of Anthropology*. New York: G. Braziller, 1960.

Meagher, M. M. *The Bison of Yellowstone Park*. National Park Service Scientific Monograph Series No. 1. Washington, D.C.: Government Printing Office, 1973.

Medicine Crow, J. *From the Heart of the Crow Country: The Crow Indians's Own Stories*, edited by H. J. Viola. New York: Orion Books, 1992.

Medicine Horse, M. H. *A Dictionary of Everyday Crow*. Crow Agency, Mont.: Bilingual Materials Development Center, 1887.

Merrill, M. D. *Yellowstone and the Great West: Journals, Letters, and Images from the 1871 Hayden Expedition*. Lincoln: University of Nebraska Press, 1999.

Meyer, J. L. *The Spirit of Yellowstone: The Cultural Evolution of a National Park*. Lanham, Md.: Rowman & Littlefield, 1996.

Miles, John C. *Guardians of the Parks: A History of the National Parks and Conservation Association*. Washington, D.C.: Taylor and Francis, 1995.

Miller, D. R. "The Assiniboines and Their Lands: The Frameworks of a Primordial Tie." *Chicago Anthropology Exchange* 14, nos. 1-2 (1981): 99–129.

Miller, H., E. Harrison, and P. Pichette. *Coyote Tales of the Montana Salish: An Exhibition Organized by the Indian Arts and Crafts Board of the United States Department of the Interior*. Rapid City, S. Dak.: Tipi Shop, 1974.

Miller, W. R. "Numic Languages." In *Handbook of North American Indians*, Vol. 11, *Great Basin*, edited by W. L. D'Azevedo, 98–106. Washington, D.C.: Smithsonian Institution, 1986.

Mills, H. B. "The Bannocks in Yellowstone National Park." *Yellowstone Nature Notes* 12 (1935): 22–23.

Milne, C. *Sacred Places in North America*. New York: Stewart, Tabor and Chany, 1995.

Moerman, D. E. "The Medicinal Flora of Native North America: An Analysis." *Journal of Ethnopharmacology* 31 (1991): 1–42.

———. *Native American Ethnobotany*. Portland, Oreg.: Timber Press, 1998.

Momaday, S. *The Way to Rainy Mountain*. Albuquerque: University of New Mexico Press, 1976.

Moodie, D. W. and B. Kaye. "The Ac Ko Mok Ki Map." *The Beaver, Magazine of the North* (Hudson's Bay Company, Winnipeg, Canada)(Spring 1977): 4–15.

Mooney, H. A. and W. Dwight Billings. "Effects of Altitude on Carbohydrate Content of Mountain Plants." *Ecology* 46, no. 5 (1965): 750–51.

Mooney, J. "The Aboriginal Population of America North of Mexico," edited by J. R. Swanton. *Smithsonian Miscellaneous Collections* 80, no. 7 (1928).

———. *Calendar History of the Kiowa Indians*. 1898. Reprint, with an introduction by J. C. Ewers, Washington, D.C.: Smithsonian Institution, 1979. Originally published in *17th Annual Report of the Bureau of American Ethnology for the Years 1892–1893*, Part 2, (1898): 129–445.

Moore, M. *Medicinal Plants of the Desert and Canyon West*. Santa Fe: Museum of New Mexico, 1989.

———. *Medicinal Plants of the Mountain West*. Santa Fe: Museum of New Mexico, 1979.

Morgan, D. L., ed. "Washakie and the Shoshoni: A Selection of Documents from the Records of the Utah Superintendency of Indian Affairs." *Annals of Wyoming* 29, no. 1 (1957): 86–102 and 29, no. 2 (1957): 195–227.

Morris, R. C. "Wyoming Indians." In *Collections of the Wyoming Historical Society*. Vol. 1. Cheyenne: Wyoming Historical Society, 1897.

Morrison, M. *Fire in Paradise: The Yellowstone Fires and the Politics of Environmentalism*. New York: Harper Collins, 1993.

Mulloy, W. "The McKean Site in Northwestern Wyoming." *Southwestern Journal of Anthropology* 10, no. 4 (1954): 432–60.

———. *A Preliminary Historical Outline for the Northwestern Plains*. University of Wyoming Publications 22, no. 1. Laramie: University of Wyoming, 1958.

Murphey, E. Van Allen. *Indian Uses of Native Plants*. Palm Desert, Calif.: Desert Printers, 1959. Reprint, Fort Bragg, Calif.: Mendicino County Historical Society, 1969.

Murphy, R. F. and Y. Murphy. "Northern Shoshone and Bannock." In *Handbook of North American Indians*, Vol. 11., *Great Basin*, edited by W. L. D'Azevedo, 284–307. Washington, D.C.: Smithsonian Institution, 1986.

——. "Shoshone-Bannock Subsistence and Society." *University of California Anthropological Records* 16, no. 7 (1960): 293–338.

Nabhan, G. P. *Enduring Seeds: Native American Agriculture and Wild Plant Conservation*. San Francisco, Calif.: North Point Press, 1989.

Nabokov, P. *Cultivating Themselves: The Inter-play of Crow Indian Religion and History*. Ph.D. diss., University of California, Berkeley, 1988. Ann Arbor, Mich.: University Microfilms.

——. *Native American Testimony*. New York: Viking, 1991.

——. *Two Leggings: The Making of a Crow Warrior*. Lincoln: University of Nebraska Press, 1967.

National Park Service. *Nez Perce Plant Uses*. 2-page leaflet, Nez Perce National Historical Park, USDI National Park Service., n.d.

Nelson, A. "New Plants from Wyoming - XII." *Bulletin of the Torrey Botanical Club* 27, no. 5 (1900): 258–74.

——. *Spring Flora of the Intermountain States*. Boston: Ginn and Company, 1912.

Nickerson, G. S. "Some Data on Plains and Great Basin Indian Uses of Certain Native Plants." *Tebiwa, Journal of the Idaho Museum of Natural History* 9, no. 1 (1966): 45–51.

Norris, P. W. *The Calumet of the Coteau and other Poetical Legends of the Border*. Philadelphia: Lippincott & Co., 1883.

Norton, H. J. *Wonder-Land Illustrated; Or Horseback Rides Through the Yellowstone National Park*. Virginia City, Mont.: Harry J. Norton, 1873.

Nye, W. S. *Bad Medicine and Good: Tales of the Kiowas*. Norman: University of Oklahoma Press, 1962.

O'Brien, J. M. "On Events and Nonevents: 'Vanishing' Indians in the Nineteenth Century New England." In *Native North American Cultures and Representations*, edited by S. Kan and P. Turner Strong. Lincoln: University of Nebraska Press, forthcoming.

Old Coyote, L. Mickey, and H. Smith. *Apsalooka: The Crow Nation Then and Now, Children of the Large Beaked Bird*. Greensburg, Penn.: McDonald/Sward Publishing, 1993.

Olden, S. E. *Shoshone Folk Lore, as Discovered from the Rev. John Roberts, a Hidden Hero, on the Wind River Indian Reservation in Wyoming*. Milwaukee: Morehouse Publishing, 1923.

Opler, M. E. "The Apachean Culture Pattern and Its Origins." In *Handbook of North American Indians*, Vol. 10, *Southwest*, edited by Alfonso Ortiz, 368–92. Washington, D.C.: Smithsonian Institution, 1983.

Ortner, S. B. *Sherpas Through Their Rituals*. Cambridge Studies in Cultural Systems 2. Cambridge: Cambridge University Press, 1978.

Owens, Louis. "Burning the Shelter." In *Mixed Blood Messages: Literature, Film, Family, Place*. Norman: University of Oklahoma Press, 1998.

Palmer, G. B. "Coeur d' Alene." In *Handbook of North American Indians*, Vol. 12, *Plateau*, edited by D. E. Walker, Jr., 313–26. Washington D.C.: Smithsonian Institution, 1998.

Parsons, E. C. *Kiowa Tales*. New York: American Folk-lore Society, G. E. Stechert and Co., Agents, 1929.

Patten, J. L. "Buffalo Hunting with the Shoshone Indians, in 1874 in the Big Horn Basin, Wyoming." *Annals of Wyoming* 4, no. 2 (1926): 296–302.

Patten J. I. "Last Great Hunt of Washakie and his Band." *Wind River Mountaineer* 9, no. 1 (January-March). Lander, Wyo.: Pioneer Museum, 1993.

Paul, J. H., C. T. Barnes, and E. Cannon Porter. *Farm Friends and Spring Flowers*. Salt Lake City, Utah: The Desert News, 1913.

Pearce, S. M. *Museum Studies in Material Culture*. Washington, D.C.: Smithsonian Institution, 1991.

Phillips, C. "Chief Joseph's Gun." *Yellowstone Nature Notes* 2, no. 1 (1925): 2.

Phillips, P. C., ed. *W. A. Ferris: Life in the Rocky Mountains (Diary of the Wanderings of a Trapper in the Years 1831–1832)*. Denver: Old West Publishing, 1940.

Plummer, N. B. *The Crow Tribe of Indians*. American Indian Ethnohistory: Plains Indians. New York: Garland Publishing, 1974.

Powell, J. W. *Exploration of the Colorado River of the West and Its Tributaries, Explored in 1869–1872, Under the Direction of the Secretary of the Smithsonian Institution*. Washington, D.C.: Government Printing Office, 1875.

———. "Indian Linguistic Families of America North of Mexico." In *7th Annual Report of the Bureau of American Ethnology for the Years 1883–1884*, 1–142. Washington, D.C.: Government Printing Office, 1891.

Prucha, F. P. *The Indians in American Society: From the Revolutionary War to the Present*. Berkeley and Los Angeles: University of California Press, 1985.

Pyne, S. J. *Fire in America*. Princeton, N.J.: Princeton University Press, 1982.

Rabinow, P. "Representations are Social Facts: Modernity and Post Modernity in Anthropology." In *Writing Culture: The Poetics and Politics of Ethnography*, edited by J. Clifford and G. Marcus. Berkeley and Los Angeles: University of California Press, 1986.

Raftery, J. H. "Historical Sketch of Yellowstone National Park." *Annals of Wyoming* 15, no. 2 (1943): 101–32.

Ramsey, J. *Coyote Was Going There: Indian Literature of the Oregon Country*. Seattle: University of Washington Press, 1977.

———. *Reading the Fire: Essays in the Traditional Indian Literature of the Far West*. Lincoln: University of Nebraska Press, 1983.

Ray, V. F. *Cultural Relations in the Plateau of Northwestern America*. Frederick Webb Hodge Anniversary Fund Publications, vol. 3. Los Angeles: Southwest Museum, 1939. Reprint, New York: AMS Press, 1978.

———. *The Sanpoil and Nespelem: Salishan Peoples of Northeastern Washington*. University of Washington Publications in Anthropology, vol. 5. Seattle: University of Washington Press, 1933. Reprint, New York: AMS Press, 1980.

Reeves, B. "How Old is the Old North Trail?" *Archaeology in Montana* 31, no. 2 (1990): 1–18.

Replogle, W. F. "Great Bannock Trails." *Naturalist* 10, no. 2 (1959).

———. *Yellowstone's Bannock Indian Trails*. Yellowstone Park, Wyo.: Yellowstone Library and Museum Association, 1956.

Rici, D. "Basin-Plateau Culture Relations in Light of Finds from Marmes Rockshelter in the Lower Snake River Region of the Southern Columbia Plateau." *NARN* 4, no. 1 (1970): 82–98.

Rogers, E. S. and J. G. E. Smith. "Environment and Culture in the Shield and Mackenzie Borderlands." In *Handbook of North American Indians*. Vol. 6, *Subarctic*, edited by June Helm, 130–45. Washington D.C.: Smithsonian Institution, 1981.

Rollinson, J. K. *Hoofprints of a Cowboy and U.S. Ranger: Pony Trails in Wyoming*. Caldwell, Idaho: Caxton Printers, 1941.

Roosevelt, T. R. "An Elk Hunt at Two-Ocean Pass." *The Century Magazine* 44 (1892): 713–19.

Ross, A. *The Fur Hunters of the Far West: A Narrative of Adventure in the Oregon and Rocky Mountains.* 2 vols. London: Smith, Elder and Co., 1855. Reprint, Chicago: R. R. Donnelley & Sons, 1924.

Ruby, R. H. and J. A. Brown. *Dreamer-Prophets of the Columbia Plateau: Smohalla and Skolaskin.* Norman: University of Oklahoma Press, 1989.

Ruggles, R. I. *A Country So Interesting: The Hudson's Bay Company and Two Centuries of Mapping, 1670–1870.* Rupert's Land Record Society. Montreal: McGill-Queen's University Press, 1991.

Runte, A. *National Parks: The American Experience.* 2nd ed. Lincoln: University of Nebraska Press, 1987.

Russell, Charles Lord. *Diary of a Visit to the United States of America in the Year 1883.* New York: U.S. Catholic Historical Society, 1910.

Russell, O. *Journal of a Trapper,* edited by Aubrey L. Haines. Portland: Oregon Historical Society, 1955. Reprint, Lincoln: University of Nebraska Press, 1964. Originally published as *Journal of a Trapper; or, Nine Years in the Rocky Mountains: 1834–1843,* edited by L. A. York. Boise, Idaho: Syms-York Co., 1914; 2nd. ed., 1921.

Ruxton, G. F. *Life in the Far West,* edited by L. R. Hafen. Norman: University of Oklahoma Press, 1951.

Saklani, A. and D. K. Upreti. "Folk Uses of Some Lichens in Sikkim." *Journal of Ethnopharmacology* 37 (1992): 229–33.

Salmonson, J. A. *Phantom Waters: Northwest Legends of Rivers, Lakes and Shores.* Seattle: Sasquatch Books, 1995.

Sanborn, W. B. "Indian Artifacts at the Norris Geyser Basin." *Yellowstone Nature Notes* 23 (1949): 6–8.

Sanders, Jeffrey. Review of *Indian Country, God's Country: Native Americans and the National Parks,* by Philip Burnham. *American Indian Culture and Research Journal* 24, no. 4 (2000): 198.

Schoolcraft, H. R. *Historical and Statistical Information Respecting the History, Condition and Prospects of the Indians of the United States.* Bureau of Indian Affairs Part I. Washington, D.C.: Government Printing Office, 1851.

Schreier, C. *Yellowstone Explorers Guide.* Moose, Wyo.: Homestead Publishing, 1983.

Schullery, P. *Searching for Yellowstone: Ecology and Wonder in the Last Wilderness.* Boston: Houghton Mifflin, 1997.

Schullery, P. and L. H. Whittlesey. "Greater Yellowstone Carnivores: A History of Changing Attitudes." In *Carnivores in Ecosystems: The Yellowstone Experience,* edited by T. W. Clark, A. Peyton Curlee, S. C. Minta, and P. M. Kareiva. New Haven: Yale University Press, 1999.

Schultz, J. W. *Blackfeet and Buffalo: Memories of Life Among the Indians,* edited by K. C. Seele. Norman: University of Oklahoma Press, 1962.

Schultz, J. W. and J. L. Donaldson. *The Sun God's Children.* Boston: Houghton Mifflin, 1930.

Scott, H. L. "Notes on the Kado or Sun Dance of the Kiowa." *American Anthropologist* 13 (1911): 345–79.

Scully, V. *A Treasury of American Indian Herbs: Their Lore and Their Use for Food, Drugs and Medicine.* New York: Crown Publishers, 1970.

Sears, J. *Sacred Places: American Tourist Attractions in the Nineteenth Century.* New York: Oxford University Press, 1989.

Seton, E. T. *Lives of Game Animals.* Garden City, N.Y.: Doubleday, Doran and Company, 1929.

Shalinsky, Audrey C. "Ritual Pageantry in the American West; A Wyoming Case Study." *Great Plains Quarterly* 6 (1986): 21-33.

Sharman, H. G. *The Cave on the Yellowstone or Early Life in the Rockies.* Chicago: Scroll Publishing, 1902.

Shaw, R. J. *Field Guide to the Vascular Plants of Grand Teton National Park and Teton County, Wyoming.* Logan, Utah: Utah State University Press, 1976.

———. *Plants of Yellowstone and Grand Teton National Parks.* Salt Lake City: Wheelwright Press, 1981.

Shimkin, D. B. "Childhood and Development Among the Wind River Shoshone." *University of California Anthropological Records* 5, no. 5 (1947): 289–325.

———. "Comanche-Shoshone Words of Acculturation 1786–1848." *Journal of the Steward Anthropological Society* 2 (1980): 195–248.

———. "Dynamics of Recent Wind River Shoshone History." *American Anthropologist* 44 (1942): 451–62.

———. "Eastern Shoshone." In *Handbook of North American Indians.* Vol. 11, *Great Basin*, edited by W. L. D'Azevedo, 308–35. Washington, D.C.: Smithsonian Institution, 1986.

———. "Shoshone-Comanche Origins and Migrations." In *Proceedings of the 6th Pacific Congress of the Pacific Science Association, 1939.* Vol. 4, 17–25. Berkeley: University of California Press, 1940.

———. "Wind River Shoshone Ethnogeography." *University of California Anthropological Records* 5, no. 4 (1947): 245–90.

———. "Wind River Shoshone Literary Forms: An Introduction." *Journal of the Washington Academy of Sciences* 37, no. 10 (1947): 329–76.

———. *The Wind River Shoshone Sun Dance.* Anthropological Papers 41, Bureau of American Ethnology Bulletin 151, 195–484. Washington, D.C.: Government Printing Office, 1953.

Shimkin, D. B. and R. M. Reid. "Socio-Cultural Persistence Among Shoshone of the Carson River Basin." In *Languages and Cultures of Western North America: Essays in Honor of Sven S. Liljeblad,* edited by E. H. Swanson, Jr., 172–200. Pocatello: Idaho State University Press, 1970.

Shippee, J. M. "Wickiups of Yellowstone Park." *Plains Anthropologist* 16 (1971): 74–75.

Sholly, D. R. and S. M. Newman. *Guardians of Yellowstone: An Intimate Look at the Challenges of Protecting America's Foremost Wilderness Park.* New York: William Morrow and Company, 1991.

Shortt, Mack W. "Museum of the Rockies Archaeological Research in the Canyons of the Yellowstone." *Yellowstone Science* 9, no. 2 (2001): 16-20.

Shortt, Mack W. "Record of Early People on Yellowstone Lake: Cody Complex Occupation at Osprey Beach." *Yellowstone Science* 11, no. 4 (2003): 2-9.

Silversides, B. *The Face Pullers: Photographing Native Canadians, 1871–1939.* Saskatoon, SK, Canada: Fifth House Publishers, 1994.

Skarsten, M. O. "George Drouillard." In *The Mountain Men and The Fur Trade of the Far West,* Vol. 4, edited by L. R. Hafen. Glendale, Calif.: Arthur H. Clark, 1966.

Skinner, C. M. *Myths & Legends of Our Own Land.* Philadelphia and London: J. P. Lippincott Co., 1896.

Skinner, M. P. *The Yellowstone Nature Book.* Chicago: A. C. McClurg & Co., 1926.

Soule, M. E. and G. Lease, eds. *Reinventing Nature? Responses to Postmodern Deconstruction.* Washington, D.C.: Island Press, 1995.

"Sources of Bow Material," *The Wind River Rendezvous* 21, no. 2 (1991): 6–7.

Southworth, Michael. "Landscapes for Learning: Studies in Experimental Interpretation and Exploration," working paper, Institute of Urban and Regional Development, University of California, Berkeley, 1992.

Spence, M. D. *Dispossessing the Wilderness: Indian Removal and the Making of the National Parks*. New York: Oxford University Press, 1999.

———. "Dispossessing the Wilderness: Yosemite Indians and the National Park Ideal, 1864–1930." *Pacific Historical Review* 65 (1996): 27–59.

The Spirit World. The American Indian Series. H. Woodhead, series ed. Alexandria, Virg.: Time-Life Books, 1992.

Stands in Timber, J. and M. Liberty. *Cheyenne Memories*. Lincoln: University of Nebraska Press, 1967.

Statham, D. S. "A Biogeographic Model of Camas and Its Role in the Aboriginal Economy of the Northern Shoshoni in Idaho." *Tebiwa, Journal of the Idaho Museum of Natural History* 18, no. 1 (1976): 59–80.

Steinhart, P. "Ecological Saints." *Audubon* 86, no. 4 (1984): 8–9.

Steward, J. H. *Basin-Plateau Aboriginal Sociopolitical Groups*. Bureau of American Ethnology Bulletin 120. Washington, D.C.: Government Printing Office, 1938. Reprint, Salt Lake City: University of Utah Press, 1970.

———. *The Blackfoot*. Berkeley: National Park Service Field Division of Education, 1934.

———. "Culture Element Distributions. XXIII: Northern and Gosiute Shoshoni." *University of California Anthropological Records* 8, no. 3 (1943): 263–392.

———. "The Foundations of Basin-Plateau Shoshonean Society." In *Languages and Cultures of Western North America: Essays in Honor of Sven S. Liljeblad*, edited by E. H. Swanson, Jr., 113–51. Pocatello: Idaho State University Press, 1970.

———. *Indian Tribes of Sequoia National Park Region*. Berkeley: U.S. Department of the Interior, National Park Service, Field Division of Education, n.d.

———. "Linguistic Distribution and Political Groups of the Great Basin Shoshoneans." *American Anthropologist* 34, no. 4 (1937): 625–34.

Stewart, O. C. *Peyote Religion: A History*. Norman: University of Oklahoma Press, 1987.

———. "The Question of Bannock Territory." In *Languages and Cultures of Western North America: Essays in Honor of Sven S. Liljeblad*, edited by E. H. Swanson, Jr., 201–31. Pocatello: Idaho State University Press, 1970.

———. "The Shoshoni: Their History and Social Organization." *Idaho Yesterdays* 9, no. 3 (1965): 2–5, 28.

———. "Tribal Distributions and Boundaries in the Great Basin." In *The Current Status of Anthropological Research in the Great Basin: 1964*, edited by W. L. D'Azevedo et al., 167–238. Desert Research Institute Social Sciences and Humanities Publications 1. Reno: University of Nevada, 1966.

Stickney, P. F. "Early Development of Vegetation Following Holocaustic Fire in Northern Rocky Mountain Forests." *Northwest Science* 64, no. 5 (1990): 243–46.

Stocking, G. W., ed. *Objects and Others: Essays on Museums and Material Culture*. Madison: University of Wisconsin Press, 1985.

Suagee, D. B. "American Indian Religious Freedom and Cultural Resources Management: Protecting Mother Earth's Caretakers." *American Indian Law Review* 10 (1982): 1.

Sucec, Rosemary and Dan Reinhart. "Trout Ecosystems and Cultural Traditions." *The Buffalo Chip*, Resource Management Newsletter, Yellowstone National Park, June-July (2000): 1.

Swanson, E. H., Jr. "Problems in Shoshone Chronology." *Idaho Yesterdays* 1, no. 4 (1958): 21.

————. *Birch Creek, Human Ecology in the Cool Desert of the Northern Rocky Mountains 9,000 B.C.-A.D. 1850.* Pocatello: Idaho State University Press, 1972.

Swanson, E. H., Jr. and G. Muto. "Recent Environmental Changes in the Northern Great Basin." *Tebiwa, Journal of the Idaho Museum of Natural History* 18, no. 1 (1975): 49–57.

Swanton, J. R. *The Indian Tribes of North America.* Bureau of American Ethnology Bulletin 145. Washington, D.C.: Government Printing Office, 1952.

Sweet, M. *Common Edible and Useful Plants of the West.* Happy Camp, Calif.: Naturegraph, 1976.

Synge, G. M. *A Ride through Wonderland.* London: Sampson, Low, Marston, & Company, 1892.

Szczawinski, A. F. and G. A. Hardy. *Common Edible Plants of British Columbia.* Handbook No. 20. Victoria, BC, Canada: Provincial Museum of Natural History and Anthropology, 1967.

Tétényi, P. *Infraspecific Chemical Taxa of Medicinal Plants.* Budapest: Akadémiai Kiadó, 1970.

Thomas, David Hurst. *Skull Wars: Kennewick Man, Archaeology, and the Battle for Native American Identity.* New York: Basic Books, 2000.

Thompson, D. *David Thompson's Narrative of His Explorations in Western America: 1784–1812,* edited by J. B. Tyrrell. Toronto: The Champlain Society, 1916.

Thompson, E. M. Schultz and W. Leigh Thompson. *Beaver Dick: The Honor and the Heartbreak.* Laramie, Wyo.: Jelm Mt. Press, 1982.

Thompson, G. A. "Fire in Wilderness Areas." In *Proceedings of the 3rd Annual Tall Timbers Fire Ecology Conference,* 105–10. Talahassee, Fla.: Tall Timbers Research Station, 1964.

Thompson, S. *Tales of the North American Indians.* Bloomington: Indiana University Press, 1966.

Thoreau, Henry David. "Chesuncook." *Atlantic Monthly* 2 (1858): 317.

Thornton, R. *American Indian Holocaust and Survival: A Population History Since 1492.* Norman: University of Oklahoma Press, 1987.

Thwaites, R. G., ed. *Original Journals of the Lewis and Clark expedition 1804–1806,* 8 vols. New York: Arno Press, 1904–1906.

Topping, E. S. *The Chronicles of the Yellowstone: An Accurate, Comprehensive History.* St. Paul, Minn.: Pioneer Press, 1888.

Torgler, K. "Continuous Artifact Tradition from the Middle Archaic to the Historical Present: Analyses of Lithics and Pottery from Selected Sites in Southeast Idaho." *Tebiwa, Journal of the Idaho Museum of Natural History* 25, no. 1 (1995): 80–107.

Trenholm, V. C. and M. Carley. *The Shoshonis: Sentinels of the Rockies.* Norman: University of Oklahoma Press, 1964.

Turner, N. J. and R. J. Hebda. "Contemporary Use of Bark for Medicine by Two Salishan Native Elders of Southeast Vancouver Island, Canada." *Journal of Ethnopharmacology* 29 (1990): 59–72.

Turner, N. J., L. C. Thompson, M. T. Thompson, and A. Z. York. *Thompson Ethnobotany: Knowledge and Usage of Plants by the Thompson Indians of British Columbia.* Victoria, BC, Canada: Royal British Columbia Museum, 1990.

Turney-High, H. H. "Ethnography of the Kutenai." *Memoirs of the American Anthropological Association* 56 (1941).

————. "The Flatheads of Montana." *Memoirs of the American Anthropological Association* 48 (1937).

Ulebaker, D. H. "The Sources and Methodology for Mooney's Estimates of North American Indian Population of the Americas in 1492." In *The Native Population of the Americas in 1492*. 2nd ed., edited by W. M. Denevan. Madison: University of Wisconsin Press, 1992.

Urbanek, M. B. *Wyoming Place Names*. Missoula, Mont.: Mountain Press Publishing, 1988.

Utley, R. M. *The Indian Frontier of the American West, 1846–1890*. Histories of the American Frontier. Albuquerque: University of New Mexico Press, 1984.

———. *Frontier Regulars: The United States Army and the Indian, 1866–1891*. New York: Macmillan, 1973. Reprint, Lincoln: University of Nebraska Press, 1984.

Vander, J. "Ghost Dance Songs and Religion of a Wind River Shoshone Woman." *Monograph Series in Ethnomusicology* No. 4. Los Angeles: University of California, 1986.

———. *Shoshone Ghost Dance Religion: Poetry, Songs and Great Basin Context*. Urbana: University of Illinois Press, 1997.

Vestal, P. A. and R. E. Schultes. *The Economic Botany of the Kiowa Indians as it Relates to the History of the Tribe*. Cambridge, Mass.: Botanical Museum, 1939.

Vinton, S. *John Colter, Discoverer of Yellowstone Park*. New York: Edward Eberstadt, 1926.

Voeglin, E. W. "Kiowa-Crow Mythological Affiliations." *American Anthropologist* 35 (1933): 470–74.

Voget, F. W. *The Shoshoni-Crow Sundance*. Norman: University of Oklahoma Press, 1984.

Voth, H. H. and C. P. Russell. *Yellowstone National Park: A Bibliography*. Rev. ed. Berkeley: National Park Service, Western Museum Laboratories, 1940.

Wagner, G. D. and W. A. Allen. *Blankets and Moccasins: Plenty Coups and His People, The Crows*. Caldwell, Idaho: Caxton Printers, 1933. Reprint, Lincoln: University of Nebraska Press, 1987.

Walgamott, C. S. *Six Decades Back*. Idaho Yesterdays. Caldwell, Idaho: Caxton Printers, 1936. Reprint, Moscow, Idaho: University of Idaho Press, 1990.

Walker, D. E., Jr. *Blood of the Monster: The Nez Perce Coyote Cycle*. Worland, Wyo.: High Plains Publishing, 1994.

———. *Conflict and Schism in the Nez Perce Acculturation: A Study of Religion and Politics*. Moscow, Idaho: University of Idaho Press, 1985.

———. "Lemhi Shoshone-Bannock Reliance on Anadromous and Other Fish Resources." *Northwest Anthropological Research* 27, no. 2 (1993): 215–50.

———. "The Shoshone-Bannock: The Anthropological Reassessment." *Northwest Anthropological Research* 27, no. 2 (1993): 139–60.

Washburn, W. E. "Ethnohistory: History in the Round." *Ethnohistory* 8 (1961): 31–48.

Wax, R. H. and R. K. Thomas. "American Indians and White People." In *Native Americans Today: Sociological Perspectives,* edited by H. M. Bahr, B. A. Chadwick, and R. C. Day, 31–42. New York: Harper and Row, 1972.

Webb, W. E. *Buffalo Lands: An Authentic Account of the Discoveries, Adventures and Mishaps of a Scientific and Sporting Party in the Wild West*. Philadelphia: George Maclean, 1874.

Wedel, M. M. and R. J. DeMallie. "The Ethnohistorical Approach in Plains Studies." In *Anthropology on the Great Plains*, edited by W. R. Wood and M. Liberty, 110–28. Lincoln: University of Nebraska Press, 1980.

Wedel, W. R. "Earthenware and Steatite Vessels from Northern Wyoming." *American Antiquity* 19, no. 4 (1954): 403–409.

Wedel, W. R., W. M. Husted, and J. H. Moss. "Mummy Caves Prehistoric Record from the Rocky Mountains." *Science* 160 (1968): 184–86.

Weeks, R. *Pachee Goyo: History and Legends from the Shoshone*. Laramie, Wyo.: Jelm Mt. Press, 1981.

Weisel, G. F. *Men and Trade on the Northwest Frontier as Shown by the Fort Owen Ledger.* Montana State University Studies, Vol. 2. Missoula: Montana State University Press, 1955.

———. "The Rams Horn Tree and other medicine trees of the Flathead Indians." *Montana: Magazine of Western History* 1, no. 3 (1951): 5–11.

Wells, M. W. Introduction to *The Northern Shoshoni*, by B. D. Madsen. Caldwell, Idaho: Caxton Printers, 1980.

West, P. C. and S. Brechlin. *Resident Peoples and National Parks.* Tucson: University of Arizona Press, 1991.

White, M. C. *David Thompson's Journals Relating to Montana & Adjacent Regions, 1808–1812.* Missoula: Montana State University Press, 1950.

White, R. *It's Your Misfortune and None of My Own: A New History of the American West.* Norman: University of Oklahoma Press, 1991.

Whittlesey, L. H. "*Yellowstone Place Names.*" Helena: Montana Historical Society, 1988.

Wilfong, C. *Following the Nez Perce Trail.* Corvallis, Ore.: Oregon State University Press, 1990.

Wilkinson, C. F. *The Eagle Bird: Mapping a New West.* New York: Vintage Books, 1993.

Willard, T. *Edible and Medicinal Plants of the Rocky Mountains and Neighbouring Territories.* Calgary, AB, Canada: Wild Rose College of Natural Healing, 1992.

Williams, K. *Eating Wild Plants.* Missoula, Mont.: Mountain Press Publishing, 1984.

Williams, P. L. "Reflections of Wash-A-Kie, Chief of the Shoshones." *Utah Historical Quarterly* 1 (1928): 101–106.

Wilson, E. N. *The White Indian Boy; or, The Story of Uncle Nick Among the Shoshones.* Yonkers-on-Hudson, N.Y.: World Book Co., 1919. Reprint, Rapid City, S. Dak.: Fenske Printers, 1985.

Wingate, G. W. *Through the Yellowstone Park on Horseback.* New York: O. Judd Company, 1886.

Wissler, C. *The American Indian: An Introduction to the Anthropology of the New World.* New York: D. C. McMurtrie, 1917.

———. "The Influence of the Horse in the Development of Plains Culture." *American Anthropologist* 16 (1914): 1–25.

Wister, O. "Old Yellowstone Days." *Harper's Monthly*, March 1936, 471–80.

Witt, D. H., J. E. Marsh, and R. B. Bovey. *Mosses, Lichens & Ferns of Northwest North America.* Edmonton, AB, Canada: Lone Pine, 1988; Seattle: University of Washington Press, 1988.

"Wonderland: A Journey through the Yellowstone National Park." Copy in the Buffalo Bill Historical Center Library, Cody, Wyo., 1884.

Wood, W. R. and T. D. Thiessen. *Early Fur Trade on the Northern Plains: Canadian Traders among the Mandan and Hidatsa Indians, 1738–1818.* Norman: University of Oklahoma Press, 1985.

Wright, G. A. "High Country Adaptations." *Plains Anthropologist* 25, no. 89 (1980): 181–97.

———. "Notes on Chronological Problems on the Northwestern Plains and Adjacent High Country." *Plains Anthropologist* 27, no. 96 (1982): 145–60.

———. *People of the High Country: Jackson Hole Before the Settlers.* American University Studies. Vol. 7. New York: Peter Lang, 1984.

———. "The Shoshonean Migration Problem." *Plains Anthropologist* 23, no. 80 (1978): 113–37.

Wright, G. A. and Jane B. Dirks. "Myth as Environmental Message." *Ethnos* 3–4 (1983): 160–76.

Writers Program, W. P. A. *Montana: A State Guide Book.* New York: Viking, 1939.

——. *Wyoming: A Guide to Its History, Highways, and People.* New York: Oxford University Press, 1941.

Wuerthner, G. *Yellowstone and the Fires of Change.* Salt Lake City: Haggis House Publications, 1988.

Wyoming Geological Association Guidebook. Archeological Research in Yellowstone National Park. Thirty-Third Annual Field Conference (1982): 11.

Yellow Wolf. *Yellow Wolf, His Own Story.* Caldwell, Idaho: Caxton Printers, 1983.

Yen, M.-H., C.-C. Lin, C.-H. Chuang, and S.-Y. Liu. "Evaluation of Root Quality of *Bupleurum* Species by TLC Scanner and the Liver Protective Effects of 'Xiao-chai-hu-tang' Prepared Using Three Different *Bupleurum* Species." *Journal of Ethnopharmacology* 34 (1991): 155–65.

Newspaper Articles

Beal, S. M. "The Snake River Stork Country." *Rexburg Idaho Journal.* 1935.

Bellinghausen, P. "Sheepeater People." *Billings (Mont.) Gazette,* 24 July 1995.

Billings (Mont.) Gazette. 6 July 1995, 4B.

——. 20 July 1997.

Bozeman (Mont.) Avant Courier. 28 November 1878.

——. 19 June 1879, A2.

Bonar, J. "Sheepeaters Were Doomed by Smallpox." *Billings (Mont.) Gazette.* 9 July 1979.

Brock, W. "Indian Icehouse." *(Twin Falls, Idaho) Times News.* 15 September 1996.

Casper (Wyo.) Star-Tribune. 20 March 1997.

Cheyenne (Wyo.) Daily Leader. 3 March 1870.

Ellsworth, Spencer. "A Visit to Wonderland." *Lacan (Illinois) Home Journal.* 25 October 1882, C3.

Frank Leslie's Illustrated Newspaper. "Protect the National Park." 27 April 1889.

Great Falls Tribune. 24 August 1926.

Hardin (Mont.) Tribune. 13 January 1933.

Helena (Mont.) Daily Herald. 18 May 1870.

(Boise) Idaho Statesman. 6 October 1876.

Livingston (Mont.) Enterprise. "The Redman's Welcome to Villard." 28 March 1884.

——. 31 July 1927.

Los Angeles Times. 3 August 1997, M4.

Louisville (Kent.) Courier Journal. 18 April 1884, 12.

Mills, J. H. "The Grand Rounds: A Fortnight in the National Park." *Deerlodge (Mont.) New Northwest* 12 October 1872.

Milstein, M. "Unearthing of Kill Site a First for Yellowstone." *The Lincoln (Nebr.) Star.* 24 September 1993.

New York Times. 13 April 1997, 18.

——. 23 June 1998, B9.

Stille, Alexander. "In the 'Greened' World, It Isn't Easy To Be Human." *The New York Times,* 15 July 2000, A17.

Stromnes, J. "Bitterroots Becoming Elusive, but Salish People Keeping Traditional Harvest Alive." *Montana Life,* 5 May 1996. Missoulian.

Trumbull, W. "The Washburn Yellowstone Expedition No. 1." *(San Fran.) Overland Monthly.* 6 May 1871, 431–37.

Wind River (Wyo.) Mountaineer. Jan-March 1991, vol.7, no.1.

Unpublished Materials

Adams, R. "Pipes and Bowls: Steatite Artifacts from Wyoming and the Region." Master's thesis, University of Wyoming, Laramie, 1992.

Anastasio, A. "Intergroup Relations in the Southern Plateau." Ph.D. diss., University of Chicago, 1955.

Barrett, S. W. "Relationship of Indian-Caused Fires to the Ecology of Western Montana Forests." Master's thesis, University of Montana, 1981.

Boschi, Father S. J. "Grammar of the Absaroki or Crow." Duplicated at St. Charles, Pryor, Mont. Record made by Father T. Meagher, 1898.

Caslick, J. W. "Bighorn Sheep in Yellowstone: A Literature Review and Some Suggestions for Management, 1993." Unpublished manuscript on file with Resource Management, Yellowstone National Park, Wyo.

Conner, S. W. "Wigwam Creek Tipis: Supplement #1." Report on file at Yellowstone National Park Library, Mammoth, Wyo.

———. Letter Report on Lava Creek Wickiups. In Stuart Conner Files, Billings, Mont.

Curtis, E. S. Curtis Papers, Box 4B/Unlabeled Pile #1, Folder #14, n.d. L. A. County Museum, Seaver Center Library, Los Angeles, Calif.

Davis, L. B. "The Prehistoric Use of Obsidian in the Northwestern Plains." Ph.D. diss., Department of Archaeology, University of Calgary, Calgary, 1972.

Flathead Cultural Committee. "Flathead Plant and Animal Names," 1995. Unpublished document in Flathead Cultural Committee Files, St. Ignatius, Mont.

Francis, J. E. "Root Procurement in the Upper Green River Basin: Archaeological Investigations at 48SU1002." Paper presented at the Second Biennial Rocky Mountain Anthropological Conference, Steamboat Springs, Colo., 1995.

Friedman, I. and K. P. Cannon. "Hydration Rate of Obsidian in Yellowstone National Park." Paper presented at the Second Biennial Rocky Mountain Anthropological Conference. Steamboat Springs, Colo., 1995.

Gilliland, H. "The Flood as told to Hap Gilliland," 1972. Council for Indian Education, Billings, Mont.

Haag, W. G. "Aboriginal Dog Remains from Yellowstone National Park," 1956. Manuscript on file, Yellowstone Library, Mammoth, Wyo.

Hadly, E. "Late Holocene Mammalian Fauna of Lamar Cave and Its Implications for Ecosystems Dynamics in Yellowstone National Park, Wyoming." Master's thesis, Northern Arizona University, Flagstaff, 1990.

Haines, A. L. "A Supplementary Report on High-Altitude Indian Occupation Sites near the North Boundary of Yellowstone National Park," 1965. Typescript on file in Yellowstone National Park Archives, Mammoth, Wyo.

———. Letter to Lee H. Whittlesey, 19 September 1977. Yellowstone National Park Archives, Mammoth, Wyo.

Henderson, A. B. "Journal of the Yellowstone Expedition of 1866 Under Captain Jeff Standifer." Original in the Beinecke Library, Yale University, New Haven; copy at Yellowstone National Park Research Library, Mammoth, Wyo.

Hoffman, J. J. "A Preliminary Archaeological Survey of Yellowstone National Park." Master's thesis, Montana State University, Bozeman, 1961.

Hogan, B. H. "Two High Altitude Game Trap Sites in Montana." Master's thesis, University of Montana, Missoula, 1974.

Horr, H. R. Letter to Secretary of Interior. 25 May 1874. Records of the Office of the Secretary of Interior Relating to Yellowstone National park, 1872–1886. (File microcopy no. 62, roll 1), National Archives, Wash.

Hough, E. "Yellowstone." St. Paul, Minn.: Northern Pacific Railway, 1933.

Howard, E. R. "Livestock and Buffalo History." W. P. A. Papers, 1936–1941. Merrill G. Burlingame Special Collections, Montana State University, Bozeman.

Hughes, S. "Test Excavations at Soapy Dale Lodge (48HO107)." Bureau of Land Management, Worland District, Wyo, 1994.

———. "Synthesis of the Mummy Cave Materials: 1994." Manuscript on file with Worland, Wyo. Bureau of Land Management, 1994.

Hultkrantz, Å. "The Sheepeaters of Wyoming: Culture History and Religion Among Some Shoshoni Mountain Indians," n.d. Handwritten manuscript in 2 volumes, in author's possession.

———. "Wind River Shoshone Fieldnotes," 1948-58. Manuscripts in author's possession.

Husted, W. M. and R. Edgar. "An Archaeology of Mummy Cave Wyoming: An Introduction to Shoshonean Prehistory," 1978. Unpublished manuscript on file at the Buffalo Bill Historical Center, Cody, Wyo.

Johnson, A. M. and K. A. Lippincott. "1988 Post-Fire Archaeological Assessment Prehistoric Sites, Yellowstone National Park," 1989. On file at Cultural Resources Division, Yellowstone National Park, Mammoth, Wyo.

Johnson, T. "The Enos Family and Wind River Shoshone Society: A Historical Analysis." Ph.D. diss., University of Illinois, Urbana Champaign, 1975.

Kay, C. E. "The Northern Yellowstone Elk Herd: A Critical Evaluation of the Natural Regulation Paradigm." Ph.D. diss., University of Utah, 1990.

Krueger, C. G. "Eighteen Months in a Wyoming Tie Camp: 1928–1929," n.d. Manuscript on file at Shoshone National Forest, Cody, Wyo.

Lanning, C. M. *A Grammar and Vocabulary of the Blackfoot Language*. Fort Benton, Montana Territory, 1882. Self-published, on file with the Montana State Historical Society, Helena, Mont.

Liljeblad, S. "Indian Peoples in Idaho." Pocatello: Idaho State College, 1957.

Loeb, B. "Classic Intermontane Beadwork of the Crow and Plateau Tribes." Ph.D. diss., University of Washington, Seattle, 1983.

Marler, G. Unpublished manuscript, 1973. On file at Yellowstone Research Library, Mammoth, Wyo.

McCleary, T. P. "Plants Utilized by the Crow Indians," 1995. (List of plant scientific names, Crow term, and translation, where available.) In author's possession.

Medicine Crow, J. Letter to Phil G. Schlamp, Helena National Forest, 20 February 1980. On file with the Carbon County Historical Society, Red Lodge, Mont.

Missionary of the Society of Jesus. "A Dictionary of the Numipu or Nez Perce Language, Part I: English-Nez Perce," 1895. St Ignatius Mission, Mont.

Napton, L. K. "Canyon & Valley Preliminary Archaeological Survey of the Gallatin Area Montana." Master's thesis, University of Montana, Missoula, 1966.

Old Coyote, H. and B. Old Coyote. "Crow Stories." (I. Saga of Red Bear, II. Story of Spotted Horse, III. Story of Rabbit Child), 1985. Little Big Horn College, Crow Tribal Archives. Crow Agency, Mont.

Old Horn, D. and T. McLeary. "Apsaalooke Social and Family Structure," 1995. Little Bighorn College, Crow Agency, Mont.

Phillips, C. "The Indians of the Yellowstone Country." In *Yellowstone Ranger Nature Manual*, 1927, 32-39. On file in the Yellowstone National Park library, Mammoth, Wyo. Mimeographed.

Ravndal, V. "A General Description of the Social and Cultural Environment Surrounding the Bison/Burcellosis Issue in the Great Yellowstone Ecosystem." Draft manuscript submitted to the U.S. National Park Service, 6 April 1997.

Reeve, S. A. "Root Crops and Prehistoric Social Process in the Snake River Headwaters, Northwestern Wyoming." Ph.D. diss., State University of New York, Albany, 1986.

Rollinson, J. K. "Northern Pacific Transport Company: Sunlight Basin Sightseeing Tour from Cody, Wyoming to Silver Gate, Montana," n.d. Manuscript in Buffalo Bill Historical Center, Cody, Wyo.

Russell, C. P. "A Summary of Relationships of Certain Indian Tribes to Yellowstone National Park." Typescript on file at Yellowstone National Park Library, Mammoth, Wyo.

Samuelson, A. E. "Archaeological Investigations in the Grant Village—West Thumb Area of Yellowstone National Park, Wyoming." Master's thesis, State University of New York at Albany, 1981.

Schaeffer, C. Claude Schaeffer Papers, Glenbow Institute, Calgary, Canada, n.d.

Schoen, J. R. and D. T. Vlchek. "Steatite Procurement and Source Areas in Western Wyoming." Paper presented at the Northwestern Plains Archaeological Symposium, Billings, Mont., 1991.

Scott, H. L. Hugh L. Scott Papers. National Anthropological Archives Manuscript 2932. Box 2, Kiowa folder, Washington, D.C., n.d.

Shimkin, D. B. Unpublished field notes on the Eastern Shoshone, 1937-1938. Demitri Boris Shimkin Papers, 1890–1993. American Heritage Center, University of Wyoming, Laramie. Accession Number 9942, Box 1–3.

———. "Some Interactions of Culture, Needs and Personality among the Wind River Shoshone." Ph.D. diss., University of California, Berkeley, 1939.

Simmons, W. S. "From Manifest Destiny to the Melting Pot: The Life and Times of Charlotte Mitchell Wampanoag," n.d.

Sowers, T. "Petroglyphs and Pictographs of Dinwoody," 1939. Typescript (185 pp. and 85 photographs) on file at American Heritage Center, University of Wyoming, Laramie.

Spence, M. D. "Dispossessing the Wilderness: The Preservationist Ideal, Indian Removal, and National Parks." Ph.D. diss., University of California, Santa Barbara, 1996.

Spence, M. D. "First Wilderness: Native Use of the Yellowstone Basin and Indian Removal from Yellowstone National Park." Paper presented at the Environmental Cultures Conference, Victoria, BC, Canada, 1996.

Stubbs, R. D. "An Investigation of the Edible and Medicinal Plants Used by the Flathead Indians." Master's thesis, University of Montana, Missoula, 1966.

Tallbull, W. "Bison Boundaries: Traditions in Transition." Paper presented at A Cinnabar Symposium. Montana State University, Bozeman, 1 February 1992.

Tschirgi, F. "The Tenderfoot," 1904. Manuscript on file at the Big Horn County Library and Montana Room, Parmly Library, Billings, Mont.

Upham, E. A. and S. Annie. "Excursion with the Raymond Party to the Yellowstone National Park in September, 1892," 1892. Manuscript in the Buffalo Bill Historical Center Archives, Cody, Wyo.

Walker, D. and J. E. Francis. "Legend Rock Petroglyph Site (48H04), Wyoming: 1988 Archaeological Investigations," 1989. Manuscript on file at Office of State Archaeologist, Department of Anthropology, University of Wyoming, Laramie.

Walpole, K. V. "Bennett Butte, 'Bivouc of the Dead': A Narrative of 'Miles Fight on the Clark's Fork' and Analysis of a Monumental Historical Mystery," 1997. Buffalo Bill Historical Center, Cody, Wyo.

Weixelman, J. "The Power to Evoke Wonder: Native Americans and the Geysers of Yellowstone National Park," 1992, project director Tom Tankersley, Park Historian.

National Park Service, Yellowstone National Park. Submitted to Wyoming Council for the Humanities, Laramie, Project #145–91.

Whipple, J. "Draft Vascular Plant Species List: Yellowstone National Park," 1991. On file in the Herbarium, Yellowstone National Park, Mammoth, Wyo.

Whittlesey, L. H. "Yellowstone's Horse-and-Buggy Tour Guides: Interpreting the Grand Old Park, 1872–1920," 1996. Manuscript in author's possession.

Willey, P. and P. Key. "Analysis of Human Skeletons from Yellowstone National Park." University Foundation, California State University, Chico, Calif. Manuscript prepared for the Midwest Archeological Center, National Park Service, Order No. PX-61159-0012.

Woods, J. C. "Manufacturing and Use Damage on Pressure-flaked Stone Tools." Master's thesis, Idaho State University, Pocatello, 1987.

Works Progress Administration. "Questionnaires for Park County, Montana," 1941. Special Collections, Mansfield Library, University of Montana, Missoula.

Interview

Lucas, T. Personal Communication. Lander, Wyo., 8 July 1995.

Video

Smith, D. J. (producer). *The Sheepeaters: Keepers of the Past.* Bozeman, Mont.: Earthtalk Studios, 1990.

Index

CPSIA information can be obtained
at www.ICGtesting.com
Printed in the USA
BVHW012220301220
596806BV00012B/121